LAW OF
THE EUROPEAN
COMMUNITY

THE FOUNDATION STUDIES IN LAW SERIES

Series Adviser – Paul Richards

The books in this series are written for law students for the foundation subjects required to be studied on both law degrees and postgraduate common professional examination courses. Each text concentrates on developing a basic framework for the subject and as such is designed to be accessible and readable, a format especially suitable for part-time courses, CPE and distance-learning courses, as well as more traditional full-time courses where teaching is becoming increasingly student-centred and modularised. These basic texts are intended to be used in conjunction with other sources, such as law reports, case books and statutory materials.

Paul Richards, LLB, PhD, PGCE is a Principal Lecturer in Law
at the University of Huddersfield.

LAW OF CONTRACT

CRIMINAL LAW

LAND LAW

LAW OF TORT

TRUSTS AND EQUITY

CONSTITUTIONAL AND ADMINISTRATIVE LAW

LAW OF THE EUROPEAN COMMUNITY

LAW OF THE EUROPEAN COMMUNITY

THIRD EDITION

Christopher Vincenzi

Formerly Huddersfield University

John Fairhurst

Huddersfield University

An imprint of **Pearson Education**

Harlow, England · London · New York · Reading, Massachusetts · San Francisco
Toronto · Don Mills, Ontario · Sydney · Tokyo · Singapore · Hong Kong · Seoul
Taipei · Cape Town · Madrid · Mexico City · Amsterdam · Munich · Paris · Milan

Pearson Education Limited
Edinburgh Gate
Harlow
Essex CM20 2JE
England

and Associated Companies around the world

Visit us on the World Wide Web at:
www.pearsoneduc.com

First published in 1996
Second edition published under the Financial Times/Pitman Publishing imprint 1999
Third edition 2002

ISBN 0 582 43813 6

British Library Cataloguing in Publication Data
A catalogue record for this book is available
from the British Library

Library of Congress Cataloging-in-Publication Data

10 9 8 7 6 5 4 3 2 1
05 04 03 02 01

Typeset in 10/12.5pt Sabon by 7
Printed in Great Britain
by Henry Ling Ltd, at the Dorset Press, Dorchester, Dorset

CONTENTS

PART I · CONSTITUTIONAL AND ADMINISTRATIVE LAW OF THE EUROPEAN COMMUNITIES AND THE EUROPEAN UNION

1 AN INTRODUCTION TO THE EUROPEAN COMMUNITIES AND THE EUROPEAN UNION

The European Coal and Steel Community · The European Economic Community and the European Atomic Energy Community · The merger of the institutions · Enlargement · Future enlargement · The Single European Act · The Treaty on European Union · The Treaty of Amsterdam · The Treaty of Nice 2000 · A two-speed Europe? · The European Economic Area · The European Convention on Human Rights, the Council of Europe and the Court of Human Rights: a structure outside the Communities and the Union

PREFACE TO THE FIRST EDITION

Over the last few years the number of books on European Community law has proliferated, and it might seem that there could not be any need for yet another. The breadth and depth of Community law has, however, meant that all those books, especially those primarily written for students, have had to be selective, emphasising either the institutional and administrative aspects of Community law, or selecting a limited range of substantive topics, such as social and employment policy, free movement of persons, competition or agriculture. The tendency, until recently, has been to treat the working of the Community and the application of Community law as essentially matters for the Community institutions. Community law tended to seem a somewhat exotic subject for common law students, located somewhere between international law, constitutional law and jurisprudence. Decisions of the European Court of Justice on the need for effective judicial protection in the national courts, and the growing realisation in those courts that much of what appeared to be national legislation had, in fact, originated in Community measures, have brought the importance of Community law home to practising lawyers in the United Kingdom.

This has resulted in Community law becoming a 'core' subject for those hoping to qualify as a solicitor. The widening legislative competence of the Community, so that Community law now reaches into almost every aspect of law, both public and private, has meant that an understanding of the fundamentals of Community law is essential for every working lawyer. In making a selection of topics for this book I have, therefore, had three principal aims. The first is to provide an account of the institutions of the Community and the selected topics in a way which I hope is accessible to those who have not already studied other areas of law in depth. The second is to provide a selection of topics of substantive Community law in the areas of free movement of persons, goods and services, competition law and policy which, though far from exhaustive, provide illustrations of much wider principles of Community law, how these relate to the national legal systems, and how they can be applied in areas of Community law which have not been examined. The third, and most important, distinctive aim of the book is to illustrate the links between Community institutions and the government, legislature and judiciary of the United Kingdom, including the effect of Community law on the law within the United Kingdom.

I have endeavoured to look at how Community principles of the supremacy of Community law and the direct effect of directives have been applied by our courts. Specific sections, and in some cases, whole chapters, have been devoted to show how the United Kingdom has met, and in some cases failed to meet, its obligations under Community law in the areas of substantive law which have been examined. This will, I hope, help the reader to see how Community law is integrated into our own and how far it has developed so as to give effect to Community rights. Even though only a necessarily limited range of topics has been covered, it is hoped that these will provide the reader with a good grounding in those areas. There is, however, a further reading section at the end of each chapter providing titles of books and articles in which the issues covered can be explored in more depth. I have endeavoured to state the law as at 1 November 1995.

I acknowledge, with thanks, permission by the Incorporated Council of Law Reporting for England and Wales to publish extracts from the *Law Reports Appeal Cases* and the *Weekly Law Reports*; by Blackstone Press Ltd in relation to an extract from *Textbook on Constitutional and Administrative Law* (2nd Edition) (1995) by Brian Thompson; by Butterworths for consent to publish an extract from *An Introduction to Intellectual Property Law* (1995) by Jeremy Phillips and Alison Firth, and extracts from the *All England Law Reports* and the *New Law Journal*; and for leave from Kluwer Academic Publishers to publish an extract from an article by Judge Federico Mancini published in the *Common Market Law Review*. I am also grateful to Advocate-General Francis Jacobs and the *European Advocate* for permission to publish extracts from an article in the Winter 1994 edition of that journal, and to Professor Terence Daintith, Professor Noreen Burrows, Hilary Hiram and John Wiley & Sons for consent to publish extracts from *Implementing EC Law in the United Kingdom: Structures for Indirect Rule* (1995). Extracts from judgments of the European Court of Justice and the Court of First Instance are taken with leave of the publishers either from the summaries of the judgments published by the Court or from the official reports.

I am also most grateful to my publishers and especially to Patrick Bond and Julianne Mulholland for all their help and advice. Finally, the greatest debt I owe is to my wife Ruth, without whose support and continuing encouragement this book would never have been completed.

Christopher Vincenzi
June 1996

PREFACE TO THE THIRD EDITION

Following Chris Vincenzi's retirement as editor, I have stepped into the breach to revise and update the second edition. Throughout this new edition, I have included recent Community legislation and legislative proposals, and recent judgments of the Court of Justice and Court of First Instance, where these seemed relevant.

Since the second edition of this book was published the Member States negotiated a further amending Treaty, the Treaty of Nice, during December 2000. This Treaty was formally signed during February 2001 and will come into force once it has been ratified by all Member States; this is unlikely to be before 2002. The primary purpose of the Treaty of Nice was to undertake the necessary institutional reforms in preparation for enlargement of the European Union to an anticipated membership of 27. Part I (which has been retitled Constitutional and Administrative Law of the European Communities and the European Union) has been revised to incorporate the amendments which will be made to the constitutional structure of the European Union and the Communities once the Treaty of Nice comes into force, and to provide the reader with the current state of play as far as Union enlargement is concerned. What was Part V in the previous edition (Remedies at Community and National Level) has been transferred into the more extensive Part I, to give the reader a thorough understanding of the constitutional and administrative law of the European Union and the Communities before undertaking the study of substantive Community law in Parts II to IV.

Apart from the amendments which will be made by the Treaty of Nice to the founding Treaties and the Treaty on European Union, Part I has been substantially revised and updated. Following an introduction to the European Communities and the European Union in Chapter 1, Chapter 2 (previously Chapter 4) is now devoted to the Sources of Community Law. The rationale for this is that I consider it preferable for the reader to have an understanding of sources of law, before embarking upon a discussion of the institutions (Chapter 3) and the decision-making process (Chapter 4). There is now a separate chapter on the Court of Justice and Court of First Instance, together with their methods of interpretation (Chapter 5). The previous Chapter 6, Fundamental Rights and the ECHR in the Community, has been incorporated into the new Chapter 5, as it is through the case law of the ECJ and the CFI that the fundamental rights and application of the ECHR have evolved. Chapters 6–8 are devoted to the previous three chapters (21–23) which were included in Part V. Chapter 9 consists of a discussion of the principles of supremacy, direct and indirect effect, and state liability and their application in English courts. The final chapter of Part I (Chapter 10) is devoted to the application of Community law in English courts and the adapting of remedies to the requirements of Community law.

The latter three Parts of the book (Parts II to IV) have retained their previous titles: Free Movement of Persons and Services and Rights of Establishment (Part II, Chapters 11–16); Free Movement of Goods (Part III, Chapters 17–18); and Competition Law

(Part IV, Chapters 19–22). In these latter three parts of the book in particular, there has been an increased use of extracts of ECJ and CFI judgements to give the reader a deeper exposure to the methodology adopted by the ECJ and CFI in its development of the Community's substantive law.

A particular feature of this new edition is the inclusion of relevant internet sites to enable the reader to keep abreast of current developments. In addition I shall be providing the publisher's with material to be placed on their website in order to keep the reader up-to-date.

I would like to thank Paul Richards (series editor) and Chris Vincenzi for providing me with the opportunity to write this third edition; to Pat Bond (aquisitions editor) and Louise Lakey (desk editor) for their help and support; and to Gwyneth Pitt (Head of Law at Huddersfield) for her unending support and encouragement, and for ensuring I had the necessary time to deliver the manuscript on schedule.

I have endeavoured to state the law as at 1 January 2001.

John Fairhurst
January 2001

ACKNOWLEDGEMENTS

We are grateful to the following for permission to reproduce copyright material:

Butterworths publishers for the use of extracts from the All England Law Reports and the Industrial Relations Law Reports, reproduced by permission of The Butterworths Division of Reed Elsevier (UK) Limited © IRLR; the European Communities for permission to reproduce extracts from the European Court Reports, various Community publications and publications available through its Europa Web Site; the Incorporated Council of Law Reporting for England and Wales for permission to reproduce extracts from the Weekly Law Reports; Sweet & Maxwell publishers for permission to reproduce extracts from the Common Law Reports.

Whilst every effort has been made to trace the owners of copyright material, in a few cases this has proved impossible and we take this opportunity to offer our apologies to any copyright holders whose rights we may have unwittingly infringed.

A Companion Web Site accompanies
Law of the European Community, 3rd Edition
by Mr Chris Vincenzi and Mr John Fairhurst

Visit the *Foundation Studies in Law Series* Companion Website at *www.booksites.net/fsls* to find valuable teaching and learning material including:

For Students:
- Study material designed to help you improve your results
- Regular updates to ensure your knowledge is up-to-date
- Weblinks to useful legal resources on the World Wide Web
- Search for specific information on the site

For Lecturers:
- All of the above
- A syllabus manager that will build and host a course web page

TABLE OF CASES BEFORE THE EUROPEAN COURT OF JUSTICE AND THE COURT OF FIRST INSTANCE (NUMERICAL)

Note: 'Ct Rep' and the subsequent numbers refer to the issue number and year of Summaries of Judgments issued by the Press and Information Division of the European Court of Justice.

TABLE OF CASES BEFORE THE EUROPEAN COURT OF JUSTICE AND THE COURT OF FIRST INSTANCE
(ALPHABETICAL)

Note: 'Ct Rep' and the subsequent numbers refer to the issue number and year of Summaries of Judgments issued by the Press and Information Division of the European Court of Justice.

TABLE OF CASES BEFORE THE EUROPEAN COURT OF HUMAN RIGHTS

TABLE OF CASES BEFORE
NATIONAL COURTS

TABLE OF EUROPEAN COMMISSION DECISIONS

TABLE OF EUROPEAN COMMUNITY TREATIES

TABLE OF EQUIVALENCES REFERRED TO IN ARTICLE 12 OF THE TREATY OF AMSTERDAM (RENUMBERED ARTICLES OF THE TREATY OF ROME)*

A. Treaty on European Union

Previous numbering	New numbering
Title I	Title I
Article A	Article 1
Article B	Article 2
Article C	Article 3
Article D	Article 4
Article E	Article 5
Article F	Article 6
Article F.1[1]	Article 7
Title II	Title II
Article G	Article 8
Title III	Title III
Article H	Article 9
Title IV	Title IV
Article I	Article 10
Title V[2]	Title V
Article J.1	Article 11
Article J.2	Article 12
Article J.3	Article 13
Article J.4	Article 14
Article J.5	Article 15
Article J.6	Article 16
Article J.7	Article 17
Article J.8	Article 18
Article J.9	Article 19
Article J.10	Article 20
Article J.11	Article 21
Article J.12	Article 22
Article J.13	Article 23
Article J.14	Article 24

*©European Communities (1999)

Excerpt from the Treaty of Amsterdam reproduced by permission of the publishers, the Office for Official Publications of the European Communities.

[1]New Article introduced by the Treaty of Amsterdam.
[2]Title restructured by the Treaty of Amsterdam.

Previous numbering	New numbering
Title V[2]	Title V
Article J.15	Article 25
Article J.16	Article 26
Article J.17	Article 27
Article J.18	Article 28
Title VI[2]	Title VI
Article K.1	Article 29
Article K.2	Article 30
Article K.3	Article 31
Article K.4	Article 32
Article K.5	Article 33
Article K.6	Article 34
Article K.7	Article 35
Article K.8	Article 36
Article K.9	Article 37
Article K.10	Article 38
Article K.11	Article 39
Article K.12	Article 40
Article K.13	Article 41
Article K.14	Article 42
Title VIa[1]	Title VII
Article K.15[2]	Article 43
Article K.16[2]	Article 44
Article K.17[2]	Article 45
Title VII	Title VIII
Article L	Article 46
Article M	Article 47
Article N	Article 48
Article O	Article 49
Article P	Article 50
Article Q	Article 51
Article R	Article 52
Article S	Article 53

[1]New Title introduced by the Treaty of Amsterdam.
[2]New Article introduced by the Treaty of Amsterdam.

B. Treaty establishing the European Community

Previous numbering	New numbering
Part One	Part One
Article 1	Article 1
Article 2	Article 2
Article 3	Article 3
Article 3a	Article 4
Article 3b	Article 5
Article 3c[2]	Article 6
Article 4	Article 7
Article 4a	Article 8
Article 4b	Article 9
Article 5	Article 10
Article 5a[2]	Article 11
Article 6	Article 12
Article 6a[2]	Article 13
Article 7 (repealed)	—
Article 7a	Article 14
Article 7b (repealed)	—
Article 7c	Article 15
Article 7d[2]	Article 16
Part Two	Part Two
Article 8	Article 17
Article 8a	Article 18
Article 8b	Article 19
Article 8c	Article 20
Article 8d	Article 21
Article 8e	Article 22
Part Three Title I	Part Three Title I
Article 9	Article 23
Article 10	Article 24
Article 11 (repealed)	—
Chapter 1 Section 1 (deleted)	Chapter 1 —
Article 12	Article 25
Article 13 (repealed)	—
Article 14 (repealed)	—
Article 15 (repealed)	—
Article 16 (repealed)	—
Article 17 (repealed)	—
[Section 2 (deleted)]	
Article 18 (repealed)	—
Article 19 (repealed)	—

[1]New Title introduced by the Treaty of Amsterdam.
[2]New Article introduced by the Treaty of Amsterdam.

Previous numbering	New numbering
Article 20 (repealed)	—
Article 21 (repealed)	—
Article 22 (repealed)	—
Article 23 (repealed)	—
Article 24 (repealed)	—
Article 26 (repealed)	—
Article 27 (repealed)	—
Article 28	Article 26
Article 29	Article 27
Chapter 2	Chapter 2
Article 30	Article 28
Article 31 (repealed)	—
Article 32 (repealed)	—
Article 33 (repealed)	—
Article 34	Article 29
Article 35 (repealed)	—
Article 36	Article 30
Article 37	Article 31
Title II	Title II
Article 38	Article 32
Article 39	Article 33
Article 40	Article 34
Article 41	Article 35
Article 42	Article 36
Article 43	Article 37
Article 44 (repealed)	—
Article 45 (repealed)	—
Article 46	Article 38
Article 47 (repealed)	—
Title III Chapter 1	Title III Chapter 1
Article 48	Article 39
Article 49	Article 40
Article 50	Article 41
Article 51	Article 42
Chapter 2	Chapter 2
Article 52	Article 43
Article 53 (repealed)	—
Article 54	Article 44
Article 55	Article 45
Article 56	Article 46
Article 57	Article 47
Article 58	Article 48

Previous numbering	New numbering
Chapter 3	Chapter 3
Article 59	Article 49
Article 60	Article 50
Article 61	Article 51
Article 62 (repealed)	—
Article 63	Article 52
Article 64	Article 53
Article 65	Article 54
Article 66	Article 55
Chapter 4	Chapter 4
Article 67 (repealed)	—
Article 68 (repealed)	—
Article 69 (repealed)	—
Article 70 (repealed)	—
Article 71 (repealed)	—
Article 72 (repealed)	—
Article 73 (repealed)	—
Article 73a (repealed)	—
Article 73b	Article 56
Article 73c	Article 57
Article 73d	Article 58
Article 73e (repealed)	—
Article 73f	Article 59
Article 73g	Article 60
Article 73h (repealed)	—
Title IIIa[1]	Title IV
Article 73i[2]	Article 61
Article 73j[2]	Article 62
Article 73k[2]	Article 63
Article 73l[2]	Article 64
Article 73m[2]	Article 65
Article 73n[2]	Article 66
Article 73o[2]	Article 67
Article 73p[2]	Article 68
Article 73q[2]	Article 69
Title IV	Title V
Article 74	Article 70
Article 75	Article 71
Article 76	Article 72
Article 77	Article 73
Article 78	Article 74
Article 79	Article 75
Article 80	Article 76
Article 81	Article 77

[1]New Title introduced by the Treaty of Amsterdam.
[2]New Article introduced by the Treaty of Amsterdam.

Previous numbering	New numbering
Title IV	Title V
Article 82	Article 78
Article 83	Article 79
Article 84	Article 80
Title V	Title VI
Chapter 1	Chapter 1
Section 1	Section 1
Article 85	Article 81
Article 86	Article 82
Article 87	Article 83
Article 88	Article 84
Article 89	Article 85
Article 90	Article 86
[Section 2 (deleted)]	—
Article 91 (repealed)	—
Section 3	Section 2
Article 92	Article 87
Article 93	Article 88
Article 94	Article 89
Chapter 2	Chapter 2
Article 95	Article 90
Article 96	Article 91
Article 97 (repealed)	—
Article 98	Article 92
Article 99	Article 93
Chapter 3	Chapter 3
Article 100	Article 94
Article 100a	Article 95
Article 100b (repealed)	—
Article 100c (repealed)	—
Article 100d (repealed)	—
Article 101	Article 96
Article 102	Article 97
Title VI	Title VII
Chapter 1	Chapter 1
Article 102a	Article 98
Article 103	Article 99
Article 103a	Article 100
Article 104	Article 101
Article 104a	Article 102
Article 104b	Article 103
Article 104c	Article 104

Previous numbering	New numbering
Chapter 2	Chapter 2
Article 105	Article 105
Article 105a	Article 106
Article 106	Article 107
Article 107	Article 108
Article 108	Article 109
Article 108a	Article 110
Article 109	Article 111
Chapter 3	Chapter 3
Article 109a	Article 112
Article 109b	Article 113
Article 109c	Article 114
Article 109d	Article 115
Chapter 4	Chapter 4
Article 109e	Article 116
Article 109f	Article 117
Article 109g	Article 118
Article 109h	Article 119
Article 109i	Article 120
Article 109j	Article 121
Article 109k	Article 122
Article 109l	Article 123
Article 109m	Article 124
Title VIa[1]	Title VIII
Article 109n[2]	Article 125
Article 109o[2]	Article 126
Article 109p[2]	Article 127
Article 109q[2]	Article 128
Article 109r[2]	Article 129
Article 109s[2]	Article 130
Title VII	Title IX
Article 110	Article 131
Article 111 (repealed)	—
Article 112	Article 132
Article 113	Article 133
Article 114 (repealed)	—
Article 115	Article 134
Title VIIa[1]	Title X
Article 116[2]	Article 135

[1]New Title introduced by the Treaty of Amsterdam.
[2]New Article introduced by the Treaty of Amsterdam.

Previous numbering	New numbering
Title VIII	Title XI
Chapter 1[1]	Chapter 1
Article 117	Article 136
Article 118	Article 137
Article 118a	Article 138
Article 118b	Article 139
Article 118c	Article 140
Article 119	Article 141
Article 119a	Article 142
Article 120	Article 143
Article 121	Article 144
Article 122	Article 145
Chapter 2	Chapter 2
Article 123	Article 146
Article 124	Article 147
Article 125	Article 148
Chapter 3	Chapter 3
Article 126	Article 149
Article 127	Article 150
Title IX	Title XII
Article 128	Article 151
Title X	Title XIII
Article 129	Article 152
Title XI	Title XIV
Article 129a	Article 153
Title XII	Title XV
Article 129b	Article 154
Article 129c	Article 155
Article 129d	Article 156
Title XIII	Title XVI
Article 130	Article 157
Title XIV	Title XVII
Article 130a	Article 158
Article 130b	Article 159
Article 130c	Article 160
Article 130d	Article 161
Article 130e	Article 162

[1]Chapter 1 restructured by the Treaty of Amsterdam.

Previous numbering	New numbering
Title XV	Title XVIII
Article 130f	Article 163
Article 130g	Article 164
Article 130h	Article 165
Article 130i	Article 166
Article 130j	Article 167
Article 130k	Article 168
Article 130l	Article 169
Article 130m	Article 170
Article 130n	Article 171
Article 130o	Article 172
Article 130p	Article 173
Article 130q (repealed)	—
Title XVI	Title XIX
Article 130r	Article 174
Article 130s	Article 175
Article 130t	Article 176
Title XVII	Title XX
Article 130u	Article 177
Article 130v	Article 178
Article 130w	Article 179
Article 130x	Article 180
Article 130y	Article 181
Part Four	Part Four
Article 131	Article 182
Article 132	Article 183
Article 133	Article 184
Article 134	Article 185
Article 135	Article 186
Article 136	Article 187
Article 136a	Article 188
Part Five Title I Chapter 1 Section 1	Part Five Title I Chapter 1 Section 1
Article 137	Article 189
Article 138	Article 190
Article 138a	Article 191
Article 138b	Article 192
Article 138c	Article 193
Article 138d	Article 194
Article 138e	Article 195
Article 139	Article 196
Article 140	Article 197

Previous numbering	New numbering
Article 141	Article 198
Article 142	Article 199
Article 143	Article 200
Article 144	Article 201
Section 2	Section 2
Article 145	Article 202
Article 146	Article 203
Article 147	Article 204
Article 148	Article 205
Article 149 (repealed)	—
Article 150	Article 206
Article 151	Article 207
Article 152	Article 208
Article 153	Article 209
Article 154	Article 210
Section 3	Section 3
Article 155	Article 211
Article 156	Article 212
Article 157	Article 213
Article 158	Article 214
Article 159	Article 215
Article 160	Article 216
Article 161	Article 217
Article 162	Article 218
Article 163	Article 219
Section 4	Section 4
Article 164	Article 220
Article 165	Article 221
Article 166	Article 222
Article 167	Article 223
Article 168	Article 224
Article 168a	Article 225
Article 169	Article 226
Article 170	Article 227
Article 171	Article 228
Article 172	Article 229
Article 173	Article 230
Article 174	Article 231
Article 175	Article 232
Article 176	Article 233
Article 177	Article 234
Article 178	Article 235
Article 179	Article 236
Article 180	Article 237
Article 181	Article 238
Article 182	Article 239
Article 183	Article 240
Article 184	Article 241

Previous numbering	New numbering
Article 185	Article 242
Article 186	Article 243
Article 187	Article 244
Article 188	Article 245
Section 5	Section 5
Article 188a	Article 246
Article 188b	Article 247
Article 188c	Article 248
Chapter 2	Chapter 2
Article 189	Article 249
Article 189a	Article 250
Article 189b	Article 251
Article 189c	Article 252
Article 190	Article 253
Article 191	Article 254
Article 191a[1]	Article 255
Article 192	Article 256
Chapter 3	Chapter 3
Article 193	Article 257
Article 194	Article 258
Article 195	Article 259
Article 196	Article 260
Article 197	Article 261
Article 198	Article 262
Chapter 4	Chapter 4
Article 198a	Article 263
Article 198b	Article 264
Article 198c	Article 265
Chapter 5	Chapter 5
Article 198d	Article 266
Article 198e	Article 267
Title II	Title II
Article 199	Article 268
Article 200 (repealed)	—
Article 201	Article 269
Article 201a	Article 270
Article 202	Article 271
Article 203	Article 272
Article 204	Article 273
Article 205	Article 274
Article 205a	Article 275
Article 206	Article 276

[1]New Article introduced by the Treaty of Amsterdam.

Previous numbering	New numbering
Article 206a (repealed)	—
Article 207	Article 277
Article 208	Article 278
Article 209	Article 279
Article 209a	Article 280
Part Six	Part Six
Article 210	Article 281
Article 211	Article 282
Article 212[1]	Article 283
Article 213	Article 284
Article 213a[1]	Article 285
Article 213b[1]	Article 286
Article 214	Article 287
Article 215	Article 288
Article 216	Article 289
Article 217	Article 290
Article 218[1]	Article 291
Article 219	Article 292
Article 220	Article 293
Article 221	Article 294
Article 222	Article 295
Article 223	Article 296
Article 224	Article 297
Article 225	Article 298
Article 226 (repealed)	—
Article 227	Article 299
Article 228	Article 300
Article 228a	Article 301
Article 229	Article 302
Article 230	Article 303
Article 231	Article 304
Article 232	Article 305
Article 233	Article 306
Article 234	Article 307
Article 235	Article 308
Article 236[1]	Article 309
Article 237 (repealed)	—
Article 238	Article 310
Article 239	Article 311
Article 240	Article 312
Article 241 (repealed)	—
Article 242 (repealed)	—
Article 243 (repealed)	—
Article 244 (repealed)	—
Article 245 (repealed)	—
Article 246 (repealed)	—

[1]New Article introduced by the Treaty of Amsterdam.

TABLE OF OTHER TREATIES

TABLE OF EUROPEAN COMMUNITY REGULATIONS

TABLE OF EUROPEAN COMMUNITY DIRECTIVES

RULES OF PROCEDURE OF THE EUROPEAN COURT OF JUSTICE

TABLE OF UNITED KINGDOM STATUTES

TABLE OF UNITED KINGDOM STATUTORY INSTRUMENTS

LIST OF ABBREVIATIONS

AC	Appeal Cases
ACP	African Caribbean Pacific states
AJCL	American Journal of Comparative Law
AJIL	American Journal of International Law
All ER	All England Law Reports
Anglo-Am LRev	Anglo-American Law Review
BDMA	British Direct Mailing Association
Bull EC	Bulletin of the European Communities
BYIL	British Yearbook of International Law
CAP	Common Agricultural Policy
CE	Compulsory Expenditure
CEEs	Charges having an equivalent effect to a customs duty
CEN	European Committee for Standardisation
CENELEC	European Committee of Electrotechnical Standardisation
CFI	Court of First Instance
CFSP	Common Foreign and Security Policy
CJHA	Co-operation in Justice and Home Affairs
CLJ	Cambridge Law Journal
CLP	Current Legal Problems
CMLR	Common Market Law Reports
CML Rev	Common Market Law Review
COM	Common Organisation of the Market or Commission Document
COREPER	Committee of Permanent Representatives *(Comite des Representants Permanents)*
DG	Directorate General
EAGGF	European Agricultural Guidance and Guarantee Fund (often referred to as FEOGA - *Fonds europden d'orientation et de garantie agricole*)
EC	European Community
ECB	European Central Bank
ECHR	European Convention on Human Rights
ECJ	European Court of Justice
ECLR	European Competition Law Review
ECOFIN	Council of Economic and Finance Ministers
ECOSOC	Economic and Social Committee
ECR	European Court Reports
ECSC	European Coal and Steel Community
ECU	European Currency Unit
EEA	European Economic Area
EEC	European Economic Community
EELR	European Environmental Law Review
EFTA	European Free Trade Association
EHRR	European Human Rights Reports Review
EIPL	European Intellectual Property Law
EL Rev	European Law Review
EP	European Parliament

EPC	European Political Co-operation
EPL	European Public Law
ESCB	European System of Central Banks
EU	European Union
Euratom	European Atomic Energy Community
FamLaw	Family Law
FAO	Food and Agriculture Organisation of the United Nations
FSR	Fleet Street Reports
GATT	General Agreement on Tariffs and Trade
GNP	Gross National Product
HarvLR or Harvard LR	Harvard Law Review
HRLJ	Human Rights Law Journal
IAT	Immigration Appeals Tribunal
IBL	International Business Lawyer
ICLQ	International and Comparative Law Quarterly
IGC	Intergovernmental Conference
IndLJ	Industrial Law Journal
Int Lawyer	International Lawyer
IRLR	Industrial Relations Law Reports
JBL	Journal of Business Law
JCMS	Journal of Common Market Studies
JESP	Journal of European Social Policy
JHA	Justice and Home Affairs
JLIS	Journal of Law and Information Science
JLS	Journal of Law and Society
JPL	Journal of Planning and Environmental Law
JSWL	Journal of Social Welfare Law (now JSWFL – Journal of Social Welfare and Family Law)
LIEI	Legal Issues of European Integration
LQR	Law Quarterly Review
MCA	Monetary Compensatory Amount
MEQR	Measure having Equivalent Effect to Quantitative Restrictions
MEP	Member of the European Parliament
MGQ	Maximum Guaranteed Quantities
MLR	Modern Law Review
NATO	North Atlantic Treaty Organization
NCE	Non-Compulsory Expenditure
NILQ	Northern Ireland Legal Quarterly
NLJ	New Law Journal
OECD	Organisation for Economic Cooperation and Development
OJ	Official Journal of the European Communities
OJLS	Oxford Journal of Legal Studies
PA	Public Administration
PL	Public Law
PPLR	Public Procurement Law Review
QMV	Qualified Majority Voting
SCA	Special Committee on Agriculture
SEA	Single European Act
SJ	Solicitors' Journal
SRWT	Société Regionale Walloon du Transport
TEU	Treaty on European Union

ToA	Treaty of Amsterdam
ToN	Treaty of Nice
WLR	Weekly Law Reports
Yale LJ	Yale Law Journal
YEL	Yearbook of European Law

Part I

CONSTITUTIONAL AND ADMINISTRATIVE LAW OF THE EUROPEAN COMMUNITIES AND THE EUROPEAN UNION

Chapter 1

AN INTRODUCTION TO THE EUROPEAN COMMUNITIES AND THE EUROPEAN UNION

The European Communities came into existence in the aftermath of the Second World War, but the impetus for their creation, to a large extent, came from a desire not to repeat the mistakes made by the victorious powers in the inter-war years. The Treaty of Versailles of 1919 recognised the new nation-states of Central and Eastern Europe that had emerged following the collapse of the Austro-Hungarian and Ottoman empires. It also imposed heavy reparations on Germany, which the new Weimar Republic was unable to pay. The hyper-inflation that followed, and the crash of 1929, wiped out the savings of the large German middle class and pushed unemployment in Germany to more than 40 per cent of the labour force (Hobsbawm, 1994). The instability that this created led directly to the rise of the Nazi Party and the outbreak of the Second World War. It also gravely affected the economies of the other Western European powers. The United Kingdom, France and Italy, the victors who were the architects of Versailles, suffered almost as much as the vanquished from its consequences. Attempts at protecting national economies by tariff barriers were largely unsuccessful and did little more than maintain the economies of Western Europe in a state of stagnation until they were lifted by preparations for another World War. The experience of the inter-war years made clear beyond doubt that it was no longer possible for the states of Western Europe, including states like the United Kingdom and France which still had large colonial markets, to operate their national economies without regard to the effect on their immediate neighbours.

Another important lesson of the First World War and its aftermath was learned from the failure of linked defence treaties and the new League of Nations to avert war. The French, above all, grasped the importance of binding Germany's coal and steel industry, the sinews of her war machine, into a new political and economic alliance. At the same time, fear of the apparently expansionist Soviet Union that now occupied the whole of Eastern and Central Europe, including East Germany, impelled the democratic states of Western Europe and North America to come together in 1949 into the North Atlantic Treaty Organisation. West Germany did not join NATO until October 1954 (The Paris Agreements, NATO Facts and Figures, Brussels 1971). The United States of America, instead of withdrawing from Europe as it had in 1919, was a founder member of the new defence organisation and took a major part in European rehabilitation and reconstruction. Millions of dollars were poured into West Germany in grants and loans under the Marshall Plan, and it started on a rapid economic recovery. Other European states were also assisted under the Plan.

The recognition of the reality and, indeed, the need for mutual interdependence by Western European states, created a receptive atmosphere for resurgent ideas about European political unity. These were expressed with force and vision by Winston Churchill (former UK Prime Minister) at Zurich in September 1946, when he proposed a 'sovereign remedy' to European tensions. He proposed the creation of a 'European family, or as much of it as we can, and provide it with a structure under which it can dwell in peace, in safety and in freedom. We must build a kind of United States of Europe'. Although he did not envisage the United Kingdom becoming a member of this 'European family', he stated that the first step in its creation should be based on a partnership between France and Germany. This would have required an imaginative leap by the French, who were only just beginning to recover from German occupation and who had been the victims of three wars of aggression by Germany. The idea of European federation, based on a Franco-German partnership, was, however, taken up with enthusiasm by two French politicians, Jean Monnet and Robert Schumann, the former with responsibility for French economic planning and the latter as Foreign Minister. The first step in the construction of a new European order was the creation of the European Coal and Steel Community.

THE EUROPEAN COAL AND STEEL COMMUNITY

Less than four years after Churchill made his Zurich speech, Robert Schumann (the French Foreign Minister) stated on 9 May 1950 that a United Europe was essential for the maintenance of world peace. He further stated that a European alliance was essential and that would require the century-old opposition between France and Germany to be eliminated. He proposed that the first stage on this road to European integration would require the whole of France and Germany's coal and steel production to be placed under one authority. His proposal provided that other countries within Europe could partici-pate in the organisation which would be created.

France, Germany, Italy and the Benelux countries (i.e. Belgium, The Netherlands and Luxembourg) accepted the proposal in principle and negotiations started immediately. The United Kingdom was not a party to these negotiations, as it was not yet interested in joining the European family (at this time the United Kingdom still had strong connections with the Commonwealth). The negotiations progressed rapidly, and less than one year later, on 18 April 1951, the Treaty Establishing the European Coal and Steel Community (ECSC) was signed by these six countries in Paris. Because it was signed in Paris it is often referred to as the Treaty of Paris; however, its official title is 'The Treaty Establishing the ECSC'. Ratification of the Treaty by the six states was a mere formality.

Following ratification, the Treaty entered into force on 25 July 1952, thus establishing the ECSC. This Community is still in existence. It is one of the three Communities which are collectively referred to as the European Communities; this shall be discussed further below.

Earlier in this discussion of the historical evolvement of the European Communities, it was stated that European integration was necessary to ensure world peace. So how did the ECSC further this aim? Coal and steel were, in the 1950s, essential com-ponents in the production of arms and munitions. Thus, by depriving France and

Germany of their independence in the production of these commodities, it was widely believed that future conflicts between France and Germany would be avoided. However, the Preamble to the Treaty made it quite clear that the long-term aims of the participants went a great deal further than the control of the production of coal and steel. The Treaty recognised that 'Europe can be built only through practical achievements which will first of all create solidarity, and through the establishment of common bases for economic solidarity'. The participants were 'resolved to substitute for age-old rivalries the merging of their essential interests; to create, by establishing an economic community, the basis for a deeper and broader community among peoples long divided by bloody conflicts' (Preamble). There was little UK enthusiasm for involvement, and successive UK governments (including the then Conservative administration headed by Winston Churchill) were prepared to support only the loosest association with their Continental neighbours. These fell far short of the aspirations of the six founding states and, for two decades, the United Kingdom remained on the sidelines of Community developments.

The ECSC Treaty created five institutions:

- an executive, called the High Authority;
- a Consultative Committee attached to the High Authority;
- a Special Council of Ministers;
- an Assembly; and
- a Court of Justice.

The most striking thing about the new Community was the fact that it had legal personality and a High Authority that was to be responsible for policy relating to the coal and steel industries in the Member States and which had the power to make decisions directly affecting the economic agents in each country without regard to the wishes of the governments of those states. Investment in the coal and steel industries was to be influenced by the High Authority, though not subject to much control. Powers were reserved to regulate prices and production, but only if there were crises of shortage or over-production. There was also a social dimension to the new community: policies were to be framed for training, housing and redeployment. Competition was, at the same time, to be stimulated by rules on price transparency, as well as anti-trust laws on US lines. These decisions could be enforced against the Member States in the new Court of Justice.

THE EUROPEAN ECONOMIC COMMUNITY AND THE EUROPEAN ATOMIC ENERGY COMMUNITY

Three of the founding states of the ECSC (Belgium, The Netherlands and Luxembourg) had already formed themselves into the Benelux customs union. From 1 January 1948, customs barriers were removed between Belgium, The Netherlands and Luxembourg and a common customs tariff was agreed between them in relation to the outside world. The effect of this was that goods could freely pass between the three countries, with minimal formalities. Customs duties levied on goods originating within the three countries were abolished and goods entering from outside would have a uniform customs tariff applied to them. In 1954 they also authorised a free flow of capital, which meant a freedom of investment and unrestricted transfer of currency within the three countries, and in 1956 they accepted free movement of labour. The internal trade of these countries between 1948–1956 increased by 50 per cent. This mini-common market proved to be profitable to all the three countries involved and its success whetted the appetites of neighbouring states and led to pressure to project this experiment on a European scale.

That pressure created the political climate for a much more ambitious project. On 25 March 1957 the EEC Treaty was signed in Rome by the six founding states of the ECSC, the aim being to establish a European Economic Community (EEC) in goods, labour, capital and services among these six states. The Common Market established by the EEC Treaty was, at the time, the biggest free trade area in the world. At the same time, a Treaty Establishing the European Atomic Energy Community (Euratom) for cooperation in the use of atomic energy was signed. The United Kingdom participated in the initial negotiations for both Treaties but withdrew because of fears of loss of national sovereignty and damage to favourable trading links with the Common-wealth. The EEC and Euratom Treaties came into force on 1 July 1958, following their ratification by the six states. This resulted in the existence of three communities (each of which is still in existence): EEC, ECSC and Euratom, which are collectively referred to as the European Communities.

The Preamble to the EEC Treaty set out the objective of the contracting parties:

> to lay the foundations of an ever closer union among the peoples of Europe ... to ensure the economic and social progress of their countries by common action to eliminate the barriers which divide Europe ... [to secure] the constant improvement of the living and working conditions of their peoples ... [and] to strengthen the unity of their economies and to ensure their harmonious development by reducing differences existing between various regions ... [and] by means of a common commercial policy, to [secure] the progressive abolition of restrictions on international trade.

The common market, which was created by the EEC Treaty, covered the whole economic field except those areas falling within the scope of the ECSC or Euratom. It involved the creation of a customs union, which required the abolition of all customs duties and quantitative restrictions in trade between the Member States, a common external tariff, and provisions for the free movement of labour, business and capital. These objectives reflected what had already largely been achieved in the Benelux states, the aim being to create, on a Community scale, economic conditions similar to those in the market of a single state; similar to the position in the United Kingdom where goods, persons, services and capital can move freely between England, Scotland, Wales and Northern Ireland.

As initially formulated, Art 3 of the EEC Treaty vested the Community with power to pursue the following activities:

- the elimination, as between Member States, of customs duties and of quantitative restrictions on the import and export of goods, and of all other measures having equivalent effect;
- the establishment of a common customs tariff and a common commercial policy towards third countries;

- the abolition, as between Member States, of obstacles to the free movement of persons, services and capital;
- the adoption of a common agricultural policy;
- the adoption of a common transport policy;
- the creation of a Community competition policy;
- the approximation of the laws of the Member States to the extent required for the proper functioning of the common market; and
- the association of overseas countries and territories in order to increase trade and promote economic development.

Article 3 was vital to empower the Community (through its institutions) to pursue these *economic* activities and thus secure the four features of the common market discussed above, i.e. the free movement of goods, labour, business and capital.

The main institutions of the EEC – the Commission, the Council of Ministers, the Assembly and the Court of Justice – were modelled on those of the ECSC, and the Community had a similar legal structure.

In contrast, the object of Euratom was to develop nuclear energy, distribute it within the Community and sell the surplus to the outside world. For political reasons originally associated with France's nuclear weapons programme and, subsequently, as a result of widespread doubts about the safety and viability of nuclear power, Euratom never developed as originally envisaged. Euratom has, however, remained an important focus for research and the promotion of nuclear safety.

THE MERGER OF THE INSTITUTIONS

One of the consequences of the new Treaties was that there were now three Communities, with three sets of Councils and Commissions, roughly corresponding to each other in function. It became clear that this made little sense. By comparison, immediately following the signing of the EEC and Euratom Treaties, agreement was reached so that there would be only one Parliamentary Assembly and one Court of Justice for the ECSC, EEC and Euratom. For some time after the new Treaties came into effect, however, there remained separate Councils of Ministers and separate executive bodies – a High Authority in the case of the ECSC and a Commission each for the EEC and Euratom.

On 8 April 1965, the simplification of the institutional structure of the Communities was completed by the signature of a Merger Treaty, the result of which was that there was thereafter one Council, one European Commission, one European Court of Justice and one Assembly (later to be renamed the European Parliament) for all three Communities.

ENLARGEMENT

The United Kingdom's response to the creation of the EEC in 1958 was to propose a much looser 'free trade area'. This proposal was not welcomed by the Community, but in 1959 it resulted in the creation of a rival organisation, the European Free Trade Association (EFTA), comprising Austria, Denmark, Norway, Portugal, Sweden,

Switzerland and the United Kingdom. Although trade increased between these states, the EFTA lacked the structure and coherence of the EEC, and its members' economies grew only modestly by comparison. By 1961, the UK Government had realised that its failure to join the European Communities had been a mistake and, in that year, the Macmillan Government applied for membership. After prolonged negotiations, the application, which needed the unanimous agreement of the Member States, was vetoed by the French President, General de Gaulle. The French were reluctant to accept the United Kingdom's membership because it was feared that the United Kingdom would attempt to retain preferences for Commonwealth trade and that the UK Government was, politically, too close to the United States of America. They were afraid that the special relationship between the United Kingdom and the United States of America would obstruct French efforts to create a European defence community free from US dominance. A further attempt was made by the Government of Harold Wilson in 1967, but this was again vetoed by the French. In 1970 a third application was made by the Heath Government and on this occasion the application was successful. The Treaty of Accession was signed on 22 January 1972 and the United Kingdom, together with Denmark and Ireland, became members of the European Communities on 1 January 1973. Norway, which had participated in the accession negotiations, did not join, as a result of a hostile national referendum.

The Treaty of Accession bound the new Member States to accept the three Treaties and to accept the existing rules of the Communities. The UK Parliament, after a debate that split both the Conservative and Labour parties, enacted the European Communities Act 1972, which was intended to give effect to both present and future Community law in the United Kingdom. Divisions within the Labour Party about membership of the European Communities led the newly elected Labour Government to promise a referendum. This was held in 1975 and resulted in endorsement of continuing membership by a majority of almost 2:1.

Danish, Irish and UK membership was followed by Greece in 1981 and Spain and Portugal in 1986. Three of the remaining EFTA members – Finland, Austria and Sweden – joined the Communities on 1 January 1995. Norway, having once more successfully negotiated terms for entry, again failed to join after another adverse national referendum. Western European states currently outside the European Communities are: Iceland, Liechtenstein, Norway and Switzerland.

FUTURE ENLARGEMENT

Applications for membership of the European Communities (and the European Union) have been addressed to the European Council by:

- Turkey   April 1987
- Cyprus   July 1990
- Switzerland   May 1992
- Hungary   March 1994
- Poland   April 1994
- Romania   June 1995
- Slovakia   June 1995

- Latvia   October 1995
- Estonia   November 1995
- Lithuania   December 1995
- Bulgaria   December 1995
- Czech Republic   January 1996
- Slovenia   January 1996.

During April 1998 the EU opened negotiations on membership with six countries with a view to their becoming full members within the foreseeable future:

- Cyprus
- Czech Republic
- Estonia
- Hungary
- Poland
- Slovenia.

As part of the Community's Agenda 2000 package, the European Commission is stepping up preparations for these six countries, and others, to join the Communities. On 8 November 2000 the Commission published a Strategy Paper together with a report on the progress of each individual country. The paper aims to step up the momentum of negotiations with all 13 candidate countries, which could end in 2002 for those at the most advanced stage. The Strategy Paper 2000 concluded as follows:

> In the light of the above the Commission recommends to the European Council to conclude that:
>
> - accession negotiations should progress following the indicative priority schedules for 2001 and 2002 contained in the proposed 'road map', whereby all requests for transitional measures and other outstanding issues will be addressed by the Union with the most advanced countries at the latest by June 2002;
> - the 'road map' will allow the Union to address requests for transitional measures which are acceptable or negotiable and may include transition measures in the interests of the Union;
> - to permit further progress in the accession negotiations when a limited number of problems cannot be solved rapidly, these will be 'set aside' to be revisited later, thus facilitating a clear identification of outstanding issues and permitting the corresponding chapters to be provisionally closed;
> - while maintaining the principle of differentiation, this approach should permit the conclusion of negotiations in the course of 2002 with those candidate countries who fulfil all the criteria for membership, thus putting the Union in a position to welcome new Member States from the end of 2002;
> - Bulgaria, Latvia, Lithuania, Malta, Romania and Slovakia should prepare their position papers on those chapters which they consider to be ready for negotiation, taking into account their state of preparation and the proposed 'road map'. On this basis, the Commission will assess whether the opening of these chapters to negotiation can be recommended. This should allow the most advanced candidates to open negotiations in all areas of the *acquis* as early as possible in 2001;
> - incorporation of the *acquis* by the candidate States in their legislation, and adaptation

of their capacity effectively to implement and enforce it, remain the key conditions for progressing in the negotiations. The Commission will thus continue to monitor negotiating countries' commitments;

- the Accession Partnerships remain the central pre-accession strategy instruments. Short-term priorities of the 1999 Partnerships not fully met yet should be implemented rapidly whilst the medium-term priorities are applicable. They will form the basis for programming pre-accession assistance in 2001;
- negotiations for further additional reciprocal trade concessions in the field of agricultural products should be launched in the framework of the Europe Agreements, with a view to enhancing trade relations and to preparing for accession in this important area;
- to facilitate the participation of all candidate countries in the Community programmes, framework decisions should be adopted for Central and Eastern European countries and bilateral agreements concluded with Cyprus, Malta and Turkey;
- although Turkey does not yet meet the conditions for opening negotiations, the following actions are necessary in order to implement the pre-accession strategy:
  - continuing political dialogue, in line with the Helsinki European Council conclusions;
  - monitoring the implementation of the Accession Partnership in the context of the Association Agreement mechanisms now in place;
  - continue preparing the process of analytical examination of the *acquis* and deciding on further steps after reporting to the European Council on progress achieved;
  - preparing a single financial framework for assistance as soon as possible;
  - preparing a bilateral agreement for facilitating its participation in Community programmes;
- the European Conference should continue to be used as the framework for discussing the future of the Union with the candidate countries;
- the Commission's proposed communication strategy should be implemented as a matter of priority in order to allay fears of enlargement, to inform about its benefits and to win over citizens' support.

The Strategy Paper 2000, and the full reports of the progress of the individual countries, is available on the Internet at: http://europa.eu.int/comm/enlargement.

The Treaty of Nice 2000, once it comes into force, will introduce institutional reform in preparation for enlargement of the Communities to 27 Member States. This includes all 13 applicants for membership (see above) excluding Turkey. It is anticipated that the first wave of enlargement will take place by 2004 at the latest.

THE SINGLE EUROPEAN ACT

The Single European Act (SEA) was a response to both development and the lack of it in the three Communities and was the first major amendment to the founding Treaties. The SEA is *not* a UK Act of Parliament; it is a Treaty which was concluded between the Member States, the purpose of which was to amend the three founding Treaties: ECSC, EEC and Euratom. It was signed in February 1986 and came into force on 1 July 1987.

A European Union?

The Preamble to the SEA set out the Member States' commitment to transform relations as a whole between the Member States into a European Union; a Union which would have activities way beyond the solely economic sphere. Political cooperation between the Member States was considered to be of paramount importance in the creation of this European Union.

The SEA separated provisions relating to political cooperation from those relating to economic integration. Those provisions relating to economic integration were to be implemented by amending the founding EEC Treaty. However, in relation to political cooperation, those provisions were to be implemented outside the existing Treaty. It was provided for the representatives of the Member States (i.e. Prime Minister/President; Foreign Secretary) to meet regularly for the purpose of drawing up common political objectives (through a body to be referred to as 'The European Council').

Therefore at one level (the economic level) policies were implemented through the structure of the European Economic Community (having its own special methods of decision making and enforcement), whereas political policies were achieved outside of this structure, through cooperation between the Member States; a kind of inter-governmental arrangement, which would not bind the Member States unless *all* the Member States were in agreement.

The main amendments made to the EEC Treaty consisted of the following.

Completing the internal market and new policy objectives

Since the signing of the Treaties in the 1950s, concerns about war in Western Europe and mass unemployment tended, by the mid-1970s and early 1980s, to have given way to pressure for greater consumer protection and protection at work. There were also growing anxieties about the degradation of the natural environment. The response to these new concerns was initially tackled at a national level, rather than Community level, which resulted in a whole range of different national standards for both goods and industrial production that seriously threatened the growth in a genuinely common market in goods and services. The development of a multiplicity of national standards was accompanied by a slowing down of the economies of all the Member States, following the explosion in oil prices in 1973. Implementing the recommendations of the Commission's White Paper, *Completing the Internal Market* (1985), the SEA attempted to tackle this problem on two fronts. It extended the competence of the EEC to enable it to legislate for the whole area of the Community on: environmental matters, economic and social cohesion, and in the fields of health and safety; consumer protection; academic, professional and vocational qualifications; public procurement (i.e. competition for public contracts); VAT; excise duties and frontier controls; and research and technological development. It also aimed to give the completion of the Common Market a new boost by setting a target for creating a new internal market by removing all the remaining legal, technical and physical obstacles to the free movement of goods, persons, services and capital by 1 January 1993. This objective was set out in Art 8a of the EEC Treaty (added by the SEA), where the internal market was described as 'an area without internal frontiers in which the free movement of goods, persons, services and capital is ensured' (Art 8a was renumbered Art 7a by the Treaty on European Union and Art 14 by the Treaty of Amsterdam (see below)).

Increasing the European Parliament's legislative powers

Until 1979 members of the European Assembly were nominated by their national parliaments. The first direct elections to the newly named European Parliament took place in June 1979 (see Chapter 3), and their effect was that the Parliament became the only directly elected European institution. It had, at the same time, only a consultative status in the legislative process (see Chapter 4). It was often said that the European Commission proposed legislation and the Council of Ministers disposed of it (i.e. adopted it). This situation generated pressure on the Member States to address the 'democratic deficit' in the Communities' decision making. The SEA added a new 'cooperation procedure' to the Treaties, giving the Parliament a much more important role in the legislative process in four areas:

● prohibition of discrimination on the grounds of nationality (now Art 12 EC Treaty, previously Art 6);
● the achievement of the free movement of workers (now Art 40 EC Treaty, formerly Art 49);
● promotion of the right of establishment (now Art 44 EC Treaty, formerly Art 54); and
● measures for implementation of the internal market (now Art 95 EC Treaty, formerly Art 100a).

This new legislative procedure required the Council of Ministers to cooperate with the Parliament. The Parliament would for the first time have a real input into the legislative process (being able to propose amendments). In addition to Parliamentary input, legislative measures in these four areas could be adopted by the Council by 'qualified majority' rather than unanimity, thus overriding the objections of a Member State. The legislative process will be considered in detail in Chapter 4.

THE TREATY ON EUROPEAN UNION

The next step in the constitutional development of the Communities was the Treaty on European Union (TEU), which was negotiated at Maastricht and signed on 7 February 1992. It came into force on 1 November 1993 once it had been ratified by the Member States. A summary of the main provisions is followed by a more substantive discussion of the key features of the TEU.

Summary

The Treaty was intended to extend further the competencies of the Communities by creating two new 'pillars' outside the legally binding, formal decision-making processes of the three 'old' Communities, which continued to exist. The two new 'pillars' of the European Union were Common Foreign and Security Policy and Cooperation in the fields of Justice and Home Affairs. These two pillars of the Union were really only intergovernmental in character, and, like the foreign policy provisions of the SEA, created a broad framework for cooperation rather than a process for the making of binding rules. The whole structure – including the old Communities and the two new pillars – was called 'the European Union' (EU).

Of more constitutional and legal significance were the amendments to the EEC Treaty. The EEC became simply 'the European Community' (EC), marking the legal recognition of the reality that the activities and competencies of the former economic Community ranged far beyond its original economic goals. The European Parliament's cooperative powers were enlarged further by the conciliation procedure which, for the first time, gave the Parliament the power to veto legislation in certain circumstances. The reunification of Germany in 1990 was reflected by increased representation in the Parliament, so that Germany now had the largest group of MEPs. It did not, however, gain any more votes in the qualified majority voting procedure within the Council of Ministers (see Chapter 4). A further institution was also created, the Committee of the Regions, having a role analogous to the Economic and Social Committee (see Chapter 3).

The central economic feature of the TEU was the section designed to lead to economic and monetary union by three stages. The United Kingdom and Denmark opted out of compulsory participation in the third stage. The United Kingdom also refused to participate in the social chapter, which incorporated principles previously agreed by the heads of government in the Community Charter of Fundamental Social Rights of Workers in Strasbourg in December 1989 on behalf of all the Member States, except the United Kingdom.

Some of the key features of the TEU will be considered further, below.

The TEU provisions

The TEU consisted of seven *titles* as follows:

- Title I: Common provisions *(Arts A to F)*
- Title II: Provisions amending the EEC Treaty *(Art G)*
- Title III: Provisions amending the ECSC Treaty *(Art H)*
- Title IV: Provisions amending the Euratom Treaty *(Art I)*
- Title V: Provisions on a Common Foreign and Security Policy *(Arts J.1 to J.11)*
- Title VI: Provisions on Cooperation in Justice and Home Affairs *(Arts K.1 to K.9)*
- Title VII: Final Provisions *(Arts L to S)*

Titles II, III and IV of the TEU simply amended the three founding Treaties (as previously amended by the SEA).

The European Union

Title I contained common provisions which set out the basic objectives of the TEU. This title did not amend the founding Treaties, but simply set out the basic aims and principles of the newly formed European Union.

The three pillars of the European Union

Article A TEU provided for the establishing of a European Union:

> The Union shall be founded on the European Communities, supplemented by the policies and forms of cooperation established by this Treaty.

It followed from this that the European Union (EU) was to be founded upon three pillars:

- The European Communities – EC; ECSC; Euratom
- Common Foreign and Security Policy – Title V (Art J)
- Cooperation in Justice and Home Affairs – Title VI (Art K).

The structure of the European Union could be represented diagrammatically as shown in Figure 1.1.

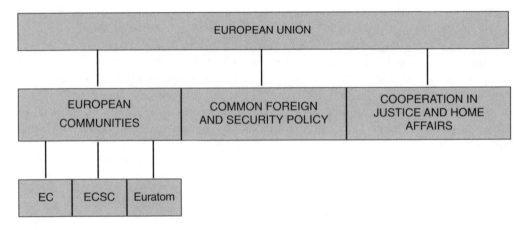

Figure 1.1 The structure of the European Union

Objectives of the European Union

Article B set out the objectives of the Union, some of which mirrored those contained in the founding Treaties as amended.

Protection of human rights

Article F(2) TEU provided that the Union would respect fundamental rights 'as guaranteed by the European Convention for the Protection of Human Rights and Fundamental Freedoms ... as general principles of Community law'.

However, Art L TEU provided that all the common provisions (which included Art F(2) TEU) were not justiciable by the European Court of Justice, i.e. the Court did not have the power to rule on their application or validity. Despite this, it was possible that the Court of Justice would take the common provisions into account, including Art F(2), when interpreting the founding Treaties, as amended. This is considered further in Chapter 5.

The two intergovernmental pillars

The second and third pillars of the Union, not being inserted into the amended founding Treaties, remained outside the formal structures of the European Communities. These two pillars, as previously mentioned, related to a Common Foreign and Security Policy and to Cooperation in the fields of Justice and Home Affairs.

Although being intergovernmental in nature, and thus falling outside the formal Community structure, they did have a connection in that some of the Community institutions (in particular the Council of Ministers) played a part in these policy areas.

It was argued that, over a period of time, these two pillars would be subsumed into the formal Community structure. This would be achieved by amending the founding Treaties. If this happened, all Community institutions could play a part in these policy areas, perhaps with a greater role for the European Parliament. Germany's former Chancellor Kohl favoured this approach. This approach had already occurred in relation to the Single European Currency policy, which had initially been introduced on an intergovernmental basis by the SEA, but was subsequently incorporated into the formal EC structure (with its own special decision-making and enforcement powers) following amendments to the EC Treaty by the TEU. This policy is now governed by Arts 98–124 EC (previously Arts 102a–109m pre-Treaty of Amsterdam).

Under the TEU, prior to its amendment by the Treaty of Amsterdam, the Court of Justice was excluded from exercising its powers in matters dealt with under these two pillars (except for certain *very limited* exceptions) – Art L TEU.

As its name suggests, the second pillar (Common Foreign and Security Policy) provides for joint foreign action and security (i.e. defence) action by the Member States. This action would be adopted by a *unanimous* vote of the Council of Ministers. However, there was provision for the Council to provide that certain decisions could be taken by a qualified majority vote (see Art J.3, para 2 TEU). There was minimal involvement of the Parliament and the Commission in the process. Art L TEU excluded the Court of Justice from ruling on these provisions.

The third pillar (Cooperation in Justice and Home Affairs) provided for cooperation in policy areas such as asylum, immigration, 'third country' nationals, international crime (e.g. drug trafficking) and various forms of judicial cooperation. Action would again be taken by the Council of Ministers acting unanimously, with very limited provision for qualified majority voting (see Art K.4, para 3 TEU). There was very little involvement of the Parliament and the Commission. Once again, Art L TEU applied to exclude the Court of Justice from ruling on these provisions.

Amendments to the EEC Treaty

Following amendments made by the TEU, as will be discussed below, the EEC Treaty covered tasks and activities which were not purely economic-based and therefore the TEU amended the title of the EEC Treaty to simply EC (i.e. European Community) Treaty. From here on the EEC Treaty will be referred to as the EC Treaty.

The EC Treaty is the most important of the three founding Treaties. Amendments made to the EC Treaty by Art G (i.e. Title II) TEU were as follows:

- the creation of a citizenship of the European Union (former Art 8 EC Treaty, now Art 17 following renumbering by the Treaty of Amsterdam (see below));
- common economic and monetary policy, with a timetable for the implementation of a common currency (formerly Arts 102a–109m EC Treaty, now Arts 98–124);
- the adoption of the principle of subsidiarity (formerly Art 3b EC Treaty, now Art 5);
- the amendment of the decision-making process – extension of qualified majority voting for the adoption of Council acts into new policy areas, and further powers given to Parliament; and
- new areas of tasks and activities were introduced (Arts 2 and 3 EC Treaty were amended).

Articles 2 and 3 EC Treaty, as amended by the TEU, extended the tasks and activities of the European Community beyond the purely economic and incorporated political and social goals. Article 2 (post-TEU, but pre-Treaty of Amsterdam) provided that:

> The Community shall have as its task, by establishing a common market and an economic and monetary union and by implementing the common policies or activities referred to in Articles 3 and 3a, to promote throughout the Community a harmonious and balanced development of economic activities, sustainable and non-inflationary growth respecting the environment, a high degree of convergence of economic performance, a high level of employment and of social protection, the raising of the standard of living and quality of life, and economic and social cohesion and solidarity among Member States.

Article 3 (post-TEU, but pre-Treaty of Amsterdam) provided that:

> For the purposes set out in Article 2, the activities of the Community shall include, as provided in this Treaty and in accordance with the timetable set out therein:
>
> (a) the elimination, as between Member States, of customs duties and quantitative restrictions on the import and export of goods, and of all measures having equivalent effect;
> (b) a common commercial policy;
> (c) an internal market characterised by the abolition, as between Member States, of obstacles to the free movement of goods, persons, services and capital;
> (d) measures concerning the entry and movement of persons in the internal market as provided for in Article 100c;
> (e) a common policy in the sphere of agriculture and fisheries;
> (f) a common policy in the sphere of transport;
> (g) a system ensuring that competition in the internal market is not distorted;
> (h) the approximation of the laws of the Member States to the extent required for the functioning of the common market;
> (i) a policy in the social sphere comprising a European Social Fund;
> (j) the strengthening of economic and social cohesion;
> (k) a policy in the sphere of the environment;
> (l) the strengthening of the competitiveness of Community industry;
> (m) the promotion of research and technological development;
> (n) encouragement for the establishment and development of trans-European networks;
> (o) a contribution to the attainment of a high level of health protection;
> (p) a contribution to education and training of quality and to the flowering of the cultures of the Member States;

(q) a policy in the sphere of development cooperation;

(r) the association of the overseas countries and territories in order to increase trade and promote jointly economic and social development;

(s) a contribution to the strengthening of consumer protection;

(t) measures in the spheres of energy, civil protection and tourism.

Article 2 provided that the Community's tasks included the promotion of 'a high level of employment and of social protection, the raising of the standard of living and quality of life, and economic and social cohesion and solidarity'. This is indicative of the fact that the European Community now had tasks and activities which were not purely economic-based, hence its amendment from EEC to EC.

Protocols

Annexed to the EC Treaty as amended by the TEU were a number of protocols. Protocols form part of the Treaty by virtue of Art 311 EC Treaty (previously Art 239):

> The protocols annexed to this Treaty by common accord of the Member States shall form an integral part thereof.

Two highly controversial protocols provided for the United Kingdom to opt out of certain Community policies which the UK Government of the day found unacceptable:

Protocol on social policy

All the Member States, except the United Kingdom's Conservative Government, wanted the EC Treaty amended to provide greater Community competence to legislate in the area of social policy (e.g. employee protection rights). The United Kingdom objected to this and would not compromise its position. Therefore, the United Kingdom agreed to a protocol providing for the remaining Member States to enter into an agreement which would permit them to have recourse to the Community institutions and Treaty procedures and mechanisms in adopting acts and decisions in the social policy area not otherwise covered by the Treaties. This agreement was annexed to the protocol (and was labelled: Agreement on Social Policy).

Following the election of a Labour Government in the United Kingdom on 1 May 1997, it was announced that the United Kingdom would no longer retain its opt-out, and would take the necessary steps to be bound by the Agreement. This was put into effect by the Treaty of Amsterdam incorporating an amended version of the Social Agreement into the EC Treaty (this is discussed further, below).

Protocol on certain provisions relating to the United Kingdom of Great Britain and Northern Ireland

Under the SEA, economic and monetary policy, including working towards a single European currency, was introduced outside the formal structures of the Communities, to be dealt with on an intergovernmental basis. Thus each Member State retained direct control of its destiny. However, the TEU amended the EC Treaty to provide for this policy area (including a timetable for the introduction of a single European currency) to be dealt with under the formal structure of the Communities, thus removing such control from the Member States. The United Kingdom was not ready to sign up to full economic and monetary union, being somewhat cautious about agreeing to the single currency timetable.

This protocol provides that the United Kingdom will not be:

> ... obliged or committed to move to the third stage of Economic and Monetary Union without a separate decision to do so by its Government and Parliament.

It is often referred to as the United Kingdom's opt-out from the single currency, but it is more akin to an 'opt-in'. Denmark has a similar opt-out to the United Kingdom's (this is provided for by the 'Protocol on certain provisions relating to Denmark'). Denmark rejected entry to the single currency in a referendum held on 28 September 2000 by a 53 per cent to 46 per cent majority. Sweden negotiated a similar opt-out to the United Kingdom and Denmark when it became a member of the Community on 1 January 1995.

The third stage was the final stage on the road to Monetary Union, when the Member States decided which of them had met the criteria laid down in the Treaty for the forming of a common currency. The third stage started on 1 January 1999 (see Art 121(4) (previously Art 109j(4)) EC Treaty). All Member States satisfied the criteria, except Greece. However, Greece has now been adjudged to have satisfied the economic criteria and will join the original 11 qualifying states.

A European Central Bank has been established which sets a common European interest rate for these 12 Member States. The currencies of these 12 Member States have fixed conversion rates, quoted in Euros. On 1 January 2002 foreign exchange operations will be completed in Euros, and Euro banknotes and coins will be placed in circulation. On 1 July 2002 national currencies in these 12 Member States will no longer be legal tender and all transactions will be completed in Euros.

The current UK Government has indicated its desire to join the single currency, but this will be subject to a positive vote of approval by the UK electorate in a referendum. This referendum will not be held before the next general election which will be held on 7 June 2001. Therefore, for the foreseeable future, the United Kingdom, Denmark and Sweden will remain outside the Euro-zone.

THE TREATY OF AMSTERDAM

The Treaty of Amsterdam (ToA) was agreed by the Member States in June 1997 and was formally signed by the Member States in Amsterdam on 2 October 1997. This Treaty was concluded on behalf of the United Kingdom by the Labour Government which had been elected to office on 1 May 1997. The Treaty came into force on 1 May 1999 once it had been ratified by all 15 Member States. A summary of the main provisions is followed by a more substantive discussion of the key features of the Treaty.

Summary

It was anticipated that the 1997 Treaty of Amsterdam (ToA) would take the first major steps towards restructuring the institutions of the European Union. This was widely seen as essential if the institutions, which were originally set up for a European Community of six states, were to continue functioning effectively in an enlarged European Union of 20 plus states. In the event, the Treaty achieved little in the way of institutional reform. A limit was set on the number of MEPs in the European Parliament, the powers of the President of the Commission were made more specific and the administrative support for the Council of Ministers was strengthened. The difficult decisions, which further enlargement will inevitably bring, were postponed. These decisions have been addressed, to a large extent, by the Treaty of Nice (see below).

The ToA did, however, broaden the objectives of the Union, moving it further away from the narrower economic base of its early years. There are now specific commitments to a number of important non-economic goals, with much more emphasis placed on the rights and duties of Union citizenship, and the Union's commitment to human and civil rights. Decisions within the Union are now to be taken 'as openly as possible', and as closely as possible to the citizen. The Union now firmly proclaims, in the common provisions of the revised Treaty on European Union, that it is founded on respect for human rights, democracy and the rule of law, and respect for these principles has been made a condition of application for membership. Under a new Art 7 TEU, the rights of Member States can now be suspended if the Council of Ministers finds that a Member State has been in 'serious and persistent breach' of its obligation to respect civil, political and human rights. Article 2 EC Treaty now describes equality between men and women as one of the principal objects of the Community. Article 13 EC Treaty now expressly confers power on the Community to legislate to combat discrimination based on sex, racial or ethnic origin, religion or belief, disability, age or sexual orientation. Environmental protection has become one of the principal aims of the Community.

The TEU had created a three-pillar structure for the Union, under which the old Communities (the EC, ECSC and Euratom) comprised the first pillar, Common Foreign and Security Policy (CFSP) the second, and Justice and Home Affairs (JHA) the third. Under the TEU, only the first pillar of the old Communities used the legally binding decision-making structures described in Chapter 4. Decisions made under the other two pillars were taken 'intergovernmentally', i.e. politically, and they could not be enforced or challenged in the Court of Justice. The sharpness of this division between legally binding decisions and the political decision-making process has, unfortunately, been blurred by the ToA. A large part of JHA (third pillar) has been brought within the Communities (first pillar) framework. Decisions in what remains of the third pillar (Police Cooperation in Criminal Matters) now have a limited input from the European Parliament and potential involvement by the Court of Justice. Decision-making in relation to the second pillar (CFSP) remains political, outside the formal, legally binding Community decision-making structure. Important changes were also made in the Communities (first pillar) decision-making structure, giving the European Parliament even greater powers to amend and block legislative proposals. These changes are examined in Chapter 4. For anyone with any prior knowledge of Community law, the most obvious change wrought by the ToA is the renumbering of the EC Treaty. All the familiar landmarks have gone: the obligation of Member States to observe Community law is now Art 10 EC Treaty, and not Art 5; proceedings against Member States are to be brought under Art 226 EC Treaty, and not Art 169; references to the Court of Justice under what used to be Art 177 EC Treaty are now to be brought under Art 234. The wording of these provisions remains identical in most cases. A table of equivalent provisions is published at the beginning of this book. Care must be taken when using old textbooks, and referring even to recent cases of the Court of Justice, in marrying the old provisions up to the new. The new numbering structure contained in Art 12 ToA came into effect on 1 May 1999. For some time, however, it will be necessary to be aware of both the old and new numbering. Subsequent chapters of this book are based on the new Treaty numbers but, where relevant, cross references to the old Treaty numbers are made.

ToA provisions

The Treaty is divided into three parts:

- Part One (Arts 1–5) contains substantive amendments to, *inter alia*, the TEU and the EC Treaty.
- Part Two (Arts 6–11) contains provisions to simplify the TEU and Community Treaties, which includes the deleting of lapsed provisions.
- Part Three (Arts 12–15) contains general and final provisions, which includes provisions which renumber articles of the TEU and the EC Treaty. This renumbering will create some confusion because case law of the Court of Justice and legislation which predates the coming into force of the ToA will refer to the old numbering.

Amendments made to the TEU by the ToA will be considered first, followed by those made to the EC Treaty.

Amendments to the TEU

The TEU articles have been renumbered by the ToA. Amendments made will be considered under the relevant Titles of the TEU.

Title I – Common provisions

The articles of Title I have been renumbered from Arts A–F TEU to 1–7 TEU; the provisions themselves have also been amended. In particular, Art 6(1) TEU now provides that:

> The Union is founded on the principles of liberty, democracy, respect for human rights and fundamental freedoms, and the rule of law, principles which are upheld by the Member States.

A new Art 6(3) TEU provides that:

> The Union shall respect the national identities of its Member States.

A new Art 7 TEU has been inserted which provides for the Council of Ministers to suspend certain rights under the Treaty (including voting rights) of any Member State if the Council determines that the Member State has committed a 'serious and persistent breach' of the Art 6 TEU principles.

As discussed above, the former Art F(2) TEU (now Art 6(2)) provides that:

> The Union shall respect fundamental rights as guaranteed by the European Convention of Human Rights and Fundamental Freedoms ... as general principles of Community law.

The former Art L TEU provided that all the common provisions (which included the former Art F(2)) were not justiciable by the Court of Justice. Article L TEU has been renumbered Art 46 and has been amended by the ToA to provide that Art 6(2) TEU shall now be justiciable by the Court of Justice, meaning that the Court can explicitly take account of the Convention rights.

Titles II, III, IV – Amendments to the founding Treaties

The articles of Titles II, III and IV have simply been renumbered from Arts G, H and I TEU, to Arts 8, 9 and 10 TEU, respectively.

The three pillars of the European Union

It was discussed above that the EU was founded upon three pillars:

- The European Communities – EC; ECSC; Euratom
- Common Foreign and Security Policy (Title V)
- Cooperation in Justice and Home Affairs (Title VI).

The major substantive change made by the ToA is to amend this structure and incorporate part of the third pillar (Justice and Home Affairs) into the EC Treaty, thus forming part of the first pillar. This will be discussed further below, when considering the amendments made to the EC Treaty by the ToA.

Title V – Common Foreign and Security Policy

The articles of Title V have been renumbered from J.1–J.11 TEU to Arts 11–28 TEU. This remains the second pillar of the EU. Although the ToA has made some amendments to the main provisions of Title V, the role of the European Parliament has not changed and the exclusion of the Court of Justice from adjudicating on the provisions remains. The Secretary General of the Council of Ministers will now act as the 'High Representative' (i.e. the spokesperson) for the Common Foreign and Security Policy.

Title VI – Police and Judicial Cooperation in Criminal Matters

The articles of Title VI have been renumbered from K.1–K.9 TEU to Arts 29–42 TEU. This is the third pillar of the EU and, as discussed above, it should be noted that the title has changed from 'Cooperation in Justice and Home Affairs' to 'Police and Judicial Cooperation in Criminal Matters'. This is to reflect the fact that those provisions of the former third pillar relating to visas, asylum, immigration and other policies relating to the free movement of persons have been incorporated into the EC Treaty with the insertion of a new Title VI EC Treaty.

The new third pillar states the Union's objective as being able to 'provide citizens with a high level of safety within an area of freedom, security and justice' (Art 29 TEU), and to develop 'common action' among the Member States in the field of police and judicial cooperation and by preventing and combating racism and xenophobia.

Article 29 TEU stipulates that this will be achieved by:

> Preventing and combating crime, organised or otherwise, in particular terrorism, trafficking in persons and offences against children, illicit drug trafficking and illicit arms trafficking, corruption and fraud ...

The European Parliament is given an increased consultative role in the decision-making process and the Court of Justice will generally have jurisdiction over most of the provisions. The diagram in Figure 1.2 illustrates the structure of the EU, following the ToA's amendments to the third pillar.

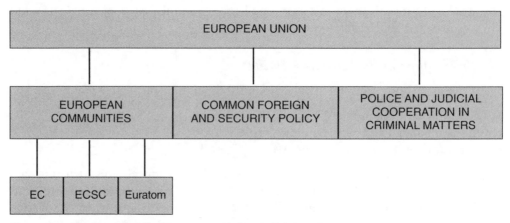

Figure 1.2 Structure of the European Union following ToA

Title VII – Closer cooperation

This new title was inserted into the TEU by the ToA and contains three articles (Arts 43–45) which enable Member States to establish closer cooperation between themselves and to use the institutions, procedures and mechanisms of the TEU and EC Treaty. However, Art 43(c) TEU provides that these provisions can only be used as a 'last resort where the objectives of the ... Treaties could not be attained by applying the relevant procedures laid down therein'.

These provisions will therefore allow flexibility in the future development of the ECs and the EU, recognising the right of Member States to 'opt-out' from *new* policy initiatives not otherwise covered by the Treaties (this formalises the situation whereby the United Kingdom opted out of the Social Policy Agreement and single currency, for example).

A similar flexibility clause has been inserted into the EC Treaty (Art 11 (see below)).

Title VIII – Final provisions

The articles of Title VIII have been renumbered from L–S TEU to Arts 46–53 TEU. Article 49 TEU (previously Art O) has amended the procedure for the admission of new Member States. New Member States must have respect for the fundamental principles set out in Art 6 TEU (see above); the Council of Ministers will act unanimously after receiving the opinion of the Commission and the assent of the European Parliament.

Amendments to the EC Treaty

Article 2 EC Treaty has been amended to include new tasks:

- promotion of equality between men and women
- a high level of protection and improvement of the quality of the environment
- promotion of a high degree of competitiveness
- economic development which must be 'sustainable' as well as 'balanced and harmonious'.

The new Art 2 EC Treaty provides that:

> The Community shall have as its task, by establishing a common market and an economic and monetary union and by implementing common policies or activities referred to in Articles 3 and 4, to promote throughout the Community a harmonious, balanced and sustainable development of economic activities, a high level of employment and of social protection, equality between men and women, sustainable and non inflationary growth, a high degree of competitiveness and convergence of economic performance, a high level of protection and improvement of the quality of the environment, the raising of the standard of living and quality of life, and economic and social cohesion and solidarity among Member States.

Article 3 EC Treaty lists the activities of the Community which can be undertaken in order to achieve the tasks set out in Art 2. Article 3 has been amended to include a new activity (the other activities already cover the new Art 2 tasks):

> The promotion of coordination between employment policies of the Member States with a view to enhancing their effectiveness by developing a coordinated strategy for employment.

A new Art 3(2) EC Treaty provides that:

> In all the activities referred to in this Article, the Community shall aim to eliminate inequalities, and to promote equality, between men and women.

The other main amendments to the EC Treaty by the ToA include:

- Article 11 EC Treaty inserts a flexibility clause similar to that in Title VII TEU (discussed above) allowing Member States to establish closer cooperation between themselves and to make use of the institutions, procedures and mechanisms laid down in the EC Treaty, provided the cooperation proposed does not, *inter alia*, 'concern areas which fall within the exclusive competence of the Community'.
- Article 13 EC Treaty (previously Art 6a) provides a new non-discriminatory provision which confers legislative competence on the Community to combat

discrimination based on sex, racial or ethnic origin, religion or belief, disability, age, or sexual orientation.

● Articles 61–69 (Title IV) EC Treaty incorporate part of the former third pillar of the European Union which covers visas, asylum, immigration and other policies relating to the free movement of persons.

● Articles 125–130 (Title VIII) EC Treaty insert a new title on employment, reflecting the new activity set out in Art 3 EC Treaty.

● Articles 136–143 EC Treaty incorporate an amended version of the Social Policy Agreement, which will apply to *all* Member States; at Amsterdam the newly elected United Kingdom Labour Government agreed to end its opt-out.

● Titles XIII and XIV EC Treaty on public health and consumer protection, respectively, have been enhanced.

● The decision-making process has been amended and the European Parliament has been given a greater role in more policy areas.

● Minor amendments have been made to the composition and/or role of some of the Community institutions.

Conclusion

The TEU provided for the European Union to be founded upon three pillars; these pillars were amended by the ToA. We are primarily concerned with the first pillar, i.e. the European Communities pillar. The European Communities comprise three separate and distinct Communities, the most important being the European Community (formerly called the European Economic Community) which was established by the Treaty Establishing the European Community.

Even though we confine ourselves to a consideration of the EC Treaty, it should not be forgotten that the ECs and the EU have evolved over a period of less than 50 years. During this time the change that has been brought about has resulted in more, not less, integration. What started off as a predominantly economic market now has a political and social agenda. Each time the founding Treaties are amended the end result is that more areas of competence are transferred by the Member States to the Community.

THE TREATY OF NICE 2000

The Treaty of Nice (ToN) was agreed by the Member States in December 2000. It was formally signed by the Member States on 26 February 2001 and will come into force once it has been ratified by them. Given this fact, this book is written on the basis that the ToN is not in force. However, changes which will be made once it comes into force will be discussed, where relevant, in subsequent chapters.

A summary of the main amendments which will be made to the EC Treaty and TEU by the ToN follows.

Institutional reform

The main reason for a new Treaty amending the EC Treaty and TEU was to reform the institutions in preparation for enlargement of membership of the Communities.

The EC Treaty will be amended to enable an enlarged membership of up to 27 Member States. The changes made will be discussed in Chapters 3 to 5.

Fundamental rights

Article 7 TEU provides for the suspension of a Member State's Treaty rights where there has been a 'serious and persistent' breach of the Art 6(1) TEU principles (i.e. the principles of liberty, democracy, respect for human rights and fundamental freedoms, and the rule of law). The ToN amends Art 7 to provide that the suspension can be imposed where the Council of Ministers votes by a four-fifths majority of its membership. Prior to the ToN it had required a unanimous vote by the Council. The role of the other institutions in this process has not been changed.

Security and defence

Article 25 TEU provides for the monitoring of the international situation within the areas covered by the second pillar (Common Foreign and Security Policy), and the development of associated policies. In a meeting of the European Council, immediately prior to the meeting where the ToN was agreed, a policy for the establishment of a European rapid reaction force was adopted. This 60,000-strong force will be used primarily for peacekeeping and emergency missions within the region. A declaration has been annexed to the ToN which states that the rapid reaction force should become operational quickly, and that a decision should be taken as soon as possible in 2001 to ensure that this occurs.

Eurojust

Articles 29 and 31 TEU have been amended to provide that in the application of the third pillar (provisions on Police and Judicial Cooperation in Criminal Matters) there shall be cooperation with, *inter alia*, the European Judicial Cooperation Unit (Eurojust). A declaration specifies that Eurojust shall comprise national prosecutors and magistrates (or police officers of equivalent competence) who are detached from each Member State.

Enhanced cooperation

Articles 43–45 (Title VII) TEU will be substantially amended to further the prospect of a minimum of eight Member States establishing closer cooperation between themselves and to use the institutions, procedures and mechanisms of the TEU and EC Treaty. Like the existing provisions, the amended provisions provide that closer cooperation can be undertaken only if it is 'aimed at furthering the objectives of the Union and the Community, at protecting and serving its interests'. The new provision also requires that 'enhanced cooperation may be engaged in only as a last resort, when it has been established within the Council that the objectives of such cooperation cannot be attained within a reasonable period by applying the relevant provisions of the Treaties'. This is discussed further, below.

New policies

Few new policies have been introduced, although some polices have been refined. One new policy concerns economic, financial and technical cooperation with third states following the insertion of a new Title XXI EC Treaty. It is stated that this new policy shall 'contribute to the general objective of developing and consolidating democracy and the rule of law, and to that of respecting human rights and fundamental freedoms'.

Decision-making process

Some legal bases for the adoption of secondary Community instruments (see Chapter 2) which originally required a unanimous vote by the Council of Ministers in order to be adopted, have been amended to provide for their adoption by a qualified majority. In addition the role of the Parliament has been enhanced.

A TWO-SPEED EUROPE?

The idea of a 'two-speed Europe' was much canvassed before the Amsterdam Conference. This would mean that those states who were keen to embrace closer political and economic cooperation would be free to do so, while the other, more reluctant states could follow at their own pace. To some extent, this had already happened in relation to Monetary Union, with the United Kingdom, Denmark and Sweden negotiating opt-outs (see above).

The ToA went some way to giving formal recognition to this kind of 'variable geometry'. Under the new Art 11 EC Treaty, the Council of Ministers may authorise 'closer cooperation' between Member States. The Council is to act on a proposal from the Commission. The use of Art 11 is, however, strictly limited and closer cooperation between Member States cannot be undertaken if the area in question is already part of the Community's exclusive competence – i.e. if it affects Community policies, actions or programmes; if it would lead to discrimination between nationals of Member States; or if it would restrict trade between Member States. It is very doubtful, given these limitations, if much use will be made of the new provision and it is unlikely that the Commission will want to initiate such a process of separate development. This will arguably remain the case once the amendments made by the ToN come into force (see above).

There are two main reasons for this. First, a European Union in which there are different rules between the 'outer' and 'inner' areas will be extremely difficult to operate in practice, and many of these difficulties are going to become apparent between those states who have adopted the single currency, in the so-called 'Euroland', and those outside it. In fact, it is likely that the new currency will be extensively used even outside the Euro states. The Commission will be unlikely to wish to exacerbate these difficulties by having yet another body of rules operating in different parts of the Union. Second, any further development of an inner 'core' of Member States moving towards greater integration will tend to accentuate what is already a tendency in the Union: the already serious drift of commerce and industry towards the geographical centre of Western Europe. If Germany, with the most powerful economy and the largest market of all the Member States, is in the 'inner circle' businesses will tend to re-establish themselves nearer to the heart of Europe. Businesses from outside the Union seeking to jump over the Community's external tariff wall will tend to look to the centre rather than to states on the periphery for new locations. There are already indications that, despite the greater enthusiasm shown by the Labour Government for the European enterprise, the United Kingdom's failure to join the single currency in the first wave is making it less attractive to external investment. For both these reasons, the Commission is likely to set its face against any further measures which may make the integration of European markets more rather than less difficult, which is likely to be the case if any body of rules is adopted which applies only in part of the Union.

THE EUROPEAN ECONOMIC AREA

The remaining EFTA (European Free Trade Association) states continued to work together as a free-trade area after the departure of Ireland, Denmark and the United Kingdom in 1973. On 2 May 1992 the then seven EFTA states, and the EC and its Member States signed an agreement to establish the European Economic Area (EEA). This agreement, which some initially saw as an alternative to full membership of the European Communities, was intended to integrate the EFTA states *economically* into the Community without giving them a role in its institutions. The EEA gave the EFTA states access for their goods, services, workers and capital to the markets of the Community. Equally, the same facilities were granted by EFTA states in their territories to Member States of the Community. Only Switzerland refused to participate in the EEA, after a hostile national referendum. In this new trading area, all the rules of the EC apply, although the Member States of EFTA are not represented in any of the EC institutions and do not participate in the EC's decision-making process. There are, however, four new bodies to coordinate the functioning of this new trading area:

- the EEA Council;
- Joint Committee;
- Joint Parliamentary Committee; and
- Consultative Committee.

The EEA came into effect on 1 January 1994. On 1 January 1995, three of the remaining EFTA members became full members of the EU, so that the EEA states now comprise existing 15 EU Member States, together with Iceland, Liechtenstein and Norway.

THE EUROPEAN CONVENTION ON HUMAN RIGHTS, THE COUNCIL OF EUROPE AND THE COURT OF HUMAN RIGHTS: A STRUCTURE OUTSIDE THE COMMUNITIES AND THE UNION

It is important to distinguish the international structure created by the European Convention on Human Rights from the quite separate supranational institutions of the EC. Newspapers talk loosely about taking a case 'to Europe', without identifying whether or not the case is a human rights matter involving the Convention on Human

Rights and to be dealt with by the Court of Human Rights in Strasbourg, or a matter of Community law to be referred to the Court of Justice in Luxembourg. Decisions made by the Human Rights Court are not legally binding on national courts, although they will be taken into account by these courts. Decisions by the Court of Justice are legally binding on all national courts.

The European Convention on Human Rights was drafted in 1950 under the auspices of the Council of Europe, an international organisation composed of 21 Western European states. It is intended to uphold common political traditions of individual civil liberties and the rule of law. All the Member States of the EC are members together with the emerging democracies of Eastern Europe. Although the Convention became part of English law on 2 October 2000 under the Human Rights Act 1998, the Convention does *not* automatically prevail where there is a clear conflict, whereas, as we shall see (in Chapter 9), under some circumstances Community obligations *are* part of national law *and* prevail over it in the event of conflict.

Decisions of the Court of Human Rights may result in compensation being paid by the UK Government to victims of human rights abuses, but such decisions are not binding on the Government, and may simply be ignored. The Court of Justice, like national courts, takes account of the Convention when interpreting Community law. Unlike national courts, however, the Court of Justice treats the Convention as a source of basic Community law principles (see Chapter 5). The European Convention on Human Rights has been formally accepted in the TEU as part of the Community's fundamental principles, but it has no application under Community law to matters outside the Community's legal competence, and thus the recognition of the provisions of the Convention as a source of law falls far short of full incorporation into Community law. Although the Convention is recognised by the ToA as an important source of Community law, it remains the case that it is only important when interpreting and applying *Community* law. However, although the Convention has only a limited application to Community law, the decision by the United Kingdom to incorporate the Convention by the Human Rights Act 1998 means that it will be unlawful for courts or tribunals and any person whose functions are of a public nature in the United Kingdom to act in a way which is incompatible with Convention rights. Unlike the position of Community law, however, which has immediate primacy, if there is a clear conflict between a United Kingdom statute and one of the articles of the Convention, the United Kingdom courts will only be able to make a 'declaration of incompatability'. Ministers will then have to ensure that the offending legislation is amended to give full effect to the Convention.

Further reading

Craig, P., 'The Treaty of Amsterdam: a brief guide' [1998] PL 351.
Craig, P. and De Burca, G. (1998) *EU Law Text, Cases and Materials* (2nd edn), OUP, Chapter 1.
Dehousse, R., 'European Institutional Architecture after Amsterdam' (1998) 35 CML Rev 595.
Duff, A. (1997) *Reforming the European Union*, The Federal Trust, Chapters 1 and 2.
Hobsbawm, E. (1994) *Age of Extremes: The Short Twentieth Century*, Michael Joseph, Chapters 2, 3 and 8.
Lasok, D. (1998) *Law and Institutions of the European Union*, Butterworths, Chapter 1.

Mancini, G.F., 'The Making of a Constitution for Europe' (1989) 26 CML Rev 595.

Meyring, B., 'Intergovernmentalism and Supranationality: two stereotypes for a complex reality' (1997) 22 EL Rev 221.

Peers, S., 'Taking Supremacy Seriously' (1998) 23 EL Rev 146.

Steiner, J. and Woods, L. (2000) *Textbook on EC Law* (7th edn), Blackstone Press, Chapter 1.

Szyszczak, E., 'Making Europe more relevant to its Citizens' (1996) 21 EL Rev 351.

Tillotson, J. (2000) *European Community Law: Text, Cases and Materials* (3rd edn), Cavendish Publishing Ltd, Chapters 1–3.

Usher, J.A., 'Variable Geometry or Concentric Circles: Patterns for the European Union' (1996) 46 ICLQ 243.

Verhoeven, A., 'How Democratic Need European Union Members Be?' (1998) 23 EL Rev 217.

Weatherill, S., (2000) *Cases and Materials on EC Law* (5th edn), Blackstone Press, Chapter 1.

Weigall, D. and Stirk, A. (eds) (1992) *The Origins and Development of the European Community*, Leicester University Press.

Chapter 2

SOURCES OF COMMUNITY LAW

THE SOURCES

There are six principal sources of Community law:

- The Treaties establishing the three European Communities and the European Union.
- Secondary legislation (and 'soft law') made under the Treaties.
- Related Treaties made between the Member States.
- International Treaties negotiated by the Community under powers conferred on it by the Treaties.
- Decisions of the European Court of Justice.
- General principles of law and fundamental rights upon which the constitutional laws of the Member States are based.

THE TREATIES ESTABLISHING THE COMMUNITIES AND THE UNION

The three founding Treaties, as amended principally by the SEA, TEU, ToA and ToN, together with the TEU which established the European Union, form the constitution of the European Communities and the Union and are therefore an important source of Community law. The EC Treaty is the most extensive of the three founding Treaties and will be considered further. Although the EC Treaty does not purport to create the constitution of a federal state, it does, in some respects, have that effect, and has been interpreted in that way by the Court of Justice. In Opinion 1/91 on the Draft Agreement between the EEC (renamed EC by the TEU) and EFTA (the European Free Trade Association (see Chapter 1)) the Court said:

> The EEC Treaty [renamed the EC Treaty by the TEU], albeit concluded in the form of an international agreement, nonetheless constitutes the constitutional charter of a Community based on the rule of law. As the Court of Justice has consistently held, the Community Treaties established a new legal order for the benefit of which the States had limited their sovereign rights, in ever wider fields, and the subjects of which comprised not only the Member States but also their nationals.
>
> The essential characteristics of the Community legal order which had thus been established were, in particular, its primacy over the law of Member States and the direct effect of a whole series of provisions which were applicable to their nationals and to the Member States themselves. ([1991] ECR 6079)

However, the Treaty, although fulfilling many of the functions of a constitution for the Community, still falls far short of creating a federal state and although Community law prevails in Member States, the Community depends on the courts and the enforcement agencies of the Member States to implement it. There is no Community police or military force, and defence and foreign policy remain in the hands of national governments; although important steps were taken in the TEU, ToA and ToN to coordinate action in those areas, as well as in the area of drugs enforcement, illegal immigration and justice and home affairs. These areas are, ultimately, still a matter of national policy over which Member States retain final control in their territories. In a federal state, defence and foreign policy would be the sole prerogative of the central, federal government. The Community is, therefore, at the most, only an embryonic federal state.

The Treaty most nearly resembles a constitution in the way in which it defines the competence of the Community itself, and each of its constituent parts, and, to a lesser extent, the rights of its citizens. Although the Treaty does not contain a complete catalogue of citizens' rights, it does confer a number of rights which can be enforced directly in the national courts. Ultimately, the Court of Justice acts as guarantor of those rights and has, in fact, quite consciously used this doctrine of direct enforcement to empower citizens in their own courts and, if need be, against their own governments (Mancini, 1989; Lenaerts, 1991). A whole range of Treaty provisions have been held to create directly enforceable rights, among them the right not to be discriminated against on grounds of nationality (Art 12 EC Treaty), the right to equal pay for work of equal value, regardless of gender (Art 141), the right to seek work and remain as a worker in another Member State (Art 39), the right to receive and provide services (Art 49), the right not to be subjected to import taxes (Art 25) and the right to take action against another undertaking for breach of the competition rules (Art 82; *Garden Cottage Foods* v *Milk Marketing Board* [1984] AC 130). This principle of direct enforcement is considered in detail later (see Chapter 9).

Advocate-General Jacobs suggested that the 1996 Intergovernmental Conference might be the occasion at which the Member States could draw together all the fundamental rules of the Community into a single document. The way to do this would be:

> ... To strip out from the Maastricht morass those basic Treaty provisions governing the competencies of the Community, the competencies of the institutions, and the fundamental principles of the Community legal order, which could then be incorporated in a basic text as an incipient constitution, and one which could be amended only by a special procedure, so that the current allocation of competencies was effectively protected against amendment by the ordinary legislative procedure; while many of the other Treaty provisions could be relegated to an instrument of a less fundamental status. (Jacobs, F., 'The European Court of Justice: some thoughts on its past and future', *The European Advocate*, Winter 1994/1995, p. 2.)

However, the Member States adopted the more modest proposal of the Court of Justice, calling for the 'codifying and streamlining of the constitutive Treaties' (para 23 of the Report of the Court of Justice on Certain Aspects of the Treaty of European Union (May 1995) – see now, Declaration 42 ToA, on the 'Consolidation of the Treaties').

The EC Treaty

The EC Treaty, being the most substantive of the three founding Treaties, requires further consideration. As the Court of Justice stated in Opinion 1/91 (see above): '... the Community Treaties established a new legal order for the benefit of which the States had limited their sovereign rights, in ever wider fields'. The reference to 'ever wider fields' in part refers to the limited nature of the Community's competence, in that it can act only in those policy areas where the Member States have given the power (through the EC Treaty) for it to act, but also recognises the fact that each time the Treaty has been amended the result has been that the powers of the Community have been enhanced, through for example the inclusion of more policy areas. In order to understand the extent of the EC's legal competence it is essential to be familiar with the contents of the Treaty itself. A useful starting point is to consider the index to the EC Treaty as amended by subsequent Treaties (e.g. the SEA, TEU, ToA and ToN).

Index to the EC Treaty

The index to the EC Treaty, following amendments made to it by the SEA, TEU and ToA (but pre-ToN) is as follows:

Preamble
Part One   Principles (Arts 1–16)
Part Two   Citizenship of the Union (Arts 17–22)
Part Three   Community Policies
                         Title I   *Free Movement of Goods (Arts 25–31)*
                                        Chapter 1   The Customs Union (Arts 25–27)
                                        Chapter 2   Prohibitions of Quantitative Restrictions (Arts 28–31)
                         Title II   *Agriculture (Arts 32–38)*
                         Title III   *Free Movement of Persons, Services and Capital (Arts 39–60)*
                                            Chapter 1   Workers (Arts 39–42)
                                          Chapter 2   Right of Establishment (Arts 43–48)
                                          Chapter 3   Services (Arts 49–55)
                                          Chapter 4   Capital and Payments (Arts 56–60)
                         Title IV   *Visas, Asylum, Immigration and Other Policies (Arts 61–69)*
                         Title V   *Transport (Arts 70–80)*
                         Title VI   *Common Rules on Comp, Tax, Approx of Laws (Arts 81–97)*
                                          Chapter 1   Rules on Competition (Arts 81–89)
                                          Chapter 2   Tax Provisions (Arts 90–93)
                                          Chapter 3   Approximation of Laws (Arts 94–97)
                         Title VII   *Economic and Monetary Policy (Arts 98–124)*
                                            Chapter 1   Economic Policy (Arts 98–104)
                                          Chapter 2   Monetary Policy (Arts 105–111)
                                          Chapter 3   Institutional Provisions (Arts 112–115)
                                          Chapter 4   Transitional Provisions (Arts 116–124)
                         Title VIII   *Employment (Arts 125–130)*
                         Title IX   *Common Commercial Policy (Arts 131–134)*
                         Title X   *Customs Cooperation (Arts 135)*
                         Title XI   *Social Policy, Educ, Voc Training and Youth (Arts 136–150)*
                                          Chapter 1   Social Provisions (Arts 136–145)

The full text of the EC Treaty, as amended, can be accessed on the official EUR-Lex website, at: http://europa.eu.int/eur-lex/en/treaties.index.html.

The Treaty is followed by a number of protocols, declarations and agreements. Protocols are given legal effect within the Community legal system by Art 311 EC Treaty, which provides that:

> The Protocols annexed to this Treaty by common accord of the Member States shall form an integral part thereof.

Declarations and agreements may be legally effective within the Community legal system, if they are adopted by the Council of Ministers (as most are). The agreement taken at the Edinburgh Summit, for example, following Denmark's rejection of the TEU in a referendum, is an example of a non-legally enforceable agreement. At this summit a Decision and Declaration on Denmark was taken, not by the Council, but by the Heads of State and Governments meeting within the European Council. This is more akin to an international agreement and does not form part of the Community legal system.

In Chapter 1 there was a brief discussion of Part One of the Treaty (Principles), considering in particular Art 2 (the task of the Community) and Art 3 (the activities of the Community to achieve the Art 2 tasks). Articles 2 and 3 set out the broad aims and objectives of the Community; aims and objectives which include not only economic policies but also social and political policies. But how does the Community operate? Is it run by the Member States?

Article 7 EC Treaty – Institutions of the Community

Article 7 EC Treaty (previously Art 4) provides that:

1. The tasks entrusted to the Community shall be carried out by the following institutions:

   – a European Parliament,
   – a Council,
   – a Commission,
   – a Court of Justice,
   – a Court of Auditors.

   Each institution shall act within the limits of the powers conferred upon it by this Treaty.
2. The Council and the Commission shall be assisted by an Economic and Social Committee and a Committee of the Regions acting in an advisory capacity.

Article 7 EC Treaty creates five institutions which are responsible for carrying out the aims and objectives of the Community as set out in Arts 2 and 3 of the Treaty and the other provisions within it. It is provided that each of these institutions must act within the powers granted to them under the Treaty. There will be a more in-depth discussion of this in subsequent chapters; suffice to say at this point that the founding Treaty (as amended) is the constitution of the Community: it created institutions to run the Community and defined the powers of each Community institution (see, for example, Part Five, EC Treaty). If any institution exceeds its powers as defined, any resultant act can be struck down as being *ultra vires*, i.e. in excess of its powers.

In the next three chapters it will be noted that in addition to these five institutions, the Treaty provides for other named bodies to be created, and defines their role. Two such bodies are specifically named in Art 7(2) EC Treaty (i.e. the Economic and Social Committee, and the Committee of the Regions).

Community policies

Part Three of the EC Treaty amplifies the broad Arts 2 and 3 aims and objectives of the Community by setting out, in more detail, the substantive Community policies. For example, in Title I 'Free Movement of Goods', seven articles are concerned specifically with this policy area:

- Article 2: 'The Community shall have as its task, by establishing a common market ...'
- Article 3: 'For the purposes set out in Article 2, the activities of the Community shall include ...

  (c) an internal market characterised by the abolition, as between Member States, of obstacles to the free movement of goods ...'

- Articles 25–31 (previously 9–37): Free Movement of Goods – set out the detailed provisions relating to this policy area.

In order to understand the nature and functioning of the Community, the policy area 'Free Movement of Persons' will be briefly considered. The provisions are contained in Part Three, Title III, Chapter One (Arts 39–42 (previously Arts 48–51)) of the EC Treaty.

- Article 2: 'The Community shall have as its task, by establishing a common market ...'
- Article 3: 'For the purposes set out in Article 2, the activities of the Community shall include ...

  (c) an internal market characterised by the abolition, as between Member States, of obstacles to the free movement of ... persons ...'

- Articles 39–42 (previously Arts 48–51): Free Movement of Workers – set out the detailed provisions relating to this policy area.

Article 39 EC Treaty (previously Art 48) defines the policy area in more detail than Arts 2 and 3, but it is still stated in quite broad terms. The first thing to note about Art 39 is that it is limited to the free movement of *workers*, not persons generally. Article 39 (previously Art 48) provides:

1. Freedom of movement for workers shall be secured within the Community.
2. Such freedom of movement shall entail the abolition of any discrimination based on nationality between workers of the Member States as regards employment, remuneration and other conditions of work and employment.
3. It shall entail the right, subject to limitations justified on grounds of public policy, public security or public health:
   (a) to accept offers of employment actually made;
   (b) to move freely within the territory of Member States for this purpose;
   (c) to stay in a Member State for the purpose of employment in accordance with the provisions governing the employment of nationals of that State laid down by law, regulation or administrative action;
   (d) to remain in the territory of a Member State after having been employed in that State, subject to conditions which shall be embodied in implementing regulations to be drawn up by the Commission.
4. The provisions of this Article shall not apply to employment in the public service.

Article 40 (previously Art 49) provides for the Council to issue directives or to make regulations setting out the measures required to bring about the free movement of workers as defined in Art 39 (previously Art 48). Article 40 (previously Art 49) provides:

The Council shall ... issue directives or make regulations setting out the measures required to bring about freedom of movement for workers, as defined in Article 39 ...

In many instances, the EC Treaty provides a framework of broad policies, which are to be supplemented by further *measures* to be adopted by certain Community institutions. In the case of Art 40, the measures are directives and regulations, and the institution which will adopt the directive or regulation is the Council. The institutions will be considered further in the next three chapters. The measures which may be adopted are the next source of Community law.

SECONDARY LEGISLATION (AND 'SOFT LAW')
MADE UNDER THE TREATIES

Article 249 EC Treaty (previously Art 189) sets out the different types of Community legislative acts:

> In order to carry out their task and in accordance with the provisions of this Treaty, the European Parliament acting jointly with the Council, the Council and the Commission, shall make regulations, issue directives, take decisions, make recommendations or deliver opinions.

The role of the institutions in the legislative process will be considered in Chapter 4. The different types of act have different consequences:

- A *regulation* shall have general application. It shall be binding in its entirety and directly applicable in all Member States (Art 249, para 2).
- A *directive* shall be binding, as to the result to be achieved, upon each Member State to which it is addressed, but shall leave to the national authorities the choice of form and methods (Art 249, para 3).
- A *decision* shall be binding in its entirety upon those to whom it is addressed (Art 249, para 4).
- *Recommendations* and *opinions* shall have no binding force (Art 249, para 5).

Regulations

Article 249 EC Treaty (previously Art 189) provides that a regulation shall be binding upon all Member States and is *directly applicable* within all such states. Article 254 (previously Art 191) provides that all regulations must be published in the *Official Journal*. The *Official Journal* is an official Community publication. It consists of two related series and a supplement:

- **The L series (legislation)** contains all the legislative acts whose publication is obligatory under the Treaties, as well as other acts.
- **The C series (information and notices)** covers the complete range of information other than legislation.
- **The S series** is a supplement containing invitations to tender for public works and supply contracts.

The L and C series are published daily (except Sunday) and the supplement is published every day from Tuesday to Saturday. Being a legislative act, a regulation will be published in the L series. The regulation will be cited alongside a reference such as OJ 1990 L 257/13 (this is a reference for an EC Regulation on the control of concentrations between businesses). The reference is decoded as: the L series of the *Official Journal*, Year 1990, issue number 257, page 13. The regulation enters into force on the date specified in the regulation, or if there is no such date specified, on the twentieth day following its publication in the *Official Journal* (Art 254 (previously Art 191)).

Recent issues of the *Official Journal* can be accessed on the Internet at: http://europa.eu.int/eur-lex/en/oj/index.html.

Directly applicable

As stated above, Art 249 provides that a regulation shall be *directly applicable*. Normally if a state enters into an agreement with another state, although that agreement may be binding in international law, it will only be effective in the legal system of that state if implemented in accordance with the state's constitutional requirements.

For example, if the United Kingdom entered into an agreement with France, for the agreement to be enforceable in UK courts an Act of Parliament would normally have to be enacted. The Act may transpose the agreement into the relevant Act, or it may simply refer to the agreement and provide for it to be effective in the United Kingdom.

An EC regulation is an agreement, made by an international body, the European Community. For the regulation to be incorporated into the national legal system implementing legislation would have to be enacted by the national legislature. This would be very burdensome, because the Community adopts a vast number of regulations each year. The whole Community system would very quickly grind to a halt if each regulation had to be incorporated into the national law of each of the 15 Member States before it was effective. Regulations, especially in the agricultural policy area, quite often require speedy implementation in order to have the desired effect. Such regulations would lose their effect if the Community had to await incorporation by each Member State into their respective national legal systems.

It is for this reason that the EC Treaty (Art 249) provides that a regulation shall be *directly applicable*. This means regulations shall be taken to have been incorporated into the national legal system of each of the Member States automatically, and come into force in accordance with Art 254 (see above). They are binding on anyone falling within their terms in all Member States. They require no further action by Member States, and can be applied by the courts of the Member States as soon as they become operative.

In the United Kingdom, the European Communities Act 1972 (as amended) provides for the direct applicability of EC regulations.

Directives

A directive differs from a regulation in that it applies only to those Member States to whom it is addressed; normally a directive will be addressed to all 15 Member States. A directive sets out the result to be achieved, but leaves some choice to each Member State as to the form and method of achieving the end result. A directive will quite often provide a Member State with a range of options it can choose from when implementing the measure.

A directive is not directly applicable. It requires each Member State to incorporate the directive in order to be given effect in the national legal system. In the United Kingdom, this requires the enactment of an Act of Parliament or delegated legislation.

Article 254 EC Treaty provides that directives which are addressed to all Member States (of which the vast majority are), and those which are adopted in accordance with the legislative procedure prescribed by Art 251 (the co-decision procedure (see Chapter 4)), must (like all regulations) be published in the *Official Journal*. Such directives shall come into force on the date specified in the directive or, if no date is specified, 20 days after publication in the *Official Journal* (Art 254).

All other directives (i.e. those which do not need to be published in the *Official Journal* (this will be rare)) must be communicated to the Member States to whom they are addressed. Such directives will take effect on the date of communication (Art 254(3)).

Regulation or directive?

Enabling the Community to legislate by means of either a regulation or a directive gives the Community some flexibility. Very few Treaty articles provide that a specific instrument must be used, therefore there is a choice available.

This flexibility is necessary given the difference between the instruments. As discussed above, regulations are directly applicable in that they become part of the Member States' national legal systems just as they are. It is therefore necessary for a regulation to be precise and clear. Compare this to a directive which is a much more flexible instrument. A directive sets out the result to be achieved, while leaving some degree of discretion to the Member State as to the choice of form and method for achieving that end result. However, despite this apparent flexibility, a directive may nevertheless contain very specific provisions, leaving very little discretion to the Member State.

Usually the Community institution empowered to adopt an instrument is given flexibility as to the mode of instrument chosen, be it a regulation, a directive or some other instrument. However, some Treaty articles will actually specify the model. For example, Art 89 EC Treaty (previously Art 94):

> The Council acting by a qualified majority on a proposal from the Commission and after consulting the European Parliament, may make any appropriate *regulations* for the application of Articles 87 and 88 ... (emphasis added)

Also, Art 94 EC Treaty (previously Art 100):

> The Council shall, acting unanimously on a proposal from the Commission and after consulting the European Parliament and the Economic and Social Committee, issue *directives* for the approximation of such laws, regulations or administrative provisions of the Member States as directly affect the establishment or functioning of the common market. (emphasis added)

Decisions

Article 249 EC Treaty provides that a decision is binding in its entirety on those to whom it is addressed. Article 254(3) (previously Art 191(3)) provides that a decision must be notified to the person or Member State to whom it is addressed and that it will take effect upon such notification. However, if a decision is adopted using the legislative procedure prescribed by Art 251 (previously Art 189(b) (the co-decision procedure)), the decision must be published in the *Official Journal*, and it will take effect either on the date specified in the decision or, if there is no such date specified, on the twentieth day following publication in the *Official Journal*.

The same can be said of decisions that can be said of regulations and directives, in that the Treaty articles are generally left open to allow the relevant institution to decide the actual mode of the instrument. However, some articles actually specify that the mode of the instrument shall be a decision. For example, Art 85(2) EC Treaty (previously Article 89(2)):

> If the infringement is not brought to an end, the Commission shall record such infringement of the principles in a reasoned *decision* ... (emphasis added)

Article 85(2) concerns infringement of EC competition rules.

Recommendations and opinions

Article 249 EC Treaty is quite clear that recommendations and opinions shall not have any binding force. However, the use of these two instruments may be useful to clarify matters in a formal way. Article 211 EC Treaty (previously Art 155) empowers the Commission to formulate recommendations or deliver opinions on matters dealt with in the Treaty, not only where expressly provided for, but also whenever it considers it necessary.

Although recommendations and opinions have no immediate legal force, they may achieve some legal effect as persuasive authority, if they are subsequently referred to, and taken notice of, in a decision of the Court of Justice. Measures of this kind are sometimes referred to as 'soft law' for this reason (Snyder, 1993). National courts are bound to take them into account when interpreting Community measures, where they throw light on the purpose of the legislation: *Grimaldi* v *Fonds des Maladies Professionelles* (Case C-322/88).

Legislative base

The relevant institution, so empowered by the Treaty, may choose the relevant mode for an instrument, unless the Treaty specifies that a particular mode must be used. Articles 39 and 40 EC Treaty (previously Arts 48 and 49) relating to the free movement of workers were discussed above. Article 40 provides that:

> The Council shall issue directives or make regulations setting out the measures required to bring about freedom of movement for workers, as defined in Article 39 ...

The Council has adopted a number of directives and regulations pursuant to the former Art 49 (now 40). For example:

- Regulation No. 1612/68/EEC of the Council of 15 October 1968 on Freedom of Movement for Workers within the Community [OJ Sp. Ed. 1968, No. L257/2, p. 475].
- Directive No. 68/360/EEC of the Council of 15 October 1968 on the Abolition of Restrictions on Movement and Residence within the Community for Workers of Member States and their Families [OJ Sp. Ed. 1968, No. L257/13, p. 485].

Article 40 EC Treaty is said to be the *legislative base* for the Community institutions to adopt secondary legislation in relation to the policy of free movement of workers. Whenever the institutions seek to adopt secondary legislation, the institution which makes the proposal (more often than not the European Commission) must find a relevant legislative base within the Treaty; without a legislative base they are prevented from acting.

RELATED TREATIES MADE BETWEEN MEMBER STATES

These are treaties related to the original Treaties, either amending or enlarging them. Within this category, as a source of law, are the Merger Treaties of 1965, the Single European Act 1986, the Treaty on European Union 1992, the Treaty of Amsterdam 1997, the Treaty of Nice 2000, as well as the Treaties of Accession of Denmark, Ireland and the United Kingdom in 1972, Greece in 1981, Spain and Portugal in 1986, and Austria, Finland and Sweden in 1994.

Like the Treaties themselves, the Treaties of Accession have been held to confer directly enforceable rights on individuals (*Rush Portugusa* v *Office National d'Immigration* (Case C-113/89)).

INTERNATIONAL TREATIES NEGOTIATED BY THE COMMUNITY UNDER POWERS CONFERRED BY THE TREATY

This category includes not only multilateral treaties to which the Community is a party, such as the General Agreement on Tariffs and Trade (GATT), but Association Agreements concluded by the Community with individual states. The GATT agreement was held in *International Fruit* (Case 21–24/72) to be binding on the Community, and the Court has also held that undertakings which complain to the Commission of illicit commercial practices which breach the Community's commercial policy instrument may rely upon the GATT as forming part of the rules of international law to which the instrument applies (*Fediol* (Case 70/87)).

In *Kupferberg* (Case 104/81), the Court held that Art 21 of the EEC/Portugal Association Agreement was directly enforceable in the national courts. The principle of the direct enforcement of such agreements has enabled the nationals of the states which are parties to such agreements to enforce their provisions against Member States of the Community (the principle of direct enforcement is considered further in Chapter 9). In *Kziber* (Case C-18/90), the Court has also held that parts of the EEC–Morocco Cooperation Agreement are directly enforceable (see also, *Yousfi* v *Belgium* (Case C-58/93)).

DECISIONS OF THE EUROPEAN COURT OF JUSTICE

The jurisprudence (i.e. case law) of the Court of Justice is a major source of law. It comprises not only all the formal decisions of the Court, but also the principles enunciated by it in its judgments and through opinions sought from it. The Treaties and the implementing legislation do not, between them, contain an exhaustive statement of the relevant law, and much of the work of the Court has been to put flesh on the legislative bones. The creative jurisprudence of the Court, and its willingness to interpret measures in such a way as to make them effective, to achieve the *effet utile*, has done much to assist in the attainment of the general objectives of the Treaties.

The role of the Court in developing the law of the Community will be discussed in Chapter 5.

GENERAL PRINCIPLES OF LAW AND FUNDAMENTAL RIGHTS UPON WHICH THE CONSTITUTIONAL LAWS OF THE MEMBER STATES ARE BASED

Article 6(1) TEU (as amended by the ToA) now states, unequivocally, that 'The Union is founded on the principles of liberty, democracy, respect for human rights and fundamental freedoms, and the rule of law, principles which are common to the Member States'. The importance of these principles is emphasised by the new powers conferred on the Council of Ministers by Art 7(2) TEU to suspend the voting rights of states found to be in breach.

In interpreting primary and secondary Community legislation, the Court has developed a number of general principles of law, some based on the fundamental laws of the constitutions of the Member States, some based on principles of international law and some derived directly from the European Convention on Human Rights. Although the jurisdiction of the Court of Justice is, as will be discussed in Chapter 5, limited by Art 220 EC Treaty to the interpretation of the Treaties and the subordinate legislation made under them, this is to be done in such a way as to ensure that 'the law is observed'. This has been widely interpreted to mean not only the law established by the Treaties but 'any rule of law relating to the Treaty's application' (Pescatore, 1970). The principles of the Convention are to be applied insofar as they relate to matters within the competence of the Community. It shall 'respect fundamental rights, as guaranteed by the European Convention for the Protection of Fundamental Freedoms signed in Rome on 4 November 1950 and as they result from the constitutional traditions common to Member States, as general principles of Community law' (Art 6(2) TEU).

The application of these general principles of EC law will be dealt with in detail in Chapter 5.

Further reading

Craig, P. and De Burca, G. (1998) *EU Law Text, Cases and Materials* (2nd edn), OUP, Chapter 3.

Hartley, T.C. (1998) *The Foundations of European Community Law* (4th edn), Oxford University Press.

Jowell, J., 'Is proportionality an alien concept?' [1996] 2 EPL 401.

Lasok, D. (1998) *Law and Institutions of the European Union*, Butterworths, Chapter 4.

Lenaerts, K., 'Fundamental Rights to be included in a Community Catalogue' (1991) 16 EL Rev 367.

Mancini, G.F., 'The Making of a Constitution for Europe' (1989) 26 CML Rev 595, 596.

Pescatore, P., 'Fundamental Rights and Freedoms in the System of the European Communities' [1970] AJIL 343.

Schilling, T., 'The autonomy of the Community legal order: an analysis of possible foundations' (1996) 37 Harv Int LJ 389.

Schwarze, J. (1994) *European Administrative Law*, Sweet & Maxwell.

Snyder, F., 'The Effectiveness of European Community Law: Institutions, Processes, Tools and Techniques' (1993) 56 MLR 19, 32.

Steiner, J. and Woods, L. (2000) *Textbook on EC Law* (7th edn), Blackstone Press, Chapter 3.

Tillotson, J. (2000) *European Community Law: Text, Cases and Materials* (3rd edn), Cavendish Publishing Ltd, Chapter 4.

Tridimas, T. (2000) *The General Principles of EC Law*, OUP.

Weatherill, S. (2000) *Cases and Materials on EC Law* (5th edn), Blackstone Press, Chapter 1.

Weiler, J. and Lockhart, N., 'Taking Rights Seriously: The European Court of Justice and its Fundamental Rights Jurisprudence' (1995) 32 CML Rev 579.

Chapter 3

COMMUNITY INSTITUTIONS
AND RELATED BODIES

The EC Treaty initially created four institutions to enable 'the tasks entrusted to the Community ... [to be] ... carried out' (Art 7(1) EC Treaty). Those institutions were:

- the European Commission;
- the Council of Ministers;
- the European Parliament; and
- the Court of Justice.

A fifth institution, the Court of Auditors, was added by the TEU in 1993.

Article 7(1) EC Treaty further provides that each institution is obliged to act within the limits of the powers conferred on it by the Treaty. It can, in other words, only do those things which it has been expressly authorised by the Treaty to do. The Court has, by and large, been strict in limiting the activities of the other institutions to their specified functions, although it has been more liberal when interpreting the powers of the European Parliament (*Les Verts* (Case 294/83); *Parliament* v *Council* (Case C-388/92)).

There are two other bodies which are expressly mentioned in Art 7(2) EC Treaty, but which have only an advisory function in the decision-making process: the Economic and Social Committee and the Committee of the Regions.

The work of each of the above institutions will be considered in turn in this chapter, except for the Court of Justice (and Court of First Instance) which will be considered in Chapter 5. The institutions that are to be examined are considered in the context of their role in the European Community (which, until the TEU, was called the *European Economic Community* (Art G (now Art 8) TEU)), unless otherwise stated. In this chapter, and throughout the book, the focus will be on the *European Community* and not the *European Union*. This is because the European Union created by the TEU includes not only the European Community, but also the European Coal and Steel Community and Euratom, and the non-legally binding cooperative decision-making processes of the Member States on foreign and security policy, and police and judicial cooperation in criminal matters (i.e. the second and third pillars of the EU (see Chapter 1)), which are generally outside the competence of the institutions. The focus of this book is on the institutions as the constituent parts of those Community acts which have *legal* effect. Each institution has a defined role in the decision- and law-making process, or in relation to adjudication or the audit of the Community's accounts.

The institutions do not fit easily into categories such as legislature, executive and judiciary. Although legislative, executive and judicial functions are performed by the

Community, there is no formal 'separation of powers' doctrine in-built into the Community's constitution. The competence of each institution has not remained static. Amendments to the founding Treaty have generally resulted in changes to the balance of power between these institutions: e.g. the Parliament started off as a mere debating chamber with limited supervisory powers, but following the introduction of direct elections in 1979, subsequent amendments to the EC Treaty (e.g. by the SEA, TEU, ToA and ToN) have resulted in its powers being enhanced, at the cost of some of the other institutions. This shifting of the balance of powers will be explored throughout this and the following chapter.

The detailed Treaty provisions which apply to the Community institutions are contained in Part Five of the EC Treaty. Part Five is structured as follows:

Part Five **Institutions of the Community (Arts 189–280)**
    Title I   *Provisions Governing the Institutions (Arts 189–267)*
        Chapter 1   *The Institutions (Arts 189–248)*
              Section 1   *The European Parliament (Arts 189–201)*
              Section 2   *The Council (Arts 202–210)*
              Section 3   *The Commission (Arts 211–219)*
              Section 4   *The Court of Justice (Arts 220–245)*
              Section 5   *The Court of Auditors (Arts 246–248)*
        Chapter 2   *Provisions Common to Several Institutions (Arts 249–256)*
        Chapter 3   *The Economic and Social Committee (Arts 257–262)*
        Chapter 4   *The Committee of the Regions (Arts 263–265)*
        Chapter 5   *The European Investment Bank (Arts 266–267)*

There is one body which is outside the Community's formal structure but plays an increasingly important political role in the Community. That body is the European Council.

THE EUROPEAN COUNCIL

The European Council did not exist when the Community came into being on 1 January 1958. The European Council was created following a meeting of heads of government in Paris in 1974 and received formal recognition in the Single European Act (see Chapter 1).

The role of the European Council (not to be confused with the Council of Ministers, see below) is described, in Art 4 TEU, as being to 'provide the Union with the necessary impetus for its development ... [and to] ... define the general political guidelines'. It is, essentially, a political forum in which the heads of government, meeting at least twice a year, accompanied by their foreign ministers, thrash out the political agenda for the Community in the ensuing months and years. These meetings are often referred to as European Summits. General programmes worked at in outline at these meetings are taken up and fleshed out by the European Commission and may, in some cases, form the background to a whole raft of legislation or more detailed policy making in such areas as monetary policy and the measures necessary to complete the single market. It is here also that discussions will take place on matters which fall within the second and third pillars of the European Union (i.e. Common Foreign and Security Policy; and Police and Judicial Cooperation in Criminal Matters (see Chapter 1)).

The subject matter of European Council meetings depends on a number of different factors but the following are relevant in determining what is discussed. The work of the European Council will depend, to some extent, on the political issues which currently preoccupy a majority of the heads of government. These might involve, for example, a foreign policy crisis in the Balkans, a run on the national currencies in the financial markets, or a major environmental disaster. Other items will appear regularly on the Council's agenda, such as the general economic situation, the level of unemployment, and a review of the development of the single market. The Commission will quite often be involved in bringing forward new policy initiatives, usually with some support from the head of government of the state which holds the presidency of the Council of Ministers (see below). Major initiatives have started in this way, such as those leading to the adoption of the Social Charter at the Strasbourg Summit in 1989, and the programmes that led up to the signing of the TEU in 1992, the ToA in 1997 and the ToN in 2000.

As we shall see, it is the task of the European Commission to carry forward the Community towards its goals as set out in the Treaty, but the European Council has proved a valuable means for ensuring that measures proposed by the Commission are actually approved. Once they have been accepted by the European Council they are much more likely to be accepted by the Council of Ministers since they will, in principle at least, have been accepted by the heads of the governments of which the Ministers are part.

THE EUROPEAN COMMISSION

The provisions of the EC Treaty which govern the Commission are Arts 211–219 EC Treaty (previously Arts 155–163). The Commission has a website on the official European Union's server, 'Europa': http://europa.eu.int/comm/index_en.htm.

The role of the Commission is laid down in Art 211 EC Treaty. It has four primary duties:

- to ensure that the provisions of the Treaty and the measures taken by the institutions under the Treaty are applied;
- to formulate recommendations or deliver opinions on matters dealt with in the Treaty if the Treaty either expressly requires it or if the Commission considers it necessary;
- to take part in the decision-making and legislative processes of the Community with the Council of Ministers and the European Parliament;
- to exercise the powers conferred on it by the Council of Ministers for the implementation of rules laid down by the latter.

Essentially, the Commission's function is, generally, to act as the executive of the Community and to see that Community policy is carried out, to formulate new policy and to draft legislation to give it effect, to police observance of Community rules (whether primary, in the form of Treaty provisions, or secondary, in the form of regulations, directives and decisions) and, to a lesser extent, to act as a legislative body in its own right. This fourth function is largely related to the making and enforcement of detailed rules for the implementation of the Common Agricultural Policy.

Composition

Since the entry of Austria, Finland and Sweden on 1 January 1995, the Commission has consisted of 20 Commissioners (Art 156(1) Act of Accession, Art 30 Decision 95/1/EC OJ 1995 L 1/1; this is set out in Art 213 EC Treaty). Article 213 EC Treaty further provides that only nationals of the Member States are eligible as Commission members, and the Commission must include at least one national of each of the Member States with no more than two. Although Art 213 does not stipulate this, in practice the five largest Member States (France, Germany, Italy, Spain and the United Kingdom) each has two Commissioners appointed, with one each for the remaining 10 Member States. Under Art 213 EC Treaty, the numbers can, however, be increased by a unanimous vote of the Council of Ministers.

Although it is usual for the Member States to put forward the member(s) of their nationality whom they wish to see appointed, it should be noted that the Treaty provides that members of the Commission are to be persons 'whose independence is beyond doubt' (Art 213(1) (previously Art 157(1))).

Article 213(2) (previously Art 157(2)) further provides that the members of the Commission shall:

> ... in the general interest of the Community, be completely independent in the performance of their duties. In the performance of these duties, they shall neither seek nor take instructions from any government or from any other body ... Each Member State undertakes to respect this principle and not to seek to influence the members of the Commission in the performance of their tasks.

It is thereby provided that the Commission shall act in the general interests of the Community. The Commission members are not representatives of the Member States of their nationality.

Treaty of Nice amendments

Article 4 of the Protocol on EU Enlargement, which is attached to the ToN, provides that from 1 January 2005, Art 213(1) EC Treaty will be amended to provide that the Commission shall include one national of each of the Member States. This is in preparation for enlargement of EU membership and its aim is to prevent the Commission becoming too large. This amendment will therefore reduce the five larger Member States' representation from two to one.

The article further provides that when the Union consists of 27 Member States, Art 213(1) will be further amended to provide that the number of members of the Commission shall be less than the number of Member States. The number shall be set by the Council of Ministers acting unanimously. The members shall be chosen according to a rotation system based on the principle of equality, the implementing arrangements for which shall be adopted by the Council acting unanimously.

Appointment

Article 214 EC Treaty (previously Art 158) provides for the appointment of the President and the other 19 members. The governments of the Member States nominate by *common accord* (i.e. they must all agree) the person whom they wish to appoint as President. That nomination is subject to a vote of approval by the European Parliament (this requirement was inserted by the ToA). Following President Jacques Santer's resignation on 15 March 1999, the Member States nominated Romano Prodi (former Italian Prime Minister) as President. This was endorsed by the European Parliament on 5 May 1999 by 392 votes to 72, with 41 abstentions.

The governments in *common accord* with the nominee for President then nominate the persons they wish to appoint as Commissioners (i.e. they must all agree – all 15 Member States and the nominee President). The body *as a whole* is subject to a vote of approval by the European Parliament. Once approved by the Parliament the body is appointed by *common accord* of the Member States. The members are appointed for a renewable period of five years. The previous appointments took effect on 7 January 1995; however, the President (Jacques Santer) and his 19 Commissioners resigned en masse on 15 March 1999 following a damning report by an external fraud inquiry that charged them with losing political control over the Brussels executive.

The Member States and the President-designate, Romano Prodi, announced their nominations to form the new Commission during July 1999. The 20 prospective members were informally presented to the European Parliament on 21 July 1999. Hearings with each nominee took place during the period 30 August 1999 to 7 September 1999, and the Parliament's vote of approval took place later that month. The current Commission (together with their portfolios) is as follows:

President	Romano Prodi (Italy)
Vice-President; Administrative Reform	Neil Kinnock (UK)
Vice-President; Relations with the European Parliament, and Transport and Energy	Loyola de Palacio (Spain)
Commissioner for Agriculture, Rural Development and Fisheries	Franz Fishler (Austria)
Commissioner for Research	Philippe Busquin (Belgium)
Commissioner for Development and Humanitarian Aid	Poul Nielsen (Denmark)
Commissioner for Enterprise and Information Society	Erkki Liikanen (Finland)
Commissioner for Regional Policy	Michel Barnier (France)
Commissioner for Trade	Pascal Lamy (France)
Commissioner for the Budget	Michaele Schreyer (Germany)
Commissioner for Enlargement	Gunter Verheugen (Germany)
Commissioner for Employment and Social Affairs	Anna Diamantopoulou (Greece)
Commissioner for Health and Consumer Protection	David Byrne (Ireland)
Commissioner for Competition	Mario Monti (Italy)
Commissioner for Education and Culture	Viviane Reding (Luxembourg)
Commissioner for Internal Market	Frits Bolkestein (Netherlands)
Commissioner for Justice and Home Affairs	Antonio Vitorino (Portugal)
Commissioner for Economic and Monetary Affairs	Pedro Solbes Mira (Spain)
Commissioner for Environment	Margot Wallstrom (Sweden)
Commissioner for External Relations	Chris Patten (UK)

It should be noted that the power of the Parliament to veto the appointment of the Commission is only a power to block the appointment of the Commission as a body; it cannot block the appointment of an individual member (other than blocking the President's appointment).

However, the Parliament may be able to negotiate a redistribution of portfolios to ensure that a member of which it disapproves does not have responsibility for a high profile portfolio; the Parliament may threaten to veto the appointment of the whole Commission if its request is not met.

Treaty of Nice amendments

Once the ToN comes into force, Art 214 EC Treaty will be amended to provide for the Council to act by a qualified majority (rather than unanimously) when appointing the President and other members of the Commission. The Parliament's role will remain unchanged.

Termination of office

Termination may occur by:

- expiry of period of office (Art 214(1) (previously Art 158(1))) – five years;
- death (Art 215 (previously Art 159));
- voluntary resignation (Art 215 (previously Art 159));
- compulsory resignation pursuant to Art 216 (previously Art 160): 'If any member of the Commission no longer fulfils the conditions required for the performance of his duties or if he is guilty of serious misconduct, the Court of Justice may, on application by the Council or the Commission, compulsorily retire him'; or
- compulsory collective resignation where the Parliament passes a vote of no confidence pursuant to Art 201 (previously Art 144); such a vote requires a two-thirds majority of the votes cast which must represent a majority of the total membership of the Parliament (i.e. 314 votes because there are 626 MEPs). On 15 March 1999 the dominant socialist bloc of Members of the European Parliament withdrew support for the President (Jacques Santer) and his 19 Commissioners following a damning report by an external fraud inquiry that charged them with losing political control over the Brussels executive. Their immediate resignation was demanded, and as stated above this was forthcoming. If they had not resigned a vote of no confidence would have been carried and the President and Commissioners would have been legally required to resign.

Treaty of Nice amendments

Once the ToN comes into force, Art 217 EC Treaty will be amended to provide that a member of the Commission must resign if the President requests such resignation, having first of all obtained the collective approval of the Commission. This amendment is in response to the forced collective resignation of Jacques Santer's administration during 1999. The external fraud inquiry, which precipitated the mass resignation, had pointed the finger at a couple of members who refused to resign individually. This amendment will empower the President to require an individual member's resignation.

Role of the President

The ToA inserted a new paragraph into Art 219 EC Treaty (previously Art 163) which provides that the 'Commission shall work under the political guidance of its President'. The President therefore has authority to lead the Commission and it will depend upon the President as to how influential and powerful he is. The former President, Jacques Delors, was a very influential and powerful leader, and contributed greatly to the future shaping of the Community. During the 1980s under Jacques Delors, it has been said that 'the office became a key focus of power, not just in the Commission, but in Europe as a whole. He gave the Commission a purpose and taught it to respond to his will' (Grant, 1994). Under a weak President, it becomes a fragmented bureaucracy, as demonstrated during Jacques Santer's period of office, which culminated in his resignation on 15 March 1999. Although the President has few special powers, the office is designed to deliver a powerful figure who represents the Community; this can be contrasted to that of other countries who are represented by their Head of State.

Treaty of Nice amendments

Article 217 EC Treaty will be amended once the ToN comes into force. This amendment will replace the first para of Art 219. The amended Art 217 will provide that the Commission shall work under the political guidance of its President (currently the first para of Art 219), but additionally provides that the President shall decide on the Commission's internal organisation in order to ensure that it acts consistently, efficiently and on the basis of collective responsibility. It will be explicitly provided that the President shall allocate responsibilities to individual members and can reshuffle those responsibilities during the Commission's term of office. This amendment will strengthen the hand of the President and would seem to be in response to the events leading up to the Commission's mass resignation during 1999.

Structure

Table 3.1 Structure of the Commission following ToN

COMMISSION	COMMISSIONER
DIRECTORATE-GENERAL	DIRECTOR GENERAL
DIRECTORATE	DIRECTOR
DIVISION	HEAD OF DIVISION

Each member of the Commission will be responsible for one or more policy areas (portfolios), to be allocated by the President. Each member will be assisted by a small cabinet of officials (similar to UK civil servants) whom he personally appoints. The cabinet is headed by a Chef de Cabinet, who will liaise closely with the member.

The Commission itself is divided into a number of departments labelled Directorates-General (DGs), and each DG is headed by a Director General who is individually responsible to the relevant member of the Commission. Each Directorate-General is further divided into a number of Directorates (usually between four and six) each headed by a Director. The Director is individually responsible to the relevant Director General. Each Directorate is further sub-divided into a number of Divisions each headed by a Head of Division who is individually responsible to the relevant Director.

Each Directorate-General used to be referred to by a number (e.g. DGI External Economic Affairs; DGV Employment, Industrial Relations and Social Affairs). However, in 1999 it was decided to label each DG with a clear name, in what was largely a symbolic change designed to facilitate understanding by outsiders. It was also announced that the number of DGs would be reduced from 42 to 36.

There are approximately 20,000 staff employed by the Commission; the adminis-tration of a medium-sized European city will often employ more people.

The Commission acts as a collegiate body and decisions are made by a simple majority. Once taken, they bind the Commissioners (see Chapter 4). Although, as dis-cussed above, the Commissioners are bound to act as a collegiate body on behalf of the Community rather than for the states from which they originate, it would be unrealistic to expect them to divest themselves of all political contacts with their national governments. Indeed, it would not be helpful for the Community for them to do so. They frequently use such contacts within the governments and civil services of Member States to promote Community policies, and to sound out the extent of support which new legislation might secure in the Parliament and the Council of Ministers. Tensions do, however, arise when they appear to be too assiduous in promoting the policies of their own states. Equally, they may also experience difficulties if their approach is seen by their home government as too *Communautaire*. After a period of five years, Commissioners need to be reappointed and will be nominated (or not, as the case may be) by their national state. The UK Commissioner largely responsible for creating and promoting the development of the Single Market in 1986, Lord Cockfield, is widely believed to have failed to achieve reappointment because he was seen by the then UK Prime Minister, Margaret Thatcher, as having 'gone native' in Brussels and lost sight of United Kingdom interests.

Despite this, most Commissioners see themselves as having a much freer hand in devising and promoting new policies. Unlike national politicians, they have no political platform to which they must adhere. They simply need to follow the very broad objectives established by the Treaties and, increasingly, by the European Council (see above). Although they need to promote a good working relationship with the European Parliament, there are very few issues which will unite the Parliament sufficiently to secure their removal *en bloc*.

The Commission as initiator of changes in policy and legislation

In recent years the Commission has annually adopted a *Work Programme*. The Work Programme for 2000 was adopted in February of that year (Brussels, 9.2.2000 COM(2000) 155 final) and it gives a useful indication of current priorities in the language of the Commission. At the same time, the Commission adopted a Communi-cation setting out its strategic objectives for the five years 2000–2005 (Brussels, 9.2.2000 COM(2000) 154 final):

Today's fast changing and divided world needs Europe. The European Union provides living proof that peace, stability, freedom and prosperity can be brought to a continent once torn apart by wars. Our European model shows the world that an ever closer union between peoples is possible where it is based on shared values and common objectives ... Over the next decade we will achieve complete economic integration and, even more importantly, give shape to a new, political Europe. The next five years will be decisive. We are already pushing forward with political integration by establishing an area of freedom, security and justice, and by developing common foreign, security and defence policies. Our common interests and objectives are best served by a common approach and common means ... the Commission will therefore pursue four strategic objectives in the five years ahead:

- **Promoting new forms of European governance.** This means giving people a greater say in the way Europe is run; making the institutions work more effectively and transparently, notably by reforming the Commission and setting an example for other bodies; adapting the institutions to the needs of enlargement; building new forms of partnership between the different levels of governance in Europe; and ensuring an active and distinctive European contribution to the development of global governance.
- **A stable Europe with a stronger voice in the world.** As a top priority we will work to make a success of enlargement, and to build a real policy of cooperation with our new neighbours. We will also aim at closer cooperation between European institutions and amongst the Member States and at enabling Europe to take a lead in building the new global economy.
- **A new economic and social agenda.** This means modernising our economy for the digital age in a manner which promotes employment and sustainable development, whilst remodelling our systems of social protection in order to build a fair and caring society.
- **A better quality of life.** Here we must provide effective answers to the issues which affect the daily lives of our citizens, notably the environment, food safety, consumer rights, justice and security against crime.

These are the challenges lying ahead over the next decade. As we rise to those challenges, the world will be watching. Let us make this a decade of success – the decade of Europe.

The current Work Programme and related documents can be found on the Commission's website at: http://europa.eu.int/comm/off/work.index_en.htm.

Proposals for legislation in 2000 included a directive on car construction requirements to reduce pedestrian injuries; a regulation on which Member State is responsible for determining a political asylum application; a regulation on additives used in flavourings; and a directive on the provision of air services.

Although the Commission is often described as the Community's executive, that description does less than justice to its major policy-making role. Although the Treaty does not expressly stipulate, in general terms, that law and policy changes must be initiated by the Commission, it contains a large number of references such as 'The Council ... acting on a proposal from the Commission' may draw up a programme, adopt appropriate regulations and/or directives, and so forth. The Work Programme described above is part of that process. The references in the Treaty to the role of the Commission have been interpreted as providing a more or less exclusive role for the Commission in policy initiation, so much so that the position has often been summarised by the maxim that 'the Commission proposes and the Council disposes'.

As we shall see, in Chapter 4, when considering the decision-making process, this no longer accurately reflects the position, partly because of the increasingly important role of the European Council and partly because of the much enhanced role of the European Parliament. Directorates-General, assisted by a large number of specialist advisory committees drawn from the appropriate industrial, commercial and other sectors in the Member States, take an active part in drafting new provisions. This process has been particularly visible in the measures proposed to harmonise product standards, consumer safety measures, and health and safety at work measures in the Single Market under what is now Art 95 EC Treaty.

Policy initiation takes place at many levels within the Commission. Senior Commission officials who have moved from civil service posts within their Member States are often surprised by the extent to which they are enabled to bring forward their own policy initiatives. Since there is no equivalent of a Cabinet with a political programme, either at Council of Ministers or at Commission level, there is much greater scope for even middle-ranking officials to bring forward proposals to implement the Work Programme.

As the Work Programme for 2000 indicates, the Commission also has an important external role, representing the Community in negotiations with other groups of states and trading organisations. This is specifically recognised by Art 133(3) EC Treaty which provides that:

> Where agreements with one or more States or international organisations need to be negotiated, the Commission shall make recommendations to the Council, which shall authorise the Commission to open the necessary negotiations.
>
> The Commission shall conduct these negotiations in consultation with a special committee appointed by the Council to assist the Commission in its task and within the framework of such directives as the Council may issue to it.

Under Art 133, the Commission is empowered, subject to the necessary Council approval, to negotiate world trade agreements: e.g. during 1994, GATT negotiations between the United States of America and Japan were conducted on behalf of the EC by Commissioner Leon Brittan.

The Commission represents the EU at a number of important international organisations, three of which are specifically mentioned in the EC Treaty:

- Article 302 – United Nations
- Article 303 – Council of Europe
- Article 304 – Organisation for Economic Cooperation and Development (OECD).

It is also the holder of Community funds and administers four special funds:

- the European Social Fund;
- the Cohesion Fund;
- the European Agricultural Guidance and Guarantee Fund; and
- the European Regional Development Fund.

The European Social Fund seeks mainly to expand vocational training for workers in order to promote employment and occupational mobility (Arts 146, 147 EC Treaty). Its rules were revised in 1983 to gear its activities more to current unemployment.

The Cohesion Fund was established in 1993 to provide financial support for projects in the environment and in relation to trans-European networks in the area of transport infrastructure (Art 161 EC Treaty). It was created as part of a process of transferring resources from some of the Community's wealthier states to those with less-developed economies. The four countries initially to benefit from the Cohesion Fund – those with Gross National Products (GNP) per capita at 90 per cent or less of the Community average – were Spain, Portugal, Greece and Ireland.

The European Agricultural Guidance and Guarantee Fund was set up to assist in the restructuring of national agricultural economies (Art 37 EC Treaty).

The European Regional Development Fund is intended to help to redress the main regional imbalances in the Community through participation in the development of regions which are lagging behind economically. It is also used to assist declining industrial regions, typically old coal, steel and textile areas of the Community (Art 160).

The Commission as 'Guardian of the Treaties'

This expression is used to describe the Commission's role both as the keeper of the 'soul' of the Community, maintaining its course towards its declared aims of political and economic unity, and the more mundane, but equally important, role of ensuring that the Member States honour their obligation to give effect to the Treaty and the implementing legislation (Art 10 EC Treaty). This role is discharged both through political contact and, if need be, by the initiation of proceedings against Member States under Art 226 EC Treaty (previously Art 169). The Commission is empowered by Art 226 to bring an action against a Member State which is acting in breach of Community law. This is a very important provision and will be considered in greater detail in Chapter 7. The Commission will first of all ask the defaulting Member State for its own observations on the default. The Commission will then, if the matter cannot be settled, deliver a reasoned opinion. This will set out why the Commission considers the Member State to be in breach of Community law and what it must do to remedy the situation. If the Member State still fails to act, the Commission may take proceedings against the Member State, such proceedings being brought before the Court of Justice. The action will be listed as *Commission v Member State*.

The Commission has another important policing and regulating function in relation to Arts 81 and 82 EC Treaty. As we shall see in Chapters 20 and 21, the preservation of a genuine common market within the Community of goods, services and capital is dependent not just on the collaboration of governments in removing both visible and invisible barriers, but also on the exercise, by the Community, of substantial powers to prevent large private and state undertakings using restrictive agreements, and other abuses of their dominant market position, to exclude Community-produced goods and services from domestic markets. These powers of intervention, including the power to demand information, to enter and search premises, and to impose fines and other penalties, are given to the Commission (Art 83 EC Treaty and Regulation 17/62). They are examined in detail in Chapter 22.

Access to Commission documents

The attitude towards openness and transparency has changed rapidly over the last few years within all the European institutions, including the Commission. A number of measures have been taken to open up the work of the Commission to public scrutiny, as a means of enabling citizens to take part in an informed way in the debate on the future of Europe. The Commission makes frequent use of Green Papers and White Papers. Green Papers are communications published by the Commission on a specific policy area. Primarily they are documents addressed to interested parties, organisations and individuals, who are invited to participate in a process of consultation and debate. In some cases they provide an impetus for subsequent legislation. White Papers are documents containing proposals for Community action in a specific area, which often follow a Green Paper. While Green Papers set out a range of ideas presented for public discussion and debate, White Papers contain an official set of proposals in specific policy areas and are used as vehicles for their development. These documents are available in the 11 official Community languages, and can be accessed on the Commission's website:

- Green Papers 1984–present: http://europa/eu/int/comm/off/green/index–en.htm
- White Papers 1985–present: http://europa/eu/int/comm/off/white/index–en.htm

The vast catalogue of documents available on the European Union's internet server Europa (http://europa.eu.int/index–en.htm) has added to this openness and transparency.

In accordance with the wish expressed at several European Council meetings, the Commission adopted a decision on public access to Commission documents in February 1994. This implemented a joint code of conduct between the Commission and the Council. The general principle expressed in it is that the public should have the widest possible access to documents held by these two institutions, subject to public or private interests being protected (Commission Decision 94/90/ECSC, EC, Euratom of 8 February 1994 on public access to Commission documents). Access to any document can be refused where disclosure could undermine:

- the protection of the public interest (public security, international relations, monetary stability, court proceedings, inspections and investigations);
- the protection of the individual and of privacy;
- the protection of commercial and industrial secrecy;
- the protection of the Community's financial interests; or
- the protection of confidentiality as requested by the natural or legal persons that supplied the information or as required by the legislation of the Member State that supplied the information.

Access can also be denied to protect the institution's interest in the confidentiality of its proceedings. Documents on this transparency policy can be found on the Commission's website at: http://europa.eu.int/comm/secretariat–general/sgc/acc–doc/en/index.htm.

In 1999 there were 408 formal requests made for access to Commission documents, of which 81 per cent of admissible requests were successful. Of those refused, 50.6 per cent were on the grounds of public interest, and 13 per cent were related to confidentiality of the proceedings.

Reforming the Commission

Following the previous Commission's forced removal from office, there was considered to be a need for reform to take place. The new Vice-President, Neil Kinnock, was given responsibility for the Administrative Reform of the Commission. A White Paper 'Reforming the Commission' was adopted by the Commission on 1 March 2000 (COM(2000) 200 final/2, Brussels, 5 April 2000). The White Paper, and other documents associated with the reform agenda, can be accessed on the Commission's website at: http://europa.eu.int/comm/reform/refdoc/index_en.htm.

The White Paper sets out a strategy with three related themes:

- *Reform of the way political priorities are set and resources allocated.* New policy-driven decision-taking mechanisms will ensure that activities undertaken by the Commission are carried out with the necessary human, administrative, IT and financial resources. The evaluation of results will become a routine part of management activities.
- *Important changes to human resources policy*, placing a premium on performance, continuous training and quality of management, as well as improving recruitment and career development. These changes will also place an emphasis on improving the working environment and equal opportunities, as well as the evaluation of management and staff, and will enable disciplinary matters or cases of under-performance to be dealt with properly and fairly.
- *An overhaul of financial management*, empowering each department to establish an effective internal control system appropriate to its own needs. In doing so, departments will be able to draw on the advice of the Commission's specialist services. Reform is predicated upon a precise definition of the responsibilities of each actor, and upon regular checks by the new Internal Audit Service on the quality and reliability of each internal control system.

Following adoption of the White Paper, Neil Kinnock stated:

The reasons for embarking on the arduous but very necessary process are wide-ranging. We have to close the widening gap between the tasks the Member States and Parliament expect the Commission to perform and the human and financial resources we have available and we have to deal efficiently with the enormous challenges of enlarging the Union. The 20,000 Commission staff are highly qualified – but to be fully motivated, they need to feel they serve in a world class administration. We have received clear calls from the heads of all EU governments to take all necessary measures to modernise the Commission to meet our common objectives.

The Commission is determined that the first concern of all its employees should be to provide high-quality service to the people of the European Union. Reform means that the Commission will be better equipped with the people, procedures and systems to fulfil the role and obligations laid down by the Treaties and to show that spirit of service.

The adoption of the White Paper on 1 March 2000 signals the real start in the implementation of an ambitious Action Plan. Reform cannot be completed overnight and some of it will need the Council and the European Parliament to adopt changes in the law. But the Commission wants the first effects to be visible in the near future and the entire programme in place in the second half of 2002. (http://europa.eu.int/comm/reform/index_en.htm)

A full review of the Action Plan (as set out in Part II of the White Paper) will be published in 2002 and transmitted to the Community institutions. Throughout the period of implementing the Action Plan, the Commission will produce regular monitoring reports, which will include a discussion on the qualitative impact as measured by staff feedback.

THE COUNCIL OF MINISTERS

The provisions of the EC Treaty which govern the Council of Ministers are Arts 202–210 (previously Arts 145–154). The Council has a website which can be accessed at: http://ue.eu.int/en/main.htm.

The EC Treaty refers to The Council; many commentators refer to the Council of Ministers. However, in November 1993, the Council chose to rename itself the Council of the European Union. This reflects the fact that this is the only institution which is truly an institution of all three pillars of the European Union. As discussed in Chapter 1, the other institutions have their principal role in the European Communities pillar.

Composition

The Council consists of members of the governments of the Member States 'authorised to commit the government of that Member State' (Art 203 EC Treaty). The Council is therefore made up of politicians from the Member States who are authorised to bind the Member State they represent. The membership will vary according to the matter under discussion and specialised Council meetings may have special titles. The General Affairs Council, in which the foreign ministers participate, deals with institutional and policy issues. The Council of Economic and Finance Ministers (ECOFIN) meets monthly, and covers the abolition of fiscal barriers and the coordination of the economic policies of the Member States. Agriculture ministers, transport ministers, and so forth, meet to consider policy and legislation in their areas of responsibility. The President of the European Commission, although not a member of the Council and not entitled to vote, will in practice attend these meetings, or another Commissioner may attend on his behalf.

Although Member States are normally represented by the senior minister in each department, this may not always be possible and there are occasions when Council meetings comprise ministers of different levels of seniority.

President of the Council

Article 203 EC Treaty provides for the office of President to be held in turn by each Member State for a period of six months in the order decided by the Council acting unanimously. Pursuant to Art 203, the Council decided that for the first six months of 2000 the presidency would be held by Portugal, followed, in the second half-year, by France and then by Sweden, Belgium, Spain, Denmark and Greece (Art 1 Decision 95/2/EC, OJ 1995 L 1/220).

The President is responsible for preparing the agenda for Council meetings, so that holding the presidency provides an opportunity for Member States to ensure that issues that are of importance to them are placed at the top of the agenda. There is also an element of competition between Member States, so that success or failure of a presidency will, to some extent, be judged by the volume of legislation passed during that six-month period.

Council of Ministers' meetings are normally convened by the country holding the presidency. In some cases, however, the Commission, or another Member State, may take the initiative in convening a meeting.

The government of the Member State holding the presidency is primarily responsible for arranging and chairing ministerial meetings of the Council and of its sub-committees. It also has to attempt to gain support among the other Member States for new initiatives, for maintaining their momentum once they are launched and for representing the Council's views to the other institutions. The presidency's control of the agenda allows it considerable scope to change and affect the pace of policy changes in the Community. Achievement of the policy goals set by the presidency will depend to a large extent on its ability to persuade the other Member States to go along with new initiatives, often by a process of trade-offs and mutual concessions in other, sometimes quite unrelated, policy areas. Continuity between successive presidencies is maintained by a close process of cooperation between the outgoing and incoming Member States.

Function

The function of the Council is set out in Art 202 EC Treaty in very broad terms:

> To ensure that the objectives set out in this Treaty are attained the Council shall, in accordance with the provisions of the Treaty:
>
> * ensure coordination of the general economic policies of the Member States;
> * have power to take decisions ...

Decision making remains the central role of the Council and the different methods of decision making are considered in detail in Chapter 4. Despite the increasingly important role of the Parliament, the Council is the place where final decisions will be made, in the overwhelming majority of cases. Hitherto, discussions in the Council of Ministers have been held in secret. However, Art 255 EC Treaty now confers a right of access to all Council documents for all citizens of the Union or anyone living in a Member State. Access may be limited on public policy grounds, but these limitations on citizens' rights will be interpreted strictly by the Court of Justice (*World Wildlife Fund* v *Commission* (Case T-105/95)). Decisions are made after preliminary discussions between officers of the Council Secretariat, the Commission and the Council's own subordinate body, COREPER.

COREPER

COREPER, which is the French acronym for the Committee of Permanent Representatives, plays an important role in providing continuity during the inevitable absences of relevant ministers from the Council. The Committee consists of senior national officials who are permanently located in Brussels. The Committee was originally established by Art 4 of the Merger Treaty in 1965, but it has now been formally integrated into the Community's decision-making structure by Art 207 EC Treaty. The Committee 'shall be responsible for preparing the work of the Council and for carrying out the tasks assigned to it by the Council' (Art 207(1) EC Treaty).

The Committee operates on two levels: COREPER I, which consists of the ambassadors from the Member States who are accredited to the Community in Brussels, and COREPER II, which is comprised of their deputies. The primary task of COREPER is to prepare items for discussion at Council meetings and it will be assisted in this by a whole range of specialist advisory committees. If the text of a policy statement or legislation can be agreed before the meeting, it will be tabled in Part A of the Council .genda, where it will normally be adopted without further discussion. More difficult, controversial items, on which agreement has not been possible, will appear in Part B of the agenda. In these cases the issue may, subject to the appropriate legal base, have to be decided by a qualified majority vote (see Chapter 4).

THE EUROPEAN PARLIAMENT

The provisions of the EC Treaty governing the European Parliament are Arts 189–201 (previously Arts 137–144). The European Parliament has a website which can be accessed at: http://www.europarl.eu.int/sg/tree/en/default.htm.

The EC Treaty, as it was originally drawn in 1957, included provision for 'an Assembly' whose task was to 'exercise the advisory and supervisory powers' conferred upon it (Art 189 EC Treaty). The Assembly is now called 'The European Parliament' and the words 'advisory and supervisory' have disappeared. The Parliament, which in 1979 became a directly elected body, now simply exercises the powers conferred on it by the Treaty (Art 189 EC Treaty (as amended by the TEU)). Prior to that date, its members were drawn from nominees from the national parliaments. It is currently the only directly elected institution in the Community, but the name 'Parliament' is misleading: it shares a number of important features with national parliaments and has considerable influence but it falls far short of being a real, sovereign parliament as would be understood in the United Kingdom. The principal difference is that it lacks the power both to initiate legislation and to impose taxes. Its powers have increased, however, and are likely to continue to do so following the changes to decision making made by the SEA, TEU, ToA and ToN. The increase in Parliament's powers was to counter the argument that the Community was democratically deficient because its only directly elected body had no real powers.

Composition

The Parliament consists of 626 Members of the European Parliament (MEPs) elected on different variants of proportional representation. The last elections to the European

Parliament took place in June 1999. Prior to this election, UK MEPs were elected by the first-past-the-post system as used for general elections (except in Northern Ireland where MEPs were elected by a system of proportional representation). The UK Labour Party, which was elected to government following a landslide general election victory on 1 May 1997, had stated in its manifesto that: 'We have long supported a proportional voting system for election to the European Parliament'. The European Parliamentary Elections Act 1999 was duly passed and was in force in time for the June 1999 MEP elections. The Act divides the United Kingdom into electoral regions:

- England – 9 regions – 71 MEPs
- Scotland – 1 region – 8 MEPs
- Wales – 1 region – 5 MEPs
- Northern Ireland – 1 region – 3 MEPs.

The system (which took place within the United Kingdom for the first time on 10 June 1999) provides that in each region within England, Scotland and Wales, MEPs are elected by a regional list system. The electorate votes either for a registered party (e.g. Labour, Conservatives, etc. – i.e. a closed party list system) or an individual candidate who stands as an independent. The first seat is allocated to the party or individual candidate with the greatest number of votes. The second and subsequent seats are allocated in the same way, but the number of votes given to a party to which one or more seats have already been allocated is divided by the number of seats allocated PLUS 1.

Northern Ireland uses a different system, which is the same as that used for elections to the Northern Ireland Assembly.

Table 3.2 provides the United Kingdom's election results in the European Parliamentary elections in 1994 (which used the first-past-the-post system) and 1999 (which used this new system).

Table 3.2 UK results in European Parliamentary elections 1994 and 1999

Parties	1994			1999		
	% vote	% seats	Seats	% vote	% seats	Seats
Labour	44.24	73.81	62	28.03	34.53	29
Conservatives	27.83	21.43	18	35.77	42.86	36
Lib Dems	16.72	2.38	2	12.66	11.9	10
SNP	3.19	2.38	2	2.68	2.38	2
Greens	3.24	0	0	6.25	2.38	2
Plaid Cymru	1.06	0	0	1.85	2.38	2
UK Ind. Party				6.96	3.57	3
Pro-Euro Cons.				1.38	0	0
Others	3.72	0	0	3.72	0	0

The system has effectively taken away some of the discrepancies which the first-past-the-post system had created. In 1994, the Labour Party had seen its proportion of the UK quota of MEPs reach 73.81 per cent based upon a 44.24 per cent share of the vote. However, in 1999 its proportion of seats had decreased to 34.53 per cent, although this was based upon a much reduced share of the vote: 28.03 per cent.

The number of MEPs was increased in 1993 from 518 to 567. The smaller Member States, such as Luxembourg and Denmark, did not see any increase, while Spain's MEPs increased by 4, France, Italy and the UK by 6 and Germany achieved the largest increase, 18, to reflect her much enlarged population following reunification in 1990 (OJ 1993 L 33/15). Following the accession of Austria, Finland and Sweden on 1 January 1995, the number of MEPs was further increased by 21 for Austria, 16 for Finland and 22 for Sweden (Art 11 Act of Accession; Art 5 Decision 95/1/EC, OJ 1995 L 1/1). The number of MEPs will be increased on the further enlargement of the EU; however, the ToA amended the EC Treaty to provide a maximum number of 700 MEPs (Art 189 EC Treaty). This will be discussed further below.

The current allocation of MEPs is as follows:

- 99 – Germany
- 87 – France, Italy, United Kingdom
- 64 – Spain
- 31 – Netherlands
- 25 – Belgium, Greece, Portugal
- 22 – Sweden
- 21 – Austria
- 16 – Denmark, Finland
- 15 – Ireland
- 6 – Luxembourg.

The number of MEPs allocated to each Member State is not in proportion to its population: the United Kingdom has one MEP per 670,000 citizens; Ireland one per 233,000; and Luxembourg one per 67,000. However, Art 190(2) EC Treaty has been amended by the ToA to provide that in the event of an amendment being made to the number of MEPs allocated to each Member State, then 'the number of representatives elected in each Member State must ensure appropriate representation of the peoples of the States brought together in the Community'.

Treaty of Nice amendments

Article 189 EC Treaty will be amended once the ToN comes into force to provide that the number of MEPs shall not exceed 732. This is an increase from the 700 inserted by the ToA and is in preparation for further enlargement of EU membership. The Protocol on EU Enlargement, which is attached to the ToN, provides that Art 190(2) EC Treaty will be amended on 1 January 2004 to provide that the number of MEPs will be as follows (Art 2, Protocol):

- 99 – Germany
- 72 – France, Italy, UK
- 50 – Spain
- 25 – Netherlands
- 22 – Belgium, Greece, Portugal

- 18 – Sweden
- 17 – Austria
- 13 – Denmark, Finland
- 12 – Ireland
- 6 – Luxembourg.

Only Germany and Luxembourg retain the same number of MEPs as before, with all other Member States having their representation reduced. This new membership will take effect for the 2004–2009 Parliament, and will additionally include all new Member States who have signed accession treaties by 1 January 2004 at the latest. However, if the total number of MEPs is less than 732, there shall be a pro-rata correction so that the total number is as near to 732 as possible. However, in this case, no Member State will be allocated more MEPs than they currently have.

Annex II to the Protocol provides that once membership of the EU has increased to 27 Member States, representation in the European Parliament will be as follows:

- 99 – Germany
- 72 – France, Italy, UK
- 50 – Poland, Spain
- 33 – Romania
- 25 – Netherlands
- 22 – Belgium, Greece, Portugal
- 20 – Czech Republic, Hungary
- 18 – Sweden
- 17 – Austria, Bulgaria
- 13 – Denmark, Finland, Slovakia
- 12 – Ireland, Lithuania
- 8 – Latvia
- 7 – Slovenia
- 6 – Cyprus, Estonia, Luxembourg
- 5 – Malta
- **TOTAL 732.**

Political groups

MEPs are elected for a term of five years. They stand as members of national political parties, but sit within broad political, rather than national, groupings in the Parliament. As at 6 December 2000 the political groups were represented within the Parliament as follows: the European People's Party and European Democrats (which includes the UK Conservative Party MEPs) had 232 members; the Party of European Socialists (which includes the UK Labour Party MEPs) 178 members; the European Liberal, Democratic and Reformist Group (which includes the UK Liberal Democrat MEPs) 52; the Greens/European Free Alliance 48; the European United Left/Nordic Green Left 42; the Union for Europe of the Nations 30; the Technical Group of Independents 18; and the Europe of Democracies and Diversities 16. Nine members were not attached to any group, including the Northern Ireland MEP, the Reverend Ian Paisley (European Parliament Session News, Briefing, 11–15 December 2000, p. 26).

Under the EC Treaty (as amended by the TEU), political parties at European level are now recognised as 'a factor for integration within the Union' and 'contribute to forming a European awareness and to expressing the political will of the citizens of the Union' (Art 191 EC Treaty).

Political activity in the European Parliament largely takes place through the groups. Under the current Rules of Procedure (14th edn, June 1999) a political group must comprise MEPs from more than one Member State (rule 29(2)). The minimum number of MEPs required to form a political group is 23 if they come from two Member States, 18 if they come from three Member States, and 14 if they come from four or more Member States. There are a number of reasons why groups have developed. Primarily they are formed to provide mutual ideological support and identification. In addition, there are organisational benefits, including funds for administrative and research purposes which are better deployed in support of groups than for individuals. There are also advantages in the conduct of Parliamentary business that stem from group status, since the Parliament arranges much of its business around the groups. Although non-attached members are not formally excluded, and indeed are guaranteed many rights under the Rules of Procedure, they can, in practice, be disadvantaged in the distribution of committee chairmanships or in the preparation of the agendas for plenary sessions (i.e. meetings of the full Parliament).

A section of the Parliament's website is set aside for the political groups, each of which publishes a plethora of information. The political groups area can be accessed at: http://www.europarl.eu.int/groups/default.htm.

Treaty of Nice amendments

Once the ToN comes into force, Art 191 EC Treaty will be amended to require the Council of Ministers to adopt regulations governing political parties and in particular regarding their funding.

Parliamentary meetings

The Parliament holds plenary sessions (i.e. all 626 MEPs congregating together in one chamber) in Strasbourg, committee meetings in Brussels and is serviced by staff located in Luxembourg. A new building has been erected in Brussels for full Parliamentary sessions but the European Council meeting in Edinburgh in December 1992 confirmed that the Parliament would remain in Strasbourg. A new Parliament building was opened in Strasbourg in December 1999 to ensure that the chamber could accommodate all 626 MEPs. Enlargement of Community membership, and the resultant increase in the number of MEPs, meant that the previous chamber was too small. A decision by the Parliament to increase the number of plenary sessions held in Brussels was struck down by the Court of Justice in October 1997 (*France* v *European Parliament* (Case C-345/95)). MEPs and officials will continue to live a highly peripatetic existence, largely because the Parliament is a major employer and the Member States cannot agree on a single, permanent site for it.

Except in August, the Parliament sits for one week in each month, usually in Strasbourg. It occasionally sits for additional periods to discuss special items, such as the budget. Between the monthly part-sessions, two weeks are set aside for meetings of the Parliamentary Committees, and the third week for meetings of the political groups.

Full details of the Parliamentary agenda and post-session report are available on the Parliament's website at: http://www.europarl.eu.int/dg3/sdp/brief/en.

Committee meetings

The Parliament has a large range of specialist committees. Some will be permanent, while others are *ad hoc* (i.e. set up to consider a particular matter). The committees cover such matters as Legal Affairs and the Internal Market; Foreign Affairs, Human Rights, Common Security and Defence Policy; Women's Rights and Equal Opportunities; Employment and Social Affairs; Constitutional Affairs; Petitions.

Much of the Parliament's legislative groundwork will be conducted in committee. When the Parliament receives a request from the Council or Commission for an opinion, approval, or assent the request will be sent to the relevant committee for a report to be prepared for full debate and vote in the chamber. The committee will appoint a member to be responsible for preparing the report. This person is called the 'Rapporteur'. The Rapporteur will lead the debate when the report of the committee comes before the full Parliament (i.e. when the Parliament sits in plenary session in Strasbourg).

The committees follow legislative and policy matters in detail and, as they usually meet *in camera* (i.e. the public are excluded from their meetings unless invited to attend by the Chairman), they are given confidential information, both by Commission officials and by the independent experts and representatives of pressure groups who appear before them.

Powers of the Parliament

There are three main powers exercised by the Parliament:

- participation in the legislative processes of the Community;
- acting as the budgetary authority; and
- supervision of the Commission.

In addition to these formal processes, the Parliament takes an active part in the political life of Europe, commissioning reports, passing resolutions on social and political issues, human rights, defence and foreign policy, and on many other matters. It can, however, do little more than express a view on the issues about which the majority of MEPs are concerned.

The TEU strengthened the position of the Parliament by the addition of Art 192 to the EC Treaty, which provides that it may:

> ... request the Commission to submit any appropriate proposal on matters on which it considers that a Community act is required for the purposes of implementing this Treaty.

The Parliament also gained the important power under the SEA (now Art 49 TEU) of approval of new Member States. This is, potentially, an important bargaining counter in relation to the acquisition by the Parliament of more powers, although the opportunity was not taken at the time of the accession of Austria, Finland and Sweden in 1995. The TEU also gave the Parliament the power to set up *Committees of Inquiry* to 'investigate alleged contraventions or maladministration in the implementation of Community law' (Art 193 EC Treaty), and to appoint a *Parliamentary Ombudsman* to investigate complaints about any of the other institutions, except the Court of Justice and the Court of First Instance acting judicially (Art 195 EC Treaty). Jacob Söderman was appointed the first European Ombudsman by the European Parliament in 1995. He can investigate complaints against the Community institutions of maladministration, which includes such things as unfairness, discrimination, abuse of power, lack or refusal of information or unnecessary delay. The Parliamentary Ombudsman has his own area on the Parliament's website which can be accessed at: http://www.euro-ombudsman.eu.int/home/en/default.htm.

The role of Parliament in the law-making process is discussed in Chapter 4.

The Budget

In relation to the budget, the Parliament has an important function, which it shares with the Council of Ministers. The Community's budget is drafted by the Commission and placed before the Council of Ministers and Parliament before 1 September each year. This is necessary because the Community's financial year runs from 1 January to 31 December. The budget is divided into two parts: compulsory expenditure (CE) and non-compulsory expenditure (NCE). Compulsory expenditure relates to those items where the expenditure is required by the Treaty, chiefly the Common Agricultural Policy, which usually absorbs almost 50 per cent of the total budget, whereas NCE covers such items as social and regional policy, research and aid to non-European Union countries in Central and Eastern Europe.

The Treaty gives the Parliament wide powers to amend NCE items, but its powers to modify CE items are more limited under Art 272 EC Treaty. The Parliament may, however, acting by a majority of its members (i.e. at least 314, because there are 626 MEPs), which must also represent a two-thirds majority of the votes actually cast, reject the whole of the draft budget and ask for a new draft to be submitted to it (Art 272(8) EC Treaty). If that happens, the Community institutions have to continue on a month-by-month basis, spending no more than one-twelfth per month of the last year's budget until a new budget is approved (Art 273 EC Treaty).

Supervision of the Commission

There is close and continuous contact between the Commissioners and the Parliament. Although Commissioners are not members of the Parliament, they frequently take part in debates where legislation is under discussion, and they will often attend the specialist committees of the Parliament to deal with detailed points arising from Commission proposals. Under the Treaty, they have the right to attend and to be heard (Art 197 EC Treaty).

Commissioners have a duty to respond, orally or in writing, to questions put to them by MEPs (Art 197 EC Treaty). Since 1974, this has become formalised into a Westminster-type Question Time during every week when the Parliament is in full session (rule 43, Rules of Procedure). Outside plenary sessions, there are regular exchanges between the Commission, the various Parliamentary Committees and individual MEPs.

The Parliament has the right to dismiss the Commission *en bloc* under the EC Treaty (Art 201 EC Treaty). Although it has never done so, it effectively forced the previous Commission from office when the Parliament threatened to use its censuring powers; the Commission accepted defeat and resigned, rather than face the humiliation of a certain defeat.

It has been said that: 'The Commission pays a great deal of attention to the views of the Parliament' (Pinder, 1991). Since the TEU this position has been reinforced by the requirement that the new Commission, before it starts its term of office, is subject to a vote of approval by the Parliament (Art 214(2) EC Treaty). Individual Commissioners in the previous administration were subjected to intensive questioning in American-style appointment committees of the Parliament in the run up to the taking of office in early 1995, and one, Padraig Flynn, the Commissioner for Social Affairs, gave up the chair of the Commission's women's rights committee to the President of the Commission, Jacques Santer, as a result (*Guardian*, 31 October 1995).

As we have seen, the Commission's work programme is put together and implemented in close conjunction with the Parliament, and there is a considerable coincidence of interest to both the Commission and the Parliament in developing Community-wide policies. Where these fail to materialise, it is often as a result of the more nationally orientated policies of the Member States, reflected in the Council of Ministers. One of the most striking examples of this is the failure of the Community to develop a common transport policy, as required by Art 70 EC Treaty. The failure of the Council to make progress on the policy led to the initiation of proceedings in the Court of Justice (under Art 232 EC Treaty) by the Parliament with the support of the Commission. Regrettably, perhaps, the Court of Justice declared that the provisions of Art 70 were not sufficiently precise to create a legally enforceable obligation (*European Parliament* v *Council* (Case 13/83)). The consequences of that case are, perhaps, evident in the fact that, more than 15 years after the decision, there is still no Community transport policy.

Enlargement of the powers of the European Parliament

The most obvious difference between the European Parliament and national parliaments is its inability to initiate legislation. As we will see in Chapter 4, although the Parliament has, in most cases, the right to be consulted, such consultation may mean no more than the right to comment on a draft prepared by the Commission. Under some Treaty provisions there is no right of consultation at all, although Commission and Council practice is, nonetheless, to seek the Parliament's views. In other cases, especially in relation to decisions in the field of economic and monetary policy, the Parliament has no more than the right to be informed of the decision reached by the Council of Ministers (Arts 99(2) and 104(11) EC Treaty). Even where the Parliament's opinion must be sought, there remains considerable scope for rejection of its views by the Council of Ministers, provided that the Parliament's opinion is properly considered by the Council. It was widely felt that these limitations were inappropriate for the only democratically elected institution in the Union, and that the Treaty of Amsterdam should have conferred on the Parliament the right to draft and initiate legislation, and to be involved at every level as a co-decision maker;

but most Member States, including the United Kingdom, were opposed to extending the powers of the Parliament in this way. Nevertheless, the role of the Parliament in the legislative process has been strengthened following amendments to the EC Treaty by the SEA, TEU, ToA and ToN (see Chapter 4).

There is also felt to be a 'democratic deficit' in relation to the Parliament's inability to dismiss individual Commissioners and to make Ministers account to the Parliament for their decisions in the Council of Ministers. Although Council documents are now available after meetings, discussion in the Council still takes place in more or less complete secrecy, and there is considerable support, largely among MEPs, for a Minister from the Council to be required to attend the Parliamentary debate and to report back to the Parliament at the conclusion of the ministerial meeting. Although there is some support for these proposals in Germany and The Netherlands, the UK Government has remained firmly opposed to them, on the grounds that they would further undermine the powers of the Westminster Parliament to which national ministers are, in the last resort, solely accountable.

COURT OF AUDITORS

The Court was established by an amendment to the Treaties in 1975 (second Budgetary Treaty 1975). It is not, strictly speaking, a court – more an audit commission – and is responsible for the external audit of the general budget of the European Communities and of the operating budget of the ECSC. The internal audit is the responsibility of the Financial Controller of each institution.

The Court came into being partly as a result of the desire of some of the newer Member States to establish more effective audit arrangements and partly as a result of the desire of the Parliament to have greater power in the financial affairs of the Communities. An independent audit body is seen by Parliament as an important part in establishing greater financial control. It had, initially, the status of a separate body but, since the TEU came into effect in 1993, it has been classed by Art 7 EC Treaty as one of the institutions of the Community.

The Court consists of 15 full-time members who are chosen by the Council of Ministers (after consulting the European Parliament) from among persons who have had relevant auditing experience and whose independence is beyond doubt (Art 247(2) EC Treaty, Art 22 Act of Accession, Art 13 Decision 95/1/EC). The 15 members include one each from Austria, Finland and Sweden, who were appointed in February 1995 (OJ 1995 L 50).

The Court of Auditors has its own website at: http://www.eca.eu.int/EN/menu.htm.

THE ECONOMIC AND SOCIAL COMMITTEE ('ECOSOC')

This Committee was established by Art 257 EC Treaty and Art 165 Euratom to assist the Council and the Commission in an advisory capacity. The Committee consists of 'representatives of the various categories of economic and social activity, in particular, representatives of producers, farmers, carriers, workers, dealers, craftsmen, professional occupations and representatives of the general public'.

The Committee has its own website at: http://www.ces.eu.int/en/acs/fr_acs_default.htm.

The 222 members of the Committee are appointed by the Council of Ministers, acting unanimously, for a period of four years (Art 259 EC Treaty, Art 23 Act of Accession, Art 14 Decision 95/1/EC) and they may be reappointed. Membership is allocated according to the size of the Member States as follows:

- 24 – France, Germany, Italy and UK
- 21 – Spain
- 12 – Austria, Belgium, Greece, Netherlands, Portugal and Sweden
- 9 – Denmark, Finland and Ireland
- 6 – Luxembourg

Members of the Committee must be completely independent 'in the general interests of the Community'. The members serve on three interest groups of Employers, Workers and General Interest, although they are prohibited from being bound by any mandate from that group in their own state or any other (Art 259 EC Treaty). The appointment of members is from a list of candidates provided by each Member State, and is to take account of the need to ensure adequate representation of the various categories of economic and social activity. The Court of Justice has held that adequate representation must be ensured at Community level but that, because of the limited number of seats available, it is not possible to guarantee that all the elements from every category of economic and social activity are represented by nationals from each Member State (*CIDA* v *Council* (Case 297/86)).

Treaty of Nice amendments

Once the ToN comes into force, Art 257 EC Treaty will be amended to provide that the Committee shall consist of representatives 'of the various economic and social components of organised civil society, and in particular representatives of producers, farmers, carriers, workers, dealers, craftsmen, professional occupations, consumers and the general public'. Consumers will therefore be explicitly included for the first time.

Article 258 will also be amended, to provide that the number of members shall not exceed 350. Annex II to the Protocol on EU Enlargement, which is annexed to the ToN, provides that once EU membership has been enlarged to 27 Member States, membership of the Committee will be as follows:

- 24 – France, Germany, Italy, UK
- 21 – Poland, Spain
- 15 – Romania
- 12 – Austria, Belgium, Bulgaria, Czech Republic, Greece, Hungary, Netherlands, Portugal, Sweden
- 9 – Denmark, Finland, Ireland, Lithuania, Slovakia
- 7 – Estonia, Latvia, Slovenia
- 6 – Cyprus, Luxembourg
- 5 – Malta
- **TOTAL 344.**

Function of the Committee

The Economic and Social Committee (ECOSOC) is not recognised by Art 7 EC Treaty as being one of the institutions of the Community, although it receives a mention in Art 7(2). A requirement in Art 24 of the Merger Treaty that the Council consult 'other institutions' when adopting or amending staff regulations was held not to apply to ECOSOC (*Adam* v *Commission* (Case 828/79)). It must be consulted by the Council or the Commission where the Treaty provides for it, and in other cases consultation is at the discretion of those institutions. When the Committee is consulted, it responds by the submission of an opinion to the Commission and Council. These institutions can, if they wish, impose a deadline for the submission of an opinion, but this must not be less than one month (Art 262 EC Treaty). Failure to deliver an opinion cannot prevent further action by the institutions. The Committee also has the right to submit opinions on its own initiative where it considers such action appropriate (Art 262). Opinions of ECOSOC are prepared by a Section designated by the Chairman and then discussed and adopted at plenary sessions of the full Committee which are held during the last seven days of the month (Title II ECOSOC's Rules of Procedure). Although the Committee's opinions are not legally binding, the expertise of the Committee's membership does mean that they carry considerable weight with the institutions. Where the Treaty requires consultation of ECOSOC, failure to do so could lead to the annulment of a measure by the Court of Justice, on the basis of failure to meet an essential procedural requirement. The ToA amended the EC Treaty to create a new right for the European Parliament to consult ECOSOC (Art 262, fourth indent EC Treaty).

THE COMMITTEE OF THE REGIONS

The Committee of the Regions was set up as an advisory body by the TEU (Art 263 EC Treaty) and, like ECOSOC, it is not recognised by Art 7 EC Treaty as one of the Community institutions, although it is mentioned in Art 7(2). It was intended to represent a move towards more region-orientated decision making, and to bring the Community and the European Union closer to the peoples of Europe, as required by Art 1 TEU. The Committee has its own website at: http://www.cor.eu.int.

The Committee consists of 222 representatives of regional and representative bodies in the Member States, with the same allocation of members to each state as ECOSOC. Its basic role is comparable to ECOSOC: the members of the Committee, whose principal role is to deliver opinions on legislation when consulted by the Council of Ministers and to issue own-initiative opinions in appropriate cases, are completely independent in the performance of their duties and act in the general interests of the Community.

The Committee must be consulted in relation to proposed legislation on culture (Art 151(5) EC Treaty), public health (Art 152(4) EC Treaty), economic and social cohesion (Arts 158–162 EC Treaty) and environmental policy (Arts 174 and 175 EC Treaty).

Treaty of Nice amendments

Article 263 EC Treaty will be amended once the ToN comes into force to provide that the Committee shall consist of representatives 'of regional and local bodies *who either hold a regional or local authority electoral mandate or are politically accountable to an elected assembly*' (emphasis added). As the emphasised words indicate, members will in future need to have an electoral mandate to represent citizens at a local level. Where a member's mandate comes to an end, their membership of the Committee shall automatically terminate.

Like ECOSOC, membership shall be limited to 350 (Art 263 EC Treaty). Annex II to the Protocol on EU Enlargement, which is annexed to the ToN, provides for the allocation of seats once EU membership has been enlarged to 27 Member States. Allocation is exactly the same as for ECOSOC.

THE EUROPEAN CENTRAL BANK AND THE EUROPEAN INVESTMENT BANK

The European Central Bank (ECB) was established by Art 8 EC Treaty. It is an innovation of the TEU and is linked to the establishment of a European System of Central Banks. The ECB was set up as part of the progression towards European Monetary Union. It is not a Community institution within the definition of Art 7 EC Treaty. It can, however, enact legislation, impose fines, submit opinions and be consulted within its field of operation (Title VII EC Treaty: Arts 105, 106, 107 and 110).

The European Investment Bank (EIB) was established by Art 9 EC Treaty and is the Union's long-term lending bank and the regional development bank for Europe. It makes grants and loans to projects affecting more than one Member State, where they cannot be funded sufficiently from within those Member States themselves.

The European Investment Bank has its own website at: http://eib.eu.int.

Further reading

Craig, P. and De Burca, G. (1998) *EU Law Text, Cases and Materials* (2nd edn), OUP, Chapter 2.

Dehousse, R., 'European Institutional Architecture after Amsterdam: Parliamentary System or Regulatory Structure?' (1998) 35 CML Rev 595.

Duff, A., Pinder, J. and Pryce, R. (1994) *Maastricht and Beyond*, Federal Trust.

Dunnett, D.R.R. (1994) 'Legal and Institutional Issues Affecting Economic and Monetary Union', in O'Keefe, D. and Twomey, P. (eds), *Legal Issues of the Maastricht Treaty*, Chancery Publications.

Edwards, G. and Spence, D. (1997) *The European Commission*, Cartermill International Ltd.

Grant, C., 'The House that Jacques Built', *Independent*, 29 June 1994.

Harlow, C., 'A Community of Interests? Making the Most of European Law' (1992) 55 MLR 331.

Hartley, T.C., (1998) *The Foundations of European Community Law* (4th edn), OUP, Chapter 1.

Pinder, J. (1991) *The European Community*, OUP.

Shepherd, M., 'The European Parliament: laying the foundations for awareness and support' 50 *Parliamentary Affairs* 438.

Söderman, J., 'A Thousand and one Complaints: The European Ombudsman en Route' [1997] 3 EPL 351.

Steiner, J. and Woods, L. (2000) *Textbook on EC Law* (7th edn), Blackstone Press, Chapter 2.

Tillotson, J. (2000) *European Union Law: Text, Cases and Materials* (3rd edn), Cavendish Publishing, Chapter 5.

Chapter 4

THE DECISION-MAKING PROCESS

Decision making is central to the effective functioning of the Community. Decisions made by Community institutions may relate to the implementation of a policy, such as enlargement of the Community, or the adoption of a trade agreement with other states, or they may be part of a number of different legislative programmes. The type of process will be determined by the subject matter of the decision, as interpreted by the European Commission, which will then choose the appropriate legislative base in the Treaties (see below). That choice will decide what institutions and other bodies will be involved in the process, the voting system used in the Council of Ministers and the extent to which the Parliament will be able to influence the content of the measure and, in some cases, whether it is approved at all. Although, as we have seen in Chapter 3, the European Council plays a growing role in setting policy goals, the task of translating those goals into specific policy decisions and legislation still belongs almost exclusively to the Commission. The European Parliament does now have the power under Art 192 EC Treaty to suggest new areas for legislation, but the decision on whether or not to bring forward such legislation and in what form is for the Commission alone. Apart from a few exceptional situations where the Council may act on its own initiative (i.e. Arts 113 and 210 EC Treaty), in most cases the EC Treaty provides that it shall act on a proposal from the Commission.

DIALOGUE BETWEEN COMMISSION, COUNCIL AND PARLIAMENT

The virtual monopoly which the Commission enjoys over the legislative process could cause serious problems. If it submits no proposals, the Council is paralysed and the progress of the Community comes to a halt, whether in the field of agriculture, transport, commercial policy or the environment. However, except for a period of relative stagnation during the economic crisis of the 1970s, the Commission has always been active in promoting the development of the Community through a series of legislative programmes. As we have seen in Chapter 3, the Commission outlines its annual work programme early in the year. The programme provides a framework of policy and legislative objectives. The Commission then brings forward a series of proposals within that programme. Once a proposal is lodged, a dialogue begins between Commission officials and the representatives of the Council in COREPER. This will continue until the legislation has passed through all its stages and it has finally been approved by the Council. Where the legislative process requires Parliamentary involvement, the Commission will similarly open a dialogue with the Parliament.

LEGISLATIVE PROPOSALS

Legislative proposals may result from the implementation of a wide programme of action, such as that laid down in the plans for the Single European Market, or the Social Chapter (which was incorporated into the EC Treaty by the ToA), or in response to particular circumstances calling for specific legislation. The appropriate Directorate-General, assisted by one of the Commission's advisory committees, will prepare the first draft, which will initially be approved by the appropriate Commissioner holding the relevant portfolio. The views of these advisory committees, which will contain representatives of industrial, commercial and social interests in Member States, are not in any sense binding on the Commission. The proposal will then be passed for consideration by the Commission voting as a collegiate body, on a simple majority basis.

Legislative base

Before considering formulating a draft proposal, the Commission must ensure it has the necessary power, i.e. it must find a legislative base within the relevant Treaty. When Arts 39 and 40 EC Treaty (previously Arts 48 and 49) were discussed in Chapter 2, it was noted that the Commission was empowered to propose legislation in relation to the free movement of workers. The extent of this power is set out in Art 40 and must not be exceeded, i.e. 'The Council shall issue directives or make regulations setting out the measures required to bring about freedom of movement for workers, as defined in Article 39'. If it is exceeded, the resulting instrument may be struck down by the Court of Justice as being *ultra vires*, i.e. in excess of power (see below).

It should be noted that Art 308 EC Treaty (previously Art 235) provides a general legislative power, where the Treaty has not otherwise granted the necessary powers, and provided that the proposal is necessary to attain one of the objectives of the Community. Article 308 provides that:

> If action by the Community should prove necessary to attain, in the course of the operation of the common market, one of the objectives of the Community and this Treaty has not provided the necessary powers, the Council shall, acting unanimously on a proposal from the Commission and after consulting the European Parliament, take the appropriate measures.

However, it should be noted from this that the Commission proposal must be backed by *all* the Member States (excluding any abstentions) because the Council must act *unanimously*.

VOTING PROCEDURES

The Commission

Decisions by the Commission on whether or not to adopt a proposal are taken by a simple majority of the Commissioners. Although the initiative for specific measures will be taken up by the appropriate Directorate-General, other Commissioners have no power to delegate approval of the details of that measure to that Commissioner. The Court made the position clear in *Commission v BASF and Others* (Case C-137/92P):

The functioning of the Commission is governed by the principle of collegiate responsibility. The principle of collegiate responsibility is based on the equal participation of the Commissioners in the adoption of decisions, from which it follows in particular that decisions should be the subject of collective deliberation and that all the members of the college of Commissioners should bear collective responsibility at political level for all decisions adopted.

The European Parliament

Except as otherwise provided in the Treaties, the European Parliament acts by an *absolute majority of the votes cast* (Art 198 EC Treaty, Art 111 Euratom Treaty). This is sometimes referred to as a simple majority, so that abstentions by MEPs within the chamber, and MEPs not present, are not taken into account. However, some Treaty articles provide for something more than an absolute majority of the votes cast: e.g. Art 252(c) EC Treaty provides that 'The European Parliament may ... [vote] by *an absolute majority of its component* members' (emphasis added). There are 626 MEPs, therefore a minimum of 314 votes will be required. Article 201 (a censure motion against the Commission) requires a 'two-thirds majority of the votes cast, representing a majority of the Members of the European Parliament'. The second limb of this is similar to that under Art 252, in that there must be at least 314 votes in favour. However, the first limb provides an additional hurdle which needs to be overcome: of the votes cast, there must be a two-thirds majority in favour. To illustrate this, on a vote under Art 201, if 610 MEPs voted, with 400 in favour and 210 against, although the second limb would have been satisfied, the first limb would not (because the majority in favour is less than two-thirds of the votes cast). Similarly, if 300 MEPs vote, with 250 in favour and 50 against, although this time the first limb has been satisfied, the second limb has not (because it requires a minimum of 314 votes in favour in any event).

A quorum exists when one-third of the current MEPs are present in the Chamber (rule 126(2), Rules of Procedure 1999). However, all votes are valid whatever the number of voters, unless the President of the Parliament, acting on a request made by at least 32 MEPs, ascertains that, at the moment of voting, the quorum is not present. In that case, the vote is placed on the agenda of the next sitting (rule 126(3), Rules of Procedure).The right to vote is a personal right and there is no right to vote by proxy (rule 132). Although members of the European Council and Commissioners have the right to attend debates of the European Parliament and to participate in the discussion, they have no right to vote (Art 23 ECSC Treaty, Art 197 EC Treaty, Art 110 Euratom Treaty).

The Council of Ministers

The Treaties set up three voting methods in the Council:

- simple majority;
- qualified majority; and
- unanimity.

All three methods have been in existence since the earliest days of the Community.

Simple majority

Although Art 205(1) EC Treaty provides that simple majority voting is the system to be used unless otherwise provided in the Treaty, the Treaty almost invariably provides for some other system. Under this system, one vote is allocated to each Member State, and the decision is simply made in favour of the largest number of votes cast. It is largely used for the establishment of sub-committees of the Council and for procedural matters.

Qualified majority

Qualified majority voting (QMV) is a system of voting, weighted according to the population size of the Member State (Art 205(2) EC Treaty). Under this system votes are allocated as follows:

- 10 – France, Germany, Italy, UK
- 8 – Spain
- 5 – Netherlands, Portugal, Greece, Belgium
- 4 – Sweden, Austria
- 3 – Denmark, Ireland, Finland
- 2 – Luxembourg.

To secure approval by a qualified majority, a measure proposed by the Commission will need to be supported by at least 62 votes. In other cases the 62 votes in favour must be cast by at least 10 Member States (Art 205(2) EC Treaty, Art 15 Act of Accession, Art 8 Decision 95/1 OJ 1995 L 1/1). Conversely, to block a proposal, opponents need to secure more than 25 votes. Following the accession of Austria, Finland and Sweden, the number of Members who have to be present to enable the Council to vote has been increased from six to eight (OJ 1995 L 31). Since the largest Member States can muster only 40 votes between them, they are not in a position to force through legislation which tends to favour them, without the support of some, at least, of the smaller states. The majority of decisions were made by qualified majority vote even before the SEA. There was, however, a substantial increase in qualified majority voting following the inclusion of Art 95 EC Treaty, which was intended to secure more rapid decision making in the run up to the Single Market (see below).

Unanimity

Unanimity is reserved for the most important decisions, or those for which Member States are least prepared to pool their national sovereignty. Although this effectively gives Member States a veto, that veto must be exercised for a measure to be blocked. Abstention by Members present or represented does not prevent the adoption of an act which requires unanimity (Art 205(3) EC Treaty). Unanimity is, for example, required for the admission of new states (Art 49 EC Treaty as amended by TEU), and for approval of any other matter within the competence of the Community for which the Treaty does not provide a legal base (Art 308 EC Treaty, see above).

Treaty of Nice amendments

Article 3 of the Protocol on EU Enlargement, which is annexed to the ToN, provides that the qualified majority voting procedure contained in Art 205 EC Treaty will be amended on 1 January 2005. This is to prepare the Community for EU enlargement and is intended to give enhanced voting rights to the larger Member States. The weighting of votes for the existing Member States will be amended as follows:

- 29 – France, Germany, Italy, UK
- 27 – Spain
- 13 – Netherlands
- 12 – Portugal, Greece, Belgium
- 10 – Sweden, Austria
- 7 – Denmark, Ireland, Finland
- 4 – Luxembourg.

Acts of the Council shall, following the amendment, require at least 170 votes in favour, which must be cast by at least a majority of the Member States. If the proposal is not made by the Commission, then the minimum 170 votes must be cast by at least two-thirds of the Member States. The 170-vote threshold will be amended as new Member States are admitted to the European Union.

A new provision, designed to take into account the population of the Member States, provides that when a decision is to be adopted by the Council, acting by a qualified majority, a Member State can request verification that the qualified majority comprises at least 62 per cent of the total population of the European Union. If this condition is shown not to have been met, then the decision in question shall not be adopted.

Annex II to the Protocol provides for the weighting of votes in an enlarged Union of 27 Member States:

- 29 – France, Germany, Italy, UK
- 27 – Poland, Spain
- 14 – Romania
- 13 – Netherlands
- 12 – Belgium, Czech Republic, Greece, Hungary, Portugal
- 10 – Austria, Bulgaria, Sweden
- 7 – Denmark, Finland, Ireland, Lithuania, Slovakia
- 4 – Cyprus, Estonia, Latvia, Luxembourg, Slovenia
- 3 – Malta.

With 27 Member States, the number of votes required to adopt a measure will increase to 258. The requirement for a majority of Member States to vote in favour in respect of a Commission proposal and two-thirds otherwise, will be unaffected, as will the 62 per cent population verification measure.

THE LUXEMBOURG ACCORDS

The Accords, or the Luxembourg Compromise, were the result of an impasse between France and the other Member States in relation to farm prices in 1965. The decision had to be determined, under the Treaty, by a qualified majority vote. The French insisted on the right to secure a unanimous decision in cases such as this, where a vital national interest was at stake. The other Member States could not agree. France then remained absent from all but technical meetings of the Council for seven months, and important decision making in the Community virtually drew to a halt. The Accords were negotiated in a reconvened meeting of the Council in January 1966. The three points that emerged from this meeting, as far as voting procedures are concerned, were as follows:

1   Where, in the case of decisions which may be taken by majority vote on a proposal of the Commission, very important interests of one or more partners are at stake, the members of Council will endeavour, within a reasonable time, to reach solutions which can be adopted by all the members of the Council while respecting their mutual interests and those of the Community, in accordance with Art 2 of the Treaty.
2   With regard to the preceding paragraph, the French delegation considers that where very important interests are at stake the discussion must be continued until unanimous agreement is reached.
3   The six delegates note that there is a divergence of views on what should be done in the event of a failure to reach complete agreement.

The six delegations concluded by observing that the divergence noted in point 3 did not prevent the Community's work from being resumed in accordance with the normal procedure. There are a number of things to be said about the Accords. In the first place, the title 'Accord' is inappropriate. There was, in fact, no agreement, only an agreement to disagree. Secondly, the Accords have no standing in law. Insofar as they purport to amend the voting procedure laid down by the Treaty in certain circumstances, they cannot be effective. Changes to the text and substance of the EC Treaty have to be accomplished in the appropriate form, after consultation with the Parliament and the Commission. This was not done in the case of the Accords. The Commission has never accepted that the Accords had any validity, and has disassociated itself from them (Bull EC 5 1982, p. 8).

Pierre Pescatore, a former judge of the Court of Justice, has described the Accords as 'a mere press release', without the least force of law (Pescatore, 1987). The Court has, moreover, stated (but not in the context of the Accords) that 'the rules regarding the manner in which the Community institutions arrive at their decisions [i.e. by a qualified majority vote or by unanimity] are laid down in the Treaty and are not at the disposal of the Member States or of the institutions themselves' (*United Kingdom* v *Council* (Case 68/86)). Successive UK Governments have, however, from the time of UK entry in 1973 until the conclusion of the Maastricht negotiations on the TEU, and after, assured the British public that 'on issues of vital national interest, Britain retains the right to veto any legislation' (Sir Geoffrey Howe, HC Deb Vol 96 Col 320, 23 April 1986). There is, however, no right to veto proposed legislation. What there has been is a willingness, in some cases where Member States appear to be in difficulties in relation to a domestic political situation, to refrain from pressing to a qualified majority vote where the Treaty authorises it.

The Accords have undoubtedly encouraged Member States to reach a compromise wherever possible. The formal invocation of the Accords has been rare, and has not always achieved the desired result. In 1982, for example, when the United Kingdom sought to block the adoption of an agricultural price package in order to put pressure on the other Member States to agree upon a reduction of the United Kingdom's contributions, its purported 'veto' was ignored and a vote was taken. However, in 1985, Germany invoked the Accords to forestall an increase in cereal prices, and was successful. It is significant that no state which has been overridden, following an appeal to the Accords, has ever taken the decision to the Court of Justice. The trend in voting procedures in recent Treaty changes has been, as we shall see, to more qualified majority voting and less unanimous decision taking, and it is likely that appeals to vital national interests under the Accords will become even rarer than at present.

THE IOANNINA DECLARATION

Some recognition of the continuing need to take into account the genuine difficulties of some Member States when a qualified majority vote is to be taken was shown early in 1994. Under a declaration made in March 1994 at the Ioannina Summit, if members of the Council representing a total of between 23 and 26 votes indicate their intention to oppose the adoption by the Council of a decision by a qualified majority vote, the Council is committed to do all in its power to reach, within a reasonable time, and without infringing the obligatory time limits in Arts 251 and 252 EC Treaty procedures (see below), a satisfactory solution that could be adopted by at least 65 votes (Bull EU 3 1994, p. 65: OJ 1994 C 105/1 as amended by Council Decision of 1 January 1995).

This does no more than provide an opportunity to delay a qualified majority vote, but cannot prevent one from being held, because the new Treaty time limits are still to be respected. The Declaration does, unlike the Luxembourg Accords, have the force of law. It was intended to continue to apply until the amendments to the Treaties following the Intergovernmental Conference of 1996 came into effect, but it was continued by the Treaty of Amsterdam until the next enlargement of the Community (Declaration 50, ToA). Although the Declaration was given legal effect by a Decision of the Council of Ministers, its vagueness must mean that it is most unlikely to be the subject of litigation in the Court of Justice.

THE LEGISLATIVE PROCESS

Due to allegations that the Community was democratically deficient, the powers of the Parliament were broadened by the SEA, broadened further by the TEU, and still further by the ToA and ToN.

There are six separate and distinct methods of enacting Community legislation, each of which will be considered. In addition, the Council has power to delegate its legislative powers to the Commission; under Art 211 EC Treaty the Commission shall 'exercise the powers conferred on it by the Council for the implementation of the rules laid down by the latter'.

Commission acting alone

The Commission is, in very limited policy areas, empowered by the EC Treaty to enact legislation. One example is Art 86(3) EC Treaty (previously Art 90(3)), which provides that:

> The Commission shall ensure the application of the provisions of this Article and shall, where necessary, address appropriate directives or decisions to Member States.

This article is concerned with the role of the state in relation to public bodies or other bodies, to which the state has granted special or exclusive rights (e.g. privatised industries: water, gas, electricity, etc.). The Commission has adopted the following directive pursuant to the former Art 90(3) (now Art 86(3)) power:

- Directive 80/723/EEC on the transparency of financial relations between Member States and public undertakings (OJ 1980 L 195/35).

Council and Commission acting alone

There are a number of policy areas where the EC Treaty provides for the Council to adopt a Commission proposal without the involvement of any other institution (in particular the Parliament). Although there is no formal duty to consult with the Parliament, consultation may (and usually will) occur.

However, if there is no consultation there is nothing the Parliament can do; the legislative measure will be effective. The relevant Treaty article (i.e. the legislative base) will specify the voting mode to be used by the Council (i.e. qualified majority or unanimity; otherwise simple majority). Some of the policy areas where this method for adopting an act is prescribed are of major importance. The areas (pre-ToN) are:

- Article 26 EC Treaty (previously Art 28) relating to the fixing of Common Customs Tariff duties – the Council acts by a qualified majority.
- Article 45 EC Treaty (previously Art 55) relating to derogations from the right of establishment – the Council acts by a qualified majority.
- Article 49 EC Treaty (previously Art 59) relating to the extension of provisions on the freedom to provide services to nationals of third countries who provide services within the Community – the Council acts by a qualified majority.
- Articles 57 and 60 EC Treaty (previously Arts 73c and 73g) relating to the free movement of capital – the Council acts by a qualified majority.
- Article 96 EC Treaty (previously Art 101) relating to harmonisation of laws necessary to eliminate a distortion in competition – the Council acts by a qualified majority.
- Articles 99 and 104 EC Treaty (previously Arts 103 and 104c) relating to Economic and Monetary policy – the Council acts by a qualified majority.
- Article 133 (previously Art 113) relating to implementation of the Common Commercial Policy – the Council acts by a qualified majority.
- Article 301 (previously Art 228a) relating to economic sanctions against a third country – the Council acts by a qualified majority.

For example, Article 301 EC Treaty provides that:

> the Council shall act by a qualified majority on a proposal from the Commission.

Council, Commission and consultation with Parliament

From the earliest days of the Community, this was the commonest legislative procedure in the Treaty, and the only one which gave the Parliament a significant role in the process. New procedures were introduced by both the SEA and the TEU to give the Parliament a greater involvement. Article 249 EC Treaty refers to the making of regulations and directives, the taking of decisions, the making of recommendations or the delivery of opinions, as a joint function of the Parliament and the Council, and the Council and the Commission. However, the Parliament is still far from being a joint legislator in the sense known to national legislatures. Under this procedure, measures are proposed by the Commission, the Parliament is consulted and delivers an opinion and the Council of Ministers makes the final decision. The opinion is prepared by the Rapporteur of one of the Parliament's specialist committees (see Chapter 3). Its preparation follows the hearing of evidence by the Committee from specialist advisers, interested individuals and organisations, and members of the officials of the Directorate-General originally responsible for the drafting of the proposal. Although the Council of Ministers is free not to follow the opinion of Parliament, the consultation must be genuine. Parliament must have a proper opportunity to respond to the proposal. This was recognised as an essential procedural requirement by the Court of Justice in *Roquette Frères* v *Council* (Case 138/79):

> The consultation provided for in ... the Treaty is the means which allows the Parliament to play an actual part in the legislative process of the Community. Such power represents an essential factor in the institutional balance intended by the Treaty. Although limited, it reflects at Community level the fundamental principle that the peoples should take part in the exercise of power through the intermediary of a representative assembly. Due consultation of the Parliament in the cases provided for by the Treaty therefore constitutes an essential formality disregard of which means that the measure concerned is void. ([1980] ECR 3333 at 3360)

This principle was further developed to require reconsultation when a measure on which Parliament had already given an opinion was subsequently changed. In *European Parliament* v *Council* (Case C-65/90) the Court of Justice said that further consultation was required unless the amendments essentially corresponded to the wishes already expressed by the Parliament. In *European Parliament* v *Council* (Case C-388/92) the Court held that the obligation arose to reconsult 'on each occasion when the text finally adopted, viewed as a whole, departs substantially from the text on which Parliament has already been consulted'. On that basis the Court found that the Council had disregarded the prerogatives of Parliament and annulled a Regulation on the operation by non-resident carriers of transport services in Member States (Reg 2454/92/EC). However, consultation is a two-way process. Where Parliament wilfully fails to respond it cannot subsequently complain that its views have not been taken into account. In *European Parliament* v *Council* (Case C-65/93), the Council had informed the Parliament of the urgent need for approval of draft regulations on tariff preference relating to agricultural products to be made under Art 43 EC Treaty (now Art 37(2)). Having agreed to deal with the draft regulations as a matter of urgency, Parliament then decided to adjourn discussion of them for reasons wholly unconnected with their content. They were subsequently adopted by the Council without having received the Parliament's opinion. The Parliament sought to annul the regulations on the ground of failure of consultation. The Court rejected the application:

> Inter-institutional dialogue, on which the consultation procedure in particular is based, is subject to the same mutual duties of sincere cooperation as those which govern relations between Member States and the Community institutions. By adopting that course of action [adjournment of consideration of the draft regulation] the Parliament failed to discharge its obligation to cooperate sincerely with the Council. ... In those circumstances the Parliament is not entitled to complain of the Council's failure to await its opinion before adopting the contested regulation ...

Although the Council should not come to a final decision without giving the Parliament an opportunity to respond, it does not have to suspend all discussion until it receives that opinion (*European Parliament* v *Council* (Case C-417/93)).

This mode of legislating has been retained for the adoption of legislation in certain policy areas (pre-ToN):

- Article 19 (previously Art 8b) concerns the right of EU citizens to vote and stand in local elections, and European Parliament elections – the Council acts unanimously.
- Article 22 (previously Art 8e) relates to provisions increasing the rights of an EU citizen – the Council acts unanimously.
- Article 89 (previously Art 94) relates to the grant of State Aids – the Council acts by a qualified majority.
- Article 93 (previously Art 99) concerns the harmonisation of indirect taxes – the Council acts unanimously.
- Article 94 (previously Art 100) provides for the approximation of national laws which directly affect the operation of the common market – the Council acts unanimously.
- Article 107(6) (previously Art 106(6)) relates to the adoption of certain provisions contained in the Statute of the European System of Central Banks (ESCB) – the Council acts by a qualified majority.
- Article 175(2) (previously Art 130s(2)) provides for fiscal planning and energy measures affecting the environment – the Council acts unanimously.

New provisions inserted into the EC Treaty by the ToA also provide for the Council to adopt legislation, upon a Commission proposal and having consulted with the European Parliament:

- Article 13 provides for measures to be adopted to combat various discriminatory conduct – the Council acts unanimously.
- Article 67(1) concerns visas, etc. – the Council acts unanimously.
- Article 128 concerns employment – the Council acts by a qualified majority.

The Treaty article (i.e. the legislative base) will specify the voting mechanism to be used in Council for the adoption of the measure (as stated above, unanimously or by a qualified majority). There may be a duty to consult other bodies, e.g. the Economic and Social Committee. For example, Art 128(2) provides:

> ... the Council, acting by a qualified majority on a proposal from the Commission and after consulting the European Parliament, the Economic and Social Committee, the Committee of the Regions and the Employment Committee referred to in Article 130 ...

If this was the full extent of Parliament's involvement in the legislative process, it could quite genuinely be questioned whether or not the Community was democratically deficient; the only directly elected institution, composed of 'representatives of the Peoples of the States brought together in the Community' (Art 189 EC Treaty (previously Art 137)), has no real say in the legislative process. It was for this reason that the SEA, TEU and ToA increased the involvement of the European Parliament in the legislative process.

Council, Commission and European Parliament – Article 252 (previously Art 189c) cooperation procedure

The election of a European Parliament by direct franchise for the first time in 1979 produced pressure to address the Community's 'democratic deficit'. The Community institutions were seen as essentially undemocratic, in that the only body that was directly accountable to an electorate played only a peripheral part in the legislative process. Parliament attacked the issue by commissioning a report on wholesale constitutional reform of the Community. That report, the Spinelli Report, appeared in 1984 and, although many of the recommendations were not taken up by the Commission, an attempt was made in the SEA to address the issue of lack of significant Parliamentary input. This was the cooperation procedure, now called (rather obscurely in the Treaty since the TEU) the 'procedure referred to in Article 252', but still widely known as 'the cooperation procedure'.

This procedure starts off similar to the consultation procedure, whereby the Commission makes a proposal which is submitted to the Council and the Parliament. The Parliament gives its opinion to the Council, which, acting by a qualified majority, adopts a common position. However, if the Council's common position amends the Commission's proposal, the Council must act unanimously (Art 250(1) EC Treaty (previously Art 189a(1))). This common position is then forwarded to the Parliament together with the Council's reasons as to why it has adopted the position. The Commission also informs the Parliament as to its opinion on the Council's common position. This will be the second occasion on which Parliament considers the matter and it is therefore said that the procedure provides Parliament with a Second Reading.

The Parliament has three months from receipt of the above to take action, with the following results:

- if the Parliament approves the common position or does nothing then the Council, within three months, shall adopt the proposal, in accordance with the common position. If the Council fails to act within this three months, the proposal shall be deemed not to have been adopted;
- if the Parliament rejects the common position by an *absolute majority of its membership* (i.e. 314, because there are 626 MEPs) then the Council can, within three months, only adopt the act by unanimity; or
- if the Parliament proposes amendments to the common position by an absolute majority of its membership then the Commission has one month within which to re-examine its proposal and the Parliament's amendments to the common position. The Commission shall forward its re-examined proposal to the Council together

with any of the Parliament's amendments which it has not accepted, and the reasons why it has not accepted them. Following this the Council may:
– adopt the re-examined proposal acting by a qualified majority;
– amend the re-examined proposal acting unanimously; or
– adopt any of Parliament's amendments not accepted by the Commission, acting unanimously.

The Council must act within three months, otherwise the proposal will be deemed not to have been adopted.

Under this procedure there is a duty on the Council, after Parliament's First Reading, to inform the Parliament why it has adopted its common position. This will include reasons why, if applicable, it has rejected Parliament's opinion. The Commission is under a duty to inform the Parliament, after the Second Reading, why it rejects any of its proposed amendments to the common position, if applicable.

In the final analysis, the Commission can reject the Parliament's proposals (except that it does not have a say if Parliament rejects the common position), and the Council can override Parliament and the Commission provided it acts unanimously. It may be appreciated, therefore, that although under this procedure Parliament's involvement in the legislative process is more significant, real legislative power still lies with the Council. It is for this reason that Parliament pushed for enhanced legislative powers in the build up to the TEU and ToA.

The policy areas in which the Art 252 (previously Art 189c) procedure applies are now very limited because the ToA transferred the majority of provisions into the Art 251 (previously Art 189b) procedure, discussed below, which gives the European Parliament an enhanced role in the legislative process. The following provisions continue to be governed by Art 252 (pre-ToN):

● Articles 102, 103 and 106 EC Treaty (previously Arts 104a, 104b and 105a) which concern aspects of economic and monetary policy.

For example, Art 106(2) EC Treaty (previously Art 105a(2)) provides that:

> The Council, acting in accordance with the procedure referred to in Article 252 ...

Council, Commission and Parliament – Article 251 (previously Art 189b) co-decision procedure

The TEU introduced a new decision-making procedure, called 'co-decision making', which gave substantial new powers of amendment and, ultimately, a veto to the European Parliament. This system has been simplified and much extended by the ToA, so that it now applies to a large majority of legislative decisions made by the Community. This procedure was amended by the ToA and renumbered Art 251 from 189b; it must be applied wherever the legal base provides that an act shall be adopted 'in accordance with the procedure referred to in Article 251'.

The procedure starts off very similar to the Art 252 (previously Art 189c) proce-dure, in that the Commission proposal is submitted to both the Council and the Parliament. The Parliament gives its opinion on the proposal to the Council. The Council may adopt the proposal by a qualified majority:

- if it approves *all* the amendments contained in the European Parliament's opinion; or
- if the European Parliament does not propose any amendments.

Otherwise, the Council, by a qualified majority, adopts a common position. Remember, however, that Art 250(1) (previously Art 189c(1)) provides that if the Council amends the Commission's proposal it must be unanimous.

The common position is communicated to the Parliament, together with the Council's reasons as to why it adopted the common position. This will obviously include reasons as to why the Council rejects the Parliament's opinion, in whole or in part (if applicable). The Commission informs the Parliament as to its view on the Council's common position. Within three months of the common position being communicated to Parliament, if Parliament either fails to take a decision, or approves the common position, the Council will be deemed to adopt the act in accordance with the common position. Alternatively, within this three-month period, Parliament may:

- by an *absolute majority of its membership* (i.e. 314, because there are 626 MEPs), reject the common position, in which case the act is deemed *not* to have been adopted (i.e. a veto); or
- by an *absolute majority of its membership*, propose amendments to the common position.

Where amendments have been proposed by Parliament, the amended text is forwarded to both the Council and the Commission. The Commission then delivers an opinion on the amendments. It will adopt one of three positions; it may:

- accept them all;
- reject them all; or
- accept some and reject others.

Within three months of receiving the Parliament's amended text, the Council may:

- approve all the amendments of the Parliament and adopt the act. It will do so by qualified majority if the Commission has also accepted all the amendments, by unanimity if the Commission has rejected all the amendments, and by a mixture of the two if the Commission has accepted some (qualified majority) and rejected others (unanimity). In this case the act is adopted; or
- fail to adopt the act, in which case a Conciliation Committee may be convened.

The Conciliation Committee consists of an equal number of representatives from the Council and the Parliament. Their task is to agree a joint text. This will be reached by the Council representatives acting by a qualified majority and the Parliament representatives acting by a majority. The Commission will act as mediator to encourage the parties to reach an agreement. There are two possibilities on the outcome of the Conciliation Committee. If, within six weeks of its being convened, the Committee:

- approves a joint text, then the act will be adopted in accordance with the joint text, by the Parliament acting by an absolute majority of the votes cast (i.e. simple majority) and the Council acting by a qualified majority. The act will be deemed not adopted if approval is not obtained from either institution; or

- does not approve a joint text, then the act is deemed not to have been adopted unless positive action is taken.

There are provisions in Art 251 (previously Art 189b(7)) for the above periods of three months and six weeks to be extended by one month and two weeks respectively.

It is no doubt appreciated by now that this is a very complicated and cumbersome procedure. It is necessary to understand that this is a reflection of the competing interests between the three institutions involved in the legislative process. The Parliament demands more powers, but the Council resists such demands. However, Art 251 has shifted some power from the Council to the Parliament because now the Parliament can actually veto a proposal, although Parliament cannot demand that its amendments be accepted. The Parliament ultimately either has to accept the proposal in totality or reject it in totality; it is therefore a negative power rather than a true (positive) legislative power.

The Art 251 procedure can be viewed as a balancing act of competing interests. The Commission will resist any inroad into its role as policy developer and initiator. Article 251 has made an inroad into the Commission's territory because, if a Conciliation Committee is set up, the Council and Parliament can agree a joint text by qualified majority and simple majority respectively. This joint text may amend the Commission's proposal; such amendments would have required unanimity by the Council pursuant to Art 250(1) (previously Art 189a(1)); however, this provision does not apply to these provisions of Art 251. The joint text (if agreed) can then be adopted by the whole Council acting by a qualified majority and the Parliament acting by a majority of the votes cast.

While the Art 251 procedure is an important development in the evolvement of Parliament's legislative powers, it should be remembered that:

- it only involves an ultimate power to veto;
- the Parliament must cooperate with the Council in order to seek its agreement to amendments (or at least seek a qualified majority if the matter proceeds to a Conciliation Committee); and
- it is limited to certain policy areas, although the policy areas have been substantially extended by amendments made by the ToA.

The pre-ToA policy areas governed by Art 251 included:

- Article 40 (previously Art 49) – free movement of workers.
- Article 44 (previously Art 54) – freedom of establishment.
- Article 47 (previously Art 57) – mutual recognition of qualifications.
- Article 95 (previously Art 100a) – completion of the internal market.
- Article 151(5) (previously Art 128(5)) – incentive measures relating to culture.
- Article 152(4) (previously Art 129(4)) – incentive measures relating to public health.
- Article 175 (previously Art 130s(3)) – certain areas of environmental policy.

The post-ToA (but pre-ToN) policy areas governed by Art 251 include:

- Article 71 (previously Art 75) – transport.
- Article 148 (previously Art 125) – provisions relating to the European Social Fund.
- Article 162 (previously Art 130e) – provisions relating to the European Regional Development Fund.

For example, Art 40 EC Treaty provides that:

> The Council shall, acting in accordance with the procedure referred to in Article 251 ...

Council, Commission and assent of Parliament

This quite simply provides for an act to be adopted by the Council (by a qualified majority or unanimously) upon a proposal by the Commission and 'after obtaining the assent of the Parliament'. The Parliament will only need to act by a *majority of the votes cast* and this procedure is a true co-decision of the two institutions – the Council and Parliament – there is no special majority required in the Parliament.

This assent procedure was introduced by the SEA and, subsequent to the ToA amendments, currently applies to the following (pre-ToN):

- Article 105(6) EC Treaty – certain functions of the European Central Bank (ECB).
- Article 107(5) EC Treaty – amendments to the Statute of the European System of Central Banks.
- Article 161 EC Treaty – application of structure and cohesion funds.
- Article 190(4) EC Treaty – uniform election procedures for MEPs.
- Article 300(3) EC Treaty – making of association agreements with foreign states.
- Article 49 TEU (previously Article O) – enlarging membership of the Communities.

For example, Art 105(6) provides:

> The Council may, acting unanimously ... and after receiving the assent of the European Parliament ...

THE INVOLVEMENT OF THE BRITISH PARLIAMENT

National parliaments become involved in the decision-making process at two, or sometimes three, points in the process. In the first place, draft directives and regulations are sent for scrutiny by national parliaments at the same time as they are sent to the European Parliament. They are examined at Westminster by a Select Committee on European Legislation which reports to the House of Commons on their political and legal consequences. In addition, more general discussion takes place about Community legislative proposals before the biennial meetings of the European Council.

Where the Select Committee recommends that further consideration should be given to any particular proposal, it will be referred to a Standing Committee. The United Kingdom Government has given an undertaking to Parliament that it will not approve proposals for legislation in the Council of Ministers if they are awaiting consideration by the House or are still subject to scrutiny. However, ministers may agree to proposals which:

- are subject to scrutiny if they are confidential, routine, trivial or substantially the same as an item which has already been scrutinised;
- are awaiting consideration but the Select Committee has indicated that agreement could be given; or
- are either awaiting consideration or are still subject to scrutiny, and the minister

has special reasons why agreement should be given, provided that these reasons are given at the first opportunity (HC Debates Vol 178 Col 399, 24 October 1990).

By a Declaration annexed to the TEU, Member States committed themselves to ensuring that 'national parliaments receive Commission proposals for legislation in good time for information or possible examination' (Declaration 13 TEU). According to a 1996 report of the Select Committee, this did not happen. Decisions are often made by the Council of Ministers on the basis of a French text for which no English translation is available, and the Select Committee frequently only sees the English translation *after* the measure has been approved by the Council of Ministers. Members of the Select Committee expressed concern that the Brussels legislative process was operating beyond the scrutiny of national parliaments. They demanded that there should be a minimum four weeks' notice period between an official text of a document being available in the appropriate language in every national capital and a decision being taken on the document by the Council of Ministers: *The Intergovern-mental Conference 1996: The Agenda; Democracy and Efficiency: the Role of National Parliaments,* 24th report, Vol 1, Select Committee on European Legislation: Session 1994–95 (HMSO). Some progress was made in this area in Amsterdam.

A Protocol attached to the EC Treaty by the ToA requires all Community Green and White Papers to be promptly forwarded to national parliaments, and legislative proposals to be forwarded 'in good time'. Not less than six weeks should elapse after a proposal is made available in all the languages of the Community before its adoption by the Council of Ministers (CM 3780, p. 89). It remains to be seen whether this Protocol will be given real effect by the Court of Justice striking down a measure which has not been properly communicated to national parliaments.

THE APPROPRIATE LEGISLATIVE BASE

In almost every case, as the initiator of the legislative process, the choice of legislative base is made by the Commission. It is not always clear – especially in relation to proposals that touch on a number of different activities – which Treaty provision, and hence, which decision-making process, is appropriate. Article 5 EC Treaty provides that the Community shall act within the limits of the powers conferred on it by the Treaty and the objectives of the Treaty. When legislating, the Commission is bound to give reasons for its proposal, the legal basis on which it is made and the process through which it passed, including the institutions and other bodies who participated in the decision (Art 253 EC Treaty). This information is normally contained in the preamble to the measure. Prior to the SEA, the choice of legislative base rarely gave rise to controversy. However, disputes have arisen subsequently, largely either because Member States contested the competence of the Community to legislate at all, or because a legal base was chosen allowing for a qualified majority vote within the Council of Ministers, when some states demanded a basis requiring unanimity and the opportunity to block the measure by a national veto (see above).

Defects in the legal base may be one of three kinds:

● lack of competence of the Community;
● lack of competence of an institution;

- inappropriate Treaty provision for the subject-matter of the legislation.

The Court of Justice has not yet found that a proposed action is without a Community base, but some challenges to the powers of institutions to take action have been successful. In *Germany* v *Commission* (Case 281/85) Germany, France, The Netherlands and the United Kingdom sought to annul a decision made by the Commission in relation to migration policy from non-Member States. Although free movement of persons is central to the working of the Community, the law is, as we shall see (Chapters 11 and 12), largely directed at the facilitation of free movement by EU citizens and their families (but see now the enlarged powers of the Community under Arts 62 and 65 EC Treaty in relation to immigration from outside the Community). It was argued by the applicant states that neither the old Art 118 EC (which then related to social policy) nor any other Treaty provision empowered the Commission to adopt a binding decision. The Court of Justice held that the Commission did have the power to consult with Member States on the impact of third state immigration on the employment market, and how this was affecting Community workers, but that it did not have the power to make a binding measure restricting the way in which Member States could regulate immigration into their territories from outside the Community. The Commission will generally choose the legislative base offering the best chance of approval for a measure, if there is at least an arguable alternative. The Court stated in *Commission* v *Council* (*Generalised Tariff Preferences*) (Case 45/86) that:

> The choice of a legal base for a measure may not depend simply on an institution's conviction as to the objective pursued but must be based on objective factors which are amenable to judicial review.

In *Commission* v *Council* (Case C-300/89), a conflict arose, between the Council on the one hand and the Parliament and the Commission on the other, as to the choice of the appropriate legislative base. The Commission (supported by the Parliament) applied to the Court of Justice for the annulment of Directive 89/428 on procedures for harmonising the programmes for the reduction and elimination of pollution caused by waste from the titanium dioxide industry. The Commission had proposed that the directive should be based on Art 100a EC Treaty (now Art 95), which involved the Council acting by a qualified majority in cooperation with the Parliament. However, despite the Parliament's objections, the Council adopted the directive on the basis of environmental policy, pursuant to the former Art 130s EC Treaty. This article provided at the time (but see, now, Art 175 EC Treaty) that decisions in Council should be taken unanimously, and only after consultation with the European Parliament. The Court decided that Art 100a, which provided that decisions should be taken by qualified majority in Council, in cooperation with the European Parliament, was the appropriate legal basis. Although the directive had the dual objectives of environmental protection and the removal of distortions of competition by establishing harmonised production conditions, it was not possible to have recourse to two legislative bases, and the unanimity rule in Art 130s was incompatible with the cooperation procedure in Article 100a. The decision has a strong political flavour:

> [20] The very purpose of the cooperation procedure, which is to increase the involvement of the European Parliament in the legislative process of the Community would thus be

jeopardised. As the Court stated in its judgment in *Roquette Frères* v *Council* (Case 138/79) and *Maizena* v *Council* (Case C-139/79), para 34, that participation reflects a fundamental democratic principle that the peoples should take part in the exercise of power through the intermediary of a representative assembly.

The Commission has continued to show a disinclination to use Treaty provisions on which decisions in the Council are to be taken unanimously, and a preference for articles for which qualified majority voting is the appropriate procedure in the Council of Ministers. An example can be found in the field of higher education. The Court of Justice had decided in *Gravier* v *City of Liège* (Case 293/83) that the then Art 128 EC Treaty, which contained some fairly general provisions on the promotion of a common vocational training policy, created a directly enforceable right of access to vocational training in other Member States. As a Treaty right, it was to be delivered in accordance with the principles of equality contained in Art 7 EC Treaty (now Art 12).

The former Arts 7 and 128 EC Treaty were, therefore, taken as the basis for a new directive on student mobility (Directive 90/366). Article 7 provided for measures to eliminate discrimination on grounds of nationality to be decided by a qualified majority vote, and it was on this basis that the measure was proposed. The Council of Ministers substituted Art 235 EC Treaty (now Art 308) as the legal base, on the grounds that since Art 128 contained no voting procedure, the residual voting system in Art 235 (a unanimous vote) was more appropriate. Although the directive was unanimously approved by the Council of Ministers, its legal base was challenged by the Parliament, since it did not want to see a precedent established of unanimous decision making in relation to future educational measures. The Court of Justice upheld the challenge on the basis that the measure was, fundamentally, about equal access to vocational training, and that Art 7, which required only a qualified majority vote, was the proper legal basis. The Court ordered that the directive be annulled and a new measure be proposed with Art 7 as the legislative base (*European Parliament* v *Council* (Case C-295/90); see Directive 93/96 EC).

SUBSIDIARITY

A relatively new feature of Community law is the recognition in the EC Treaty, following amendment by the TEU, of a national dimension to the decision-making process. Article 5 EC Treaty now provides that:

> The Community shall act within the limits of the powers conferred upon it by this Treaty and of the objectives assigned to it therein. In areas which do not fall within its exclusive competence, the Community shall take action, in accordance with the principle of subsidiarity, only if and in so far as the objectives of the proposed action cannot be sufficiently achieved by the Member States and can, therefore, by reason of the scale or effects of the proposed action, be better achieved by the Community. Any action by the Community shall not go beyond what is necessary to achieve the objectives of this Treaty.

Although subsidiarity is not a new concept for the Community, the TEU made it a central criterion to be applied by the Commission in proposing new legislation. Hitherto, subsidiarity had been implicit in Art 249 EC Treaty in relation to the implementation of directives, where the Community set the objectives, and the Member

States chose the 'manner and form of implementation'. It was first made specific by the then Art 130(4) in relation to the environment, where legislation was only to be introduced where the environmental objectives could 'be attained better at Community level than at the level of individual Member States'. Article 5 EC Treaty makes the principle applicable to all new legislation where the issue of competing competencies arises.

At the Edinburgh European Council Meeting of October 1993, it was decided that the Commission should consult more widely before proposing legislation and should include in the recitals to any new measure, besides the legislative base, its justification for initiating the measure, under the subsidiarity principle. If legislation had to be made at Community level, directives were to be preferred to regulations and 'framework directives' (allowing Member States considerable leeway in the manner of implementation) to specific and detailed directives (Toth, 1994). ¹

As part of the process of implementing the new subsidiarity principle, the Commission embarked on a so-called bonfire of measures and the abandonment of some legislative programmes, with a view to the policies which they were intended to implement being carried out at national level. It announced the withdrawal of proposals for more than 15 directives, including proposals on the liability of suppliers of services (COM (90) 482), minimum standards for the keeping of animals in zoos, speed limits for motor vehicles and maximum alcohol levels for vehicle drivers (Bull EU 6 1994, p. 26).

There are, however, both legal and practical limits to the implementing of policies at national level, as envisaged in Art 5. Article 5 refers to matters which are not within the exclusive competence of the Community, implying that there are matters of shared competence. Such a concept is fundamentally at odds with basic principles of Community law. The Community either has competence, in which case it has the power to legislate in a way which must take precedence over national legislation, or it has no competence, in which case the question of whether or not the decision should be taken at Community or national level does not arise. Essentially, the issue is about how Community policies are to be implemented and enforced, and how much discretion is to be given to national governments. It is, however, arguable that the inclusion of the new areas of competence in the TEU, at the same time as the recognition of a joint competence of Community and Member States, suggests that in the new areas of competence, questions of who is to make decisions as well as who is to implement them, and how, will arise.

It is at the national level that practical difficulties arise. Long experience has shown that there are major divergences in the extent of implementation of Community law by Member States. The briefest examination of the European Court Reports and the Annual Report of the Commission indicates the scale of the problem. The Commission's annual report on monitoring the application of Community law is available on the Internet at: http://europa.eu.int/comm/off/rep/index_en.htm.

If more legislation and more enforcement are to take place at state level, there will be even greater local variations in the degree of regulation in each Member State. The 'level playing field' for business may then become even less attainable. On a practical level, the regulation of air and water quality, which clearly may involve the environments of a number of Member States, can be carried out effectively only if the same environmental quality is to be maintained at Community level. The Court of Justice may be called upon to decide, according to the effects or scale of a measure, whether its objectives could be 'sufficiently' achieved by legislation in the Member States. It may have to apply conflicting criteria. Pollution control may be most effectively managed at local level, but given the extent of water and air pollution in Europe, the scale could require a Community *standard* of air and water quality and action at Community level to see that it is secured in Member States. Whether a practical assessment to determine the appropriate level of action is possible, or whether it is an apposite exercise for a court of law, is yet to be demonstrated.

Ironically, subsidiarity was championed by those Member States, among them the United Kingdom, that were concerned about the centralising of decision making in Brussels, and the apparent movement of the Community towards a federal structure. If the Court of Justice has to determine which decisions can and should be taken at the centre, and which at national level by national parliaments, then Art 5 could become the cornerstone in the constitution of a new federal Europe. Subsidiarity was again discussed at the Amsterdam Conference in 1997 and some attempt was made to build the principle into the decision-making process. A Protocol added to the ToA provides as follows:

> Subsidiarity is a dynamic concept and should be applied in the light of the objectives set out in the Treaty. It allows Community action within the limits of its powers to be expanded where circumstances so require, and conversely, to be restricted or discontinued where it is no longer justified.

The Protocol requires every proposed piece of Community legislation to state how it complies with the principle of subsidiarity and proportionality (see Chapter 5) and why 'a Community objective can be better achieved by the Community'. Essentially, Member States retain powers only in those areas where the Treaties confer no powers on the Community, or where the Community has general powers in a given area but has not yet chosen to act. Once it does act, its measures prevail over national rules, and it has exclusive competence.

Further reading

Bradley, K., 'Comitology and the Law: Through a Glass Darkly' (1992) 29 CML Rev 695.

Chalmers, D. and Szyszczak, E. (1998) *European Union Law*, Vol I, Ashgate/Dartmouth.

Craig, P. and De Burca, G. (1998) *EU Law Text, Cases and Materials* (2nd edn), OUP, Chapter 3.

Curtin, D., 'The Constitutional Structure of the Union: A Europe of Bits and Pieces' (1993) 30 CML Rev 17.

Hartley, T.C. (1998) *The Foundations of European Community Law* (4th edn), OUP, Chapter 1.

Hosli, M., 'Coalitions and Power: Effects of qualified majority voting on the Council of the European Union' (1996) 34 JCMS 255.

The Intergovernmental Conference 1996: The Agenda; Democracy and Efficiency; the Role of National Parliaments, 24th Report, Vol 1, Select Committee on European Legislation: Session 1994–95, HMSO.

Lang, J. Temple, 'Community Constitutional Law: Article 5 EEC Treaty' (1990) 27 CML Rev 645.

Langrish, S., 'The Treaty of Amsterdam: Selected Highlights' (1998) 23 EL Rev 3.

Nicholl, W., 'The Code of Conduct of the Commission towards the European Parliament' (1996) 34 JCMS 275.

Nugent, N. (1994) *The Government and Politics of the European Union*, Macmillan, Chapters 5 and 11.

O'Keefe, D. and Twomey, P. (eds) (1994) *Legal Issues of the Maastricht Treaty*, Chancery Publications, Chapters 3–5, 11.

Pescatore, P., 'Some Critical Remarks on the Single European Act' (1987) CML Rev 9, 13.

Steiner, J. and Woods, L. (2000) *Textbook on EC Law* (7th edn), Blackstone Press, Chapter 3.

Tillotson, J. (2000) *European Community Law: Text, Cases and Materials* (3rd edn), Cavendish Publishing Ltd, Chapters 5 and 6.

Timmermans, Ch., 'How can one improve the quality of Community legislation?' (1997) 34 CML Rev 1229.

Toth, A.G. (1994) 'A Legal Analysis of Subsidiarity', in O'Keefe, D. and Twomey, P. (eds) *Legal Issues of the Maastricht Treaty*, Chancery Publications.

Toth, A.G. (1995) *The Oxford Encyclopaedia of European Community Law*, Clarendon Press.

Weatherill, S. (2000) *Cases and Materials on EC Law* (5th edn), Blackstone Press, Chapter 1.

Chapter 5

THE EUROPEAN COURT OF JUSTICE AND THE COURT OF FIRST INSTANCE

Article 7(1) EC Treaty (previously Art 4(1)) refers to this institution as the Court of Justice (it may also be referred to as the European Court, or European Court of Justice). It should not be confused with the European Court of Human Rights, which is not a Community institution and does not have jurisdiction to adjudicate on Community law. The European Court of Human Rights has jurisdiction to adjudicate on breaches of the European Convention on Human Rights, of which the United Kingdom is a signatory (see Chapter 1). The Court of Justice is permanently in session in Luxembourg and vacations are fixed according to the workload; the European Court of Human Rights sits in Strasbourg.

The Court of Justice plays a pivotal role in the Community. Some of the legal principles which govern the way the Community functions are not found in the Treaty or the legislative acts made under it, but they are to be found in the case law of the Court. This will be considered further in this chapter and Chapter 9.

The Court of Justice is itself governed by the founding Treaties as amended, and the Statutes of the Court of Justice which are appended to the Treaties as protocols. The Statute annexed to the EC Treaty has the title: 'Protocol on the Statute of the Court of Justice of the European Community', as amended by Council Decision 94/993 (OJ 1994 L 397/1). Detailed effect is given to the Statute by the Court's Rules of Procedure. The third paragraph of Art 245 EC Treaty provides that 'the Court of Justice shall adopt its rules of procedure. These shall require the unanimous approval of the Council'. The current Rules were adopted on 19 June 1991 (OJ 1991 L 176/1, with corrigendum in OJ 1992 L 383/117) and were amended on 21 February 1995 (OJ 1995 L 44/61), 11 March 1997 (OJ 1997 L 103/1, with corrigendum in OJ 1997 L 351/72), and most recently 16 May 2000 (OJ 2000 L 122/43). The last amendments came into effect on 1 July 2000 and were designed to improve the conduct of procedures, to expedite (i.e. accelerate) the treatment of certain references for a preliminary ruling which are of exceptional urgency, and to adapt the Rules to the amendments introduced by the ToA. In its submission to the Nice 2000 Intergovernmental Conference the Court of Justice and the Court of First Instance (see below) requested the power to amend their Rules of Procedure themselves:

> In an enlarged Union, the requirement that amendments to the Rules of Procedure of the Court of Justice and the Court of First Instance be unanimously approved by the Council may give rise to a lack of flexibility which is incompatible with the need for the courts to

adapt to their new work. Such inflexibility is unnecessary, particularly since most of the procedural provisions having any special importance in terms of institutional considerations or matters of policy are contained in the Statute. It will also be noted that other courts, such as the International Court of Justice and the European Court of Human Rights, have the power to adopt their own rules of procedure.

The Court of Justice and the Court of First Instance therefore propose the removal of the words 'Those rules shall require the unanimous approval of the Council' from the end of the third paragraph of Article 245 and the end of Article 225(4). (*Contribution by the Court of Justice and the Court of First Instance to the Intergovernmental Conference*, Luxembourg, 2000)

Although the ToN did not accommodate the Court's request, once the ToN comes into force (which is unlikely to be before 2002), Art 223 will be amended to provide that the Council's approval of the Court's rules of procedure shall be by a qualified majority vote rather than by unanimity. The ToN will make other amendments affecting the composition, rules and procedures of both the Court of Justice and Court of First Instance, which will be discussed below. In addition, a new Statute will come into force alongside the ToN.

The provisions of the EC Treaty applicable to the Court of Justice are Articles 220–245 (previously Arts 164–188). The Court of Justice has a website which can be accessed at: http://www.curia.eu.int/en/index.htm.

ORGANISATION OF THE COURT OF JUSTICE

Members

The Court shall consist of 15 judges (Art 221 EC Treaty (previously Art 165)) assisted by 8 Advocates-General (Art 222 EC Treaty (previously Art 166)). Article 223 (previously Art 167) provides that both:

> shall be chosen from persons whose independence is beyond doubt and who possess the qualifications required for appointment to the highest judicial offices in their respective countries or who are jurisconsults of recognised competence.

The requirements for these appointments are therefore not intended to be confined to those who have made a career in the courts and are destined for, or already sit, on the bench in their Member State. Appointments may also be made from the ranks of distinguished academic lawyers or 'jurisconsults of recognised competence'.

Although the Treaty does not contain any provisions regarding the nomination and nationality of judges and Advocates-General, it has been the practice that each Member State nominates one judge who is a national, and each of the four larger states (France, Germany, Italy and the United Kingdom) has done the same in relation to four of the Advocates-General. However, on the accession of Austria, Finland and Sweden, a Declaration was made by the Member States in relation to the allocation of the posts of Advocates-General. Under the Declaration, France, Germany, Italy, Spain and the United Kingdom will be allocated a 'permanent' Advocate-General each. Spanish, Irish and Italian Advocates-General were appointed from 1 January 1995, and replacements for the non-permanent posts will be filled by the Member States taking part in rotation, in alphabetical order (Joint Declaration 1 January 1995, OJ 1995 L 1/21).

A new judge is required to take an oath to perform his duties impartially and conscientiously and to preserve the secrecy of the deliberations of the Court. He also signs a solemn declaration to behave with integrity and discretion in relation to the acceptance of benefits after he has left office (Arts 2 and 4 Protocol on the Statute of the Court of Justice). Judges may not hold any political and administrative office and may not follow any other occupation, paid or unpaid, during their period of office (Art 4 Statute).

Membership of the Court has been increased as a matter of course as the Community has enlarged. The Court expressed anxiety about the indefinite application of this policy in its submission to the 1996 Intergovernmental Conference. In relation to membership, two factors must be balanced:

> On the one hand, any significant increase in the number of judges might mean that the plenary session of the Court would cross the invisible boundary between a collegiate body and a deliberative assembly. Moreover, as the great majority of cases would be heard by Chambers, this increase would pose a threat to the consistency of the case law.
>
> On the other hand, the presence of members from all the national legal systems on the Court is undoubtedly conducive to harmonious development of Community case law, taking into account concepts regarded as fundamental in the various Member States and thus enhancing the acceptability of the solutions arrived at. It may also be considered that the presence of a judge from each of the Member States enhances the legitimacy of the Court.

Article 15 of the Statute provides that a decision of the Court of Justice is valid only if an uneven number of judges sit in on the deliberations. Article 26(1) of the Rules provides that where, by reason of a judge being absent or prevented from attending, there is an even number of judges, the most junior judge will abstain from taking part in the deliberations. This is because the Court of Justice delivers a single judgment, to be agreed by majority vote if necessary; it is therefore necessary to have an uneven number of judges to avoid a tied vote. Prior to the accession of Austria, Finland, and Sweden to the Community on 1 January 1995, there were 12 Member States, and therefore only 12 judges (i.e. one nominated by each of the 12 Member States); it was agreed that a thirteenth judge would be nominated by the five largest Member States (i.e. France, Germany, Italy, Spain and the United Kingdom). However, on 1 January 1995 when membership of the Community grew to 15, three new judges were nominated (one from each of the new Member States). This would have increased the number of judges to 16 (an even number). For this reason, the 'extra' judge who had been nominated by the five largest Member States was made an Advocate-General for a temporary period. Article 222 (previously Art 166) therefore provides: 'however a ninth Advocate-General shall be appointed as from 1 January 1995 until 6 October 2000'.

Article 223 EC Treaty (previously Art 167) provides for the appointments to be for a renewable six-year term. Appointment and reappointment of the judges and Advocates-General is staggered, taking place every three years. It has been argued that this necessity to seek reappointment could threaten the impartiality of the judiciary, because if a particular judge acts against the interests of the Member State of his nationality it is likely he would not be nominated for reselection. Accordingly, there may be pressure on the judge to be sympathetic to national issues. This argument may be rejected because the Court delivers one judgment, and therefore it is impossible for a Member State to ascertain the actual views of their nominee (see below). The same, however, could not be said of Advocates-General, the role of whom shall be considered below.

The UK judge is David A. O. Edward, who has been a member since 10 March 1992, having previously been a judge of the Court of First Instance (from 1 September 1989 to 10 March 1992). He is a QC (Scotland) and an academic.

The UK Advocate-General is Francis Jacobs. He has occupied the post since 7 October 1988. He is a QC and an academic.

Treaty of Nice amendments

Once the ToN comes into force, Art 221 EC Treaty will be amended to provide that the Court of Justice will consist of one judge from each Member State. Article 222 EC Treaty will provide for eight Advocates-General to assist the Court, and that if the Court requests the number to be increased, the Council may do so acting unanimously.

President of the Court

Article 223 EC Treaty (previously Art 167) provides for the election by the judges of a President for a term of three years, which may be renewed. The current President is Mr Gill Carlos Rodriguez Iglesias from Spain. He has occupied the post since 7 October 1994. His Presidency was renewed for the period from 7 October 1997 to 6 October 2000 and has since been extended to 6 October 2003.

The President directs the judicial business and administration of the Court: thus he presides at hearings of the full court, fixes and extends time limits for lodging pleadings, documents, etc., and usually deals with interlocutory applications (i.e. applications within the course of the proceedings, prior to the full hearing).

Article 9(2) of the Rules provides for the President to appoint a Judge-Rapporteur to each case before the Court. The function of the Judge-Rapporteur is to manage the case throughout its progression through the Court's system. The Judge-Rapporteur will be responsible for drafting the final judgment.

Treaty of Nice amendments

Article 13 of the Statute of the Court of Justice, which will come into force at the same time as the ToN, provides that the Council (acting unanimously) may provide for the appointment of Assistant Rapporteurs to assist the Judge-Rapporteur. These assistants will be legally qualified persons and shall be appointed by the Council.

Advocate-General

The title 'Advocate' is something of a misnomer, because the Advocate-General represents no one and does not present a case on anyone's behalf. Although not a judge, the Advocate-General enjoys equal status with the judges. For that reason, the Report by the Court of Justice to the Intergovernmental Conference (IGC) in 1996 suggested that Advocates-General should be able to take part in the election of the President of the Court, but the recommendation was not acted upon. Once the President has assigned a Judge-Rapporteur to a case, the First Advocate-General (Art 10(2) of the Rules provides for the office of First Advocate-General to rotate annually among the Advocates-General) assigns an Advocate-General to the case. Thus each case will have one Judge-Rapporteur and one Advocate-General.

Article 222 (previously Art 166) prescribes the role of the Advocate-General as being:

> to make, in open court, reasoned submissions on cases brought before the Court of Justice, in order to assist the Court in the performance of the task assigned to it in Article 220 [previously Art 164].

The various Court stages will be considered below. Once all the formal stages have been completed, but before the judges deliberate upon their judgment, the Advocate-General will prepare his personal opinion as to the decision the Court should reach, which he will deliver in open court. He is an independent adviser to the Court.

The recommendation in the Opinion is not binding on the Court, or on the parties, and the Court is free to follow it or not, as it chooses. However, in spite of their non-binding nature, the Opinions of Advocates-General carry considerable weight on account of the very high standard of the legal analysis which they contain and are frequently cited in the Court as well as in legal writing as persuasive sources of authority.

The Opinion is fully reasoned. It normally deals with every aspect of the case, and will generally be much longer and more wide-ranging than the judgment of the Court. It will usually attempt to set the case in a broader context than the issues which divide the parties. It will set out the relevant facts and any applicable legislation (e.g. Treaty articles, regulations, directives, etc.), the issues that have been raised will be discussed, there will be a full review of any relevant past case law of the Court, and it will conclude with a recommendation for a solution which the Court may adopt.

An Opinion that is particularly persuasive may strongly influence the Court, especially if it suggests creating a new principle, or departing from a previous decision of the Court. In the vast majority of cases, judgments of the Court will follow the Opinion. However, for example, in *Paola Faccini Dori v Recreb SRL* (Case C-91/92) the Court did not follow the Advocate-General's Opinion; in this case the Advocate-General recommended a departure from existing case law of the Court, which the Court was not minded to depart from.

The reasoning of the Court's judgment may not be as clear and fully argued as the Advocate-General's Opinion, due to the fact that the Court must reach a single judgment. The Opinion therefore may be persuasive in future cases on broadly the same theme. The Opinion will be published together with the judgment in the European Court Reports (the official Community law reports, abbreviated to ECR) and both are also available on the internet at: http://www.curia.eu.int/en/jurisp/index.htm.

Treaty of Nice amendments

Article 20 of the new Statute of the Court of Justice will provide that, after hearing the Advocate-General assigned to a particular case, if the Court considers that the case raises no new point of law, it may decide to determine the case without a submission from the Advocate-General. This is already incorporated into the current Rules of Procedure (see below).

Registrar

Article 224 EC Treaty (previously Art 168) provides that:

> The Court of Justice shall appoint its Registrar and lay down the rules governing his service.

The Rules provide for him to be appointed for a six-year renewable term (Art 12, Rules). The current Registrar is Roger Grass from France. He has been in post since 10 February 1994.

The Registrar heads the Registry, which is responsible for the filing of documents, distribution of documents to relevant parties, etc. The Registrar is also responsible for the administration of the Court of Justice, and is directly responsible to the President of the Court.

Chambers

Article 221 EC Treaty (previously Art 165) provides that:

> The Court of Justice shall sit in plenary session [i.e. all 15 judges sitting together, subject to the rules on quorum]. It may, however, form chambers, each consisting of three, five or seven Judges, either to undertake certain preparatory inquiries or to adjudicate on particular categories of cases in accordance with rules laid down for these purposes.
>
> The Court of Justice shall sit in plenary session when a Member State or Community institution that is a party to the proceedings so requests.

Article 15 of the Statute provides that decisions are valid only where there is an uneven number of judges sitting in the deliberations. Decisions of the full Court (i.e. in plenary session) are valid if nine judges are sitting, and decisions of chambers consisting of three or five judges are valid if three judges are sitting, while chambers of seven will be valid if five are sitting.

Article 95(1) of the Rules provides that any type of case may be assigned to a chamber:

> ... in so far as the difficulty or the importance of the case or particular circumstances are not such as to require that the Court decide it in plenary session.

However, a Member State or Community institution which is a party to a case can demand that the case be heard by the full Court (Article 221, third indent, EC Treaty (previously Art 165)), i.e. sitting in plenary session.

Treaty of Nice amendments

Once the ToN comes into force, Art 221 EC Treaty will be amended to provide for the sitting of the Court in chambers, in a new Grand Chamber, and in plenary session (i.e. the full Court).

Article 16 of the new Statute will provide that the Court shall form chambers of three or five judges (thus dispensing with the seven-judge chamber). The Grand Chamber shall consist of 11 judges and shall sit whenever a Member State or Community institution that is a party to the proceedings so requests. Where it is considered that a case before it is of exceptional importance, the Court may decide, after hearing the Advocate-General, to refer the case to the plenary session.

Article 17 of the new Statute will provide that decisions of the chambers consisting of three or five judges shall be valid only if they are taken by three judges; those of the Grand Chamber valid only if nine judges are sitting; and those of the full Court valid only if 11 judges are sitting.

Language

The case may be conducted in any one of the Community's 11 official languages (Danish, Dutch, English, Finnish, French, German, Greek, Italian, Portuguese, Spanish, Swedish). It may also be conducted in Irish (Art 29(1), Rules). It is for the applicant to choose the language (Art 29(2), Rules). This is overridden by Art 29(2)(a) of the Rules, which provides that where the defendant is a Member State or a natural or legal person with the nationality of a Member State, then the case shall be conducted in the official language of that state. References for a preliminary ruling pursuant to Art 234 EC Treaty (previously Art 177) (see Chapter 6) shall be conducted in the language of the referring national court (Art 29(2), Rules).

The Court itself will use French as its working language. This is despite a majority of citizens of the Member States now speaking English rather than French. It is hardly surprising, however, that French was chosen as the working language because when the first Community (the ECSC) was created by the six founding Member States, French was the official language of three of them (France, Belgium and Luxembourg).

Procedure of the Court

The rules concerning the procedure of the Court are laid down in the Protocol on the Statute of the Court annexed to the EC Treaty and the Rules of Procedure (see above). It must be understood that the process is essentially inquisitorial. Unlike an English adversarial process, the procedure of the Court, after the initiation of the case by one or more of the parties, is Court-led: it can request the parties to provide documents and statements; witnesses are heard at the instigation of the Court. Their evidence is part of the investigation by the Judge-Rapporteur and not, as in an English case, part of the oral hearing. The procedure in a direct action (as opposed to a reference under Art 234 EC Treaty, which is considered in Chapter 6) generally has four stages:

- written proceedings
- preparatory inquiry
- oral hearing
- judgment.

Written proceedings

Article 18 of the Statute provides that:

The written procedure shall consist of the communication to the parties and to the institutions of the Community whose decisions are in dispute, of applications, statements of case, defences and observations, and of replies, if any, as well as of all papers and documents in support or of certified copies of them.

Direct actions are initiated by the applicant filing an application (this is known as a 'pleading') at the Court's registry in accordance with Art 38 of the Rules. At this stage, the case may be assigned to a chamber, and a Judge-Rapporteur and Advocate-General will be appointed. Articles 39 and 40 of the Rules require the Registrar to serve the application on the defendant and any Community institution affected, following which the defendant has one month within which to lodge his defence, if any (this is also known as a 'pleading').

After the close of pleadings, the defendant can argue separately that the application is not admissible, e.g. he may argue that the proceedings were not issued within any relevant time limit. The Court may hear this application at this stage and, if successful, the action will be struck out. Alternatively, the Court may decide to hear the argument as to admissibility at the substantive hearing (i.e. the hearing of the main application).

Preparatory inquiry

It is at this stage that the Court takes over the future direction of the case. Unlike the English legal system, the Court will decide what evidence is required. Article 45(1) of the Rules provides that:

> The Court, after hearing the Advocate-General, shall prescribe the measures of inquiry that it considers appropriate by means of an order setting out the facts to be proved.

At the close of pleadings, the Judge-Rapporteur prepares a report which considers the issues of fact. The Court will decide at an administrative meeting what evidence is required to prove the facts which have not otherwise been agreed by the applicant and the defendant. Article 45(2) of the Rules provides that the following measures of inquiry may be adopted:

- the personal appearance of the parties
- a request for information and production of documents
- oral testimony
- the commissioning of an expert's report
- an inspection of the place or thing in question.

Article 47 of the Rules provides that if a witness is called, the witness is a witness of the Court. The parties do not have the right to call witnesses; they would have to request the Court to call a witness. The witness may be examined by the judges, the Advocate-General and the parties.

Oral hearing

Articles 55 to 62 of the Rules govern the procedural aspects associated with the oral procedure. Once the preparatory inquiry has been concluded, the President of the Court fixes the date for the public hearing. A few days before the hearing the Judge-

Rapporteur issues his report for the hearing. This sets out the facts of the case and summarises the arguments of the parties. Copies of the report are given to all the judges in the chamber and the parties, and are made available to members of the public before the hearing.

The oral proceedings are brief compared to those in an English court in a contested action. They consist of the addresses by counsel for the parties and the Opinion of the Advocate-General. There is usually a gap of some months between the conclusion of the addresses and the delivery of the Opinion to the reconvened Court. Addresses by counsel tend to be quite brief. They are expected to have lodged a copy of their submission before the hearing, and will normally use their address to emphasise their strongest arguments and to attack the weakest points in those of their opponents. The judges will quite frequently challenge points made, but the cut and thrust of forensic debate is somewhat blunted by the need for instant translation by interpreters as the argument proceeds.

Following the addresses the Advocate-General prepares his Opinion, which will be delivered in open court at some future date. Although he takes no part in the discussions between the judges which precede the judgment, his Opinion will have a significant influence on their decision. The Court has held that it is not open to the parties to submit written observations in response to the Advocate-General's Opinion: *Emesa Sugar (Free Zone) NV v Aruba* (Case C-17/98). Immediately after delivery of the Opinion the Court goes into deliberation.

Article 44a of the Rules, which provides for the oral procedure, was amended on 1 July 2000 (OJ 2000 L 122/43). The new Art 44a provides that:

> Without prejudice to any special provisions laid down in these Rules, the procedure before the Court shall also include an oral part. However, after the pleadings referred to in Article 40(1) [i.e. service of a defence] and, as the case may be, in Article 41(1) have been lodged, the Court, acting on a report from the Judge-Rapporteur and after hearing the Advocate-General, and if none of the parties have submitted an application setting out the reasons for which he wishes to be heard, may decide otherwise ...

The effect of this provision is that the Court can decide to dispense with the oral procedure, having received a report from the Judge-Rapporteur, and having listened to the Advocate-General and the parties to the case. This will be reflected in Art 20 of the new Statute of the Court of Justice which will come into force at the same time as the ToN (see above).

Judgment

Articles 63 to 68 of the Rules govern the procedural aspects associated with the delivering of a judgment. Judgment is always reserved by the Court, i.e. it goes into secret deliberation and will deliver its judgment in open court at some future date. This is necessary, because a single judgment is delivered. The deliberation may be lengthy, taking many weeks (or months) to conclude.

A draft judgment will be prepared by the Judge-Rapporteur. This draft will form the basis of the deliberations. It may be necessary to go through the judgment sentence by sentence, voting on individual sentences. The votes of the judges are taken in ascending order of seniority: this is to ensure that the younger judges do not merely follow their seniors. The judgment may be short on reasons, or it may include differing (maybe conflicting) reasons, in order to obtain the necessary majority. It will be recalled (from above) that Art 15 of the Statute provides that a judgment will be valid only if an uneven number of judges sit in on the deliberations.

The deliberations will be conducted in French, and the judgment will be drafted in French, being translated into the language of the hearing (the authentic version of the judgment) once agreed.

Publication of judgments

The formal ruling (the 'operative part') of the judgment is published in the *Official Journal*. The whole of the judgment together with the Advocate-General's Opinion will be published in the official European Court Reports (ECR). The reports are published in the 11 official languages. They are not published in Irish, Irish not being one of the official languages. The series of reports are distinguished by colour, the English version being purple.

The correct mode of citation is for the case number to precede the title, followed by the year of publication of the judgment in square brackets, the abbreviation ECR, and ending with the page number of the report – e.g. Case 20/59 *Italy v High Authority* [1960] ECR 423.

Since the Court of First Instance was established (see below), cases before that court are prefixed with a capital letter 'T' (from the French version of 'Tribunal') and those of the Court of Justice by 'C'. From 1990, the volumes of law reports are divided into two sections, so that the page number is now preceded by the numeral 'I' for cases before the Court of Justice and the numeral 'II' for cases before the Court of First Instance: e.g. Case C-79/89 *Brown Boveri v Hauptzollamt Mannheim* [1991] ECR I-1853, which was also reported at [1993] 1 CMLR 814. The two sections may be bound in two separate volumes depending upon the number of cases reported.

Due to the fact that judgments are always drafted in French, the bound French volume will usually be available six months following the end of the month to which it relates. There are 11 monthly paperback volumes: no judgments are delivered in August. They will subsequently be bound into one yearly volume. Following certain changes at the Court of Justice (for example, it has decided not to publish the Report for the Hearing in all the official languages) the printed volumes should be available in all languages quite soon after publication of the French version. It had previously been two years later.

Judgments are available from the Court's Registry (at a charge) on the day of the judgment, or very shortly thereafter. Judgments (and Opinions of Advocates-Generals) are now available on the Internet (free of charge) soon after the judgment is delivered, although there can be some delay in obtaining an Advocate-General's Opinion prior to the judgment. These can be accessed on the Internet at: http://europa.eu.int/jurisp/ cgi-bin/ form.pl?lang=en.

An alternative means of accessing the Court's case law is through electronic and online databases such as EuroLaw. There are several independent unofficial law reports, e.g. the Common Market Law Reports (CMLR). The advantage of these reports is that, because they employ their own translators, a case may appear in them before it appears in the official ECR. The cases published are selective. The judgments may omit the Advocate-General's Opinion and will rarely include the Report for the Hearing. The downside is that their translations may differ from the version of the official report (ECR). When conducting research or litigation, it is always advisable to refer to the ECRs; alternatives should be used only if the official report is not available because it has not yet been published.

Some important cases may be reported in the domestic law reports, e.g. All ER, Weekly Law Reports, etc.

ToA renumbering of Treaties – future citation

As a consequence of the renumbering of the Treaties provided for by the Treaty of Amsterdam, the Court of Justice has opted for a uniform system for citing provisions of the Treaty (see *Proceedings of the Court of Justice and the Court of First Instance of the European Communities* 7–11 December 1998 No. 31/98):

> In their pre-ToA versions, the Community Treaties (ECSC, Euratom, EC) and the TEU numbered their respective provisions differently to each other.
>
> They used Roman and Arabic numerals (ECSC and Euratom Treaties) or a combination of Roman and Arabic numerals and letters of the alphabet (EC and TEU).
>
> Article 12 of the ToA provides that, as from 1 May 1999 (the date it came into force), the provisions (articles, chapters and sections) of the EC Treaty and TEU are to be renumbered in Arabic numerals.
>
> The amendment of those Treaties involved not only an amendment of their content and the insertion of new provisions, but also the renumbering of most of the already existing provisions.
>
> This could obviously cause confusion in the mind of the user between the version of an article before the entry into force of the ToA and that subsequent to that date, as well as confusion between the provisions of the EC Treaty and the TEU, which are ever more frequently bound to be cited in the same document.
>
> The Court of Justice has therefore decided, in the interests of clarity and consistency, to implement a uniform system of citation of the provisions of the four Treaties in the judgments of the Court and the Opinions of the Advocates-General.
>
> Thus, from 1 May 1999, references to the provisions of the Treaties are to consist of an Arabic numeral designating the article plus two letters designating the Treaty, for example 'Article 2 EC' refers to Article 2 of the EC Treaty.
>
> In English, each of the four Treaties will be designated by two letters:
>
> - ECSC   CS
> - Euratom Treaty   EA
> - EC Treaty   EC
> - Treaty on European Union   EU
>
> These rules are to be applied in all cases brought *after* 1 May 1999 which concern the renumbered provisions.
>
> However, the Court of Justice has provided for a transitional period. The Court has adopted different rules of citation for documents relating to cases brought *before* 1 May 1999 and for cases brought *after* 1 May 1999 but concerning the Treaties as they applied before this date. These transitional rules are as follows:

- Where an article has simply been renumbered with no change to its wording, the example to be followed is '*Article 81 EC (ex Article 85)*'
- Where the article has been both renumbered and amended but the version concerned is that prior to the amendment, the formula used is '*Article 51 of the EC Treaty (now, after amendment, Article 41 EC)*'
- Where the article has been repealed by the ToA, it should be referred to as, for example, '*Article 53 of the EC Treaty (repealed by the Treaty of Amsterdam)*'.

PRECEDENT

The doctrine of precedent (*stare decisis*) does not apply to the Court of Justice. However, the Court does generally follow its own previous decisions; this is necessary for the sake of legal certainty. Nonetheless, faced with a very persuasive Advocate-General's Opinion, the Court may be persuaded to deviate from its past case law (e.g. to develop a new Community legal principle). The Court may, of its own volition, depart from its own previous case law: e.g. on policy grounds.

An example of a departure from its past case law is illustrated in *Criminal Proceedings against Keck and Mithouard* (Cases C-267 and 268/91), in which the Court of Justice held:

14. ... the Court considers it necessary to re-examine and clarify its case law on this matter ...

16. ... contrary to what has previously been decided ...

It is usual for lawyers to cite previous case law when arguing a point of law before the Court. Indeed, the Advocate-General in his Opinion, and the Court in its judgment, will generally refer to previous cases. It may be difficult, if not impossible, to extract a *ratio decidendi* (i.e. principle of law applied to the facts) from the judgment because of the style of the Court's single judgment.

METHODS OF INTERPRETATION

The task of the Court of Justice is stated simply in all three Treaties. It '... shall ensure that in the interpretation and application of [the] Treaty the law is observed' (Art 220 EC Treaty). The sources of the law to which the Court has to give effect are diverse (and have been considered in detail in Chapter 2). Many of the Treaty provisions, and some of the implementing legislation, are expressed in the broadest terms, and the Court of Justice plays a crucial role in developing the law and constitution of the Community. It emphasised the importance and the breadth of that role in its submission to the Intergovernmental Conference of 1996:

The Court ... carries out tasks which, in the legal systems of the Member States, are those of the constitutional courts, the courts of general jurisdiction or the administrative courts or tribunals, as the case may be.

In its constitutional role, the Court rules on the respective powers of the Communities and of the Member States, and on those of the Communities in relation to other forms of cooperation within the framework of the Union and, generally, determines the scope of the provisions of the Treaties whose observance it is its duty to ensure. It ensures that the delimitation of powers between the institutions is safeguarded, thereby helping to maintain the institutional balance. It examines whether fundamental rights and general principles of law have been observed by the institutions, and by the Member States when their actions fall within the scope of Community law. It rules on the relationship between Community law and national law and on the reciprocal obligations between the Member States and the Community institutions. Finally, it may be called upon to judge whether international commitments envisaged by the Communities are compatible with the Treaties. (*Report of the Court of Justice on Certain Aspects of the Application of the Treaty on European Union for the Purposes of the 1996 Intergovernmental Conference* (May 1995))

In this section, the methods of interpretation which the Court of Justice employs when interpreting Community law, be it the Treaty, a regulation, directive, etc., will be considered. This 'European way' of interpretation is totally different to that employed by the English judiciary. This was recognised by Lord Denning sitting in the Court of Appeal in *Bulmer* v *Bollinger* [1974] 3 WLR 202, when he stated:

> The [EC] Treaty is quite unlike any of the enactments to which we have become accustomed ... It lays down general principles. It expresses its aims and purposes. All in sentences of moderate length and commendable style. But it lacks precision. It uses words and phrases without defining what they mean. An English lawyer would look for an interpretation clause, but he would look in vain. There is none. All the way through the Treaty there are gaps and lacunae. These have to be filled by the judges, or by regulations or directives.
>
> It is the European way ... Seeing these differences, what are the English courts to do when they are faced with a problem of interpretation? They must follow the European pattern. No longer must they argue about the precise grammatical sense. They must look to the purpose and intent ... They must divine the spirit of the Treaty and gain inspiration from it. If they find a gap, they must fill it as best they can ... These are the principles, as I understand it, on which the European Court acts.

This approach of Lord Denning has its source in s 3(1), European Communities Act 1972, which provides:

> For the purposes of all legal proceedings any question as to the meaning or effect of any of the Treaties, or as to the validity, meaning or effect of any Community instrument, shall be treated as a question of law (and, if not referred to the European Court, be for determination as such in accordance with the principles laid down by and any relevant decision of the European Court or any court attached thereto).

The 'principles laid down by ... the European Court' is certainly wide enough to include the Court of Justice's method of interpretation. The European Communities Act 1972 was enacted by the UK Parliament to enable the United Kingdom to become a Member State of the Communities with effect from 1 January 1973.

The Court employs four separate methods of interpretation, each of which will be considered below:

- literal
- historical
- contextual
- teleological.

It has emerged that the last two (and the last one in particular) are most often employed by the Court of Justice, these two being novel to the English judiciary.

Literal interpretation

This rule is commonly used by the English judiciary in interpreting national legislation. You begin with the words of the text and give them their natural, plain meaning. The Court of Justice may refuse to employ this method, even where the words of the measure in question appear to be perfectly clear (see, e.g., *Commission* v *Council* (Case 22/70)).

Literal interpretation may be more difficult for the Court of Justice to apply because of the lack of interpretation sections in the relevant legislative measure. It will therefore be left to judicial interpretation to develop the meanings of certain words and phrases. Examples from the EC Treaty which have required interpretation include:

- 'charges having equivalent effect' (Arts 23 and 25 (previously Arts 9 and 12)).
- 'worker' (Art 39 (previously Art 48)).
- 'public policy' (Art 39 (previously Art 48)).
- 'abuse of a dominant position' (Art 82 (previously Art 86)).

Secondary legislation may be drafted more specifically (especially regulations which are to be directly applicable as they stand (see Chapter 2)). Nevertheless, the Court of Justice may apply one of the other methods rather than the literal method.

Historical interpretation

Historical interpretation requires a consideration of the subjective intention of the author of the text. This will involve an examination of the preliminary debates. This may be equated with the English mischief rule, where the judiciary seek to establish the legislative intent, i.e. ascertain why the legislation was enacted; what its purpose was conceived to be at the time of enactment.

Historical interpretation is little used by the Court of Justice. Generally it is not prepared to examine records of debates, and it should be remembered that meetings of the Council and Commission are secret, although there is now a greater tendency to openness and transparency. With regard to regulations, directives and decisions, Art 253 EC Treaty (previously Art 190) provides that reasons on which they are based must be given, i.e. the reasons as to why they have been enacted. These reasons will be contained in the preamble. The Court of Justice may be guided by these historical reasons in ascertaining the legislative intention of the Commission and the Council. They are often referred to in judgments of the Court of Justice. In *Markus* v *Hauptzollamt Hamburg-Jonas* (Case 14/69) the Court of Justice held that:

> ... according to the seventh recital of the preamble to the regulation in question ... the eight recital of the same preamble states ... It must therefore be assumed that the authors of the first paragraph of Article 16 intended ... The solution is confirmed by the penultimate recital of the preamble to the said regulation according to which ...

Contextual interpretation

This method is extensively used by the Court of Justice in interpreting the Treaties and secondary legislation. It involves placing the provision within its context and interpreting it in relation to the other provisions. A particular paragraph of a directive or regulation, etc., must be considered not in isolation, but within the context of the whole instrument. In interpreting an article of the Treaty the Court of Justice may have regard to 'the general scheme of the Treaty as a whole' (*Commission* v *Luxembourg and Belgium* (Cases 2 & 3/62)). In this case the Court of Justice was considering the former Art 12 (now Art 25), which provides that:

> Customs duties on imports and exports and charges having equivalent effect shall be prohibited between Member States. This prohibition shall also apply to customs duties of a fiscal nature.

The Court held that:

> The position of those Articles [former Arts 9 and 12 (now Arts 23 and 25)] towards the beginning of that Part of the Treaty dealing with the 'Foundations of the Community' – [former] Article 9 [now Art 23] being placed at the beginning of the Title relating to 'Free Movement of Goods' and [former] Article 12 [now Art 25] at the beginning of the section dealing with the 'Elimination of Customs Duties' – is sufficient to emphasise the essential nature of the prohibitions which they impose.

The Court of Justice, relying upon the 'general scheme' of these provisions and of the Treaty as a whole, went on to state that there was:

> a general intention to prohibit not only measures which obviously take the form of the classic customs duty but also all those which, presented under other names or introduced by the indirect means of other procedures, would lead to the same discriminatory or protective results as customs duties.

The Court gave a wide interpretation to the general words 'charges having equivalent effect', whereas an English Court may have applied the *ejusdem generis* rule to limit its scope: i.e. where specific categories are followed by general words, then the general words are limited to the context of the specific categories. The Court of Justice used the general expression as a catch-all provision, looking at the specific provision in context and in relation to the Treaty as a whole, the aim of which is to abolish all restrictions on the free movement of goods.

Teleological interpretation

In adopting this method, the Court in interpreting the provision in question will be guided by the aims and objectives of the Community as a whole. As we have seen in Chapter 1, the EC Treaty sets out a broad programme rather than a detailed plan. The preamble to the Treaty and some of the introductory articles (especially Arts 2 and 3) set out the broad aims and objectives of the Community, in very general terms. In interpreting the Treaties or other Community legislation, the Court of Justice may be guided by these overarching aims and objectives (the grand scheme), thus adopting a teleological approach.

Therefore, the contextual approach considers a specific section of a provision in the context of all the sections of that provision, whereas the teleological approach goes outside the actual provision and considers the whole purpose, the aims and objectives, of the Community and the Union.

The Court has become accustomed to interpreting Community law teleologically, by reference to the broad policy objectives of the Treaty, rather than, as would an English court, by the meaning of the words before it and their immediate context. It has, for example, been accepted that the European Parliament has the right to bring an action for annulment against the Council or Commission, although only Member States, the Council and affected individuals were specifically given such a right in Art 230(1) EC Treaty. The Court of Justice held that not to imply such a right for the Parliament would deprive it of the legal means with which to protect its privileges against incursions by the other institutions (*Parliament* v *Council* (Case C-70/88)). Article 230 EC Treaty, indent 3 (as amended by the TEU), now gives the Parliament the right to take such an action to protect its prerogatives. The Court has also extended the right of free movement of workers to those looking for work, even though the relevant Art 39 EC Treaty appears to confer the right only on those to whom an offer of work has actually been made. The Court of Justice felt that the object of the Treaty to secure the free movement of labour would not be achieved if only those with an offer of employment from another Member State were enabled to move (*Procureur du Roi* v *Royer* (Case 48/75)). In these, and in many other matters, the Court has used its interpretative powers to put flesh on the bones of Treaty provisions, and to do so in such a way as to facilitate the effective development of the Community.

Underlying these decisions is what can only be described as the *policy* of the Court. All national courts have unstated policy objectives, such as the maintenance of the rule of law or the discouragement of what is seen as anti-social behaviour. The law will be interpreted as far as possible to achieve those ends. The Court's objectives are more clearly discernible. Broadly, the Court's policies could be said to consist of strengthening the Union's structure, increasing the scope and effectiveness of Community law and enhancing the powers of the Community institutions. The series of cases in which the Parliament's ability to bring proceedings to protect its prerogatives has effectively been extended beyond those powers conferred by the EC Treaty, and the decisions under which its consultative role has been enhanced, all reflect the concern of the Court to ensure that the Community's only democratically elected institution is given proper weight in the decision-making process.

The Court's policy of securing greater effectiveness for Community law is achieved partly by interpreting the law in such a way that it achieves the broader objectives of the Treaty, even if this has to be done, in some cases, by ignoring the express words of the Community legislation. It can also be seen in the doctrine of the direct effect of directives (see Chapter 9) under which the measures originally intended to bind only the governments of Member States have become the means by which individuals can secure their rights in national courts. In pursuit of the same policy objective, remedies in national courts, which were originally seen as being of purely national concern and beyond the competence of the Court, are now judged by the Court in terms of their effectiveness to secure the implementation of Community law. If they are not effective, they must be set aside and an effective remedy provided: *R* v *Secretary of State for Transport, ex parte Factortame* (Case C-213/89 – see Chapter 10).

GENERAL PRINCIPLES OF LAW AND FUNDAMENTAL RIGHTS UPON WHICH THE CONSTITUTIONAL LAWS OF THE MEMBER STATES ARE BASED

Article 6(1) TEU (as amended by ToA) now states, unequivocally, that 'The Union is founded on the principles of liberty, democracy, respect for human rights and fundamental freedoms, and the rule of law, principles which are common to the Member States'. The importance of these principles is emphasised by the new powers conferred on the Council of Ministers by Art 7(2) TEU to suspend the voting rights of states found to be in breach.

In interpreting primary and secondary Community legislation, the Court has developed a number of general principles of law, some based on the fundamental laws of the constitutions of the Member States, some based on principles of international law and some derived directly from the European Convention on Human Rights. Although the jurisdiction of the Court of Justice is, as we have seen, limited by Art 220 EC Treaty to the interpretation of the Treaties and the subordinate legislation made under them, this is to be done in such a way as to ensure that 'the law is observed'. This has been widely interpreted to mean not only the law established by the Treaties but 'any rule of law relating to the Treaty's application' (Pescatore, 1970). The principles of the Convention are to be applied insofar as they relate to matters within the competence of the Community. It shall 'respect fundamental rights, as guaranteed by the European Convention for the Protection of Human Rights and Fundamental Freedoms signed in Rome on 4 November 1950 and as they result from the constitutional traditions common to Member States, as general principles of Community law' (Art 6(2) TEU).

Human rights

Article 6 TEU (as amended by the ToA) declares that:

(1) The Union is founded on the principles of liberty, democracy, respect for human rights and fundamental freedoms, and the rule of law, principles which are common to the Member States.

(2) The Union shall respect fundamental rights, as guaranteed by the European Convention for the Protection of Human Rights and Fundamental Freedoms signed in Rome on 4 November 1950 and as they result from the constitutional traditions common to the Member States, as general principles of Community Law.

The effect of Art 6 is to give formal recognition in the Treaty to what has been part of the jurisprudence of the Court since *Stauder* (Case 29/69). In that case the Court declared that 'fundamental human rights are enshrined in the general principles of Community law and protected by the Court'. In *A* v *Commission* (Case T-10/93) the Court of First Instance noted the commitment in Art F.2 (now Art 6 TEU) to respect the fundamental rights guaranteed by the Convention and said, repeating the words of the Court of Justice in the *ERT* case (Case C-260/89), 'the Court draws inspiration from the constitutional traditions common to Member States and from the guidelines supplied by international treaties for the protection of human rights on which Member States have collaborated or of which they are signatories' (see, in particular, the judgment in *Nold* v *Commission* (Case 4/73)). The European Convention on Human Rights (ECHR) has special significance in that respect (see, in particular *Johnston* v *Chief Constable of the Royal Ulster Constabulary* (Case 222/84)). It follows that, as the Court held in its judgment in *Wachauf* v *Germany* (Case 5/88), the Community cannot accept measures which are incompatible with observance of the human rights thus recognised and guaranteed.

What this means is that when there is a conflict between a national law which is, for example, intended to implement Community law, but does so in such a way as to breach the Convention, the Court will rule the national measure as contrary to Community law. In the *Johnston* case, national measures intended to prohibit sexual discrimination in Northern Ireland and to provide a remedy for those alleging discriminatory behaviour, were held contrary to Community law because the Court held that they did not give complainants an effective remedy as required by Art 13 of the Convention. It must, however, be emphasised that the Court of Justice can only rule on compatibility between the Convention and Community law in those areas of national law affected by Community law. It could not, for example, rule on the compatibility of a criminal trial in a Member State with the Convention's provisions on fair process, where the trial was unrelated to any rules of Community law, even though the individual involved was a citizen of the Union (*Kremzow* v *Austria* (Case C-299/95)). The Court defined the limits of its powers in *Demirel* v *Stadt Schwabisch Gmund* (Case 12/86). The Court, it said,

> has no power to examine the *compatibility with the European Convention on Human Rights of national legislation lying outside the scope of Community law*. (emphasis added)

The application of the Convention and the development of the jurisprudence of fundamental rights has been a somewhat erratic process, depending very much on the kind of cases which have come before the Court. Some provisions of the Convention, particularly those relating to due process under Art 6 ECHR, have been discussed frequently by the Court, while others, such as that relating to the right to life, hardly at all. Fundamental rights have been drawn both from the Convention and from the constitutions of the Member States; rights and freedoms recognised by national constitutions as being 'fundamental' both in the sense that they protect and promote the most essential human values, such as the dignity, the personality, the intellectual and physical integrity, or the economic and social wellbeing of the individual, and in the sense that they are inseparably attached to the person. The Court has emphasised its commitment to human rights in general on several occasions, over a period of 30 years, starting with *Stauder* (Case 29/69). However, until the Treaty on European Union came into effect in 1993, there were no specific provisions for the protection of human rights as such, in the Treaties. It is arguable that the Court has been reluctant to take on the protection of fundamental rights, and did so largely to protect the supremacy of its jurisdiction:

> Reading an unwritten bill of rights into Community law is indeed the most striking contribution the Court made to the development of a new constitution for Europe. This statement should be qualified in two respects. First ... that contribution was forced on the court from outside, by the German and, later, the Italian Constitutional Courts. Second, the court's effort to safeguard the fundamental rights of the Community citizens stopped at the threshold of national legislations. (Mancini, 1989)

Even where a right is recognised by the Court as a fundamental Community right, that recognition is not conclusive. The designation by the Court of a right as 'fundamental' does not always mean that all other rules must give way before it. In some circumstances, one 'fundamental' right may have to give way to another which the Court regards as even more important. Much will depend on the context in which the 'fundamental' right is called upon, and the nature of the right itself.

The right to property and the freedom to choose a trade or profession

This right is contained in Art 1 of the First Protocol ECHR (1952 Cmd 9221) (and see *Nold* v *Commission* (Case 4/73)). The Court of Justice has declared 'The right to property is guaranteed in the Community legal order' (*Hauer* v *Land Rheinland-Pflaz* (Case 44/79)). In *Wachauf* (Case 5/88), a German tenant farmer was deprived of his right to compensation under Regulation 857/84 for loss of a milk quota, as a result of the way in which the German Government had interpreted the regulation. He argued that this amounted to expropriation without compensation. The case was referred to the Court of Justice which held:

> It must be observed that Community rules which, upon the expiry of the lease, had the effect of depriving the lessee, without compensation, of the fruits of his labour and of his investments in the tenanted holding would be incompatible with the requirements of the protection of fundamental rights in the Community legal order. Since those requirements are also binding on Member States when they implement Community rules, the Member States must, as far as possible, apply those rules in accordance with those requirements.

However, the Court held in *R* v *Ministry of Agriculture, ex parte Bostock* (Case C-2/92), that where a lessor 'inherited' the benefit of a milk quota, neither the milk quota scheme itself nor the Community principles of fundamental rights required a Member State to introduce a scheme for compensation for the outgoing lessee, nor did they confer directly on the lessee a right to such compensation.

In *Commission* v *Germany* (Case C-280/93), the Court affirmed that both the right to property and the freedom to pursue a trade or business formed part of the general principles of Community law. But those principles were not absolute, and

> had to be viewed in relation to their social function. Consequently, the exercise of the right to property and the freedom to pursue a trade or profession could be restricted, particularly in the context of a common organisation of a market, provided that those restrictions in fact corresponded to objectives of general interest pursued by the Community and did not constitute a disproportionate and intolerable interference, impairing the very substance of the rights guaranteed.

In relation to access to a trade or profession, the principle of equality should ensure equal access to available employment and the professions between Community citizens and nationals of the host state (see *Thieffry* (Case 71/76)). In *UNECTEF* v *Heylens* (Case 222/86), the Court said that 'free access to employment is a fundamental right which the Treaty confers individually on each worker of the Community' ([1987] ECR 4098 at 4117).

The right to carry on an economic activity

This is closely tied to the right to property. The Court has held that the right to property is guaranteed in the Community legal order. However, it has also decided that a Community-imposed restriction on the planting of vines constitutes a legitimate exception to the principle, which is recognised in the constitutions of Member States (see *Hauer* (Case 44/79), *Eridania* (Case 230/78) and *S M Winsersett* v *Land Rheinland-Pflaz* (Case C-306/93)).

Freedom of trade

In *Procureur de la République* v *ADBHU* (Case 240/83), the Court of Justice said that:

> It should be borne in mind that the principles of free movement of goods and freedom of competition, together with freedom of trade as a fundamental right, are general principles of Community law of which the Court ensures observance.

The Court has held on several occasions that the right for goods to be allowed access to markets in other Member States under Art 28 EC Treaty is, subject to the exceptions in Art 30, a directly enforceable right. This decision elevates that right to a fundamental principle, in the face of which inconsistent Community and national legislation must generally give way. But, the freedom to trade is not absolute, and may have to give way to the imperatives of the Single Market (see *Commission* v *Germany* (above)).

The right to an effective judicial remedy before national courts (Arts 6, 13 ECHR)

This has become one of the most developed fundamental principles in the jurisprudence of the Court of Justice. In *Johnston* v *Chief Constable of the RUC* (Case 222/84), the RUC maintained a general policy of refraining from issuing firearms to female members of the force. The policy was defended on the ground, *inter alia*, that Art 53, Sex Discrimination (Northern Ireland) Order 1976 (SI 1976/1042 (NI 15)) permitted sex discrimination for the purpose of 'safeguarding national security or of protecting public safety or public order'. A certificate issued by the Secretary of State was to be 'conclusive evidence' that the action was necessary on security grounds. The complainant argued that the rule effectively barred her promotion, and that Directive 76/207 should take priority over national law. Article 6 of the directive provided that complainants should be able to 'pursue their claims by judicial process'. On a reference to the Court of Justice, the Court held that the national tribunal had to be given enough information to determine whether or not the policy of the Chief

Constable was objectively justified. This was necessary in the interests of effective judicial control:

> The requirements of judicial control stipulated by that Article [Art 6 Dir 76/207] reflect a general principle of law which underlines the constitutional traditions common to the Member States. That principle is also laid down in Articles 6 and 13 of the European Convention of Human Rights and Fundamental Freedoms ... As the European Parliament, Council and Commission recognised in their joint declaration of 5 April 1977 (OJ 1977 C 103 p. 1) and as the Court has recognised in its own decisions, the principles on which the Convention is based must be taken into consideration in Community law.

This approach was endorsed by the European Court of Human Rights in *Tinnelly & Sons Ltd and McElduff* v *United Kingdom*. The Court declared, in relation to similar Northern Ireland legislation permitting discrimination on religious grounds:

> The right of a court guaranteed by Article 6.1 ... cannot be replaced by the *ipse dixit* of the executive even if national security considerations constitute a highly material aspect of the case.

The principle of effective judicial control and effective remedies underlies several decisions relating to difficulties encountered by individuals in seeking to establish themselves in businesses and professions in other Member States. These require that sufficient reasons must be given for official decisions, to enable them to be challenged in court, should the need arise. Where:

> it is ... a question of securing the effective protection of a fundamental right conferred by the Treaty on Community workers, the latter must ... be able to defend that right under the best possible conditions and have the possibility of deciding, with a full knowledge of the relevant facts, whether there is any point in their applying to the courts. (See *UNECTEF* v *Heylens* (Case 222/86) and *Pecastaing* (Case 98/79) (A-G Capotorti))

The right to due judicial process also involves a fair investigative process in accordance with the Convention when the European Commission is investigating alleged breaches of competition law. In interpreting its investigative powers under Regulation 17/62, the Commission has to have regard to the Convention and, particularly, the rights of the defence to be informed of the matters under investigation (see *Hoechst* v *Commission* (Case 46/87)). This principle has come to be known as 'equality of arms' (*Solvay SA* v *Commission* (Case T-30/91)). The same principle entitles protection to be given to certain communications between the person under investigation and his lawyer (see *Australia Mining & Smelting Ltd* v *Commission* (Case 155/79)).

The protection of family life, home and family correspondence (Art 8 ECHR)

In *National Panasonic* (Case 136/79), the Court of Justice held that the principles of Art 8 ECHR were applicable to an investigation by the Commission of an alleged anti-competitive practice, but held that the exception in Art 8.2 justified the action taken by the Commission under Regulation 17/62.

In *X* v *Commission* (Case C-404/92), the applicant had applied for an appointment as a temporary member of the Commission's staff. He had agreed to undergo the normal medical examination but had refused to be subjected to a test which might disclose whether or not he carried the AIDS virus. The Court of Justice held that he was entitled to do so:

> The right to respect for private life, embodied in Art 8 ECHR and deriving from the common constitutional traditions of the Member States, is one of the fundamental rights protected by the legal order of the Community. It includes in particular a person's right to keep his state of health secret.

The right of Community citizens in other Member States to have only those restrictions imposed on them in other Member States as are necessary in the interests of national security or public safety in a democratic society (Art 2 Fourth Protocol ECHR)

This right has a wide application. The position of European Union citizens in other Member States, in relation to their human rights, has been described in the most comprehensive terms by Advocate-General Jacobs in *Christos Konstantinidis v Stadt Altensteig-Standesamt* (Case C-168/91):

> In my opinion, a Community national who goes to another Member State as a worker or a self-employed person under Articles 48, 52 or 59 [now Articles 39, 43 or 49] of the Treaty is entitled ... to assume that, wherever he goes to earn his living in the European Community, he will be treated in accordance with a common code of fundamental values, in particular those laid down in the European Convention on Human Rights. In other words, he is entitled to say 'civis Europeus sum' and to invoke that status in order to oppose any violation of his fundamental rights.

The principle applies, *a fortiori*, since the creation of European Union citizenship by Art 17 EC Treaty, as this carries with it, under Art 18, a general right of residence anywhere in the Community for those holding it, subject only to the limitations contained in the Treaty and in the implementing legislation (see Chapters 11–13).

Prohibition of discrimination on the grounds of sex in relation to pay and working conditions (Art 14 ECHR)

This is now one of the principal objectives of the Community (Art 3(2) EC Treaty which is more specifically spelt out in Art 141 EC Treaty). In *P/S and Cornwall County Council* (C-13/94), a case involving the dismissal of a transsexual, the Court of Justice held that the right not to be discriminated against on grounds of sex is 'simply the expression, in the relevant field, of the principle of equality, which is one of the fundamental principles of Community law'. However, since the Court was not prepared to regard cohabitees of the same sex as being in an 'equal' situation, the principle of equality did not apply to them (*Grant v South-Western Trains* (Case C-249/96)). Despite this decision, the creation by the ToA of a power for the Council of Ministers in Art 13 EC Treaty to 'combat' discrimination on grounds of sexual orientation, could well persuade the Court of Justice that the situation of same-sex couples is now an 'equal' situation.

Freedom of expression (Art 10 ECHR)

The relationship to freedom of expression has been considered on several occasions by the Court in the context of freedom to provide and receive services, and in relation to the establishment of businesses in other Member States. In *Elleneki Radiophonia Tileorasi* (ERT) (Case C-260/89) the Court had to consider a challenge by an independent broadcasting company to the monopoly of the state broadcasting company. Greek law forbade any party other than the state television company from broadcasting television programmes within Greek territory. The defendant company defied the ban and, when prosecuted, pleaded in their defence that the television monopoly was contrary both to Community law (*inter alia*, on the free movement of goods and services) and to Art 10 ECHR. The Greek Government defended the television monopoly as a public policy derogation from the free movement of goods and services under Art 66 (now Art 55) EC Treaty. The Court accepted that these derogations were subject to the Convention and said:

> When a Member State invokes Articles 56 and 66 of the Treaty [now Articles 46 and 55] in order to justify rules which hinder the free movement of services, this justification, which is provided for in Community law, must be interpreted in the light of general principles of law, notably fundamental rights ... The limitations imposed on the power of Member States to apply the provisions of Articles 66 and 56 [now Articles 55 and 46] of the Treaty, for reasons of public order, public security and public health must be understood in the light of the general principles of freedom of expression, enshrined in Article 10 of the Convention. (para 45)

Access to information is an important corollary to the effective exercise both of freedom of expression (Art 10 ECHR) and of the right to know the basis of a decision under the general rules requiring a fair decision-making process. Article 253 EC Treaty (formerly Art 190) has long required that reasons for all decisions by Community institutions be given. The ToA has gone further, conferring a right of information on consumers (Art 153 EC Treaty), and a right of access for all EU citizens and those resident in the Community to documents produced by the institutions (Art 255(3) EC Treaty). The right of access is, however, subject to the rules made by each body. The Court of First Instance has already recognised that the policy decision of the Commission to make its documents available could be subject to its power to withhold documents on grounds of public security, international relations, monetary stability, court proceedings and investigations, but these limitations must be specifically justified in the case of each document, and interpreted strictly (*Van der Wal* v *Commission* (Case T-83/96)).

Freedom of religion (Art 9 ECHR)

In *Prais* v *The Council* (Case 130/75), the question of religious discrimination came before the Court. It concerned a woman of Jewish faith who wished to obtain a post as a Community official. She did not mention her faith in her application form, but when she was informed that she would have to sit a competitive examination on a particular day, she explained that she could not do so because it was an important Jewish festival. She asked to be able to take the examination on another day. She was refused, because the Council decided that it was essential for all candidates to sit the examination on the same day. The Court upheld the decision of the Council, because it had not been told, in advance, about the difficulty. The Court accepted, as did the Council, that freedom of religion was a general principle of Community law, but decided that it had not been breached in this case.

Freedom of trade union activity including the right to join and form staff associations

Union Syndicale v *Council* (Case 175/73) recognised the right to trade union membership. It is doubtful if this right extends to a right to engage in industrial action, although Art 13 of the Community Charter of the Fundamental Social Rights of Workers of 1989 provides that the worker shall have the right:

> to resort to collective action in the event of a conflict of interests and shall have the right to strike, subject to the obligations arising under national regulations and collective agreements.

These rights are now, by implication, recognised by all Member States (Art 136 EC Treaty, added by ToA 1997). Individuals benefiting from the protection of Community law are entitled to participate equally in trade unions and staff associations, and should not be penalised for taking part in legitimate trade union activity (see *Rutili* (Case 36/75) and *Association de Soutien aux Traveilleurs Immigrés* (Case C-213/90)). This includes the right to vote and stand for office in such bodies (*Commission* v *Luxembourg* (Case C-118/92)). The European Court of Human Rights, in *Schmidt and Dahlstom*, held that the European Convention on Human Rights safeguards the freedom to protect the occupational interests of trade union members by trade union action, but leaves each state a free choice of the means to be used to this end. Article 8, Regulation 1612/68, which gives migrant workers equal rights with national workers as far as membership of trade unions and the election to office in them is concerned, refers only to 'the rights attaching' to such membership, without further elaboration.

Fundamental rights and the United Kingdom's Human Rights Act 1998

Applying the rule of supremacy of Community law (see Chapter 9), the principles referred to in this chapter must be recognised and implemented by the courts of the United Kingdom as part of its national law. In addition, since the incorporation of the Convention into the law of England, Wales, Scotland and Northern Ireland by the Human Rights Act 1998, all public bodies, including courts and tribunals, and even private bodies implementing public law, will have to abide by the principles of the Convention. Therefore Convention rights may be applied either as a matter of Community law, where they concern a measure within the competence of the Community, or under national law, following the procedures set out in the Act, where Community law is not involved.

The following are additional general principles which have been embraced by the Court of Justice in interpreting and applying Community law.

Proportionality

This is a general principle imported from German law, and is often invoked to determine whether a piece of subordinate legislation or an action purported to be taken under the Treaties goes beyond what is necessary to achieve the declared, lawful objects. It holds that 'the individual should not have his freedom of action limited beyond the degree necessary for the public interest' (*Internationale Handelsgesellschaft* (Case 11/70)). The principle applies in relation to action by the Community in the sphere of legislation, to determine whether a regulation has, for example, gone beyond what was necessary to achieve the aim contained in the enabling Treaty provision, or whether a Community institution has exceeded the necessary action to be taken in relation to an infraction of Community law. It may thus be invoked to challenge fines imposed by undertakings found by the Commission to have breached the competition rules in Arts 81 and 82 EC Treaty.

It is also applicable to action by Member States in relation to permitted derogations from Community law. While, for example, restrictions on imports from other Member States, and also other measures having an equivalent effect, are prohibited by Art 28 EC Treaty, an exception is permitted under Art 30 in relation to action taken on the grounds of, *inter alia*, public health. A total ban on a product will in almost every case be disproportionate, while some sampling and testing, in proportion to the degree of the perceived risk, may be legitimate. Excessive action may constitute a disguised restriction on trade (*Commission* v *Germany (Re Crayfish Imports)* (Case C-131/93)). The rule applies similarly in relation to restrictions on free movement of workers. Some rules relating to registration of foreigners are permitted, including their application to EU citizens, but the imposition of penalties for breach of those rules involving deportation would be disproportionate, since they would render the exercise of the very right of free movement itself ineffective (*R* v *Pieck* (Case 157/79)).

The principle of equality

The EC Treaty includes three specific types of prohibition against discrimination:

- prohibition against discrimination on grounds of nationality in Art 12 EC Treaty;
- prohibition of discrimination between producers and consumers in relation to the operation of the Common Agricultural Policy under Art 34(2) EC Treaty; and
- entitlement to equal pay for work of equal value for both men and women under Art 141 EC Treaty.

Article 2 EC Treaty was amended by the ToA to set a new general goal of 'equality between men and women'. Hitherto, this objective was confined to the workplace. Article 13 EC Treaty creates a new power for the Council of Ministers but 'within the limits of the powers conferred upon it by the Community...[to] take appropriate action to combat discrimination based on sex, racial or ethnic origin, religion or belief, disability, age or sexual orientation'.

Although this provision does not contain a *prohibition* against these types of discrimination, the existence of a power to *combat* them is likely to mean that the Court of Justice's decision in *Grant* v *South-Western Trains Ltd* (Case C-249/96) is

unlikely to be followed (see above). The Court had ruled that the equal pay requirements of the former Art 119 EC Treaty (now Art 141) did not oblige an employer to
grant special travel concessions, normally given to spouses and cohabitees of
employees, to a same-sex partner.

The principle of equality has been recognised by the Court as one of general
application and requires that comparable situations should not be treated differently
and different situations should not be treated in the same way unless such differentiation is objectively justified (*Graff* v *Hauptzollamt Köln-Rheinau* (Case C-351/92)).
Besides the specific Treaty provisions, the Court has held that the fixing and collection
of the financial charges making up the Community's own resources are governed by
the general principle of equality (*Grosoli* (Case 131/73)), as is the allocation of
Community tariff quotas by the Member States (*Krohn* (Case 165/84)).

The principle is also evident in the Court's requirement of equality of arms under
which undertakings which are subject to investigation by the Commission for breach
of competition law should have full knowledge of the allegations and evidence in the
Commission's file (*Solvay SA* v *Commission* (Case T-30/91)).

Legal certainty and non-retroactivity

This is a general principle of law familiar to all the legal systems of the Member States.
In its broadest sense, it means that 'Community legislation must be unequivocal and its
application must be predictable for those who are subject to it' (*Kloppenburg* (Case
70/81)). It means, for example, that the principle of the indirect effect of directives
does not apply in relation to national provisions with criminal sanctions, since the
need for legal certainty requires that the effect of national criminal law should be
absolutely clear to those subject to it. In *Kolpinghuis Nijmegen* (Case 80/86), the
Court said that the national court's obligation to interpret domestic law to comply with
EC law was 'limited by the general principles of law which form part of Community
law, and in particular, the principles of legal certainty and non-retroactivity' (see
Chapter 9).

Legitimate expectation

This principle is based on the concept that 'trust in the Community's legal order must
be respected' (*Deuka* (Case 5/75) (A-G Trabucchi)). Under the principle, 'assurances
relied on in good faith should be honoured' (*Compagnie Continentale* v *Council* (Case
169/73) (A-G Trabucchi)). It is closely linked to the principle of legal certainty. The
relationship of the two principles is well illustrated by the case of *Mulder* (Case
120/86) (Sharpston, 1990).

In order to stabilise milk production, Community rules required dairy farmers to enter
into a five-year non-marketing agreement, in exchange for which they were to receive a
premium. In 1984, the Community introduced a system of milk quotas, under which
milk producers would have to pay a super levy on milk produced in excess of their
quota in any one year. Those who had entered into the non-marketing agreement for
1983 were not allowed any quota, because there was no provision in the regulations
for them to do so. Having suspended production for the non-marketing period, they

were effectively excluded from subsequent milk production. A farmer excluded in this way challenged the validity of the regulations. The Court held that:

> where such a producer, as in the present case, has been encouraged by a Community measure to suspend marketing for a limited period in the general interest and against payment of a premium, he may legitimately expect not to be subject, upon the expiry of his undertaking, to restrictions which specifically affect him because he has availed himself of the possibilities offered by the Community provisions.

The principle of legitimate expectation goes to ensure a fair process, however, and it cannot fetter the Community's freedom of action. The balance is not always easily struck, but the issues involved in doing so were applied by Sedley J in *R* v *Ministry of Agriculture and Fisheries, ex parte Hamble Fisheries* [1995] 2 All ER 714:

> The principle of legal certainty and the protection of legitimate expectation are fundamental to European Community law. Yet these principles are merely general maxims derived from the notion that the Community is based on the rule of law and can be applied to individual cases only if expressed in enforceable rules. Moreover, in most instances there are other principles which run counter to legal certainty and the protection of legitimate expectations; here the right balance will need to be struck. For instance, in the field of Community legislation the need for changes in the law can conflict with the expectation of those affected by such a change that the previous legal situation will remain in force ...

In *R* v *Ministry of Agriculture and Fisheries, ex parte Hamble Fisheries* the court decided that the legitimate expectations of the holders of fishing licences had not been infringed when the Ministry introduced a more restrictive fishing licensing policy to protect the remaining fish stocks allocated to the United Kingdom under the EC quota system. The Court of First Instance has held that operators in the Community's agricultural markets cannot have a legitimate expectation that an existing situation will prevail since the Community's intervention in these markets involves constant adjustments to meet changes in the economic situation (*O'Dwyer and Others* v *Council* (Cases T-466, 469, 473 and 477/93)).

Natural justice

This is a concept derived from English administrative law, but closely linked to the American 'due process'. It is sometimes used by the Court of Justice to mean no more than 'fairness', and is not always distinguishable from 'equity'. In the English administrative law sense, it implies, however, two basic principles: the right to an unbiased hearing and the right to be heard before the making of a potentially adverse decision affecting the person concerned (see, for example, *Ridge* v *Baldwin* [1964] AC 40). In a staff case, the Court of Justice has stated the principle as:

> a general principle of good administration to the effect that an administration which has to take decisions, even legally, which cause serious detriment to the person concerned, must allow the latter to make known their point of view, unless there is a serious reason for not doing so. (*Kuhner* (Case 33/79))

The principle is explicit in relation to decisions affecting an individual's free movement rights on public policy, public security and public health grounds (Arts 5–7, Directive 64/221), and implicit in other decisions affecting the exercise of those rights. It involves the right to be given full reasons for the decision in order that they may be challenged. The right to natural justice is thus closely linked to the right to an effective remedy:

> Where, as in this case, it is more particularly a question of securing the effective protection of a fundamental right conferred by the Treaty on Community workers, the latter must ... be able to defend that right under the best possible conditions and have the possibility of deciding, with a full knowledge of the relevant facts, whether there is any point in their applying to the courts. (*UNECTEF* v *Heylens and Others* (Case 222/86), para 15)

Charter of Fundamental Rights of the European Union

The Charter was signed by the 15 Member States during December 2000 at the meeting of the European Council held in Nice, France. The Charter is not legally binding, but, despite the protestations of the United Kingdom Government, it is highly probable that the Court of Justice will draw on its provisions when interpreting and applying Community law. A Declaration annexed to the ToN provides that an Intergovernmental Conference will be held in 2004 to consider, *inter alia*, the status of the Charter.

The Charter combines in a single text the civil, political, economic, social and societal rights which have previously been laid down in a variety of international, European and national sources. It includes rights of dignity (e.g. the right to life); freedoms (e.g. respect for private and family life; freedom of assembly and of association); equality (e.g. respect for cultural, religious and linguistic diversity); solidarity (e.g. right of collective bargaining and action); citizens' rights (e.g. freedom of movement and residence); and justice (e.g. presumption of innocence and right of defence).

On 7 December 2000, the President of the European Commission (Romano Prodi) stated:

> In the eyes of the European Commission, by proclaiming the Charter of fundamental rights, the European Union institutions have committed themselves to respecting the Charter in everything they do and in every policy they promote. The Charter is *the* instrument to verify respect for fundamental rights by the EU institutions and the Member States where they act under Union law.
>
> The citizens of Europe can rely on the Commission to ensure that the Charter will be respected in all aspects of the Union's activity, both internally and in its relations with third countries.
>
> In signing this Charter in the name of the Commission and looking towards the future, I am convinced that this proclamation paves the way for the creation of a solid basis for the evolution of the protection of fundamental rights in the Union. On this basis, the protection of fundamental rights will be able to evolve and strengthen. On this basis too, it will be possible to envisage calmly how to incorporate the Charter in the founding treaties of the Union. The Commission would like to see this happening as soon as possible. (IP/00/1423)

THE COURT OF FIRST INSTANCE

To cope with the great increase in the work of the Court of Justice, the SEA provided for the creation of a new Court of First Instance (CFI) to be attached to the Court of Justice (Art 225 EC Treaty). Article 225 EC Treaty provides for the determination of the categories of case which can be heard by the CFI. Article 225(1) expressly provides that the CFI 'shall not be competent to hear and determine questions referred for a preliminary ruling under Article 234 [EC Treaty]'. The Decision establishing the CFI (Council Decision 88/591 ECSC, EC OJ 1988 L 319/1) laid down four categories of cases which could be heard by the new Court:

1   Staff cases.
2   Actions by undertakings (but not by Community institutions or Member States) against the Commission concerning individual acts relating to the ECSC Treaty provisions on levies, production controls, price regulation or competition.
3   Actions by natural or legal persons against a Community institution relating to the implementation of the EC competition rules applicable to undertakings.
4   Damages claims by natural or legal persons where the damage is alleged to arise from an act or failure to act which is the subject of an action under 1, 2, or 3 above or from breach of contract (Art 4 Decision 88/591).

Following amendments made to the EC Treaty by the TEU, one further important category has been added:

5   Claims brought by natural and legal persons under Arts 230 and 232 EC Treaty (including anti-dumping cases) for judicial review. The Court has no competence to hear applications by institutions or Member States. There had been resistance by some Member States to the transfer from the Court of Justice to CFI of the anti-dumping cases, but this change over was finally effected in March 1994 (Art 225 and Council Decision 93/350 OJ 1993 L 144/21).

In addition, Art 4 of Decision 88/591 provides for the CFI to have unlimited jurisdiction in relation to penalties, and gives it jurisdiction to suspend measures and to grant interim relief during the course of proceedings.

Staff cases have long been seen as more suitable for a first instance court, rather than the Court of Justice which is, essentially, a constitutional-type court. Employment lawyers have been appointed to sit on these cases, which largely concern the interpretation of individual employment contracts of staff employed by the institutions, staff regulations and related matters of fact (Art 236 EC Treaty).

Coal and steel cases relate to actions brought by coal and steel undertakings against the Commission. Most of these relate to restrictions on production imposed by the Commission to prevent over-production of steel during the recession in the early 1980s. The number of such cases has considerably diminished.

Most of the competition cases arise from challenges to decisions by the Commission relating to Arts 81 and 82 EC Treaty and, especially, the level of fines imposed for uncompetitive practices (see Chapters 20–22).

Finally, challenges to Community institutions for failure to act or for unlawful action can now be brought by individuals and undertakings in the CFI. These actions, which are similar to applications for judicial review in the English courts, can still be brought only by Member States and by other institutions in the Court of Justice.

Treaty of Nice amendments

Once it comes into force, the ToN will substantially change the structure, functions, rules and procedures of the Court of First Instance. This is considered to be essential given the fact that it currently takes about two years finally to determine a case; with the prospect of an enlarged membership of 27 Member States, reform is all the more necessary.

Article 220 EC Treaty will provide for judicial panels to be attached to the CFI. By Art 225a, the Council, acting unanimously, may set up these panels to hear and determine at first instance certain classes of action or proceeding brought in specific areas. Decisions of the panel may be subject to a right of appeal on points of law (and in certain circumstances matters of fact) to the CFI. Article 225(2) EC Treaty will provide that the Court of Justice may exceptionally review a decision of the CFI (where the CFI has acted as a court of appeal from a judicial panel) where there is a serious risk to the unity or consistency of Community law. The members of the judicial panels will be appointed by the Council, acting unanimously. A Declaration attached to the ToN provides that the Court and the Commission should prepare as swiftly as possible a draft decision establishing a judicial panel which is competent to deliver judgments at first instance on disputes between the Community and its servants (i.e. actions pursuant to Art 236 EC Treaty).

In addition to the introduction of judicial panels, the jurisdiction of the CFI will be increased. Article 225 EC Treaty will provide that the CFI shall have jurisdiction to hear and determine at first instance actions or proceedings referred to in Arts 230, 232, 235, 236 and 238 EC Treaty with the exception of those which have already been assigned to a judicial panel, and also of those reserved in the Court's Statute for hearing before the Court of Justice. It also provides that the Statute may provide for the CFI to have jurisdiction for other classes of action or proceeding. As before, a right of appeal from a decision of the CFI to the Court of Justice shall be possible only on a point of law.

A major shift from the CFI's previous competence will be provided by Art 225(3) EC Treaty, which will give the CFI jurisdiction to hear and determine questions referred for a preliminary ruling under Art 234 EC Treaty, in specified areas laid down in the Court's Statute. In such a situation, if the CFI considers that the case requires a decision of principle likely to affect the unity or consistency of Community law, it may refer the case to the Court of Justice for a ruling. In addition, CFI decisions may exceptionally be subject to review by the Court of Justice, under the conditions and within the limits laid down by the Court's Statute, where there is a serious risk of the unity or consistency of Community law being affected.

A Declaration annexed to the ToN calls on the Court of Justice and the Commission to give overall consideration as soon as possible to the division of competence between the Court of Justice and the CFI, in particular in the area of direct actions, and to submit suitable proposals for change.

Article 62 of the new Statute, which will come into force alongside the ToN, provides that in the cases provided for in the new Art 225(2) and (3) EC Treaty, if the Court of Justice's First Advocate-General considers that there is a serious risk of the unity or consistency of Community law being affected, he may propose that the Court of Justice review the decision of the CFI. The proposal by the First Advocate-General must be made within one month of delivery of the CFI's decision. Within one month of receiving the proposal, the Court of Justice has to decide whether or not to review the decision.

Membership of the Court of First Instance

Although it is attached to the Court of Justice, the CFI is staffed by judges who are separately appointed according to slightly different criteria. This partly relates to the type of work allocated to the CFI, and partly to the role of the CFI in hearing evidence and determining questions of fact.

Article 225(3) EC Treaty provides that the 15 Members of the CFI shall be chosen from persons whose independence is beyond doubt and who 'possess the ability required for appointment to judicial office' (Art 21, Act of Accession; Art 12, Decision 95/1/EC). Like the members of the Court of Justice, members of the CFI are appointed by common accord of the governments of the Member States for terms of six years, with partial renewal of membership every three years. The first members of the CFI were appointed on 1 September 1989 by a Decision of the governments (Decision 89/452/EEC, Euratom, ECSC, OJ 1989 L 220/76). To ensure partial renewal every three years, half of the new members had to be appointed for only three years. The allocation of the first terms was chosen by lot.

Treaty of Nice amendments

Article 224 EC Treaty will provide that the CFI shall consist of *at least* one judge from each Member State. The number of judges will be determined by the Court's Statute. This therefore provides the possibility of increasing the CFI's membership in the light of the shifting of jurisdiction from the Court of Justice to the CFI. Given the increasing competence of the CFI, it would not be sensible to increase the workload of the CFI while at the same time standing still in terms of members. As discussed above, there is a safeguard that cases before the CFI can be referred to, or reviewed by, the Court of Justice in certain circumstances.

Article 50 of the new Statute will provide that the CFI may sit in chambers of three or five judges. The Rules of Procedure can determine when the CFI may sit in plenary session or even be constituted by a single judge. As with the Court of Justice, there are provisions for the establishing of a Grand Chamber of 11 judges.

THE JURISDICTION OF THE EUROPEAN COURT OF JUSTICE AND THE COURT OF FIRST INSTANCE

Besides the general function of ensuring that Community law is observed, the Court of Justice and the CFI (the Courts) have a number of other tasks. Since the Courts, like the other Community institutions, can act only within the limits of their powers, they have jurisdiction only where jurisdiction has been expressly conferred upon them (Art 3 ECSC, Art 7 EC, Art 3 Euratom). This means that the Courts have, unlike English courts, no 'residual' or 'inherent' powers and, consequently, cannot hear cases not expressly falling within their jurisdiction. It has, for example, been held that judicial protection cannot be afforded to private individuals who might otherwise be deprived of all legal redress at both national and Community level (*Schlieker* v *HA* (Case 12/63)), since there is no express provision authorising them to do so. The Courts were specifically excluded by the ToA from ruling on any measure or decision relating to the maintenance of law and order and the safeguarding of internal security in a Member State (Art 68(2) EC Treaty). The Court of Justice has also recently ruled that, in hearing appeals from the CFI, it has no jurisdiction to review the facts established by the CFI (*John Deere Ltd* v *Commission* (Case C-7/95)). More recently, however, the Court of Justice has shown greater flexibility in ruling on cases which it might, hitherto, have refused to adjudicate (*Imm Zwartveld* (Case 2/88); *Dzodzi* v *Belgium* (Case C-297/88)).

The main heads of jurisdiction for the Court of Justice are as follows:

- To establish whether or not a Member State has failed to fulfil an obligation under the Treaty. Actions for this purpose can be brought by the Commission under Art 226 EC Treaty, or a Member State under Art 227. These actions are considered in detail in Chapter 7.
- To exercise unlimited jurisdiction with regard to penalties in actions brought by the Commission under Arts 228(1) and 229 EC Treaty.
- To review the legality of an act, or of a failure to act, of, *inter alia*, the Council, the Commission, or the Parliament, at the request of Member States, the Council or the Commission. Applications by the Parliament and the European Central Bank are limited to the protection of their prerogatives (Arts 230 and 231 EC Treaty (as amended by TEU) and Art 9 of the Protocol on the Statute of the European System of Central Banks and of the European Central Bank).
- To give preliminary rulings under Art 234 EC Treaty at the request of a national court or tribunal (see Chapter 6).
- To grant compensation for damage caused by the institutions in actions brought by Member States, and natural and legal persons under Arts 235 and 288 EC Treaty (see Chapter 8).
- To act as a Court of Appeal from the CFI under Art 225(1) EC Treaty.

Further reading

Arnull, A., 'Does the Court of Justice have an Inherent Jurisdiction?' (1990) 27 CML Rev 683.

Besselink, L., 'Entrapped by the maximum standard: On fundamental rights, pluralism and subsidiarity in the European Union' (1998) 35 CML Rev 629.

Brown, N. and Jacobs F. (1994) *The Court of Justice of the European Communities* (4th edn), Sweet & Maxwell.

Coppel, J. and O'Neill, A., 'The European Court of Justice: Taking Rights Seriously?' [1992] Legal Studies 227.

Craig, P. and De Burca, G. (1998) *EU Law Text, Cases and Materials* (2nd edn), OUP, Chapters 2 and 7.

Hall, 'The European Convention on Human Rights and Public Exceptions to the Free Movement of Workers under the EEC Treaty' (1991) 10 EL Rev 466.

Hartley, T.C. (1998) *The Foundations of European Community Law* (3rd edn), Oxford University Press, Chapter 2.

Jacobs, F., 'The European Court of Justice: Some Thoughts on its Past and Future', *The European Advocate*, Winter 1994–95, p. 2.

Jacobs, F.G. and White R.C.A. (1996) *The European Convention on Human Rights*, Clarendon Press.

Lenaerts, K., 'Fundamental Rights to be Included in a Community Catalogue' (1991) 16 EL Rev 367.

Mancini, G.F., 'The Making of a Constitution for Europe' (1989) 26 CML Rev 595.

March Hunnings, N. (1996) *The European Courts*, Cartermill International Ltd.

Millett, T. (1990) *The Court of First Instance of the European Communities*, Butterworths.

Pescatore, P., 'Fundamental Rights and Freedoms in the System of the European Communities' [1970] AJIL 343.

Schermers, H., 'Is there a Fundamental Human Right to Strike?' (1989) 9 YEL 225.

Schermers, H., 'The European Communities Bound by Fundamental Human Rights' (1990) 27 CML Rev 249.

Sharpston, E., 'Legitimate Expectation and Economic Reality' (1990) 15 EL Rev 103.

Shaw, J. (1994) 'Twin-track Social Europe – the Inside Track', in O'Keefe, D. and Twomey P. (eds) *Legal Issues of the Maastricht Treaty*, Wiley Chancery Laws.

Steiner, J. and Woods, L. (2000) *Textbook on EC Law* (7th edn), Blackstone Press, Chapters 2 and 6.

Tillotson, J. (2000) *European Community Law: Text, Cases and Materials* (3rd edn), Cavendish Publishing Ltd, Chapter 7.

Toth, A.G., 'The European Union and Human Rights: The Way Forward' (1997) 34 CML Rev 491.

Tridimas, T. (2000) *The General Principles of EC Law*, OUP.

Tridimas, T., 'The Court of Justice and Judicial Activism' (1996) 21 EL Rev 199.

Weatherill, S. (2000) *Cases and Materials on EC Law* (5th edn) Blackstone Press, Chapter 1.

Chapter 6

PRELIMINARY RULING JURISDICTION OF THE COURT OF JUSTICE

ARTICLE 234 EC TREATY

National courts perform a crucial role in administering and applying Community law. The Court of Justice has developed an important body of case law on the application of directly enforceable Community provisions in the courts of Member States (see Chapter 9), but it depends on the national courts to cooperate with it to make those provisions effective. As the Court said in _Simmenthal_ (Case 106/77):

> A national court which is called upon, within the limits of its jurisdiction, to apply provisions of Community law is under a duty to give full effect to those provisions, if necessary refusing of its own motion to apply any conflicting provisions of national legislation, even if adopted subsequently, and it is not necessary for the court to request or await the prior setting aside of such provisions by legislative or other constitutional means.

There is a clear danger that, given the disparate national legal traditions of the Member States, Community law will develop differently in the national courts. If this were to happen, individuals and businesses would be operating under different rules and many of the benefits of an open Community and a genuine common market would be lost. The Community has, therefore, a fundamental interest in ensuring that its law has the same meaning and effect in all the Member States. The only effective way of doing this is to provide that ultimate authority for deciding the meaning of Community law should reside in one court. That court is, of course, the Court of Justice. The best way to ensure the harmonious development of Community law would have been to have established the Court of Justice as a final Court of Appeal on matters of Community law. That course seemed to constitute too direct a challenge to the supremacy of national legal systems, and was rejected by the founders of the Community. They opted, instead, for a system of references by national courts. Article 234 EC Treaty (previously Art 177), which establishes the preliminary reference procedure, is the only provision of the Treaty which expressly acknowledges the enforcement role of the courts of the Member States.

The Court of Justice has recognised that there is some concern about the effectiveness of the system because of the time which such references take. However, in its Report to the 1996 Intergovernmental Conference ('Report of the Court of Justice on certain aspects of the application of the Treaty on European Union', Luxembourg, May 1995) it unequivocally rejected suggestions that the scope for references be limited:

> To limit access to the Court would have the effect of jeopardising the uniform application and interpretation of Community law. But that is not all. The preliminary ruling system is the veritable cornerstone of the operation of the internal market, since it plays a fundamental role in ensuring that the law established by the Treaties retains its Community character with a view to guaranteeing that the law has the same effect in all circumstances in all the Member States of the European Union. Any weakening, even if only potential, of the uniform application and interpretation of Community law throughout the Union would be liable to give rise to distortions of competition and discrimination between economic operators, thus jeopardising equality of opportunity between those operators and consequently the proper functioning of the internal market.

However, the Court's position soon changed in the light of its increasing case load and resulting delays. The Court of Justice and Court of First Instance issued a discussion paper in May 1999, which was submitted to the Commission in January 2000: 'The Future of the Judicial System of the European Union (Proposals and Reflections)'. The paper is available in full on the Internet: http://curia.eu.int/en/txts/intergov/index.htm.

This paper includes statistics for cases which came before the Court of Justice between 1 January 1990 and 31 December 1998 (see Annex I to the paper). With regard to references for a preliminary ruling the statistics are as shown in Table 6.1.

Table 6.1 Cases coming before ECJ for preliminary ruling (1990–98)

	1990	1991	1992	1993	1994	1995	1996	1997	1998
Cases brought	141	186	162	204	203	251	256	239	264
Cases completed	162	131	157	196	163	162	205	301	246
Cases pending	209	264	269	277	317	406	457	395	413
Duration (in months)	17.4	18.2	18.8	20.4	18.0	20.5	20.8	21.4	21.4

Given this increase in the cases which have been brought before the Court of Justice pursuant to Art 234 EC Treaty, and the resulting increase in the time period between lodging the case and final judgment, it is perhaps not surprising that the Court has changed its view, especially with the prospect of an enlarged Community membership in the not too distant future. Further discussion of this paper will appear at the end of the chapter.

To ensure that national courts are fully aware of the circumstances and the manner in which references should be made under Art 234, the Court of Justice issued a *Note of Guidance on References by National Courts for Preliminary Rulings* in December 1996 ([1997] 1 CMLR 78). The *Guidance* is not legally binding, but it summarises the case law of the Court and provides a clear indication of how a case ought to be prepared for reference by a national court. This guidance is included towards the end of the chapter.

REFERENCES FROM NATIONAL COURTS UNDER ARTICLE 234 EC TREATY

Article 234 EC Treaty envisages a partnership role between the Court of Justice and the national court, with jurisdiction divided between the Court of Justice, which interprets the law, and the national courts, which apply it. It must be emphasised that Art 234 references have a different function to an appeal. In an appeal, the initiative lies with the parties, and if the appeal is successful the appellate court can substitute its own decision for that of the lower court. In a reference, however, it is the lower court itself which takes the decision to refer the case. The Court of Justice rules on the issues which have been raised, but it is then for the lower court to apply the ruling of the Court of Justice to the facts of the case before it. At the end of the day, the decision in that case will be that of the national court. The whole object of the reference procedure is to retain the independence of the national courts, while at the same time preventing 'a body of national case law not in accord with the rules of Community law from coming into existence in any Member State' (*Hoffmann La Roche* v *Centrafarm* (Case 107/76)). It must, however, be emphasised that in many instances the national court will be able to give judgment *without* making a reference to the Court of Justice. National courts do so throughout the Community, quite properly, in many hundreds of cases each day.

Article 234 provides:

The Court of Justice shall have jurisdiction to give preliminary rulings concerning:

(a)   the interpretation of this Treaty;
(b)   the validity and interpretation of acts of the institutions of the Community and of the ECB [i.e. the European Central Bank];
(c)   the interpretation of the statutes of bodies established by an act of the Council, where those statutes so provide.

Where such a question is raised before any court or tribunal of a Member State, that court or tribunal may, if it considers that a decision on the question is necessary to enable it to give judgment, request the Court of Justice to give a ruling thereon.

Where any such question is raised in a case pending before a court or tribunal of a Member State against whose decisions there is no judicial remedy under national law, that court or tribunal shall bring the matter before the Court of Justice.

What matters can be the subject of a reference under Art 234?

Article 234 refers to three kinds of provisions which can be the subject of a reference to the Court for a preliminary ruling on interpretation and validity:

(a)   the interpretation of the Treaty;
(b)   the validity and interpretation of acts of the institutions of the Community and of the ECB;
(c)   the interpretation of the statutes of bodies established by an act of the Council, where those statutes so provide.

The most common of these will now be considered.

Interpretation of the Treaty

'Interpretation of the Treaty' covers any part of the EC Treaty, the amending Treaties and the Treaties of Accession, the last normally being made expressly subject to Art 234. In the case of the United Kingdom's entry to the Community, this was achieved by Art 1(3) of the Treaty of Accession of 1972 (*Department of Health and Social Security* v *Barr and Montrose Holdings Ltd* (Case C-355/89)).

Parts of the Treaty on European Union relating to Common Foreign and Security Policy, and Police and Judicial Cooperation in Criminal Matters (i.e. the second and third pillars of the European Union (see Chapter 1)) are excluded from the referral procedure (Art 46 TEU): *Grau Gomis* (Case C-167/94R).

Acts of the institutions of the Community

'Community acts' includes not only legally binding acts, such as regulations, directives and decisions, but also opinions and recommendations where these are relevant to the interpretation of Community law by the courts of Member States: *Frecassetti* (Case 113/75); *Grimaldi* v *Fonds des Maladies Professionelles* (Case C-322/88). In *Deutsche Shell AG* v *Hauptzollamt Hamburg* (Case C-188/91), the Court of Justice held that 'arrangements' made by a joint committee responsible for implementing a convention on a common transit policy between the EEC and EFTA formed 'part of the Community legal order'. The Court noted that the fact that a Community legal measure lacked compulsory effect did not exclude the Court from giving a legal ruling on it, because national courts were obliged to take it into account when interpreting the convention.

In the *Deutsche Shell* case the Court of Justice emphasised that it did not have jurisdiction under Art 234 to give a ruling on the compatibility of a national measure with Community law. However, it does in fact come very close to doing so. Characteristically, it will describe the national measure in hypothetical terms and state that, if there was such a measure, it would not be compatible with Community law! Although the Court can only give a ruling on the interpretation (and validity – see below) of *Community* law, it has been prepared to rule on the meaning of *national* provisions which are not intended to implement Community law but which are based on the wording of a Community provision: *Gmurzynska-Bscher* (Case C-231/89).

With regard to 'Community acts', the Court has power to give preliminary rulings concerning their *validity* in addition to their interpretation. However, it should be noted that the Court does not have the power to question the validity of the Treaties. 'Validity' relates to the question of whether or not the act is void (i.e. of no effect). It may, for example, have been made *ultra vires* (where, for example, the opinion of the European Parliament has not been obtained despite the relevant Treaty article requiring this). Consider the following scenario: a levy is imposed by a regulation; it may be provided in the regulation for the levy to be collected by a national agency. An individual may be sued when he refuses to pay the levy. In his defence he may argue that the regulation is not valid because a procedural step in the legislative process has not been followed. The national court may refer the matter to the Court of Justice pursuant to Art 234 to ascertain if the regulation (i.e. a Community act) is valid. The Court of Justice will make the ruling and pass the case back to the national court. The national court will then apply the law as determined by the Court of Justice. If the Court of Justice rules that the regulation is invalid, the national court will be obliged to rule in favour of the defendant. As we shall note in Chapter 8, this indirect way of challenging the validity of a Community act is a much more effective mechanism than the restricted power to challenge such an act directly under Art 230 EC Treaty (previously Art 173).

Which courts or tribunals are able to refer?

Depending on the status of the court or tribunal, some *may*, while others *must* refer questions of interpretation of the Treaty or interpretation/validity of Community acts to the Court of Justice. Before discussing the issue of which courts and tribunals have a discretion to refer, and which are under an obligation to make a referral, it is necessary to ask which courts or tribunals should consider the possibility of a reference under Art 234. Article 234 refers to 'any court or tribunal of a Member State' so that, at first glance, it would appear that references can only be made by courts and tribunals within the state's judicial structure. However, the essential elements to determine the status of the body in relation to Art 234 are its power to make legally binding decisions, its independence from the parties and the recognition of its decision-making function by the state. To be able to make references under Art 234 it will have to satisfy all these criteria. An arbitrator, although conferred with a power by contract to make legally binding decisions on the parties, and also being independent of the parties, lacks the official state recognition to make his decisions 'judicial' in character, and he cannot, therefore, make a reference under Art 234 (*Nordsee v Reederei Mond* (Case 102/81)). However, an arbitration board or a disciplinary body which is recognised by the state as having a function in making legally binding decisions in relation to an industry or a professional body may well be a 'court or tribunal' for the purposes of Art 234 (*Broekmeulen v Huisarts Registratie Commissie* (Case 246/80)).

The *Broekmeulen* case concerned a Dutch body called the Appeals Committee for General Medicine. This body heard appeals from the Dutch body responsible for registering persons seeking to practise medicine in The Netherlands; without registration, it was practicably impossible to practise. Both of these bodies were established by the Royal Netherlands Society for the Promotion of Medicine, a private association, but recognised indirectly in some Dutch legal provisions. The Appeals Committee was not a court or tribunal under Dutch law. It followed an adversarial procedure and allowed legal representation.

The applicant was a Dutch national and had qualified in Belgium. He wanted to practice in The Netherlands and applied for registration. This was refused and he appealed. The case was referred to the Court of Justice pursuant to the former Art 177 (now Art 234) and the question arose whether the Appeals Committee was a 'court or tribunal of a Member State'. If it was not, then the Court of Justice would not have jurisdiction to give a preliminary ruling. The Court of Justice stated that:

> 17. In order to deal with the question of applicability in the present case of Article 177 of the Treaty [now Article 234], it should be noted that it is incumbent upon Member States to take the necessary steps to ensure within their own territory the provisions adopted by the Community institutions are implemented in their entirety. *If, under the legal system of*

a Member State, the task of implementing such provisions is assigned to a professional body acting under a degree of governmental supervision, and if that body, in conjunction with the public authorities concerned, creates appeal procedures which may affect the exercise of rights granted by Community law, it is imperative, in order to ensure the proper functioning of Community law, that the Court should have an opportunity of ruling on issues of interpretation and validity arising out of such proceedings.

18. As a result of all the foregoing considerations and in the absence, in practice, of any right of appeal to the ordinary courts, the Appeals Committee, which operates with the consent of the public authorities and with their cooperation, and which, after an adversarial procedure, delivers decisions which are recognised as final, must, in a matter involving the application of Community law, be considered as a court or tribunal of a Member State within the meaning of Article 177 of the Treaty [now Article 234]. Therefore, the Court has jurisdiction to reply to the question asked. (emphasis added)

Even a national court determining an appeal against an arbitration award, not according to law but according to what is 'fair and reasonable', may be regarded as a 'court' for the purposes of Art 234 (*Municipality of Almelo and Others v Energiebedvijf NV* (Case C-394/92)). A court delivering an advisory 'opinion' may be a 'court or tribunal' for the purposes of Art 234. In *Garofalo and Others v Ministero del Sanita and Others* (Joined Cases C-69–79/96) an opinion delivered by the Italian Consiglio del Stato to the Italian President, although not binding on him, was held to be a proper subject for a reference under Art 234. In the United Kingdom, besides references from magistrates' courts, Crown Courts and county courts, there have also been references from VAT tribunals, employment tribunals and the Social Security Commissioners.

What is the appropriate stage in the proceedings for a reference?

A reference to the Court of Justice may be made at any stage in the proceedings, even before a full hearing, either during the interim stage (i.e. a hearing on a preliminary matter before the full hearing) or where the case is being dealt with in the absence of one of the parties (*Simmenthal v Amministrazione delle Finanze dello Stato* (Case 70/77); *Balocchi v Ministero delle Finanze dello Stato* (Case C-10/92)). The Court does, however, think it desirable that an *inter partes* hearing (i.e. a hearing where all the parties are invited to take part in the proceedings) takes place before the reference, if that is possible (*Eurico Italia Srl v Ente Nazionale Risi* (Case C-332/92)).

Although the Court of Justice will not hear arguments that the national court or tribunal should not, under national law, have made the reference (*Reina v Landeskreditbank Baden-Württemberg* (Case 65/81)), it does expect the case to have reached a stage at which the relevant facts have been established and the issues identified on which the assistance of the Court of Justice is required:

It might be convenient, in certain circumstances, for the facts in the case to be established and for questions of purely national law to be settled at the time the reference is made to the Court of Justice so as to enable the latter to take cognisance of all the features of fact and of law which may be relevant. (*Irish Creamery Milk Suppliers Association v Ireland* (Case 36/80))

In *Telemarsicabruzzo SpA* (Joined Cases C-320–322/90), the Court refused to give a ruling, stating that the need to give a practical interpretation of Community law requires the national court to define the factual and legal framework in which the questions it puts arise, or that at least it explains the factual assumptions on which those questions are based. Neither had been done in this case. In *Venntveld* (Case C-316/93), however, although all the relevant facts were not included, the Court held that there was sufficient information in the case file and in the pleadings to give a preliminary ruling.

A discretion to refer

The second paragraph of Art 234 EC Treaty provides that:

> Where such a question is raised before any court or tribunal of a Member State, that court or tribunal *may*, if it considers that a decision on the question is necessary to enable it to give judgment, request the Court of Justice to give a ruling thereon. (emphasis added)

It contemplates a situation in which the national court or tribunal considers that it is 'necessary' to refer a question to the Court of Justice to enable it to give judgment in the case. In such a case, it *may* refer the question to the Court. The question to be referred must relate to one of the matters considered above (e.g. interpretation of the Treaty or the interpretation/validity of a regulation, directive or decision). Therefore, before the discretion to refer arises, the national court must be of the view that 'a decision on the question is *necessary* in order to enable it to give judgment' (emphasis added (see below)). The decision on whether or not to make a reference is essentially a matter for the national courts. The Court has said:

> In the context of the division of judicial functions between national courts and the Court of Justice, provided for by Article 177 [now Art 234], the Court of Justice gives preliminary rulings without, in principle, needing to enquire as to the circumstances which led to the national court submitting questions to it ... The only exception to that principle would be in cases in which it appeared that the procedure provided for in Article 177 had been abused and where the question submitted sought, in reality, to lead the Court of Justice to make a ruling on the basis of an artificial dispute, or where it is obvious that the provision of Community law submitted to the Court of Justice could not be applied. (*Dzodzi* v *Belgium* (Joined Cases C-297/88 and C-197/89))

In *Dzodzi*, the Court of Justice allowed a reference where the national court needed a ruling to determine a question of national law in an area of law that was outside the competence of the Community but which had been based on Community law.

Although the national court has the discretion to assess the need for a reference, it should explain how it has come to the conclusion that a reference is necessary, so that the Court of Justice can be satisfied that it has the jurisdiction to deal with the matter (*Foglia* v *Novello* (No. 2) (Case 244/80)). Once it is satisfied that it has the jurisdiction to deal with a reference, the Court is, in principle, bound to give a ruling. It cannot refuse to do so on the basis that, if its ruling were to have the effect of annulling a Community or national provision, this would create a 'legal vacuum' in a Member State. It then would be for the national court to interpret national law in such a way as to fill any gap (*Gmurzynska* (Case C-231/89); *Helmig and Others* (Joined Cases C-399, 409 & 425/92 and C-34, 50 & 78/93)). However, the national court does have 'the widest discretion' (*Rheinmuhlen* (Case 166/73), paras 3 and 4); the power to make a reference arises 'as soon as the judge perceives either of his own motion or at the request of the parties that the litigation depends on a point referred to in the first paragraph of Art 177 [now Art 234]'. However, even if the judge decided that it was 'necessary' to make a referral, he has a total discretion whether or not to do so (see below).

If one of the parties to the national proceedings withdraws from them, the Court of Justice cannot, however, continue to deliver a judgment on the reference, because such a judgment would then no longer be 'necessary' for the outcome of the case (*Teres Zabala Erasun and Others* v *Instituto Nacional de Empleo* (Joined Cases C-422–424/93)). Even if a superior national court has decided the issue, the lower court is not precluded from making a reference by national rules. Although the national court has a discretion to refer, or not, where it is a lower court and where its decisions are subject to appeal (see below), it has little real discretion in cases where its decision depends on the disputed *validity* of a Community measure. It has itself no power to declare the Community measure invalid, so it has no choice but to refer the matter to the Court of Justice for a ruling on its validity (*Foto-Frost* (Case 314/85)).

When *must* a reference to the Court of Justice be made?

The third paragraph of Art 234 EC Treaty provides that:

> Where any such question is raised in a case pending before a court or tribunal of a Member State against whose decisions there is no judicial remedy under national law, that court or tribunal *shall* bring the matter before the Court of Justice. (emphasis added)

Therefore, a court or tribunal which satisfies the above criteria has no discretion; it is *required* to refer the case to the Court of Justice for a preliminary ruling. The criteria are as follows.

No judicial remedy under national law

The concept of 'no judicial remedy under national law' clearly includes situations where there is no further appeal. That situation may arise where the court is, like the House of Lords, the highest in the hierarchy of courts. It may also arise in specific cases where an appeal is denied from a court which is very low in the hierarchy. In some jurisdictions, for example, there may be no appeal where the amount claimed or the value of the goods concerned is below a certain figure. In the landmark case of *Costa* v *ENEL* (Case 6/64), the amount claimed was less than £2. There was no appeal from the magistrate's decision because of the smallness of the sum. The magistrate was, therefore, under Art 177 (now Art 234) obliged to refer the question before him to the Court of Justice. In the more recent case of *Parfums Christian Dior BV* v *Evora BV* (Case C-337/95), the Dutch Court of Appeal (the *Hoge Raad*) had the power to refer a question on trade mark law to the Benelux Court, the highest court for points of law affecting the Benelux Agreement. The Court of Justice held that, if the *Hoge Raad* decided *not* to refer the case to the Benelux Court, it was *obliged* to refer the case to the Court of Justice. If it did refer the case to the Benelux Court, the Benelux Court was itself, as the ultimate court *in that case*, obliged to refer the matter to the Court of Justice.

In English courts, a reference may have to be made where the court concerned, although not the final court of appeal, refuses leave (i.e. permission) to appeal, and where the upper court also refuses it. The avenue for an appeal would then be totally blocked. To illustrate this, in the English legal system a litigant whose case comes before the Court of Appeal can request leave to appeal to the House of Lords if he loses the case. If the Court of Appeal refuses leave to appeal, the litigant can then request it from the House of Lords. If the House of Lords also refuses leave, then in that particular case, the Court of Appeal constitutes the 'court ... against whose decisions there is no judicial remedy'. Therefore the Court of Appeal, if it considers it *necessary* to make the referral, has no discretion; it must refer the case to the Court of Justice for a preliminary ruling.

In the English courts the term 'judicial remedy' is wide enough to include applications for judicial review. Even when, therefore, there is no appeal from, say, the Immigration Appeal Tribunal, its decisions are subject to judicial review and may subsequently be referred to the Court of Justice in the course of those judicial review proceedings (see, for example, *R v Immigration Appeal Tribunal, ex parte Antonissen* (Case C-292/89)). In such a case, it would appear that there is no obligation on the tribunal to refer and an English tribunal has, in fact, refused to refer a case because it has held that it was not obliged to do so because of the availability of judicial review of its decisions (*Re a Holiday in Italy* [1975] 1 CMLR 184 (National Insurance Commissioner)). This point has still to be decided by the Court of Justice.

Having considered the concept of 'no judicial remedy' the other two criteria are as follows.

'Where any such question is raised'

This was considered above, and includes a question relating to the interpretation of the Treaty or the interpretation/validity of a Community act (i.e. a regulation, directive or decision).

'A decision on the question is necessary to enable it to give judgment'

It will be noted that there is no express reference to this in the third paragraph of Art 234, although there is such a reference in the second paragraph. However, the Court of Justice has stated that it is also applicable to the third paragraph:

> 10. ... it follows from the relationship between the second and third paragraphs of Article 177 [now Art 234] that the courts or tribunals referred to in paragraph 3 have the same discretion as any other national court or tribunal to ascertain whether a decision on a question of Community law is necessary to enable them to give judgment. (*CILFIT* (Case 283/81))

To conclude this section, a court or tribunal which satisfies the above three criteria has no discretion; it must refer the question to the Court of Justice for a preliminary ruling.

Is it *necessary* to make the referral?

As discussed above, a court or tribunal will have a discretion (pursuant to the second paragraph of Art 234) or be under an obligation (pursuant to the third paragraph) to refer a case to the Court of Justice for a preliminary ruling only if it 'considers a decision on the question to be *necessary* to enable it to give judgment' (emphasis added). There may be a number of reasons why the court or tribunal does not consider it *necessary* to have the question answered by the Court of Justice. We shall consider two of these reasons.

The development of precedent

Not every question concerning the interpretation of Community law that is relevant to the outcome of a case requires a reference under Art 234. In Chapter 5 it was stated that the doctrine of precedent does not apply to the Court of Justice, but the Court generally follows its own previous decisions for the sake of legal certainty. This has been acknowledged by the Court of Justice in the application of Art 234; the Court has stated that:

> the authority of an interpretation under Article 177 [now Art 234] already given by the Court may deprive the obligation of its purpose and thus empty it of its substance. Such is the case when the question raised is materially identical with a question which has already been the subject of a preliminary ruling in a similar case. (*CILFIT* (Case 283/81))

The Court of Justice has therefore held that it may not be *necessary* to make a referral to it because the question may already have been answered in a previous case (e.g. the Court of Justice may already have interpreted the relevant Treaty article). However, a national court can refer any question on interpretation or validity, whether or not the Court of Justice has ruled on the point. The case before the national court may raise some new fact or argument. However, if it does not raise any new fact or argument, the Court may, in its ruling, simply restate the substance of the earlier case, as it did in *Da Costa* (Cases 28–30/62):

> The questions of interpretation posed in this case are identical with those settled [in the case of *Van Gend en Loos*] and no new factor has been presented to the Court. In these circumstances the Tariefcommissie must be referred to the previous judgment.

It would appear that the Court of Justice is actively encouraging national courts to apply the Court's previous decisions: thus a system of precedent is emerging by default. This is apparent in *International Chemical Corporation* (Case 66/80). The Court of Justice had previously ruled in a former Art 177 referral (now Art 234 referral) that Regulation 563/76 was invalid. The *International Chemical Corporation* case concerned the validity of this regulation and the Italian court referred the matter to the Court of Justice asking whether the previous decision that the regulation was invalid applied only to that particular case, or whether it was effective in any subsequent litigation. The Court of Justice held that the purpose of the former Art 177 (now Art 234) was to ensure that Community law was applied uniformly by national courts. Uniform application did not only concern the interpretation of Community law, it also concerned the validity of a Community act. It said that in the previous case, the ruling that the regulation in question was void was addressed to the national court making the reference. However, since it was declared to be void, any other national court could likewise regard the act as void for the purposes of a judgment which it had to give.

It should be noted, however, that the Court of Justice is the sole arbitrator upon the *validity* of an act of the Community institutions. To decide otherwise would put the objective of uniform application of Community law at risk. It is not open to a national court to declare an act of the Community (e.g. a regulation or directive) to be void, unless the Court of Justice has decided this in an earlier judgment (see *Firma Foto-Frost* (Case 314/85)).

The doctrine of acte clair

In *CILFIT* (Case 283/81), the Court of Justice also held that even a court which is bound by the mandatory reference provisions in the third paragraph of Art 234 is not obliged to refer a case where the answer to a question of interpretation of Community law is 'so obvious as to leave no scope for any reasonable doubt' (para 16). This situation of an apparently transparent interpretative point is normally referred to in Community law as *acte clair*. The Court described in *CILFIT* the circumstances in which a reference should be made:

16. Finally, the correct application of Community law may be so obvious as to leave no scope for reasonable doubt as to the manner in which the question raised is to be resolved. Before it comes to the conclusion that such is the case, the national court or tribunal must be convinced that the matter is equally obvious to the Courts of the other Member States and to the Court of Justice. Only if those conditions are satisfied, may the national court or tribunal refrain from submitting the question to the Court of Justice and take upon itself the responsibility for resolving it.

17. However, the existence of such a possibility must be assessed on the basis of the characteristic feature of Community law and the particular difficulties to which its interpretation gives rise.

18. To begin with, it must be borne in mind that Community legislation is drafted in several languages and that the different language versions are equally authentic. An interpretation of a provision of Community law thus involves a comparison of the different language versions.

19. It must also be borne in mind, even where the different language versions are entirely in accord with one another, that *Community law uses terminology which is peculiar to it*. Furthermore, it must be emphasised that *legal concepts do not necessarily have the same meaning in Community law and in the law of the various Member States*.

20. Finally, every provision of Community law must be placed in its context and interpreted in the light of the provisions of Community law as a whole, regard being had to the objectives thereof and to its state of evolution at the date on which the provision in question is to be applied. (emphasis added)

We have considered (in Chapter 5) the approach adopted by the Court of Justice when interpreting Community law; suffice to say at this point, the Court of Justice does not interpret such law literally, but generally favours a contextual or teleological application. Quite often the interpretation of the Court could not have been predicted. Hence, although the Court of Justice has given permission to national courts to apply the *acte clair* doctrine, the national court must do so with the utmost caution.

The responsibility imposed on a court in declining to refer a question which, by virtue of the lack of possibility for further appeal or review of its decisions, it, *prima facie*, ought to refer, is thus an onerous one. An English judge has recognised the

> ... advantages enjoyed by the Court of Justice. It has a panoramic view of the Community and its institutions, a detailed knowledge of the treaties and of much subordinate legislation made under them, and an intimate familiarity with the functioning of the Community market which no national judge denied the collective experience of the Court of Justice could hope to achieve. (Bingham J in *Customs and Excise Commissioners* v *Samex* [1983] 3 CMLR 194)

Other English courts have not been so mindful of their limitations. *R* v *London Boroughs Transport Committee, ex parte Freight Transport Association* [1991] 3 All ER 915 involved the interpretation of directives on vehicle brake construction and the powers of national authorities to impose further restrictions on vehicles. The House of Lords refused to make a reference although the issues were complex. Lord Templeman noted that 'no plausible grounds had been advanced for a reference to the European Court'. The refusal to refer has been criticised, and one of the parties made a complaint to the Commission about the refusal (see Weatherill, 1992). The case is not, however, indicative of a general unwillingness to refer cases by the House of Lords, as the *Factortame* and the equal treatment cases demonstrate (*R* v *Secretary of State for Transport, ex parte Factortame (No. 1)* (Case C-221/89); *R* v *Secretary of State for Transport, ex parte Factortame (No. 2)* (Case C-213/89); *Webb* v *EMO Cargo* [1993] 1 WLR 49; *R* v *Secretary of State for Employment, ex parte EOC* [1995] 1 CMLR 345). There is, however, continuing evidence of a reluctance to refer by English courts and tribunals, not least because of the time which such references take (see, for example: *Johnson* v *Chief Adjudication Officer* [1994] 1 CMLR 829 (CA); *Gould and Cullen* v *Commissioners of Customs and Excise (VAT Tribunal)* [1994] 1 CMLR 347; *R* v *Ministry of Agriculture, Fisheries and Food, ex parte Portman Agrochemicals Ltd* [1994] 1 CMLR 18 (QBD)). As discussed above, there is one situation in which *any* national court *must* refer a question to the Court of Justice. In its *Note of Guidance* (see below) the Court declares that it 'has jurisdiction to rule on the validity of acts of Community institutions. National courts may *reject* a plea challenging the validity of such an act. But where a national court (*even one whose decision is still subject to appeal*) intends to question the validity of a Community act, it *must* refer the question to the Court of Justice' (*Foto-Frost* v *Hauptzollamt Lubeck-Ost* (Case 314/85)) (emphasis added).

Simplified procedure and expedited hearing

The Rules of Procedure of the Court of Justice were amended with effect from 1 July 2000 to include a simplified procedure for certain types of case referred to it under Art 234, and in other situations to provide for an accelerated procedure (OJ 2000 L 122/43).

The simplified procedure will be applied to those questions referred to the Court which are identical to questions that have been answered previously, where the answer to the question can be clearly deduced from existing case law or where the answer admits of no reasonable doubt. The new Art 104(3) of the Rules provides that:

> Where a question referred to the Court for a preliminary hearing is identical to a question on which the Court has already ruled, where the answer to such a question may be clearly deduced from existing case law or where the answer to the question admits of no reasonable doubt, the Court may, after informing the court or tribunal which referred the question to it, hearing any observations submitted by the persons referred to in Article 20 of the EC Statute, Article 21 of the Euratom Statute and Article 103(3) of these Rules and hearing the Advocate-General, give its decision by reasoned order in which, if appropriate, reference is made to its previous judgment or to the relevant case law.

The accelerated procedure has been introduced by Art 104a of the Rules, which provides that:

> At the request of the national court, the President may exceptionally decide, on a proposal from the Judge-Rapporteur and after hearing the Advocate-General, to apply an accelerated procedure derogating from the provisions of these Rules to a reference for a preliminary ruling, where the circumstances referred to establish that a ruling on the question put to the Court is a matter of exceptional urgency.
>
> In that event, the President may immediately fix the date for the hearing, which shall be notified to the parties in the main proceedings and to the other persons referred to in Article 20 of the EC Statute, Article 21 of the Euratom Statute and Article 103(3) of these Rules when the decision making the reference is served.
>
> The parties and other interested persons referred to in the preceding paragraph may lodge statements of case or written observations within a period prescribed by the President, which shall not be less than 15 days. The President may request the parties and other interested persons to restrict the matters addressed in their statement of case or written observations to the essential points of law raised by the question referred.
>
> The statements of case or written observations, if any, shall be notified to the parties and to other persons referred to above prior to the hearing.
>
> The Court shall rule after hearing the Advocate-General.

Pending the outcome of the reference

As discussed above, it may be as long as two years before a decision on a reference under Art 234 is available from the Court of Justice. The Court of Justice has jurisdiction under Art 243 EC Treaty to 'prescribe any interim measures' and will sometimes do so where the legality of a Community measure is being challenged under Art 230 EC Treaty (see Chapter 8). Under Art 234, the validity of any act of the institutions may be raised in a reference. The following questions need to be addressed: Can the allegedly invalid Community measure be suspended by the national court pending the outcome of the reference? Will the Court of Justice suspend it? Should national courts suspend national legislation which is alleged to conflict with Community law or which implements a Community measure whose validity is disputed?

The Court of Justice may use its power under Art 243 to order a Member State to cease pursuing a course of conduct which *prima facie* breaches Community law, and which is requested by a party to the proceedings (*Commission* v *United Kingdom (Re Nationality of Fishermen)* (Case 246/89R); *Commission* v *Germany* (Case C-195/90)). This will normally be an interim measure in the course of Art 226 proceedings against a Member State (see Chapter 7). Alternatively, national courts may be required to suspend a provision of national law which, arguably, conflicts with Community law (see *Factortame*, above). Although the criteria for granting interim relief are national (in the United Kingdom, according to the American Cynamid formula (*American Cynamid* v *Ethicon* [1975] AC 397)), presumptions about the validity of primary national law should not act as a bar to its interim suspension.

The position with regard to the suspension of national measures implementing a provision of Community law the validity of which is challenged was discussed by the Court of Justice in *Zuckerfabrik Suderdithmarschen* v *HZA Itzehoe* (Case C-143/88). The Court declared that, to enable Art 234 references to work effectively, national courts must have the power to grant interim relief, where a national measure is disputed on the grounds of the validity of the Community measure on which it is based, on the same grounds as when the compatibility of a national measure with Community law is contested. The national court has to be careful before doing so, however:

> Where a national court or tribunal has serious doubts about the validity of a Community act on which a national measure is based, it may, in exceptional circumstances, temporarily suspend application of the latter measure or grant other interim relief with respect to it. It must then refer the question of validity to the Court of Justice, stating the reasons for which it considers that the Community act is not valid.

National courts can apply national criteria for weighing up, in the particular circumstances, whether or not to grant suspensory relief, but the national measures must be effective in providing the necessary remedies to protect rights conferred by Community law (*Factortame (No. 2)* (Case C-213/89)) and to prevent 'irreparable damage' to the person seeking relief, pending the outcome of the reference (*Atlanta Fruchthandelsgesellschaft GmbH* v *Bundesamt für Ernährung und Forstwirtschaft* (Case C-465/93)).

Interpretation or application

Article 234 EC Treaty empowers the Court of Justice to interpret Community law, but not to apply it to the facts of a case. The application of the law to the facts is the role of the national court. This is the division of the powers between the two courts. The national court, if it considers a decision of the Court of Justice is necessary in order for it to give a judgment, refers the matter to the Court of Justice, requesting an answer to a given question (or series of questions) concerning the interpretation or validity of Community law. The Court of Justice answers the question(s) and sends the case back to the national court for the national court to apply the law to the facts of the case. However, this distinction may become blurred in practice.

Cristini (Case 32/75), for example, concerned the meaning of Art 7(2), Regulation 1612/68, which provides that a Community worker who is working in another Member State should be entitled to the same 'social advantages' as workers of that Member

State. Large *French* families were allowed reduced fares on the railways. The question put before the Court of Justice by the French court was whether this was a 'social advantage' within the meaning of the regulation and thus should be available to large families of all Member State nationals working in France. The Court of Justice stated that it was not empowered to decide the actual case, it being its duty simply to interpret the provision of the regulation in question. The Court, however, went on to hold that the concept of 'social advantage' included this type of fare reduction offered by the French Railways. In reality, the Court of Justice not only interpreted Community law, but also applied it to the particular facts. However, to be fair to the Court, in answering the national court's question it would have been difficult for the Court of Justice to have done anything else.

NOTE FOR GUIDANCE ON REFERENCES BY NATIONAL COURTS FOR PRELIMINARY RULINGS

As discussed above, the Court of Justice has issued guidance ([1997] 1 CMLR 78) to national courts and tribunals on the operation of Art 234. It is set out in full below:

The development of the Community legal order is largely the result of cooperation between the Court of Justice of the European Communities and the national courts and tribunals through the preliminary ruling procedure under Article 234 of the EC Treaty and the corresponding provisions of the ECSC and Euratom Treaties. [A preliminary ruling procedure is also provided for by protocols to several conventions concluded by the Member States, in particular the Brussels Convention on Jurisdiction and the Enforcement of Judgments in Civil and Commercial Matters.]

In order to make this cooperation more effective, and so enable the Court of Justice better to meet the requirements of national courts by providing helpful answers to preliminary questions, this Note for Guidance is addressed to all interested parties, in particular to all national courts and tribunals.

It must be emphasised that the Note is for guidance only and has no binding or interpretative effect in relation to the provisions governing the preliminary ruling procedure. It merely contains practical information which, in the light of experience in applying the preliminary ruling procedure, may help to prevent the kind of difficulties which the Court has sometimes encountered.

1. Any court or tribunal of a Member State may ask the Court of Justice to interpret a rule of Community law, whether contained in the Treaties or in acts of secondary law, if it considers that this is necessary for it to give judgment in a case pending before it.

   Courts or tribunals against whose decisions there is no judicial remedy under national law must refer questions of interpretation arising before them to the Court of Justice, unless the Court has already ruled on the point or unless the correct application of the rule of Community law is obvious. [Judgment in Case 283/81 *CILFIT* v *Ministry of Health* [1982] ECR 3415]

2. The Court of Justice has jurisdiction to rule on the validity of acts of the Community institutions. National courts or tribunals may reject a plea challenging the validity of such an act. But where a national court (even one whose decision is still subject to appeal) intends to question the validity of a Community act, it must refer that question to the Court of Justice. [Judgment in Case 314/85 *Foto-Frost* v *Hauptzollamt Lubeck-Ost* [1987] ECR 4199]

   Where, however, a national court or tribunal has serious doubts about the validity of a Community act on which a national measure is based, it may, in exceptional cases, temporarily suspend application of the latter measure or grant other interim relief with respect to it. It must then refer the question of validity to the Court of Justice, stating the reasons for which it considers that the Community act is not valid. [Judgments in Joined Cases C-143/88 and C-92/89 *Zuckerfabrik Suderdithmarschen and Zuckerfabrik*]

3. Questions referred for a preliminary ruling must be limited to the interpretation or validity of a provision of Community law, since the Court of Justice does not have jurisdiction to interpret national law or assess its validity. It is for the referring court or tribunal to apply the relevant rule of Community law in the specific case pending before it.

4. The order of the national court or tribunal referring a question to the Court of Justice for a preliminary ruling may be in any form allowed by national procedural law. Reference of a question or questions to the Court of Justice generally involves stay of the national proceedings until the Court has given its ruling, but the decision to stay proceedings is one which it is for the national court alone to take in accordance with its own national law.

5. The order for reference containing the question or questions referred to the Court will have to be translated by the Court's translators into the other official languages of the Community. Questions concerning the interpretation or validity of Community law are frequently of general interest and the Member States and Community institutions are entitled to submit observations. It is therefore desirable that the reference should be drafted as clearly and precisely as possible.

6. The order for reference should contain a statement of reasons which is succinct but sufficiently complete to give the Court, and those to whom it must be notified (the Member States, the Commission and in certain cases the Council and the European Parliament), a clear understanding of the factual and legal context of the main proceedings. [Judgment in Joined Cases C-320–322/90 *Telemarsicabruzzo* [1993] ECR I-393]

   In particular it should include:

   • a statement of the facts which are essential to a full understanding of the legal significance of the main proceedings;
   • an exposition of the national law which may be applicable;
   • a statement of the reasons which have prompted the national court to refer the question or questions to the Court of Justice; and
   • where appropriate, a summary of the arguments of the parties.

   The aim should be to put the Court of Justice in a position to give the national court an answer which will be of assistance to it.

   The order for reference should also be accompanied by copies of any documents needed for a proper understanding of the case, especially the text of the applicable national provisions. However, as the case-file or documents annexed to the order for reference are not always translated in full into the other official languages of the Community, the national court should ensure that the order for reference itself includes all the relevant information.

7. A national court or tribunal may refer a question to the Court of Justice as soon as it finds that a ruling on the point or points of interpretation or validity is necessary to enable it to give judgment. It must be stressed, however, that it is not for the Court of Justice to decide issues of fact or to resolve disputes as to the interpretation or application of rules of national law. It is therefore desirable that a decision to refer should not be taken until the national proceedings have reached a stage where the national court is able to define, if only as a working hypothesis, the factual and legal context of the question; on any view, the administration of justice is likely to be best served if the reference is not made until both sides have been heard. [Judgment in Case 70/77 *Simmenthal* v *Amministrazione delle Finanze dello Stato* [1978] ECR 1453]

8. The order for reference and the relevant documents should be sent by the national court directly to the Court of Justice, by registered post, addressed to:

The Registry
Court of Justice of the European Communities
L-2925 Luxembourg
Telephone (352) 43031

The Court Registry will remain in contact with the national court until judgment is given, and will send copies of the various documents (written observations, Report for the Hearing, Opinion of the Advocate General). The Court will also send its judgment to the national court. The Court would appreciate being informed about the application of its judgment in the national proceedings and being sent a copy of the national court's final decision.

9. Proceedings for a preliminary ruling before the Court of Justice are free of charge. The Court does not rule on costs.

THE FUTURE OF THE JUDICIAL SYSTEM OF THE EUROPEAN UNION

As discussed above, the Court of Justice and Court of First Instance issued a discussion paper in May 1999, which was submitted to the Commission in January 2000: 'The Future of the Judicial System of the European Union (Proposals and Reflections)'. Chapter IV, part 3, of this report contained the Courts' thoughts on possible changes to the judicial system in relation to references for a preliminary ruling pursuant to Art 234. The discussion is topical and therefore has been included below:

Reform of the system of references for a preliminary ruling

The constant growth in the number of references for preliminary rulings emanating from courts and tribunals of the Member States carries with it a serious risk that the Court of Justice will be overwhelmed by its case-load. If current trends continue without any reform of the machinery for dealing with cases, not only will proceedings become more protracted, to the detriment of the proper working of the preliminary ruling system, but the Court of Justice will also be obliged to conduct its deliberations with such dispatch that it will no longer be able to apply to cases the thorough consideration necessary for it to give a useful reply to the questions referred.

It is highly likely that the impact of its decisions will diminish as their number increases and as they deal more frequently with questions of secondary importance or of interest only in the context of the case concerned.

This would seriously undermine those functions which have become most characteristic of its role within the Community legal order, namely to guarantee respect for the distribution of powers between the Community and its Member States and between the Community institutions, the uniformity and consistency of Community law and to contribute to the harmonious development of the law within the Union.

If the Court of Justice is to continue to fulfil those essential tasks, it will be necessary to reform the preliminary ruling system in such a way as to curtail the number of cases to be dealt with each year.

Various kinds of measures could be contemplated to reduce the number of references for preliminary rulings which the Court of Justice is called upon to determine.

(i) *Limitation of the national courts empowered to make references to the Court of Justice*

The two existing options would be (a) to reserve the power to make references to supreme courts alone or (b) to exclude only courts of first instance.

In its 1995 Report, referred to above, the Court of Justice stated that 'to limit access to the Court would have the effect of jeopardising the uniform application and interpretation of Community law throughout the Union, and could deprive individuals of effective judicial protection and undermine the unity of the case-law'.

Although the specific nature of the rules contained in Title IV of the EC Treaty (visas, asylum, immigration and other policies related to free movement of persons) and of the Conventions adopted by the Council under the third pillar (justice and home affairs) justified derogations in the Treaty of Amsterdam from the principle that all courts and tribunals are to have the power to make references to the Court of Justice, that solution cannot be directly transposed to the rules concerning the internal market and to joint policies and actions.

In its Report, the Court of Justice stated: 'The preliminary ruling system is the veritable cornerstone of the operation of the internal market, since it plays a fundamental role in ensuring that the law established by the Treaties retains its Community character with a view to guaranteeing that that law has the same effect in all circumstances in all the Member States of the European Union. Any weakening, even if only potential, of the uniform application and interpretation of Community law throughout the Union would be liable to give rise to distortions of competition and discrimination between economic operators, thus jeopardising equality of opportunity as between those operators and consequently the proper functioning of the internal market.

One of the Court's essential tasks is to ensure just such a uniform interpretation, and it discharges that duty by answering the questions put to it by the national courts and tribunals'.

For those reasons, it seems necessary for all national courts and tribunals to retain the right to refer questions to the Court of Justice. Although national courts and tribunals against whose decisions an appeal may lie under domestic law should be encouraged to apply Community law themselves, and not to resort too hastily to the solution afforded by a reference to the Court of Justice, the fact remains that the uniform application of Community law frequently depends on the answer to a question of interpretation raised before a national court not having to await the outcome of appeal proceedings but being given by the Court of Justice at the outset, so that the case law can become established at an early stage in the Member States of the Union.

To deprive certain courts and tribunals of the right to refer questions to the Court of Justice would also be undesirable from the point of view of procedural economy. It would result in proceedings being brought before supreme courts in the Member States solely in order to enable the parties to seek a referral to the Court of Justice.

(ii) *The introduction of a filtering system*

This would enable the Court of Justice to decide which of the questions referred needed to be answered by it on account of, for example, their novelty, complexity or importance.

Such a mechanism, designed to weed out at a preliminary stage cases of lesser importance from the point of view of the uniformity and development of Community law, is radically different in nature from the procedure enabling the Court of Justice to rule by way of an order on certain questions referred for a preliminary ruling.

To confer on the Court of Justice the power to assess the expediency of examining questions referred to it for a preliminary ruling, and thus to reduce the number of answers to be given, would undoubtedly have a number of advantages.

The introduction of such a filtering system would prompt national courts and tribunals to exercise selectivity in choosing which questions to refer, and would thus encourage them to exercise yet more fully their functions as Community courts of general jurisdiction.

Moreover, the existence of a filtering mechanism would enable the Court of Justice to concentrate wholly upon questions which are fundamental from the point of view of the uniformity and development of Community law. Lastly, the ensuing reduction in the number of cases would help to reduce the translation work-load, by removing the need to translate observations lodged in written proceedings.

The effectiveness of such a power of selection would depend on its scope and on the conditions governing its exercise. In order effectively to stem the inflow of references for preliminary rulings, there would be a need for selection criteria capable of being applied in a flexible and prudent manner.

However, the introduction of a filtering mechanism in this area would involve drawbacks which should not be underestimated. Even if such a mechanism were applicable only to courts and tribunals which may, but are not bound to, refer questions to the Court of Justice, this might distort the 'judicial cooperation' which has become established in the Community and which 'requires the national court and the Court of Justice, both keeping within their respective jurisdiction, (…) to make direct and complementary contributions to the working out of a decision' (judgment in Case 16/65 *Schwarze v Einfuhr-und Vorratsstelle Getreide* [1965] ECR 877).

That cooperation is founded, in principle, on the assumption that the Court of Justice will answer any question referred by a national court or tribunal which fulfils the conditions of admissibility. If that assumption can no longer be made, national courts and tribunals might well refrain from referring questions to the Court of Justice, in order to avoid the risk of their references being rejected for lack of interest. Such a development would jeopardise the machinery for ensuring that Community law is interpreted uniformly throughout the Member States.

In order to mitigate the drawbacks of a filtering mechanism, a system could be set up whereby the national court would be requested to include in its decision a proposed reply to the question referred. That would lessen the adverse effect of the filtering mechanism on the cooperation between the national court and the Court of Justice, while the proposed reply could at the same time serve as the basis for deciding which questions need to be answered by the Court of Justice and which can be answered in the terms indicated.

A more radical variant of the system would be to alter the preliminary ruling procedure so that national courts which are not bound to refer questions to the Court of Justice would be required, before making any reference, first to give judgment in cases raising questions concerning the interpretation of Community law. It would then be open to any party to the proceedings to request the national court to forward its judgment to the Court of Justice and to make a reference for a ruling on those points of Community law in respect of which that party contests the validity of the judgment given. This would give the Court of Justice the opportunity of assessing, at the filtering stage, whether it needed to give its own ruling on the interpretation of Community law arrived at in the contested judgment.

Such a procedure, resembling an appeal in cassation, would facilitate the task of the Court of Justice. It would enable the Court to give its ruling on the reference in full knowledge of the national context, both factual and legal, in which the points of Community law raised in the case in question fall to be interpreted.

However, such a procedure would involve a fundamental change in the way in which the preliminary ruling system currently operates. Judicial cooperation between the national courts and the Court of Justice would be transformed into a hierarchical system, in which it would be for the parties to an action to decide whether to require the national court to make a reference to the Court of Justice, and in which the national court would be bound, depending on the circumstances, to revise its earlier judgment so as to bring it into line with a ruling given by the Court of Justice. From the point of view of national procedural law, this aspect of the system would doubtless raise problems which could not easily be resolved.

Lastly, a party who was not satisfied with a judgment given by a national court might well be more eager to seek a ruling from the Court of Justice if only in order to defer enforcement of the judgment than the referring court itself.

Thus, a system of filtering references for preliminary rulings even one more flexible than that just envisaged would not be easy to reconcile with the principle of mutual cooperation between the national courts and the Court of Justice which is a feature of the preliminary ruling procedure and which, by ensuring uniformity and consistency in the interpretation of Community law, has made such a major contribution to the proper working of the internal market. Nevertheless, a mechanism giving the Court of Justice the power to assess the appropriateness of a reference would constitute a possible solution to the problem of an excessive case-load. From that point of view, there is much to be said for a more thorough examination of such a mechanism and of the ways of implementing it.

(iii) *Conferral on the Court of First Instance of jurisdiction in preliminary ruling proceedings*

The difficulties attending a transfer to the Court of First Instance of jurisdiction in proceedings for a preliminary ruling have been indicated by the Court of Justice in its 1995 Report, referred to above. Despite those difficulties, the idea of such a transfer should not be rejected out of hand.

Conferral on the Court of First Instance of jurisdiction in this area would have the effect of transferring to it part of the work-load, even though it will itself have to contend with an influx of direct actions far exceeding the limits of its current capacity. Such a transfer would need to be accompanied by a corresponding increase in the number of judges.

It would also be necessary to ensure, by means of machinery for referrals and/or appeals in cases involving points of general legal interest, that the most important questions always come before the Court of Justice in the end.

Similar reasoning could apply to the idea of transferring jurisdiction in preliminary ruling proceedings to specialised courts, should such courts be set up in the future.

(iv) *The creation or designation, in each Member State, of decentralised judicial bodies responsible for dealing with references for preliminary rulings from courts within their area of territorial jurisdiction*

Such bodies, specialising in Community law, would be closer than the Court of Justice to the national legal system in which the questions referred were to be answered. Furthermore, they would operate in the language or languages of the State concerned, thereby affording the national courts and tribunals the widest possible access to the preliminary ruling procedure by avoiding the congestion resulting from the need for translation.

Those courts could have the status either of a Community or of a national body. Whatever the status chosen, the important factor would be to maintain the benefit gained from a substantial reduction in the translation burden borne by the Court of Justice.

A system of that kind, which would entail a very significant change from the existing mechanism, would undeniably involve major drawbacks as regards the maintenance of uniformity in the interpretation and application of Community law.

Any reorganisation of the preliminary ruling procedure on a national or regional basis, regardless of whether jurisdiction is conferred on national or on Community courts, involves a serious risk of shattering the unity of Community law, which constitutes one of the corner-stones of the Union and which will become still more vital and vulnerable as a result of enlargement of the Union. Jurisdiction to determine the final and binding interpretation of a Community rule, as well as the validity of that rule, should therefore be vested in a single court covering the whole of the Union.

However, certain measures may be envisaged which would reduce the risks inherent in a decentralised system. First, the national judicial bodies to be set up should have the power to refer to the Court of Justice any question of interpretation which raises legal issues of general relevance to the unity or development of Community law. Furthermore, provision would need to be made for the possibility of appealing to the Court of Justice 'on a point of general legal interest', in accordance with detailed procedures to be laid down, against preliminary rulings given by those bodies. This would, in effect, create a decentralised filtering system in this area which would nevertheless remain subject to review by the Court of Justice.

Certain problems could arise, however, as a result of the links between those courts and the various national legal systems, which diverge considerably from one another, at any rate if they are accorded the status of national courts. In order to ensure that their decisions are sufficiently authoritative in the national legal order, they would need to be established at the highest level of the judicial hierarchy of the Member States. Consequently, the Member States would have to decide to which of their supreme courts such a judicial body should be attached; alternatively, if that proved impossible to decide, it would be necessary to establish a forum common to the highest courts of the State concerned.

Subject to that, the Court of Justice considers that, whilst the difficulties connected with the implementation of a system for the decentralisation of the preliminary ruling procedure should not be underestimated, in-depth consideration should nevertheless be given to a system of that kind and to its various detailed aspects.

As discussed above, the Court's Rules of Procedure have been amended to provide for a simplified procedure in cases where the question which has been referred is identical to a question which has been previously answered by the Court. This is designed to reduce the Court's workload.

At the Intergovernmental Conference in Nice, during December 2000, the Treaty of Nice was agreed. This Treaty, once it comes into force, addresses some of the issues raised by the Court in its discussion paper above. The ToN, as discussed in Chapter 5, opts for a sharing of the Art 234 jurisdiction between the Court of Justice and the CFI.

Once the ToN comes into force, which is unlikely to be before 2002, Art 225(3) EC Treaty will give the CFI jurisdiction to hear and determine questions referred for a preliminary ruling under Art 234 EC Treaty, in specified areas laid down in the Court's Statute. In such a situation, if the CFI considers that the case requires a decision of principle likely to affect the unity or consistency of Community law, it may refer the case to the Court of Justice for a ruling. In addition, CFI decisions may exceptionally be subject to review by the Court of Justice, under the conditions and within the limits laid down by the Court's Statute, where there is a serious risk of the unity or consistency of Community law being affected.

A Declaration annexed to the ToN calls on the Court of Justice and the Commission to give overall consideration as soon as possible to the division of competence between the Court of Justice and the CFI.

Article 62 of the new Statute, which will come into force alongside the ToN, provides that in the cases provided for in, *inter alia*, the new Art 225(3) EC Treaty, if the Court of Justice's First Advocate-General considers that there is a serious risk of the unity or consistency of Community law being affected, he may propose that the Court of Justice review the decision of the CFI. The proposal by the First Advocate-General must be made within one month of delivery of the CFI's decision. Within one month of receiving the proposal, the Court of Justice has to decide whether or not to review the decision.

Further reading

Anderson, D. (1995) *References to the European Court*, Sweet & Maxwell.

Arnull, A., 'The Use and Abuse of Article 177 EEC' (1989) 52 MLR 622.

Arnull, A., 'References to the European Court' (1990) 15 EL Rev 375.

Barnard, C. and Sharpston, E., 'The changing face of Article 177 References' (1997) 34 CML Rev 1113.

Brown, L.N. and Jacobs, F. (1994) *The Court of Justice of the European Communities* (4th edn), Sweet & Maxwell, Chapter 9.

Craig, P. and De Burca, G. (1998) *EU Law Text, Cases and Materials* (2nd edn), OUP, Chapter 10.

D'Sa, R. (1994) *European Community Law and Civil Remedies in England and Wales*, Sweet & Maxwell, Chapters 9 and 10, pp. 46–58.

Hartley, T.C. (1998) *The Foundations of European Community Law* (4th edn), Clarendon Press, Chapter 9.

Jacobs, F., 'The European Court of Justice: some Thoughts on its Past and its Future', *The European Advocate* (1994/95), p. 2.

Maher, I. (1995) 'A Question of Conflict: The Higher English Courts and the Implementation of European Community Law', in Daintith T. (ed.) *Implementing EC Law in the United Kingdom: Structures for Indirect Rule*, John Wiley and Sons.

Mancini, F. and Keeling, D., 'From CILFIT to ERT: The Constitutional Challenge Facing the European Court' (1991) 11 YEL 1.

O'Neill, M., 'Article 177 and limits to the right to refer: an end to confusion' (1996) 2 EPL 375.

Rasmussen, H., 'The European Court's Acte Clair Strategy in CILFIT' (1984) 9 CML Rev 242.

Steiner, J. (1995) *Enforcing EC Law*, Blackstone Press, Chapters 6 and 7.

Steiner, J. and Woods, L. (2000) *Textbook on EC Law* (7th edn), Blackstone Press, Chapter 27.

Tillotson, J. (2000) *European Community Law: Text, Cases and Materials* (3rd edn), Cavendish Publishing Ltd, Chapter 9.

Vincenzi, C. (1995) 'Private Initiative and Public Control in the Regulatory Process', in Daintith, T. (ed.) *Implementing EC Law in the United Kingdom: Structures for Indirect Rule*, John Wiley and Sons.

Weatherill, S., 'Regulating the Internal Market: Result Orientation in the House of Lords' (1992) 17 EL Rev 299, 318.

Weatherill, S. (2000) *Cases and Materials on EC Law* (5th edn), Blackstone Press, Chapter 4.

Chapter 7

DIRECT ACTIONS AGAINST MEMBER STATES

ARTICLES 226–228 EC TREATY

THE OBLIGATION OF MEMBER STATES UNDER THE EC TREATY

Member States have a general duty, under Art 10 EC Treaty (previously Art 5), to 'take all appropriate measures, whether general or particular, to ensure fulfilment of the obligations arising out of this [EC] Treaty or resulting from action taken by the institutions of the Community. They shall facilitate the achievement of the Community's tasks'. The obligation to observe Community law extends beyond the Treaties and secondary legislation to agreements made by the Community with other states under Art 300(1) EC Treaty (*SZ Service* (Case 192/89), para 13; First EEA Case Opinion 1/94). This positive duty to do what is required of them both under the Treaty and under legislation enacted by the institutions is underpinned by a negative obligation in the second limb of Art 10 to 'abstain from any measure which could jeopardise the attainment of the objectives of this Treaty'. The Commission, in order 'to ensure the proper functioning and development of the common market' shall ensure 'that the provisions of this Treaty and the measures taken by the institutions pursuant thereto are applied' (Art 211 EC Treaty (previously Art 155)).

The obligation to observe Community law binds, as shall be seen in the discussion on the direct enforcement of directives (referred to as the principle of 'direct effect'), not only the state but organs and emanations of the state (see Chapter 9). Those organs include government departments, state-funded and regulated agencies providing public services, state governments in federal systems (the *Länder*, for example, in Germany), local authorities (*Costanzo* (Case 103/88), *Johnston* v *RUC* (Case 222/84)), and the courts. All are, potentially, the subject of enforcement proceedings, although the actual defendant in each case will be the state itself. There have, as yet, been no proceedings where courts have refused to follow or apply principles of Community law, although these have occasionally been called for (see *Minister of the Interior* v *Cohn-Bendit (Conseil d'Etat)* [1980] 1 CMLR 543, where the French *Conseil d'Etat* refused to follow the decision of the Court of Justice in *Van Duyn* v *Home Office* (Case 41/74) and give direct enforcement to Directive 64/221). In these cases the Court of Justice has preferred to rely on establishing a cooperative relationship with national courts and achieving the necessary change in the approach of the national court by persuasion rather than by litigation.

In some cases where action is required, lack of Commission resources may limit or delay its response to unlawful action or inaction by Member States. A more appropriate response than a Commission initiative may be reliance by individuals on the direct enforcement of Treaty and other Community provisions in the courts of the offending Member State (see Chapter 9). Despite the liberal interpretation of the Treaties and the secondary legislation by the Court of Justice, not every Community provision is sufficiently clear, precise and unconditional to be directly effective. In addition, individuals may not have the means to start proceedings or to obtain the evidence to prove a breach. Action by individuals in the courts of the state alleged to have breached Community law does not preclude action by the Commission in the Court of Justice. In 1977 the UK Government banned the importation of main crop potatoes. A Dutch potato exporter challenged this by applying for a declaration in the English High Court that the ban breached Art 28 EC Treaty. A reference was made to the Court of Justice under Art 234 EC Treaty which confirmed that the ban was indeed unlawful. A parallel case was also brought by the Commission in the Court of Justice under Art 226 EC Treaty (*Meijer* v *Department of Trade* (Case 118/78); *Commission* v *United Kingdom* (Case 231/78)).

Action by the Commission: Article 226 EC Treaty

If an individual is unable or unwilling to commence proceedings in relation to the alleged breach, there may be no practical alternative to action by the Commission. The Commission has the power to commence proceedings. Where Member States fail to implement Community law, or fail to eliminate obstacles to its implementation, it can take the necessary action under Art 226 EC Treaty (previously Art 169):

> If the Commission considers that a Member State has failed to fulfil an obligation under this Treaty, it shall deliver a reasoned opinion on the matter after giving the State concerned the opportunity to submit its observations.
>
> If the State concerned does not comply with the opinion within the period laid down by the Commission the latter may bring the matter before the Court of Justice.

Action by another Member State: Article 227 EC Treaty

As an alternative to Art 226, action can be commenced by other Member States under Art 227 EC Treaty (previously Art 170):

> A Member State which considers that another Member State has failed to fulfil an obligation under this Treaty may bring the matter before the Court of Justice.
>
> Before a Member State brings an action against another Member State for an alleged infringement of an obligation under this Treaty, it shall bring the matter before the Commission.
>
> The Commission shall deliver a reasoned opinion after each of the States concerned has been given the opportunity to submit its own case and its observations on that of the other party both orally and in writing.
>
> If the Commission has not delivered an opinion within three months of the date on which the matter was brought before it, the absence of such opinion shall not prevent the matter from being brought before the Court of Justice.

Member States have shown a marked reluctance to use Art 227, and although states have quite frequently brought breaches of Community law to the attention of the Commission, it could be politically damaging for a complainant to take action all the way to the Court of Justice. The increased use of qualified majority voting has made the governments of Member States more aware of the need to retain the goodwill of fellow states. A very public confrontation in the Court of Justice is not likely to be regarded as helpful. In fact, only one case has come to judgment in the life of the Community: *France v United Kingdom* (Case 141/78). For that reason, any action in the Court of Justice that results from a complaint to the Commission about the failure of a Member State to meet its obligations is likely to brought under Art 226.

Nevertheless, Art 227 can be usefully employed by a Member State to focus the Commission's mind to take action under Art 226. During 1999, when the Community lifted the worldwide ban on UK beef (which had originally been imposed for health reasons), France (and Germany) refused to comply and allow UK beef to enter its market. The United Kingdom informed the Commission that it intended to take action against France under Art 227. The Commission, which had been involved in negotiations with France in an attempt to resolve the dispute, eventually decided to take action against France under Art 226, and thus prevent the United Kingdom from taking its own independent action under Art 227.

THE STAGES OF ARTICLE 226 PROCEEDINGS

The administrative stage

Suspected breaches of Community law generally come to the notice of the Commission as a result of the complaints of individuals or businesses affected by the breach. The first stage is usually an informal inquiry by letter to the government of the Member State concerned to ascertain the relevant facts. Member States have a legal duty to cooperate with Commission investigations into alleged breaches by them (*Commission* v *Spain* (Case C-375/92)).

In *Greece v Commission* (Case 240/86), the Commission was investigating the possible breach by Greece of certain Treaty articles relating to the free movement of goods. It requested certain information which Greece refused to give. Accordingly the Commission could not ascertain whether Greece was in breach of the Treaty. The Commission initiated Art 226 proceedings against Greece claiming Greece was in breach of its duty under the former Art 5 EC Treaty (now Art 10) because of its failure to cooperate with the Commission. The Court of Justice held that Greece was in breach of the former Art 5 (now Art 10).

Accordingly, if the Commission requires information from a Member State to enable it to ascertain if that Member State is in breach of its Community obligations, it will have to pursue Art 226 proceedings for breach of Art 10 EC Treaty if the Member State refuses to cooperate. If successful, the Member State will have to 'take the necessary measures to comply with the judgment' (Art 228(1) EC Treaty) and thus hand the information over. If this information discloses a breach, the Commission will have to start fresh Art 226 proceedings with regard to this breach.

Commission's discretion or obligation?

Article 226 EC Treaty provides that:

> ... If the Commission *considers* ... it *shall* deliver a reasoned opinion ... [the Commission] *may* bring the matter before the Court of Justice. (emphasis added)

The Commission does not have to carry out a formal investigation, but it does at least have to 'consider' whether or not there may have been a breach. Where the Commission does consider that there has been a breach, it must, after giving the Member State an opportunity to submit observations on the suspected breach, deliver a reasoned opinion to the government of the state concerned. The reasoned opinion will often follow prolonged correspondence between the Member State and the Commission. The Commission will have to decide, at some stage in its discussions with (or, in some cases, non-cooperation by) Member States, whether or not to proceed to delivery of a formal opinion which will stipulate a date by which time the necessary remedial action should have taken place. The Commission may decide to take no further action if it considers the breach is not serious and that its resources would be better applied to other infractions.

It would seem that the Commission does have a discretion, but it also has a duty under Art 226. It must consider the possibility of whether or not there has been a breach and it must take the most appropriate action. This may be to decide not to commence proceedings. Advocate-General Roemer gave some indication of the appropriate considerations which the Commission should have in mind in *Commission v France* (Case 7/71). He said that it might be justifiable not to start formal proceedings where there is a possibility that an amicable settlement may be achieved if formal proceedings are delayed, where the effects of the violation are only minor, where there is a major political crisis which could be aggravated if proceedings are commenced in relation to relatively minor matters and where there is a possibility that the Community provision in issue might be altered in the near future. As the Advocate-General noted in this case, Member States resent proceedings being brought against them and the Commission is not always anxious, on this account alone, to take action. Many breaches go for years without being remedied. For example, the United Kingdom Government failed to implement Directive 64/221 for more than 20 years after it had been held to have been in default in *Van Duyn* (see now, the Immigration (European Economic Area) Order 1994, SI 1994/1895 (which has been replaced by SI 2000/ 2326) – see Chapter 16); while the French Government was, in 1996, again before the Court of Justice for failing to amend its Code du Travail Maritime, 22 years after the Court in *Commission v France (Re French Merchant Seamen)* (Case 167/73) had held that it breached Arts 12 and 39 EC Treaty (*Commission v France* (Case C-334/94), and see *Commission v Belgium* (Case C-37/93) (similar restrictions on Belgian ships)). Some of the cases on which action has not been taken involve immigration and social issues which tend to be more politically sensitive.

Despite the embarrassment which Art 226 proceedings may occasionally cause to Member States, the Commission has shown an increasing willingness to use them and has employed Art 226 as part of the process of achieving the single market. In its Seventeenth Annual Report on Monitoring the Application of Community Law

(COM (2000) 92 final, 23 June 2000) the Commission reported that pursuant to Art 226 EC Treaty, during 1999, 1,075 letters of formal notification had been issued compared to 1,101 during 1998 and 1,461 during 1997; 460 reasoned opinions were issued during 1999 compared to 675 during 1998 and 334 during 1997; and 178 cases were referred to the Court of Justice during 1999, compared to 123 during 1998 and 121 during 1997.

The only Member State not to have had a case referred to the Court of Justice pursuant to Art 226 during 1999 was Finland (however, it had been issued with five reasoned opinions and 44 letters of formal notice). The Member State with the greatest number of referrals to the Court during 1999 was France with 35, closely followed by Italy with 32. During 1999 the United Kingdom had eight alleged infringements referred to the Court, and during the same period it was issued with 61 letters of formal notice and 33 reasoned opinions.

The Commission's report is available on the Internet at: http://europa.eu.int/comm/off/rep/index en.htm.

The reasoned opinion

If the Commission decides that a violation of Community law has occurred it must record the infringement in a reasoned opinion or decision served on the offending Member State. In arriving at that opinion the Commission must take into account the replies to its inquiries from the state and any defences which may have been advanced. The Court of Justice has said that an opportunity to submit such observations before a reasoned opinion is served is an essential procedural requirement. A failure to observe it may invalidate the whole process (*Commission* v *Italy* (Case 31/69), para 13).

Types of infringement

A large number of infringements concern either the failure to implement directives or a failure to implement them properly, or to observe their terms when implemented. Other infringements may involve direct breaches of Treaty provisions. Whether or not there is an infringement will often depend on the nature and effect of national legal provisions and of the administrative steps taken to give effect to the Community provision, and it is on these legal and factual issues that many disputes with the Commission over implementation occur. A few examples will serve to indicate the diversity of the actions brought by the Commission under Art 226 and the issues involved.

In *Commission* v *United Kingdom* (Case C-337/89) proceedings were brought by the Commission against the United Kingdom for failing to legislate to implement Directive 80/778 to ensure that water used for food production met the maximum nitrate levels in the directive. The UK Government argued that most food production was carried out with water from the domestic supply and that legislation was not necessary. The Court of Justice upheld the Commission's view that, in the absence of a specific derogation in the directive, all water used for food production should be made to comply. However, in *Commission* v *Belgium* (Case C-376/90), the Court rejected the Commission's interpretation of Directive 80/836/Euratom which required the adoption of national laws protecting the general public and workers against specified levels of ionising radiation. The Commission considered that Member States were not allowed to fix different dose limits to those laid down in the directive, even if they were stricter than those specified. The Court disagreed, holding that the directive only laid down maximum exposure levels and Belgium was not, therefore, in breach for enacting lower permitted exposure levels.

It will also be a breach by the Member State if, while implementing the directive, it does not provide an effective remedy or uses means which cannot be relied upon by individuals in the national courts. Directive 77/187 protects employees who are employed by undertakings which are transferred to new owners. The Directive had been implemented in the United Kingdom by the Transfer of Undertakings (Protection of Employment) Regulations 1981 (SI 1981/1794) and, *inter alia*, provided for consultation with employees' representatives. The United Kingdom's implementing regulations, however, provided no means for recognising such employee representatives. Effectively, in the United Kingdom the duty to consult could be negated by a refusal of the employer to recognise employee representatives and there was no effective remedy for this failure to consult. The Court of Justice held that where a Community directive does not specifically provide any penalty for an infringement, Art 10 EC Treaty requires the Member States to guarantee the application and effectiveness of Community law. For that purpose, while the choice of penalties remains within the discretion of the Member State, it must ensure in particular that infringements of Community law are penalised under conditions, both procedural and substantive, which are analogous to those applicable to infringements of national law of a similar nature and importance and which, in any event, make the penalty effective, proportionate and dissuasive (*Commission* v *United Kingdom* (Case C-382/92), para 55).

Contents of the opinion

The opinion must set out the Community provision and specific details of the breach, together with a response to the Member State's arguments that there has been compliance or attempting to justify delay in compliance, and it must detail the steps to be taken by the Member State to correct its infringement. The opinion has to be more fully reasoned than a legislative act under Art 253 EC Treaty (*Commission* v *Germany (Re Brennwein)* (Case 24/62)).

Time limit

The Commission must also set a time limit within which the Member State must end its violation. The Court of Justice has held that a Member State must be given a 'reasonable period of time' within which to comply with the opinion and thus negate the Commission's power to institute proceedings before the Court of Justice (*Commission* v *Ireland* (Case 74/82)).

It is normal practice for a Member State to be given at least two months to respond to a reasoned opinion, but a shorter period might be permissible in certain cases. In the recent case of the French ban on British beef, the Commission issued a letter of formal notice to France on 16 November 1999. The Commission gave France only two weeks to explain its continued ban. Following the expiry of this two-week period a reasoned opinion was served on France (giving an equally short period within which to lift the ban) and proceedings were subsequently issued in the Court of Justice.

Effect of complying with the reasoned opinion

If a Member State complies with the reasoned opinion within the time limit laid down, the Commission does not have the power to bring the matter before the Court of Justice. This in effect gives the Member State a period of grace within which it is protected from the threat of legal proceedings. If the Commission does subsequently bring proceedings, it has the obligation of proving that the violation was not ended before the expiry of the time limit (*Commission* v *Belgium* (Case 298/86)). In *Commission* v *Italy* (Case 7/61), the Court of Justice stated:

> It is true that the second paragraph of Article 169 [now Art 226] gives the Commission the right to bring the matter before the Court only if the State concerned does not comply with the Commission's opinion within the period laid down by the Commission, the period being such as to allow the State in question to regularise its position in accordance with the provisions of the Treaty.
>
> However, if the Member State does not comply with the opinion within the prescribed period, there is no question that the Commission has the right to obtain the Court's judgment on that Member State's failure to fulfil the obligations flowing from the Treaty.

The effect of this can be appreciated by considering the situation where a Member State fails to implement a directive within the time limit stipulated in the directive. Once this time limit has expired the Commission may move swiftly against the defaulting Member State. If it has still failed to implement it by the date specified in the reasoned opinion, the Commission may take enforcement action in the Court of Justice irrespective of whether the Member State subsequently implements the directive. However, if the directive has been implemented within the time period laid down within the reasoned opinion, no further action can be taken pursuant to Art 226.

Take as an example the case of the Working Time Directive 93/104 (OJ 1993 L 307/18) which should have been implemented by all Member States by 23 November 1996. The United Kingdom failed to implement it on time. The Directive provides rights for individual workers (e.g. four weeks' paid annual leave, minimum daily and weekly rest periods and a 48-hour maximum working week; all of which are subject to certain exceptions and derogations). A relatively short breach by the United Kingdom would have an enormous impact on an indeterminate number of workers. The United Kingdom implemented the Directive by the Working Time Regulations 1998 (SI 1998/1833) which came into force on 1 October 1998 (almost two years after the date stipulated in the Directive). The Commission had taken no action against the United Kingdom under Art 226; even if it had done, provided the directive had been implemented before expiry of the time limit laid down in the reasoned opinion, the United Kingdom could not have been hauled before the Court of Justice. A sceptic could therefore argue that a Member State may view the period from the date of implementation specified in the directive, to expiry of the reasoned opinion, as an extra period of time within which to implement the directive (although see Chapter 9 for the development of principles by the Court of Justice, which in certain situations empower citizens to enforce their Community law rights in national courts, and ultimately to claim damages from the state if loss has been suffered due to the Member State's breach of Community law). Two other examples will further illustrate this point.

Commission v *United Kingdom* (Cases C-382 & 383/92) concerned the Acquired Rights Directive 77/187 (OJ 1977 L 61/27), which had been implemented in the United Kingdom by delegated legislation: the Transfer of Undertakings (Protection of Employment) Regulations 1981 (SI 1981/1974). The aim of this directive, *inter alia*, was to ensure that when a business or part of a business was transferred to another party (e.g. sold), the employees would continue in the employment of the new employer on the same conditions as before (i.e. same hours of work, pay, etc.). Any dismissal connected with the transfer would be unlawful.

Article 1 of the directive provided it would apply to an 'undertaking, business or part of a business'. This was transposed into reg 2(1) of the UK regulations as applying to an undertaking, which would include any trade or business 'but not including any undertaking ... which is not in the nature of a commercial venture'.

The English courts held that a local authority was not 'in the nature of a commercial venture', because it was not a profit-making organisation, and therefore the regulations did not apply. Accordingly, where part of a local authority's activities was transferred to a private contractor, because the regulations did not apply, the employees could be dismissed lawfully, or those re-employed could have their pay reduced, etc. Therefore, where, following a competitive tender, responsibility for refuse collection was transferred to a private contractor, the employees affected would be the former local authority refuse collectors.

Following subsequent rulings of the Court of Justice on the interpretation of the directive, it became clear that the directive applied in these circumstances and therefore the United Kingdom had incorrectly implemented the directive by providing that it would not apply to undertakings 'not in the nature of a commercial venture' (see, for example, *Dr Sophie Redmond Stichting Foundation* v *Bartol and Others* (Case C-29/91)).

The Commission initiated Art 226 proceedings against the United Kingdom once the time limit specified in the reasoned opinion had expired. Although the United Kingdom had remedied the breach by the time the matter reached the Court of Justice, the Court nevertheless found the United Kingdom in breach of its obligations under the Treaty, i.e. to implement the directive correctly by the date of implementation specified in the directive.

A more recent example of a possible breach of Community law, through the wrongful implementation of a directive, is provided in *R* v *Secretary of State for Trade and Industry, ex parte Trades Union Congress* [2000] IRLR 565, which concerns the Parental Leave Directive 96/34. Under the directive, parents of children under five years of age have the right to, *inter alia*, 13 weeks' unpaid leave. The United Kingdom implemented the directive by the Maternity and Parental Leave Regulations 1999 (SI 1999/3312), but by reg 13(3) the right to parental leave was limited to children born or adopted after the commencement of the regulations, namely 15 December 1999. It was argued that this was an incorrect implementation and that the right should be made available to parents of all children under the age of five, it being irrelevant whether or not they were born after 15 December 1999.

The Commission had not instituted proceedings against the United Kingdom pursuant to Art 226, and therefore the case is not directly relevant to the Art 226 process. Instead, the TUC issued judicial review proceedings in the Divisional Court against the UK Government, arguing that there had been an incorrect implementation. This case is therefore included simply to provide an example of a case involving a possible wrongful implementation of a directive, and of the consequences of the alleged breach.

Evidence adduced at the hearing indicated that the regulations excluded the right of 2.7 million parents of children under the age of five, but who had been born before 15 December 1999, from the right to take unpaid parental leave. The European Commission had already taken issue with Ireland, whose legislation included a similar exclusion to the United Kingdom's. Ireland subsequently amended its legislation to remove this exclusion.

The Divisional Court exercised its discretion to make a referral to the Court of Justice pursuant to Art 234, for guidance on the interpretation of the directive (see Chapter 6).

Altering the subject matter

When the case comes before the Court of Justice, the Commission cannot rely on matters which have not been included in the reasoned opinion (*Commission* v *Belgium* (Case 186/85), para 13).

This is the case even if both parties consent. In *Commission* v *Italy* (Case 7/69), after the date for complying with a reasoned opinion which had been served on Italy had expired, the Commission started enforcement proceedings in the Court of Justice. After starting these proceedings, Italy amended its law in an attempt to comply with the reasoned opinion, but the Commission still considered Italy to be in breach of Community law. Both parties agreed that the Court of Justice should decide whether the new Italian law complied with Community obligations, rather than adjudicate on Italy's initial breach.

The Court of Justice refused to consider this question. The nature of the proceedings could not be altered, even by consent. The subject matter of the Commission's complaint had changed significantly since it had issued the reasoned opinion, the issuing of which is a compulsory part of the Art 226 procedure. The proceedings (as set out in the reasoned opinion) only concerned a default existing at the time the proceedings were initiated. What transpired afterwards was irrelevant for the current proceedings. If the Commission wished to have the new law tested, the full Art 226 proceedings must be started afresh, i.e. formal letter, reasoned opinion, enforcement proceedings.

Disclosure of draft reasoned opinion

In *Bavarian Lager Company Ltd* v *Commission of the European Communities* (Case T-309/97), the Court of First Instance of the European Communities held that the European Commission was not obliged to disclose a draft reasoned opinion which it subsequently decided not to serve on a Member State because it was satisfied with the action taken by that Member State to remedy the alleged breach of Community law. The Court of First Instance stated:

The Joint Code of Conduct concerning access to Council and Commission documents (OJ 1993 L 340/4) laid down the general principle that the public was to have the widest access to documents held by the Commission and the Council, and on the basis of that and Case T-105/95 *United Kingdom* v *Commission* [1997] ECR II-313, the applicant [Bavarian Lager Company Ltd] asserted that it had a right to access to the document in issue [i.e. the draft reasoned opinion].

The grounds which could be relied on by a Community institution to reject an application for access were listed in the Code of Conduct which provided, *inter alia*:

> 'The institutions will refuse access to any documents where disclosure could undermine the protection of the public interest (public security, … inspections and investigations) …'

It was on that exception that the Commission grounded its refusal.

The applicant classified the document to which it sought access as a reasoned opinion, but that was wrong in fact and in law.

The document was in fact a draft reasoned opinion drawn up by Commission staff after the members of the Commission had decided to deliver a reasoned opinion.

In view of the decision to suspend the procedure, that document was in the end never signed by the Commissioner responsible or communicated to the Member State.

The procedure initiated under article 169 [now 226] thus only got as far as the stage of inspection and investigation and never reached the stage where the Commission delivered a reasoned opinion, and the 'opinion' remained a purely preparatory document.

The Member States were entitled to expect confidentiality from the Commission during investigations which could lead to an infringement procedure, and the disclosure of documents relating thereto, during the negotiations between the Commission and the Member State concerned, could jeopardise the purpose of the infringement procedures: to enable the Member State to comply of its own accord with the requirements of the Treaty or, if appropriate, to justify its position.

The safeguarding of that objective warranted, under the heading of the protection of the public interest, the refusal of access to a preparatory document relating to the investigation stage of the article 169 [now 226] procedure.

On those grounds the CFI dismissed the application.

The judicial stage

The Commission does not have to commence proceedings immediately on the expiry of the period specified in its opinion. In one case it waited six years before commencing proceedings (*Commission* v *Germany* (Case C-422/92)). It is envisaged that the Commission may wish to give the offending state more time to take the necessary remedial action (*Commission* v *France* (Case 7/71), para 5).

Member States have attempted to rely upon a number of defences to breaches of Community law, but the Court has not, generally, been receptive. In relation to non-transposition of directives, it is frequently argued either that there has been a shortage of parliamentary time or, alternatively, that transposition is not necessary because the terms of the directive are, in fact, observed and conflicting national legislative provisions are not adhered to. The first defence was resolutely disposed of by the Court in *Commission* v *Belgium* (Case 77/69). Belgium had imposed a discriminatory tax on wood which violated Art 95 EC Treaty (now Art 90) (see Chapter 17). A draft law to amend the tax scheme had been laid before the Belgian Parliament, but had fallen when the Parliament was dissolved. The Belgian Government argued that these were matters out of its control and it had been prevented from legislating by *force majeure*. The Court was curt in its dismissal of the argument:

> The obligations arising from Article 95 [now Art 90] of the Treaty devolve upon States as such and the liability of a Member State under Article 169 [now Art 226] arises whatever the agency of the State whose action or inaction is the cause of the failure to fulfil its obligations, even in the case of a constitutionally independent institution. The objection raised by the defendant cannot therefore be sustained. (paras 15 and 16) (see also *Commission* v *Belgium* (Case 1/86))

Nor is the fact that the requirements imposed by a directive are difficult to meet accepted as a defence. In *Commission* v *United Kingdom* (Case C-56/90), the United Kingdom attempted to justify its failure to take all necessary measures to ensure that bathing beaches in Blackpool and Southport met the environmental and health standards set by Directive 76/160 by arguing that implementation was made more difficult by local circumstances. The Court said that, even assuming that absolute physical impossibility to carry out the obligations imposed by the Directive might justify failure to fulfil them, the United Kingdom had not established such impossibility in this case. Nor can Member States qualify their obligations imposed by directives in response to the demands of 'special' local circumstances or particular economic or social interest groups. In *Commission* v *Hellenic Republic* (Case C-45/91), the Greek Government attempted to justify its failure to implement a directive on the safe disposal of toxic waste because of 'opposition by the local population'. The Court commented that it had consistently held that a Member State cannot rely on an internal situation to justify disregard of its obligations. Similar defences relating to local conditions have been advanced, and rejected, in two Art 226 proceedings following the failure of Member States to implement Directive 79/409 on the protection of wild birds (*Commission* v *Netherlands (Re Protection of Wild Birds)* (Case 339/87); *Commission* v *Spain* (Case C-355/90)).

In *Commission* v *Greece* (Case C-105/91), the Greek Government defended its admittedly unlawful and discriminatory tax on foreign vehicles by arguing that the Greek vehicles concerned constituted no more than 10 per cent of the internal demand and that there was no manifest discrimination. The Court rejected the defence on the ground that it had consistently held that a Member State was guilty of a failure to fulfil its obligations under the Treaty regardless of the frequency or the scale of the infringement. The defence that a directive or regulation is observed in practice or 'administratively' where there are conflicting national provisions has also been rejected by the Court on a number of occasions (*Commission* v *Italy* (Case 166/82); *Commission* v *Germany (Re Nursing Directives)* (Case 29/84); *Commission* v *United Kingdom (Re Tachographs)* (Case 128/78)). However, the use of existing, legally binding provisions of national law may be acceptable if they provide an effective means of implementing the directive. Such legislation may, therefore, provide a defence to non-implementation (*Commission* v *Netherlands* (Case C-190/90)). Individuals must, nonetheless, be able to rely on a text of national law that accurately reflects their rights and on which they can rely in the event of a judicial challenge (*Commission* v *France* (Case 167/73)). For this reason, a Community obligation cannot be implemented by the government of a Member State simply by accepting assurances from the bodies affected that they will meet the terms of the Community provision. It is suggested, therefore, that *R* v *Secretary of State for the Environment, ex parte Friends of the Earth* [1994] 2 CMLR 760, in which Schiemann J held that an undertaking from water authorities given to the Secretary of State that they would meet Community requirements on water quality was an acceptable way of meeting the United Kingdom's Community obligations, is probably wrongly decided.

ARTICLE 228 – PECUNIARY PENALTY

Once judgment has been given against a Member State, failure to observe the terms of that judgment will constitute a further breach of Art 228 EC Treaty (previously Art 171). A number of judgments have not been implemented for as long as five years after the hearing (Audretsch, 1986). The Treaty on European Union significantly strengthened the hand of the Court of Justice in those cases in which Member States are found to have breached Community law. Article 228 (as amended by the TEU) provides:

1 If the Court of Justice finds that a Member State has failed to fulfil an obligation under this Treaty, the State shall be required to take the necessary measures to comply with the judgment of the Court of Justice.

2 If the Commission considers that the Member State concerned has not taken such measures it shall, after giving that State the opportunity to submit its observations, issue a reasoned opinion specifying the points on which the Member State concerned has not complied with the judgment of the Court of Justice.

   If the Member State concerned fails to take the necessary measures to comply with the Court's judgment within the time limit laid down by the Commission, the latter may bring the case before the Court of Justice. In so doing it shall specify the amount of the lump sum or penalty to be paid by the Member State concerned which it considers appropriate in the circumstances.

   If the Court of Justice finds that the Member State concerned has not complied with its judgment it may impose a lump sum or penalty payment on it.

   This procedure shall be without prejudice to Article 227.

Following a judgment of the Court pursuant to Art 226, the Member State is obliged to take the necessary measures to give effect to the judgment (Art 228(1)). This may require national legislation being implemented, amended or repealed to remedy the breach of Community law. If the Member State fails to comply with the judgment it will be in breach of its Art 228(1) duty. The Commission is then empowered by Art 228(2) to initiate fresh enforcement proceedings for breach of Art 228(1). The three Art 226 stages will apply (Art 228(2)). If the Commission decides to implement stage three (i.e. referral to the Court of Justice), the Commission will recommend a lump sum or penalty payment which should be imposed against the defaulting Member State. However, this is only a recommendation; the Court of Justice can levy any amount it wishes. There is no upper limit.

Prior to the TEU, Art 228(2) carried no sanction. All the Court of Justice was empowered to do was to make a declaration that a Member State was acting in breach of its Community law obligations. The incorporation of financial sanctions into the Art 228 procedure strengthens the Commission's hand in ensuring that Member States comply with their Community obligations. However, the Commission will still seek to resolve the conflict informally; it will explore every possible avenue before initiating Court proceedings.

On 8 January 1997 the Commission agreed a procedure with regard to recommending to the Court the use of penalties in the future (OJ 1997 C 63/2). It starts with a basic penalty of 55 euros per day, which will be multiplied by factors to account for the gravity of the breach, the length of time it has lasted and the relative wealth of the state. The United Kingdom would face a minimum daily penalty of 90,000 euros and a maximum of 537,500 euros. France and Germany have larger economies and therefore would face increased penalties, while Italy would be liable to a slightly lower penalty.

The Court of Justice has subsequently imposed a financial penalty on a Member State in Art 228(2) proceedings and commented upon the Commission's pecuniary penalty guidelines. In *Commission v Hellenic Republic* (Case C-387/97), Greece had failed to fulfil its obligations under Art 4, Directive 75/442 on waste (OJ 1975 L 194/39) and Art 5, Directive 78/319 on toxic and dangerous waste (OJ 1978 L 84/43), whereby Member States had to take measures to ensure that, respectively, waste and toxic and dangerous waste were disposed of without endangering human health and harming the environment. In addition Greece had failed to comply with Art 6, Directive 74/442 and Art 12, Directive 78/319, whereby the competent authorities were required to draw up plans in relation to waste disposal.

The Commission received a complaint in September 1987 about the uncontrolled tipping in the mouth of the River Kouroupitos in Chania, Crete, of waste including household refuse, refuse from military bases, hospitals and clinics, and residues from salt factories, poultry farms, slaughterhouses and industrial sites. The Commission brought the matter to the attention of the Greek Government which in reply referred, *inter alia*, to the opposition of the Chania population to the creation of new landfill sites in the area.

The Commission in due course brought proceedings under the former Art 169 EC Treaty (now Art 226) which culminated in the judgment in Case C-45/91, given on 7 April 1992. In finding against Greece, the Court of Justice pointed out, *inter alia*, that a Member State could not plead internal circumstances such as difficulties of implementation to justify a failure to comply with obligations laid down by Community law (see above).

After further communications between the Commission and the Greek Government between 1993 and 1996, the Commission issued a reasoned opinion to the effect that, by continuing not to draw up or implement requisite waste disposal plans, Greece had failed to comply with the 1992 judgment. The Commission therefore brought an action under Art 171(2) EC Treaty (now Art 228(2)).

In its judgment, the Court of Justice concluded that waste was still being tipped into the Kouroupitos in an uncontrolled and unlawful manner, and, although the Greek Government had stated that it was going to end the operation of the Chania tip after August 1988 and create new disposal sites, that had still not been done.

It had not been proved that Greece had failed to comply with the judgment in Case

C-45/91 in relation to Art 5, Directive 78/319, but in other respects that judgment had not been complied with.

The Court of Justice stated that Art 171(2) (now Art 228(2)) did not specify the period within which a judgment had to be complied with, but the importance of immediate and uniform application of Community law meant that the process of compliance had to be initiated at once and completed as soon as possible.

In the absence of provisions in the Treaty, the Court stated that the Commission could adopt guidelines for determining how the lump sums or penalty payments which it intended to propose to the Court were calculated, so as in particular to ensure equal treatment between the Member States. The Court of Justice then referred to the Commission's guidelines and continued:

> The Commission's suggestion that account should be taken both of the gross domestic product of the Member State concerned, and of the number of votes in the Council, appeared appropriate in that it enabled that State's ability to pay to be reflected while keeping the variation between Member States within a reasonable range.
>
> Those suggestions could not bind the court but were a useful point of reference.
>
> First, since the principal aim of penalty payments was that the Member State should remedy the breach of obligations as soon as possible, a penalty payment had to be set that was appropriate to the circumstances and proportionate both to the breach which had been found and to the State's ability to pay.
>
> Second, the degree of urgency that the Member State should fulfil its obligations could vary in accordance with the breach.
>
> *In that light, and as the Commission had suggested, the basic criteria which were to be taken into account in order to ensure that penalty payments had coercive force and Community law was applied uniformly and effectively were, in principle, the duration of the infringement, its degree of seriousness and the ability of the Member State to pay.*
>
> *In applying those criteria, regard should be had in particular to the effects of the failure to comply on private and public interests, and to the urgency of getting the Member State to fulfil its obligations.*
>
> In the present case, having regard to the nature of the breaches of obligations, which continued to the present day, a penalty payment was the means best suited to the circumstances.
>
> The duration of the infringement was considerable, as was its degree of seriousness and in particular the effect on private and public interests, given, *inter alia*, that the failure to comply with the obligation in article 4 of Directive 75/442 could, by the very nature of that obligation, directly endanger human health and harm the environment. (emphasis added)

The Court ordered Greece to pay to the Commission, into the account of 'EC own resources', a penalty payment of 20,000 euros for each day of delay in implementing the measures necessary to comply with the judgment in Case C-45/91 from delivery of the present judgment (4 July 2000) until the judgment in Case C-45/91 had been complied with. The interesting point here is that the Court only applied the daily penalty from the date of the current judgment and not 'a reasonable period' after its initial judgment when it had been held that Greece was in breach of its Community law obligations (7 April 1992).

The potency of the amended Art 228 is clearly amplified in the above case. It is further evidenced by the fact that in 1997 two cases were settled as soon as the

Commission had commenced proceedings for the imposition of a fine (Fifteenth Annual Report on Monitoring the Application of Community Law, 27 May 1998, COM (1998) final, OJ 1998 C 250/01).

INTERIM MEASURES

Breaches of Community law may occur inadvertently or intentionally. In the former case, Member States will normally take remedial action when the breach is brought to their attention by the Commission. In the latter, Member States may risk action by the Commission when they are confronted by internal political pressures which they cannot, or will not, resist. They will often do so in the hope that, by the time the Commission commences proceedings, a solution can be found and the illegal action can be terminated. Such considerations appear to have motivated the French Government in the ban it imposed on the import of lamb and mutton from other Member States, principally the United Kingdom (*Commission v France (Re Sheepmeat)* (Case 232/78)). Similar considerations seem, at least, to have been in the mind of the French Government during 1999 when it refused to lift the ban on the sale of UK beef. A worldwide ban had earlier been imposed by the Community in response to concerns about UK beef being affected by Bovine Spongiform Encephalitis (BSE) or 'mad cow disease'. When the ban was lifted during 1999 the French refused to comply, and the Commission has since issued proceedings against France pursuant to Art 226.

Given that several years may elapse between the initial complaint to the Commission and the hearing before the Court of Justice, the Commission, in circumstances where continuing damage is being caused while the case is processed, may apply to the Court for interim relief. Interim relief may be granted by the Court under Art 243 EC Treaty (previously Art 186), which simply states:

> The Court of Justice may in any cases before it prescribe any necessary interim measures.

The speed of the relief available is demonstrated by *Commission v Ireland* (Case 61/77R). In this case, Ireland had introduced fisheries conservation measures which the Commission regarded as contrary to the Treaty. It commenced Art 226 proceedings and, at the same time, made an application for an interim order requiring Ireland to suspend the operation of the legislation. Only nine days later the Court gave judgment. It doubted the validity of the Irish legislation on grounds of discrimination and, after several adjournments to promote a settlement, ordered the Irish Government to suspend the measures within five days. The case of *Commission v United Kingdom* (Case C-246/89R), also arose out of pressure to conserve diminishing fishing stocks. The UK Government, concerned about fishing vessels from other Member States operating in UK waters under UK 'flags of convenience' to gain access to UK fishing quotas, enacted the Merchant Shipping Act 1988. The Act confined the issue of fishing licences to companies registered in the United Kingdom and whose owners or shareholders were UK nationals or were ordinarily resident in the United Kingdom. The Act was clearly discriminatory under Art 7 EC Treaty (now Art 12), and it was an obstacle to establishment under Art 43 EC Treaty. The UK Government argued that the measures were necessary to protect the UK fishing quota. Pending the hearing of the case, could the Spanish shipowners who had challenged the licensing system continue to fish? The Court of Justice noted that the owners of the vessels were suffering heavy losses while their ships remained idle, and would soon have to sell them under very adverse conditions. *Prima facie*, the companies had a right to continue in business and, given the urgency of the situation, the Court ordered the United Kingdom to suspend the relevant provisions of the Merchant Shipping Act 1988. The Court of Justice subsequently found that there was unlawful discrimination (*Factortame* (Case C-221/89)).

In another case, *Commission v Germany* (Case C-195/90R), the Federal Republic had imposed a new tax on heavy goods vehicles with a view to encouraging greater use of water transport on the country's inland waterways. The tax, which was to be imposed largely for environmental reasons, was to take effect on 1 July 1990. The Commission applied for what was, in effect, an *ex parte* interim order from the President of the Court, which was ordered on 28 June, pending the full hearing of the interim application. Under the Court's Rules of Procedure, applicants need to state grounds indicating, first, a *prima facie* case establishing the breach of the law alleged and, secondly, urgency and the need for the interim measures.

On the law allegedly infringed, the Commission argued that the new German tax breached the 'stand-still' provisions of Art 72 EC Treaty, which were intended to protect the present position until a common Community transport policy was adopted under Art 70. It also breached Art 90 EC Treaty (the prohibition against discriminatory taxation – see Chapter 17), since the charge, although payable by all vehicles of the appropriate weight, was offset in relation to German vehicles by a reduction in German vehicle tax. The Court accepted that these arguments constituted a sufficiently strong case to meet the first requirement of the Rules of Procedure. But were the circumstances sufficiently urgent for interim relief? The Court has laid down that the urgency of an application for an interim measure is to be assessed in the light of the extent to which an interim order is necessary to avoid serious and irreparable damage (*Commission v Greece* (Case C-170/94R)). The Commission argued that the new German tax would disrupt its attempts to create a common transport policy and would drive a number of carriers out of business before the full proceedings could be heard. The German Government insisted that if the tax was suspended it would suffer irreparable damage in the loss of tax, which could not be recovered subsequently if the tax was found to be lawful in the main proceedings. The Court accepted the Commission's argument of the need to protect the status quo and the need to avoid irreparable damage to transport undertakings. The German Government could hardly be said to be suffering a loss to its exchequer, since the tax had never existed before. The interim order to suspend the operation of the new tax was, therefore, confirmed.

A more recent application for interim relief arose out of the award of contracts to replace old buses in Belgium and the alleged breach of the procedures laid down in Directive 90/531 by the Société Regionale Walloon du Transport (SRWT). The contract had been awarded (wrongly, the Commission maintained) and the delivery of the first buses was due to take place before the full hearing could take place. The Commission argued that there was a risk of serious and irreparable damage, in that the award of the contract and the first deliveries would confront the Commission, guardian of the treaties responsible for the application of Community law, with a *fait accompli*, and would create the conditions for a serious and immediate threat to the Community legal order. The Court agreed that the failure to comply with a directive applicable to a public contract constituted a serious threat to Community legality, and that a declaration at the conclusion of Art 226 proceedings could not cancel the damage suffered. However, the Court felt that an applicant for interim relief should act with due diligence. The Commission took more than two months to apply for relief after one of the unsuccessful tenderers had informed it of the situation. The formal contract was, in the meantime, concluded. Relief was, accordingly, refused to the Commission (*Commission* v *Belgium* (Case C-87/94)).

OTHER ACTIONS AGAINST MEMBER STATES

The power of the Commission to take cases directly to the Court of Justice where a Member State has granted aid to an undertaking in breach of Art 87 EC Treaty, will be considered in Chapter 19. Failure to abolish the offending aid within the time specified will entitle the Commission to proceed without giving a reasoned opinion as required under Arts 226 and 227.

There are also special powers given to the Commission under Art 95(9) EC Treaty to enable it to bring Member States before the Court of Justice without going through the Art 226 procedure in cases where a Member State has used its power to derogate from a harmonising directive on grounds of major needs or protection of the environment or the working environment. This can be done where the Commission believes that the Member State is using its power of derogation improperly.

Further reading

Audretsch, H.A.H. (1986) *Supervision in European Community Law* (2nd edn), North Holland.

Barav, A., 'Failure of Member States to Fulfil their Obligations under Community Law' (1975) 12 CML Rev 369.

Craig, P. and De Burca, G. (1998) *EU Law Text, Cases and Materials* (2nd edn), OUP, Chapter 9.

Dashwood, A. and White, R., 'Enforcement Actions and Articles 169 & 170' (1989) 14 EL Rev 388.

Gray, C., 'Interim Measures of Protection in the European Court' (1979) 4 EL Rev 80.

Harding, C., 'Member State Enforcement of European Community Measures: the Chimera of "Effective Enforcement"' (1997) 4 MJ 5.

Hartley, T.C. (1998) *The Foundations of European Community Law* (4th edn), Oxford University Press, Chapter 10.

Snyder, F., 'The Effectiveness of European Community Law: Institutions, Processes, Tools and Techniques' (1993) 56 MLR 19.

Steiner, J. and Woods, L. (2000) *Textbook on EC Law* (7th edn), Blackstone Press, Chapter 28.

Tillotson, J. (2000) *European Community Law: Text, Cases and Materials* (3rd edn), Cavendish Publishing Ltd, Chapter 20.

Van den Bossche, 'In Search of Remedies for Non-compliance: The Experience of the European Community' (1996) 3 MJ 371.

Weatherill, S. (2000) *Cases and Materials on EC Law* (5th edn), Blackstone Press, Chapter 17.

Chapter 8

JUDICIAL REVIEW OF ACTS OF COMMUNITY INSTITUTIONS

Although the Community does not have a formal constitution, the EC Treaty confers specific powers and duties on each of the institutions and establishes what the Court of Justice has, on a number of occasions, referred to as 'a new legal order' (Opinion 1/91 [1991] ECR I-6079). Each of the institutions has a limited competence and must carry out its functions in the way specified in the Treaty and according to general principles of Community law (Art 7(1) EC Treaty).

LEGALITY OF COMMUNITY ACTS: ARTICLE 230 EC TREATY

If an institution exceeds its powers or uses them unlawfully, its acts may be subject to review by the Court of Justice under Art 230 (as amended by the ToA):

> The Court of Justice shall review the legality of acts adopted jointly by the European Parliament and the Council, of acts of the Council, of the Commission and of the European Central Bank, other than recommendations and opinions, and of acts of the European Parliament intended to produce legal effects *vis-à-vis* third parties.
>
> It shall for this purpose have jurisdiction in actions brought by a Member State, the Council or the Commission on grounds of lack of competence, infringement of an essential procedural requirement, infringement of this Treaty or of any rule of law relating to its application, or misuse of powers.
>
> The Court shall have jurisdiction under the same conditions in actions brought by the European Parliament, by the Court of Auditors and by the ECB for the purpose of protecting their prerogatives.
>
> Any natural or legal person may, under the same conditions, institute proceedings against a decision addressed to that person or against a decision which, although in the form of a regulation or a decision addressed to another person, is of direct and individual concern to the former. The proceedings provided for in this Article shall be instituted within two months of the publication of the measure, or of its notification to the plaintiff, or, in the absence thereof, of the day on which it came to the knowledge of the latter, as the case may be.

The terms of Art 230 raise *five* questions which need to be answered:

1 What acts may be reviewed?
2 Who may challenge them, i.e. who has, in the language of English administrative law, the *locus standi* to mount a challenge?
3 When is an action barred by lapse of time?

4   What are the grounds for challenge?
5   What are the consequences of an annulment?

Reviewable acts

Not every act of an institution may be reviewed. *Prima facie*, it is only those acts which Art 249 EC Treaty defines as legally binding – namely regulations, directives and decisions – which are subject to review. Opinions and recommendations are not reviewable. Other acts, however, not specified in Art 249, have been treated by the Court of Justice as subject to review. In *Commission* v *Council* (Case 22/70), the Court held that a resolution passed by the Council to participate in a European Transport Agreement was reviewable under Art 230. It refused to interpret Art 249 restrictively, and declared that 'an action for annulment must ... be available in the case of all measures adopted by the institutions, whatever their nature and form, which are intended to have legal effects'. The Court of Justice has frequently emphasised that the determining factor is whether or not an act has legal consequences, no matter how it has been arrived at:

> In order to ascertain whether the measures in question are acts within the meaning of Article 173 [now Art 230] it is necessary ... to look to their substance. According to the consistent case law of the Court any measure the legal effects of which are binding on, and capable of affecting the interests of, the applicant by bringing about a distinct change in his legal position is an act or decision which may be the subject of an action under Article 173 [now Art 230] for a declaration that it is void. However, the form in which such acts or decisions are cast is, in principle, immaterial as regards the question whether they are open to challenge under that article. (*IBM* v *Commission* (Case 60/81))

It is, however, often difficult to distinguish between form and substance. An act may not have any legal consequence precisely because it has not been adopted in the form required. In *Air France* v *Commission* (Case T-3/93) the Commissioner responsible for competition policy, Sir Leon Brittan, had issued a press statement about the merger between Dan Air and British Airways, declaring that it would result in a sufficient concentration of air transport to have a Community dimension. Air France's attempt to challenge the statement failed at the first hurdle, because the statement had not been adopted by the whole Commission and did not have the *form* of a legal act. It could, therefore, have no legal consequences (see also *Nefarma* v *Commission* (Case T-113/89)).

As it was originally drawn, Art 230 made no mention of measures adopted by the European Parliament. Despite this, the Court of Justice held, in *Parti Ecologiste ('Les Verts')* v *European Parliament* (Case 294/83) that measures adopted by the Parliament intended to have legal effects *vis-à-vis* third parties were subject to annulment under Art 230 (see also *Luxembourg* v *European Parliament* (Case C-213/88)). The Court has also held that a declaration made by the President of the Parliament at the conclusion of the debate by Parliament on the Community's budget has the character of a legal act and is also subject to annulment (*Council* v *Parliament* (Case 34/86); *Council* v *European Parliament* (Case C-284/90)). Measures taken by the Parliament affecting third parties are now specifically subject to review as a result of amendments made to Art 230 by the TEU. A measure adopted by the Court of Auditors has also been held to be reviewable under Art 230 (*Maurissen and others* v *Court of Auditors* (Cases 193 & 194/87)). A decision by the Commission to close the file on a complaint alleging breach of Art 82 EC Treaty has also been held to be a 'decision' reviewable under Art 230 (*SFEI and Others* v *Commission* (Case C-39/93P)).

Although the acts of the Council are reviewable, the representatives of the Member States must be acting *as* the Council for Art 230 to apply. In *Parliament* v *Council* (Cases C-181/91 & C-248/91), the Parliament attempted to challenge a decision made at a Council meeting granting special aid to Bangladesh. The Court of Justice held that acts adopted by representatives of the Member States acting not as members of the Council but as representatives of their governments, amounted to the collective exercise of the competencies of the Member States. They were not, therefore, acts of the Council and were not, consequently, subject to review by the Court of Justice.

Some acts are specifically excluded from review. Article 35(5) TEU (as amended by the ToA) provides, for example, that the Court of Justice shall have no jurisdiction to review the validity or proportionality of operations carried out by the police or other law enforcement services of a Member State. The Court has, however, decided that it does have jurisdiction to determine the *scope* of such exclusions. In *Svenska Journalist-forbundet* v *Council of European Union* (Case T-174/95), the Court of First Instance ruled that, although it could not rule on the substance of decisions contained in Council documents, it did have jurisdiction to review the refusal to journalists of access to the documents themselves. It accordingly annulled a decision by the Council refusing access to certain documents concerning the European Police Office.

Who may apply for review?

Privileged applicants

Article 230 confers specific and unlimited rights of challenge on Member States, the Council of Ministers and the Commission. The European Parliament, the Court of Auditors and the European Central Bank have more limited rights of challenge to enable them to protect their prerogatives. Their powers to do so reflect decisions of the Court of Justice made on the basis of Art 230 in relation to the Parliament as it was originally framed, before amendment by the Treaty on European Union. Member States may apply for review, even though they have no direct or indirect interest in the subject matter of the case but, for example, are concerned that the appropriate procedure should be used (*Italy* v *Commission* (Case 41/83)).

Non-privileged applicant

The fourth paragraph of Art 230 confers a right of challenge on 'any natural or legal person', although this right is much more limited than that of Member States and Community institutions. A 'natural or legal person' is entitled only to challenge:

- a decision addressed to himself; or
- a decision, in the form of a regulation or a decision addressed to another person, which is *of direct and individual concern to himself.*

Community law has had as much difficulty as English law in defining who has a sufficient interest to be recognised by the Court of Justice as being a proper person for judicial review purposes. Many decisions which are subject to challenge are made by the Commission in relation to competition law, and are challenged by those against whom they are made. Individuals who have, for example, complained that the conduct of an undertaking infringes Art 82 EC Treaty, where the Commission refuses to investigate the complaint, will have standing to challenge that refusal (*Demo-Studio Schmidt* v *Commission* (Case 210/81); compare, *Lord Bethell* v *Commission* (Case 246/81)). The concept of 'direct and individual concern' has been narrowly construed by the Court of First Instance in relation to decisions made by the Commission. It denied the *locus standi* of employees' representatives to challenge Commission decisions approving mergers which were likely to result in redundancies. In both *Comité Central d'Enterprise de la Société Générale des Grandes Sources and Others* v *Commission* and *Comité Centrale d'Enterprise de la Société Anonyme Vittel and Others* v *Commission* (Case T-96/92), the Court held that the employee representatives had standing to challenge the decisions of the Commission only insofar as the mergers that would result following the Commission's approval affected rights of representation of the employee organisations concerned. The Court was not satisfied that redundancies were an inevitable consequence of the mergers. Even if they were, the effect on the *representatives* of the redundancies would 'only be of an indirect nature' and they did not, therefore, have standing to challenge the decisions. On this basis, inhabitants of Tahiti who were likely to be affected by radioactive fallout caused by French nuclear tests in 1995, were held by the Court of First Instance to be unable to challenge a decision by the Commission not to intercede with the French Government under powers conferred on it by the Euratom Treaty. The Court held that the applicants could not show that they would suffer greater effects from the fallout than 'all other persons residing in Polynesia' (*Danielsson and Others* v *Commission* (Case T-219/95R)). Even individuals who the Court acknowledged ought to have been consulted as a matter of good environmental practice before a decision was made, were held not to have standing to challenge the decision when it was made because the regulation did not give them a *right* to challenge it: *Associazone Agricoltori di Rovigo* v *Commission* (Case C-142/95). Some greater flexibility has, however, recently been shown by the Court of First Instance in allowing a journalist to apply for annulment of a decision refusing access to documents without requiring him to show a special interest above others affected by the refusal (*Svenska Journalistforbundet* v *Council of the European Union* (Case T-174/95)).

An adopted regulation may have an adverse effect upon a small group of individuals or commercial undertakings. Will they have the standing to challenge it under Art 230? If the regulation is of a general kind, the answer will be in the negative. However, in the case of anti-dumping regulations, the Court recently accepted the standing of a company to challenge a regulation of a general character (*Codorniu* (Case C-309/89)). If the regulation is intended to affect a specific group of undertakings, it may be 'a conglomeration of individual decisions ... under the guise of a regulation', and those affected may have the status to challenge it (*International Fruit Co* v *Commission* (Case 41/70)). Conversely, if a regulation is a genuine one, the fact that it affects a small group of undertakings positively, and the complainant negatively, does not give the complainant the right to bring Art 230 proceedings (*Campo Ebro SA* v *Council* (Case T-472/93)).

The fact that a decision, although addressed to a Member State, will have a direct effect on a specific undertaking, and where the decision is made with that undertaking in mind (e.g. in relation to a proposed state aid), will clearly give that undertaking standing to mount a challenge to that decision (*Philip Morris Holland* v *Commission* (Case 730/79); *Intermills* (Case 323/82)). This will be the case even if the complainant may not benefit from the state aid if the state concerned decides otherwise, provided that the possibility of non-payment by the state is 'purely theoretical' (*ASPEC* v *Commission* (Case T-435/93)). If, however, a decision is not of 'individual concern' to an undertaking, although it may be adversely affected by it, that undertaking will not be regarded as having sufficient standing (*Plaumann* v *Commission* (Case 25/62)). Many of the cases show a nervousness on the part of the Court to 'opening the flood-gates' to a multiplicity of claims by bodies adversely affected by Community legislation, and they are not wholly consistent. It should be noted, though, that, in its Report to the 1996 Intergovernmental Conference (May 1995), the Court expressed its own misgivings about the present law on standing:

> It may be asked ... whether the right to bring an action for annulment under Article 173 [now Art 230] of the EC Treaty (and the corresponding provisions of the other Treaties), which individuals enjoy only in regard to acts of direct and individual concern is sufficient to guarantee for them effective judicial protection against possible infringements of their fundamental rights arising from the legislative activity of the institutions. (p. 12)

No amendments were made by the Treaty of Amsterdam, however, to relax the rules on standing for individual applicants, and there remains a growing discrepancy between Community and English law, with the latter showing an increasing tendency to flexibility, not least in cases involving English institutions and the interpretation and application of Community law (see, e.g., *R* v *Minister of Agriculture, Fisheries and Food, ex parte Compassion in World Farming Ltd* (Case-1/96)).

Time limits

Article 230(4) provides that proceedings should be instituted within two months of:

- the publication of the measure; or
- its notification to the claimant; or, in the absence thereof
- the day on which it came to the knowledge of the latter, as the case may be.

The two-month period expires at the end of the day in the last month which bears the same number as the day of the occurrence of the event which caused time to start running (*Misset* v *Council* (Case 152/85)). So, for example, if the measure had been published in the *Official Journal* on 2 February 2001, the two-month period would expire at midnight on 2 April 2001. The Court of First Instance has held that where an applicant lets the time limit for bringing an action against a decision unequivocally affecting his interests expire, he cannot start time running again by asking the institution to reconsider its decision and then start proceedings against the confirmation of the decision (*Cobrecaf SA* v *Commission* (Case T-514/93)). The expiry of the period of time allowed for bringing proceedings will not be fatal if the applicant can rely on the second paragraph of the Statute of the Court, which provides:

> No right shall be prejudiced in consequence of the expiry of the time limit if the party concerned proves the existence of unforeseeable circumstances or of force majeure.

The Court of Justice has, however, shown reluctance in allowing applications outside the statutory time limits. Time limits do not apply where the issue of the legality of a Community measure is raised in Art 234 EC Treaty proceedings (see below). However, a national court cannot refer a case under Art 234 to the Court of Justice where the applicant could have challenged the Community measure within the time limit under Art 230, but failed to do so (*TWD Deggendorf* (Case C-188/92); see Chapter 6).

The legal basis for a challenge

Article 230 provides four possible bases for a challenge. These are:

- lack of competence;
- infringement of an essential procedural requirement;
- infringement of the Treaty or any rule of law relating to its application; and
- misuse of powers.

These are not mutually exclusive and two or even three may be cited together in an application for judicial review.

Lack of competence

This corresponds in English law to substantive *ultra vires*; a body can only do that which it is authorised to do by law. A number of challenges have been mounted on the grounds that the Commission has chosen the wrong legal base for a legislative proposal (see *Commission v Council (Re Titanium Dioxide Waste)* (Case C-300/89)) or a decision. In *Germany, France, Netherlands, Denmark and the United Kingdom v Commission* (Cases 281, 283–285, 287/85) the Commission had adopted a decision under Art 137 EC Treaty (then Art 118) under which Member States were required to consult with the Commission on measures relating to the integration of workers from states outside the Community. The Court of Justice held that the social policy objects of Art 137 were confined to measures that affected migrants from other Member States, and did not extend, as this decision purported to do, to measures affecting only migrants from states outside the Community.

There are not a great many challenges which are successful on this basis, but an example is *France v Commission* (Case C-327/91), where the Commission had concluded an agreement with the United States of America to promote cooperation and coordination and to lessen the possibility of conflict between the parties in the application of their competition laws. The case concerned the competence of the Commission to conclude the agreement. In a challenge by the French Government, the Court held that the Commission did not have the competence to do so. Under Art 228 EC Treaty (before amendment by the TEU) the Commission had the power to negotiate agreements with states outside the Community or with international organisations, but they had to be concluded by the Council.

Infringement of an essential procedural requirement

This is probably the most oft-cited basis of challenge and is equivalent in English law to procedural *ultra vires*. It comprises breaches of both formal procedural requirements laid down in the EC Treaty and in secondary legislation and the more informal rules of fairness required by general principles of Community law (see Chapter 5). The most important general procedural requirement in the EC Treaty is that laid down in Art 253, under which secondary legislation must state the reasons on which it is based. The Court of First Instance has emphasised the importance of this provision:

> According to a consistent line of case law, the purpose of the obligation to state the reasons on which an individual decision is based is to enable the Community judicature to review the legality of the decision and to provide the person concerned with sufficient information to make it possible to ascertain whether the decision is well founded or whether it is vitiated by a defect which may permit its legality to be contested. The extent of that obligation depends on the nature of the measure in question and on the context in which it was adopted. (*Eugénio Branco Ld* v *Commission* (Case T-85/94))

In this case, and two similar previous cases, the Court annulled Commission decisions withdrawing approval or partial support of projects financed by the European Social Fund. Besides the obligation imposed by Art 253 EC Treaty, there was also a breach of the requirement imposed by Art 6(1), Regulation 2950/83 under which the Commission, before deciding to suspend, reduce or withdraw fund aid, had to give the relevant Member State the opportunity to comment (*Consorgan Lda* v *Commission* (Case C-181/90); *Socurte Ld and Others* v *Commission* (Cases T-432, 434/93)).

Breach of a procedural requirement may be so fundamental that the decision or other measure may be void *ab initio*, i.e. the decision will be held to have never existed. In *Commission* v *BASF AG and Others* (Case C-137/92P), the Court of First Instance had dismissed as inadmissible actions for annulment of a measure which purported to have been taken by the Commission under Art 81 EC Treaty, on the ground that the measure was 'non-existent'. The Court of Justice allowed an appeal. The Court stated that acts of the Community institutions are presumed to be lawful and accordingly produce legal effects, even if they are tainted by irregularities, until such time as they are annulled or withdrawn. However, it held that there are some acts which are so tainted by irregularity, whose gravity is so obvious, that they cannot be tolerated by the Community legal order. They must be treated as having no legal effect, even provisional. The Court said that such a conclusion, with all its potentially serious consequences, should be reached only in 'quite extreme circumstances'. In this case, both the operative part of the decision and the reasons for it had been adopted by a single Commissioner and three of the texts of the decision in the relevant languages had never been seen by the full Commission, contrary to the Commission's Rules of Procedure. It amounted to breach of an essential procedural requirement and was consequently annulled by the Court under Art 230. The decision of the Commission had not, however, been 'non-existent'.

Infringement of the Treaty or any rule relating to its application

There is an obvious overlap between Art 253 EC Treaty, the need to give reasons, procedural requirements and the general principles of fairness and natural justice which are fundamental principles of Community law. In addition there are also the rights set out in the European Convention on Human Rights, together with the principles of non-discrimination, proportionality, legitimate expectation, respect for property rights and equal treatment (see Chapter 5). These latter rights and principles are not absolute and may, in appropriate circumstances, have to give way to restrictions imposed in the interest of the common organisation of the market, 'provided that those restrictions in fact correspond to objectives of general interest pursued by the Community, and do not constitute a disproportionate and intolerable interference, impairing the very substance of the rights guaranteed' (*Germany* v *Commission (Re Banana Market)* (Case C-280/93)).

Misuse of powers

This ground for challenge stems from the French *détournement de pouvoir*. This is the equivalent, in English administrative law, of using a power conferred for an improper or illegitimate purpose. Since the power is itself lawful, a challenger must prove a subjective matter, the purpose for which it has been used (*Netherlands* v *High Authority* (Case 6/54)). Since outsiders are not privy to the reasons for institutional decisions unless they are made public, most of the few successful cases have relied on published documents, or the reasons given under Art 253 EC Treaty, which indicate that the institution has misunderstood the purpose for which a power has been conferred on it (*Giuffrida* v *Council* (Case 105/75)).

The United Kingdom's challenge to the Working Time Directive: a case study

In 1990, the Commission proposed a directive to regulate working time, under the health and safety provisions of the former Art 118a EC Treaty (now Art 137 (OJ 1990 C 254/4)). The legislative procedure which applied to Art 118a was the cooperation procedure (see Chapter 4). The Working Time Directive 93/104 was adopted by the Council, acting by a qualified majority, on 23 November 1993, with an implementation date of 23 November 1996 (OJ 1993 L 307/18). Eleven of the then 12 Member States voted in favour; the United Kingdom abstained and indicated that it would challenge the legality of the directive.

On 8 March 1994 the United Kingdom brought an action under Art 173 EC Treaty (now Art 230) for the annulment of the directive and, in the alternative, the annulment of specific parts of the directive including, *inter alia*, the second sentence of Art 5 of the directive. The second sentence of Art 5 provided that the minimum weekly rest period should 'in principle include Sunday'. In *United Kingdom* v *Council of the European Union* (Case C-84/94), in support of its action, the United Kingdom relied on four pleas:

1   that the legal base of the directive was defective;

2   breach of the principle of proportionality;
3   misuse of powers; and
4   infringement of essential procedural requirements.

Defective legal base

The main thrust of the United Kingdom's argument centred around the first plea that the directive was not concerned with the improvement of the health and safety of workers and therefore should not have been adopted under Art 118a (now Art 137). It was contended that the correct legal base was either Art 100 (now Art 94) or Art 235 (now Art 308), which both required unanimity within the Council of Ministers.

Article 100 (now Art 94) empowers the Council of Ministers to adopt directives which directly affect the establishment or functioning of the common market, by a *unanimous* vote. Article 100a (now Art 95) derogates from Art 100 (now Art 94) in that it empowers the Council of Ministers to adopt directives which directly affect the establishment or functioning of the internal market by a *qualified majority* while specifically excluding provisions 'relating to the rights and interests of employed persons'.

The United Kingdom first argued that provisions which related to the rights and interests of employed persons and which directly affected the internal or common market would as a general rule have to be enacted under Art 100 (now Art 94). The Court of Justice rejected this submission. It held that Art 118a (now Art 137) is a more specific legal base than Arts 100 (now Art 94) and 100a (now Art 95) and this is confirmed by the actual wording of Art 100a(1) (now Art 95(1)) which states that its provisions apply 'save where otherwise provided in this Treaty'. Therefore the more specific legal base of Art 118a (now Art 137) was to be preferred.

Secondly, the United Kingdom argued that a strict interpretation of Art 118a (now Art 137) only permitted the adoption of directives which had a genuine and objective link to the health and safety of workers and which therefore related to physical conditions and risks at the workplace. This did not apply to measures concerning, in particular, weekly working time (Art 6 of the Directive), paid annual leave (Art 7) and rest periods (Arts 4 and 5) whose connection with the health and safety of workers was tenuous. The United Kingdom's alternative plea was for the annulment of these specific provisions. This was also rejected by the Court of Justice, which held that a broad scope was to be given to health and safety. This was supported by reference to the Constitution of the World Health Organisation (to which all the Member States belong): health is there defined as 'a state of complete physical, mental and social well-being which does not consist only in the absence of illness or infirmity'. The United Kingdom additionally argued that the reference to the adoption of 'minimum requirements' in Art 118a(2) (now Art 137(2)) empowered the Council of Ministers only to adopt measures which were at a level acceptable to all Member States, and which constituted a minimum benchmark. This was similarly rejected by the Court. The reference to 'minimum requirements' enabled Member States to adopt more stringent measures than those contained in the directive, as confirmed by Art 118a(3) (now Art 137(5)).

Thirdly, it was argued by the United Kingdom that Art 118a (now Art 137) did not empower the Council to adopt directives which deal with the question of health and safety in a 'generalised, unspecific and unscientific manner'. The United Kingdom supported this argument with reference to previous directives which had been adopted under Art 118a (now Art 137), which covered specific areas of activity. The Court likewise rejected this argument. Past practice of the Council cannot create a precedent binding on the Community institutions with regard to the correct legal basis. In any event, the Health and Safety Framework Directive 89/391 (OJ 1989 L 183/1), which had been adopted under Art 118a (now Art 137), had a general, unspecific scope.

The Court of Justice concluded that 'where the principal aim of the measure in question is the protection of the health and safety of workers, Article118a (now Art 137) must be used, albeit such a measure may have ancillary effects on the establishment and functioning of the internal market'.

Having set out the legal basis for the adoption of a directive under Art 118a (now Art 137), the Court examined whether, in the particular circumstances of this case, the Working Time Directive had been properly adopted under this article. The Court noted that the approach taken by the directive, viewing the organisation of working time essentially in terms of the favourable impact it may have on the health and safety of workers, was apparent from its preamble. While it could not be denied that the directive might affect employment, its essential and overriding objective was one of health and safety. However, the Court did not accept that choosing Sunday as the weekly rest day (Art 5, second sentence) was more closely connected to the health and safety of workers than any other day of the week. The Court therefore upheld this part of the United Kingdom's alternative claim; the second sentence of Art 5, which could be severed from the other provisions of the directive, was annulled.

With regard to Art 235 EC Treaty (now Art 308), the Court of Justice simply noted that the article could be used as the legal basis for a measure only where no other Treaty provision conferred on the Community institutions the necessary power to adopt it; this was not the case here.

Breach of the principle of proportionality

First, the United Kingdom argued that not all measures which may 'improve' the level of the health and safety protection of workers constitute minimum requirements. This was rejected by the Court of Justice which reiterated the point made above that the concept of 'minimum requirements' does not limit Community action to the lowest level of protection provided by the various Member States, but means a Member State can adopt provisions more stringent than those of the directive.

Secondly, it was argued by the United Kingdom that the application of the principle of proportionality would require the directive's objective of safeguarding the health and safety of workers to be attained by measures which were less restrictive and involved fewer obstacles to the competitiveness of industry and the earning capacity of individuals. The Court held that the Council, acting as legislature, must be allowed a wide discretion where it was making social policy choices and was required to carry out complex assessments. The Court would only rule the measure to be disproportionate if the exercise of the Council's discretion had been vitiated by manifest error or misuse of powers, or if it had manifestly exceeded the limits of its power. This could not be proven and was therefore rejected by the Court.

Thirdly, the United Kingdom argued that a measure will only be proportionate if it complies with the principle of subsidiarity. It is for the Community institutions to demonstrate that the aims of the directive could be better achieved at Community level rather than national level. The Court held that it had been demonstrated that Community action was necessary to adopt minimum requirements with the objective of raising the level of the health and safety protection of workers.

Misuse of powers

Misuse of powers is defined by the Court of Justice as the adoption of a measure with the exclusive or main purpose of achieving an end other than that stated, or evading a procedure specifically prescribed by the Treaty. The Court had already held that Art 118a (now Art 137) was the appropriate legal base and therefore this plea was also dismissed.

Infringement of essential procedural requirements

The United Kingdom argued that the directive was inadequately reasoned because there was a failure to demonstrate a connection between the health and safety of workers and the provisions of the directive. Many of the provisions were concerned with improving the living and working conditions of workers, or the internal market, rather than the health and safety of workers. This was rejected; the various recitals in the preamble to the directive clearly reasoned the connection between the provisions and the health and safety of workers. There was no necessity to include in the preamble specific references to scientific material justifying the adoption of the various provisions.

Consequences of annulment

Under Art 231 EC Treaty:

> If the action is well founded, the Court of Justice shall declare the act concerned to be void. In the case of a regulation, however, the Court of Justice shall, if it considers this necessary, state which of the effects of the regulation which it has declared void shall be considered as definitive.

Under Art 233 EC Treaty:

> The institution or institutions whose act has been declared void or whose failure to act has been declared contrary to the Treaty shall be required to take the necessary measures to comply with the judgment of the Court of Justice.
>
> The obligation shall not affect any obligation which may result from the application of the second paragraph of Article 288.

Since decisions and other acts having legal consequences will affect only single undertakings or individuals or groups of undertakings, the Court of Justice, if it finds the decision or other act to be void, will declare it to be void from the moment of delivery of the judgment. It can, of course, declare an act non-existent, but, as can be seen in the *BASF Case* (Case C-137/92), it is reluctant to do this because of the disruption which this may cause to actions which may have been based on the assumption that the act was valid. The second paragraph of Art 230 enables the Court to declare part of a decision void. In the case of Community legislation, it will frequently declare that, for example, the provisions of an annulled directive or regulation will remain effective until a new regulation is adopted (see, e.g., the Court's declaration on annulling Directive 90/366 on students' rights in *European Parliament* v *Council* (Case C-295/90), and on Council Regulation 2454/92 on transport undertakings operating in other Member States in *European Parliament* v *Council* (Case C-388/92)).

Article 233 requires the institution concerned to take the necessary remedial action to correct the failure which has been established by the judgment of the Court. There is no time limit for this, but the Court has held that such steps should be taken within a reasonable period from the date of the judgment (*European Parliament* v *Council* (Case 13/83)).

INDIRECT CHALLENGE TO A COMMUNITY ACT UNDER ARTICLES 241 AND 234 EC TREATY

The legality of a Community act may become an issue in proceedings in which the object is not the Community act itself but some action of an institution which purports to be based upon it. The issue can be raised only if it is relevant to the proceedings (*Italy* v *Commission* (Case 32/65)). Attacks on the legality of Community acts in this way are normally called indirect challenges and they may result in the judicial review of the legality of Community acts long after the time has passed for an application for review under Art 230. The issue of legality may arise in both the Court of Justice and the Court of First Instance at Community level or in national courts. Where it arises at Community level it is subject to the rules laid down in Art 241 EC Treaty which provides:

> Notwithstanding the expiry of the period laid down in the third paragraph of Article 230, any party may, in proceedings in which a regulation of the Council or of the Commission is in issue, plead the grounds specified in the first paragraph of Article 230 in order to invoke before the Court of Justice the inapplicability of that regulation.

The first point to note is that an indirect challenge in this way is only available in relation to regulations and cannot, therefore, be used in relation to other Community acts having legal effect. Secondly, the effect of Art 241 is limited to proceedings brought before the Court of Justice (*Wöhrmann* v *Commission* (Case 31/62)). Although Art 241 excludes an indirect challenge to other acts having legal effect, this rule may, in some cases, be circumvented where the issue arises in a national court. The question of the legality of the Community measure may then be raised, as we have already noted in connection with time limits under Art 230, in the national court and referred to the Court of Justice under Art 234 EC Treaty. The operation of Art 234 was examined in Chapter 6; the relevant part of that article enables national courts to ask for a preliminary ruling, *inter alia*, in relation to 'the validity ... of acts of the institutions of the Community'.

If a national body purports to act on the basis of, for example, a decision or a directive which is invalid, a party to the proceedings may ask the national court to refer the question of the validity of that measure to the Court of Justice. Such a reference will be necessary if the issue arises, because national courts have no power themselves to rule on the validity of a Community measure (*Foto-frost* v *HZA Lübeck-Ost* (Case 314/85)). An important restriction on that principle is, however, the rule laid down by the Court in *TWD Deggendorf* (Case C-188/92). In that case the Court held that no indirect challenge to a Commission decision could be made under Art 234 where the party had been informed of the Commission decision and could 'without doubt' have challenged it directly before the Court of Justice under Art 230, but had not done so.

CHALLENGING A FAILURE TO ACT

Institutions may act unlawfully not only by exceeding or abusing their powers, but by failing to carry out a duty imposed on them by the Treaty or some other provision having legal effect. This form of inaction may result in proceedings brought under Art 232 EC Treaty:

> Should the European Parliament, the Council or the Commission, in infringement of this Treaty, fail to act, the Member States and the other institutions of the Community may bring an action before the Court of Justice to have the infringement established.
>
> The action shall be admissible only if the institution concerned has first been called upon to act. If, within two months of being called upon, the institution concerned has not defined its position, the action may be brought within a further period of two months.
>
> Any natural or legal person may, under the conditions laid down in the preceding paragraphs, complain to the Court of Justice that an institution of the Community has failed to address to that person any act other than a recommendation or an opinion.
>
> The Court of Justice shall have jurisdiction, under the same conditions, in actions or proceedings brought by the European Central Bank in the areas falling within the latter's field of competence and in actions and proceedings brought against the latter.

Standing to challenge a failure to act

The position of 'privileged' applicants (i.e. Member States and institutions) who can bring proceedings under Art 232 irrespective of any particular interest, and 'non-privileged' applicants (i.e. legal and natural persons) who need to establish a special interest, is the same under Art 232 as in relation to challenges under Art 230. The Court has, in fact, stated that 'in the system of legal remedies provided for by the Treaty, there is a close relationship between the right of action given in Article 173 [now Art 230] ... and that based on Article 175 [now Art 232]' (*European Parliament* v *Council (Re Transport Policy)* (Case 13/83)).

Scope for challenge

There have not been many successful actions brought on this basis. Many of the duties which are conferred on the institutions involve both a duty and a discretion of whether, and how, to exercise that duty. To satisfy Art 232, the institution needs, generally, only to have addressed the issue and defined its position. In the case of natural or legal persons, if the only outcome of the institution's deliberations will be an opinion or a recommendation, a failure to produce either is not a failure which can be dealt with by Art 232. Where there is a clear duty to act, as there is imposed on the

Commission by Art 85(1) EC Treaty in relation to breaches of Arts 81 and 82, a statement by the Commission that it is not going to respond to a complaint might give grounds for an action under Art 232, after the appropriate warning has been given. For example, in *Ladbroke Racing (Deutschland) GmbH* v *Commission* (Case T-74/92), Ladbroke had complained to the Commission about a denial of access for the televising of horse racing, alleging a breach of Arts 81 and 82 EC Treaty by German and French companies in the horse racing and communications businesses. After deciding to investigate the complaint in December 1990, the Commission had still not defined its position on the alleged breach of Art 82 by June 1992, when it was formally requested to do so. The Court of First Instance found that there was a breach following the instigation of Art 232 proceedings. The Commission could have either initiated the procedure for establishing a breach of Art 82, dismissed the complaint in a formal letter to the complainant or made a reasoned decision not to pursue the complaint on the ground of a lack of Community interest. It had, however, done none of these things. If there is a refusal to pursue an investigation, it may in itself constitute a decision which is best attacked under Art 230 (*SFEI and Others* v *Commission* (Case C-39/93P)).

The difficulty of launching a successful action under Art 232 is illustrated by the *Transport Policy* case ((Case 13/83) – see above) concerning Arts 70 and 71 EC Treaty that require the Council to adopt a common transport policy for the Community. More than 20 years after the Treaty had come into force no such policy had been adopted, and the Parliament brought proceedings against the Council for failure to act under Art 232, after a number of requests had been made to the Council for progress in this area. The Court of Justice agreed that the Council had been 'called upon to act, by the Parliament, as required by Article 175(2) EC Treaty [now Art 232], and had produced equivocal replies as to what, if any, action it proposed to take'. The requirement in Arts 70 and 71 EC Treaty was not sufficiently precise, however, to amount to an enforceable obligation. Other cases have failed because the Court decided that all that was required was an opinion (*Chevally* v *Commission* (Case 15/70)), or because the decision which the applicant required was not to be addressed to him (*Lord Bethell* v *Commission* (Case 246/81)).

CLAIMS FOR DAMAGES AGAINST COMMUNITY INSTITUTIONS FOR UNLAWFUL ACTS

Article 233 EC Treaty specifically preserves the question of non-contractual liability as a separate issue from the legality or otherwise of institutional acts. As in English law, the fact that a public body has acted unlawfully does not, *per se*, mean that the body concerned is under a duty to compensate those adversely affected by its action, although a court does have the power to order the payment of compensation at the conclusion of an application for judicial review. Whether or not damages are payable under Community law depends on the way in which the Court of Justice, which under Art 235 EC Treaty has exclusive jurisdiction over damages claims against the institutions, has interpreted the provisions of Art 288 EC Treaty. The liability of Community institutions in contract will generally be governed by the law of the Member State where the institution is situated. Liability in non-contractual matters (tort, in English law) is governed by Art 288, second indent, which provides that:

In the case of non-contractual liability, the Community shall, in accordance with the general principles common to the laws of the Member States, make good any damage caused by its institutions or by its servants in the performance of their duties.

The Court laid down some basic rules for liability in *Lütticke* v *Commission* (Case 4/69). There must be actual damage to the claimant and a causal link between the damage and the alleged unlawful conduct of the institution. Fault is not an essential element in liability, in the sense that the institution does not have to be conscious of any wrongdoing. The only type of fault that need be established is an unlawful act by the relevant institution. Where there is a positive duty to do something, there must be an omission to do it and where there is a discretion, it must have been exercised in an unlawful way. The wrongdoing is likely to have been the result of carelessness, failure to make appropriate inquiries or the giving of misleading information. The conduct giving rise to a claim under Art 288 will usually amount to no more than *faute de service* or poor administrative practice causing loss to the claimant. The scope for liability is much wider than under English law, however, and institutions can be liable for wrongful legislative acts. This liability is, however, limited by the so-called *Schöppenstedt formula* (*Zückerfabrik Schöppenstedt* v *Council* (Case 5/71)). Under the formula the Court held that 'the Community does not incur liability on account of a legislative measure which involves choices of economic policy unless a sufficiently serious breach of a superior rule of law for the protection of the individual has occurred' (*HNL* v *Council and Commission* (Case 83/77), para 4; *Unifruit Hellas* v *Commission* (Case T-489/93)).

Adams v *Commission* (Case 145/83) illustrates the circumstances in which an institution may be liable. Stanley Adams was employed by Hoffmann La Roche, one of the largest pharmaceutical companies in Europe. Although the company was based in Switzerland, its products were widely sold throughout the Community, and it came to the attention of Adams that the company, which dominated parts of the pharmaceutical market, appeared to be engaged in a number of abuses. He passed various documents to the Commission, requesting that it did not identify him, and the documents subsequently enabled the Commission to establish the existence of the abuses and to fine the company (*Hoffmann La Roche* v *Commission* (Case 85/76)). During the course of exchanges with the company the Commission sent it copies of various documents supplied by Adams. Some of these documents contained marks and other indications which identified Adams as the informant. As a consequence, he was arrested and charged under Swiss law for the criminal offence of breach of employee confidentiality and economic espionage. He was prevented from communicating with his wife during his detention and she committed suicide. His conviction subsequently led to the collapse of a business he had established in Italy (see Hunnings, 1987).

Adams later brought proceedings against the Commission for breach of its duty of confidentiality under what is now Art 287 EC Treaty and Art 20 of Regulation 17/62. The Court of Justice found that the Commission had breached that duty of confidentiality by handing over the documents to Hoffmann La Roche, and had compounded the damage to Adams by failing to warn him of the company's intention to institute criminal proceedings against him which it learned of some months before his arrest by the Swiss police. The Commission was held liable for non-contractual damage under Art 288, but the damages payable to Adams were reduced by half, because he had failed to inform the Commission of the possibility that he might be identified from the documents and had returned to Switzerland without enquiring of the Commission whether he might be at risk from doing so.

The Court has not developed a comprehensive set of principles concerning the type and extent of damages which may be recovered, but certain rules have emerged in the case law. Actual financial loss that results from the unlawful action by the Commission may be recovered, but it must be established that this results directly from the unlawful conduct (*Dumortier Frères* v *Council* (Case 64/76)). The Court has also awarded damages for shock, disturbance and uneasiness in Community staff cases (*Algera* v *Common Assembly* (Case 7/56)).

Difficulties may arise where a national authority has acted on what subsequently transpires to have been an unlawful act by a Community institution. Who is liable? Should the injured party sue the institution which promulgated the unlawful act, or the national institution which implemented it, or both? Where the claimant's loss has occurred as a result of being obliged to pay money under an unlawful act, and he is claiming restitution, he will be expected to claim in the national courts against the national institution (*Vreugdenhil* v *Commission* (Case C-282/90)). Where there is no remedy in the national courts, claims can be brought against the relevant institution in the Court of Justice (*Krohn* v *Commission* (Case 175/84), paras 24–29).

Further reading

Arnull, A., 'Private applicants and the action for annulment under Art 173 of the EC Treaty' (1995) 32 CML Rev 7.

Brealey, M. and Hoskins, M. (1994) *Remedies in EC Law*, Longman.

Craig, P. and De Burca, G. (1998) *EU Law Text, Cases and Materials* (2nd edn), OUP, Chapters 11–12.

Greaves, R.M., 'Locus Standi under Article 173 when Seeking Annulment of a Regulation' (1986) 11 EL Rev 119.

Harlow, C., 'Towards a Theory of Access for the European Court of Justice' (1992) 12 YEL 213.

Hartley, T.C. (1998) *The Foundations of European Community Law, Pt IV* (4th edn), Oxford University Press, Chapters 11–17.

Hunnings, N.M., 'The Stanley Adams Affair or the Biter Bit' (1987) 24 CML Rev 65.

Lewis, A.D.E., 'Joint and Several Liability of the European Communities and National Authorities' (1980) *Current Legal Problems* 99.

Nehl, P.H. (1998) *Principles of Administrative Procedure in EC Law*, Hart Publishing.

Schermers, H.G., Mead, P. and Heukels, T., (eds) (1988) *Non-Contractual Liability of the European Communities*, Nijhoff Publications.

Steiner, J. (1995) *Enforcing EC Law*, Blackstone Press.

Steiner, J. and Woods, L. (2000) *Textbook on EC Law* (7th edn), Blackstone Press, Chapters 29–33.

Tillotson, J. (2000) *European Community Law: Text, Cases and Materials* (3rd edn), Cavendish Publishing Ltd, Chapters 1–3.

Weatherill, S. (2000) *Cases and Materials on EC Law* (5th edn), Blackstone Press, Chapter 19.

Wils, W., 'Concurrent Liability of the Community and a Member State' (1992) 17 EL Rev 191.

Chapter 9

PRINCIPLES OF SUPREMACY, DIRECT EFFECT, INDIRECT EFFECT AND STATE LIABILITY

THE SUPREMACY OF COMMUNITY LAW

Nowhere in the Treaty is there a reference to the supremacy of Community law. However, the Court of Justice has consistently held that this principle of supremacy is implied into the Treaty. In *Flaminio Costa* v *ENEL* (Case 6/64) the Court addressed this issue of supremacy. In an oft-quoted statement, the Court held ([1964] ECR 585 at 593) that:

> By creating a Community of unlimited duration, having its own institutions, its own personality, its own legal capacity and capacity of representation on the international plane and, more particularly, real powers stemming from a limitation of sovereignty or a transfer of powers from the States of the Community, *the Member States have limited their sovereign rights*, albeit within limited fields, and have thus *created a body of law which binds both their nationals and themselves*. (emphasis added)

ARTICLE 226 EC TREATY – INEFFECTIVE MEANS OF ENFORCEMENT

As discussed in Chapter 7, Art 226 EC Treaty (previously Art 169) expressly provides a mechanism for infraction proceedings to be initiated by the Commission against a defaulting Member State to ensure the state complies with its Community law obligations. The weakness in the Art 226 EC Treaty procedure, as initially formulated, was that there was no provision for imposing a penalty on a defaulting Member State; it proved ineffective in dealing with a recalcitrant Member State. However, as discussed in Chapter 7, following amendments made to the EC Treaty by the TEU, if a Member State fails to comply with a declaration made by the Court of Justice that it is in breach of Community law, the Commission may take action against that state under Art 228(2) EC Treaty. In this instance the Court of Justice can impose a financial penalty on the defaulting Member State.

An additional weakness is the article's failure sufficiently to safeguard the rights of individuals (e.g. a compensation order cannot be made against the defaulting Member State in favour of an aggrieved individual). The United Kingdom, for example, may have failed to implement a directive or may have implemented it incorrectly. With regard to employment-related directives, the purpose of such directives is to provide protection for employees. Breach of such a directive may have a significant impact upon an indeterminate number of workers. The fact that the United Kingdom may be hauled before the Court of Justice will be of little comfort to this group of persons deprived of their rights under Community law. The fact that Community law is considered by the Court of Justice to be supreme means nothing. It does not repair the possible damage suffered by them, unless they are provided with rights which they can enforce in the courts of Member States.

The impact on individuals can be illustrated by considering the Working Time Directive 93/104 (OJ 1993 L 307/18) which should have been implemented by all Member States by 23 November 1996. The United Kingdom failed to implement it on time. The directive provides rights for individual workers (e.g. four weeks' paid annual leave, minimum daily and weekly rest periods and a 48-hour maximum working week; all of which are subject to certain exceptions and derogations). A relatively short breach by the United Kingdom could have an enormous impact on an indeterminate number of workers. The United Kingdom implemented the directive by the Working Time Regulations 1998 (SI 1998/1833) which came into force on 1 October 1998 (almos. two years after the date stipulated in the directive). The Commission had taken no action against the United Kingdom under Art 226. Even if it had done, provided the United Kingdom had implemented the directive before expiry of the time limit laid down in the reasoned opinion, the United Kingdom could not have been brought before the Court of Justice. Even if the Court had ruled against the United Kingdom, it would not have had the power to award compensation to those workers whose rights had been infringed by the United Kingdom's failure to implement the directive.

DEVELOPMENT OF COMMUNITY LAW PRINCIPLES

In an attempt to address the problem of ineffective individual rights, the Court of Justice developed principles whereby an aggrieved national of a Member State would be afforded rights based upon Community law which could, in certain circumstances, be enforced in the courts of Member States. These rights are enshrined in the three principles of direct effect, indirect effect and *Francovich* damages against the state.

These principles have been established by the Court of Justice following referrals to it from national courts pursuant to Art 234 EC Treaty (previously Art 177) (see Chapter 6). These three principles will be considered further.

THE PRINCIPLE OF DIRECT EFFECT

The Court of Justice developed the principle of direct effect in *Van Gend en Loos* v *Nederlandse Administratie der Belastingen* (Case 26/62). The facts are quite mundane, but the consequences of the decision have been highly significant in the development of Community law.

Van Gend en Loos had imported ureaformaldehyde from Germany into The Netherlands. It had been charged a customs duty. This breached the rules on the free movement of goods between Member States, and in particular Art 12 (now Art 25) EC Treaty. Van Gend claimed reimbursement from the Dutch Government in the Dutch courts. The court referred the question of whether or not the claimant could rely on Art 12 in the national court to the Court of Justice.

The Court of Justice first of all addressed the general question of whether Treaty provisions could confer directly effective rights on individuals. It decided that they could:

> The Community constitutes a new legal order of international law for the benefit of which the States have limited their sovereign rights, albeit within limited fields, and the subjects of which comprise not only the Member States but also their nationals. *Independently of the legislation of Member States Community law therefore not only imposes obligations on individuals but is also intended to confer on them rights which become part of their legal heritage. These rights arise not only where they are expressly granted by the Treaty, but also by reason of obligations which the Treaty imposes in a clearly defined way upon individuals as well as upon Member States* and upon institutions of the Community. (emphasis added)

Effective supervision

Prior to *Van Gend en Loos* the accepted method of enforcement was, as stated above, for the Commission to issue infraction proceedings against the defaulting Member State under Art 169 (now Art 226). However, even if such proceedings proved successful, this would have been of no assistance to Van Gend en Loos. It would not have resulted in the repayment to it of the customs duty levied in breach of Community law. The Court accordingly dismissed the suggestion (by Belgium, The Netherlands and (West) Germany) that, because there existed machinery under former Art 169 to bring offending states before the Court of Justice, this must preclude the possibility of the use of Treaty provisions before national courts:

> the argument based on Articles 169 and 170 of the Treaty [now Articles 226 and 227] put forward by the three Governments ... is misconceived. The fact that these Articles of the Treaty enable the Commission and the Member States to bring before the Court a State which has not fulfilled its obligations does not mean that individuals cannot plead these obligations, should the occasion arise, before a national court, any more than the fact that the Treaty places at the disposal of the Commission ways of ensuring that obligations imposed upon those subject to the Treaty are observed, precludes the possibility, in actions between individuals before a national court, of pleading infringement of these obligations. ... *The vigilance of individuals concerned to protect their rights amounts to an effective supervision in addition to the supervision entrusted by Articles 169 and 170 [now 226 and 227] to the diligence of the Commission and of the Member States.* (emphasis added)

In this landmark judgment the Court of Justice created the principle of direct effect which was based upon the premise that the Treaty created rights for citizens of Member States which, if enforced by them in the courts of the Member States, would provide an additional supervisory function to that already contained in the former Arts 169 and 170 EC Treaty (now Arts 226 and 227).

The scope of direct effect

The Court of Justice, in establishing the general principle of direct effect, limited its scope only to those provisions which were *sufficiently precise and unconditional*. This has been applied quite flexibly by the Court and has resulted in articles of the Treaty and provisions of directives being held to be directly effective by the Court in circumstances where a national court could have been excused from coming to the opposite conclusion.

Before considering the three forms of Community legislation (EC Treaty, regulations and directives) separately, the following examples give an indication of the Court of Justice's approach in determining whether or not a provision is *sufficiently precise and unconditional*.

Sufficiently precise

In *Van Duyn* v *Home Office* (Case 41/74) the Court of Justice held that Art 3(1) of the Residence and Public Policy, Security and Health Directive (64/221, OJ Sp. Ed. 1964 850/64 p. 117), which provides that 'measures taken on the grounds of *public policy* or of *public security* shall be based exclusively on the personal conduct of the individual concerned', was sufficiently precise to be capable of having direct effect, despite the fact that the scope of 'public policy' and 'public security' would require determination by the Court.

Similarly, in *Defrenne* v *SABENA* (Case 43/75) the Court of Justice held that the former Art 119 EC Treaty (now Art 141), which set out a principle that men and women 'should receive equal pay for equal work', was sufficiently precise to be capable of having direct effect despite the fact that the scope of 'equal pay' and 'equal work' would likewise have to be determined by the Court.

Unconditional

A Community provision is 'unconditional' where it is not subject, in its implementation or effects, to any additional measure by either the Community institutions or Member States.

In *Van Gend en Loos* v *Administratie der Belastingen* (Case 26/62), the former Art 12 EC Treaty (now Art 25) was held by the Court of Justice to be unconditional because it imposed a negative obligation on Member States to 'refrain from introducing between themselves any new customs duties on imports and exports ... and from increasing those which they already apply in their trade with each other'. It was not qualified by any reservation on the part of the Member States which would make its implementation conditional upon a positive legislative measure enacted under national law.

This case can be contrasted with *Costa* v *ENEL* (Case 6/64), where the Court of Justice held, *inter alia*, that the former Art 102 EC Treaty (now Art 97) was not unconditional. The former Art 102 provided that, where a Member State intended to adopt or amend its laws in such a way that there was a reason to fear this might cause distortion of the conditions of competition in the common market, there was an obligation of prior consultation between the Member State and the Commission. It was held that this was *not* unconditional because it was subject to additional measures in the form of 'prior consultation' and therefore was not capable of having direct effect.

Treaty articles

As a general principle, treaties and international agreements are not capable, in international law, of conferring rights on individuals in the courts of their own state. However, as discussed above, the Court of Justice has developed the principle of direct effect to provide otherwise as regards Community law (*Van Gend en Loos* v *Nederlandse Administratie der Belastingen* (Case 26/62)).

The principle of direct effect was established in *Van Gend* but its application was still unclear. Certain Treaty provisions were to be enforceable against Member States, provided that the obligations imposed were 'clear' and 'unconditional'. These were necessary preconditions, because many Treaty provisions are set out in the most general terms and do not appear to impose a commitment to do anything. Sometimes they express no more than a statement or an aspiration. Article 191 EC Treaty, for example, provides that 'Political parties at European level are important as a factor for integration within the Union'. Following *Van Gend*, and largely on the basis of the chance appearance of appropriate cases before it, the Court of Justice has developed its criteria for determining whether particular Treaty provisions have direct effect, and if so, against whom.

In *Van Gend* the Court had found that the former Art 12 EC Treaty (now Art 25) was directly effective against the state. It had reached this position to some extent, at least, on the basis that the state had entered into a commitment when it signed the Treaty. That commitment was owed not only to the other Member States as parties, but also to its own citizens as actual or potential beneficiaries of the Treaty. However, the decision left unresolved the status of Treaty provisions between private citizens. Could a private citizen rely on an article of the Treaty, provided that it was sufficiently clear, precise and unconditional, against another private citizen or undertaking? The Court did not give an unequivocal reply to this question until 13 years later in *Defrenne* v *SABENA* (Case 43/75).

The case involved a claim by an air stewardess against her employer for equal pay to that received by male stewards. Article 119 EC Treaty (now Art 141) provided that 'Each Member State shall during the first stage ensure and subsequently maintain the application of the principle that men and women should receive equal pay for equal work'. Belgium had not enacted legislation to bring this about. Could the claimant rely on Art 119 in her national court? The case was referred to the Court of Justice on a reference under Art 177 (now Art 234) (see Chapter 6).

The Court dismissed the suggestion that the wording of the article confined the obligation to the Member State itself:

> [35] In its reference to 'Member States', Article 119 [now Art 141] is alluding to those States in the exercise of all those of their functions which may usefully contribute to the implementation of the principle of equal pay ... Thus ... this provision is far from merely referring the matter to the powers of the national legislative authorities. Therefore, the reference to 'Member States' in Article 119 cannot be interpreted as excluding the intervention of the courts in the direct application of the Treaty ... Since Article 119 is mandatory in nature, the prohibition on discrimination between men and women applies not only to the action of public authorities, *but also extends to all agreements which are*

intended to regulate paid labour collectively, as well as to contracts between individuals.
(emphasis added)

The effect of the decision in *Defrenne* was, therefore, that the former Art 119 (now Art 141) could be used between individuals in relation to a contract of employment. Some articles of the Treaty could thus be vertically effective (i.e. directly effective against the state, as in *Van Gend*) or both vertically and horizontally effective (i.e. directly effective between private individuals and the state, and between individuals) according to their wording and the context. In subsequent years the Court has found the former Art 7 EC Treaty (now Art 12), prohibiting discrimination on grounds of nationality, to be both vertically and horizontally effective. It was so held in *Cowan v The French Treasury* (Case 186/87) to enable a British tourist, who had been attacked and injured in Paris, to obtain equal treatment in relation to payments of criminal injuries compensation by the French Government. In *Walrave and Koch v Association Union Cycliste Internationale* (Case 36/74), the Court of Justice held that:

> prohibition of such discrimination does not only apply to the acts of public authorities, but extends likewise to rules of any other nature aimed at regulating in a collective manner gainful employment and the provision of services.

Other Treaty provisions have also been held to be both horizontally and vertically effective, including Arts 28 and 29 (prohibiting the imposition of restrictions on the export and import of goods: *Dansk Supermarked* (Case 58/80)), Art 39 (free movement of workers: *Donà v Mantero* (Case 13/76)), Arts 43 and 49 (the right of establishment of businesses and professions and the right to provide services: *Thieffry v Paris Bar Association* (Case 71/76)), and Arts 81 and 82 (the prohibition of restrictive agreements and the abuse of a monopoly position: *Brasseries de Haecht* (Case 48/72); *Marty* (Case 37/79)). The accumulation of case law in relation to a number of these provisions has resulted in a subtle change in the terminology of the Court of Justice. In the jurisprudence of the Court, many of these Treaty provisions, especially those relating to freedom of movement, have come to be regarded not merely as directly effective Treaty provisions at the suit of individuals in national courts, but also as *fundamental rights* of Community citizens. Direct effect has come to be regarded as fundamentally important to the development of the Community. As a judge of the Court of Justice has declared: 'Without direct effect, we should have a very different Community today – a more obscure, more remote Community barely distinguishable from so many other international organisations whose existence passes unnoticed by ordinary citizens' (Mancini and Keeling, 1994).

Regulations

The EC Treaty provides in Art 249(2) that 'A regulation shall have general application. It shall be binding in its entirety and directly applicable'. The reference to 'directly applicable' means that no domestic legislation is needed to incorporate or transpose that type of Community law into national law. Community regulations are thus part of UK law without any further need of implementation. Indeed, any attempt at express incorporation is illegal, unless it is explicitly or implicitly required by the regulation itself (*Fratelli Variola SpA v Amministrazione Italiana delle Finanze*

(Case 34/73)). Whether or not a directly applicable measure is 'directly effective' (i.e. is capable of creating individual rights which a national court must recognise) will depend on the terms of the regulation; it must satisfy the 'sufficiently precise and unconditional' test (see above). In practice, many are directly effective and are a fruitful source of individual rights (see e.g., Regulation 1612/68 on employment rights of migrant workers, and Regulation 1408/71 on social security benefits for those employed and self-employed in other Member States; see also Chapters 12 and 14). Regulations which satisfy the 'sufficiently precise and unconditional' test will be both vertically and horizontally effective.

Implementation of directives

Directives were not originally seen as being capable of creating directly effective rights. In contrast to regulations, they are not described as having direct applicability:

> A directive shall be binding, as to the result to be achieved, upon each Member State to which it is addressed, but shall leave to the national authorities the choice of form and method. (Art 249 EC Treaty (third indent))

Directives are thus not directed, like regulations, at the world at large but at Member States. That did not, of course, in the case of Treaty articles in *Defrenne*, deter the Court from finding that individuals could also be bound by them. But, unlike Treaty articles, directives are always conditional. They depend, under Art 249 EC Treaty, on the Member State giving effect to them. They have, since the inception of the Treaty, been a form of legislative subsidiarity, giving the Member State the option of the way in which it will legislate to meet the Community's objectives. The problem, as it became clear to both the Commission and the Court of Justice, was that Member States either simply did not implement directives by the date set for them, or implemented them in such a way as to fail, in whole or in part, to achieve their objectives.

Implementation does not mean that a directive must be directly transposed into national law. The Court described the Member States' obligations in *Commission* v *Germany (Re Nursing Directives)* (Case 29/84), para 23:

> The implementation of a directive does not necessarily require legislative action in each Member State. In particular, the existence of general principles of constitutional and administrative law may render the implementation by specific legislation superfluous, provided, however, that those principles guarantee that the national authorities will, in fact, apply the directive fully, and where the directive is intended to create rights for individuals, the legal position arising from those principles is sufficiently clear and precise, and the persons concerned are made fully aware of their rights, and, where appropriate, are afforded the possibility of relying upon them before national courts.

Although legislation may not always be necessary in relation to directives which are not intended to confer rights on individuals, the vast majority have either that intention, or at least that effect if implemented. In such cases, the issue of circular letters, urging a change of policy, or a change in administrative practice, will not constitute implementation. Such practices, which may alter from time to time at the whim of the authority, and be quite unknown to the ordinary citizen, completely lack the certainty and transparency which Community law demands (*Commission* v *Belgium* (Case 102/79)).

A failure to implement fully often results in a complaint by interested individuals and groups to the relevant Directorate-General in the Commission. This will usually be followed by protracted correspondence between the Commission and the offending state. If this is unsuccessful, formal Art 226 EC Treaty proceedings may be instituted by the Commission in the Court of Justice. Finally, if non-implementation persists, the case may come to a hearing before the Court and the Court may impose a penalty on the Member State if its judgment is not complied with (Arts 226, 228 EC Treaty; see Chapter 7). The process, from first complaint to judgment, may take several years. Enforcement procedures, given the limited resources of the Commission, can only be a partial solution to the problem. Until all Member States have implemented a directive, however, those states who fail to do so may gain an unfair competitive advantage. Many directives, particularly those aimed at reducing environmental pollution, can significantly increase business costs. In addition, individuals may be deprived of rights which Community law has been enacted to create for them. It is this situation to which the Court of Justice responded in its approach to unimplemented (or incorrectly implemented) directives.

Direct effect of directives

It is clear from the wording of Art 249 EC Treaty that directives were not to be directly applicable in the same way as regulations. They required Member States to act to give the directives effect in their territories. However, in *Grad* (Case 9/70) the Court suggested, in a case turning on the effect of a regulation, that a directive might have some effect in a state where it had not been implemented by the due date. In *Van Duyn* v *Home Office* (Case 41/74), the Court took its first important step towards recognising the direct effect of a directive.

The claimant in the case, Ms Van Duyn, a Dutch national, was a member of the Church of Scientology. She wished to enter the United Kingdom to work at the headquarters of the organisation. She was refused leave to enter. The United Kingdom Government had decided some years previously that the Church of Scientology was an undesirable organisation, although no steps had been taken against it, except to publicise the Government's view.

Prima facie, Ms Van Duyn, as a worker, had a right of entry under Art 39 EC Treaty. That right was, and remains, subject to the right of the host state to exclude and expel on public policy and public security grounds. The limits of the powers of the host state to derogate from its Treaty obligation on these grounds, and the extent of the procedural rights of those affected by such a decision, are set out in Directive 64/221. In particular, Art 3(1) of the directive provided that a decision should be based 'exclusively on the personal conduct of the individual concerned'. Ms Van Duyn argued that membership of an organisation could not be 'personal conduct' under Art 3(1). The UK Government maintained that its power to refuse entry could not be limited in this way, because the United Kingdom had not yet implemented Directive 64/221 (it remained unimplemented for another 20 years: see Chapter 16). The case was referred to the Court of Justice under the former Art 177 EC Treaty (now Art 234), where the Court refused to accept the position taken by the UK Government:

> The United Kingdom observes that, since Article 189 [now Art 249] of the Treaty distinguishes between the effects ascribed to regulations, directives and decisions, it must therefore be presumed that the Council, in issuing a directive rather than making a regulation, must have intended that the directive should have had an effect other than that of a regulation and accordingly that the former should not be directly applicable ... However ... it does not follow from this that other categories of acts mentioned in that article can never have similar effects. It would be incompatible with the binding effect attributed to a directive by Article 189 to exclude, in principle, the possibility that the obligation which it imposes may be invoked by those concerned. In particular, where the Community authorities have, by directive, imposed on Member States the obligation to pursue a particular course of conduct, the useful effect of such an act would be weakened if individuals were prevented from relying on it before their national courts and if the latter were prevented from taking it into consideration as an element of Community law.

The guiding principle adopted in *Van Duyn* is that of ensuring the *effet utile* (the useful effect) of a measure in the territories and courts of Member States. In addition to this pragmatic approach, there was another, implied principle that is known to continental as well as to common law lawyers but was not mentioned in the case. That is the equitable doctrine of estoppel, or the continental doctrine of the impermissibility of reliance on one's own turpitude. On this principle, it is not open to a Member State to defend itself against a claim by an individual by raising its own failure to implement a directive as a defence (Advocate-General Van Gerven in *Barber* (Case C-262/88)). Once the deadline for implementing a directive had passed, and not before (see *Ratti* (Case 148/78)), an individual could enforce the directive against the government of the state which had failed to implement it. It was thus *vertically* effective.

Not every directive is, however, effective in this way. As the Court said in *Van Duyn*, 'it is necessary to examine in every case, whether the nature, general scheme and wording of the provision in question are capable of having direct effects'; are the provisions 'unconditional and sufficiently precise?' (*Becker* (Case 8/81)).

Directives – 'sufficiently precise and unconditional'

The fact that a directive requires Member States to perform a positive act to implement it, does not in itself prevent it from being capable of being unconditional.

The Court of Justice held in *Francovich* v *Republic of Italy* (Cases C-6&9/90) that in the case of employment-related directives in general, in order to be sufficiently precise and unconditional, it is necessary to be able to:

- identify the persons who are entitled to the right;
- ascertain the content of that right; and
- identify the person/body liable to provide that right.

A similar approach was adopted by the Court of Justice in *Kampelmann* v *Landschaftsverband Westfalen-Lippe* (Cases C-253–258/96) in which it was held that

Art 2(2)(c), Directive 91/583 (OJ 1991 L 288/32), which imposed an obligation on employers to inform their employees of the conditions applicable to their contract or employment relationship, was sufficiently clear and precise to be capable of having direct effect.

The *Francovich* case concerned Directive 80/987 (OJ 1980 L 283/23) which sought to protect employees on their employers' insolvency. The persons entitled to the rights under this directive were employees (Art 2(2) of the directive refers to national law for the definition of the terms 'employee' and 'employer'). The Court of Justice held this was sufficiently precise to allow a national judge to ascertain whether an applicant had the status of employee under national law and whether the applicant was excluded from the scope of the directive under the specific exclusions set out therein.

The content of the right was more problematic. In implementing the directive, the Member State was given a number of choices, which included, *inter alia*:

- Choice of date from which the payment of wages would accrue. As a result Member States could limit the payment of wages to periods of three months or eight weeks.
- A discretion to set a liability ceiling so that payment of wages would not exceed a certain sum.

Given these legislative choices it would appear that the directive was not uncondititional or sufficiently precise. However, the Court of Justice held that it was possible to calculate the *minimum* guarantee provided for by the directive which would impose the least burden on the body liable to provide the benefit (i.e. the 'guarantee institution'). With regard to the discretion to set a liability ceiling, the Court of Justice held that this discretion would not be available, however, unless the Member State had actually implemented the directive and taken advantage of the derogation in its implementing legislation.

The identity of the person/body liable to provide the benefit was subject to the Member State making a legislative choice as to whether the body should be public or private, or whether it would be publicly or privately funded. Under the directive, Member States enjoyed a wide discretion with regard to the functioning and financing of the 'guarantee institution'. The Member State had to identify the institution which would be liable to provide the benefit. The Court of Justice held this provision was not sufficiently precise or unconditional and therefore the directive was not capable of having direct effect.

The state ...

As discussed above, the Court of Justice held that a directive which satisfied the 'sufficiently precise and unconditional' test could be enforced against the state (i.e. vertical effect). It was not until 1986 in *Marshall* v *Southampton Area Health Authority* (Case 152/84) that the Court finally, and explicitly, held that directives could *not* be enforced against private individuals and legal persons. The Court of Justice declared that a directive may only be directly effective against the *state*. After considering the effect of the third paragraph of the former Art 189 (now Art 249), the Court stated (at paras 46 and 48) that:

a Member State which has not adopted the implementing measures required by the directive within the prescribed period may not plead, as against individuals, its own failure to perform the obligations which the directive entails. ... According to Article 189 [now Art 249] ... the binding nature of a directive ... exists only in relation to 'each Member State to which it is addressed'. It follows that a directive may not of itself impose obligations on an individual and that a provision of a directive may not be relied upon as such against such a person.

The Court of Justice's reasoning for distinguishing between vertical and horizontal effect is based upon the fact that the former Art 189 (now Art 249) does not provide for directives to bind individuals and therefore it would be unfair for the Court to give them such an effect. The Court of Justice, however, is anxious to prevent a Member State from defending an action on the basis of its own wrongdoing.

So, if the directive is sufficiently precise and unconditional, the individual can enforce the unimplemented directive against the state. But what constitutes 'the state'? Under Art 10 EC Treaty, the obligation to implement Community law binds the Member States. The Court has been prepared to give that term a broad interpretation. Initially, it referred to the state exercising various functions and it was not necessary that it should be engaged in activities normally carried on by (or associated with) the state, such as operating immigration controls, collecting taxes, enforcing public health measures. Directives were enforceable against it, in addition, when it was, say, simply acting as an employer.

In *Marshall* v *Southampton Area Health Authority* (Case 152/84), the claimant was employed by the Health Authority. She wished to retire at 65, the same age as her male colleagues. The rules of the authority required her to retire at the age of 60. She was dismissed on the grounds of her age at 62, and brought proceedings against the Authority on grounds of unfair dismissal. Discrimination on grounds of sex in relation to conditions of employment is prohibited by Directive 76/207. The Sex Discrimination Act 1975, which had been enacted to implement the directive while it was still in draft form, contained an exception, allowing differential male and female retirement ages. There was no such exception in the directive. To that extent, therefore, the United Kingdom had failed to implement the directive. Could Ms Marshall enforce it against the Health Authority? The Court of Justice, on a referral under Art 177 EC Treaty (now Art 234), held that she could.

The Court decided that the Health Authority in this case was bound:

> Where a person involved in legal proceedings is able to rely on a directive as against the State, he may do so regardless of the capacity in which the latter is acting, whether employer or public authority. In either case it is necessary to prevent the State from taking advantage of its own failure to comply with Community law.

The Court added that it was for the national courts to determine the status of a body for the purposes of determining whether a directive can be directly effective against it. It has, however, continued to give guidance. It decided in *Costanzo* v *Comune di Milano* (Case 103/88) that 'the state' included 'all organs of the administration, including decentralised authorities such as municipalities'. How 'decentralised' a body could be and still be bound was considered by the Court in *Foster* v *British Gas* (Case C-188/89).

... or emanation of the state

In *Foster*, the House of Lords requested a preliminary ruling from the Court of Justice, pursuant to the former Art 177 EC Treaty (now Art 234), on the question of whether the British Gas Corporation (BGC) was, at the material time, a body of such a type that individuals could directly enforce a directive against it in the national courts and tribunals. At the material time, BGC had not been privatised (it was privatised on 24 August 1986 by the Gas Act 1986). Foster was employed by BGC and was made to retire on attaining the age of 60. This was in line with company policy which required women to retire at the age of 60 and men at the age of 65. Under English law, s 6(2)(b) of the Sex Discrimination Act 1975, which was in force at the material time, made it unlawful for any employer to discriminate against a woman employed in Great Britain 'by dismissing her or subjecting her to any other detriment'. However, s 6(4) provided that s 6(2) did not apply to 'provisions in relation to death or retirement'. Section 6(4) was repealed with effect from 7 November 1986, by s 2 of the Sex Discrimination Act 1986.

Foster therefore sought to rely upon Art 5(1) of the Equal Treatment Directive (Council Directive 76/207) which provides that:

> Application of the principle of equal treatment with regard to working conditions, including the conditions governing dismissals, means that men and women shall be guaranteed the same conditions without discrimination on grounds of sex.

In the *Marshall* case, which was factually similar to this case, the Court of Justice interpreted Art 5(1) as meaning that such a general policy of discriminatory retirement ages constituted discrimination on grounds of sex, contrary to the directive, which could be relied upon against a state authority. Foster's application to an employment tribunal was dismissed on the ground the BGC was not a state authority within the meaning of *Marshall* and therefore the directive could not be relied upon against it. This decision was subsequently confirmed by both the Employment Appeal Tribunal and the Court of Appeal. The question of 'state authority' was critical to the outcome of the case, hence the House of Lords' referral of such question to the Court of Justice.

The Court of Justice (at para 20) developed a test to be applied to ascertain if the body against whom a directive was sought to be enforced was an *emanation of the state*:

> a body, whatever its legal form, which has been made responsible, pursuant to a measure adopted by the State, for providing a public service under the control of the State and has for that purpose special powers beyond those which result from the normal rules applicable in relations between individuals *is included* in any event among the bodies against which the provisions of a directive capable of having direct effect may be relied upon. (emphasis added)

The three *Foster* criteria can be summarised as:

- provision of a public service;
- under state control; and
- having special powers.

The case was then returned to the House of Lords for the test to be applied to the facts of the case. Lord Templeman was of the view that there was no justification for a narrow or strained construction of the Court of Justice's ruling (see *(No. 2)* [1991] 2 AC 306 at 315, paras E–F). He further stated (at p. 315, paras G–H):

> I decline to apply the ruling of the European Court of Justice, couched in terms of broad principle and purposive language characteristic of Community law, in a manner which is ... sometimes applied to an enactment of the United Kingdom ... I can find no warrant in the present circumstances for the limited and speculative approach of [British Gas plc] and have no means of judging whether the relevant provisions of the Directive are enforceable against the BGC save by applying the plain words of the ruling of the European Court of Justice.

Lord Templeman reviewed the regulatory provisions under the Gas Act 1972 whereby the Secretary of State was authorised to make regulations and whereby the BGC was obliged to develop and maintain a gas supply for the United Kingdom (see s 2, Gas Act 1972) and he concluded (at p. 313, para F):

> Thus the BGC was a body which was made responsible pursuant to a measure adopted by the State [i.e. the Gas Act 1972] for providing a public service.

He further held (at p. 314, para B) that the BGC performed its public service under the control of the state:

> The BGC was not independent, its members were appointed by the State; the BGC was responsible to the minister acting on behalf of the State, and the BGC was subject to directions given by the Secretary of State.

By s 29 of the Gas Act 1972 BGC was afforded a monopoly for the supply of gas. This was sufficient for it to satisfy the Court's third criteria that the BGC had conferred upon it 'special powers beyond those which result from the normal rules applicable in relations between individuals' (at p. 314, para D).

The House of Lords held that the BGC satisfied the three criteria established by the Court of Justice and therefore the BGC was an 'emanation of the state' against which the directive could be enforced. The inconsistent provisions of the Sex Discrimination Act 1975 would be overridden.

Three important post-*Foster* cases in the United Kingdom have considered the concept of 'emanation of the state' and the application of the *Foster* test.

The first case, *Doughty v Rolls-Royce plc* [1992] CMLR 1045, was factually similar to the *Marshall* and *Foster* cases. Ms Doughty was compulsorily retired at age 60, in accordance with company policy that women retire at 60 whereas men retire only at 65. As considered above, such discrimination was, at the material time, expressly permitted under English law. Doughty sought to rely upon the Equal Treatment Directive. The question before the Court of Appeal was whether or not Rolls-Royce was an emanation of the state. Lord Justice Mustill gave the leading judgment with which Lord Justice Butler-Sloss and Sir John Megaw agreed.

Mustill LJ quoted extensively from the employment tribunal's findings of fact as to the nature of Rolls-Royce, which at the material time had not been privatised (see p. 1048, para 8). All of Rolls-Royce's shares were held on behalf of the Crown; the ultimate power in relation to the company and its business rested with the shareholder (i.e. the Crown) by virtue of its ability to pass resolutions in General Meeting. In December 1980 a 'Memorandum of Understanding with Rolls-Royce – Relationship with Government' was issued. This provided that the Government had three separate roles in its relationship with Rolls-Royce:

- that of 100 per cent shareholder;
- that of principal customer for the development and production of military engines; and
- that of its overall sponsorship of the aerospace industry.

The employment tribunal held that Rolls-Royce was an emanation of the state because as 100 per cent shareholder it had the power to require the directors to alter the contracts of employment of the company's employees so as to comply with the directive.

This decision was reversed by the Employment Appeal Tribunal ([1987] IRLR 447), which held that the crucial question was whether or not Rolls-Royce could be said to be an organ or agent of the state carrying out a state function (see paras 11–12).

The appeal to the Court of Appeal was heard after the decisions of the Court of Justice and the House of Lords in *Foster*. Mustill LJ stated that the *Foster* test was not intended to be an exhaustive statement for determining the status of the entity, but, nevertheless, it was Mustill LJ's opinion that in a case which was factually similar to *Foster*, the test:

> ... *must always be the starting point and will usually be the finishing point.* If all the factors identified by the Court are present it is likely to require something very unusual to produce the result that an entity is not to be identified with the State. Conversely, although the absence of a factor will not necessarily be fatal, it will need the addition of something else, not contemplated by the formula ...(para 24) (emphasis added)

Mustill LJ went on to examine whether or not the three *Foster* criteria were satisfied. He accepted that the second criterion, requiring the service to be provided under the control of the state, was satisfied. However, he stated that if this point had been crucial to the outcome it would have required detailed examination. He stated that with regard to this criterion, the relevant question was whether the public *service* (rather than the *body* providing the service) was under the state's control. He concluded that the other two criteria were not satisfied: Rolls-Royce could not be said to have been made responsible for providing a public service, pursuant to a measure adopted by the state, nor was there any evidence that Rolls-Royce possessed or exercised any 'special powers'.

Accordingly, Doughty could not enforce the directive against Rolls-Royce, because Rolls-Royce was deemed not to be an emanation of the state.

The second case, *Griffin and Others* v *South West Water Services Ltd* [1995] IRLR 15, centred around the question of whether the provisions of the Collective Redundancies Directive 92/129 could be enforced directly against the privatised company, South West Water (SWW). The High Court first considered the question of whether SWW was an emanation of the state. It was common ground between the parties that the correct approach was to consider whether the three *Foster* criteria were fulfilled. Blackburne J relied upon Mustill LJ's dicta in *Doughty* that the *Foster* criteria must be the starting point and will usually be the finishing point. In deciding the question,

Blackburne J conducted a detailed examination of the powers and duties conferred upon the newly privatised SWW and of the control to which it was subject.

It was common ground between the parties that the first criterion, the 'public service' condition, and the third criterion, the 'special powers' condition, were fulfilled. The crucial question was whether or not the second criterion, the 'state control' condition, was satisfied. Blackburne J, as did Mustill LJ in *Doughty*, made it clear (at para 94) that:

> The question is not whether the body in question is under the control of the State, but whether the public service in question is under the control of the State ... It is also irrelevant that the body does not carry out any of the traditional functions of the State and is not an agent of the State ... It is irrelevant too that the State does not possess day-to-day control over the activities of the body.

The question therefore was whether or not the public services of water and sewerage provision performed by SWW were under the control of the state. There were a whole number of powers available to the Secretary of State and the Director General of Water Services (see paras 96–110) to conclude that the public service of water and sewerage provision performed by SWW were under the control of the state, thus fulfilling the 'control' condition.

The three *Foster* criteria being satisfied, SWW was an emanation of the state, a body against which the directive was capable of being enforced. It should be noted that, as discussed above, the directive could therefore be directly enforced, provided the provisions of the directive were *sufficiently precise and unconditional*. The High Court decided the relevant provisions were *not* sufficiently precise and unconditional and therefore the directive could not be enforced against SWW.

The third and final case is that of *National Union of Teachers and Others* v *The Governing Body of St Mary's Church of England (Aided) Junior School and Others* [1997] IRLR 242. The individual applicants had been employed at a school that was closed down, following which a new school was established under the control of a temporary governing body. The applicants were not re-employed. It was argued by the applicants that the Acquired Rights Directive 77/187 applied automatically to transfer their contracts of employment and therefore their dismissals were unlawful. It was common ground that, at the material time, English law would not assist the applicants.

To determine whether the governing body was an emanation of the state, the employment tribunal applied the *Foster* test and concluded that it did not satisfy the 'special powers' criterion. The directive could therefore not be directly enforced against the governing body as it was not an emanation of the state. The appeal to the Employment Appeal Tribunal ([1995] ICR 317) was dismissed. The Court of Appeal unanimously allowed the appeal. The leading judgment was delivered by Schiemann LJ.

Schiemann LJ quite correctly recognised that the Court of Justice had not established a test which could be applied to all situations. Although each party to the case had relied upon the *Foster* test, he stated that:

> It is clear from the wording of paragraph 20 [of the Court's judgment in *Foster*] and in particular the words 'is included among' that the formula there used was not intended to be an exclusive formula.

The governing body relied heavily upon the Court of Appeal's decision in *Doughty*, and in particular on Mustill LJ's observation that in a case of the same general type as *Foster*, the test formulated by the Court of Justice will always be the starting point and will usually be the finishing point. However, Schiemann LJ was of the view that this case was not of the same general type as that of *Foster*:

> That case and *Rolls-Royce* were both concerned with commercial undertakings in which the Government had a stake. The present case is not concerned with any commercial undertaking but rather with the provision of what would generally in the Community be regarded as the provision of a public service.

He said that the Employment Appeal Tribunal was wrong in applying the *Foster* test as if it was a statutory definition. Even though the parties had relied upon the test, Schiemann LJ did not think it was appropriate to apply it in a similar fashion to the Appeal Tribunal. Nevertheless, in view of the parties' submissions, he made his own observations on the application of the three *Foster* criteria to the particular facts.

The first two criteria – 'public service' provision and 'state control' – were fulfilled. However, he was not satisfied that the governing body had 'special powers'. Despite this reservation, he held that the governing body was an emanation of the state. He was no doubt influenced by the benefit accruing to the local education authority if the appeal was dismissed:

> The financial position is that the failure to transpose the Directive will, if the present appeal is dismissed, have the effect of allowing the local education authority and the State to benefit from the failure to transpose the Directive. The Rolls-Royce case indicates that the mere fact that some incidental benefit may arise to the State from a failure to implement a directive does not necessarily bring the doctrine of vertical effect into play. In the present case the benefit is direct to the local education authority, as is conceded because of the provisions of s 46 of the Education Reform Act 1988, and the local education authority, as is further conceded, is an emanation of the State for the purposes of the doctrine of direct vertical effect.

Section 46 of the 1988 Act provided that local education authorities were responsible for redundancy payments.

The nature of the service being provided and the fact that the body providing the service was financially dependent upon the local education authority were indicative of the outcome of the case. Schiemann LJ quite correctly departed from a strict application of the *Foster* test, preferring to address the question on the basis that the state should not benefit from its own failure to implement a directive.

The Court of Justice has subsequently delivered a judgment which considers the *Foster* test further. In *Kampelmann* v *Landschaftsverband Westfalen-Lippe* (Cases C-253–258/96) the Court of Justice held that, in accordance with its *Foster* v *British Gas plc* judgment:

> 46. … a directive … may … be relied on against organisations or bodies which are subject to the authority or control of the State *or* have special powers beyond those which result from the normal rules applicable to relations between individuals, such as local or regional authorities *or* other bodies which, irrespective of their legal form, have been given responsibility by the public authorities and under their supervision, for providing a public service. (emphasis added)

Although the Court of Justice stated that this judgment was in line with its *Foster* judgment, it could represent an important departure. In the operative part of *Foster* the three criteria were stated to be cumulative, whereas in the *Kampelmann* judgment the Court of Justice sets out the criteria as alternatives. If this is subsequently reaffirmed by the Court of Justice as a departure from *Foster* then the bodies and organisations against which a directive may be capable of having direct effect could be extended. However, this would require the Court explicitly to depart from its previous reasoning as to why a directive should be enforceable vertically only (i.e. to prevent a Member State from profiting from its own failure to implement (or correctly implement) a directive).

Directives: horizontal effect?

Paola Faccini Dori v *Recreb SRL* (Case C-91/92) concerned the direct effect of an EC directive: was it directly effective horizontally? Could Miss Faccini Dori rely upon it in the national (Italian) court against a private company (not being an emanation of the state) even though at the material time the directive had not been transposed into national law?

On 9 February 1994 the opinion of Advocate-General Lenz was delivered at a sitting of the full Court. The Advocate-General recognised that the Court of Justice had consistently held that directives could not have direct effect in relations between individuals, and that for reasons of legal certainty this should be maintained with regard to situations in the past. However, as regards the future, the Advocate-General was of the opinion that those provisions of a directive which are sufficiently precise and unconditional should have direct effect: for future cases the Community should recognise that directives may be directly effective both vertically and horizontally.

As discussed in Chapter 5, the Court of Justice is not bound by the doctrine of precedent and accordingly could have departed from its own previous decisions. However, for the sake of legal certainty the Court generally follows and builds upon its own previous case law. The Court of Justice rejected the Advocate-General's opinion. The Court stated that ever since the *Marshall* case it had been held that a directive could not of itself impose obligations on an individual. Accordingly, a directive could not be relied upon against such an individual. This appears to have settled the issue, certainly for the foreseeable future.

THE PRINCIPLE OF INDIRECT EFFECT

The obvious limitation of the application of the direct effect of directives is that, however generously the Court of Justice has interpreted 'emanation of the state' in favour of individual claimants, the term clearly cannot apply to the private commercial employer. The anomaly created between public and private employment in relation to the direct effect of Directive 76/207 on equal employment rights was most starkly thrown into relief by two cases which came before the Court of Justice in 1984 (*Von Colson* (Case 14/83), and *Harz* v *Deutsche Tradax* (Case 79/83)). Ms Von Colson was employed by the prison service and Ms Harz by a private company. Both cases were referred to the Court of Justice by the (West) German Labour Court. Germany had implemented Directive 76/207, but the German law provided only nominal and not proper compensation as required by the directive (see *Marshall (No. 2)* (Case C-271/91)). Clearly, Ms Von Colson could enforce the directive vertically against her employer and obtain full compensation for the discrimination she had suffered, but Ms Harz could not. The Court adopted a novel approach that would have the effect of enabling both claimants to recover compensation.

The Court's starting point was Art 10 EC Treaty (previously Art 5): the obligation of Member States to take all appropriate measures to give effect to Community law 'is binding on all the authorities of Member States including, for matters within their jurisdiction, the courts. It follows that, in applying the national law ... national courts are required to interpret their national law in the light of the wording and the purpose of the directive in order to achieve the result referred to in the third paragraph of Art 189 EC Treaty [now Art 249]'. The German courts therefore had to 'interpret' the national law on sexual discrimination in such a way that there was no limit on proper compensation to which injured parties were entitled. On this basis, the German court which had referred the case could award proper compensation to both claimants. *Von Colson* dealt with a case which turned on the interpretation of legislation put into place to implement the directive in question. Was this new interpretative doctrine confined to cases where the Member State had implemented the directive but had done so incorrectly? The Court answered this question in the negative in *Marleasing SA v La Commercial SA* (Case C-106/89). In *Marleasing* a Spanish court was confronted with a national law on the constitution of companies which conflicted with an EC Company Directive 68/71. The directive had not been implemented in Spain. The Court of Justice, nevertheless, held that:

> in applying national law, whether the provisions concerned *pre-date* or post-date the directive, the national court asked to interpret national law is bound to do so in every way possible in the light of the text and the aims of the directive to achieve the results envisaged by it and thus comply with Article 189(3) of the Treaty. (emphasis added)

A national court, might, therefore, be required to 'interpret' a provision of national law that preceded the directive by many years, and which had been enacted with quite different considerations in mind. The extent of this interpretative obligation has caused particular problems for the UK courts. These are considered below. The Court of Justice has made it clear that the courts of Member States should act on the presumption that relevant national legislation, whether passed before or after the relevant directive, was intended to implement it. However, whether this is in fact possible, in the light of the wording of the national provision, is essentially a matter of interpretation by those courts (*Wagner Miret* (Case 334/92)).

There is one exception to the obligation to interpret national law in conformity with an unimplemented directive. That is where the national measure, which ought to be interpreted in this way, imposes criminal liability. The Court held in *Arcaro* (Case C-168/95) that no obligation could be imposed on an individual by an untransposed directive. Nor could there be any liability in criminal law of persons who act in contravention of that directive's provisions. The Court has, however, held that a person can be convicted of a driving offence in a national court, even where that conviction rests upon evidence obtained under national legislation made in breach of a Community directive (*Lemmens* (Case C-226/97)).

THE PRINCIPLE OF STATE LIABILITY

The possibility of taking action against the state for failing to implement a directive was first considered in *Francovich and Bonifaci* v *Republic of Italy* (Cases C-6 & 9/90). The case arose after an Italian company went into liquidation, leaving Mr Francovich and other employees with unpaid arrears of salary. Directive 80/987 required Member States to set up a compensation scheme for employees in these circumstances, but Italy had not established one. Mr Francovich therefore wanted compensation from the Italian Government. The case was referred to the Court of Justice. The Court was asked whether the directive had direct effect, whether the Member State was liable for the damage arising from its failure to implement the directive, and to what extent it was liable for damages for violation of its obligations under Community law.

The Court decided that the directive was insufficiently precise to have direct effect (see above). However, it emphasised that the EC Treaty creates a legal order which is binding upon Member States and citizens. The *effet utile* of Community law would be diminished if individuals were not able to obtain damages after suffering loss incurred because of a violation of Community law by a Member State. There was an implied obligation under the former Art 5 EC Treaty (now Art 10) to compensate individuals affected by such a violation. The Court held that, in cases such as this, where there was a violation of the state's obligation to implement Community law under Art 189 EC Treaty (now Art 249), there was a right to compensation from the state, provided that three conditions were satisfied:

- The result which had to be attained by the directive involved rights conferred on individuals.
- The content of those rights could be identified from the provisions of the directive.
- There must exist a causal link between the failure by the Member State to fulfil its obligations and the damage suffered by the person affected.

The Court did not decide how the extent of liability was to be determined as this was to be a matter for national law. National procedures had, however, 'to ensure the full protection of rights which individuals might derive from Community law'. In this particular case, the failure of Italy to implement the directive in question had already been established by the Court. Generally, there will not be a defence to simple non-implementation because, whatever practical difficulties there may be, the obligation to implement is strict (*Commission* v *Belgium* (Case 1/86)).

The Court has developed the concept of state liability and entitlement to damages in a number of recent judgments.

Legislative acts

The first judgment to be delivered was that involving the joined cases: *Brasserie du Pêcheur* v *Germany*; *R* v *Secretary of State for Transport, ex parte Factortame Ltd and Others* (Cases C-46 & 48/93). Both cases concerned directly effective Treaty articles which had been breached. The former case concerned a pre-existing German law which breached the former Art 30 EC Treaty (now Art 28), and the latter a United Kingdom Act of Parliament which was enacted in breach of, *inter alia*, the former Art 52 EC Treaty (now Art 43). The claimants sought damages against the respective states for the *legislature's* breach of Community law. The national courts referred a number of questions to the Court for a preliminary ruling pursuant to the former Art 177 EC Treaty (now Art 234).

The first question in both cases concerned whether or not the *Francovich* principle of state liability would oblige Member States to make good damage caused to individuals by a breach of Community law by the state legislature, no matter what form that breach took. In assessing this question, the Court of Justice initially stated that it was irrelevant that the breach concerned a directly effective Treaty article and that it was irrelevant what organ of state was responsible for the breach:

> 31. ... the Court held in *Francovich and Others*, at paragraph 35, that the principle of State liability for loss and damage caused to individuals as a result of breaches of Community law for which it can be held responsible is inherent in the system of the Treaty.
> 32. It follows that that principle holds good for any case in which a Member State breaches Community law, whatever be the organ of the State whose act or omission was responsible for the breach.

The Court of Justice then gave consideration to the conditions under which state liability may be incurred. Reiterating its *Francovich* judgment, the Court stated that:

> 38. Although Community law imposes State liability, the conditions under which that liability gives rise to a right to reparation depend on the nature of the breach of Community law giving rise to the loss and damage.

In examining the facts of the two cases, the Court of Justice stated that the national legislatures had a wide discretion in the relevant fields of activity. Where there is such a wide discretion, three conditions must be met in order to incur state liability (at para 51):

- the rule of law infringed must be intended to *confer rights on individuals*;
- the breach must be *sufficiently serious*; and
- there must be a *direct causal link* between the breach of the obligation resting on the state and the damage sustained by the injured parties.

The former Arts 30 and 52 EC Treaty (now Arts 28 and 43) are directly effective and therefore the first condition is satisfied *per se*. It is the second condition which is the most interesting. The Court of Justice stated that the decisive test for finding that a breach of Community law is *sufficiently serious* is whether the Member State 'manifestly and gravely disregarded the limits on its discretion' (at para 55). The Court of Justice then set out a number of factors which may be taken into consideration by the national court when assessing whether or not there was such a manifest and grave disregard by the Member State of the limit on its discretion:

> 56. *The factors* which the competent court may take into consideration *include the clarity and precision* of the rule breached, *the measure of discretion* left by that rule to the

national or Community authorities, *whether the infringement and the damage caused was intentional or involuntary*, whether any error of law was *excusable or inexcusable*, the fact that the *position taken by a Community institution* may have contributed towards the omission, and the *adoption or retention of national measures or practices contrary to Community law.*

57. On any view, a breach of Community law will clearly be sufficiently serious if it has persisted despite a judgment finding the infringement in question to be established, or a preliminary ruling or settled case law of the Court on the matter from which it is clear that the conduct in question constituted an infringement. (emphasis added)

The *Factortame* case then returned to the UK court for it to apply the three conditions of state liability. The case reached the House of Lords (*R v Secretary of State for Transport, ex parte Factortame Ltd and Others (No. 5)* [1999] 3 WLR 1062 *The Times*, 3 November). The House of Lords held that the adoption of legislation which was discriminatory on the ground of nationality in respect of the registration of British fishing vessels, in breach of clear and unambiguous rules of European Community law, was *sufficiently serious* to give rise to liability in damages to individuals who suffered loss as a consequence. Factortame would then have to prove their losses (i.e. prove that there was a *direct causal link* between the breach and the damage they had sustained). On 29 November 1999, *The Times* reported that the Government faced a £100 million bill for damages and costs in this particular case.

Legislative act – incorrect implementation of a directive

The second case, *R v HM Treasury, ex parte British Telecommunications PLC* (Case C-392/93), concerned the incorrect implementation of a directive by the United Kingdom, a situation in which a Member State does not enjoy a wide discretion (the former Art 189(3) (now Art 249(3)) requires a Member State to implement a directive within the time period laid down). In its judgment the Court of Justice (at para 39) restated the three conditions in the previous joined cases. Where a Member State acts in a field in which it has a wide discretion in the taking of legislative decisions, for the defaulting Member State to incur liability:

> the rule of law infringed must be intended to confer rights on individuals; the breach must be sufficiently serious; and there must be a direct causal link between the breach … and the damage sustained.

The Court of Justice held (at para 40) that this restrictive approach was equally applicable to the facts of this case, where the United Kingdom had incorrectly transposed a directive. Once again the Court stated that it was for the national court to determine whether or not there was a *sufficiently serious* breach. However, because the Court of Justice had all the necessary facts before it, it went on to advise the national court as to the determination of the factual situation.

In the *Brasserie du Pêcheur* and *Factortame* joined cases the Court of Justice held (at para 56) that one of the relevant factors was the clarity and precision of the rule breached. In this case the directive was imprecisely worded and was reasonably capable of bearing the interpretation given to it by the United Kingdom. Moreover, the United Kingdom had acted in good faith (at para 43). The Court of Justice noted that this interpretation was shared by other Member States and 'was not manifestly contrary to the wording of the directive or to the objective pursued by it' (at para 43).

Additionally, there had been no case law from the Court of Justice to guide the United Kingdom. The Commission had not questioned the United Kingdom's implementing legislation. In those circumstances, the Court of Justice held that the breach could not be regarded as *sufficiently serious*.

Executive act – breach of the Treaty

The third case again involved the United Kingdom courts: *R v Ministry of Agriculture, Fisheries and Food, ex parte Hedley Lomas (Ireland) Ltd* (Case C-5/94). In this case the Ministry refused licences for the exporting of livestock to Spain for slaughter because it was of the view that Spain was acting contrary to Directive 74/557 which concerns the stunning of animals before slaughter. Unlike the previous cases, this involved an act of the executive rather than an act of the legislature. The Court of Justice held that the refusal by the Ministry was a quantitative restriction contrary to the former Art 34 EC Treaty (now Art 29) which could not be justified under the former Art 36 (now Art 30). The United Kingdom was therefore in breach of Community law.

In reaching its judgment, the Court of Justice restated that part of its judgment in *Brasserie du Pêcheur* and *Factortame* where it held that in a field in which a Member State has a wide discretion to make legislative choices, a defaulting Member State will incur liability where three conditions are satisfied:

> 25. ... the rule of law infringed must be intended to confer rights on individuals; the breach must be sufficiently serious; and there must be a direct causal link between the breach of the obligation resting on the State and the damage sustained by the injured parties.

In an attempt to impose a common standard for state liability throughout the Community, the Court of Justice held that:

> 26. Those three conditions are also applicable in the circumstances of this case.

This was despite the fact that the breach did not involve a legislative act and despite the fact the Member State did not enjoy a wide discretion. It should be recalled, however, that under the former Art 5 EC Treaty (now Art 10), Member States have an obligation to:

> take all appropriate measures ... to ensure fulfilment of the obligations arising out of this Treaty.

The Court of Justice held that the United Kingdom's Ministry was in breach of the former Art 34 EC Treaty (now Art 29); the breach could not be justified under the former Art 36 (now Art 30). Although the Court of Justice introduced the three conditions in order to impose a uniform test for state liability throughout the Community, it acknowledged that the concept of 'sufficiently serious breach' will vary, depending upon the facts of the case. With regard to this particular case, the Court of Justice stated:

28. ... where, at the time when it committed the infringement, the Member State in question was not called upon to make any legislative choices and had only considerably reduced, or even no, discretion, *the mere infringement of Community law may be sufficient to establish the existence of a sufficiently serious breach*. (emphasis added)

Failure to implement a directive – *Francovich* revisited

The final case, *Dillenkofer and others* v *Federal Republic of Germany* (Joined Cases C-178, 179 & 188–190/94), concerned Germany's failure to transpose Directive 90/314/EEC. This case was therefore factually similar to *Francovich*. In *Francovich* the Court of Justice did *not* make it a condition that the breach of Community law must be sufficiently serious in order for state liability to be incurred. However, in this case, the Court of Justice stated that this was a condition, but by the very nature of the breach (i.e. a complete disregard of the Member State's obligation under the former Art 189(3) EC Treaty (now Art 249(3))) the breach was sufficiently serious *per se* (i.e. automatically).

Conclusion

The *Dillenkofer* case completes the post-*Francovich* case law insofar as it has established that the conditions relating to state liability are fixed no matter what the nature of the breach, thus ensuring uniform application of the principle throughout the 15 Member States. It will be for the national court to determine whether or not the breach is, on its facts, sufficiently serious. As we have seen in the cases discussed, this may be a difficult question to answer and the factors to be taken into consideration will vary depending upon the particular circumstances of the case. In *Brasserie du Pêcheur* and *Factortame* the Court set out, at paras 56–57, some factors to be taken into account when determining this question with regard to legislative acts. However, the Court of Justice determined that fault, i.e. intention or negligence, is not in itself one of the conditions which it is necessary to satisfy in order for state liability to be established. Two later cases applying the principle of state liability are:

- *Denkavit and Others* (Cases C-283, 291 & 292/94)
- *Brinkmann Tabakfabriken GmbH* v *Skatteministeriet* (Case C-319/96)

APPLICATION OF THE PRINCIPLES OF DIRECT AND INDIRECT EFFECT IN UNITED KINGDOM COURTS

Treaty provisions

Under the law and practice within the United Kingdom, the EC Treaty, like any other Treaty, is effective in that country only after it is incorporated into the domestic legal system, and will be effective only to the extent of its incorporation by the Westminster Parliament (*Blackburn* v *Attorney-General* [1971] 2 All ER 1380 at 1382; Lord Denning MR). The United Kingdom's accession to the European Community was given effect in national law by the European Communities Act 1972. The implementation of Community rights will, therefore, depend on the extent to which Community law has been fully incorporated by the Act, and the extent to which the United Kingdom courts are prepared to interpret national law in conformity with Community obligations (*R* v *Secretary for Foreign and Commonwealth Office, ex parte Rees-Mogg* [1994] 1 CMLR 101 (QBD); s 2(1), European Communities Act 1972).

Only those provisions which 'in accordance with the Treaties are *without further enactment* to be given legal effect ... shall be ... enforced, allowed, and followed' in UK courts (s 2(1), European Communities Act 1972 (emphasis added)). Section 3(1) of the 1972 Act provides that:

> For the purposes of all legal proceedings any question as to the meaning or effect of any of the Treaties, or as to the validity, meaning or effect of any Community instrument, shall be treated as a question of law and, if not referred to the European Court, be for determination as such in accordance with the principles laid down by and any relevant decision of the European Court or of any Court attached thereto.

Under s 2(1), UK courts have not had any difficulty in giving effect to Treaty provisions or regulations, since 'in accordance with the Treaties' both are to be given legal effect without further legislative enactment. Thus, the directly effective provisions of the former Art 119 EC Treaty (now Art 141) on equal pay were, in *Macarthys Ltd* v *Smith* (Case 129/79), held to prevail over the Equal Pay Act 1970. The Court of Appeal held that it was bound to give effect to the former Art 119 because it was directly effective. Lord Denning MR expressed the position in this way:

> The provisions of Article 119 of the EEC Treaty [now Art 141 EC Treaty] take priority over anything in our English statute on equal pay which is inconsistent with Article 119. *That priority is given by our law. It is given by the European Communities Act 1972 itself.* ([1981] QB 180 at 200–1) (emphasis added)

There was no difficulty where the legislation of the United Kingdom Parliament could be construed in accordance with Community law. The problem came where national law had been enacted after UK membership in a way that clearly conflicted with a directly effective Treaty provision. In *Macarthys* Lord Denning had said that:

> If the time should come when our Parliament deliberately passes an Act with the intention of repudiating the Treaty or any provision in it – and says so in express terms – then I should have thought that it would be the duty of our courts to follow the statute of our Parliament. ([1979] ICR 785 at 789)

When the House of Lords was confronted with the Merchant Shipping Act 1988, which had been enacted to prevent Spanish fishermen from 'quota hopping' into UK fishing areas, the moment seemed to have arrived. It was fairly clear that these measures discriminated on grounds of nationality against the right of Spanish fishing businesses to establish themselves in the United Kingdom in accordance with the directly effective former Arts 7 and 52 (now Arts 12 and 43) EC Treaty. The House of Lords was, however, prepared, following a reference to the Court of Justice, to hold the Act to be without effect to the extent of the conflict. 'It is the duty of a United Kingdom court', said Lord Bridge in his speech, 'when delivering final judgment, to override any rule of national law found to be in conflict with any directly enforceable rule of Community law' (*R* v *Secretary of State for Transport, ex parte Factortame* [1991] 1 AC 603 at 659).

Directly effective directives

British courts have experienced some difficulty with directly effective directives. As we have seen, *prima facie*, directives are not directly applicable, and so do not fall into that category of Community provisions which, without further enactment, are to be given legal effect under s 2(1) of the European Communities Act 1972. However, where they have been held by the Court of Justice to create directly effective rights they have been applied vertically against emanations of the state by the United Kingdom courts, following references to the Court of Justice, as in *Marshall* and *Foster* v *British Gas* (see above). However, as discussed above, United Kingdom courts have had some difficulty in determining the scope of state emanation (see *Doughty*, *Griffin* and *NUT*).

Despite this difficulty with state emanation, where United Kingdom courts have determined that a directive can be enforced against a state or state emanation body, United Kingdom courts have complied fully with the principle. The House of Lords has even held parts of the Trade Union and Labour Relations Act 1978 to be incompatible with a directly effective directive (Directive 76/207) in *Equal Opportunities Commission* v *Secretary of State for Employment* [1994] 1 All ER 910.

Indirect effect

Where a statute has been enacted to implement a directive, the courts have shown themselves capable of creative interpretation, on the basis that Parliament would have intended that the statute be interpreted in conformity with the directive, even if it had been misunderstood at the time of enactment. In *Litster* v *Forth Dry Dock* [1989] 2 WLR 634, the House of Lords had to consider Directive 77/187, which is intended to protect workers dismissed in connection with a business transfer. The directive had been implemented by the Transfer of Undertakings (Protection of Employment) Regulations 1981 (SI 1981/1794). The UK regulations did not, however, protect employees who had been dismissed immediately before the transfer of the undertaking. Several decisions of the Court of Justice had held that workers dismissed immediately before the transfer were to be treated as having been employed by the undertaking at the time when it took place. The House of Lords decided that it was the duty of the UK court to give the UK regulation 'a construction which accords with the decisions of the European Court upon the corresponding provisions of the directive to which the regulation was intended to give effect' (Lord Keith).

The House of Lords took a different line in *Duke* v *GEC Reliance* [1988] 2 WLR 359. The case turned on the legality of different retirement ages for men and women, the same point as in *Marshall* and *Foster*, above. In this case, though, the employer was a private undertaking, and the question of vertical effect could not arise. Did the court have to interpret the Sex Discrimination Act 1975 in accordance with the Equal Treatment Directive dated 9 February 1976? The House of Lords decided that it did not. Parliament had passed the Act in the belief that it was entitled to have discriminatory retirement ages even when the directive (which was then in draft) came into effect.

> Of course a UK court will always be willing and anxious to conclude that United Kingdom law is consistent with Community law. Where an Act is passed for the purpose of giving effect to an obligation imposed by a directive or other instrument a British court will seldom encounter difficulty in concluding that the language of the Act is effective for the intended purpose. But the construction of a British Act of Parliament is a matter of judgment to be determined by British courts and to be derived from the language of the legislation considered in the light of the circumstances prevailing at the date of the enactment ... It would be most unfair to the respondent to distort the construction of the Sex Discrimination Act 1975 in order to accommodate the Equal Treatment Directive 1976 as construed by the European Court of Justice in the 1986 *Marshall* case. (Lord Templeman)

This decision has been criticised, however. Lord Slynn, a former Lord Advocate, and now a Lord of Appeal, has expressed the anxiety of United Kingdom judges on the issue:

> I find it difficult to say that a statute of 1870 must be interpreted in the light of a 1991 directive. If the former is in conflict with the latter, it is not for the judges to strain language but for Governments to introduce new legislation. (Slynn, 1992, p. 124)

Although this observation is consistent with United Kingdom constitutional principles, it is at odds with the judgment of the Court of Justice in *Simmenthal* (Case 106/77):

> Every national court must, in a case within its jurisdiction, apply Community law in its entirety and protect rights which the latter confers on individuals and must accordingly set aside any provision of national law which may conflict with it, whether prior or subsequent to the Community rule.

The application of the principle by the United Kingdom, post-*Marleasing*, is usefully illustrated by the approach adopted by the House of Lords in *Webb v EMO Cargo (UK) Ltd* [1995] IRLR 647. Ms Webb was employed to cover for Ms Stewart while she was on maternity leave. Ms Webb later discovered that she herself was pregnant and that she would not be able to provide the requisite cover during Ms Stewart's maternity leave. EMO Cargo dismissed Ms Webb who subsequently made a complaint that she had been discriminated against on grounds of sex. Under domestic legislation, s 1(1) of the Sex Discrimination Act 1975 ('the 1975 Act') states that:

> A person discriminates against a woman in any circumstances relevant for the purposes of ... this Act if –
> (a) on the ground of her sex he treats her less favourably than he treats or would treat a man ...

Section 5 of the 1975 Act provides that:

> (3) A comparison of the cases of persons of different sex or marital status under sections 1(1) or 3(1) ... must be such that the relevant circumstances in the one case are the same, or not materially different, in the other.

Section 6(2) further provides that:

> It is unlawful for a person, in the case of a woman employed by him at an establishment in Great Britain, to discriminate against her –
>
> ...
>
> (b) by dismissing her, or subjecting her to any other detriment.

An employment tribunal dismissed her complaint. It held that the correct approach was to compare the treatment of Ms Webb with that which would have been accorded to a man in comparable circumstances. If a man had told his employer that he would be absent from work for a similar period, there is very little doubt that likewise he would have been dismissed. Accordingly, Ms Webb's dismissal was not on the ground of her sex (under s 1(1) of the 1975 Act) and she was not treated less favourably than EMO Cargo would have treated a man.

The Employment Appeal Tribunal ([1990] IRLR 124) dismissed Ms Webb's appeal, as did the Court of Appeal ([1992] IRLR 116). The Court of Appeal stated that it was necessary to determine whether a man with a condition as nearly comparable to that of Ms Webb (i.e. pregnancy) which had the same practical effect upon his ability to do the job would, or would not, have been dismissed; this was an application of s 5(3) of the 1975 Act.

On appeal to the House of Lords ([1993] IRLR 27), Lord Keith of Kinkel held (at para 8) that there was no direct application of a gender-based criterion:

> If [Ms Webb's] expected date of confinement had not been so very close to that of Valerie Stewart she would not have been dismissed. It was her expected non-availability during the period when she was needed to cover for Valerie Stewart which was the critical factor.

Lord Keith discussed the application of s 5(3) of the 1975 Act to ascertain whether it was legitimate to compare the non-availability of a man for medical reasons. He concluded that the relevant circumstance for the purpose of s 5(3) was the expected unavailability at the material time. The precise reason (i.e. pregnancy) was not relevant, nor was it relevant that this reason was a condition only capable of affecting women, therefore (at para 11):

> on a proper construction of the relevant provisions of the 1975 Act the dismissal did not ... constitute direct unlawful discrimination.

However, the *Marleasing* interpretative obligation was acknowledged by Lord Keith, who stated (at para 21) that it applied:

> Whether the domestic legislation came after or, as in this case, preceded the Directive.

Directive 76/207 (the Equal Treatment Directive) applies to the same area of activity – sex discrimination – as the 1975 Act. Article 2(1) provides that:

> For the purposes of the following provisions, the principle of equal treatment shall mean that there shall be no discrimination whatsoever on grounds of sex either directly or indirectly by reference in particular to marital or family status.

Article 5(1) provides that:

> Application of the principle of equal treatment with regard to working conditions,

including the conditions governing dismissal, means that men and women shall be guaranteed the same conditions without discrimination on grounds of sex.

Lord Keith thought it was necessary to refer the matter to the Court of Justice for a preliminary ruling, pursuant to the former Art 177 EC Treaty (now Art 234), to ascertain if, on the facts of the case, there was a breach of the directive. If there was, then the House of Lords would be required to decide if the 1975 Act could be construed in such a way as to accord with the Court's decision. The Court of Justice (Case C-32/93 [1994] IRLR 482) held (at para 29) that Ms Webb's dismissal contravened the directive:

Article 2(1) read with Article 5(1) of Directive 76/207 precludes dismissal of an employee who is recruited for an unlimited term with a view, initially, to replacing another employee during the latter's maternity leave and who cannot do so because, shortly after recruitment, she is found herself to be pregnant.

The Court of Justice was clearly influenced by the fact that Ms Webb was not simply taken on to cover for the maternity leave. She was initially employed some months prior to Ms Stewart's expected maternity leave, in order that she could be trained. It was intended to retain her following Ms Stewart's return to work. The Court of Justice decided that the contract of employment was for an unlimited duration rather than for a specific period directly related to the length of Ms Stewart's maternity leave. The case was then referred back to the House of Lords (*(No. 2)* [1995] IRLR 647), where Lord Keith observed (at para 11) that:

The ruling of the European Court proceeds on an interpretation of the broad principles dealt with in Articles 2(1) and 5(1) of the Directive 76/207/EEC. Sections 1(1)(a) and 5(3) of the Act of 1975 set out a more precise test of unlawful discrimination and the problem is how to fit the terms of that test into the ruling.

What the House of Lords was seeking to ascertain (at para 2) was whether it was:

... possible to construe the relevant provisions of the Act of 1975 so as to accord with the ruling of the European Court.

Lord Keith held (at para 11) that it was possible to interpret s 5(3) in such a fashion:

in a case where a woman is engaged for an indefinite period, the fact that the reason why she will be temporarily unavailable for work at a time when to her knowledge her services will be particularly required is pregnancy is a circumstance relevant to her case, being a circumstance which could not be present in the case of a hypothetical man.

The House of Lords held that Ms Webb's dismissal constituted direct sex discrimination contrary to the 1975 Act and remitted the case back to the employment tribunal for compensation to be assessed. The application of *Marleasing* was possible in this case because it did not involve *distorting* the meaning of the Act, an Act which preceded the directive. The Act was simply interpreted purposively by the House of Lords so as to accord with the wording and purpose of the directive.

Clearly, the *Duke* case and those cases subsequent to it are not in conflict with this decision. In the former cases, Parliament expressly permitted the discriminatory retirement ages complained of. To have decided otherwise would have required the court to *distort* the clear wording of the Sex Discrimination Act 1975.

UNIMPLEMENTED DIRECTIVES: A CONTINUING PROBLEM

The approach adopted by the Court to individuals affected by the non-implementation of directives was, as we have seen, a pragmatic response to a perceived problem of inequality between Member States. Those states which failed to implement directives on time might actually enjoy an advantage over those states which had shouldered the burden which the directive had imposed. Individuals in the non-implementing state would be deprived of the benefits which the directive was intended to confer upon them. Despite the increase in Art 226 EC Treaty proceedings, bringing defaulting Member States before the Court is a slow and only partial solution to the problem (see Chapter 7). Even if it achieves belated implementation of the directive, it cannot provide compensation to those individuals who have been deprived for many years of its beneficial effect. The creation, in the first instance, of the doctrine of vertical effect, the right to enforce the directive against the defaulting Member State, and a gradual enlargement of that right by the Court so that enforcement is now possible against a whole range of state or state-sponsored bodies, has provided a valuable weapon in the hands of intended beneficiaries.

The failure of the Court of Justice to grasp the nettle and to give directives horizontal direct effect between individuals in *Marshall* and *Faccini Dori* has only partly been mitigated by the development of the interpretative obligation of indirect effect expounded in *Harz* and *Marleasing*. This approach depends very much on the willingness of national courts to engage in creative interpretation of national legislation. At the present time the Court seems reluctant, as it demonstrated in *Wagner Miret* (Case C-334/92), to be more specific in defining the nature of the national court's interpretative obligation. The Court of Justice has made it clear that it expects individuals who cannot establish the vertical effect of a directive, or who are unsuccessful in persuading a national court to give it interpretative effect, to claim damages against their own Member State. This will involve a direct claim against the Member State for its failure to implement on the basis of the Court's decisions in *Brasserie du Pêcheur* and *Factortame* (Cases C-46 & 48/93). It may, as in *Faccini Dori*, require the individual to commence a whole new legal action, after having failed to establish the interpretative effect of the directive against another individual.

The criteria for determining the extent of fault of a Member State for non-implementation are still being developed by the Court of Justice. However, a claim against a Member State cannot be regarded as a wholly satisfactory substitute for the enforcement of a directive against those who were intended to be bound by it. The Member State may have believed, in good faith, that it had taken all necessary steps to implement the directive, and it may be hard to establish that the breach was 'sufficiently serious'. Even if this can be established, damages may not constitute a satisfactory remedy for, say, the failure to set up an area of environmental protection, as required by an unimplemented directive. The losers may be the local community as a whole rather than an individual and it may be impossible to establish any causal link, as required by *Francovich*, between the failure to implement the directive and any specific loss suffered by an individual. These difficulties will probably remain unless and until the Court accepts that unimplemented directives may have horizontal as well as vertical direct effect.

ENFORCEMENT OF A DIRECTIVE IN THE NATIONAL COURTS: THE CORRECT APPROACH

When considering a case on the enforcement of a Community directive in the national courts, the following issues should be considered in this order:

1   Is the directive directly enforceable (i.e. is it sufficiently precise and unconditional *and* is it being enforced against the state or an emanation of the state)? If it is not directly effective, then:

2   Is the directive indirectly effective (i.e. will the national courts comply with their *Marleasing* interpretative obligation and interpret national law in such a way as to comply with the wording and purpose of the directive)? If it is not indirectly effective, then:

3   Is it possible to claim *Francovich* damages from the state because of the state's failure to implement (or correctly implement) the directive?

Obviously it will be necessary to consider direct enforcement of the directive only if it has not been implemented by the Member State or it has been implemented incorrectly. If the directive has been correctly implemented then the national implementing legislation can be applied (in the United Kingdom this will be through either an Act of Parliament or delegated legislation). Flowcharts summarising this approach are laid out in Figures 9.1a–9.1c.

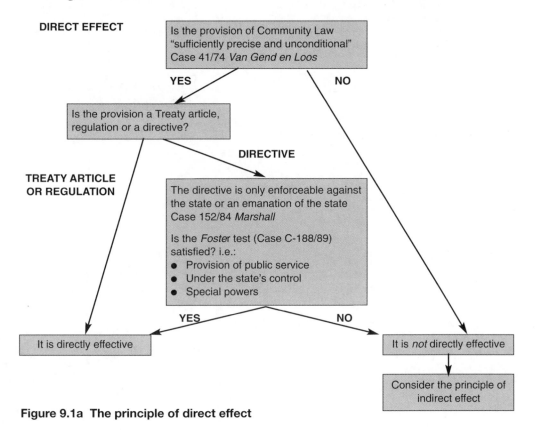

Figure 9.1a The principle of direct effect

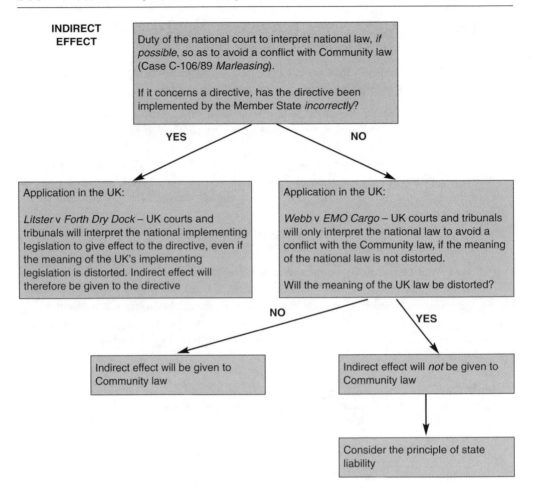

Figure 9.1b The principle of indirect effect

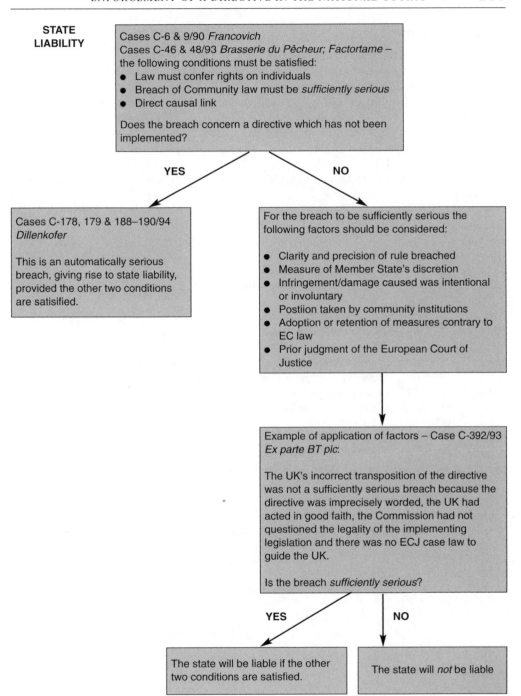

STATE LIABILITY

Cases C-6 & 9/90 *Francovich*
Cases C-46 & 48/93 *Brasserie du Pêcheur; Factortame* –
the following conditions must be satisfied:
- Law must confer rights on individuals
- Breach of Community law must be *sufficiently serious*
- Direct causal link

Does the breach concern a directive which has not been implemented?

YES

NO

Cases C-178, 179 & 188–190/94
Dillenkofer

This is an automatically serious breach, giving rise to state liability, provided the other two conditions are satisified.

For the breach to be sufficiently serious the following factors should be considered:

- Clarity and precision of rule breached
- Measure of Member State's discretion
- Infringement/damage caused was intentional or involuntary
- Postiion taken by community institutions
- Adoption or retention of measures contrary to EC law
- Prior judgment of the European Court of Justice

Example of application of factors – Case C-392/93
Ex parte BT plc:

The UK's incorrect transposition of the directive was not a sufficiently serious breach because the directive was imprecisely worded, the UK had acted in good faith, the Commission had not questioned the legality of the implementing legislation and there was no ECJ case law to guide the UK.

Is the breach *sufficiently serious*?

YES

NO

The state will be liable if the other two conditions are satisfied.

The state will *not* be liable

Figure 9.1c The principle of state liability

Further reading

Bebr, G., 'Case note on *Francovich*' (1992) 29 CML Rev 557.

De Burca, G., 'Giving Effect to European Community Directives' (1992) 55 MLR 215.

Caranta, R., 'Government Liability after *Francovich*' (1993) 52 CLJ 272.

Convery, J., 'State Liability in the United Kingdom after *Brasserie du Pêcheur*' (1997) 34 CML Rev 603.

Coppel, J., 'Rights, Duties and the End of *Marshall*' (1994) 57 MLR 859.

Craig, P.P., 'Directives: Direct, Indirect Effect and the Construction of National Legislation' (1997) 22 EL Rev 519.

Craig, P. and De Burca, G. (1998) *EU Law Text, Cases and Materials* (2nd edn), OUP, Chapters 4 and 6.

Curtin, D., 'The Province of Government: Delimiting the Direct Effect of Directives in the Common Law Context' (1990) 15 EL Rev 195.

Hartley, T.C. (1998) *The Foundations of European Community Law* (4th edn), Oxford University Press, Chapter 7.

Howells, 'European Directives: The Emerging Dilemmas' (1991) MLR 456.

Mancini, G.F. and Keeling, D.T., 'Democracy and the European Court of Justice' (1994) 57 MLR 175, 183.

Mead, P., 'The Obligation to Apply European Law: Is *Duke* Dead?' (1991) 16 EL Rev 490.

Robinson, W., 'Annotations on Case C-91/92 *Paola Faccini Dori* v *Recreb s.r.l.*' (1995) 32 CML Rev 629.

Slynn, G. (1992) *Introducing a New Legal Order*, Sweet & Maxwell, p. 124.

Snyder, F., 'The Effectiveness of European Community Law: Institutions, Processes, Tools and Techniques' (1993) 56 MLR 19.

Steiner, J., 'From Direct Effects of *Francovich*: Shifting Means of Enforcement of Community Law' (1993) 18 EL Rev 3.

Steiner, J. and Woods, L. (2000) *Textbook on EC Law* (7th edn), Blackstone Press, Chapters 4 and 5.

Szyszczak, E., 'United Kingdom: Judicial Review of the Public Acts' (1998) 23 EL Rev 89.

Tillotson, J. (2000) *European Community Law: Text, Cases and Materials* (3rd edn), Cavendish Publishing Ltd, Chapter 8.

Tridimas, T., 'Horizontal Effect of Directives: A Missed Opportunity' (1994) 19 EL Rev 621.

Weatherill, S. (2000) *Cases and Materials on EC Law* (5th edn), Blackstone Press, Chapters 2 and 3.

Chapter 10

APPLYING COMMUNITY LAW IN THE ENGLISH COURTS: ADAPTING ENGLISH REMEDIES TO THE REQUIREMENTS OF COMMUNITY LAW

Some consideration was given in Chapter 9 to the approach of English courts towards the enforcement of unimplemented directives, and that approach is complicated by the uniquely British concept of parliamentary sovereignty and the less distinctive, but equally difficult, separation of powers between legislature and judiciary. The same problems are apparent when the prospective claimant seeks an appropriate avenue for the enforcement of a right derived from Community law or the redress of a wrong resulting from its breach in the courts of England and Wales.

The effectiveness of remedies in national courts has become an increasing pre-occupation of the Court of Justice, and the Court has moved from its original position on national remedies. In *Comet v Produktschap voor Siergewassen* (Case 45/76), it held that the remedy to deal with a breach of Community law should be 'no less effective' than that available to protect a right derived from national law and should not make it impossible in practice to obtain relief. This comparative standard with a very low irreducible minimum does not fully take into account the deficiencies of national legal remedies which may place all kinds of obstacles in the path of a claimant seeking to enforce a Community right. Although the way in which national courts operate is, in theory at least, outside the competence of Community law, the practical effects of deficiencies in national legal systems have led the Court of Justice to put an increasing emphasis on the duty of cooperation in Art 10 EC Treaty, and the extent to which it binds national courts. Consequently, the Court of Justice took a stronger line in *R v Secretary of State for Transport, ex parte Factortame (No. 2)* (Case C-213/89). In this case, where the House of Lords had declared that national law did not allow an interim order against the Crown to suspend the operation of the Merchant Shipping Act 1988, the Court held that the national court must 'set aside' any national rule which precluded it from granting interim relief. In *Johnston v Chief Constable of the RUC* (Case 222/84), the Court specifically adopted Art 13 of the European Convention on Human Rights as a fundamental principle of Community law. Article 13 provides that:

Everyone whose rights and freedoms as set forth in this Convention are violated shall have an effective remedy before a national authority notwithstanding that the violation has been committed by persons acting in an official capacity.

The effect of the Court's judgment in the *Factortame* case is that there is now a necessary implication in Community law that 'an appropriate legal remedy must be created if one does not exist' (Advocate-General Mischo in *Francovich* v *Italy* (Case C-6/90)). Community legislation may also prescribe the type of remedy and the amount of damages that should be awarded (see, e.g., Directives 93/37 and 93/38 on public procurement contracts). Some directives may specify the bodies or types of bodies which should have the standing to challenge decisions infringing the directive (Directive 93/12 (unfair consumer contract terms)). Directives have, more recently, also tended to make specific requirements as to penalties, with a view to ensuring that national implementing legislation contains real deterrent sanctions (see, e.g., Directive 92/59 (Product Safety) and Directive 89/592 (Insider Dealing)). Where there is no penalty prescribed by Community law, the Court has held that national law should provide a penalty that is 'effective, proportionate and dissuasive' (*Commission* v *United Kingdom* (Case C-382/92)).

PUBLIC LAW REMEDIES: JUDICIAL REVIEW

The obligation to implement Community law in the United Kingdom falls primarily on the Government and the various agencies which it has chosen to carry out the functions of public administration. In English law, all bodies which exercise public powers, whether conferred by statute or common law, and whether public or private in origin, are subject to control and review by the courts (*Council of Civil Service Unions* v *Minister for the Civil Service* [1985] AC 374; *R* v *Panel on Takeovers and Mergers, ex parte Datafin plc* [1987] QB 815). In relation to Community law, that process of control and review extends to decisions made about the implementation of Community law. If the decision relates to the exercise of a power conferred on a subordinate body to legislate by way of delegated legislation, the court may intervene to prevent an abuse of those delegated legislative powers (*R* v *HM Treasury, ex parte Smedley* [1985] QB 657). If, on the other hand, the decision is by Parliament itself on the scope and content of primary legislation then the decision on whether or not to legislate, and in what form, is not subject to any control or review by the courts (*Blackburn* v *Attorney-General* [1971] 1 WLR 137; *R* v *Secretary of State for Foreign and Commonwealth Affairs, ex parte Rees-Mogg* [1993] 3 CMLR 101).

It is now accepted by the English courts that they are able to rule on the compatibility of English law with Community law (*Factortame Ltd* v *Secretary of State for Transport* [1989] 2 All ER 692). The appropriate remedy in such a case is a declaration on the extent of incompatibility (*R* v *Secretary of State for Employment, ex parte EOC* [1994] 2 WLR 409). Although a court in judicial review proceedings has the power to award damages, they may be awarded only where these would be available in an ordinary *private* action (e.g. breach of contract, etc.). This position has obviously been affected by the decision of the House of Lords in *R* v *Secretary of State for Transport, ex parte Factortame and Others (No. 5)* [1999] 3 WLR 1062 *The Times*, 3 November, where the House of Lords held that the United Kingdom's breach of

Community law was 'sufficiently serious', rendering the UK Government liable to the claimants for all losses which flowed from the breach.

CLAIMS IN TORT AGAINST THE STATE

As we have seen in Chapter 9, the Court of Justice has held on many occasions that, subject to Treaty provisions being sufficiently clear, precise and unconditional, such provisions could create rights which were enforceable at the suit of individuals in the courts of Member States (*Van Gend en Loos* (Case 26/62)). The application of this doctrine in relation to those Treaty provisions found to be directly effective has to be worked out in the national courts according to substantive and procedural national rules. In English law, where damages are claimed, this has meant that the breach of Community law has had either to be recognised as a new tort, or incorporated within the bounds of an old one.

In *Bourgoin* v *Ministry of Agriculture, Fisheries and Food (MAFF)* [1985] 3 All ER 385, the proceedings arose out of a ban imposed by the Ministry on the importation of turkeys from France in the run-up to Christmas 1981. The ban was imposed, ostensibly, on animal health grounds, but in *Commission* v *United Kingdom* (Case 40/82) the Court of Justice held that the real reason behind the ban was a desire to protect the home market from foreign competition. It was not, therefore, justified under Art 30 EC Treaty. Bourgoin was an importer who suffered considerable loss by the action of the UK Government. He brought an action in damages, claiming infringement of Art 28 EC Treaty as a breach of statutory duty, breach of an innominate tort, or for misfeasance in public office. The Court of Appeal held, by a majority, that the only appropriate remedy was judicial review and that damages would not be available. Although the House of Lords had held, in *Garden Cottage Foods Ltd* v *Milk Marketing Board* [1984] AC 130, that a breach of Art 82 EC Treaty gave rise to a claim for breach of statutory duty, a breach of Art 28 by a public authority was different. Article 28 did not confer private rights, simply a right to ensure that a public duty was performed. That duty could be enforced in judicial review proceedings and, in accordance with general principles of administrative law, damages would not normally be available. Since the decision of the Court of Justice in *Brasserie du Pêcheur SA* v *Germany* ((Case 46/93) – see Chapter 9) this view is no longer tenable. The question to be determined by the national court is whether or not the breach in question is 'sufficiently serious' and, if it is, whether there is a sufficient causative link between the breach and the damage suffered.

It is now clear, as a matter of English law, that a person who argues that he has suffered a loss as a result of a breach of a public law duty is not compelled to proceed by way of judicial review, with its highly restrictive three-month time limit for the commencement of proceedings. Provided that he can show a particular loss, he does not need to prove a breach of a duty giving rise to a claim in tort, or the existence of a contract to bring a private action (*Roy* v *Kensington and Chelsea and Westminster FPC* [1992] 1 AC 624; The Law Commission, HC 669, *Administrative Law: Judicial Review and Statutory Appeals*, para 3.15, 24 October 1994). There seems little doubt that a person who has suffered loss as a result of a breach by a public body of a Treaty provision or a legally binding act of the institutions of the Community, and who can satisfy the criteria laid down by the Court of Justice in *Brasserie du Pêcheur*, will be able to succeed in the English courts (see view expressed *obiter* by Lord Goff in *Kirklees MBC* v *Wickes* [1993] AC 227).

CLAIMS IN TORT BETWEEN PRIVATE INDIVIDUALS FOR BREACHES OF TREATY PROVISIONS

Individuals who have suffered loss as a result of breach of a directly effective provision of the Treaty can claim damages against another individual who has caused that loss. This is clearly the case in relation to Art 82 EC Treaty (*Garden Cottage Foods* v *Milk Marketing Board* [1984] AC 130). Damages may also be payable in English courts for breach of Art 81 EC Treaty (*H.J. Banks and Co Ltd* v *British Coal Corporation* (Case C-128/92); *MTV Europe* v *BMG Records (UK) Ltd* [1995] 1 CMLR 437). Individuals are also clearly entitled to damages for discriminatory treatment at work in breach of Art 141 EC Treaty, or on grounds of Community nationality under Art 12 EC Treaty. An individual might, for example, wish not only to secure equal treatment, but to obtain damages where national law precluded them. As can be seen in *Defrenne* v *SABENA* (Case 43/75), an individual may make such a claim for compensation for loss of equal pay simply on the basis of the Treaty provision (*Macarthys Ltd* v *Smith* (Case 129/79)).

Any national limitations on the extent of compensation payable in cases of sex discrimination should not be observed where they prevent the claimant from being adequately compensated for the damage suffered. Although the decision in *Marshall* v *Southampton and South-West Hampshire Area Health Authority (No. 2)* (Case 271/91) was limited to the interpretation of Art 6, Directive 76/207 in relation to the amount of damages payable, the principles laid down are wide enough to cover other claims against the state and emanations of the state (see Woolridge and D'Sa, 1993). This view is supported by the Court's decision in *Commission* v *United Kingdom* (Case C-382/92), where the Court held that the United Kingdom's implementation of Directives 77/187 (Transfer of Undertakings) and 75/129 (Consultation on Redundancy) did not provide sufficient compensation for workers affected by a breach of the rules by the employer. The Court held that the compensation payable under the Employment Protection Act 1975, which purported to implement Directive 75/129, was potentially so little as to deprive the measure of its practical effect:

> Where a Community directive does not specifically provide any penalty for an infringement or refers for that purpose to national laws, regulations and administrative provisions, Article 5 of the Treaty [now Art 10] requires the Member States to take all measures necessary to guarantee the application and effectiveness of Community law. For that purpose, while the choice of penalties remains within their discretion, *they must ensure in particular that infringements of Community law are penalised under conditions, both procedural and substantive, which are analogous to those applicable of a similar nature and which, in any event, make the penalty effective, proportionate and dissuasive.* (emphasis added)

Although the Court was speaking of 'penalties', it is clear from the circumstances of the case that it had in mind both criminal sanctions and civil damages which could, in appropriate circumstances, be punitive in nature. It would seem from the words in italics that the Court has now moved on from merely requiring equivalent remedies. Where the national remedy is not effective, the remedy for the breach of Community law should be *effective, proportionate and dissuasive*. This principle will apply whether or not the defendant is the state, an emanation of the state or a private individual or undertaking.

COMMUNITY LAW AS THE BASIS FOR A CLAIM IN CONTRACT, A DEFENCE IN BREACH OF CONTRACT PROCEEDINGS, AND FOR CLAIMS IN QUASI-CONTRACT

Community law may be used to found or assist in a claim for breach of contract in English courts. Under Art 141 EC Treaty, for example, discriminatory provisions in collective agreements are made unlawful and any contract, therefore, which incorporates the terms of such a discriminatory agreement will be void insofar as it offends Art 141 (*Defrenne* v *SABENA* (above)). Community law may also be used as a defence to a claim for breach of contract. If an individual is sued for breach of a contract which, for example, infringes the prohibition on restrictive agreements in Art 81(1) EC Treaty, he may raise the issue of validity of the agreement under Community law as a defence (*Brasserie de Haecht* v *Wilkin* (Case 23/67); *Society of Lloyds* v *Clementson* [1995] 1 CMLR 693).

In *Amministrazione delle Finanze* v *San Giorgio* (Case 199/82), the Court of Justice decided that an individual is entitled to recover charges that have been levied on him contrary to a directly effective provision of Community law. The right of recovery was a necessary adjunct to the right to equal treatment. National law should, therefore, enable individuals who have been wrongly taxed or charged in this way to recover the payments which they have made. So, for example, an EU citizen in receipt of educational services must not be charged a different fee to home students (*Gravier* v *City of Liège* (Case 293/83)), nor may importers be levied for tax at a rate which exceeds that payable in respect of home-produced goods of the same kind (Art 90 EC Treaty). When this happens, the individuals affected should be able to recover the sums overpaid.

The rule laid down by the Court of Justice in *San Giorgio* conflicted with an established rule of English law that a person who has paid money under a mistake of fact can generally recover it, but a person who has paid money under a mistake of law cannot, generally, do so (Goff and Jones, 1993; Tettenborn, 1993; D'Sa, 1994). However, mistake of law is narrowly construed so that, for example, a payment made on the basis of a misunderstanding about a rule of foreign law is regarded as a mistake of fact. Community law is not 'foreign law', of course, since it is incorporated into English law and must be treated as a question of law and not fact (*R* v *Goldstein* [1983] 1 CMLR 252). The House of Lords narrowed the rule further, so that money paid to a public body in response to an unlawful demand on the basis of a mistake of law is now recoverable (*Woolwich Equitable Building Society* v *IRC* [1992] 3 WLR 366). Referring to the right to recovery in relation to money wrongfully paid under Community law, Lord Goff of Chievely remarked:

At a time when Community law is becoming increasingly important, it would be strange if the right of the citizens to recover overpaid charges were to be more restricted under domestic law than it is under Community law.

A similar extension of Community principles into the wider application of the common law followed the decision of the Court of Justice in *Factortame* that interim orders should bind the Crown, when the House of Lords subsequently held that such orders were available even in cases not involving Community law (*Re M* [1994] 1 AC 377).

COMMUNITY LAW AS A DEFENCE IN CRIMINAL PROCEEDINGS

Many of the landmark decisions of Community law have been made by the Court of Justice on references from national courts during the course of criminal proceedings. In *Procureur du Roi* v *Dassonville* (Case 8/74), the defendant was prosecuted for selling Scotch whisky without supplying purchasers with a certificate of origin. The Court held that the legislation under which he was prosecuted was incompatible with Art 28 EC Treaty and as a consequence the national court would, therefore, have been obliged to have dismissed the charge against him. Similarly, the defendants in *R* v *Henn and Darby* (Case 34/79) were able to raise in their prosecution a potential breach of Art 28 EC Treaty, although the Court of Justice held that the UK legislation was justifiable under Art 30 EC Treaty.

In the English courts, so-called Euro-defences have been successfully raised in criminal proceedings for 'overstaying', contrary to the Immigration Act 1971. In *R* v *Pieck* (Case 157/79) the charge against the defendant had to be dismissed because the requirement imposed on the defendant to obtain 'leave' for his continuing residence was held to be contrary to the rights of residence conferred on him by Art 39 EC Treaty (see also *R* v *Kirk* (Case 63/83)). Also, where Community law provides a defence in an unimplemented directive, the defendant may rely upon it (*Pubblico Ministero* v *Ratti* (Case 148/78)). On the other hand, prosecutors cannot rely on an unimplemented directive to interpret the criminal law in such a way as to secure a conviction. This offends the Community principle of legal certainty and non-retroactivity (*Officier van Justitie* v *Kolpinghuis Nijmegen BV* (Case 80/86)).

Euro-defences, using Art 28 EC Treaty, had been widely attempted by businesses prosecuted under the Shops Act 1950, until this avenue was finally closed by the Court of Justice in *Stoke-on-Trent and Norwich City Councils* v *B & Q* (Case C-169/91). Prosecutions are, in any event, much less likely following the liberalising of Sunday trading in England and Wales by the Sunday Trading Act 1994. The scope for the use of Art 28 to defeat prosecutions under national laws aimed at consumer protection has also been considerably diminished by the decision of the Court of Justice to exclude from the scope of Art 28 'selling arrangements' which are unlikely to affect trade between states, in *Keck and Mithouard* (Cases C-267 & 268/91); see Chapter 18.

Further reading

Convery, J., 'State Liability in the United Kingdom after *Brasserie du Pêcheur*' (1997) 34 CML Rev 603.

Craig, P. and De Burca, G. (1998) *EU Law Text, Cases and Materials* (2nd edn), OUP, Chapter 5.

D'Sa, R. (1994) *European Community Law and Civil Remedies in England and Wales*, Sweet & Maxwell, Chapters 9 and 10.

Harlow, C. (1982) *Compensation and Government Torts*, Sweet & Maxwell.

Hartley, T.C. (1998) *The Foundations of European Community Law* (4th edn), Clarendon Press, Chapters 7 and 8.

Maher, I. (1995) 'A Question of Conflict: The Higher English Courts and the Implementation of European Community Law', in Daintith T. (ed.) *Implementing EC Law in the United Kingdom: Structures for Indirect Rule*, John Wiley and Sons.

Steiner, J. (1995) *Enforcing EC Law*, Blackstone Press.

Tettenborn, A. (1993) *Law of Restitution*, pp. 36–38.

Vincenzi, C. (1995) 'Private Initiative and Public Control in the Regulatory Process', in Daintith, T. (ed.) *Implementing EC Law in the United Kingdom: Structures for Indirect Rule*, John Wiley and Sons.

Woolridge, F. and D'Sa, R., 'Damages for Breaches of Community Directives: The Decision in Marshall (No. 2)' (1993) *European Business Law Review*, Vol 4, No. 11.

Part II

THE FREE MOVEMENT OF PERSONS AND SERVICES, AND RIGHTS OF ESTABLISHMENT

Chapter 11

EUROPEAN CITIZENSHIP AND FREE MOVEMENT RIGHTS

The free movement of persons has been a cornerstone of the European Community since its inception. That freedom was not, initially, an entitlement for citizens of Member States to move anywhere in the Community for any purpose, but was linked to a number of specific economic activities (Arts 39–42 (workers), Arts 43–48 (rights of establishment) and Arts 49–55 (services)). Each of these Treaty provisions has been elaborated by detailed secondary legislation. The rights of individuals and undertakings in the three principal categories are examined in more detail in Chapter 12 (workers) and Chapter 13 (services and establishment).

Free movement rights must be seen in the context of three important developments of recent years. The first of these are the measures taken to create the Single European Market which shall, under Art 14(2) EC Treaty, 'comprise an area without internal frontiers in which the free movement of goods, persons, services and capital is ensured'. Although Art 14(2) creates a commitment for the Community to remove border restrictions, it is not clear whether the provision has direct effect. In *R v Secretary of State for the Home Office, ex parte Flynn* [1995] 3 CMLR 397, McCullough J held that it did not match the criteria for having direct effect. It imposed no obligation on Member States, 'let alone one which is clear and precise'. He therefore refused a claim by the applicant, an EU citizen, that he had been unlawfully detained for questioning at Dover. This decision was subsequently upheld in the Court of Appeal.

The second development is the European Economic Area Agreement, under which all the free movement rights enjoyed under the EC Treaty were extended to the remaining states of EFTA (except Switzerland), under the agreement which came into effect on 1 January 1994. Citizens of the Union and their families, and citizens of the participating EFTA states (currently Iceland, Liechtenstein and Norway) and their families, enjoy the full free movement rights of the Treaty and of the implementing legislation in all the territories of the EC and the participating EFTA states.

The third, and most significant, development is the creation of EU citizenship by the Treaty on European Union (Art 17 EC Treaty). Under Art 18(1):

> Every citizen of the Union shall have the right to move and to reside freely within the territory of the Member States, *subject to the limitations and conditions laid down in this Treaty and by the measures adopted to give it effect.* (emphasis added)

The words in italics, which have been added for emphasis, make it clear that the citizenship of the Union does not bring any new free movement rights into being but formally attaches the existing rights, with all the qualifications and exceptions, to the new citizenship. The most that might be said about EU citizenship and free movement is that possession of such citizenship raises a presumption of a right of entry or residence which will have to be rebutted by the host state if those rights are to be refused or terminated. The Treaty envisages the existing rights as a basis for further development, and authorises further measures 'to strengthen or add to the rights' (Art 18(1)). The scope of EU citizenship was a central issue in *R v Home Secretary, ex parte Vitale and Do Amaral* [1995] All ER (EC) 946. The applicants, both EU citizens, were resident in the United Kingdom and had been in receipt of income support for a number of months. They had not found work and, in the view of the Department of Employment, they were not seeking it. They were therefore asked to leave the country. They argued that, irrespective of the truth of the allegations, they were entitled to remain simply as EU citizens. Judge J rejected this argument:

> Article 8a [EC Treaty, now Art 18(1)] provides two distinct rights, the right to move freely within the territory and the right to reside freely. Neither right is free-standing nor absolute. It is expressly and unequivocally subject to the limitations and conditions contained in the Treaty. Moreover it is clear from the provisions in Article 8a(2) [now Art 18(2)] and, more significantly, Article 8e [now Art 22], that provisions may be adopted in due course 'to strengthen or add to the rights laid down' in the part of the Treaty devoted to 'citizenship'. In effect, therefore, the existence of limitations and the potential for extending the rights of citizens are acknowledged in Article 8e as well as Article 8a. So Article 8a does not provide every citizen of the Union with an open-ended right to reside freely within every Member State.

The decision of the Divisional Court in *Vitale* was upheld by the Court of Appeal ([1996] All ER (EC) 461). This view of the limited scope of Art 8a (now Art 18(1)) received some support from the Court of Justice in *Kremzow v Austria* (Case C-299/95). The claimant argued that, as a citizen of the Union, he was entitled to the protection of Community law in relation to criminal proceedings which had been brought against him. The Court of Justice held, on a reference from the national court, that the mere fact of his European Union citizenship was 'not a sufficient connection with Community law to justify the application of Community provisions'. The Court was, however, more recently prepared to hold that an EU citizen who had been *permitted* by the host state to remain there (where she had no right to remain under *Community law*) was entitled, as an EU citizen, to equal treatment in relation to welfare and other benefits in line with nationals of the host state. It left open the question of whether a person who is no longer engaged in the activities of a worker or a self-employed person might still enjoy an independent right of residence as an EU citizen (*Sala v Freistaat Bayern* (Case C-85/96)).

Freedom of movement was seen, in the early days of the Community, as the means by which labour and skills shortages in one Member State could be met out of a surplus of labour and skills in another. That approach was subsequently modified, both in later implementing legislation, and by decisions of the Court of Justice. The Court has interpreted the Treaty and the implementing provisions generously. The application of Art 39(3)(a) EC Treaty, which appears to confer a right to go to another Member State only on those able to 'accept offers of employment *actually made*' (emphasis added), to work-seekers, is perhaps one of the most remarkable examples of creative interpretation (*Procureur du Roi v Royer* (Case 48/75)). Although each of the free movement rights depended, until the 1990s (see the general right of residence created by Directive 90/364, Chapter 13), on a specific economic activity, the Court has tended to develop a body of general principles applicable to all those exercising free movement rights.

Most importantly, all free movement rights are directly effective and enforceable in the courts of Member States as fundamental rights. The entry or residence of those exercising them is not dependent upon any consent or leave given by the host state. Provided that an individual is engaged in an activity which confers Community rights of entry or residence, the host state cannot terminate that right of residence (*R* v *Pieck* (Case 157/79)). There are exceptions to rights of entry and residence in cases where the individual constitutes a threat to public policy, public security and public health under Arts 39(3), 46(1) and Directive 64/221. These powers of Member States to derogate from individual rights of free movement have, however, been interpreted strictly by the Court (see *Adoui and Cornuaille* v *Belgian State* (Cases 115 & 116/81), and Chapter 15).

Since free movement rights are fundamental rights, the Court of Justice has held that they must be transparent in national legislation. Incompatible provisions of national law which, for example, exclude the employment of foreign nationals, even though they are not, in practice, applied in the case of EU citizens, must be amended to make it absolutely clear that EU citizens enjoy equal access (*Commission* v *France (Re French Merchant Seamen)* (Case 167/73)). It is not sufficient that Community rights should be enjoyed by virtue of administrative concessions. Those enjoying such rights must be made aware of them, and be able, should the need arise, to rely upon them before a court of law (*Commission* v *Germany (Re Nursing Directives)* (Case 29/84)).

Decisions affecting the exercise by an individual of free movement rights should spell out the reasons for them, to enable an effective legal challenge to be made. The procedures for challenging any denial of such rights, whether on the basis of public policy, public security or public health, under Directive 64/221 (see Chapter 15), or on any other ground, should follow the Community principles of fairness and the provisions of the European Convention on Human Rights (*UNECTEF* v *Heylens and Others* (Case 222/86)). The provisions of the Convention are now directly applicable to the exercise of Community rights (Art 6(2) TEU). Failure to deliver those rights can give rise to a claim in damages against the Member State concerned.

Non-discrimination on grounds of nationality (Art 12 EC Treaty) is another fundamental principle of Community law that is important in the exercise of free movement rights. The detailed provisions of Regulation 1612/68 relating to equal access to employment and to other benefits enable the worker and his family to integrate into the host state, but there is no parallel legislation relating to the self-employed and to those providing and receiving services. Decisions of the Court relating to access to housing and the criminal process, which have been secured for workers under Regulation 1612/68 (Arts 7(2) and 9), have, however, been achieved for the self-employed and the recipients of services by a creative use of Art 12 EC Treaty (see *Commission* v *Italy* (Case 63/86) and *Cowan* v *Le Trésor Public* (Case 186/87)). Article 12 does, however, apply only to matters covered by the Treaty, and any aspect of an individual's life which may affect his entry into or residence in another Member State as a beneficiary of Community law.

The free movement rights will also be enhanced by measures adopted pursuant to Art 13 EC Treaty. Article 13 is the legal base for the adoption of measures to 'combat discrimination based on sex, racial or ethnic origin, religion or belief, disability, age or sexual orientation', provided such measures do not exceed the powers of the Community as conferred upon it by the EC Treaty. In other words, measures can be adopted to combat discrimination provided they are in furtherance of the existing powers of the Community.

On 29 June 2000, pursuant to Art 13 EC Treaty, the Council adopted Directive 2000/43/EC (OJ 2000 L 180/22) which implemented the principle of equal treatment between persons irrespective of racial or ethnic origin. The directive has to be implemented by 19 July 2003. The principle of equal treatment prohibits direct or indirect discrimination based on racial or ethnic origin (Art 1). It applies to EU and non-EU citizens and covers both public and private sectors in relation to employment, self-employment, education, social protection including social security and healthcare, social advantages, and access to and supply of goods and services (Art 3(1)). The prohibition of racial or ethnic discrimination does not, however, cover national provisions relating to the entry into and residence of third-country nationals (Art 13(2)). The directive does not, therefore, extend the free movement provisions, *per se*, to non-EU citizens (see below).

Again pursuant to Art 13 EC Treaty, the Commission has recently proposed a directive to establish a general framework for equal treatment in employment and occupation. If adopted, the directive will prohibit direct and indirect discrimination as regards access to employment and occupation on grounds of religion or belief, disability, age or sexual orientation. It will apply to both the public and private sectors. As with Directive 2000/43, this directive will apply to EU and non-EU citizens, but likewise, the prohibition will not cover national provisions relating to the entry into and residence of third-country nationals (Art 13(2)). The directive will not, therefore, extend the free movement provisions, *per se*, to non-EU citizens (see below).

Although discrimination in relation to both employment and self-employment is generally prohibited, restrictions on the employment of EU nationals in 'the public service' are permitted by Art 39(4) EC Treaty. There are similar provisions relating to the self-employed, who may be refused participation in activities which 'are connected, even occasionally, with the exercise of official authority', in Art 45 EC Treaty. There is no definition in the Treaty or the secondary legislation of either 'the public service' or 'the exercise of official authority', but both exceptions have been narrowly interpreted by the Court. The mere fact that the employer is the state is not conclusive. It is the nature of the employment which is the determining factor (*Lawrie-Blum* v *Land Baden-Württemberg* (Case 66/85); see Chapters 12 and 13).

To benefit from Community free movement rights, a person must be, or have been, a migrant in some sense or other. A person who has not left his own state, and does not intend to do so, cannot be a beneficiary (*Iorio* (Case 298/84)). However, this may change in relation to family reunification. Article 63(3)(a) EC Treaty, which was inserted by the Treaty of Amsterdam, enables measures to be adopted on immigration policy concerning the 'conditions of entry and residence, and standards on procedures for the issue by Member States of long term visas and residence permits, including those for the purpose of family reunion'. Pursuant to Art 63(3)(a), the Commission has recently proposed a directive on the right to family reunification. The proposed directive establishes a right to family reunification for the benefit of third-country nationals who are residing lawfully within a Member State, and also to EU citizens who do not exercise their free movement rights. For the purpose of the current discussion, it is the latter which is relevant. The aim of the provision is to 'avoid discriminating between citizens of the Union' who exercise their right to free movement and those who do not. In order to achieve this, it is necessary to provide for 'the family reunification of citizens of the Union residing in countries of which they are nationals to be governed by the rules of Community law relating to free movement' (para 12, Preamble). Accordingly, if this directive is adopted, an EU citizen who has not exercised his free movement rights in another Member State will have the right to have specified family members installed with him. This right will override any less generous national provisions.

In the meantime, however, he can be a worker or a self-employed person *vis-à-vis* his own state if he works abroad for a period and then returns home. He may then enjoy the family rights of a Community migrant against his own state, which will override the more restrictive national provisions (*Morson* v *Netherlands* (Case 35/82); *R* v *IAT and Surinder Singh* (Case C-370/90)). A person who has not left his own state may still benefit from free movement rights if, for example, he has arranged employment in another Member State, or wishes to establish a business there. He will be entitled to be issued with a travel document and cannot, subject to the public policy/security/health exception, be prevented from leaving (Art 2(1) and (2), Directives 68/360 and 73/148; see Chapters 12, 13 and 15).

OTHER RIGHTS DERIVED FROM CITIZENSHIP OF THE UNION

The creation of EU citizenship is part of a broader programme of enhancement of individual political and social rights in the European context called a 'Peoples' Europe' (Second Addonino Report on a Peoples' Europe, Bull EC Supplement, 7/85, p. 18). As part of that programme, which is intended to give European citizens both a greater sense of identity as Europeans and a number of new tangible rights, EU citizenship confers other benefits in addition to the general right of residence. It is not possible to discuss them in detail here, but broadly they comprise: a right to vote and stand as a candidate in local (but not national) and European Parliamentary elections in other Member States where the EU citizen is resident, a right to diplomatic representation outside the Community from any of the other Member States in territories where the citizen's own state has no consulate or embassy, a right to petition the European Parliament, a right to apply for assistance to the European Parliamentary Ombudsman, and a right of access to documents held by the Community institutions. The right to apply to the Ombudsman is not confined to EU citizens but is open to 'any natural or legal person residing or having its registered office in a Member State' (Art 195(1) EC Treaty).

Although European citizenship has created a general right of entry and residence for all those holding the nationality of a Member State, that right is defined by reference to the existing miscellany of largely economically related rights of free movement contained in the EC Treaty and elaborated in secondary legislation. The subsequent chapters will examine the scope of those rights, identify the beneficiaries and the extent to which Member States are permitted to derogate from them. European citizenship is the primary avenue by which those rights are acquired, but Community law also confers more limited rights on those who are not citizens of the Union.

FREE MOVEMENT RIGHTS OF NON-UNION CITIZENS

Nationals of third states outside the Community can enjoy a number of important free movement rights under Treaties made with it. Besides the full range of free movement rights enjoyed by Iceland, Liechtenstein and Norway under the EEA Agreement discussed above, family members of Community workers, the self-employed and other beneficiaries of free movement rights who are nationals of other states have the right to install themselves with the person entitled to the free movement right. Host states may demand that such individuals obtain a visa, but 'every facility' should be given to enable them to obtain one (Art 3(2), Directive 68/360). Once installed with the principal beneficiary, the spouse or other family member is entitled to access to employment and equal treatment as if he or she was a European Union citizen (*Gül* v *Regierungspräsident Düsseldorf* (Case 131/85)).

More limited rights are enjoyed by the beneficiaries of Association Agreements made with the Community. Such agreements have been held by the Court to be directly effective (*Kupferberg* (Case 104/81)). The rights in these cases are normally limited to equal treatment in employment and social security after admission, but they do not entitle the beneficiaries to enter. Such rights have been recognised in this way under the EC–Turkey Agreement (*Kus* v *Landeshauptstadt Wiesbaden* (Case C-237/91); *Eroglu* v *Baden-Württemberg* (Case C-355/93)), and under the EC–Morocco Cooperation Agreement (*Bahia Kziber* v *ONEM* (Case C-18/90); *Yousfi* v *Belgium* (Case C-58/93)). There are other agreements with, *inter alia*, Tunisia, Algeria, Poland, the Czech Republic, Hungary, Romania, Slovakia and Cyprus which contain provisions that could be used by nationals of those states while working in the Community.

Other third state nationals may benefit from Community free movement rights in a different way. As we shall see, undertakings established in one Member State have the right to go to another, either to provide a service or to become established there (Arts 43, 49 EC Treaty). To enable the undertaking to carry out its activities in the host state it is entitled to take its workforce with it whatever their nationality. Such employees should be admitted without any requirement of a work permit in the host state and should be entitled to remain there until the business of the undertaking is complete. On this basis, the French immigration authorities have been obliged to allow non-EC workers employed by Portuguese and Belgian companies to work without any further restrictions than those already imposed in the state of origin of the undertaking (*Rush Portuguesa Lda* (Case C-113/89); *Van der Elst* v *OMI* (Case C-43/93)). This right is, in essence, the right of the undertaking rather than the right of the worker and, if challenged, should, in principle, have to be asserted by the undertaking in the courts of the Member State. Advocate-General Tesauro, in his opinion in *Van der Elst* (above), did, however, describe the workers in the *Rush Portuguesa* case as having a *derived* right in relation to entry and employment, although he did not argue that it could be asserted by them personally (p. 3813). Somewhat surprisingly, the United Kingdom's Immigration Appeal Tribunal has held that the right of the employing company in the United Kingdom can be the subject of an application for judicial review by the *employee* (*Pasha* v *Home Office* [1993] 2 CMLR 350).

Third state nationals given leave to enter any Member State may, under a 1995 regulation, be issued with a EU visa and be able to travel anywhere in the EU for a period of up to three months. The visa may be issued by any Member State, but it is in a standard form for use in all the Member States (Art 63(3) EC Treaty, Council Regulation 1683/95, OJ 1995 L 164). In addition, such nationals will benefit from Directive 2000/43/EC prohibiting discrimination on grounds of racial or ethnic origin (see above). They will also benefit from the proposed directive prohibiting direct and indirect discrimination as regards access to employment and occupation on grounds of religion or belief, disability, age or sexual orientation; and from the proposed directive on family reunification (if adopted; see above).

Further reading

Albors-Llorens, A. *et al*. 'CELS (Cambridge) EC Treaty Project: Part II Citizenship of the Union' (1997) 22 EL Rev 436.

Closa, C., 'The Concept of Citizenship in the Treaty of European Union' (1992) 29 CML Rev 1137.

Closa, C., 'Citizenship of the Union and Nationality of Member States' (1995) 32 CML Rev 487.

Craig, P. and De Burca, G. (1998) *EU Law Text, Cases and Materials* (2nd edn), OUP, pp. 719–725.

Handoll, J. (1995) *Free Movement of Persons in the European Union*, John Wiley and Sons, Chapter 9.

Hardy, S. and McCarthy, J., 'After Amsterdam: EU Citizenship – Myth or Reality?' (1997) *Immigration and Nationality Law and Practice*, Vol II, No. 4, p. 118.

Hartley, T.C. (1991) 'Free Movement of Persons' Pt II in Green, N., Hartley, T.C. and Usher, J.A., *The Legal Foundation of the Single European Market*, Clarendon Press.

Hedemann-Robinson, M., 'New Electoral and Political Rights in the Community', *New Law Journal*, 9 April 1994, p. 564.

O'Keefe, D. (1994) 'Union Citizenship', in O'Keefe, D. and Twomey, P. (eds) *Legal Issues of the Maastricht Treaty*, Wiley Chancery Laws.

O'Keefe, D., 'The Free Movement of Persons in the Single Market' (1992) 13 EL Rev 3.

O'Leary, S., 'The Relationship Between Community Citizenship and the Protection of Fundamental Rights in Community Law' (1995) 32 CML Rev 487, p. 519.

O'Leary, S. (1996) *The Evolving Concept of Community Citizenship*, Kluwer.

Shaw, J., 'The Many Pasts and Futures of Citizenship the European Union' (1997) 22 EL Rev 554.

Vincenzi, C., 'European Citizenship and Free Movement Rights in the United Kingdom', *Public Law*, Summer 1995, p. 259.

Weatherill, S. (2000) *Cases and Materials on EC Law* (5th edn), Blackstone Press, pp. 398–404.

Chapter 12

FREE MOVEMENT OF WORKERS

INTRODUCTION

The free movement of workers is of great economic and social importance to the Community. Although the right to move to other Member States in an employed capacity was originally seen as no more than an economic function whereby a surplus of labour and skills in one part of the Community could meet a shortage in another, the worker was soon recognised in the Community's legislation, and in the decisions of the Court of Justice, as more than merely a unit of labour. The right to move under what is now Art 39 EC Treaty was seen as 'a fundamental right' which was to be 'exercised in freedom and dignity' (Preamble to Regulation 1612/68). 'The migrant worker is not to be viewed as a mere source of labour, but as a human being' (Advocate-General Trabucchi in *Mr and Mrs F v Belgian State* (Case 7/75)).

The exercise of the migrant worker's rights is to be facilitated in the workplace and in the broader social context of the host Member State. The implementing legislation and the jurisprudence of the Court is directed at securing the worker's departure from his state of origin and his entry, residence and integration, in the widest sense, into the economic and social fabric of the host Member State. Article 39 is directly effective, not only at the instance of the worker but also, the Court of Justice has held, by his employer (*Clean Car Autoservice GmbH v Landeshauptmann von Wien* (Case C-350/96)).

Consideration begins with Art 39 EC Treaty (previously Art 48) and the rights of workers:

1. Freedom of movement of workers shall be secured within the Community.

2. Such freedom of movement shall entail the abolition of any discrimination based on nationality between workers of the Member States as regards employment, remuneration and other conditions of work and employment.

3. It shall entail the right, subject to limitations justified on grounds of public policy, public security or public health:
(a) to accept offers of employment actually made;
(b) to move freely within the territory of Member States for this purpose;
(c) to stay in a Member State for the purpose of employment in accordance with the provisions governing the employment of nationals of that State laid down by law, regulation or administrative action;
(d) to remain in the territory of a Member State after having been employed in that State, subject to conditions which shall be embodied in implementing regulations to be drawn up by the Commission.

4. The provisions of this Article shall not apply to employment in the public service.

The importance of the principles of free movement and of non-discrimination have been emphasised time and again by the Court of Justice. In relation to non-discrimination, Art 39 sets out the general Art 12 EC Treaty anti-discrimination principle, but specifically in relation to workers. Art 12 provides that:

> Within the scope of application of this Treaty, and without prejudice to any special provisions contained therein, any discrimination on grounds of nationality shall be prohibited ...

Secondary legislation

Article 40 EC Treaty (previously Art 49) provides for secondary legislation to be adopted to bring about the freedoms set out in Art 39:

> The Council shall ... issue directives or make regulations setting out the measures required to bring about freedom of movement for workers, as defined in Article 39 ...

Several directives and regulations have been adopted under the former Art 49 (now Art 40), the most important of which will be discussed below.

Reverse discrimination

The rights of free movement, which are conferred on workers and their families by the above-mentioned Treaty provisions and secondary legislation, will apply only to 'Community' workers.

The provisions do not prohibit discrimination in a totally 'internal' situation: i.e. national workers cannot claim rights in their own Member State which workers who are nationals of other Member States could claim there. In *R v Saunders* (Case 175/78), the Court of Justice held that because there was no factor connecting Saunders with any of the situations envisaged by Community law, Saunders could not rely upon the former Art 48 (now Art 39) to challenge a binding over order which effectively excluded her from part of the national territory. There was a similar outcome in *Morson and Jhanjan v Netherlands* (Cases 35 & 36/82) where two Dutch nationals were working in the their home state, The Netherlands. They wanted to bring their parents (Surinamese nationals) into The Netherlands to live with them. Had they been members of any other EU country, working in The Netherlands, their parents would have been covered by Art 10, Regulation 1612/68 (this provision is considered in detail later) and would have been able to join their children. However, their children were nationals working in their own Member State, who had not exercised their right of free movement within the Community, and therefore Community law did not apply: i.e. it was a totally internal situation. This was confirmed by the Court of Justice in *Land Nordrhein-Westfalen v Uecker; Jacquei v Land Nordrhein-Westfalen* (Cases C-64 & 65/96).

However, the facts of *R v Immigration Appeal Tribunal and Surinder Singh, ex parte Secretary of State for the Home Department* (Case C-370/90) were different.

An Indian national married a British national. They both worked in Germany before returning to the United Kingdom some years later. The United Kingdom argued that the spouse's right to re-enter the United Kingdom derived from national law *not* Community law (i.e. it was an internal situation). The Court of Justice considered the period of work in another Member State, and stated as follows.

19. A national of a Member State might be deterred from leaving his country of origin in order to pursue an activity as an employed or self-employed person as envisaged by the Treaty in the territory of another Member State if, on returning to the Member State of which he is a national in order to pursue an activity there as an employed or self-employed person, the conditions of his entry were not at least equivalent to those which he would enjoy under the Treaty or secondary law in the territory of another Member State.

20. He would in particular be deterred from so doing if his spouse and children were not also permitted to enter and reside in the territory of his Member State of origin under conditions at least equivalent to those granted them by Community law in the territory of another Member State.

The Court held that the Community law provisions on the free movement of workers can be relied upon by a worker against the Member State of which he is a national *provided* he has resided and been employed in another Member State. This has been confirmed subsequently by the Court of Justice: see *Terhoeve* v *Inspecteur van de Belastingdienst Particulieren/Ondernemingen Buitenland* (Case C-18/95).

As discussed in Chapter 11, pursuant to Art 63(3)(a), the Commission has proposed a directive on the right to family reunification. The directive (if adopted) will establish a right to family reunification for the benefit of third-country nationals who are residing lawfully within a Member State, and also to EU citizens who do not exercise their free movement rights. For the purpose of the current discussion, it is the latter which is relevant. The aim of the provision is to 'avoid discriminating between citizens of the Union' who exercise their right to free movement and those who do not. In order to achieve this, it is necessary to provide for 'the family reunification of citizens of the Union residing in countries of which they are nationals to be governed by the rules of Community law relating to free movement' (Preamble, para 12). Accordingly, if this directive is adopted, an EU citizen who has not exercised his free movement rights in another Member State will have the right to have specified family members installed with him. This right will override any less generous national provisions.

SCOPE OF THE TERM 'WORKER'

As discussed above, Art 39(1) EC Treaty provides that freedom of movement of workers shall be secured within the Community. It entails the abolition of any discrimination based on nationality in relation to access to employment, remuneration and other conditions of work (Art 39(2)). As discussed in Chapter 11, two recently adopted anti-discrimination directives will have an impact on, *inter alia*, EU citizens exercising their free movement rights. Article 13 EC Treaty is the legal base for the adoption of measures to 'combat discrimination based on sex, racial or ethnic origin, religion or belief, disability, age or sexual orientation', provided such measures do not exceed the powers of the Community as conferred upon it by the EC Treaty. In other words, measures can be adopted to combat discrimination provided they are in furtherance of the existing powers of the Community.

On 29 June 2000, pursuant to Art 13 EC Treaty, the Council adopted Directive 2000/43/EC (OJ 2000 L 180/22) which implemented the principle of equal treatment between persons irrespective of racial or ethnic origin. The directive has to be implemented by 19 July 2003. The principle of equal treatment prohibits direct or indirect discrimination based on racial or ethnic origin (Art 1). It applies to EU and non-EU citizens and covers both public and private sectors in relation to employment, self-employment, education, social protection including social security and healthcare, social advantages, and access to and supply of goods and services (Art 3(1)). The prohibition of racial or ethnic discrimination does not, however, cover national provisions relating to the entry and residence of third-country nationals (Art 13(2)). The directive does not, therefore, extend the free movement provisions, *per se*, to non-EU citizens.

Again pursuant to Art 13 EC Treaty, the Commission has proposed a directive to establish a general framework for equal treatment in employment and occupation. If adopted, the directive will prohibit direct and indirect discrimination as regards access to employment and occupation on grounds of religion or belief, disability, age or sexual orientation. It will apply to both the public and private sectors. As with Directive 2000/43, this directive will apply to EU and non-EU citizens, but likewise, the prohibition does not cover national provisions relating to the entry and residence of third-country nationals (Art 13(2)). The directive will not, therefore, extend the free movement provisions, *per se*, to non-EU citizens (see below).

Although the exercise of workers' rights may be made subject to national rules relating to public policy, public security and public health (as limited by the provisions of Directive 64/221 (see Chapter 15)), Art 39 EC Treaty provides that an EC worker should have the right:

- to accept offers of employment actually made;
- to move freely within the territory of Member States for this purpose;
- to stay in the Member State for the purpose of employment; and
- to remain in the territory of a Member State after having been employed in that state.

Implementing legislation has given detailed effect to these provisions. Directive 68/360 defines the rights of workers and the obligations of the immigration authorities of Member States in relation to entry, residence and the issue and revocation of residence permits. Regulation 1612/68 deals with matters relating to equal access to employment, equality of terms of employment, family, housing, educational and social rights. Regulation 1408/71 ensures that workers who are entitled to contributory and related benefits continue to enjoy them in the host state and on return to their own state. Regulation 1251/70 contains detailed provisions on rights of retirement in the state where the worker has been employed, and Directive 90/365 confers a right of retirement on employees and the self-employed in Member States other than those where the person has been employed. All of these provisions create directly effective rights and will be considered in the context of the exercise by the worker of those rights.

The range of rights accruing under Art 39 EC Treaty and the secondary legislation is dependent upon the person coming within the scope of the term 'worker'. However, neither the EC Treaty nor the secondary legislation defines 'worker', and so the Court of Justice has been left to elaborate upon its meaning. In *Lawrie-Blum* v *Land Baden-Württemberg* (Case 66/85) the Court said that:

Objectively defined, a 'worker' is a person who is obliged to provide services for another in return for monetary reward and who is subject to the direction and control of the other person as regards the way in which the work is to be done. (para 14)

This is a classic definition and simply distinguishes an employee (i.e. a person who performs under a contract *of service*) from one who is self-employed, an independent contractor (i.e. a person who performs under a contract *for services*).

In a series of cases which have come before the Court of Justice, the Court has further considered the question of the scope of 'worker'. In *Hoekstra (nee Unger)* v *Bestuur der Bedrijfsvereniging voor Detailhandel en Ambachten* (Case 75/63) the Court held that the activities which confer worker status are a matter of Community law. It is therefore for the Court to determine its meaning and scope. Had this not been the case, the result could have been an unequal application of the provisions throughout the Community: e.g. Germany's definition may not have been the same as the United Kingdom's, which may not have been the same as Greece's, etc.

In *Levin* v *Staatssecretaris van Justitie* (Case 53/81):

Mrs Levin was a British national married to a South African national. She was refused a residence permit by the Dutch authorities because it was claimed that she was not a 'worker' within the scope of the former Art 48 (now Art 39). She challenged the refusal before the Dutch courts, which referred the matter to the Court of Justice pursuant to the former Art 177 (now Art 234). The Court was asked to explain the concept of 'worker' for Community law purposes, and in particular whether it included an individual who earns an income less than the minimum required for subsistence as defined under national law. The Court stated that there was no definition of 'worker' within the Treaty or secondary legislation and that its scope was a matter of Community law:

---

11. ... [T]he terms *'worker'* and *'activity as an employed person'* may not be defined by *references to the national laws of the Member States but have a Community meaning.* If that were not the case, the Community rules on the free movement of workers would be frustrated, as the meaning of those terms could be fixed and modified unilaterally, without any control by the Community institutions, by national laws which would thus be able to exclude at will certain categories of persons from the benefit of the Treaty ...

13. In this respect it must be stressed that *these concepts define the field of application of one of the fundamental freedoms guaranteed by the Treaty and, as such, may not be interpreted restrictively ...*

15. An interpretation which reflects the full scope of these concepts is also in conformity with the objectives of the Treaty which include, according to Articles 2 and 3, the abolition, as between Member States, of obstacles to freedom of movement for persons, with the purpose *inter alia* of promoting throughout the Community a harmonious development of economic activities and a raising of the standard of living. *Since part-time employment, although it may provide an income lower than that considered to be the minimum required for subsistence, constitutes for a large number of persons an effective means of improving their living conditions, the effectiveness of Community law would be impaired and the achievement of the objectives of the Treaty would be jeopardised if the enjoyment of rights conferred by the principle of freedom of movement for workers were reserved solely to persons engaged in full-time employment and earning, as a result, a wage at least equivalent to the guaranteed minimum wage in the sector under consideration ...*

17. It should however be stated that *whilst part-time employment is not excluded from the field of application of the rules on freedom of movement for workers, those rules cover only the pursuit of effective and genuine activities, to the exclusion of activities on such a small scale as to be regarded as purely marginal and ancillary.* It follows both from the statement of principle of freedom of movement for workers and from the place occupied by the rules relating to that principle in the system of the Treaty as a whole that *those rules guarantee only the free movement of persons who pursue or are desirous of pursuing an economic activity.* (emphasis added)

As in the *Hoekstra* case, the Court made it clear that it is for the Court *not* the Member States to define the term 'worker'. The Court then went on to consider at para 15 whether or not part-time work was sufficient to bring somebody within the status of a 'worker' for Community law purposes. The Court stated that it was important to understand that part-time work was not only a valuable contribution to the economies of the Member States, but it also contributed to the raising of living standards for the individual employees concerned. The fact the work was part-time should not affect Mrs Levin's status as a 'worker' within Community law.

The Court stated at para 17 that the part-time work must constitute an 'effective and genuine' economic activity which must not be on such a small scale as to be 'purely marginal and ancillary'. This is the test to be applied to ascertain if the person is a 'worker'. The Court concluded by stating that the intention of the applicant was irrelevant. It was irrelevant that the applicant had taken up an economic activity only in order to obtain a residence permit provided that, in the words of para 17, such economic activity was 'effective and genuine' and not on such a small scale as to be 'purely marginal and ancillary'.

This was a very important case, clarifying that part-time workers could be covered by the Community law provisions on free movement of workers. It did not matter if the worker chose to supplement his income from other sources. This was taken a step further in *Kempf v Staatssecretaris van Justitie* (Case 139/85).

A German national was living and working in The Netherlands as a music teacher. She gave 12 lessons a week. She was refused a residence permit. She challenged this refusal and the national court referred the case to the Court of Justice pursuant to the former Art 177 (now Art 234). It was argued by the Dutch and Danish Governments that work providing an income below the minimum level of subsistence was not 'effective or genuine' if the person undertaking the work claimed social security benefits. If it was not 'effective or genuine' then the person would not come within the scope of 'worker' and therefore could not benefit from the rights under the Treaty or secondary legislation.

---

14. ... In that regard, *it is irrelevant whether those supplementary means of subsistence are derived from property or from the employment of a member of his family, as was the case in Levin, or whether, as in this instance, they are obtained from financial assistance drawn from the public funds of the Member State in which he resides, provided that the effective and genuine nature of his work is established.* (emphasis added)

So, once again, the Court reiterated the test to be applied in order to ascertain whether or not a person comes within the scope of 'worker': i.e. pursuit of an economic activity which is effective and genuine (and which is not purely marginal or ancillary).

In *Lawrie-Blum* (see above), the Court held that a trainee teacher qualified even though her remuneration was only nominal. The fact that the salary was less than a teacher's full salary was immaterial. What mattered was the genuinely economic nature of the work in question, and the receipt of some remuneration.

The Court has not laid down any criteria as to how much, or how little, or what kind of work, is 'effective and genuine' and not 'marginal and ancillary', although some guidance can be gained from the cases. In *Steymann* v *Staatssecretaris van Justitie* (Case 196/87), the individual was engaged in maintenance and repair work for a religious community. He received his keep, but no wages. Despite the fact that his reward was in kind rather than in cash, the Court held that he was to be considered a 'worker' under Community law. In *Bettray* v *Staatssecretaris van Justitie* (Case 344/87), however, the person concerned was engaged in paid work as part of a form of therapy. It was, therefore, ancillary. Surprisingly small amounts of work can be regarded as 'sufficient', though. In *Raulin* v *Netherlands Ministry for Education and Science* (Case 357/89), the person claiming worker status had been on an 'on call' contract for a period of eight months. During that period she actually worked as a waitress for a total of 60 hours. Nonetheless, the Court held that the brevity of her employment period did not exclude her from qualifying for worker status.

In view of the broad scope which has been given by the Court to 'worker', some Member States have expressed concern that EC nationals from Member States with less generous welfare benefit provisions would migrate to those with more generous provisions (this will be discussed further below). However, Member States have a number of options available to them in this regard. One of them, in relation to part-timers, is to provide that benefits will only be available to national and non-national workers who are 'available for full-time work'.

WORK-SEEKERS

Not every individual wishing to go to another Member State to work will already have a job arranged. On a first impression of Art 39(3) EC Treaty, people in this category would not seem to qualify for a right of free movement, since the bene-ficiaries are described as those in a position 'to accept offers of employment actually made'. However, in *Royer* (Case 48/75) the Court of Justice decided, in a remarkably creative judgment, that

> the right of nationals of a Member State to enter the territory of another Member State and reside there for the purposes intended by the Treaty – in particular to look for or pursue an occupation or activities as employed or self-employed persons, or to rejoin their spouse or family – is a right conferred directly by the Treaty, or, as the case may be, by the provisions adopted for its implementation.

Although the Court had decided in *Royer* that work-seekers were entitled to enter another Member State and look for work, it had not given any indication of how long that right should continue. For a number of years it was thought that the appropriate period was three months, partly because that was the limit of the entitlement to payment of unemployment benefit under Regulation 1408/71 (see Chapter 14), and partly because the Council of Ministers had made a declaration to that effect at the time of approval of Regulation 1612/68 and Directive 68/360 (see the opinion of Advocate-General

Lenz in *Centre Public d'Aide Sociale* v *Lebon* (Case C-316/85)). The Court rejected both bases for limiting the rights of residence of work-seekers. In *R* v *Immigration Appeal Tribunal, ex parte Antonissen* (Case C-292/89), the Court said that there was no 'necessary link between the right to unemployment benefit in the Member State of origin and the right to stay in the host State' (para 20). The declaration had 'no legal significance', since it was not part of any binding legislative provision (para 18).

The way seemed clear for an unequivocal statement by the Court on how long an individual may look for work in another Member State. The Court's response to the question only marginally clarified the issue. The facts of this case are as follows.

Antonissen was a Belgian national who came to the United Kingdom in 1984 to find work. He did not find work. In 1987 the Secretary of State decided to deport him, following his conviction and imprisonment for a drug-related offence. He sought judicial review of the decision and the case was referred to the Court of Justice. The relevant issue here concerned the length of time a person could stay in the territory of another Member State while seeking work.

---

16. In that regard, it must be pointed out in the first place that the effectiveness of Article 48 [now Art 39] is secured in so far as Community legislation or, in its absence, the legislation of a Member State gives persons concerned *a reasonable time in which to apprise themselves, in the territory of the Member State concerned, of offers of employment corresponding to their occupational qualifications and to take, where appropriate, the necessary steps in order to be engaged* ...

21. In the absence of a Community provision prescribing the period during which Community nationals seeking employment in a Member State may stay there, *a period of six months*, such as that laid down in the national legislation at issue in the main proceedings, *does not appear in principle to be insufficient to enable the persons concerned to apprise themselves, in the host Member State, of offers of employment* corresponding to their occupational qualifications and to take, where appropriate, the necessary steps in order to be engaged *and, therefore, does not jeopardise the effectiveness of the principle of free movement. However, if after the expiry of that period the person concerned provides evidence that he is continuing to* seek *employment and that he has genuine chances of being engaged, he cannot be required to leave the territory of the host Member State.* (emphasis added)

The Court held that EC nationals could enter another Member State to seek work, and that they could stay there for a *reasonable period of time* while they sought work (para 16). The Court stated that (in the context of the UK legislation existing at the material time) six months was a *reasonable period of time* to allow a person seeking work to find employment. This does not mean that a period of less than six months may not be reasonable. At the end of para 21 the Court declared that even if work has not been found at the end of this period, the EC national cannot be deported if he can show that he is still seeking work and he has genuine chances of finding work.

The Court of Justice has subsequently decided, in *Commission* v *Belgium* (Case C-344/95), that the period of *three months* allocated by Belgium to EU nationals to find work is also reasonable, provided that it can be extended if the work-seeker has a genuine chance of finding work.

Work-seekers are entitled to entry and limited rights of residence but not the full range of benefits enjoyed by those who have full worker status. Their differing entitlements are examined below.

THE WORKER'S FAMILY

It is not only the worker who will derive benefits from Community law, but also the family of the worker. However, the rights of the family are dependent upon the worker's status as a 'Community worker' (see above). Although the worker has to be an EC national, the family of the worker does not. Article 10 of Regulation 1612/68 defines workers' families:

> 1. The following shall, irrespective of their nationality, have the right to install themselves with a worker who is a national of one Member State and who is employed in the territory of another Member State:
> (a) his spouse and their descendants who are under the age of 21 or are dependants;
> (b) dependent relatives in the ascending line of the worker and his spouse.
>
> 2. Member States shall facilitate the admission of any member of the family not coming within the provisions of paragraph 1 if dependent on the worker referred to above or living under his roof in the country whence he comes.

There are four categories of persons who come within the scope of Art 10(1) and have a *right* to install themselves with the worker:

- the worker's spouse;
- his (and his spouse's) descendants (i.e. children) under the age of 21;
- his (and his spouse's) descendants (i.e. children) over the age of 21 who are dependent upon him;
- his (or his spouse's) ascendants (i.e. parents, grandparents) who are dependent upon him.

There are two categories of persons who come within the scope of Art 10(2) but who only have the right to have their admission *facilitated*:

- any dependent relative of the worker (who is not otherwise covered by Art 10(1)); or
- any relative of the worker (who is not otherwise covered by Art 10(1)) who was living under the worker's roof in the worker's Member State of origin.

The right to install, and to have admission facilitated, is subject to Art 10(3) of the Regulation:

> For the purposes of paragraphs 1 and 2, the worker must have available for his family housing considered as normal for national workers in the region where he is employed; this provision, however, must not give rise to discrimination between national workers and workers from the other Member States.

Dependants

In *Centre Public d'Aide Sociale de Courcelles* v *Lebon* (Case 316/85) the Court of Justice held that the status of dependant did not require an objective assessment as to the *need* for support, but required an assessment of the facts to ascertain whether the worker was *actually providing* support for the family member. This support could be financial or non-financial. Take the case of a disabled child of an EC worker who is over the age of 21. If this child had suffered the disability in a motor accident and had received a substantial financial settlement in subsequent civil litigation, obviously the child would not be financially dependent upon his parents. However, if the parents provided the child with other support (e.g. arranging care, etc.), this would be sufficient to come within Art 10(1)(a) of the Regulation.

Spouse

In *Netherlands* v *Reed* (Case 59/85) a UK national had travelled to The Netherlands to live with her long-term partner, who was also a UK national working in The Netherlands. The Court of Justice held that 'spouse' within Art 10(1), Regulation 1612/68 only referred to a married relationship.

Separate accommodation

In *Diatta* v *Land Berlin* (Case 267/83) the Court of Justice was faced with the question of whether or not a spouse of an EC worker could still come within the scope of Art 10(1) of the Regulation if they separated and were no longer living together.

The applicant was a Senegalese national (i.e. non-EC national) who had married a French national. Both were resident and working in Berlin. They later separated, moved into separate accommodation and she intended divorcing him. She applied for an extension to her residence permit. This was refused on the ground that she was no longer a family member of an EC national. She challenged this refusal and the national court referred the case to the Court of Justice for a preliminary ruling pursuant to Art 177 EC Treaty (now Art 234). Article 11, Regulation 1612/68 gives the member of an EC worker's family the right to take up any activity as an employed person throughout the territory of the Member State concerned, notwithstanding her nationality. The Court was asked whether a migrant worker's family must live permanently with the worker in order to qualify for a right of residence, or whether Art 11, Regulation 1612/68 gives a separate and independent right of residence.

18. In providing that a member of a migrant worker's family has the right to install himself with the worker, *Article 10 of the Regulation does not require that the member of the family in question must live permanently with the worker*, but, as is clear from Article 10(3), *only that the accommodation which the worker has available must be such as may be considered normal for the purpose of accommodating his family. A requirement that the family must live under the same roof permanently cannot be implied.*

19. In addition, such an interpretation corresponds to the spirit of Article 11 of the Regulation, which gives the member of the family the right to take up any activity as an employed person throughout the territory of the Member State concerned, even though that activity is exercised at a place some distance from the place where the migrant worker resides.

20. It must be added that the marital relationship cannot be regarded as dissolved so long as it has not been terminated by the competent authority. It is not dissolved merely

because the spouses live separately, even where they intend to divorce at a later date.
(emphasis added)

The Court did not rule that the family members had a separate and distinct right of
residence, because the family's right to reside in the host Member State was linked to
the right of the worker. However, the Court held that there was no necessity for them
to live under one roof. To decide otherwise would conflict with the right given to
family members by Art 11, Regulation 1612/68 to work within the host Member
State, notwithstanding their nationality. In this case, the EC worker was working in
Berlin in Germany. If his spouse had decided to exercise her rights under Art 11 and
work in Munich in Germany then quite clearly she would have needed to have
separate accommodation because it would be physically impossible to commute
between Berlin and Munich daily.

The application of this principle can be seen in *R v Immigration Appeal Tribunal
and Surinder Singh, ex parte Secretary of State for the Home Department* (Case C-
370/90). In this case, an Indian national married a UK national. They both worked in
Germany, subsequently returning to the United Kingdom. Following their return to
the United Kingdom they divorced. The Court of Justice held that because they were
working in Germany, the EC national was a Community worker exercising her EC
free movement rights, and therefore her Indian husband could claim rights as the
spouse of an EC worker. The Court did not comment on the effect of the divorce
because this was not relevant to the particular factual situation; they divorced *after*
they had returned to the United Kingdom.

THE EXERCISE OF WORKERS' RIGHTS

Departure from the home state

A person cannot benefit from free movement rights as a worker until he has taken
steps to leave his home state. Thus, in *Iorio* (Case 298/84), an Italian national from
Southern Italy, who complained of unequal treatment in relation to travel arrangements compared to local workers in the North, was held unable to rely on Community
law because the matter was wholly internal to Italy. A worker cannot rely on Art 39
EC Treaty unless he or she has exercised the right to free movement, or is seeking to
do so. The possibility that a person may do so at some time in the future is insufficient
(*Moser* (Case 180/83)). However, if he wishes to go to work in another Member State,
his own state is obliged to allow him to leave and to issue him with a valid identity
card or passport to enable him to do so. It cannot demand that he first obtain an exit
visa or equivalent document (Art 2(1), (2) and (3), Directive 68/360). UK nationals
are, therefore, entitled to be issued with a passport, and the directive will override the
discretion of the Foreign Secretary under the Royal Prerogative to withhold it (*R v
Secretary of State for Foreign and Commonwealth Affairs, ex parte Everett* [1989] QB
811). Limitations on departure may be imposed, however, where they are justified on
grounds of public policy, public security, or public health as defined by Community
law (see Chapter 15).

Entry

Since the creation of the Single European Market at the beginning of 1993, national frontier controls on the movement of European citizens and their families should have been removed (Art 14 EC Treaty). The removal of controls envisaged by Art 14 has not been realised. An attempt to challenge the remaining restrictions on the basis of Art 14 was, however, unsuccessful in the English High Court and the Court of Appeal in *R* v *Secretary of State for the Home Office, ex parte Flynn* (see Chapter 11). It was not intended that there would be no frontier supervision, but that routine checking of individual travel documents would be discontinued. Only where there was some basis for suspicion, justifying action on grounds of public policy, public security or public health, would the individual examination of passengers be justified. In several Member States this point has not been reached, particularly in the United Kingdom, where there is anxiety about relaxation of port controls. The permitted limitations on public policy, public security and public health are considered in Chapter 15.

Under Art 3(1), Directive 68/360, workers and their families (as defined in Art 10, Regulation 1612/68 (see above)) are entitled to enter 'simply on production of a valid identity card or passport. No entry visa or equivalent document may be demanded save from members of the family who are not nationals of a Member State'. The directive says that the Member State shall 'allow' them to enter, but the Court of Justice held in *R* v *Pieck* (Case 157/79) that beneficiaries of free movement did not require 'leave' (i.e. permission) from the host state, since the rights conferred by Art 39 EC Treaty are directly effective. Indeed, any process of granting 'leave' amounts to the imposition of an additional requirement on entry, contrary to the express words of Art 3(1), Directive 68/360. Furthermore, questioning of passengers coming to work in another Member State in relation to their ability to support themselves while there is also prohibited by Art 3(1) (*Commission* v *Netherlands* (C-68/89)). Family members who are not EU citizens may have to obtain a visa, but the host state is expected 'to accord to such persons every facility for obtaining any necessary visas' (Art 3(2), Directive 68/360).

Residence rights and residence permits

The right of residence of a worker derives from the direct effect of Art 39 EC Treaty. It cannot be subject to limitations imposed by the state, other than those justified by Community law. In effect, it means that, provided that he does nothing to warrant his expulsion, a worker has a right of residence as long as he continues in employment, or at least as long as he retains worker status. However, he is entitled to apply for a residence permit as soon as he has found work. That permit, the Court stated in *Echternach and Moritz* v *Netherlands Minister for Education and Science* (Cases 389 & 390/87), 'does not create the rights guaranteed by Community law and the lack of a permit cannot affect the exercise of those rights' (para 25).

Residence permits should be issued by the host state in such a way as to distinguish them from other permits issued to foreign nationals. Such permits should say that they are issued under Directive 68/360 and Regulation 1612/68 and should be free of charge, or, if there is a charge, it should not amount to any more than that charged to nationals of the host state for identity cards (Arts 4(2) and 9(1), Directive 68/360). Article 4(3), Directive 68/360 provides that a worker is entitled to be issued with a residence permit on production of:

- the document with which he entered the territory; and
- a confirmation of engagement issued by the employer.

Despite the clear words of this provision, the Court of Justice has held that a worker who no longer holds the original document with which he entered the country is entitled to be issued with a permit on the basis of a valid national identity card (*Giagounidis* (Case C-376/89)). Family members are entitled to be issued with a residence permit on production of the document with which they entered the territory and a document issued by the country of origin proving their relationship to the worker. In most cases these will be marriage and birth certificates, although for remoter relations a sworn declaration may be required. This will be the case where there is also an issue of whether or not they are dependent on the worker (Art 4(3)(e), Directive 68/360 and Art 10(2), Regulation 1612/68).

Workers do not have to wait until the permit is issued before they begin work (Art 5, Directive 68/360). The residence permit must be valid for the whole territory of the Member State which issued it, must be valid for at least five years from the date of issue and be automatically renewable (Art 6(1), Directive 69/360). Whether or not the worker holds a residence permit, he cannot, in any event, have his residence limited to any area in the Member State (*Rutili* (Case 36/75)). Workers who are to be employed for less than a year but for more than three months, may be issued with a permit that is valid only for the expected period of employment (Art 6(3), Directive 68/360). Residence permits cannot be withdrawn from the worker on the grounds that he is no longer in employment, either because he is involuntarily unemployed or is incapable of employment as a result of illness or accident. Whether or not an individual's unemployment is involuntary or not is a matter for the 'competent employment office' (Art 7(1), Directive 68/360).

Penalties for non-compliance with administrative formalities

The right of free movement for workers stems directly from Art 39 EC Treaty, and therefore a host Member State cannot refuse entry to a worker or deport a worker simply because he has not obtained a residence permit. This was decided by the Court of Justice in *Royer* (Case 48/75).

Royer, a French national, was working in Belgium. He was ordered to leave Belgium on the ground he was unlawfully resident there, having failed to comply with the administrative formalities requiring him to enrol on the population register. He complied with the order but subsequently returned. He was convicted of breaching the order (which prohibited his returning) and was convicted and sentenced. At a subsequent hearing the national court referred questions to the Court of Justice asking whether the right of residence was independent of the possession of a permit, and whether failure to comply with an administrative matter regarding application for a permit could constitute grounds for deportation.

28. These provisions show that the legislative authorities of the Community were aware that, while not creating new rights in favour of persons protected by Community law, the regulation and directives concerned determined the scope and detailed rules for the exercise of rights conferred directly by the Treaty.

29. It is therefore evident that the exception concerning the safeguard of public policy, security and public health contained in Articles 48(3) and 56(1) [now Arts 39(3) and 46(1)] of the Treaty must be regarded not as a condition precedent to the acquisition of the right of entry and residence but as providing the possibility, in individual cases where there is sufficient justification, of imposing restrictions on the exercise of a right derived directly from the Treaty ...

33. The grant of this [residence] permit is therefore to be regarded not as a measure giving rise to rights but as a measure by a Member State serving to prove the individual position of a national of another Member State with regard to the provisions of Community law ...

38. *The logical consequence of the foregoing is that the mere failure by a national of a Member State to complete the legal formalities concerning access, movement and residence of aliens does not justify a decision ordering expulsion.* (emphasis added)

The Court held that Community law did not prevent a Member State from adopting provisions to control non-nationals, which were backed up by penalties for non-observance, but *those sanctions must be proportionate*: i.e. they must not impose an excessive restriction on the free movement of workers. Accordingly, a fine may be proportionate (depending upon its level) but a term of imprisonment may not necessarily be so. A sanction of expulsion was not valid because it completely curtailed the Treaty right of free movement.

This issue was also considered by the Court in *Commission v Germany* (Case C-24/97).

German law required all residents to hold a valid identity document. However, the degree of fault and scale of fines imposed for a failure to hold the document differed according to nationality. A non-German EC national, who was exercising his free movement rights within Germany, and who *negligently* failed to obtain an identity document, would be liable to a fine of up to DM 5,000. In the case of a German national, an offence would be committed only if there was an *intentional* or *reckless disregard* to obtain an identity card, or a failure to produce it when required to do so, and the maximum fine that could generally be imposed was DM 1,000. The degree of fault for a non-national (i.e. negligence) compared to that of a national (i.e. intention or reckless disregard) could be proven more easily in the case of a non-national (and therefore a non-national was more likely to be found guilty of an offence than a national). The maximum fines which could be imposed were 500 per cent greater in the case of a non-national. The Commission issued Art 169 EC Treaty (now Art 226) proceedings against Germany, and the Court of Justice held that the German law breached the free movement of workers (and establishment and services (see Chapter 13)) provisions:

13. Community law does not prevent a Member State from carrying out checks on compliance with the obligation to be able to produce a residence permit at all times, provided that it imposes the same obligation on its own nationals as regards their identity card.

14. In the event of failure to comply with that obligation, the national authorities are entitled to impose penalties comparable to those attaching to minor offences committed

by their own nationals, such as those laid down in respect of failure to carry an identity card, provided that they do not impose a penalty so disproportionate that it becomes an obstacle to the free movement of workers.

15. In view of the foregoing, it must be held that, by treating nationals of other Member States residing in Germany disproportionately differently, as regards the degree of fault and the scale of fines, from German nationals when they commit a comparable infringement of the obligation to carry a valid identity document, the Federal Republic of Germany has failed to fulfil its obligation under Articles 48 [now 39], 52 [now 43] and 59 [now 49] of the Treaty, Article 4 of Directive 68/360 and Article 4 of Directive 73/148.

Articles 52 (now Art 43) and 59 (now Art 49) of the EC Treaty and Directive 73/148 applied to the freedom of establishment and the free movement of services (see Chapter 13). This case is also relevant to administrative formalities in respect of EC nationals' residency rights under those provisions. In this case, the Court simply affirmed the principles espoused in the *Royer* case (above). The operative part of the judgment can be summarised as follows:

- Member States can require EC nationals to produce residence permits, if nationals are under an obligation to produce their identity cards.
- A failure to comply can result in a penalty being imposed, but the penalty must be *comparable to those attaching to a minor offence committed by the state's own nationals.*
- However, the penalty must not be so disproportionate that it becomes an obstacle to the free movement of workers.

Restrictive administrative formalities

Administrative formalities themselves may infringe the free movement provisions if they are unduly restrictive. Although a Member State is permitted to require a Community worker to report to the police within a certain time period (in order to keep a record of population flow), that period must itself be proportionate. This was considered by the Court of Justice in *Watson and Belmann* (Case 118/75).

A British national stayed with an Italian family as an *au pair*. He failed to report his presence to the police as required under national law within three days of his arrival. The possible sanction for breach was deportation. He was charged and the Italian court referred the matter to the Court of Justice pursuant to Art 177 (now Art 234) EC Treaty, seeking advice on whether the deportation provision was compatible with Community law.

The Court ruled that Member States could adopt administrative provisions to ensure they had an exact knowledge of population movements; accordingly, a requirement to report to the police did not infringe the rules on free movement of persons. But such requirements may infringe these rules if they are unduly restrictive:

19. *In particular as regards the period within which the arrival of foreign nationals must be reported, the provisions of the Treaty are only infringed if the period fixed is unreasonable.* (emphasis added)

Rights of residence of work-seekers

Work-seekers have no right to be issued with a residence permit until they have found work. The right of EU citizens to enter another Member State to seek work has been considered above.

Loss of worker status on cessation of employment

As we have seen, a person remains a worker as long as he continues in employment. However, that status is not automatically lost when a person ceases to work. The provisions of the Treaty and the implementing legislation give little guidance on how long worker status is retained after cessation of employment. Article 39(3)(d) EC Treaty refers to the right 'to remain in the territory of a Member State after having been employed in that State, subject to conditions which shall be embodied in implementing legislation'. This is generally taken to mean the right to remain after retirement, or when the worker has become incapable of employment. Regulation 1251/70 has been made to this effect. The Court of Justice in *Lair* v *University of Hannover* (Case 39/86), referred to Art 39(3)(d) in more general terms, saying that 'migrant workers are granted certain rights linked to their status of worker even when they are no longer in the employment relationship'. It did not, however, indicate how long that status might continue. Since the right of residence is not dependent on the possession of a residence permit, it must be assumed that the provisions of Art 7(1), Directive 68/360 which exclude the loss of a residence permit, except in the event of 'voluntary' unemployment, apply no less to someone who has no such permit. This, at least, was the view of the United Kingdom Immigration Appeal Tribunal in *Lubbersen* v *Secretary of State for the Home Department* [1984] 3 CMLR 77.

The concept of 'voluntary' unemployment has had little attention from the Court of Justice, except in the context of the availability of 'social advantages' to those who retain worker status (Art 7(2), Regulation 1612/68 – see below). In connection with obtaining access to educational 'social advantages', the Court has held that a worker who leaves employment to take up a vocational course linked to his previous employment retains his status as a worker, even though he has voluntarily left that employment (*Raulin* (Case C-357/89), para 21). It is, further, likely that a worker who is voluntarily unemployed may become a work-seeker (*Tetik* v *Land Berlin* (Case C-171/95)). It would seem that the competent employment office under Art 7(1), Directive 68/360 may properly conclude that a person who refuses a reasonable offer of employment cannot genuinely be seeking work. Such a person would no longer have a right of residence, unless he has sufficient resources to bring him within the residual category of general residence rights conferred by Directive 90/364 (see Chapter 13).

EQUAL ACCESS TO EMPLOYMENT, HOUSING, EDUCATION AND SOCIAL RIGHTS UNDER REGULATION 1612/68

Equal access to employment

Regulation 1612/68 provides a wide range of directly enforceable rights designed to enable the migrant worker to obtain employment, and to provide the means by which the worker is guaranteed the possibility of improving his living and working conditions and promoting his social advancement. The right of freedom of movement, in order that it may be exercised by objective standards, in freedom and dignity, requires equality of treatment in fact and law in respect of all matters relating to the actual pursuit of activities as employed persons ... eligibility for housing ... the right to be joined by his family and the conditions for the integration of that family into the host country. (Preamble)

Articles 1, 3 and 4 of the Regulation require equal treatment in relation to applications for employment by those entitled to free movement rights and prohibit national quotas and other systems of limiting access to employment by foreign nationals. Where these exist, it is not sufficient for the Member State to issue instructions that they are not to be applied in relation to EU citizens. They must be repealed or amended so that Community workers are fully aware of their right to have access to that type of employment. In *Commission v France (Re French Merchant Seamen)* (Case 167/73), the Court held that a quota system excluding foreign deck officers from French ships, under the Code Maritime, was unlawful under both Arts 1–4, Regulation 1612/68 and Art 7 (now Art 12) EC Treaty. The Court refused to accept an assurance that it was not operated against Community nationals. Individuals needed to be able to see a clear statement of their rights in the national legislation. The Court came to a similar decision in relation to the reservation of seamen's jobs for Belgian nationals (*Commission v Belgium* (Case C-37/93)). The same principle of transparency was applied by the Court in relation to nursing posts in the German health service (*Commission v Germany (Re Nursing Directives)* (Case 29/84), para 23). The only exception to this rule is the right given to Member States by Art 39(3) EC Treaty to exclude foreign nationals (including EU citizens) from the public service. This exception is, however, very narrowly construed by the Court of Justice (see below). It is permissible to make a knowledge of the language a precondition of appointment, provided that it is necessary for the kind of post to be filled. This may be so, even if it is a language which the applicant will not be required to use to carry out the job. In *Groener v Minister of Education* (Case 379/87), the Court of Justice held that a requirement of Irish law that teachers in vocational schools in Ireland should be able to speak Gaelic was permissible under Art 3(1), Regulation 1612/68 because of the national policy to maintain and promote the national language as a means of sustaining national education and culture.

Under Regulation 1612/68, Community work-seekers are entitled to receive the same assistance as that offered to national workers from the state's employment offices (Art 5). Recruitment should not depend on medical, vocational and other criteria which are discriminatory on grounds of nationality (Art 6). The Court of Justice has held that refusal by a government department in one Member State to take into account the employment experience of a job applicant in the government service of another state amounted to unlawful discrimination (*Schöning-Kougebetopoulo v Hamburg* (Case C-15/96)). Those entitled to Community free movement rights are also entitled to equal access to any form of employment on an equal basis, even that requiring official authorisation (*Gül v Regierungspräsident Düsseldorf* (Case 131/85)). The only exception to this is in relation to the public service under Art 39(4) EC Treaty (see below).

The general prohibition on discrimination contained in Art 39(2) EC Treaty covers not only measures that directly impact on the rights of access to employment, but any conditions which may make the engagement of Community workers more difficult or result in their employment on less favourable terms. In *Allué and Others* v *Università degli studi di Venezia* (Case 33/88), the applicants challenged national legislation under which foreign language assistants' contracts at Italian universities were limited to one year, where no such limitation applied to other university teachers' contracts. There was evidence that about a quarter of those affected were from other Community states. On a preliminary reference under Art 177 (now Art 234) EC Treaty the Court held that, while it was permissible to adopt measures 'applying without distinction in order to ensure the sound management of universities ... such measures have to observe the principle of proportionality'. It concluded that the limitation constituted 'an insecurity factor' and was precluded by Art 39(2) EC Treaty.

Under Art 7(1) and (4), Regulation 1612/68, Community workers are entitled to the same treatment in relation to all conditions of employment, including pay, dismissal, reinstatement and re-employment, and they should benefit equally from the terms of any collective agreement negotiated with the management. They are entitled to participate equally in trade unions and staff associations, and should not be penalised for taking part in legitimate trade union activities (*Rutili* v *Ministre de l'Intérieur* (Case 36/75); *Association de Soutien aux Traveilleurs Immigrés* (Case C-213/90)). Restrictive contractual provisions which inhibit their re-employment in other Member States may breach Art 39 EC Treaty even if they are applied by a sporting body, such as a football association, which is not an emanation of the state, and which applies the rules to all employees of that category, irrespective of nationality (*Donà* v *Mantero* (Case 13/76) and *Bosman* (Case C-415/93)).

The public service exception

Although, as a general rule, Member States are not entitled to restrict access to any type of employment on grounds of nationality (Arts 12, 39(3) EC Treaty and Arts 1, 3, 4 and 6, Regulation 1612/68), there is one important exception. Under Art 39(4) EC Treaty, the right of equal access 'shall not apply to employment in the public service'. The term 'public service' is not defined in the Treaty or the implementing legislation and its meaning has been left to the Court of Justice. The Court has sought to limit its application, in order to give the widest employment opportunities to migrant workers.

In *Sotgiu* v *Deutsche Bundespost* (Case 152/73), Advocate-General Mayras offered a definition in his Opinion which has largely been adopted in subsequent judgments of the Court. He said:

> It is clear ... that for the interpretation of Article 48(4) [now Art 39(4)] the concept of employment in the public service cannot be defined in terms of the legal status of the holder of the post. A Community interpretation which would allow a uniform application of the exception provided for by this provision requires us therefore to have resort to factual criteria based on the duties which the post held within the administration entails and the activities actually performed by the holder of the post.

> *The exception will only be applicable if this person possesses a power of discretion with regard to individuals or if his activity involves national interests – in particular those which are concerned with the internal or external security of the State.* (emphasis added)

In *Commission* v *Belgium* (Case 149/79), the Court elaborated on the two central criteria proposed by Advocate-General Mayras. It held that the then Art 48(4)

> removes from the ambit of Article 48 (1)–(3) [now Art 39(1)–(3)] a series of posts which involve direct or indirect participation in the exercise of powers conferred by public law and duties designed to safeguard the general interests of the State or of other public authorities. Such posts in fact presume on the part of those occupying them the existence of a special relationship of allegiance to the State and reciprocity of rights and duties which form the foundation of the bond of nationality.

The Court, in fact, adopted a somewhat looser definition than that offered by Advocate-General Mayras. Instead of the limitation applying to a person with a power of discretion over individuals, the Court held that it applied to posts participating in the exercise of such powers. In other words, all those who acted under the instructions of the person vested with the public powers would be included in the exception. On this basis, the Court seems to have accepted that the posts of head technical office supervisor, principal supervisor, works supervisor, stock controller and night-watchman with the municipalities of Brussels and Auderghem fell within the exception. It is clear that a person with specific statutory powers, such as an environmental health officer, a registrar of births and deaths and a police officer, would all occupy posts in the United Kingdom falling within the exception relating to the exercise of public powers. In relation to national security and allegiance, appointments with the defence ministry dealing with issues relating to national defence, would fall within the 'allegiance' aspect of the exception. Some posts, such as a policeman at a defence establishment, would seem to fall within both.

The essential factor is the nature of the work, not the status of the employer or of the employee. In *Lawrie-Blum* v *Land Baden-Württemberg* (Case 66/85) the applicant was a trainee teacher employed by the Ministry of Education, with the status of a civil servant. The local state government argued that she came within the exception in Art 39(4), since she performed 'powers conferred by public law', including the preparation of lessons, the awarding of marks, and participation in the decision of whether or not pupils should move to a higher class. The Court rejected this argument. It held that the exception in Art 39(4) must be construed in such a way as to limit its scope to what is strictly necessary for safeguarding the interests which that provision allows Member States to protect. Access to posts could not be limited simply because the host state designated such employees as civil servants (*Bleis* v *Ministère de l'Education Nationale* (Case C-4/91)). To allow that would be to accept the power of the Member States to determine who fell within the exception of Art 39(4). The derogation permitted by Art 39(4) applies only to access to employment; it does not apply to the terms of employment once access has been permitted. It would not therefore be permissible for national and Community citizens to be engaged in the same work but on different contractual terms or conditions (*Sotgiu* v *Deutsche Bundespost* (Case 152/73); *Allué and Coonan* v *Universita di Venezia* (Case 33/88)).

The Court did not elaborate in *Lawrie-Blum* on the special qualities of public employment to which Art 39(4) is applicable, except to repeat, almost verbatim, its formulation in *Commission* v *Belgium* (above). It added that 'Those very strict conditions are not fulfilled in the case of a trainee teacher, even if he does in fact take the decisions described by the [government of] Baden-Württemberg' (para 28). Undoubtedly senior officers in the Government's Education Service would take major public policy decisions affecting education. It is, however, not clear at what level the Art 39(4) exception would start to apply. Only further decisions of the Court of Justice on specific cases can provide more detailed criteria for the application of this exception. In the meantime, the Commission issued a Notice in 1988 which indicates, provisionally at least, its view of a number of occupations in public employment which do not fall within the Art 39(4) exception. This includes posts in public health care, teaching in state education, non-military research, and public bodies involved in the administrative services. This is a far from exhaustive list, and does not, of course, have the force of law.

The public service in the United Kingdom

Until May 1991, all Civil Service posts in the United Kingdom were unavailable to all Community nationals, except Irish citizens (who are not classified as aliens under the Aliens Employment Act 1955). The 1955 Act did permit some limited exceptions, but it was far too sweeping to comply with Art 39(4), as interpreted by the Court of Justice in *Commission* v *Belgium* (above). The European Communities (Employment in the Civil Service) Order 1991 (SI 1991/1221) was brought into effect to enable citizens of Member States and their families to have access to Civil Service posts in accordance with Community law. It does not specify the posts which are to be opened up, but an internal Civil Service Circular (GC/378) listed a large number of jobs which would be open to EU citizens. The list includes bookbinders, catering staff, civil researchers, cleaners, dentists, porters, plumbers, teachers, translators and typists. However, the posts of curators in such museums as the National Gallery, the Tate Gallery, and the National Galleries of Scotland all remain closed to EU citizens.

The Circular acknowledges that the criteria for identifying posts that fall within Art 39(4) according to the concept of powers conferred by public law are difficult to apply in the United Kingdom, where the concept does not have the same meaning as in other Member States. Nevertheless, many of the posts which are still unavailable – such as that of clerical officer in the Department of Health, and museum curators – are clearly not within the narrow core of state activities envisaged by the Court of Justice in *Commission* v *Belgium* (above). Special restrictions imposed on access by Irish nationals to the Civil Service in Northern Ireland were held to be unlawful, disproportionate and not justified by what is now Art 39(4) by the High Court of Northern Ireland in *Re Katherine Colgan and Others* [1997] 1 CMLR 53.

Social advantages

Article 7(2), Regulation 1612/68 provides simply that the migrant worker 'shall enjoy the same social and tax advantages as national workers'. This provision has been a very fruitful source of rights for Community workers and their families. 'Social advantages' has been given the broadest of interpretations by the Court of Justice. In *Ministère Public* v *Even* (Case 207/78) the Court said ([1979] ECR 2019 at 2034) that:

> 'social advantages' were all those advantages which, whether or not [they] are linked to a contract of employment, are generally granted to national workers, *primarily because of their objective status as workers or by virtue of the mere fact of their residence on the national territory* and the extension of which to workers who are nationals of other Member States therefore seems suitable to facilitate their mobility. (emphasis added)

Advocate-General Mancini in his Opinion in *Gül* ([1986] ECR 1573 at 1579), above, also emphasised that the equal treatment provisions of Regulation 1612/68 are not confined to the employment relationship:

> The migrant worker is not regarded by Community law – nor is he by the internal legal systems – as a mere source of labour but is viewed as a human being. In this context the Community legislature is not concerned solely to guarantee him the right to equal pay and social benefits in connection with the employer–employee relationship, it also emphasised the need to eliminate obstacles to the mobility of the worker ... [and see, *Mr and Mrs F* v *Belgium* (Case 7/75), Opinion of A-G Trabucchi]

Adopting an approach of facilitating the removal of obstacles, and assisting the worker in the process of integrating into the social fabric of the Member State, the Court has held a very diverse range of benefits to be within the term 'social advantages'. In *Fiorinin (nee Cristini)* v *SNCF* (Case 32/75):

SNCF, the French railway company, offered a fare reduction to large families of French nationality. Cristini, an Italian national resident in France and the widow of an Italian national who had worked in France, was refused the reduction card on the basis of nationality. SNCF argued that Art 7(2), Regulation 1612/68 covered only advantages connected with the contract of employment. The national court made a former Art 177 (now Art 234) reference to the Court of Justice.

It should be noted that Cristini was entitled to remain in France under Art 3(2), Regulation 1251/70 (see below) as the spouse of a deceased worker. By Art 7 of that Regulation 'the right to equality of treatment established by Regulation 1612/68/EEC shall apply'. The Court of Justice held as follows:

> 12. ... [T]he reference to 'social advantages' in Article 7(2) cannot be interpreted restrictively.

> 13. It therefore follows that, in view of the equality of treatment which the provision seeks to achieve, the substantive area of application must be delineated so as to include all social and tax advantages, whether or not attached to the contract of employment, such as reduction in fares for large families.

> 14. It then becomes necessary to examine whether such an advantage must be granted to the widow and children after the death of the migrant worker when the national law provides that, at the request of the head of the family, each member of the family shall be issued with an identity card entitling him or her to the reduction.

> 15. If the widow and infant children of a national of the Member State in question are entitled to such cards provided that the request has been made by the father before his

death, the same must apply where the deceased father was a migrant worker and a national of another Member State.

16. It would be contrary to the purpose and the spirit of the Community rules on freedom of movement for workers to deprive the survivors of such a benefit following the death of the worker whilst granting the same benefit to the survivors of a national.

17. In this respect it is important to note the provisions of Regulation (EEC) No 1251/70 of the Commission on the right of workers to remain in the territory of a Member State after having been employed in that State.

18. Article 3(1) of that regulation provides that if a worker has acquired the right to remain in the territory of a Member State, the members of his family who are residing with him shall be entitled to remain there after his death, whilst Article 7 provides that: 'The right to equality of treatment, established by Council Regulation (EEC) No 1612/68, shall apply also to persons coming under the provisions of this regulation'.

19. *Accordingly the answer to the question should be that Article 7(2) of Regulation (EEC) No 1612/68 of the Council must be interpreted as meaning that the social advantages referred to by that provision include fare reduction cards issued by a national railway authority to large families and that this applies, even if the said advantage is only sought after the worker's death, to the benefit of his family remaining in the same Member State.* (emphasis added)

The Court held that 'social advantages' under Art 7(2) do not have to be connected with the worker's contract of employment (para 13). The Court also held that the right of equality of treatment was applicable not just to workers, but also, by virtue of Regulation 1251/70/EEC (which governs the right of workers and their families to remain in a Member State after having been employed there (see below)), to those surviving family members who had been residing with the deceased worker. In *Inzirillo v Caisse d'Allocations Familiales de l'Arrondissement de Lyon* (Case 63/76), the applicant was an Italian, working in France, who had been refused a disability allowance for his adult son. It was argued that Art 7(2), Regulation 1612/68 was not applicable because the allowance was not a social advantage to the worker (as provided for in Art 7(2)) but rather to his son. The Court held that offspring were covered by Art 10(1) of the Regulation and that an allowance for handicapped adults which a Member State awarded to its own nationals constituted a social advantage to a non-national in a case like this.

In *Mutsch* (Case 137/84), the applicant was a German national working in Belgium. He was charged with a criminal offence. In that part of Belgium, German-speaking Belgian nationals were allowed to have proceedings conducted in German. Mutsch was denied this right as a non-Belgian citizen, but the Court of Justice held that he was entitled to this facility as a 'social advantage' under Art 7(2).

Netherlands v Reed (Case 59/85) was considered above with regard to family members, but it provides an interesting illustration of how Art 7(2) may come to the aid of a worker where other provisions may not assist. The case concerned a British national who travelled to The Netherlands to live with her long-term partner, who was also a British national working in The Netherlands. The Court held that 'spouse' within Art 10(1), Regulation 1612/68 only referred to a married relationship. However, the problem was resolved by relying upon Art 7(2) of the Regulation on the specific facts of the case. In Dutch law, a foreigner who had a stable relationship with a working national was treated as that person's spouse. The Court held that this constituted a 'social advantage' within Art 7(2), as it would further the policy of free movement of persons.

The tax advantages referred to in Art 7(2), Regulation 1612/68 were held in *Biehl* (Case C-175/88) and *Schumacker* (Case C-279/93) to require that different rates of tax payable by residents and non-residents could not be applied to workers from other Member States.

Retaining worker status

The advantages to which migrant workers are entitled continue even after they have ceased employment, provided that they retain worker status. Thus, a worker who is not voluntarily unemployed can claim payments of 'social assistance' from the state. He is excluded from claiming them as social security benefits under Art 4(4), Regulation 1408/71 (see Chapter 14), but the Court held in *Scrivner* v *Centre Public d'Aide Sociale de Chastre* (Case 122/84) that 'a social benefit guaranteeing a minimum means of subsistence in a general manner' constituted a social advantage and the applicant was, therefore, entitled to the Belgian payment, MINIMEX, on this basis, despite the fact that national rules restricted it to Belgian citizens. Similarly, a person who loses her job and takes up an educational course is entitled to an educational grant as a social advantage (*Lair* v *University of Hannover* (Case 39/86)). This will be the case even if the worker gives up her job voluntarily, provided that there is a link between the job and the course that is undertaken (*Raulin* (Case C-357/89), paras 18 and 22).

Limits of Article 7(2)

Article 7(2), Regulation 1612/68 has been held to cover all social advantages whether or not they are actually linked to the employment, and even where they are only of indirect benefit to the worker himself. But the Court of Justice has made it clear that Art 7(2) can be invoked only where the advantage is actually of some direct or indirect benefit to the worker, and not just to a family member or dependant. In *Centre Public d'aide Sociale de Courcelles* v *Lebon* (Case 316/85) the Court of Justice stated:

> 12. However, the members of a worker's family, within the meaning of Article 10 of Regulation No 1612/68 qualify only indirectly for the equal treatment accorded to the worker himself by Article 7 of Regulation No 1612/68. Social Benefits such as the income guaranteed to old people by the legislation of a Member State (see the judgment of 12 July 1984 in Case 261/83 *Castelli* v *ONPTS* [1984] ECR 3199) or guaranteeing in general terms the minimum means of subsistence operate in favour of members of the worker's family only if such benefits may be regarded as a social advantage, within the meaning of Article 7(2) of Regulation No 1612/68, for the worker himself.

The Court of Justice was faced with a sensitive issue in *Ministère Public* v *Even and ONPTS* (Case 207/78).

Even was a French national working in Belgium. He received an early retirement pension from the Belgian authorities. A percentage was deducted from the pension based upon the number of years early he had received the pension. This rule was applied to all recipients, except Belgian nationals who were in receipt of a Second World War service invalidity pension granted by an Allied nation. Even was in receipt of a French war service pension and pleaded the principle of equality of treatment between nationals and non-nationals to claim the benefit of an early retirement pension without any deduction. The national court referred the matter to the Court of Justice for a preliminary ruling under the former Art 177 (now Art 234).

22. It follows from all its provisions and from the objective pursued that *the advantages which this regulation extends to workers who are nationals of other Member States are all those which, whether or not linked to a contract of employment, are generally granted to national workers primarily because of their objective status as workers or by virtue of the mere fact of their residence on the national territory and the extension of which to workers who are nationals of other Member States therefore* seems *suitable to facilitate their mobility within the Community.*

23. ... *The main reason for a benefit such as that granted by the Belgian national legislation in question to certain categories of national workers is the services which those in receipt of the benefit have rendered in wartime to their own country and its essential objective is to give those nationals an advantage by reason of the hardships suffered for that country.*

24. *Such a benefit,* which is based upon a scheme of national recognition, *cannot therefore be considered as an advantage granted to a national worker by reason primarily of his status of worker* or resident on the national territory and for that reason does not fulfil the essential characteristics of the 'social advantages' referred to in Article 7(2) of Regulation No 1612/68. (emphasis added)

The Court (at para 22) set out three factors to be taken into account when deciding whether a worker is entitled to a particular benefit in a host Member State under Art 7(2):

- status as a worker;
- residence on national territory;
- suitability of the benefit in facilitating worker mobility within the Community.

In this case the Court held that the benefit, which was linked to wartime military service, was not suitable to facilitate the free movement of workers, and therefore did not constitute a 'social advantage' (para 24). This is not surprising given the sensitive nature of what the Court was being asked to adjudicate upon, and the decision should, perhaps, be confined to its particular facts.

In *Kaba* v *Secretary of State for the Home Department* (Case C-356/98):

Mr Kaba (K), a Yugoslav national, married a French national who found work in the United Kingdom in April 1994. In 1996 K applied for indefinite leave to remain in the United Kingdom, but was refused on the ground that paragraph 255 of the Immigration Rules 1994 was not satisfied because his wife (the EC national) had only remained in the United Kingdom as an EC worker for one year and ten months and not the required four years. After four years, K's wife could apply for indefinite leave to remain in the United Kingdom, as the spouse of an EC worker. However, K challenged this refusal maintaining that there was discrimination, contrary to Art 7(2), Regulation 1612/68. This was based upon the fact that if K's wife had been a UK citizen then he would have been eligible for indefinite leave to remain in the United Kingdom after just one year, rather than the four-year requirement which applied to EC workers. The national court referred the matter to the Court of Justice.

The relevant Community rules conferred on the spouses of migrant workers who were nationals of other Member States a right of residence co-extensive with that accorded to those workers.

However, in seeking to remain in the UK, K was applying, in his capacity as the spouse of a migrant worker, for a more extensive right of residence than that conferred on the migrant worker herself.

Even if such a right constituted a social advantage within article 7(2) of Regulation 1612/68, there was still the question whether legislation such as that in issue constituted discrimination contrary to that provision.

The equal treatment rule laid down in article 7 prohibited not only overt discrimination but also all covert forms of discrimination which, by the application of other distinguishing criteria, led to the same result.

It was true that where rules made the grant of an advantage subject to the requirement that the beneficiary be present and settled in national territory, that condition was more easily met by national workers than by workers who were nationals of other Member States, but, as Community law stood at present, the right of nationals of a Member State to remain in another Member State was not unconditional.

For example, article 8a of the EC Treaty (now article 18 EC), while granting citizens of the Union the right to move freely within the Member States, expressly referred to the limitations and conditions laid down in the Treaty and the measures adopted to give it effect. Accordingly, the Member States were entitled to rely on any objective difference there might be between their own nationals and those of other Member States, when they laid down the conditions under which leave to remain indefinitely in their territory was to be granted to the spouses of such persons.

In particular, they were entitled to require the spouses of persons who did not themselves enjoy an unconditional right of residence to be resident for a longer period than that required for the spouses of persons who already enjoyed such a right, before granting the same right to them.

Once leave to remain indefinitely had been granted, no condition could be imposed on the person to whom such leave had been granted, and therefore the authorities must be able, when the application was made, to require the applicant to have established sufficiently enduring links with the State.

The Court therefore held that legislation which required spouses of migrant workers who were nationals of other Member States to have resided in the territory of that Member State for four years before they became entitled to apply for indefinite leave to remain, but which required residence of only 12 months for the spouses of persons who were settled in that territory, did not constitute discrimination contrary to Art 7(2), Regulation 1612/68. The Court therefore did not need to decide whether or not this would otherwise have been a social advantage within Art 7(2).

Social advantages for work-seekers

Access to social advantages is, however, conditional upon the acquisition of worker status. A person who has never worked in the host state will not be eligible. In *Centre Public d'Aide Sociale de Courcelles* v *Lebon* (Case 316/85), the applicant, a French national living in Belgium, claimed MINIMEX. She lived with her father, also French, who was a retired migrant worker. She no longer satisfied the 'family member' provisions of Art 10, Regulation 1612/68 because she was over the age of 21 and no longer dependent upon her father. She had never found employment. The Court held in this case that, since she was no longer dependent, she was not entitled to a social advantage as a member of his family, and could not claim such an advantage as a work-seeker in her own right:

> It must be pointed out that the right to equal treatment with regard to social and tax advantages applies only to workers. Those who move in search of employment qualify for equal treatment only as regards access to employment in accordance with Article 48 [now Art 39] of the EEC Treaty and Articles 2 and 5 of Regulation No 1612/68.

The decision is, in some ways, surprising. The Court held that she was not entitled to social advantages because these are payable only to 'workers', as compared to the benefits in Title I Regulation 1612/68, which are available to all 'nationals' of other Member States. This is certainly in keeping with the text of the Regulation. However, Ms Lebon, in seeking work, was exercising a right conferred upon her by Art 39(3) EC Treaty and, in doing so, she was entitled to expect that she would be treated by the national authorities in the same way as a fellow Belgian work-seeker, who would be entitled to be paid MINIMEX. The Court did not deal with this aspect, nor did the opinion of Advocate-General Lenz. It is likely that the decision was motivated as much by policy as by legal considerations. Some of the submissions by Member States indicated an anxiety about 'social tourism' and abuse of national welfare systems.

Education and vocational training

Migrant workers are entitled, by virtue of Art 7(3), Regulation 1612/68, to equal access with local workers to vocational schools and retraining centres. Article 12 also provides that the workers' children are to be admitted to the host state's 'general, educational, apprenticeship and vocational training courses under the same conditions as nationals of that State'.

Neither the Treaty nor any implementing measures define the meaning of vocational training, but the Court of Justice in *Gravier* v *City of Liège* (Case 293/83) said that 'any form of education which prepares for a qualification for a particular profession, trade or employment or which provides the necessary skills for such a profession, trade or employment is vocational training whatever the age and level of the pupil or student'. The applicant's course in *Gravier*, that of strip cartoon design, clearly fell into that category. The Court held in *Blaizot* (Case 24/86) that whether all, or part, of a course was 'vocational' was for the national court to decide on the facts. Academic work at university level was not excluded, provided either that the final academic examination gave the required qualification for a particular trade, profession or employment, or:

the studies in question provide specific training and skills ... [which] ... the student needs for the pursuit of a profession, trade or employment, even if no legislative or administrative provisions make the acquisition of that knowledge a prerequisite for that purpose. (para 19)

Despite the need for a course of study with at least some career-orientated skills, the Court, in *Lair* v *University of Hannover* (Case 39/86), did not appear to doubt that a course in Romance and Germanic languages, that had no immediate vocational orientation, was, nonetheless, a 'vocational course' (see Flynn, 1988).

The entitlement to equal access includes non-discrimination in relation to course fees (*Gravier*, above), so that, on any distinctions drawn by the host state between 'home' and 'foreign' students, EU citizens and their families exercising free movement rights should be classified as 'home' students. In addition, equal access applies not only to courses in the host state, but also to courses in other states, where the host state assists its own nationals in relation to attendance at foreign universities and colleges (*Matteucci* (Case 235/87)).

The educational rights of workers' children extend to a right to be admitted to the host state's primary and secondary schooling system, as well as to vocational courses in further and higher education (*Casagrande* (Case 9/74)). Besides equal treatment in relation to course fees, students are entitled to equal access to educational grants. In the case of the children of workers, this right is dependent on the child continuing as a dependant of the worker (Arts 10 and 12, Regulation 1612/68), who must remain resident in the host state, or, alternatively, the student must have acquired the status of worker himself. Both possibilities were discussed in the important case of *Brown* v *Secretary of State for Scotland* (Case 197/86).

Brown, who was a French national of Anglo-French origin, had applied for a discretionary grant from the Scottish Education Department to attend an electrical engineering course at Cambridge. Prior to the commencement of the course, he had obtained employment with an engineering company in Edinburgh for eight months. This job was described as 'pre-university industrial training'. Although he did not qualify for a grant under the Scottish regulations, he argued that he was entitled to receive one either as a social advantage in his capacity as a worker, under Art 7(2), Regulation 1612/68 or, alternatively, as a child of a worker under Art 12, since his father, although no longer resident in Scotland, had worked there as his last place of employment. He was refused on both counts and the case was referred to the Court of Justice under what is now Art 234.

Although the Court emphasised that it was for the national court to decide whether or not a particular course was 'vocational', there seems little doubt that this course met the criteria which the Court had laid down in *Blaizot* (above). It held that, although access to education, in terms of admission fees and admission criteria, was within the Treaty (and thus within the prohibition against discrimination under Art 12, Regulation 1612/68), access to educational grants was not. Article 12 did not, therefore, assist the applicant unless he qualified either as a worker or as a child of a worker. The Court, in a somewhat ambivalent decision, held that a person who

enters into an employment relationship in the host State for a period of eight months with a view to subsequently taking up university studies there in the same field of activity ... is to be regarded as a worker within the meaning of Article 7(2) of Regulation 1612/68.

That should have concluded the issue, but the Court then added (at para 27), in answer to the fourth question raised by the national court:

> it cannot be inferred from that finding that a national of a Member State will be entitled to a grant for studies in another Member State by virtue of his status as a worker where it is established that he acquired that status exclusively as a result of his being accepted for admission to university to undertake the studies in question. In such circumstances, *the employment relationship, which is the only basis for the rights deriving from Regulation No. 1612/68, is merely ancillary to the studies to be financed by the grant.* (emphasis added)

As we have seen, where the employment is 'ancillary' to some other purpose – e.g. 'therapy' as in the case of *Bettray* ((Case 344/87) above – the individual may not be regarded as a worker under either Art 39 EC Treaty or Art 7(2), Regulation 1612/68, for the purpose of social advantages. On that basis the Court, and the Advocate-General, could well have concluded that Brown was not a worker at all. His entitlement to social advantages would not, therefore, have arisen, as in the case of *Lebon*, above. It chose, however, to hold that he was both a worker and disentitled to the social advantages to which workers would normally be entitled in these circumstances! The Court had less difficulty in concluding that he could not be a child of a worker either, because he was born after his parents had ceased to work and reside in the host state.

Family rights

Regulation 1612/68 confers extensive family rights on the worker. Although much of this section has been discussed above, it is useful to reconsider the rights relating to family members of an EC worker, now that the substantive provisions under the Treaty and secondary legislation have been examined.

Once he is in employment, an EC worker may either be accompanied by, or be joined by, his spouse and their descendants who are under the age of 21 or who are dependent, and his own dependent relatives in the ascending line and those of his spouse. That means that dependent children, grandchildren, and even great-grandchildren have the right to install themselves with the worker. Likewise, parents and grandparents of both spouses, if dependent, could join the worker. Other family members not coming within the ascending or descending lines, such as aunts and uncles and nephews and nieces, if dependent on the worker, or living under his roof, should have their entry 'facilitated' (Art 10(1) and (2), Regulation 1612/68). 'Facilitation' might seem to fall short of a right to admission. However, read in conjunction with Art 1, Directive 68/360, which requires the abolition of restrictions on the free movement of workers and of 'members of their families *to whom Regulation 1612/68 applies*' (emphasis added), and Art 3, Directive 68/360, which confers a right of entry on the worker and the family members defined in Art 1 of the same directive, it would seem that they also have a right of entry. In the case of family members who are not nationals of a Member State, it is permissible that they should obtain visas before being admitted. In such cases Member States should 'accord to such persons every facility for obtaining any necessary visa' (Art 3(2), Directive 68/360).

There should be no need to prove the relationship at the point of entry, although, for the purpose of acquisition of a residence permit, proof of the relationship, normally in the form of marriage and birth certificates, and proof of the dependency in the form of documentary evidence from the state of origin, will have to be produced when the application for a residence permit is made (Art 4(3)(c)–(e), Directive 68/360). Rights of residence of spouses do not depend on their continuing cohabitation. In *Diatta v Land Berlin* (Case 267/83), the Court of Justice held that the right of residence subsisted as long as the marriage continued, irrespective of whether or not the parties to the marriage were still together. Once the marriage is dissolved, the spouse's right of residence in that capacity would appear to terminate. That was the decision of the House of Lords in *R v Secretary of State, ex parte Sandhu*, *The Times*, 10 May 1985, although Community free movement rights must be read in the light of Art 8 of the European Convention on Human Rights (respect for family life). In *Berrehab*, judgment of European Court of Human Rights, 21 June 1988, series A, No. 138, pp. 15–16, the Court held that the expulsion of a divorced husband whose child remained in Belgium, breached Art 8. The Court held that expulsion in such circumstances did not, however, automatically breach the Convention for it depended on the degree of contact between the divorced parent and the child. Thus, the person whose marriage has terminated does not automatically lose the right of residence. It will depend on whether he or she would leave children or other relatives in the state in question, and the extent to which they were, in fact, part of a close family unit (see Schermers, 1991). The Court of Justice has yet to consider the position arising on the divorce of the worker and spouse. In the context of rights of residence of a Turkish national under the EEC–Turkey Association Agreement, the Court has held that where a Turkish national was working lawfully in a Member State, the fact that his marriage to a Community national, the original basis of his right of residence, had been dissolved did not affect the legality of his continuing residence (*Kus v Landeshauptstadt Wiesbaden* (Case C-237/91); *Buyukyilmas v Secretary of State for the Home Department* (11769) 19 January 1995 (Immigration Appeal Tribunal) (unreported)).

Family free movement rights derive directly from Community law. They apply not only to EU citizens who work in other Member States in relation to those states, but also in relation to their own state where they have returned to it after having worked abroad. In *R v Immigration Appeal Tribunal and Surinder Singh* (Case C-370/90), the Court of Justice held that a national of a Member State who has gone to another Member State in order to work there as an employed person under Art 39 EC Treaty, and returns to establish himself as a self-employed person in the territory of the Member State of which he is a national, has the right to return to that state under the same conditions as are laid down by Regulation 1612/68 or Directive 68/360. That meant that the obligation under UK immigration law for a spouse to establish that the 'primary purpose' of his entry was the marriage and not to secure entry to or residence in the United Kingdom did not apply. This UK immigration rule has since been abolished.

Members of the family have a right to work in the host state. Under Art 11, Regulation 1612/68, the worker's spouse and those of his children who are under the age of 21 or dependent on him, are entitled to take up any activity as an employed person throughout the territory of the host state, even if they are not nationals of any Member State. In *Gül* (Case 131/85), the applicant sought to rely on Art 11. He was a Turkish-Cypriot doctor, married to an Englishwoman working as a hairdresser in

Germany. When he applied for authorisation to practise medicine in Germany he was refused on account of his nationality. On a reference under what is now Art 234, the Court of Justice held that, provided he had the qualifications necessary to practise in the host state, according to national legislation, he was entitled to practise his profession in that state by virtue of Art 11, Regulation 1612/68.

Housing provisions

The entry of family members is conditional upon the worker having available for them 'housing considered as normal for national workers in the region where he is employed' (Art 10(3), Regulation 1612/68). This condition is operative only at the time of the family's entry. An attempt by the German authorities to make access to reasonable housing provisions a precondition for the renewal of a resident permit was held by the Court of Justice in *Re Housing of Migrant Workers: EC Commission* v *Germany* (Case 249/86) to be unlawful. The reference to adequate housing in Art 10(3) related only to the 'installation' of the worker's family. The Court emphasised the importance of family reunion, as guaranteed by Art 8 of the European Convention on Human Rights, and the need to 'facilitate ... the integration of the worker and his family into the host Member State without any difference in treatment in relation to nationals of that State' (paras 10 and 11).

The need for equal treatment in the housing field is dealt with in Art 9, Regulation 1612/68. Under this provision, the 'worker shall enjoy all the rights and benefits accorded to national workers in matters of housing, including ownership of the housing he needs'. If his family has remained in the country whence he came, they shall be considered for this purpose as residing in the region where he is working. On this basis, the worker is entitled to be treated both for the purpose of applications for public housing, and the purchase of a private house, as having his family with him. If he loses the housing which he initially obtained for his family, through no fault of his own, he is entitled to equal access, for example, to emergency housing provision under Part III of the Housing Act 1985, in the United Kingdom. Even if he has housing in his country of origin, provided that he organised adequate housing on the arrival of the family, the family cannot be expected to return to the country of origin (compare, *De Falco* v *Crawley Borough Council* [1980] QB 460 and *R* v *Hillingdon LBC, ex parte Islam* [1981] 3 WLR 942 at 953 (HL)). The Court of Justice held in *Commission* v *Germany* (above) that the acquisition of housing solely to secure a residence permit could be penalised, if the family then moved into less suitable accommodation, but that any penalty should fall short of measures leading to expulsion (para 14).

Retirement

Article 39(3) EC Treaty confers on the worker the right to remain in the host Member State, with his family, after having been employed there. The conditions under which this right is exercisable following retirement, or premature cessation of work due to an accident at work or to a disease contracted while working, are laid down in Regulation 1251/70. The worker must have been employed for at least a year in the host state before he is entitled to retire there on reaching the age at which the state retirement pension becomes payable (Art 2(1)(a)). If the worker becomes incapable of working having been employed for more than two years in the host state, he can stay on there for as long as he likes. He can remain, irrespective of his period of residence, if he is incapacitated by an accident or disease contracted at work (Art 2(1)(b)). His family, as defined in Art 10, Regulation 1612/68, is entitled to remain as long as he does.

If the worker should die before retirement, his family is entitled to remain in the host state, provided the deceased worker had lived there continuously for more than two years. If he died as a result of an industrial accident or occupational disease, there is no qualifying period to be satisfied to enable the family to remain, nor is there such a qualifying period if the widow or widower either is a national of the host state, or was one before his or her marriage (Arts 2 and 3, Regulation 1251/70). The families of deceased workers are entitled to all the social advantages that are available to the families of active and retired workers (*Cristini* v *SNCF* (Case 32/75) (see above)). They must also be issued with a residence permit on application, valid for a period of five years, which is automatically renewable (Art 6, Regulation 1251/70).

The entitlement to retire to another Member State is not limited to those who have worked there. Under Directive 90/365, EU citizens who have worked either as employees or in a self-employed capacity in one Member State are entitled to retire to another Member State. The directive is made possible by the fact that, under Art 10, Regulation 1408/71, recipients of invalidity or old age cash benefits or pensions for accidents at work or occupational diseases are entitled to continue to receive those benefits and pensions even if they reside in the territory of a Member State other than the one that pays the benefits (see recitals of Directive 90/365, and Chapter 14). It has a more limited application, however, than Regulation 1251/70, and could result in unwary individuals getting into difficulties, especially those who retire to a Member State with a Mediterranean climate but with a less developed welfare state than that of their country of origin.

The right of residence is dependent on the retired person having, first, a retirement or other pension of an amount sufficient to avoid becoming a burden on the social security system of the host state, and secondly, an all-risks sickness insurance scheme. Pensioners are entitled to be accompanied by their families, who are, in this case, limited to spouse and dependent children and grandchildren, and dependent relatives in the ascending line of the pensioner and his spouse. Unlike Art 10(2), Regulation 1612/68, there are no provisions for the entry of collateral relatives (Art 1(2), Directive 90/365). Pensioners are entitled to be issued with residence permits, but the period of validity can be limited to two years. On application and on renewal the host state is entitled to demand proof that the individual continues to meet the subsistence and insurance criteria (Art 2(1)). Unlike those who retire in the state where they worked, the beneficiaries of this directive are not entitled to social advantages under Art 7(2), Regulation 1612/68, so they will have to meet payments for medical treatment either under their sickness insurance policy or from their own resources.

Further reading

Craig, P. and De Burca, G. (1998) *EU Law Text, Cases and Materials* (2nd edn), OUP, Chapter 16.

Daniele, L., 'Non-Discriminatory Restrictions and the Free Movement of Persons' (1997) 22 EL Rev 191.

Davies, P., 'Posted workers: Single Market or protection of national labour systems?' (1997) 34 CML Rev 571.

Farmer, P., 'Article 48 EC and the Taxation of Frontier Workers' (1995) 32 CML Rev 310.

Flynn J., 'Vocational Training in Community Law and Practice' [1988] 8 YEL 59.

Green N., Hartley T.C. and Usher, J. (1991) *The Legal Foundations of the Single European Market*, Pt II, OUP.

Handoll, J., 'Article 48(4) EEC and Non-National Access to Public Employment' (1988) 13 EL Rev 223.

Lonbay, J., 'Education and Law: The Community Context' (1989) 14 EL Rev 363.

Pickup, D., 'Reverse Discrimination and Freedom of Movement of Workers' (1986) 23 CML Rev 135.

Schermers, H. (1991) 'Human Rights and Free Movement of Persons', in Schermers, H. (ed.) *Free Movement of Persons in Europe: Legal Problems and Experiences*, Martinus Nijhoff.

Steiner, J. and Woods, L. (2000) *Textbook on EC Law* (7th edn), Blackstone Press, Chapter 20.

Watson, P., 'Notes on Free Movement of Workers' (1985) 9 EL Rev 335; (1989) 14 EL Rev 415.

Weatherill, S. (2000) *Cases and Materials on EC Law* (5th edn), Blackstone Press, Chapter 9.

Chapter 13

FREEDOM OF ESTABLISHMENT AND THE PROVISION AND RECEIPT OF SERVICES

INTRODUCTION

Individuals may wish to move to another Member State to engage in a business or profession in a self-employed capacity. Article 43 EC Treaty (previously Art 52), provides for the freedom of establishment:

> Within the framework of the provisions set out below, restrictions on the freedom of establishment of nationals of a Member State in the territory of another Member State shall be prohibited. Such prohibition shall also apply to restrictions on the setting up of agencies, branches or subsidiaries by nationals of any Member State established in the territory of any Member State.
>
> Freedom of establishment shall include the right to take up and pursue activities as self-employed persons and to set up and manage undertakings, in particular companies or firms within the meaning of the second paragraph of Article 48, under the conditions laid down for its own nationals by the law of the country where such establishment is effected, subject to the provisions of the Chapter relating to capital.

'Establishment' is not defined in the Treaty or the implementing legislation. However, Art 43 requires the abolition of restrictions on the freedom of establishment of nationals of a Member State in the territory of another Member State. Freedom of establishment includes the right of individuals and companies to set themselves up in business (a permanent or settled place of business) in a Member State. It covers the self-employed and in addition the practising of a profession or trade (e.g. lawyer, doctor, vet) on a permanent or semi-permanent basis. Naturally, a worker may seek to practise a profession in another Member State, and therefore the provisions relating to workers will apply (see Chapter 12) in addition to those of establishment which relate to recognition of the profession or trade.

Articles 49 and 50 EC Treaty provide for the abolition of restrictions on individuals to provide services in a Member State other than that in which they are established. Article 49 provides that:

> Within the framework of the provisions set out below, restrictions on freedom to provide services within the Community shall be prohibited in respect of nationals of Member States who are established in a State of the Community other than that of the person for whom the services are intended.

The Council may, acting by a qualified majority on a proposal from the Commission, extend the provisions of this Chapter to nationals of a third country who provide services and who are established within the Community.

Article 50 provides that services shall be considered to be 'services' within the meaning of the Treaty 'where they are normally provided for remuneration'. Article 50 lists such services as including activities of an industrial and commercial character, activities of craftsmen and activities of the professions. This is, however, far from being an exhaustive list. The person providing the service 'may, in order to do so, temporarily pursue his activity in the State where the service is provided'. This is 'without prejudice to the right of establishment'. There is, in fact, a close link to the right of establishment. The right to provide the service confers a right of residence as long as the service is provided.

If the service provider wishes to provide that service in the host state on a long-term basis then Art 43 will apply, and he may become established in that state. The crucial element that differentiates the service provider from the established business is the process of 'setting up'. This may involve anything from leasing or buying business premises, to acquiring a licence to run a company in the host state (see *Steinhauser* v *City of Biarritz* (Case 197/84) and *R* v *Secretary of State for Transport, ex parte Factortame* (Case C-213/89)). The Court of Justice referred to 'establishment' in the *Factortame* case as 'the actual pursuit of an economic activity through a fixed establishment for an indefinite period' (para 20).

None of the Treaty provisions confers a right to go to another Member State to *receive* services, but Directive 73/148 is more wide-ranging than Arts 43, 49 and 50 EC Treaty. It provides for the abolition of restrictions on the movement and residence of:

- nationals of a Member State who are established or who wish to establish themselves in another Member State in order to pursue activities as self-employed persons or who wish to provide services in that state; and
- nationals of Member States wishing to go to another Member State *as recipients of services*.

The scope of the Treaty provisions and the directive in relation to the provision of services, the receipt of services and the right of establishment will be examined in turn.

THE PROVISION OF SERVICES

Article 49 EC Treaty is directly effective (see, e.g., *Van Binsbergen* (Case 33/74)). It will not apply to a totally internal situation. In *Peter Jagerskiold* v *Torolf Gustafsson* (Case C-97/98):

On 29 May 1997 Mr Gustafsson (G) fished with a spinning rod in waters belonging to Mr Jagerskiold (J) in the commune of Kimoto in Finland. Two days earlier, on 27 May 1997, he had paid the fishing licence fee provided for in Finnish law, which allowed him to practise that type of fishing even in private waters.

J brought an action before the national court for a declaration that G might not, without his permission, fish with a rod in his waters, notwithstanding the fact that J had paid the fishing licence fee provided for by Finnish law. In support of his action, J argued that the Finnish law, on which the right to fish with a rod was based, was contrary to the rules of the EC Treaty concerning the free movement of goods or to those relating to the freedom to provide services. The Court held that the provisions relating to the free movement of goods did not apply, but those relating to the freedom to provide services did apply. However:

> ... concerning the provisions of the Treaty relating to the freedom to provide services, it is sufficient to observe that these provisions are not applicable to activities which are confined in all respects within a single Member State.
>
> *The legal proceedings pending before the Tingsratt are between two Finnish nationals, both established in Finland, concerning the right of one of them to fish in waters belonging to the other situated in Finland*
>
> Such a situation does not present any link to one of the situations envisaged by Community law in the field of the free provision of services. (emphasis added)

Remuneration

Only those services which are provided for remuneration entitle the providers and recipients to move to another Member State to provide and receive them. The Court of Justice in *Belgium v Humbel* (Case 263/86) said that 'the essential characteristic of remuneration is that it constitutes the countervailing financial advantage for the services in question and is normally fixed between the supplier and the recipient of the service'. It held, on this basis, that courses of study provided in the framework of a national educational system were not provided for remuneration. The situation was not affected by the fact that students had to pay a registration fee or some other charge. By establishing and maintaining a national educational system, 'the State does not intend to engage in activities for which remuneration is received, but is fulfilling its duty to its people in the social, cultural and educational fields' (paras 17 and 18). Education can, however, be a service if it is provided by a private body on a commercial basis (see *Luisi and Carbone v Ministero del Tesoro* (Case 286/83)). The services are, therefore, either of a commercial character, or they are, at least, provided in exchange for money or money's worth.

The Court of Justice has also held that there must be an *economic* link in order to come within the provisions of the Treaty. In *SPUC v Grogan* (Case C-159/90):

Ireland had a restriction on the publication of information about the provision of abortion in other Member States (abortion was (and remains) illegal in Ireland). A Students' Union in Dublin provided information about abortion services which were lawfully available in London. This practice was challenged before the Irish Courts by the Society for the Protection of Unborn Children (SPUC).

Although the Court of Justice held that the provision of abortion could constitute a service, it held that because the Students' Union was not distributing the information *on behalf of the economic operators* (i.e. the clinics providing the service (abortions)) Ireland could restrain its activity. The Students' Union had no economic link with the clinics – it was not being paid. The case may have been decided differently if the clinics themselves had been advertising their services, because clearly there would have been an *economic link*, or if the Students' Union had been acting as the agent of the clinics (and was being paid). This case was also politically sensitive given that abortion was illegal under Ireland's constitution. There could therefore have been strong policy consider-ations for the Court's decision.

Meaning of 'service'

The Court of Justice considered the meaning of 'service' in *Schindler* (Case C-275/92).

In this case, the undertakings concerned were agents of four local state lotteries in Germany. They sent letters from The Netherlands to the United Kingdom enclosing application forms with invitations to participate in the German lotteries. The letters were confiscated by Customs and Excise on the grounds that they infringed national legislation on lotteries and gaming. The Court held that the letters were not 'goods', so the restrictions did not fall to be considered under Art 29 EC Treaty.

Were they, then, a service? The Court decided that they were. The services provided by the operators of the lottery enabled purchasers of tickets to participate in a game of chance with the hope of winning, by arranging for that purpose for the stakes to be collected, the draws to be organised and the prizes for winnings to be ascertained and paid out. The services were 'normally provided for remuneration', represented by the price of the lottery ticket. They were cross-border, since they were offered in a Member State other than that in which the lottery operator was established. The Court reached a similar conclusion in relation to the offer of financial services by telephone to potential recipients in another state (*Alpine Investments BV* v *Minister van Financiën* (Case C-384/93)), and similarly in relation to the provision of insurance (*Safir* v *Skattemyndigheten i Dalarnas Lan* (Case C-118/96)).

Providers of services and their workers

The provision of services may be by sole traders, companies or partnerships. If the providers are companies, they do not need to be owned or controlled by nationals of the Member State in which they are based, nor do the employees of the company providing a service in another Member State have to be EU citizens. They should be able to operate in other Member States without restriction. In *Van der Elst* v *OMI* (Case C-43/93):

The claimant operated a demolition company which was established in Belgium. He employed a number of foreign workers, many of them from Morocco. They had work permits and were lawfully employed in Belgium. The company was engaged to carry out a demolition contract in France. Foreign employees were not permitted by the French authorities to work on the contract without French work permits. On an Art 177 reference (now Art 234), the Court of Justice held that the Belgian undertaking was providing a service under Arts 49 and 50. The question before the Court, which is relevant here, was whether the company could transfer its workforce to France to service the demolition contract.

The Court of Justice held that where a service is being provided pursuant to Arts 49 and 50 EC Treaty, the provider of the service could bring its workforce of whatever nationality to perform the task. Any attempt to impose further controls on its work-force would amount to a restriction on the provision of services and would be unlawful. The imposition of further work permit requirements would, the Court said, amount to the duplication of the procedures the company had already gone through in its home state.

Objective justification

As with the free movement of workers, if a restriction on the freedom to provide services is found to exist the Member State can seek to justify it on grounds of public policy, security or health (Art 46 EC Treaty, which is applicable by reason of Art 55). This will be considered in Chapter 15.

The freedom to provide services may also be restricted by rules which are justified by overriding reasons in the general interest, provided the rules are applied to all persons and undertakings operating in the territory of the state where the service is provided. The restriction will not be justified if the reason for the restriction is safeguarded by the rules to which the provider of the service is subject in the Member State where he is established (see, in particular, *Commission* v *Italy* (Case C-180/89), and *Commission* v *Greece* (Case C-198/89), para 18). This objective justification defence will apply only to restrictions which are indirectly discriminatory or to those which are non-discriminatory. It is similar to the application of the *Cassis* rule of reason relating to the free movement of goods (see Chapter 18).

The nature of the defence was discussed by the Court of Justice in *Van Binsbergen* v *Bestuur van de Bedrijfsvereniging voor de Metaalnijverheid* (Case 33/74).

This case concerned a restriction that the provider of the service must satisfy a residence requirement. A Dutch national acted as legal adviser to the applicant in relation to legal proceedings before a Dutch court. The legal adviser moved to Belgium during the course of the proceedings and was told that he could no longer represent the applicant because under Dutch law, only persons established in The Netherlands could act as legal advisers. The national court referred the matter to the Court of Justice under the former Art 177 (now Art 234) to determine whether or not the Dutch rule was compatible with the freedom to provide services provisions. It was undoubtedly indirectly discriminatory because it would be more difficult for a non-national to satisfy than a national. The Court ruled that this restriction was contrary to the former Art 59 (now Art 49) because it was excessive. However, it acknowledged that not every restriction would be incompatible with the former Art 59 (now Art 49):

12. However, taking into account the particular nature of the services to be provided, specific requirements imposed on the person providing the service cannot be considered incompatible with the Treaty where they have as their purpose the application of professional rules justified by the general good – in particular rules relating to the organisation, qualifications, professional ethics, supervision and liability – which are binding upon any person established in the State in which the service is provided, where the person providing the service would escape from the ambit of those rules by being established in another Member State ...

14. In accordance with those principles, the requirement that persons whose functions are to assist the administration of justice must be permanently established for professional purposes within the jurisdiction of certain courts or tribunals cannot be considered incompatible with the provisions of Articles 59 and 60 [now Arts 49 and 50], where such

requirement is objectively justified by the need to ensure observance of professional rules of conduct connected, in particular, with the administration of justice and with respect for professional ethics.

For an indirectly discriminatory or non-discriminatory restriction to the provision of a service to be compatible with Art 49 (previously Art 59) it must:

1 be adopted in pursuance of a legitimate public interest, which is not incompatible with Community aims (some of these are set out at para 12 above (e.g. observance of professional ethics));
2 be equally applicable to persons established within the state and which would be avoided if the person providing the service was established in another state;
3 be objectively justified. This involves application of the proportionality test:

   • is there a genuine need for the restriction;
   • is the restriction appropriate to achieve its aim; and
   • could the interest pursued by the restriction be satisfied by other, less restrictive means?

In *Van Binsbergen*, the Court of Justice ruled that the public interest in the proper administration of justice could be achieved by a less restrictive means. Rather than a *place of residence* within the jurisdiction, an *address for service* within the jurisdiction could have been imposed.

The Court further defined the scope of the objective justification test in *Criminal proceedings against Webb* (Case 279/80).

Webb was the manager of a company which was established in the United Kingdom and which was licensed by the UK authorities to act as an agent for the supply of manpower. The company was paid to recruit temporary technical staff for employment by a business located in The Netherlands. Webb was prosecuted for having supplied workers without the necessary licence issued by the Dutch authorities. The case was referred to the Court under the former Art 177 (now Art 234) to consider the compatibility of the licence requirement with the former Art 59 (now Art 49). In this case, the service being provided was the provision of manpower (from the United Kingdom to The Netherlands). The restriction to the freedom to provide services, which was under challenge, was the Dutch licence requirement:

---

17. In Cases 110 and 111/78 *Van Wesemael* [1979] ECR 35, the Court held that, regard being had to the particular nature of certain services, specific requirements imposed on the provider of the services cannot be considered incompatible with the Treaty where they have as their purpose the application of rules governing such activities. However, *the freedom to provide services is one of the fundamental principles of the Treaty and may be restricted only by provisions which are justified by the general good and which are imposed on all persons or undertakings operating in the said State in so far as that interest is not safeguarded by the provisions to which the provider of the service is subject in the Member State of his establishment* ...
20. Such a measure would be excessive in relation to the aim pursued, however, if the requirements to which the issue of a licence is subject coincided with the proofs and guarantees required in the State of establishment. In order to maintain the principle of freedom to provide services *the first requirement is that in considering applications for*

licences and in granting them the Member State in which the service is to be provided may not make any distinction based on the nationality of the provider of the services or the place of his establishment; the second requirement is that it must take into account the evidence and guarantees already furnished by the provider of the services for the pursuit of his activities in the Member State of his establishment. (emphasis added)

The three *Van Binsbergen* conditions are set out in para 20:

- the restriction must pursue a justified aim;
- it must be equally applicable to nationals, non-nationals and those established within and outside the Member State alike; and
- it must not be any more restrictive or burdensome than is necessary (i.e. application of the proportionality test).

This approach was followed by the Court of Justice in *Questore di Verona* v *Diego Zenatti* (Case C-67/98).

Italian law made it a criminal offence to conduct or organise games of chance, and prohibited the organisation of games or betting, which were reserved to the state or to organisations holding a state concession. Betting licences were granted by the state to two organisations, which were required to serve to promote sporting activities through investments in sports facilities, especially in the poorest regions and in the peripheral areas of large cities, and to support equine sports and the breeding of horses. The restriction was intended to satisfy social policy concerns (relating to the harmful effects of gambling) and the concern to prevent fraud. These two organisations could authorise other persons and bodies who could offer appropriate safeguards.

Mr Zenatti (Z) had acted as an intermediary in Italy for the London company SSP Overseas Betting Ltd (SSP), a licensed bookmaker. Z ran an information exchange for the Italian customers of SSP in relation to bets on foreign sports events. He would send to London, by fax or internet, forms which had been filled in by customers, together with bank transfer forms, and he would receive faxes from SSP for transmission to the same customers. Action was taken against Z because he had not been licensed to provide such a service in Italy, and he was ordered by the national court to cease the activity. However, the court referred the case to the Court of Justice (pursuant to Art 177 (now Art 234)), to consider whether the restriction was compatible with the Community law provisions on the freedom to provide services.

The Italian legislation, inasmuch as it prohibits the taking of bets by any person or body other than those which may be licensed to do so, applies without distinction to all operators who might be interested in such an activity, whether established in Italy or in another Member State.

However, such legislation constitutes an obstacle to the freedom to provide services.

The Court thus verifies whether that restriction on the freedom to provide services is permissible under the exceptions expressly provided for by the Treaty or is justified, in accordance with the case law of the Court, by overriding reasons relating to the public interest.

The legislation at issue in the main proceedings pursues objectives similar to those pursued by the United Kingdom legislation on lotteries, as identified by the Court in *Schindler*, since it seeks to prevent such gaming from being a source of private profit, to avoid risks of crime and fraud and the damaging individual and social consequences of the incitement to spend which it represents and to allow it only to the extent to which it may be socially useful as being conducive to the proper conduct of competitive sports.

Those objectives must be considered together. They concern the protection of the recipients of the service and, more generally, of consumers as well as the maintenance of order in society and have already been held to rank among those objectives which may be regarded as constituting overriding reasons relating to the public interest. Moreover, measures based on such reasons must be suitable for securing attainment of the objectives pursued and not go beyond what is necessary to attain them.

Determination of the scope of the protection which a Member State intends providing in its territory in relation to lotteries and other forms of gambling falls within the margin of appreciation which the Court recognised as being enjoyed by the national authorities. It is for those authorities to consider whether, in the context of the aim pursued, it is necessary to prohibit activities of that kind, totally or partially, or only to restrict them and lay down more or less rigorous procedures for controlling them.

The provisions adopted must be assessed solely in the light of the objectives pursued by the national authorities of the Member State concerned and of the level of protection which they seek to ensure.

The fact that the games in issue are not totally prohibited is not enough to show that the national legislation is not in reality intended to achieve the public-interest objectives at which it is purportedly aimed, which must be considered as a whole. Limited authorisation of gambling on the basis of special or exclusive rights granted or assigned to certain bodies, which has the advantage of confining the desire to gamble and the exploitation of gambling within controlled channels, of preventing the risk of fraud or crime in the context of such exploitation, and of using the resulting profits for public-interest purposes, likewise falls within the ambit of those objectives.

However, such a limitation is acceptable only if, from the outset, it reflects a concern to bring about a genuine diminution in gambling opportunities and if the financing of social activities through a levy on the proceeds of authorised games constitutes only an incidental beneficial consequence and not the real justification for the restrictive policy adopted. Even if it is not irrelevant that lotteries and other types of gambling may contribute significantly to the financing of benevolent or public-interest activities, that motive cannot in itself be regarded as an objective justification for restrictions on the freedom to provide services.

It is for the national court to verify whether, having regard to the specific rules governing its application, the national legislation is genuinely directed to realising the objectives which are capable of justifying it and whether the restrictions which it imposes do not appear disproportionate in the light of those objectives. (emphasis added)

The Court of Justice therefore held that the EC Treaty provisions on the freedom to provide services do not prevent national legislation which reserves to certain bodies the right to take bets on sporting events if that legislation is justified by social-policy objectives which are intended to limit the harmful effects of such activities and if the restrictions which it imposes are not disproportionate in relation to those objectives. The Court further held that where a contribution is made from the profits of the authorised provider to benevolent activities, that should constitute only an incidental beneficial concern. It should not be the real justification for the restriction. The justification must be based on overriding reasons relating to the public interest (e.g. confining the desire to gamble; preventing the risk of fraud or other criminal activity).

The *Van Binsbergen* case makes it clear (at para 20) that the proportionality test requires additionally that any restrictions imposed by the Member State in which the provider is established should be taken into consideration, as it may duplicate the restrictive measures. For example, where a licence is required, both Member States may have licensing requirements. Therefore the licence requirement of the Member State in which the service is to be provided may not be necessary.

In *Jean-Claude Arblade, Arblade & Fils SARL; Bernard Leloup, Serge Leloup, Sofrage SARL* (Cases C-369 & 376/96), the Court of Justice had to decide whether a company established within the Community, which provided services in another Member State and posted its own workforce in the host state for the duration of the contract, had to comply with the host state's social legislation designed to safeguard the rights of workers (e.g. a requirement that certain social and labour documents had to be kept). The Court held that clearly this constituted a restriction on the freedom to provide services within the meaning of Art 49 EC Treaty. However, it held that the restriction could be justified (and would therefore be compatible with the Treaty obligations) if it was necessary in order to safeguard, effectively and by appropriate means, the overriding public interest which the social protection of workers represents. Nevertheless, the Court stated that the national court would also have to assess whether the objective of the host state's legislation is satisfied by legislation which the service provider has to comply with in his home Member State, in which case the restriction could not be justified. This will be the case where

> the undertaking is already subject, in the Member State in which it is established, to obligations which are comparable, as regards their objective of safeguarding the interests of workers, to those imposed by the legislation of the host Member State, and which relate to the same workers and the same periods of activity.

While the Court is reluctant to recognise new 'overriding interests in the general interest', it will, in exceptional circumstances, accept that such interests enable a state to impose a total ban on the import of the service in question, even when it is permitted, within strict limitations, in the state imposing the ban (*Schindler*, above).

RECIPIENTS OF SERVICES

Article 49 EC Treaty expressly refers to the freedom to provide services but does not mention the recipient. However, secondary legislation does acknowledge the recipient: Directive 64/221 protects the position of a recipient of services who resides in or travels to another Member State for that purpose; Art 1(b), Directive 73/148 requires the abolition of restrictions on the movement and residence of nationals wishing to go to another Member State as recipients (as well as providers) of services. In *Luisi and Carbone v Ministero del Tesoro* (Cases 286/82 and 26/83), the Court of Justice held that the Treaty Articles themselves cover recipients.

The applicants were Italian nationals who were prosecuted for attempting to export more than the legal maximum of Italian currency for use abroad. They argued that they had exported it for use within the Community to pay for services as tourists and to purchase medical treatment; they argued that the currency restrictions were contrary to Community law. The Court was asked whether the restrictions were covered by the rules on the payment for services covered by the former Arts 106(1) (now 107), 59 (now 49) and 60 (now 50) of the Treaty:

---

10. By virtue of Article 59 [now Art 49] of the Treaty, restrictions on freedom to provide such services are to be abolished in respect of nationals of Member States who are established in a Member State other than that of the person for whom the service is intended. *In order to enable services to be provided, the person providing the services may go to the Member State where the person for whom it is to be provided is established or else the latter may go to the State in which the person providing the service is established. Whilst the former case is expressly mentioned in the third paragraph of Article 60 [now Art 50], which permits the person providing the service to pursue his activity temporarily in the Member State where the service is provided, the latter case is the necessary corollary thereof, which fulfils the objective of liberalising all gainful activity not covered by the free movement of goods, persons and capital ...*

14. Among the restrictions on the freedom to provide services which must be abolished, the General Programme mentions, in section C of Title III, impediments to payments for services, particularly where, according to section D of Title III and in conformity with Article 106(2) [now Art 107(2)], the provision of such services is limited only by restrictions in respect of the payments therefor ... Those provisions were implemented by Council Directive 63/340/EEC of 31 May 1963 on the abolition of all prohibitions on or obstacles to payments for services where the only restrictions on exchange of services are those governing such payments ...

15. However, both the General Programme and the aforesaid directive reserve the right for Member States to verify the nature and genuineness of transfers of funds and of payments and to take all necessary measures in order to prevent contravention of their laws and regulations, 'in particular as regards the issue of foreign currency to tourists'.

16. It follows that the freedom to provide services includes the freedom, for the recipient of services, to go to another Member State in order to receive a service there, without being obstructed by restrictions, even in relation to payments and that tourists, persons receiving medical treatment and persons travelling for the purposes of education or business are to be regarded as recipients of services. (emphasis added)

In this case the Court held that tourism itself was a service which was covered by former Art 59 (now Art 49). In *Cowan* v *Le Tresor Public* (Case 186/87), the Court of Justice declared that tourists were entitled to full equal treatment under Art 12 EC Treaty, and that equal treatment included access to the criminal process and to national provisions on criminal injuries compensation (see Weatherill, 1989). Even leisure activities pursued by providers of services from other Member States must not be subject to discriminatory treatment (*Commission* v *Greece* (Case C-62/96)).

Recipients of services are, like providers, entitled to remain only as long as the service is received. Given the breadth of the concept of 'services', it would seem that any EU citizen or national of an EEA state can remain in another Member State for as long as he is paying for a service. He may, for example, be paying for accommodation out of his own resources. As long as he is relying exclusively on his own resources, however modest, he is providing 'remuneration' and would seem to be entitled to remain under Arts 49 and 50 EC Treaty, and Directive 73/148; and see *Belgium* v *Humbel* (Case 263/86). There is a somewhat unclear dividing line between this situation and that to which the general right of residence under Directive 90/364 is applicable.

Directive 90/364

Directive 90/364 confers a right of residence on nationals of Member States who do not enjoy such a right under any other provision of Community law, and to spouses and descendants and relatives in the ascending line of the main beneficiary and his spouse who are dependent. This right of residence is open only to those who have sufficient resources to avoid becoming a burden on the social assistance system of the host state and who hold an 'all risks' sickness insurance policy (Art 1). There is no obvious distinction between individuals in this residual category and recipients of services. It may be that a person who has adequate resources can survive in another Member State without paying for services, such as by staying with a friend. But in most cases, self-sufficient individuals will also be recipients of services. It is clearly in their interest to remain in this category, because if they are identifiable as beneficiaries under Directive 90/364 they will have to provide evidence of 'all risks' health insurance, a facility which currently appears to be unavailable from any insurance company! (See Vincenzi, 1995).

THE PROVISION OF SERVICES AND RIGHTS OF ESTABLISHMENT

There is a close link between the provision of services by the self-employed and undertakings, and the establishment of businesses in another Member State: one frequently precedes the other. Thus, provisions under Arts 43–48 EC Treaty dealing with establishment, particularly the preliminaries to becoming established, will often overlap with the provision of services. Freedom of establishment includes:

> the right to take up and pursue activities as self-employed persons and to set up and manage undertakings, in particular companies and firms ... under the conditions laid down for its own nationals by the law of the country where such establishment is effected. (Art 43 EC Treaty)

'Companies and firms' means companies and firms constituted under civil or commercial law, including cooperative societies, and other legal persons governed by public or private law, save for those which are non profit-making (Art 48). Although the inclusive term 'other legal persons' would seem to exclude the English partnership, since this has no legal personality, this is not in fact the case. The rights both to provision of services and to establishment belong to both natural and legal persons. In practice, it matters not whether a partnership enjoys the right to set up branches in another Member State by virtue of being a 'legal person' or a collection of 'natural persons', provided that both have their registered office, central administration or principal place of business within the Community.

Article 43 EC Treaty draws a distinction between nationals of Member States and those already established in the territory of a Member State. Each state defines its own nationals, thereby giving them the benefits enjoyed by EU citizenship (see Chapter 11). However, an undertaking which does not have its principal office in the Community can set up agencies and branches in other Member States, provided it is established in one of the Member States.

OBSTACLES TO ESTABLISHMENT

Article 54 (now Art 44) EC Treaty provided for the drawing up of a general programme for the abolition of restrictions on freedom of establishment within the Community. The Council and Commission were to give priority treatment to activities where freedom of establishment made a particularly valuable contribution to the development of production and trade, and were to abolish administrative procedures and practices forming obstacles to establishment, and enable nationals of Member States to acquire and use land and buildings. Existing necessary safeguards for the operation of businesses and the professions were to be harmonised and coordinated.

The General Programme made under Art 54 (now Art 44) was approved in December 1961. Title III of the Programme called for the abolition of discriminatory measures which might impair access to non-wage-earning activities of Community nationals. The measures to be abolished included the following:

- Provisions which made access to a non-wage-earning activity conditional upon the issue of an official authorisation or the issue of a document, such as a foreign merchant's card or a foreign professional's card.
- The imposition of taxes or other charges which would make access to a business or profession in another Member State more difficult and costly. In *Hayes* v *Kronenberger* (Case C-323/95), for example, the Court of Justice held that a requirement that foreign litigants from other Member States pay a sum as security for costs in court proceedings, in circumstances where local nationals were not required to do so, was discriminatory and was liable to have an adverse effect on trade in goods and services between Member States.
- Provisions which barred or limited membership in companies, particularly with regard to the activities of their members.
- Restrictions imposed on foreign nationals in relation to entry into various commercial and other contracts, the right to tender or participate in public works contracts, to borrow and have access to various forms of credit and to have access to loans and grants provided by State agencies.

To give effect to the programme, the Commission drew up a wide range of directives which were intended to facilitate access to a great variety of activities, including itinerant traders, film producers, hairdressers and the providers of gas, water and electricity services. Some of these require specific periods of academic training and practical experience, while others simply require a period of self-employment and a certificate of good character (compare the provisions in Directive 86/653 on self-employed commercial agents with Directive 87/540 on carriers of goods by waterway). It was thought, initially, that until an appropriate directive was in place, national measures would continue to apply and, in many cases, would have the effect of excluding Community nationals from participating in the relevant business or occupation. The right to equality of opportunity provided in Art 43 in relation to establishment and Art 50 in relation to the provision of services relates to the conditions for establishment and self-employment in the host state. These may, in many instances, be more difficult for Community nationals to satisfy, despite their overt application to local nationals and Community nationals on the same terms.

However, the right of establishment and the right to provide services have been described by the Court of Justice as 'fundamental rights', and it has been active in asserting that businesses and the self-employed should have access to activities in Member States without hindrance or open or covert discrimination, even where there were no implementing Community measures. The difficulty, in many of these cases, is that perfectly proper national measures to protect consumers and users of professional services, or to achieve other legitimate objectives, have, in the same way as they have in the national context, been used by practitioners to exclude competitors from other Member States. The Court has often had to judge whether a national measure could be objectively justified, or whether it operated as an unlawful restriction. In *Commission* v *Italy (Re Freedom of Establishment)* (Case 168/85), it held that national provisions on tourism, the operation of pharmacies and access to the occupation of journalism, which denied access to those not holding Italian nationality, were incompatible with Arts 39, 43 and 49 EC Treaty. It was not sufficient that instructions should be issued disapplying them to Community citizens. They had to be repealed.

In *Reyners* v *Belgian State* (Case 2/74), the Court held that, like Art 39, Art 43 was directly effective. The fact that it was to be given effect over a period did not affect the right of the beneficiaries to enjoy immediate protection:

> Article 52 [now Art 43] ... imposes an obligation to attain a precise result, the fulfilment of which had to be made easier by, but not made dependent on, the implementation of a programme of progressive measures. The fact that this progression has not been adhered to leaves the obligation itself intact beyond the end of the period provided for its fulfilment. (paras 26 and 27)

This case concerned a Dutchman who had been born and educated in Belgium. He was resident in Belgium, and held a doctorate in Belgian law. He was excluded from legal practice in Belgium because he was not a Belgian. The Court of Justice held that this restriction was incompatible with Arts 12 and 43 EC Treaty.

Less direct provisions than national restrictions may also infringe the rights conferred by Arts 43, 49 and 50. In a series of cases brought by the Commission under Art 226, local restrictions on the operation of insurance services were challenged in the Court. In each of the four states concerned insurance undertakings were required to conduct their business in those states through individuals already established and authorised to practise there (*Commission* v *Denmark* (Case 252/83); *Commission* v *France* (Case 220/83); *Commission* v *Germany* (Case 205/84); *Commission* v *Ireland* (Case 206/84)). The Court accepted that, in the state of Community law prevailing at the time, the authorisation and licensing of insurance services was still a matter of the law of the host state. However, in operating its national system, the host state may not duplicate equivalent statutory conditions which have already been satisfied in the state where the business has originally been established. Until such time as national rules on company taxation are harmonised throughout the Community, it is permissible for a Member State to impose a restriction on companies, so that they cannot move their principal place of business without the consent of the national tax authorities (*R* v *HM Treasury, ex parte Daily Mail and General Trust plc* (Case 81/87)). The retention of national company taxation rules should not, however, allow Member States to operate discriminatory tax rules which operate as a barrier to the establishment of branches of foreign undertakings in their territories (*R* v *IRC, ex parte Commerzbank AG* (Case C-330/91)). A similar principle applies, pending the adoption of a common visa policy, in the case of companies which operate in other Member States and employ third state nationals (*Van der Elst* (Case C-43/93)). Although such national rules may be accepted by the Court of Justice, they will be acceptable only if they meet the qualifications laid down by the Court in the *Gebhard* case (Case C-55/94). National measures liable to hinder or make less attractive the exercise of the fundamental freedoms guaranteed by the Treaty must fulfil four conditions:

1 they must be applied in a non-discriminatory manner;
2 they must be justified by imperative requirements in the general interest;
3 they must be suitable for securing attainment of the objective which they pursue; and
4 they must not go beyond what is necessary to attain the objective.

The Treaty of Amsterdam has emphasised the presumption in favour of freedom of establishment and the right to provide services in other Member States by stating that 'the Community and the Member States ... shall take care that such services operate on the basis of principles and conditions which enable them to fulfil their missions' (Art 16 EC Treaty).

RIGHTS OF ENTRY AND RESIDENCE

Directive 73/148 was adopted under Title II of the General Programme for the abolition of restrictions on the right of establishment and the provision of services. Its provisions are similar to Directive 68/360 in relation to the entry and residence of workers. The Court of Justice does not, in fact, always draw a clear distinction between the rights of entry and residence enjoyed on the basis of being a provider or receiver of services, or being a worker (*Royer* (Case 48/75); *Watson and Belmann* (Case 118/75)). Indeed, where a person enters another Member State, he may not immediately know whether he will set up in business, provide a service or enter into employment. The last status has, however, some distinct benefits, particularly in the area of social advantages, which are not enjoyed by the self-employed (under Art 7(2), Regulation 1612/68 (see Chapter 12)).

The beneficiaries of the directive are, as indicated above, those establishing themselves or wishing to do so, and those providing and receiving services. The family members entitled to move are the spouse of the main beneficiary, their children under the age of 21, and the ascending and descending relatives of the beneficiary and spouse who are dependent on the beneficiary. Member States are also obliged to 'favour the admission' of any other members of the family of the beneficiary who are either dependent or are living under the same roof in the country of origin (Art 1). Despite the difference in terminology in relation to collateral and other relatives, Art 3, like the equivalent provision of Directive 68/360 (Art 3), provides that all the family members should have the right to enter the territory of the host state simply on production of a valid identity card or passport. Visas can be demanded for non-EU family members, but 'every facility' should be afforded to them for obtaining one (Art 3(1)).

Those providing or receiving services are entitled to remain for as long as the services are being given or received. The right is not, as with the right of workers, dependent on the issue of a residence permit (Art 4(2); *Royer* (Case 48/75)). In the case of a provider or recipient of services there is no residence permit, only a 'right of abode', which is similar to a temporary residence permit issued under Art 6(3), Directive 68/360 to workers. Those who have become established are entitled to be issued with a residence permit valid for at least five years, which is automatically renewable. The provisions for the issue and renewal of permits are very similar to those with regard to workers (see Chapter 12). There is, however, an important distinction. Although a residence permit cannot be lost where the self-employed worker becomes temporarily incapable of working because of sickness or accident (Art 4(1), Directive 73/148), it can be withdrawn where the self-employed person's business fails through no fault of his own, and he becomes 'involuntarily' unemployed (compare Art 7, Directive 68/360 (see Chapter 12)).

EQUAL TREATMENT

The self-employed, and the providers and recipients of services, do not have the benefit of Art 7(2), Regulation 1612/68 (social advantages), or of the provisions of Arts 7(1) and 9–12 of the same regulation in relation to vocational education, housing, and employment rights of family members, since the regulation applies only to workers. On the face of it, this is an important difference, since social advantages have played an important part in the jurisprudence of the Court in relation to the integration of workers and their families into the host state (see Chapter 12). There are no equivalent provisions in Directive 73/148, and its beneficiaries are obliged to look to Art 12 EC Treaty to be put on an equal footing with local nationals. The Court considerably mitigated the difference by a creative application of Art 12. It has, however, drawn the line at equality of treatment in relation to social assistance and educational grants.

In *Commission* v *Italy (Re Housing Aid)* (Case 63/86), a cheap mortgage facility, which was by Italian law confined to Italian nationals, was held by the Court of Justice to contravene Art 12 EC Treaty. In *Cowan* v *Le Tresor Public* (Case 186/87), Mr Cowan, a British citizen, was visiting Paris as a tourist (i.e. the recipient of services (see above)) when he was assaulted in the exit of a Metro station. He was held to be entitled to the same rights in relation to criminal injuries compensation as a French national. The Court confined itself to considering the availability of the compensation scheme to non-French nationals. Rather on the same basis that it had decided that equal access to the criminal process was a necessary precondition to the vindication of the rights of the worker in the criminal process (and could thus be seen to be a 'social advantage') in *Mutsch* (Case 137/84), it decided that the criminal injuries scheme should be similarly available to Mr Cowan. Presumably it would have come to the same conclusion if his attackers had been identified and his application had been for legal aid to bring proceedings against them for assault (see, Weatherill, 1989, p. 575). It is, however, difficult to predict this with confidence. Although the Court has been quick to use Art 12 EC Treaty to enable an individual to overcome obstacles, either overt or covert, to the exercise of rights conferred by Arts 43, 49 and 50 EC Treaty, it has been more reluctant to do so when the obstacle is the individual's shortage of resources (see below).

In *Commission* v *Spain* (Case C-45/93), the Court held that the principle of equal treatment extended to the right of visitors from other EU states to free admission to museums, where this facility was available to Spanish nationals.

In *Gravier* v *City of Liège* (Case 293/83), the Court held that Ms Gravier was exercising a right to receive education under what was then Art 128 EC Treaty. In the course of exercising such a right, she was entitled to benefit from Art 7 (now Art 12) EC Treaty. On that basis she should receive equal treatment in relation to payment of the university admission fee, the *minerval*, so that she would have to pay only the same amount as 'home' students (see also *Commission* v *Belgium (Re University Fees)* (Case C-47/93)). The right to equal treatment in relation to access to vocational education did not, however, extend to financial assistance to enable an individual to go to another Member State and receive a grant to support him while at a vocational school or on a vocational course. Such a right did not exist under what was then Art 128, nor under Art 12 (*Lair* v *University of Hannover* (Case 39/86)). Indeed, the right to receive education as a 'service' under Art 49 depended on the individual providing 'remuneration' for it (*Humbel* (Case 263/86), paras 8–13). However, Directive 93/96 now provides students with the right to receive vocational education in another Member State, provided that they have sufficient resources to avoid becoming a burden on the social assistance scheme of the host state (Art 1). The Directive expressly excludes any entitlement to a maintenance grant from the host state, although a maintenance grant paid by the state of origin could, of course, constitute the 'resources' which would enable the student to exercise the right.

THE OFFICIAL AUTHORITY EXCEPTION

As with Art 39, the rights of entry and residence of those entering to provide and receive services are subject to the right of the host state to derogate on grounds of public policy, public security and public health (Arts 46(1) and 55 EC Treaty). The scope of these provisions will be examined in Chapter 15. In addition, the rights enjoyed by virtue of Arts 43, 49 and 50 EC Treaty 'shall not apply ... to activities ... connected, even occasionally, with the exercise of official authority' (Art 45 EC Treaty). Like the public service exception in Art 39(4), 'the exercise of official authority' is not defined in the Treaty, but its scope was considered by the Court of Justice in *Reyners* v *Belgian State* (Case 2/74). The defendant in this case argued that the profession of avocat was exempted from the chapter of the Treaty on rights of establishment because it sometimes involved the exercise of official authority. The Court rejected the idea that an avocat, despite his occasional official duties, was necessarily concerned with the exercise of official authority:

> An extension of the exception allowed by Article 55 [now Art 45] to a whole profession would be possible only in cases where such activities were linked with that profession in such a way that freedom of establishment would result in imposing on the Member State concerned the obligation to allow the exercise, even occasionally, by nationals of functions appertaining to official authority. This extension is on the other hand not possible when, within the framework of an independent profession, the activities

connected with the exercise of official authority are separable from the professional activity in question taken as a whole. (paras 46 and 47)

The 'exercise of official authority' would seem to be analogous to the exercise of 'public service' under Art 39(4) (*Commission* v *Belgium* (Case 149/79) – see above, Chapter 12), and is likely to be as narrowly construed by the Court (see, e.g., *Commission* v *Greece* (Case C-306/89) – road traffic experts not within Art 45 exception; *Commission* v *Italy* (Case C-272/91) – the provision of computer services for the state lottery not within Art 45). More decisions of the Court are required before the full scope of this exception can be determined.

PROFESSIONAL QUALIFICATIONS

Specific harmonising directives

The lack of common qualifications in the Community, and an unwillingness to recognise diplomas and other qualifications from other states, proved a major obstacle to the exercise of free movement rights, especially for those with specialist skills. The problem was addressed by the General Programme, which resulted in the production of a whole range of harmonising directives relating to a wide range of activities (e.g. GPs, nurses, vets). The harmonising directives provide that if the professional satisfies the conditions set out within the directive, then recognition of the profession is guaranteed throughout the Community.

Mutual Recognition of Diplomas Directive 89/48

Little progress was made in relation to other traditional professions. It is generally accepted that in professions such as law, accountancy, banking and insurance the public needs to be protected against those who might misrepresent their skills and qualifications. To protect both public and professionals, many such professions are regulated by law. Regulation will cover matters such as education and training, professional conduct and disciplinary proceedings. In some Member States the regulatory process is entirely in the hands of government. In the United Kingdom and Ireland it is largely in the hands of professional bodies, operating within a statutory framework. Individuals and undertakings providing financial services will also work within a framework of self and state regulation, the trend in the United Kingdom during the 1980s and 1990s being towards self-regulation and deregulation. From the point of view of the consuming public, the self-regulation process by professionals has sometimes been seen to be as much concerned with the protection of professionals from competition as with protection of the public from abuse. It could also be perceived in a single market as a covert form of protectionism in relation to the delivery of professional services by citizens of other Member States.

The reluctance of national professional bodies to agree harmonised standards for particular occupations led the Commission to adopt a new approach in 1985, following publication of the White Paper on the single market. That approach acknowledged the need:

to provide a rapid response to the expectations of nationals of Community countries who hold higher-education diplomas awarded on completion of professional education and training issued in a Member State other than that in which they wish to pursue their profession. (Preamble to Directive 89/48)

The new approach involved both general educational criteria and the mutual recognition of educational diplomas and relevant practical experience. Directive 89/48 opened the way for entry into professional practice in other Member States for a whole new range of activities. In the United Kingdom these occupations include: actuaries, auditors, barristers, chiropodists, dieticians, physiotherapists, optometrists, civil engineers, marine architects, town planners, solicitors and teachers. There are more than 30 regulated professions listed by the Department of Trade and Industry (see Department of Trade and Industry, *EC Professional Qualifications Directive: Guidance for Competent Authorities* (1989)).

Directive 89/48 is essentially a 'residual' directive, in the sense that it does not apply to professions which are the subject of a separate harmonising directive establishing arrangements for the mutual recognition of diplomas by Member States (Art 2). It applies to 'regulated professional activity', that is, 'a professional activity, in so far as the taking up or pursuit of such an activity or one of its modes of pursuit in a Member State is subject, directly or indirectly by virtue of laws, regulations or administrative provisions, to the possession of a diploma' (Art 1). Beneficiaries of the directive are those who can show the following:

1 possession of a diploma indicating that the holder has the professional qualifications required for the taking up or pursuit of a regulated profession in one of the Member States in a self-employed capacity or as an employed person;
2 completion of a post-secondary course of at least three years' duration, or of an equivalent duration part-time, at a university or establishment of higher education or another establishment of similar level; and
3 where appropriate, that the holder of the diploma has successfully completed the professional training required in addition to the post-secondary course.

The host state may also require the holder of the diploma to provide evidence of professional experience of not more than four years where the period of education and training falls short by more than one year compared to that required in the host state. Where the education and training received by the individual in his home state differ substantially from those required in the host state, or where there is a substantial mismatch between the regulated activities in the home and host states, the host state can require the holder of the diploma either to complete an adaptation period of not more than three years, or to take an aptitude test. Except in those cases where the holder would need a precise knowledge of the law of the host state to carry on the profession, the choice of whether to undergo an adaptation period or an aptitude test belongs to the diploma holder.

Directive 89/48 has been implemented in the United Kingdom by the European Communities (Recognition of Professional Qualifications) Regulations 1991 (SI 1991/824). Under the regulations, professional bodies are obliged to recognise the qualifications of other Community professionals, to provide full reasons where this is not done in individual cases, and to set up an independent appeal tribunal before which any refusal of recognition can be challenged.

The Commission adopted a report in 1996 on the implementation of Directive 89/48 (see Brussels Agenda, February 1996, p. 3). The directive enables, *inter alia*, lawyers qualified in one jurisdiction to requalify as full members of the legal profession of another jurisdiction. The directive has been implemented in the United Kingdom by the Qualified Lawyers Transfer Regulations, which require any foreign lawyer wishing to become a solicitor to sit an aptitude test. As at Autumn 1995, only 620 lawyers had requalified in another Member State. Of these 620, the United Kingdom had admitted about 400 lawyers. According to the Commission, the low figure of 620 lawyers was partly because some Member States allowed lawyers from other Member States to practise under the title of their Member State of origin and partly because many Member States were late in implementing the directive for the legal profession. Further, the requirement for migrant lawyers to sit an aptitude test was considered by the Commission to be a disincentive.

With regard to the establishment of lawyers, Directive 98/5 was adopted at the end of 1997, the aim of which is to make it easier for lawyers to practise in other Member States. The directive, which had to be implemented by March 2000:

- permits EU lawyers to be established under their home title in another Member State
- requires them to register with an appropriate regulatory body in the host state
- gives them a right to representation within the host regulatory body
- subjects them to the rules and regulatory regime of the host regulatory body
- offers them a 'fast track' to requalification as a lawyer of the host state.

This directive has been implemented in the United Kingdom by the European Community (Lawyer's Practice) Regulations 2000 (SI 2000/1119), which came into force on 22 May 2000.

Recognition of diplomas for other professional activities: Directive 92/51

Directive 89/48 applies only to regulated professional activities where the holder has completed at least three years in higher education. There remained still a great many professional and other activities for which some further education was required, but which did not fall within the ambit of Directive 89/48. A further directive was, therefore, approved in 1992: Directive 92/51 deals with the remaining areas of professional education and training and applies to holders of diplomas which show either that the holder has successfully completed a post-secondary course of at least a year or the equivalent on a part-time basis, entry to which is on the same basis as entry into university or higher education, or that the holder has been successful in completing one of the recognised education and training courses listed in the directive. In the same way as Directive 89/48, the host state may require the diploma holder to complete an adaptation period of not more than three years or to take an aptitude test (Art 4(1)(b)).

OTHER QUALIFICATIONS

In the case of qualifications that do not fall within the specific harmonising directives which have been adopted, or the general Directives 89/48 and 92/51 described above, the basic rules (developed through the case law of the Court of Justice) on recognition and the investigation of the equivalence of qualifications will continue to apply. In these cases, the person seeking to establish himself in another Member State is relying directly on Art 43 EC Treaty. It is therefore necessary to review the case law of the Court of Justice.

In *Thieffry* v *Conseil de l'Ordre des Avocats à la Cour de Paris* (Case 71/76), a Belgian national had obtained a doctorate in law in Belgium. He practised as an advocate in Brussels (Belgium) for a number of years. His qualifications were recognised by a French university as *equivalent* to a degree in French law. He obtained a certificate stating that he was academically qualified for the profession of *avocat*. However, the French Bar refused him admission to the training stage solely on the ground that he did not have a degree in French law.

The Court held that if the applicant had already obtained what was recognised (professionally and academically) as an *equivalent qualification* and had *satisfied the necessary training requirements* then the French Bar would not have been justified in excluding him from admission solely because he did not have a French law degree. The fact that no directives had been adopted under the former Art 57 (now Art 47) EC Treaty was irrelevant.

This was taken a stage further in *UNECTEF* v *Heylens* (Case 222/86).

Heylens was a Belgian national who held a Belgian football trainer's diploma. He was taken on as the trainer of a French football team. He applied for recognition of his diploma as *equivalent* to the French diploma. His application was refused. He continued to practise as a trainer and was prosecuted by the French football trainers' union (UNECTEF). The French court referred the case to the Court of Justice under the former Art 177 (now Art 234) for a preliminary ruling, questioning the compatibility of the French system with Community law:

---

10. In the absence of harmonisation of the conditions of access to a particular occupation, the Member States are entitled to lay down the knowledge and qualifications needed in order to pursue it and to require the production of a diploma certifying that the holder has the relevant knowledge and qualifications ...

13. Since it has to reconcile the requirement as to the qualifications necessary in order to pursue a particular occupation with the requirements of the free movement of workers, *the procedure for the recognition of equivalence must enable the national authorities to assure themselves, on an objective basis, that the foreign diploma certifies that its holder has the knowledge and qualifications which are, if not identical, at least equivalent to those certified by the national diploma. That assessment of the equivalence of the foreign diploma must be effected exclusively in the light of the level of knowledge and qualifications which its holder can be assumed to possess in the light of that diploma, having regard to the nature and duration of the studies and practical training which the diploma certifies that he has carried out.* (emphasis added)

The Court of Justice held that the assessment of the equivalence of a foreign diploma must be effected exclusively in the light of the *level of knowledge and qualifications which its holder can be assumed to possess in the light of that diploma*, having regard to the *nature and duration of the studies* and *practical training which the diploma certifies that he has carried out*. This was further amplified in *Vlassopoulou v Ministerium für Justiz, Bundes-und Europaangelegenheiten Baden Württemberg* (Case C-340/89):

The applicant was a Greek who had obtained a Greek law degree and had been admitted to the Athens Bar. Most of her professional practice had been undertaken in Germany and involved the application of German law. She applied for admission to a German Bar. Her application was rejected on the ground that she lacked the necessary qualifications. The case came before the German Federal Supreme Court, who referred the matter to the Court of Justice to determine whether it was permissible to refuse admission for this reason:

15. It must be stated in this regard that, even if applied without any discrimination on the basis of nationality, national requirements concerning qualifications may have the effect of hindering nationals of the other Member States in the exercise of their right of establishment guaranteed to them by Article 52 [now Art 43] of the EEC Treaty. That could be the case if the national rules in question took no account of the knowledge and qualifications already acquired by the person concerned in another Member State.

16. Consequently, a Member State which receives a request to admit a person to a profession to which access, under national law, depends upon the possession of a diploma or a professional qualification must take into consideration the diplomas, certificates and other evidence of qualifications which the person concerned has acquired in order to exercise the same profession in another Member State by making comparison between the specialised knowledge and abilities concerned by those diplomas and the knowledge and qualifications required by the national rules.

The Court of Justice held that national authorities are required to consider any education or training received by that person which is indicated by the qualification, and to contrast that with the knowledge and skills required by the domestic qualification. If they are *equivalent* then the Member State *must* recognise the qualification. If they are not considered equivalent, then they must go on to consider the *knowledge or training received by the applicant through study or experience*; this may be sufficient to make up for what was lacking in the formal qualification (paras 19–20).

Two later cases have confirmed this approach. The first is *Colegio Oficial de Agentes de la Propriedad Inmobiliara v Aguirre, Newman and Others* (Case C-104/91):

The defendant Newman was prosecuted for practising as an estate agent in Spain without being a member of the Colegio. He had applied for membership but had received no response. He was a member of the Royal Institute of Chartered Surveyors in the United Kingdom. It should be noted that the prosecution took place before 4 January 1991, the date by which Directive 89/48 should have been implemented in Member States. The Spanish court referred to the Court of Justice the question of how far the Colegio was obliged to take into account the defendant's UK qualifications.

The Court held that, in the absence of harmonisation of the conditions of access to a particular profession, Member States were entitled to lay down the knowledge and qualifications needed in order to pursue it and to require the production of a diploma certifying that the holder had the relevant knowledge and qualifications. In this case, the Member State was required to carry out a comparative examination of professional qualifications, taking into account the differences between the national legal systems concerned.

If the comparison shows that the knowledge and qualifications correspond to the national provisions of the host state, then it is bound to accept their equivalence. If, on the other hand, the examination reveals only partial equivalence, the host state has the right to require that the person concerned should demonstrate that he has acquired the additional knowledge and qualifications needed. The host state is under an obligation to give full reasons as to the lack of equivalence. This is to enable the person to takes steps to remedy the deficiency or, if he disagrees with the decision, to challenge it in a court of law (*UNECTEF* v *Heylens* (Case 222/86); *Vlassopoulou* (Case C-340/89)).

The second case is *Fernandez de Bobadilla* v *Museo Nacional del Prado and Others* (Case C-234/97).

Ms Fernandez de Bobadilla (F) was a Spanish national. She obtained a BA in History of Art from an American university, following which she obtained a postgraduate degree in fine arts and restoration from a UK university. For the following three years, F worked for the Prado (in Madrid, Spain) as a restorer of works of art under a temporary contract. She also worked for other studios and museums.

The Prado is attached to Spain's Ministry of Culture, and a collective agreement entered into provided that the post of restorer would be available only to persons who possessed a specified qualification. This did not include the qualifications F had obtained.

F applied to have her qualifications recognised as equivalent to those specified in the collective agreement, but she was told that she would need to take additional examinations, to demonstrate that she had sufficient knowledge. She did not take these examinations.

The Prado subsequently advertised a permanent vacancy as a restorer of works of art. F applied but her application was rejected because she did not possess one of the specified qualifications. F argued that this infringed her free movement rights.

The case came before the Court of Justice, and the Court stated that if the general Directives 89/48/EEC or 92/51/EEC (see above) did not apply then:

---

28. ... Community law does not in principle preclude a public body in a Member State from restricting access to a post to candidates holding a qualification awarded by an educational establishment in that Member State or any other foreign qualification officially recognised by the competent authorities of that Member State. However, where the qualification was awarded in another Member State, the procedure for granting it official recognition must comply with the requirements of Community law.

29. The Court has already had occasion to set out, *inter alia* in Case C-340/89 *Vlassopoulou* [1991] ECR I-2357, the conditions with which the competent authorities of a Member State must comply when they receive a request to admit a person to a profession to which entry under national law depends on the possession of a diploma or professional qualification ...

31. It is clear from paragraph 16 of the judgment in *Vlassopoulou* that the competent authorities of the host Member State must take into consideration the diplomas, certificates and other evidence of qualifications which the person concerned has acquired

in order to practise that profession in another Member State by comparing the specialised knowledge and abilities certified by those diplomas with the knowledge and qualifications required by the national rules.

32. *If the comparative examination of diplomas results in the finding that the knowledge and qualifications certified by the diploma awarded in another Member State correspond to those required by the national provisions, the competent authorities of the host Member State must recognise that diploma as fulfilling the requirements laid down by its national provisions. If, on the other hand, the comparison reveals that the knowledge and qualifications certified by the foreign diploma and those required by the national provisions correspond only partially, the competent authorities are entitled to require the person concerned to show that he has acquired the knowledge and qualifications which are lacking* (judgment in *Vlassopoulou*, cited above, paragraph 19).

33. *In that regard, the competent national authorities must assess whether the knowledge acquired by the candidate, either during a course of study or by way of practical experience, is sufficient to show possession of knowledge which is lacking* (judgment in *Vlassopoulou*, cited above, paragraph 20).

34. Where no general procedure for official recognition has been laid down at national level by the host Member State, or where that procedure does not comply with the requirements of Community law as set out in paragraphs 29–33 of this judgment, it is for the public body seeking to fill the post itself to investigate whether the diploma obtained by the candidate in another Member State, together, where appropriate, with practical experience, is to be regarded as equivalent to the qualification required. (emphasis added)

The Court was undecided as to whether or not the general directives (89/48/EEC and 92/51/EEC (see above)) applied and therefore it determined the case on the basis that these two directives did not apply. It reaffirmed the old case law in paras 29–33 and stated in para 34 that it was the responsibility of the public body seeking to fill the vacancy to determine whether the foreign qualification and/or experience of the candidate was such as to afford equivalence to the qualifications specified.

This line of reasoning was followed in *Hugo Fernando Hocsman* v *Ministre de l'Emploi et de la Solidarité* (Case C-238/98).

Hocsman held a diploma of doctor of medicine awarded in 1976 by a university in Argentina. He acquired Spanish nationality in 1986, and became a French citizen in 1998. During 1980 the Spanish authorities recognised Hocsman's Argentine qualification as equivalent to the Spanish university degree in medicine and surgery, which allowed him to practise medicine in Spain and train there as a specialist. Due to the fact that he was not a Spanish national at the time of his specialist training, the qualification he was subsequently awarded (specialist in urology) was an academic title. When he became a Spanish national in 1986 he obtained authorisation to practise as a specialist in urology.

In 1990 he entered France and held various urology posts. He applied to be registered to practise general medicine, but in 1997 the French authorities rejected his application on the ground that his Argentine qualification did not entitle him to practise general medicine in France. Hocsman issued proceedings in a French court to have that decision annulled.

Although there was a directive which applied to medicine, Hocsman's Argentine qualification was not included. The French court referred the case to the Court of Justice pursuant to Art 234 EC Treaty and asked, *inter alia*, whether a person could rely on Art 43 EC Treaty where there was a directive covering the relevant profession:

The object of such [harmonising or coordinating] directives is, as appears from Article 57(1) of the Treaty [now Art 47(1)], to make it easier for persons to take up and pursue activities as self-employed persons, and hence to make the existing possibilities of taking up those activities easier for nationals of other Member States ...

The function of directives which lay down common rules and criteria for mutual recognition of diplomas is thus to introduce a system in which Member States are obliged to accept the equivalence of certain diplomas and cannot require the persons concerned to comply with requirements other than those laid down in the relevant directives.

Where the requirements such as those set out in Directive 93/16 [which gives Community recognition to specified medical training diplomas] are satisfied, mutual recognition of the diplomas in question renders superfluous their recognition under the principle referred to [i.e. as the Court held in *Haim* (see below), that in order to verify whether a training period requirement prescribed by the national rules is satisfied, the competent national authorities must take into account the professional experience of the person concerned, including that which he has acquired in another Member State]. However, that principle unquestionably remains relevant in situations not covered by such directives, as in Dr Hocsman's case.

The Court of Justice therefore held that even though there was a harmonisation directive covering medical training diplomas, Hocsman could still rely directly on Art 43. In this instance, the principles espoused by the Court in the case law considered above have to be applied to ascertain if Hocsman's qualifications and experience are sufficient to warrant recognition of his professional qualifications.

Non-EU qualifications

As with most of the Treaty provisions on the free movement of persons, neither the specific directives nor the two general directives cover non-Community nationals. Neither do they apply to qualifications obtained outside the Community. This was the issue in *Tawil-Albertini* v *Ministre des Affairs Sociales* (Case C-154/93).

The applicant was a French national. He obtained a dental qualification in the Lebanon. This qualification was later recognised in Belgium as equivalent to the Belgian dentistry qualification. He subsequently applied to the French authorities to practise in France, but his application was refused. The qualifications listed in the specific Council Directive 78/686 on the mutual recognition of dental qualifications did not include any qualification obtained outside the Community; but because his qualification had been recognised as equivalent to the Belgian Diploma, and the Belgian Diploma was included in the Directive, he argued that his qualification was also covered by the Directive.

The Court of Justice held that the mutual recognition of qualifications in dentistry was based upon minimum specific levels of competence agreed between all the Member States. Even though one Member State accepted a qualification as equivalent to its own standards, that did not bind all the other Member States. Only the qualifications listed in the specific Directive were guaranteed equivalent. Obviously, if he had obtained work experience within Belgium then, according to the decision in *Hocsman*, above, that experience would have been required to be taken into consideration, relying directly on Art 43 rather than the directive.

Haim v *Kassenzahnarztliche Vereinigung Nordrhein* (Case C-319/92) was referred to in the Court's judgment in *Hocsman*.

The applicant did not hold one of the qualifications specified in Council Directive 78/686, but had nevertheless been authorised to practise as a dentist in Germany. He applied to work on a social-security scheme in Germany, but was told that he would have to complete a further two-year training period.

He argued that his experience working for eight years as a dentist in Belgium should be taken into account. The Court cited the *Vlassopoulou* case (above) and ruled in his favour:

> 28. The competent national authority, in order to verify whether the training period requirement prescribed by the national rules is met, must take into account the professional experience of the plaintiff in the main proceedings, including that which he has acquired during his appointment as a dental practitioner of a social security scheme in another Member State.

In each of the above cases, the applicants had obtained non-Community qualifications. The *Haim* case ruled that experience within the Community must be taken into account if the Member State recognised the qualification which had been obtained from outside the Community. However, nationals of non-Member countries who are established in the Community have no rights of recognition or permission to practise under Community law. This is so even if they have obtained the professional qualification in one of the Member States and such qualification is listed in one of the earlier specific directives.

The internal situation

From the wording of Art 43 there would appear to be a limitation, in that it cannot be relied upon by a person wishing to establish himself in the Member State of his nationality. One obvious way in which a national may be disadvantaged is where he obtains a qualification in another Member State and then seeks to have it recognised in his own Member State.

In *Knoors* v *Secretary of State for Economic Affairs* (Case 115/78) the Court of Justice held that the former Art 52 (now Art 43) could be relied upon in a person's home Member State in respect of a qualification he had obtained in another Member State. However, later case law of the Court suggested that there were limitations to this. It held that the existence of a directive recognising the foreign qualification was essential: the former Art 52 (now Art 43) of itself could not assist nationals established in the Member State of their nationality. So, in *Ministère Public* v *Auer* (Case 136/78):

A French citizen obtained a vet qualification in Italy. He was not permitted to practise in France, the Italian qualification not being considered to be equivalent. There was no Community directive in force at the time. The Court of Justice held as follows:

> 20. ... Article 52 [now Art 43] concerns only – and can concern only – in each Member State the nationals of other Member States, those of the host Member State coming already, by definition, under the rules in question.

Following this decision the Council adopted Directives 78/1026 and 78/1027 which governed veterinary qualifications, thus recognising the qualification Auer had obtained. Generally, directives do not distinguish between nationals of the Member State in question. The case came before the Court of Justice for a second time, but on this occasion Auer was able to rely upon the directives (see *Auer* v *Ministère Public* (Case 271/82)).

Following the adoption of the general Directives 89/48 and 92/51 (which include most trade or professional qualifications, and which are not restricted to nationals establishing themselves in a Member State other than that of their nationality) most situations involving a *regulated profession* will be covered by the directives and therefore reliance solely on Art 43 EC Treaty will not be necessary. Accordingly, the national may rely upon the relevant directive in the Member State of his nationality with regard to qualifications and training obtained in another Member State.

However, a recent decision of the Court of Justice (considered above) has cast doubt on whether or not Case 136/78 *Auer* was correctly decided. In *Fernandez de Bobadilla* v *Museo Nacional del Prado and Others* (Case C-234/97).

Ms Fernandez de Bobadilla ('F') was a Spanish national. She obtained a BA in History of Art from an American university, following which she obtained a postgraduate degree in fine arts and restoration from a UK university. For the following three years, F worked for the Prado (in Madrid, Spain) as a restorer of works of art under a temporary contract. She also worked for other studios and museums.

The Prado did not recognise F's UK qualification when she applied for the post of restorer of works of art. F argued that this infringed her free movement rights.

The case came before the Court of Justice, and the Court stated that if Directives 89/48 or 92/51 (see above) did not apply then:

---

30. In contrast to *Vlassopoulou*, this case concerns a Spanish national seeking to practise her profession in Spain. However, if a national of a Member State, owing to the fact that he has lawfully resided on the territory of another Member State and has acquired a professional qualification there, finds himself with regard to his State of origin in a situation which may be assimilated to that of a migrant worker, he must also be entitled to enjoy the rights and freedoms guaranteed by the Treaty (see, to that effect, Case C-19/92 *Kraus* [1993] ECR I-1663, paragraphs 15 and 16).

The Court was undecided whether or not the mutual recognition of qualifications directives (89/48 and 92/51) applied, and therefore it decided the case on the basis that they did not apply. It held that even if there was no directive applicable to the test of equivalence of her qualifications, she could rely upon the general principles of Community law.

The above applies only where there is some 'Community element'. In the *Bobadilla* case, the Community element is the completion of an educational course and training in another Member State. If there is no Community element present there will be a completely/wholly internal situation, and Community law will not provide a remedy (see *Nino and Others* (Cases 54 & 91/88 and 14/89)).

RETIREMENT

There is no equivalent right to remain in the host state after a person has become established there under Art 43, in comparison to that enjoyed by workers under Art 39(3) and Regulation 1251/70 (see Chapter 12). However, Directive 75/34 is intended to put the self-employed person in the same position:

> The nature of establishment, together with the attachments formed to the countries in which they have pursued their activities, means that such persons have a definite interest in enjoying the same right to remain as that granted to workers. (Preamble)

The right to remain is to be enjoyed by all those who have pursued an activity as a self-employed person in another Member State and who have reached the age at which an old-age pension becomes payable in that state. They must have pursued the activity for at least the previous 12 months, and have lived in the state for more than three years. If no pension is payable to the self-employed in that state, then the retirement age is to be 65 (Art 2(1)(a)).

The qualifying period is shorter for a self-employed person who has worked in another state and who has become permanently incapacitated. In such cases, he has a right to remain if he has lived in the state for two years. If he ceased to work as a result of an accident at work or an occupational disease, there is no qualifying period, provided that he is entitled to an industrial injuries or similar pension payable by the host state (Art 2(1)(b)).

Those enjoying this right are entitled to retain with them those members of their family who were living with them at the date on which their right to remain became effective (Art 3(1)). Members of the family can remain after the death of the self-employed person, even if he dies before his own entitlement to remain has taken effect, provided that the individual who would have had the right had lived there for at least two years (Art 3(2)).

The self-employed, while both active and retired, are not entitled to the 'social advantages' conferred by Art 7(2), Regulation 1612/68 (see Chapter 12), but they will be entitled to equal treatment under Art 12 EC Treaty and this will entitle them to a number of benefits available in the host state. Given the reluctance of the Court to extend the principle of equal treatment to benefits, such as grants, for recipients of services (see *Lair* (Case 39/86)), it is not clear how far this principle extends. However, since Directive 75/34 is modelled closely on Regulation 1251/70, it seems likely that the retired self-employed and their families will be treated no less favourably than the beneficiaries of Regulation 1251/70 (see, e.g., *Cristini* v *SNCF* (Case 32/75) – Chapter 12).

Further reading

Capelli, F. (1993) 'The Free Movement of Professionals in the European Community', in Schermers, H. (ed.) *Free Movement of Persons in Europe: Legal Problems and Experiences,* Martinus Nijhoff, p. 437.

Craig, P. and De Burca, G. (1998) *EU Law Text, Cases and Materials* (2nd edn), OUP, Chapter 17.

Eidenmüller, H., 'Deregulating the Market for Legal Services in the European Community' (1990) 53 MLR 604.

Greaves, R. 'Advertising Restrictions and the Free Movement of Goods and Services' (1998) 34 EL Rev 305.

Green, N., Hartley, T.C. and Usher, J. (1991) *The Legal Foundations of the Single European Market*, OUP, Chapter 12.

Guild, E. (1996) *A Guide to the Right of Establishment under the Europe Agreements*, Baileys Shaw & Gillett.

Marenco, M., 'The Notion of Restriction on Freedom of Establishment and Provision of Services in the Case Law of the Court' (1991) 11 YEL 111.

Peers, S., 'Indirect Rights for Third-Country Service Providers Confirmed' (1995) 32 CML Rev 311.

Steiner, J. and Woods, L. (2000) *Textbook on EC Law* (7th edn), Blackstone Press, Chapter 21.

Van der Woude, M. and Mead, P., 'Free Movement of the Tourist in Community Law' (1988) 25 CML Rev 117.

Vincenzi, C. (1995) 'Welcoming the Well and Wealthy: the Implementation of Directive 90/364 in the United Kingdom', in Daintith, T. *Implementing EC Law in the United Kingdom: Structures for Direct Rule.*

Weatherill, S., 'Note on *Cowan v Le Tresor Public*' (1989) 25 CML Rev 563.

Weatherill, S. (2000) *Cases and Materials on EC Law* (5th edn), Blackstone Press, Chapter 10.

Wouters, J., 'Conflict of Laws and the Single Market for Financial Services' (1997) 4 MJ 161, 284.

Wouters, J. and Schneider, H. (eds) (1995) *Current Issues of Cross-border establishment of Companies in the European Union*, Maklu.

Chapter 14

SOCIAL SECURITY

All Member States of the Community have contributory social security systems, but they vary greatly in the quantity and quality of benefits which they provide. This is, potentially, a major barrier to the mobility of the employed and self-employed. A person moving to another Member State may suffer the double disadvantage of losing out on the contributions to his own national insurance scheme, with a consequent loss of benefits in his home state, and he may also find that he is not entitled to benefits in the host state because he has not contributed sufficiently or for long enough. The founders of the Community were clearly aware of this difficulty and provision was made to deal with it in what is now Art 42 EC Treaty. This facilitates the adoption of such measures in the field of social security as are necessary to provide freedom of movement for workers (and the self-employed (see below)). To this end it shall make arrangements to secure for migrant workers and their dependants:

- aggregation, for the purpose of acquiring and retaining the right to benefit and of calculating the amount of benefit, of all periods taken into account under the laws of the several countries; and
- payment of benefits to persons resident in the territories of Member States.

Article 42 is thus aimed at enabling the migrant worker to take his accrued rights with him, in the sense that his contributions and period of contribution in his home state will be taken into account in the host state, and his contributions in the host state will be taken into account in calculating his level of benefits when he returns to his home state. Given the variation in level and type of contribution in each Member State, and the dissimilarity of social security schemes, this is a complex task. It must, however, be emphasised that the scheme is not intended to equalise the level of social security benefits throughout the Community. It is simply directed at ensuring that the migrant worker gets, as far as possible, equal treatment within local social security schemes, and does not lose out in relation to entitlements due from his home state. The Court of Justice has declared that, when applying national social security law to migrant workers, the host state should interpret its own legislation in the light of the aims of Arts 32 to 42 of the Treaty. It should, as far as possible, avoid interpreting it in such a way as to discourage migrant workers from exercising their rights to freedom of movement (*Van Munster* (Case C-165/91)).

As a result of the large discrepancies between national security schemes, this area of Community law has been highly productive of litigation and the case law is considerable and complicated. This chapter will do no more than outline the general principles and provide some examples of their interpretation by the Court of Justice and their application in the United Kingdom.

The current Community rules enacted to give effect to the principles laid down in Art 42 are to be found in Regulations 1408/71 and 574/72 as amended by Regulation 2001/83, and Regulation 1247/92. Regulation 1408/71, as amended by Regulation 2001/83, contains the substantive provisions. Regulation 574/72 deals with the procedures for the operation and interrelation of national social security schemes. The most recent important legislation, Regulation 1247/92, limits the availability of national welfare provisions, and will be considered in the context of UK legislation.

The European Commission has published a guide – 'Your Social Security Rights when moving within the European Union' – which is available on its website at: europa.eu.int/comm/employment_social/fundamri/movement/guide_en.htm.

The scope of Regulation 1408/71, as amended, will first be examined.

THE BENEFICIARIES OF THE REGULATIONS

The regulations cover EU citizens who are employed or self-employed and who are, or who have been, subject to social security legislation in more than one of the Member States. Their families are also covered, together with any survivors of the worker or self-employed person after his death, provided that they were, at some stage, covered by the social security legislation of more than one Member State (Arts 1 and 2, Regulation 1408/71). Regulation 1408/71 also applies to refugees, stateless persons, and their families, as defined by Art 1 of the Geneva Convention on the Status of Refugees 1951 and Art 1 of the Convention on Stateless Persons 1954, and civil servants who are treated as such by national legislation. The term 'employed person' is much wider in scope than 'worker' under Art 39 EC Treaty, and it includes any person who is insured either voluntarily or compulsorily against one of the contingencies covered by the regulation. The fourth recital of Regulation 1408/71 refers to the wide variations in applicability of various national social security schemes, which made it desirable to establish the principle that the regulation applies to all nationals of a Member State insured under social security schemes for employed persons.

In relation to the self-employed, they are classified as such because, like the employed, they are included in a national scheme set up for the benefit of the self-employed, not because they might enjoy that status under Arts 43 and 49 EC Treaty. In *Van Roosmalen* (Case 300/84), the Court considered the meaning of 'self-employment' in the context of Regulation 1408/71.

The case concerned a missionary priest who had worked from 1955 until 1980 in what is now Zaire. He was not paid by the religious order of which he was a member but was maintained by his parishioners. The Court held that the concept of a self-employed person encompasses any person who pursues, other than under a contract of employment, the exercise of an independent trade or profession in respect of which he receives income permitting him to meet some or all of his needs. The situation is not affected by the fact that the income may be supplied by a third party – the parishioners, in this case.

The determining factor is the making of contributions to the national social security scheme. Thus, a person who goes to another Member State, not in the capacity of a worker, may still fall within the scope of the regulation. Thus, in *Hoekstra (née Unger)* (Case 75/63), a person subject to Netherlands social security legislation who fell ill during a visit to her parents in Germany was entitled to claim the cost of treatment received in that country on her return. Similarly, in *Hessische Knappschaft v Maison Singer et Fils* (Case 44/65), a German worker was killed in a road accident while on holiday in France. It was argued that the rights arising under Art 42 EC Treaty were intended to promote the freedom of movement of workers, not holidaymakers, but the Court rejected this argument. It held that nothing in Art 42 required the concept of workers to be limited strictly to that of migrant workers as such. In *Brack v Insurance Officer* (Case 17/76), the Court held that the term 'employed persons' must be applied taking into account the objectives and spirit of the regulation and Arts 39 to 42 EC Treaty on which it is based. The claimant had been covered by the British social security scheme, first as an employed person and then in a self-employed capacity. He had gone to France for health reasons, but had fallen seriously ill there. The Court held that he retained the status of an employed/self-employed person for the purposes of Art 1(a)(ii) during his stay in France.

Family members

Unlike the provisions relating to the exercise of free movement rights for workers under Art 10, Regulation 1612/68 and the self-employed under Art 1(1)(c) and (d), Directive 73/148 (see Chapters 12 and 13), the scope of family membership is not defined by Community law but is left to the Member State. Under Art 1(f), Regulation 1408/71 a member of the family is any person defined or recognised as a member of the family or 'designated as a member of the household by the legislation under which benefits are provided ... Where the said legislations regard as a member of the family or a member of the household only a person living under the same roof as the worker, this condition shall be considered satisfied if the worker in question is mainly dependent on that worker'. Although the definition of family entitlement is left to the state concerned, where the definition could constitute a barrier to worker mobility, the Court has preferred a broader definition. In *Mr and Mrs F v Belgian State* (Case 7/75), the Belgian social security scheme provided a benefit payable to parents of handicapped children. This was payable only to parents of Belgian nationality and until the age of the majority of the child. The Court held that neither condition should be applied to the child of an employed person covered by Regulation 1408/71.

An exception to the general rule has been introduced by Regulation 1247/92, amending Art 1(f), which provides a Community definition of 'family members' in the case of benefits for people with disabilities. The Court had already adopted a more liberal definition of 'family members' to include adult handicapped members who had never worked and could not do so (*Inzirillo* (Case 63/76)).

Equality of treatment

The beneficiaries of Regulation 1408/71 who are resident in the territory of one of the Member States 'shall be subject to the same obligations and enjoy the same benefits under the legislation of any Member State as the nationals of that state' except where the regulation provides otherwise (Art 3(1)). The effect of this provision is to prohibit indirect or covert discrimination. In *Commission* v *Belgium* (Case C-326/90), the Court held that the Belgian authorities had breached Art 3(1) by maintaining a requirement of a period of residence on Belgian territory which workers from other Member States subject to Belgian legislation had to fulfil in order to qualify for the grant of allowances for handicapped people, the guaranteed income for the elderly and the payment of the minimum subsistence allowance (MINIMEX). An even more direct form of discrimination occurred in *Palermo* (Case 237/78).

The case concerned a claim by an Italian woman to an allowance payable under the French Social Security Code to French women of at least 65 years of age and without sufficient means, who were married and who had brought up at least five dependent children of French nationality during a period of at least nine years before their sixteenth birthday. The French authorities did not insist on the nationality requirement in the case of the applicant herself, but refused the benefit because five of the seven children were Italian and not French.

The Court of Justice held that payment of a benefit could not be made conditional on the nationality of the claimant or her children, provided that both she and the children held the nationality of a Member State.

Discrimination may occur not only in relation to entitlement to social security benefits but also in relation to contributions. In *Allué and Coonan* (Case 33/88) a number of Community nationals employed as university teachers were obliged, as a consequence of Italian legislation, to pay their own social security contributions, whereas in the case of the ordinary salaried employees of the university, this burden was largely carried by the employer. The Court held that the practice violated Art 3(1). The Court has also said that a system of calculation of social security contributions that works less favourably in relation to trainee workers coming from another Member State in comparison to workers who come under the national educational system is unlawful because it is also discriminatory (*URSSAGF* v *Société a Responsabilité Limitée Hostellerie Le Manoir* (Case C-27/91)).

Another aspect of equality of treatment in the regulation is specifically dealt with in relation to mobility and receipt of benefits. Article 10(1), Regulation 1408/71 provides:

> Save as otherwise provided in this regulation, invalidity, old-age or survivors' cash benefits, pensions for accidents at work or occupational diseases and death grants acquired under the legislation of one or more Member State shall not be subject to any reduction, modification, suspension, withdrawal or confiscation by reason of the fact that the recipient resides in the territory of a Member State other than that in which the institution responsible for payment is situated.

The effect of Art 10(1) is that a worker or self-employed person who has, for example, contributed all his working life to a national insurance scheme in one Member State will be entitled to have that pension paid to him at the full rate, should he choose to retire to another Member State. It should be noted, however, that the right of equal treatment as it affects payment of social security and the mobility of the employed and self-employed applies only to those benefits specifically covered by Art 10(1): i.e. benefits which are 'exportable', in the sense that they are payable by the state where the contributions have been made, to the recipient in the Member State in which he or she now lives.

The principle of equality is also reflected in Directive 79/7, under which there is a prohibition against any kind of discrimination on ground of sex (Art 4(1)). The principle applies in relation to access to social security schemes, the obligation to contribute and the calculation of contributions and the calculation of benefits. This directive applies both to migrant workers and their families and to domestic claimants for social security who do not leave their own state. The equality requirement is, however, limited to schemes which relate to sickness, invalidity, old age, accidents at work and occupational diseases, unemployment and social assistance, so far as the social assistance is intended to supplement or replace one of the schemes included. The directive does not, for example, cover housing benefits (*R* v *Secretary of State for Social Security, ex parte Smithson* (Case C-243/90)). However, where a benefit is linked to employment – e.g. working families' tax credit in the United Kingdom, which is intended to bring low wages for family wage earners up to a minimum level – the position is different. The Court of Justice has held that benefits of this kind are concerned with improving access to employment. They are therefore subject to the prohibitions against discrimination in employment in Directive 76/207 (*Meyers* v *Adjudication Officer* (Case C-116/94)).

THE PRINCIPLES OF ARTICLE 42 EC TREATY

The principles underlying Art 42 EC Treaty have been elaborated by Regulation 1408/71 and by decisions of the Court.

1 Aggregation of contributions and periods of contribution

The Court has held on a number occasions that all the provisions of Regulation 1408/71 are to be interpreted in the light of Art 42 EC Treaty (see, e.g., *Reichling* v *INAMI* (Case C-406/93)). The purpose of Art 42 was to facilitate freedom of movement for workers by securing for migrant workers and their dependants 'aggregation, for the purpose of acquiring and retaining the right to benefit and of calculating the amount of benefit of all periods taken into account under the laws of the several countries' (Art 42(a)).

Article 18(b), Regulation 1408/71 contains specific provisions on aggregation in relation to sickness and maternity benefits:

> The competent institution of a Member State whose legislation makes the acquisition, retention or recovery of the right to benefits conditional upon the completion of periods of insurance, employment or residence shall, to the extent necessary, take account of periods of insurance, employment or residence completed under the legislation of any other Member State as if they were periods completed under the legislation which it administers (as amended by the Act of Accession and Regulation 2864/72).

In *Reichling*, above, for example, the Art 234 EC Treaty proceedings concerned the way in which the amount of invalidity benefit to which the claimant was entitled should be calculated under Art 46(2)(a), Regulation 1408/71. The legislation of the state where he claimed the benefit required the amount to be calculated on the basis of the amount of his remuneration which he last received in that state. He was not, in fact, working in that state when the invalidity occurred. The Court held that the competent institution of the state in which he made the claim must calculate it on the basis of the remuneration he received in the state where he last worked. In *Paraschi* v *Handelsversicherungs anstalt Württemberg* (Case C-349/87), the failure of the host Member State to take account of the circumstances of the claimant in the state of origin in calculating the qualifying period for a benefit was held to constitute discrimination in breach of both Art 39(2) EC Treaty and the aggregation provisions of Art 42 EC Treaty.

2 Exportability of benefits

Exportability is often more expressively described as 'the portability principle'. It requires that the right to receive a benefit, usually from the state of origin, attaches to a worker as he or she travels around the Community, irrespective of national boundaries. It also enables individuals to have benefits remitted to dependants who live in other Member States. It does not, however, apply to all types of benefit, but, as a general rule, only to those payable on a long-term basis. The benefits which are exportable are: unemployment, invalidity, old-age or survivors' cash benefits, pensions for accidents at work or occupational diseases, death grants and lump sum benefits granted in case of remarriage of a surviving spouse: Art 10(1), Regulation 1408/71. Unemployment benefit is, however, exportable only for three months after the individual has left the home territory: Art 69(1)(c), Regulation 1408/71. Other benefits linked to the above may also be exportable. In *Re an Emigré to the Canary Islands* [1994] 1 CMLR 717, for example, the UK Social Security Commissioners decided that a constant attendance allowance that was payable to a recipient of an invalidity allowance should be treated in the same way, and be payable to the claimant who had emigrated from the United Kingdom to the Canary Islands.

3 Prevention of overlapping benefits

The concept of overlapping benefits is closely related to exportability. It is intended to prevent a worker or a self-employed person who has qualified for an exportable benefit from receiving it from both his country of origin and the state to which he or she has emigrated.

Article 12(1), Regulation 1408/71 provides that the regulation:

> Can neither confer nor maintain the right to several benefits of the same kind for one and the same period of compulsory insurance.

This provision does not, however, apply to invalidity, old-age, death or occupational diseases payments which are awarded by the institutions of two or more Member States (Arts 41, 43(2) and (3), 46, 50, 51 and 60(1)(b), Regulation 1408/71).

In relation to those cases to which the rule against overlapping benefits applies, the position can be illustrated by a claim to unemployment benefit. A worker who is, for example, intermittently unemployed in the host state may not claim unemployment benefit as long as he is entitled to receive it from his state of origin (Art 71(2)). National legislation prohibiting the receipt of overlapping benefits is lawful, provided that it does not work more unfavourably for the claimant than Community law. Whether or not two benefits are of the same kind and do, in fact, overlap is a matter of interpretation of the national legislation by the national court (*Union National des Mutualités Socialistes* v *Aldo Del Grosso* (Case C-325/93)).

In the case of old-age, invalidity and other benefits which may be paid on an overlapping basis, it is still permissible for the state paying the largest amount of benefit to set off against what it would normally pay the amount which the beneficiary actually receives in the state where he is living. In *Bogana* v *UNMS* (Case C-193/92) the claimant, an Italian national, had worked in both Italy and Belgium. When he became incapable of working, he returned to Italy, and became entitled in both states to invalidity benefits. He was paid the Belgian benefit, less the Italian benefit, on a pro rata basis. The Court of Justice accepted this as a proper course. However, it did not accept that when an increase in payment was made in Italy to compensate beneficiaries for the deterioration in value of the Italian currency, the Belgian payments could be decreased. To allow that to happen would depreciate the real value of the claimant's total pension.

4 The types of benefit covered

Article 4(1), Regulation 1408/71 provides that:

> This regulation shall apply to all legislation concerning the following branches of social security:
> (a) sickness and maternity benefits;
> (b   invalidity benefits, including those intended for the maintenance or improvement of earning capacity;
> (c) old-age benefits;
> (d) survivors' benefits;
> (e) benefits in respect of accidents at work and occupational diseases;
> (f) death grants;
> (g) unemployment benefits;
> (h) family benefits.

The terms 'benefits' (which is used throughout Art 4(1)) and 'pensions' are defined in Art 1(t) as 'all benefits and pensions … payable out of public funds, revalorisation increases and supplementary allowances, … and also lump sum benefits which may be paid in lieu of pensions, and payments made by way of reimbursement of contributions'.

Not all benefits are covered by the regulation, though. Article 4(4) expressly excludes three types:

1 social and medical assistance;
2 benefit schemes for victims of war and its consequences;
3 special schemes for civil servants and persons treated as such.

The effect of these exclusions is that migrant workers and the self-employed in other Member States will not be entitled to the benefits listed in Art 4(1), except where they are linked to other benefits to which they are entitled under the 'double-function test' (see below).

The regulation does not provide any criteria for differentiating between 'social security' and 'social assistance'. The Court of Justice has held that benefits must satisfy two tests to come within the regulation. First, the legislation granting the benefit must place claimants in a legally defined position as a result of which they have an absolute right to benefits as opposed to a conditional right dependent upon the exercise of a discretionary power in their favour. Secondly, the benefit must cover one of the risks referred to in Art 4(1) of the regulation. The characteristic feature of social assistance is that it is discretionary and will be payable according to some nationally defined criteria indicating need. In the United Kingdom, for example, a payment such as the contribution-based jobseeker's allowance is dependent on contributions and other qualifying criteria. Once they are established, there is, as a general rule, an entitlement to payment. Payment of income support or income-based jobseeker's allowance will depend on an assessment of means, and may be withheld in certain circumstances, even when the criteria are satisfied (e.g. if a claimant is classed as voluntarily unemployed, even if available for work). Under Directive 90/364, a claim for social assistance will be indicative that an individual no longer has a right of residence under that directive.

The Commission, reflecting the jurisprudence of the Court of Justice, has laid down the following criteria for identifying social assistance:

1   The benefit must be designed to alleviate a manifest condition of need in the person concerned, established after a proper investigation into his resources and bearing in mind the standard of living in the country of residence. If cash benefits are concerned, the amount must be set, case by case, on the basis of the individual situation and means of livelihood of the person concerned.
2   The award of benefit should not be subject to any condition as to the length of employment or length of residence.
3   The fact that a benefit is non-contributory does not determine its nature as a social assistance benefit or exempt it from the rules laid down in Regulation 1408/71. In the same way, the fact that a benefit is linked to a means test is not sufficient in itself to give it the nature of a social assistance benefit: Commentary on Regulation 1408/71 in *Compendium of Community Provisions on Social Security* (1980) Commission of the European Communities, para 4084, p. 235.

Although the Court has emphasised that the list of benefits enumerated in Art 4(1) is exhaustive (see *Scrivner v Centre Public d'Aide Sociale de Chastre* (Case 122/84)), some benefits may, according to the circumstances, qualify as both social assistance and social security under the 'double-function' test.

5 The double-function test

Although the Court held in *Scrivner* that discretionary social-assistance-type benefits would fall outside the scope of Regulation 1408/71, as a result of the exclusion contained in Art 4(4), it has tended to be generous in its interpretation of the scope of Regulation 1408/71. The discretionary element which the Court established as the primary differentiation between social security and social assistance did not exclude many benefits, even though they were not within the list set out in Art 4(1), and benefits which have been described as 'of extremely dubious status as social security benefits' (Steiner (2000), p. 386) were accepted as within the scope of the regulation (*Inzirillo* (Case 63/76); *Vigier* (Case 70/80); *Palermo* (Case 237/78)). However, following *Scrivner*, in which the Court emphasised the exhaustive nature of the list in Art 4(1), Regulation 1408/71, the opportunities for claiming benefits not listed in Art 4(1) as social security benefits would seem to have diminished. In *Scrivner* the Court turned to the 'social advantages' route in Art 7(2), Regulation 1612/68 as an alternative basis for entitlement (see below, and Chapter 12),

The 'double-function test', which was one aspect of the earlier case law, would seem to have survived. It remains important because, unlike 'social advantages', a benefit which can be brought within Regulation 1408/71 will be 'exportable', whereas 'social advantages' (see below) are available only in the host state and are open only to those who have the status of worker or members of a worker's family. The 'double-function' test was established by the Court in *Frilli* (Case 1/72). In this case, the Court held that even a means-tested discretionary payment could become 'social security' rather than 'social assistance' where it was used to *supplement* a contributory old-age benefit. Thus, a supplement which, when it stood alone, might be considered to be 'social assistance', could come within the scope of the regulation where it could be regarded as a supplement to one of the listed benefits. In *Giletti* (Cases 379–381/85), the Court held that Community social security benefits could include supplements to inadequate old-age, widows' and invalidity pensions.

The 'double-function' aspect of welfare benefits, as developed in the jurisprudence of the Court, was recognised in more recent Community legislation. The preamble to Regulation 1247/92 states that it is 'necessary to take account of this [case] law', and that changes are necessary which 'take account of the special characteristics of the benefits concerned ... in order to protect the interests of migrant workers in accordance with the provisions of Article 51 [now Art 42] of the Treaty'. Social-assistance-type benefits may therefore continue to be treated as social security where they are linked to a recognised benefit under Art 4(1), Regulation 1408/71. Where there is no such linkage, a person may have an entitlement to it only, if at all, as a social advantage under Art 7(2), Regulation 1612/68 in the host state where he or she works or has worked.

The problem of classification of non-contributory benefits has partly been alleviated as a result of the extension of the scope of Regulation 1247/92 to cover a wide range of non-contributory social security benefits.

SOCIAL ASSISTANCE AND SOCIAL ADVANTAGES

The exclusion of social and medical assistance from the scope of Regulation 1408/71 was, potentially, a major obstacle to social mobility, but it reflected the anxiety of Member States about 'social tourism'. Now that EU citizenship confers a right to live anywhere in the Community, it would seem arguable, at least, that EU citizens, like citizens of the nation states, should be able to do so regardless of means. This argument, as H.C. Taschner (a Commission official) has observed, 'overlooks the fact that the social security systems of Member States still differ enormously, and any effort to harmonise these systems is met with formidable resistance, mainly by those Member States that have highly developed social security systems financed by their taxpayers ... the fear of an uncontrolled flow of persons seeking residence for no other reason than to become beneficiaries of better social security than at home was, and is, completely justified' (Taschner, 1993). There is, in fact, no evidence that 'social tourism' is a major factor in the decision to move to another Member State, but in matters of political sensitivity of this kind, the perception is more important than the reality.

Although Regulation 1408/71 excluded social assistance, the narrow definition given to that term, and the generous interpretation of the listed benefits in the ways described above, did somewhat diminish the problems caused by that exclusion. Where 'social assistance' payments could not, by the double-function test, be linked to a social security benefit, the Court of Justice developed the scope of social advantages under Art 7(2), Regulation 1612/68 to plug the gap. The scope of social advantages has already been examined in some detail in Chapter 12, but something needs to be said about Art 7(2), Regulation 1612/68 in the context of social assistance.

In *Scrivner* v *Centre Public d'Aide Sociale de Chastre* (Case 122/84), the Court had to consider the relationship between 'social assistance', which is excluded from the application of Regulation 1408/71 by Art 4(4), and 'social advantages' under Art 7(2), Regulation 1612/68.

Mr and Mrs Scrivner settled in Belgium in 1978 with their six children. In June 1982 Mr Scrivner left his employment 'for personal reasons'. It is not stated in the report what they were, but the Court seems to have assumed that they were not such as to make Mr Scrivner 'voluntarily unemployed' and therefore deprive him of his worker status (see *Raulin* (Case C-357/89), para 22). Mr Scrivner and his family were refused payment of MINIMEX (a grant to provide the minimum means of subsistence) because it was available only to those who had been resident in Belgium for at least five years. The claimants argued that the benefit fell within Regulation 1408/71, and that they should, therefore, be protected from discrimination under Art 3(1) of the regulation. The question was referred to the Court of Justice under what is now Art 234.

The Court, on this occasion adopting a more restrictive approach, held that MINIMEX did not fall within the regulation:

> The Court has stated in a number of decisions that the distinction between benefits which are excluded from the scope of Regulation 1408/71 and benefits which come within it rests entirely on factors relating to each benefit, in particular its purpose and the condition for its grant, and not whether the national legislation describes the benefit as a social security benefit or not. (para 11)

The list of benefits contained in Art 4(1) is exhaustive. Thus, a branch of social security not mentioned in the list does not fall within that category 'even if it confers upon individuals a legally defined position entitling them to benefits'. Furthermore, MINIMEX 'adopts "need" as an essential criterion for its application and *does not make any stipulations as to periods of work, contribution or affiliation to any particular social security body covering a specific risk*' (para 13, emphasis added).

The Court was, however, prepared to accept that MINIMEX was a social advantage under Art 7(2), Regulation 1612/68 and found that it could be seen to be an advantage granted to national workers 'primarily because of their objective status as workers or by virtue of the mere fact of their residence on the national territory'. In so deciding, the Court drew on the analogy of the guaranteed old people's income in *Castelli* v *ONPTS* (Case 261/83), which the Court had also found to be a social advantage under Art 7(2), Regulation 1612/68.

It must be emphasised that the right to subsistence grants of the MINIMEX type under Art 7(2) is attributable only to *workers* and not to *work-seekers,* since the provisions of Title I apply to all Community nationals, whereas Titles II and III of Regulation 1612/68 (including Art 7(2)) are confined explicitly to workers (*Centre Public d'Aide Sociale de Courcelles* v *Lebon* (Case 316/85), para 26). However, as we have seen, the term 'worker' is wide enough to cover anyone who is working, or who has worked but has lost his employment other than voluntarily. In relation to education grants for vocational education, even voluntary unemployment may not deprive an individual of worker status, provided there is a link between the work that has been abandoned and the course which the student has embarked upon (*Raulin*, above, Chapter 12).

Self-employed workers are not entitled to receive subsistence payments, or social assistance, as a social advantage since Regulation 1612/68 is applicable only to workers and their families. The equal treatment provisions of Art 12 EC Treaty are not likely to assist here, because the Court has held that grants and other such benefits are outside the scope of equal treatment of recipients of services (*Lair* (Case 39/86)). However, the distinction between having equal access to facilities to enable a person to pursue a business or a profession and equal access to grants and benefits is not always clear. In *Commission* v *Italy* (Case 63/86), the Court held that denial of housing aid to a self-employed person claiming under Arts 43 and 49 EC Treaty was unlawful as an 'obstacle to the pursuit of the occupation itself' (para 16).

The scope of the benefits covered

The range of social security schemes listed in Art 4(1), Regulation 1408/71 has been the subject of extensive litigation in the Court of Justice. A selection of cases on the main benefits will give some idea of the scope of each benefit.

Sickness and maternity benefits

The Court in *Heinze* v *Landesversicherunganstalt Rheinprovinz* (Case 14/72) held that 'sickness benefits' are not confined to benefits paid to a sick person when he is incapacitated. They include social security benefits which, without being related to earning capacity on the part of the insured person, are also granted to members of his family and which are designed principally for healing the sick person and protecting those around him. In *Commission* v *Luxembourg* (Case C-118/91), the Court held that a maternity benefit was covered by both Art 4, Regulation 1408/71 and Art 7(2), Regulation 1612/68 as a social advantage. Residence requirements breached both the principle of aggregation under Art 42 EC Treaty and the prohibition against discrimination.

Invalidity benefits

Invalidity benefit normally means a long-term contributory benefit for adults who are unfit to work. The Administrative Commission set up under Community social security rules considers that the term 'invalidity benefits' must be interpreted broadly so as to include all benefits granted to a person who is an invalid (*Re Invalidity Benefits* [1988] CMLR 1). In *Baison* (Case 24/74), the Court held that the term included a supplementary allowance, paid by a national solidarity fund, which could be awarded to individuals receiving a life pension provided by virtue of an invalidity that reduced the worker's working or earning capacity by two-thirds. In *Newton v Chief Adjudication Officer* (Case C-358/89), the Court held that an allowance paid under the legislation of a Member State which is granted on the basis of objective criteria to persons suffering from physical disablement affecting their mobility, and to the grant of which the individuals concerned have a legally protected right, must be treated as an invalidity benefit.

Old-age benefits

These are pensions payable by the state in which the pensioner has been employed, according to the law of the state in which he retired and claimed a pension (Arts 44 and 45, Regulation 1408/71). There are complex rules under Arts 46 and 47, Regulation 1408/71 on the calculation of the amount payable in respect of each Member State to which the retired worker has paid contributions. An old-age benefit will normally be a personal retirement pension 'intended to ensure that a worker has an adequate income from the date on which he or she … retires' (*Schmidt v Rijksdienst voor Pensioenen* (Case C-98/94)).

Unemployment benefits

A worker who is wholly unemployed and who satisfies the conditions of the legislation of a Member State for entitlement to benefits, and who goes to one or more Member State seeking employment, retains his right to benefit. He will, however, have had to register as unemployed in his home state, and have remained available for work there for at least four weeks (Art 69(1), Regulation 1408/71). He has to register as a person seeking work with the employment services of each of the Member States to which he goes and must subject himself to the procedures of that system. He will be entitled to benefit for three months after he last registered with the employment office of his home state (Art 69(1)(b) and (c)).

The Court held in *Kuyken* (Case 66/77) that the provisions of Arts 69 and 70 have no application to an unemployed person who has never been in employment and never been treated as an unemployed person under the relevant national legislation. However, in *Bonaffini v INPS* (Case 27/75), the Court held that:

> Article 69 … is intended solely to ensure for the migrant worker the limited and conditional preservation of the unemployment benefits of the competent State even if he goes to another Member State and this other Member State cannot, therefore, rely on mere failure to comply with the conditions prescribed under that Article to deny the worker entitlement to the benefit which he may claim under the national legislation of that State.

FUTURE DEVELOPMENTS

On 21 December 1998 the European Commission presented a proposal for a regulation on the coordination of social security systems, which would replace Regulations 1408/71 and 574/92 (COM(98) 779 final, OJ 1999 C38). The objective of the proposal is to simplify and clarify the current rules and to bring Regulation 1408/71 into line with developments in national legislation and the case law of the Court of Justice. The proposal is shorter than Regulation 1408/71 and has the advantage of rationalising the concepts, rules and procedures. Changes include:

- extension of the scope to all persons covered by the social security legislation of a Member State (such as students) and not just the active population;
- increase in the number of social security branches subject to the coordination regime so as to include new forms of benefits (such as pre-retirement benefits); and
- amendment of certain provisions on unemployment (maintenance for a certain time of the right to unemployment benefits for unemployed persons who visit another Member State to seek work, and the right of unemployed persons to benefits other than cash benefits).

There has been no rush to adopt the proposal by the Council of Ministers and it is unclear when (if at all) it will actually be adopted. Details of the proposal are available on the Commission's website at: europa.eu.int.scadplus/leg/en/cha/c10521.htm.

SOCIAL SECURITY AND SOCIAL ASSISTANCE IN THE UNITED KINGDOM

The United Kingdom's Department of Social Security has a website where information on social security benefits for EC citizens is available: www.dss.gov.uk.

Social security

The full range of benefits falling within Art 4(1), Regulation 1408/71 is available in the United Kingdom. The terms on which these benefits are available are complicated but it is possible to match a number of contributory and non-contributory benefits which will be available to Community migrant workers, assuming that the qualifying provisions under both UK and EC law are met.

The UK benefits falling within Art 4(1) currently comprise: the contribution-based jobseeker's allowance, statutory sick pay and sickness benefit, maternity allowances, benefits relating to invalidity and disability, widows' benefits, retirement pensions, industrial injuries benefits and benefits for children. In *Re an Emigré to the Canary Islands* [1994] 1 CMLR 717, the Social Security Commissioner held that attendance allowance was equivalent to invalidity benefit, and should therefore, as a benefit payable under Regulation 1408/71, continue to be paid to a claimant after he had moved to another Member State. In *Snares* v *Adjudication Officer* (Case C-20/96), however, disability living allowance was held by the Court of Justice to have been validly refused to a British citizen in Tenerife as a non-exportable benefit.

Social assistance

Since income support, income-based jobseeker's allowance and working families' tax credit are calculated according to need, they would appear to fall outside the social security criteria (see above). In relation to family credit (which has been replaced by working families' tax credit), however, the Court has stated, in relation to the form of family credit payable in Northern Ireland, that it is a Community social security benefit (*Hughes* (Case C-78/91)). The position should now be viewed in the light of the United Kingdom's declaration annexed to Regulation 1247/92, Annex II, s III L. It will continue to be the case that inclusion of a benefit in a declaration will be conclusive evidence that a benefit is within the Community social security scheme. However, the regulation enables Member States to specify in the annex non-contributory benefits which are excluded from Community law. These exclusions by a Member State are permissible only when the validity of the benefit excluded 'is confined to part of its territory'. The United Kingdom's declaration excludes specific benefits (e.g. income support and attendance allowance). The declaration also lists separately the same provisions made under Northern Ireland legislation. Whether the United Kingdom's declaration is in fact in relation to only part of its territory, as required, is certainly open to argument (see Morris, Rahal and Storey (1993), p. 289). The effect of the declaration will have to be determined by the Court of Justice. It should, however, be remembered that, even if an entitlement to the above benefits does not arise as a social security benefit, there can be no doubt that all those benefits should be paid to a European Union citizen, or other beneficiary of free movement rights, under Art 7(2), Regulation 1612/68 as a social advantage in the same circumstances in which they would be payable to a UK citizen. The fact that the benefit is included in the list lodged by the UK Government in relation to social security benefits will have no bearing on the availability of the benefit as a social advantage.

Income support

United Kingdom law is more generous than it is required to be in relation to income support (and income-based jobseeker's allowance) which, as we have seen, except where it is supplementing a social security benefit listed in Art 4(1), Regulation 1408/71, does not have to be paid to an individual who has not yet reached worker status. The Court of Justice decided in *Lebon* (Case 316/85), that work-seekers, as opposed to workers, were not entitled to the social advantages conferred by Art 7(2), Regulation 1612/68. Income support (or income-based jobseeker's allowance) can be a social advantage, but only for a person who has, for example, worked but lost his job involuntarily and thus retains his worker status (see above, Chapter 12). In the United Kingdom, an EU citizen, or other national of an EEA state, who arrives to look for work can sign on here. If he has paid sufficient contributions in his home state, he may qualify for contribution-based jobseeker's allowance and, under Art 69(1)(c), Regulation 1408/71, will be entitled to receive it for three months. He may, as he is entitled, remain to look for work for as long as six months, or even longer (*R v Immigration Appeal Tribunal, ex parte Antonissen* (Case 292/89)). In the latter half of that six-month period he may be compelled to rely on income support or income-based jobseeker's allowance.

The practice in the United Kingdom is that EU citizens and EEA nationals who come here to seek work and who have not previously worked in the United Kingdom are eligible for income support (or income-based jobseeker's allowance) for a period of up to six months. After that period, if in the opinion of the Employment Services Claimant Adviser they are no longer actively looking for work, they may be declared by the Home Office to be no longer lawfully present in the United Kingdom, and be required to leave. Their cases will then be referred to an adjudication officer and payment of income support (or income-based jobseeker's allowance) will cease (*Report by the Social Security Advisory Committee on the Income-related Benefits Schemes (Miscellaneous Amendments) (No. 3) Regulations 1994* (SI 1994/1807), Cm 2609, para 9).

Other EU citizens who come to the United Kingdom to retire, on social visits, as students or in some other non-economically active capacity will fall under the following Directives: 90/364 (economically self-sufficient), 90/365 (retired people) and 93/96 (students). All three categories have a right of residence on condition that they do not become a burden on the social assistance system of the host state. In the United Kingdom, if an EU citizen or an EEA national who is living here under the terms of one of the directives makes a claim for income support (or income-based jobseeker's allowance), he may be declared by the Home Office to be no longer lawfully present in the country and required to leave (*Report of the Social Security Advisory Committee*, para 8).

In addition, since 1994, an EU citizen or an EEA national, or a member of their families, is not entitled to receive income support (or income-based jobseeker's allowance), council tax benefit or housing benefit unless he can show that he is 'ordinarily resident' in the United Kingdom. This provision does not apply to workers 'for the purposes of Regulation 1612/68' or a person with a right of residence under Directive 68/360 or Directive 73/148 (paras 2–4, Income-related Benefits Schemes (Miscellaneous Amendments) (No. 3) Regulations 1994 (SI 1994/1807)).

Therefore, an EU national will have to satisfy the residence test, if he does not fall within one of the categories defined by the above Community provisions. This test will involve proof by the claimant: that his centre of interest lies in the United Kingdom; that he has stable employment; of his reasons for coming to this country; of the length and continuity of his residence outside the United Kingdom; and of his future intentions (para 6, *Report of Social Security Advisory Committee*). There is some doubt as to the legality of this test under Community law. If Community nationals are to be allowed these benefits while in the United Kingdom, they should receive them on the same basis as local nationals, without discrimination. Such equal treatment should operate at least in relation to those individuals who are exercising a right of residence under Community provisions, and it should not be open to Member States to impose additional requirements that discriminate covertly against Community nationals. Residence qualifications operated in relation to all applicants, both EU and non-EU, may, however, represent indirect discrimination where it is obvious that local nationals will find them much easier to satisfy than Community nationals (*Lair* (Case 39/86); *Commission* v *Belgium* (Case C-326/90)).

The relationship between claims to benefit and the exercise of free movement rights in the United Kingdom will be examined further in Chapter 16.

Further reading

Cornelissen, R., 'The principle of territoriality and the Community regulations on social security (Regs 1408/71 and 574/72)' (1996) 33 CML Rev 439.

Craig, P. and De Burca, G. (1998) *EU Law Text, Cases and Materials* (2nd edn), OUP, Chapter 19.

Moore, M., 'Freedom of Movement and Migrant Workers' Social Security: an Overview of the Court's Jurisprudence 1992–1997' (1998) 35 CML Rev 409.

Morris, P., Rahal, I. and Storey, H. (1993) *Ethnic Minorities Benefits Handbook Pt III*, Child Poverty Action Group.

Steiner, J., 'The Right to Welfare: Equality and Equity under Community Law' (1985) 10 EL Rev 21.

Steiner, J. and Woods L. (2000) *Textbook on EC Law* (7th edn), Blackstone Press, Chapter 24.

Taschner, H.C. (1993) 'Free Movement of Students, Retired Persons and other European Citizens', in Schermers, H. (ed.) *Free Movement of Persons in Europe: Legal Problems and Experiences*, Martinus Nijhoff.

Verschueren, H., 'EC Social Security Co-ordination excluding third country nationals' (1997) 34 CML Rev 991.

Watson, P., 'Minimum Income Benefits: Social Security or Social Assistance?' (1985) 10 El Rev 335.

Chapter 15

LIMITATIONS ON THE FREE MOVEMENT OF PERSONS

All the Treaty provisions conferring free movement rights, as discussed in Chapters 12 and 13, are subject to the power of national derogation on the grounds of public policy, public security and public health (Arts 39(3), 46(1) and 55 EC Treaty; Art 10, Directive 68/360; and Art 8, Directive 73/148). There is no Community definition of any of those grounds, but Directive 64/221 is intended, first, to limit the extent to which Member States are entitled to restrict rights of free movement and, second, to provide minimum standards of procedural protection for the individuals affected when Member States take such restrictive action. The scope of both aspects of the directive will be examined.

PUBLIC POLICY

The directive does not attempt to define 'public policy'. It is a term that is also found in relation to permitted restrictions on the import and export of goods under Art 30 (see Chapter 18). Member States are free to determine the scope of public policy in their territory, which may be different in each Member State. It is, for example, permissible for the Republic of Ireland to prohibit abortions on its territory, and equally acceptable under Community law for the United Kingdom to permit them. It would, however, probably not be compatible with Community law for a person to be prevented from receiving information in Ireland issued by an abortion clinic in the United Kingdom or from going to the United Kingdom to have an abortion. In *Society for the Protection of the Unborn Child Ireland Ltd* v *Grogan* (Case C-159/90), the Court held that medical termination of pregnancy, performed in accordance with the law of the state where it was carried out, constituted a service within Art 50. However, the distribution of information about the clinics in the United Kingdom was not carried out on their behalf and the Court did not adjudicate on whether the lawful public policy restrictions in one state could legitimately interfere with access to a lawful service in another. The same issue was raised in *Attorney-General* v *X and Others* [1992] 2 CMLR 277, but the case was decided by the Supreme Court of the Republic of Ireland on the basis that the young woman who wished to go to the United Kingdom for an abortion had 'an unenumerated constitutional right to travel' under Irish law, and did not, therefore, need to rely on her Community right to travel to receive a service (pp. 303, 306). Different public policy requirements in different states may result in the quite lawful prohibition of cross-border services, even where they are legitimate in one of the states concerned, provided that the prohibition is proportionate to the risk and provided it is applied equally in the receiving state to local citizens and EU citizens alike (*HM Customs and*

Excise Commissioners v *Schindler* (Case C-275/92)). 'Public policy' and 'public security' are used interchangeably, and they seem to be regarded by the Court of Justice as overlapping concepts. However, although the Court accepted in *Van Duyn* (Case 41/74) that 'the concept of public policy may vary from one country to another and from one period to another and it is, therefore, necessary ... to allow the competent national authorities an area of discretion within the limits imposed by the Treaty', in more recent years it has tended to emphasise the limitations imposed by Community law and the need for equality of treatment between local nationals and EU citizens and their families (*Commission* v *Germany, Re Housing of Migrant Workers* (Case 249/86), paras 18 and 19). An attempt to prevent an EU citizen from having access to a service relating to fertility treatment not available on policy grounds in the United Kingdom was held by the English Court of Appeal, in *R* v *The Human Fertilisation and Embryology Authority, ex parte DB* [1997] 2 WLR 806, to be disproportionate and, therefore, unlawful. It may well be that the Court of Justice would hold that, whilst the state has a broad discretion as to what services it controls on public policy grounds within its own frontiers, it would be disproportionate to prevent a citizen from receiving such services in other Member States where they are lawful.

The discretion retained by Member States in identifying the areas of public policy which may result in the restriction of free movement rights, has been substantially limited by the substantive provisions of Directive 64/221.

Scope of Directive 64/221

The directive applies to any national of a Member State or a state in the European Economic Area, and his family, who resides in or travels to another Member State either in order to pursue an activity as an employed or self-employed person or as a recipient of services (Art 1). It covers all measures concerning entry into their territory, issue or renewal of residence permits, or expulsion from their territory taken by Member States on grounds of public policy, public security or public health (Art 2). It is not confined to restricting or limiting national legislation regulating entry and residence, but the directive also applies to all administrative decisions made by states in relation to individuals exercising free movement rights on their territory (*Rutili* v *Minister of the Interior* (Case 36/75)).

The directive does not refer to departure from the home state and it is not immediately clear whether national measures taken to restrict individuals from leaving the home territory to go to another Member State fall within the directive. However, the right of individuals to depart from their own state is specifically dealt with in Art 2, Directive 68/360 in the case of workers, and Art 2, Directive 73/148 in the case of the self-employed. Both directives have been held to be directly effective (*Royer* (Case 48/75)). The exercise of all the rights conferred by both directives is made subject to the power of the Member States to derogate from them on grounds of public policy, public security and public health (Art 10, Directive 68/360) and it does, therefore, seem that the exercise of all the rights conferred by the directives are protected by Directive 64/221, including the right to depart, and the right to be issued with a travel document.

The directive refers only to public policy, public security and public health measures. Member States may decide, in some cases, that an individual, although an EU citizen, is not exercising rights conferred by the Treaty or the implementing legislation. This is a decision taken on the facts of the case. The Court of Justice has, on a number of occasions, declared that whether or not a person is a worker or a recipient of services is to be determined according to principles laid down by Community law (see, e.g., *Levin v Staatsecretaris van Justitie* (Case 53/81), para 11). In *Commission v Netherlands* (Case C-68/89), the Court held that this was a decision which could not be made by the national authorities at the point of entry, but had to be determined subsequently on the basis of activities undertaken by the individual. It seems likely that a decision, say, that an individual is not economically active and does not have sufficient resources to fall within the residual right of residence under Directive 90/364, will not be a decision made on public policy or public security grounds. It will, however, be a decision affecting the exercise of an individual's free movement rights and should therefore confer at least the minimum procedural protection guaranteed by the general principles of Community law (*UNECTEF v Heylens* (Case 222/86); and see *R v Secretary of State for the Home Office, ex parte Vitali and Do Amaral* [1995] All ER 946). If an individual does enjoy the protection of Community law, but has been a recipient of welfare benefits because of incapacity or some other reason beyond his control, expulsion to relieve the burden on public funds is prohibited by Art 2(2), Directive 64/221, which excludes any action by national authorities falling within the directive 'to service economic ends'.

Article 3(1) provides that measures taken shall be 'based exclusively on the personal conduct of the individual concerned'. Although Member States have a wide discretion in determining the type of 'personal conduct' which may form the basis for action, the Court of Justice has laid down a number of criteria by which such national restrictions must be judged. In the first place, the Court has said that the action of Member States must be assessed in the light of the European Convention on Human Rights. In *Rutili* (above) an Italian national working in France had, following political and trade union activity, been confined by a ministerial order to certain areas of France. He challenged this restriction and the case was referred to the Court under what is now Art 234 EC Treaty. The Court held that:

> The concept of public policy must, in the Community context and where, in particular, it is used as a justification for derogating from the fundamental principles of equality of treatment and freedom of movement of workers, be interpreted strictly, so that its scope cannot be interpreted unilaterally by each Member State without being subject to control by the institutions of the Community. Accordingly, restrictions cannot be imposed on the right of a national of any Member State to enter the territory of another Member State, to stay there and to move within it unless his presence constitutes a genuine and sufficiently serious threat to public policy ... Nor, under Article 8 of Regulation 1612/68, which ensures equality of treatment as regards membership of trades unions and the exercise of rights attached thereto, may the reservation relating to public policy be invoked on grounds arising from the exercise of those rights. Taken as a whole, these limitations placed on the powers of Member States in respect of control of aliens are a specific manifestation of the more general principle, enshrined in Articles 8, 9, 10 and 11 of the Convention for the Protection of Human Rights ... which provide in identical terms, that no restrictions in the interests of national security or public safety shall be placed on the rights secured by the above-quoted articles other than such as are necessary for the protection of those interests 'in a democratic society'.

The Court held in *Rutili* that free movement rights entailed a right of entry and residence in the *whole* territory of the host state, and the restrictions imposed here could not be justified in the case of Community nationals exercising free movement rights unless they were also applicable in similar circumstances to nationals of the host state.

Secondly, the conduct must be both 'personal' and 'a genuine and serious threat' to public policy. The concepts of 'personal conduct' and 'genuine and serious threat to public policy' were explored by the Court in *Van Duyn* v *Home Office* (Case 41/74). It was in this case, it may be remembered, that the Court established the principle that directives, and Directive 64/221 in particular, are vertically effective against the state which has failed to implement them (see Chapter 9).

Yvonne van Duyn, a Dutch national, was a member of the Church of Scientology. She wished to enter the United Kingdom to work for the organisation. The British Government had decided in 1968 that membership of the Church was 'socially harmful', but had not taken any steps to ban or restrict the activities which it carried on at its headquarters in East Grinstead, Sussex. Other Dutch nationals who wished to work for the organisation had, however, been excluded before British membership of the Community (*Schmidt* v *Home Office* [1969] 2 Ch 149). Ms Van Duyn was refused entry on the grounds that her membership of the organisation constituted a threat to public policy. She challenged the refusal on the grounds that membership of an organisation could not be 'personal conduct' within Art 3(1), Directive 64/221. The case was referred to the Court of Justice. The Court held that membership of an organisation could constitute 'personal conduct':

> Although a person's past associations cannot in general, justify a decision refusing him the right to move freely within the Community, it is nevertheless the case that present association, which reflects participation in the activities of the body or of the organisation as well as identification with its aims and designs, may be considered a voluntary act of the person concerned and, consequently, as part of his personal conduct within the meaning of the provision cited. (para 17)

As to whether such an organisation could be regarded as a threat to public policy when no action had been taken against it and when it operated without restriction in the United Kingdom, the Court said:

> The particular circumstances justifying recourse to the concept of public policy may vary from one country to another and from one period to another ... It follows from the above that where the competent authorities of a Member State have clearly defined their standpoint as regards the activities of a particular organisation and where, considering it to be socially harmful, they have taken administrative measures to counteract their activities the Member State cannot be required, before it can rely on the concept of public policy, to make such activities unlawful, if recourse to such a measure is not thought appropriate in the circumstances. (paras 18 and 19)

This decision was somewhat anomalous. At para 19, the Court of Justice stated that a Member State *may* be justified in taking action preventing an EC national from participating in an activity which is considered to be socially harmful, provided it has 'taken administrative measures to counteract these activities' among its own citizens. In this case, the UK Government had simply made a statement in Parliament expressing strong disapproval of the activities of the Church of Scientology. It did not seek to ban the

Church from operating in the United Kingdom, and declared that there was no power to do so.

So, this decision seemed to provide that Member States were justified in excluding or expelling Community citizens for belonging to an organisation engaged in activities which were both 'a serious threat to public policy' and, at the same time, thought by the host state not serious enough to merit even the mildest criminal sanctions when the citizens of the host state were engaged in the same activities. Whilst membership of an organisation committed to activities which clearly breach the criminal law, such as a terrorist organisation, would seem to fall squarely within the concept of 'personal conduct constituting a serious threat to public policy' (see, e.g., *Astrid Proll (No. 2)* [1988] 2 CMLR 387, IAT), membership of an organisation enjoying the full protection of the law would hardly seem to fall within the same category. Neither would such a decision seem to be compatible with the rights to freedom of thought, conscience and religion and freedom of expression enshrined in Arts 9 and 10 of the European Convention on Human Rights, which should, as the Court made clear in *Rutili* (above), inform all decisions made by Member States in relation to the exercise of free movement rights.

The wide discretion which the Court seemed to accept that Member States enjoyed in *Van Duyn* in relation to the type of prohibited conduct was subsequently limited by the Court in an important decision, *Adoui and Cornuaille* v *Belgian State* (Cases 115 & 116/81).

The applicants in this case were French nationals who worked in a Belgian café with a somewhat dubious reputation. They were refused residence in Belgium on public policy grounds. The case was referred to the Court, because 'prostitution as such is not prohibited by Belgian legislation, although the law does prohibit certain incidental activities, such as the exploitation of prostitution by third parties and various forms of incitement to debauchery' (para 6). On this occasion the Court emphasised the need, as far as possible, for equality of treatment between nationals and non-nationals exercising Community rights. Having pointed out that Member States cannot exclude or expel their own nationals, it said:

Although that difference of treatment, which bears upon the nature of the measures available, must therefore be allowed, it must nevertheless be stressed that, in a Member State, the authority empowered to adopt [public policy/public security] measures must not base the exercise of its powers on assessment of certain conduct which would have the effect of applying an arbitrary distinction to the detriment of nationals of other Member States ... Although Community law does not impose upon the Member States a uniform scale of values as regards the assessment of conduct which may be considered as contrary to public policy, it should nevertheless be stated that conduct may not be considered as being of a sufficiently serious nature to justify restrictions on the admission to or residence within the territory of a Member State of a national of another Member State in a case *where the former Member State does not adopt, with respect to the same conduct on the part of its own nationals, repressive measures or other genuine and effective measures intended to combat such conduct.* (paras 7 and 8) (emphasis added)

Had this test been imposed in the *Van Duyn* case, it seems unlikely that the outcome would have been the same since, although the Government had 'clearly defined its standpoint' on the Church of Scientology, it had, in fact, taken no 'repressive or other genuine and effective measures to combat it'. This new approach, reflecting both a standard of equality of treatment and proportionality of response, is also to be found in decisions of the Court in relation to measures taken by national authorities restricting the importation of goods, where reliance is placed on the 'public morality' derogation permitted by Art 30 EC Treaty (*Conegate Ltd* v *Customs and Excise Commissioners* (Case 121/85); see Chapter 18).

'Personal conduct' justifying action must relate exclusively to the individual on whom the restriction is imposed. In *Bonsignore* v *Oberstadtdirektor der Stadt Köln* (Case 67/74), Bonsignore, an Italian national working in Germany, had been found guilty of causing the death of his brother by the negligent handling of a firearm. Following the conviction, he was ordered by the aliens authority to be deported. It was accepted by the German authorities that there was little likelihood of the commission of further offences by the defendant. They were, however, seeking to use the deportation for its deterrent effect 'which the deportation of an alien found in illegal possession of a firearm would have in immigrant circles having regard to the resurgence of violence in large urban areas' (para 4). The matter was referred to the Court of Justice. Advocate-General Mayras emphasised, in his Opinion, that 'it is not permissible for a Community worker, even when convicted of a criminal offence, to be made into a "scapegoat" in order to deter other aliens from acting in the same way ... the concept of personal conduct must be examined not only in the light of the offences committed but also in view of the "potential criminality" of the offender'. The Court agreed with this view and held that Art 3(1), Directive 64/221 means that action taken against an individual on public policy or public security grounds 'cannot be justified on grounds extraneous to the individual case', and thus deportation as a deterrent or as a general preventive measure is prohibited.

The effect of criminal convictions

Previous criminal convictions should not 'in themselves constitute grounds' for exclusion or expulsion (Art 3(2), Directive 64/221). The Court of Justice, in *R* v *Bouchereau* (Case 30/77), was asked by Marlborough Street Magistrates' Court in London 'whether the wording of Art 3(2) of Directive 64/221 EEC, namely that previous criminal convictions shall not "in themselves" constitute grounds for the taking of measures based on public policy or public security, means that previous criminal convictions are solely relevant in so far as they manifest a present or future propensity to act in a manner contrary to public policy or public security; alternatively, the meaning to be attached to "in themselves" in Art 3(2) of Directive 64/221'.

In its reply, the Court said that Art 3(2)

> must be understood as requiring the national authorities to carry out a specific appraisal from the point of view of the interests inherent in protecting requirements of public policy which does not necessarily coincide with the appraisals which formed the basis of the criminal conviction.
>
> The existence of a previous criminal conviction can, therefore, only be taken into account in so far as the circumstances which gave rise to that conviction are evidence of personal conduct constituting a present threat to the requirements of public policy.

Although, in general, a finding that *such a threat exists implies the existence in the individual concerned of a propensity to act in the same way in the future, it is possible that past conduct alone may constitute such a threat to the requirements of public policy.* (emphasis added)

It would seem, from this somewhat obscure judgment, and the words emphasised, that what the national authorities making the decision relating to an EU citizen should be looking for is an indication of whether or not the person concerned is likely to be a future threat. Or, in other words, is there a likelihood of reoffending? That would seem to be the purpose of the assessment, despite Advocate-General Warner having referred to 'circumstances when cases do arise, exceptionally, where the personal conduct of the alien has been such that, whilst not necessarily evincing any clear propensity on his part, has caused such deep revulsion that public policy requires his departure' ([1977] ECR 1999 at 2022). There is no indication, however, that the Court of Justice agreed with Advocate-General Warner in this regard, and indeed, it had agreed with Advocate-General Mayras in an earlier case when he warned against the use of deportation to mollify public opinion: 'one cannot avoid the impression that the deportation of a foreign worker, even a national of the Common Market, satisfies the feeling of hostility, sometimes verging on xenophobia, which the commission of an offence by an alien generally causes or revives in the indigenous population' (*Bonsignore*, above).

There is very little to be said, in terms of the limitations imposed by the directive, for making a decision on the basis of public reaction to an offence. Setting aside the frequent misreporting of the circumstances of offences in the press which may well provoke a quite inappropriate response, the requirement in Art 3(1) that the decision should be 'based exclusively on the personal conduct of the offender' would seem to exclude the taking into account of such extraneous factors as the public response to the offence. What, then, did the Court mean when it said that 'past conduct alone may constitute such a threat'? A 'threat' must indicate that something may happen. A reasonable interpretation of this exceptional circumstance in which past conduct constitutes a future threat might be where the offence itself indicates some kind of mental or other disorder importing the risk of recurrent offending. As we shall see, however, the authorities will have to decide at the time when the decision is taken, by making an assessment, whether the individual still constitutes a threat at the time when the exclusion or expulsion is given effect, 'as the factors to be taken into account, particularly those concerning his conduct, are likely to change in the course of time' (*R* v *Secretary of State for the Home Department, ex parte Santillo* (Case 131/79), para 18 of judgment).

Donatella Calfa (Case C-348/96) concerned an EC national who was expelled from another Member State for life.

Ms Calfa, an Italian national, was charged with possession and use of prohibited drugs while staying as a tourist in Crete (Greece). She was found guilty and sentenced to three months' imprisonment and ordered to be expelled for life from Greek territory, in accordance with national law. The national court was under an obligation to order her expulsion for life (unless there were compelling reasons, in particular family reasons), and she would be able to return to Greece only after a period of three years, provided that the Minister of Justice in his discretion gave his approval.

Ms Calfa contested that the expulsion for life breached her Community law rights to travel to Greece as a tourist (i.e. as the recipient of services in accordance with Art 59 (now Art 49) EC Treaty). The Greek authorities argued that she could be expelled in accordance with the public policy derogation. The Greek court referred the case to the Court of Justice under what is now Art 234, seeking guidance on whether the penalty was compatible with Community law:

17. Although in principle criminal legislation is a matter for which the Member States are responsible, the Court has consistently held that Community law sets certain limits to their power, and such legislation may not restrict the fundamental freedoms guaranteed by Community law ...

18. In the present case, the penalty of expulsion for life from the territory, which is applicable to the nationals of other Member States in the event of conviction for obtaining and being in possession of drugs for their own use, clearly constitutes an obstacle to the freedom to provide services recognised in Article 59 [now Art 49] of the Treaty, since it is the very negation of that freedom. This would also be true for the other fundamental freedoms laid down in Articles 48 [now Art 39 (free movement of workers)] and 52 [now Art 43 (right of establishment)] of the Treaty and referred to by the national court.

19. It is none the less necessary to consider whether such a penalty could be justified by the public policy exception provided for in *inter alia* Article 56 [now Art 46] of the Treaty, which is relied upon by the Member State in question.

20. Article 56 [now Art 46] permits Member States to adopt, with respect to nationals of other Member States, and in particular on the grounds of public policy, measures which they cannot apply to their own nationals, inasmuch as they have no authority to expel the latter from the territory or to deny them access thereto ...

21. *Under the Court's case law, the concept of public policy may be relied upon in the event of a genuine and sufficiently serious threat to the requirements of public policy affecting one of the fundamental interests of society* (see case 30/77 *Bouchereau* [1977] ECR 1999, paragraph 35).

22. In this respect, *it must be accepted that a Member State may consider that the use of drugs constitutes a danger for society such as to justify special measures against foreign nationals who contravene its laws on drugs, in order to maintain public order.*

23. However, as the Court has repeatedly stated, the public policy exception, like all derogations from a fundamental principle of the Treaty, must be interpreted restrictively.

24. In that regard, Directive 64/221, Article 1(1) of which provides that the directive is to apply to *inter alia* any national of a Member State who travels to another Member State as a recipient of services, sets certain limits on the right of Member States to expel foreign nationals on the grounds of public policy. Article 3 of that directive states that measures taken on the grounds of public policy or of public security that have the effect of restricting the residence of a national of another Member State must be based exclusively on the personal conduct of the individual concerned. In addition, previous criminal convictions cannot in themselves constitute grounds for the taking of such measures. *It follows that the existence of a previous criminal conviction can, therefore, only be taken into account in so far as the circumstances which gave rise to that conviction are evidence of personal conduct constituting a present threat to the requirements of public policy (Bouchereau, paragraph 28).*

25. *It follows that an expulsion order could be made against a Community national such as Ms Calfa only if, besides her having committed an offence under drugs laws, her personal conduct created a genuine and sufficiently serious threat affecting one of the fundamental interests of society.*

26. In the present case, the legislation at issue in the main proceedings requires nationals of other Member States found guilty, on the national territory in which that legislation applies, of an offence under the drugs laws, to be expelled for life from that territory, unless compelling reasons, in particular family reasons, justify the continued residence in the country. The penalty can be revoked only by a decision taken at the discretion of the Minister for Justice after a period of three years.

27. Therefore, expulsion for life automatically follows a criminal conviction, without any account being taken of the personal conduct of the offender or the danger which that person represents for the requirements of public policy.

28. It follows that the conditions for the application of the public policy exception provided for in Directive 64/221, as interpreted by the Court of Justice, are not fulfilled and that *the public policy exception cannot be successfully relied upon to justify a restriction on the freedom to provide services, such as that imposed by the legislation at issue in the main proceedings.*

29. In view of the foregoing considerations, the answer to be given to the national court's questions must be that Articles 48 [now 39], 52 [now 43] and 59 [now 49] of the Treaty and Article 3 of Directive 62/221 preclude legislation which, with certain exceptions, in particular where there are family reasons, requires a Member State's courts to order the expulsion for life from its territory of nationals of other Member States found guilty on that territory of the offences of obtaining and being in possession of drugs for their own personal use. (emphasis added)

At paras 21 and 22 the Court of Justice reiterated the principles developed in its previous case law. At para 22, the Court accepted that in order to maintain public order a Member State could consider drug taking to constitute a danger to the public which could therefore justify special measures being taken against foreigners who breached its anti-drug laws. Having said that, the Court at para 25 stated that an EU citizen could be expelled only if it was shown that, in addition to breaching the anti-drug laws, their personal conduct 'created a genuine and sufficiently serious threat affecting one of the fundamental interests of society'. In any event, the Court held at para 28 that expulsion for life was not compatible with the Treaty provisions or Directive 62/221. This was the case even though there was the possibility of review of that decision after three years. It therefore would appear that a mandatory ban on readmission would not be compatible with Community law, because an EU citizen can be prevented from exercising his free movement rights only where he constitutes a genuine and sufficient threat (present or future, *not past*) to one of the fundamental interests of society.

A final point to be aware of, which was discussed in detail in Chapter 12, is that whilst it is permissible to penalise individuals exercising free movement rights who do not comply with national provisions on registration and notification of their removal to a different place, any penalties for not renewing a passport or identity card should not include expulsion from the territory or even imprisonment (Art 3(3)). 'Such penalties should not be so severe as to cause an obstacle to the freedom of entry and residence provided for in the Treaty' (*Sagulo, Brenca and Bakhouche* (Case 8/77), at para 12).

PUBLIC HEALTH MEASURES

Article 4, Directive 64/221 permits exclusion of EU citizens and their families where they are suffering from the diseases listed in the annex to the directive. The list includes diseases subject to quarantine under World Health regulations: tuberculosis in an active state, syphilis, and other infectious diseases subject to notification under the legislation of the host state. There is a separate category of diseases and disabilities which might threaten public policy and public security. These are: drug addiction, profound mental disturbance and manifest conditions of psychotic disturbance with agitation, delirium, hallucinations or confusion.

It is not permissible to carry out routine medical examinations for any of these conditions, since to do so would be to impose an additional requirement on entry prohibited by Art 3(1), Directive 68/360 (*Commission* v *Netherlands* (Case C-68/89)). Nor would it be open to a state to require production of medical or other certificates to confirm that individuals are free from infection, since this, too, would constitute a further restriction. A medical examination would, however, be lawful if a person were to be manifesting obvious symptoms of sickness which might indicate that he was suffering from one of the conditions listed in the annex to Directive 64/221. Such a situation might constitute a case where there is 'sufficient justification for imposing restrictions' (*Commission* v *Belgium (Re Belgian Passport Controls)* (Case 321/87), para 10).

Once a person has entered the Member State, the development of one of the listed diseases cannot be a ground for expulsion. Article 4(1), Directive 64/221 provides that diseases or disabilities occurring after a first residence permit has been issued shall not justify refusal to renew the residence permit or expulsion from the territory. It might, however, be implied from this that a person who contracts a listed illness before being issued with a residence permit, or where none has been applied for, can be expelled on this ground. Such a conclusion would not be compatible with the Court's frequent affirmation that the residence permit is merely proof of the right of residence, not the basis for it (see, e.g., *Echternach* (Cases 389 & 390/87)):

> The issue of such a permit does not create the rights guaranteed by Community law. (para 25)

It would also seem that expulsion following the development of an infectious disease could be regarded as a measure of a 'general preventive nature', i.e. one not relating to the personal conduct of the individual. It was for this reason, *inter alia*, that the Court held that occupation by a family of overcrowded or insanitary housing could not justify expulsion (*Commission* v *Germany (Re Housing of Migrant Workers)* (Case 249/86), para 18).

PROCEDURAL PROTECTION

Articles 5 to 9 of Directive 64/221 are intended to ensure that when action is taken against EU citizens or others exercising Community free movement rights, it is taken in accordance with minimum standards of due process. In addition, in 'each Member State nationals of other Member States should have adequate legal remedies available to them in respect of decisions of the administration' (preamble to Directive 64/221). Article 5 provides that a decision to give or refuse a residence permit should be taken as soon as possible, and in any event not later than six months from the date of application. In the meantime, 'the person concerned shall be allowed to remain temporarily in the territory pending a decision either to grant or refuse a residence permit'. The language of this provision sits somewhat awkwardly with the often repeated pronouncement of the Court that 'the issue of the permit does not create the rights guaranteed by Community law' (see *Echternach*, above). However, it is plain that an EU citizen, has, *prima facie*, a right of entry and residence under Art 18 EC Treaty. Since the onus is on the Member State to justify the denial of that right on public policy, public security or public health grounds, the individual continues to enjoy that right until he has been notified that grounds exist warranting his exclusion or expulsion, and the Member State has provided sufficient evidence to justify its actions.

Under Art 6 of the Directive, the person concerned shall be informed of the grounds of public policy, public security or public health upon which the decision taken in his case is based, unless this is contrary to the interests of the security of the state involved. Where a decision has been taken to refuse the issue or renewal of a residence permit or to expel a person from the territory, he must be officially notified of the decision. The period allowed for leaving the territory must be stated in the notification and, except in cases of urgency, the period should be not less than 15 days if a person has not yet been granted a residence permit and not less than a month in all other cases (Art 7). The person concerned is entitled to have the same legal remedies in respect of any decision concerning entry, or refusing the issue or reissue of a residence permit, or ordering expulsion from the territory, as are available to nationals of the host state in relation to acts of the administration (Art 8).

The giving of sufficient reasons

To enable an effective judicial challenge to be mounted, it is important that adequate reasons are given where a person is excluded or expelled on public policy or public security grounds (Arts 5 and 6, Directive 64/221). The reasons will need to address the relevant aspects of public policy or public security on which the decision is based. The Court in *Rutili* v *Minister of the Interior* (Case 36/75) (para 39), held that:

> this requirement means that the state concerned must, when notifying an individual of a restrictive measure adopted in his case, *give him a precise and comprehensive statement of the grounds for the decision, to enable him to take effective steps to prepare his defence.* (emphasis added)

To be comprehensive, the statement will have to indicate the way in which a person continues to constitute a threat to public policy or public security. In determining whether or not to act against an individual, national authorities must 'carry out a specific appraisal from the point of view of the interests inherent in protecting the requirements of public policy' (*R* v *Bouchereau* (Case 30/77), para 27). It is the result of that appraisal that the authorities must communicate to the individual against whom they have decided to act. If the communication does not meet these requirements then it will invalidate the decision (*R v Secretary of State for the Home Office, ex parte Dannenberg* [1984] 2 CMLR 456 (CA)).

Although Art 6, Directive 64/221 provides that an individual need not be given the reasons for a decision where this is contrary to the interests of the security of the state involved, it would probably not satisfy the Community's principle of a minimum of effective judicial control if the authority does not at least provide some justification as to why the giving of reasons would threaten national security. The Court, in *Johnston v RUC* (Case 222/84) (a sex discrimination case), held that the mere issue of a certificate by the authorities to the effect that the disclosure of information would be prejudicial to national security was not sufficient without some indication of why this should be the case. Although the decision was given in the context of the need for an effective judicial process in Art 6, Directive 76/207, the Court emphasised that it was part of a broader principle of effective judicial control ([1986] ECR 1651 at 1663). However, the English Court of Appeal, in *R v Home Secretary, ex parte Gallagher* [1994] 3 CMLR 295, thought that a recital of the relevant section of the Prevention of Terrorism (Temporary Provisions) Act 1989 as the basis of an exclusion from the United Kingdom, without more, would meet the requirements of Art 6 (*per* Steyn LJ at p. 307). In *Tinelly & Sons Ltd and McElduff v UK*, judgment of 10 July 1998, though, the European Court of Human Rights, in relation to a case involving religious discrimination in Northern Ireland, refused to accept that such an '*ipse dixit* of the Executive' would satisfy Art 6 ECHR.

The need for effective remedies

Article 9 deals with the refusal to renew a residence permit or a decision to order the expulsion of the holder of a residence permit. It provides, in three cases, that the decision must not be taken, except in cases of urgency, until an opinion has been obtained from a competent authority of the host country before which the person concerned enjoys such rights of defence and representation as are provided by domestic law. The three types of cases are, first, where there is no right of appeal to a court of law; secondly, where such an appeal lies only in respect of the legal validity of the decision; and, thirdly, where the appeal cannot have suspensory effect. The object of these provisions, collectively, is to enable an individual either to have access to an appeal body, where this exists, so that it may consider the full circumstances of an individual's case and be obliged to suspend expulsion until it has made a decision, or, where no such appeal body exists, for a competent authority to give an opinion before a decision is put into effect. Article 9(2) provides that '*the person concerned shall then be entitled to submit his defence in person*, except where this would be contrary to the interests of national security' (emphasis added). The system of review must be effective, but it needs only to be as effective as other administrative law remedies, and need not involve an appeal to an immigration appeal body to which nationals of the state involved have access: *R v Secretary of State for the Home Department, ex parte Shingara and Radiom* (Joined Cases C-65 & 111/95).

The Court considered the relationship between Arts 8 and 9 in *Procureur du Roi v Royer* (Case 48/75). The defendant, a French national, was charged with having entered Belgium illegally. He had no residence permit, nor, it seems from the facts of the case, had he applied for one. In an Art 177 (now Art 234) reference from the national court the Court of Justice was asked, *inter alia*, whether a decision ordering expulsion or a refusal to issue a residence or establishment permit may be put into effect immediately or only after remedies before national courts have been exhausted. The Court ruled that:

> Under Article 8 of Directive 64/221 any person subject to an order of expulsion from the territory shall have the same legal remedies in respect of those decisions as are available to nationals in respect of acts of the administration (para [53]). In default of this *the person concerned must, under Article 9, at the very least, be able to exercise his right of defence before a competent authority which must not be the same as that which adopted the measure restricting his freedom* [54]. It is appropriate to state in this respect that *all steps must be taken by the Member State to ensure that the safeguard of the right of appeals is in fact available to anyone against whom a restrictive measure of this kind has been adopted.*
>
> However, this guarantee would become illusory if the Member State could by the immediate execution of a decision ordering expulsion, deprive the person concerned of the opportunity of effectively making use of the remedies which he is guaranteed by Directive 64/221. In the case of the legal remedies referred to in Article 8 of Directive 64/221, the party concerned must have at least the opportunity of lodging an appeal and thus obtaining a stay of execution before the expulsion order is carried out [57]. This conclusion also follows from the link established by the directive between Articles 8 and 9 thereof in view of the fact that the procedure set out in the latter provision is obligatory, inter alia, where the legal remedies referred to in Article 8 'cannot have suspensory effect.' [58]
>
> Under Article 9, the procedure of appeal to a competent authority must precede the decision ordering expulsion, except in cases of urgency [59]. Consequently, where a legal remedy referred to in Article 8 is available the decision ordering expulsion may not be executed before the party concerned is able to avail himself of the remedy [60]. Where no such remedy is available, or where it is available but cannot have suspensory effect, the decision cannot be taken – save in cases of urgency which have been properly justified – until the party concerned has had the opportunity of appealing to the authority designated in Article 9 of the Directive 64/221 *and until that authority has reached a decision* [61]. (emphasis added)

Where an individual is relying on the national remedies referred to in Art 8, it might be thought that, since there is no provision in that Article entitling the individual to remain to present his case, there is no right in such cases to remain until the appeal authority has reached a decision, unless, of course, national law provides otherwise. This would seem to be a possible interpretation of the Court's decision in *Pecastaing* (Case 98/79). However, the relationship between Arts 8 and 9, as the Court said in *Royer* (above), is that Art 9 is complementary to Art 8 (para 12). Although Art 8 refers, ostensibly, to all those exercising free movement rights, whereas Art 9 refers only to those refused renewal of a residence permit, the Court has not used these apparent limitations to distinguish between the two provisions. Indeed, neither Royer nor Adoui, Cornuaille or Santillo were holders of residence permits, but the Court, nonetheless, indicated that they might have recourse to Art 9, without commenting on their lack of permits. This approach accords with that of the Court in *Giagounidis*

(Case C-376/89), where it disregarded the requirement of Directive 68/360 to produce the document with which he entered the country, and declared that since 'freedom of movement of workers forms one of the foundations of the Community ... the provisions laying down that freedom must be given a broad interpretation' (para 20). It was, of course, in *Royer* that the Court declared that the right of residence did not depend on the issue of a permit. It would therefore seem anomalous to make the procedural rights of those exercising free movement rights conditional upon the possession of a permit. Article 9 is, therefore, to be read as being available to remedy any deficiencies in national legislation relating to the exercise of any free movement rights under which acts of the administration can be challenged. The provisions of the Article are 'to ensure a minimum procedural safeguard for persons affected by one of the measures referred to in the three cases described in para (1) of that Article' (para 12 in *Santillo*). If, therefore, there is no right to remain until a decision is given, under national law, then such a right will be conferred by Art 9.

Article 9(1) refers to the requirement, before a final decision is taken, to obtain the opinion 'of a competent authority before which the person concerned enjoys such rights of defence and of assistance or representation as the domestic law of that country provides for'. In *Santillo* (above) the Court of Justice considered the meaning of 'competent authority'. It refers to an authority which must be independent of the administration, but it gives Member States a margin of discretion in regard to the nature of the authority (para 15). It accepted that a criminal court in Britain was such an independent authority. Whether or not an adviser appointed by the Home Secretary whose decision is under review is similarly independent was doubted by the majority of the Court of Appeal in *R v Home Secretary, ex parte Gallagher* [1994] 3 CMLR 295. The Court, having taken into account the observation of Advocate-General Capotorti in *Pecastaing* that 'the advisory authority should have no links whatsoever with the authority required to take the decision', referred the question to the Court of Justice under Art 177 (now Art 234) EC Treaty. The Court of Justice did not exclude the possibility of the competent authority being appointed by the administrative authority, provided that it is able to 'perform its duties in absolute independence' (*R v Home Secretary, ex parte Gallagher* (Case C-175/94)).

Article 9 does not provide that the opinion is binding on the administrative authority. The Court of Appeal in *Gallagher* (*per* Steyn LJ at p. 308) considered that the better view is that it is not. However, in *UNECTEF v Heylens* (Case 222/86) the Court of Justice declared, in the context of the exercise of the right of migrant workers to equal access to employment:

> the existence of a remedy of a judicial nature against any decision of a national authority refusing the benefit of that right is essential in order to secure for the individual effective protection for his right.

The concept of 'effectiveness' means that the national court must 'have the power to do everything ... to set aside national legislative provisions which might prevent ... Community rules from having full force and effect' (*R v Secretary of State for Transport, ex parte Factortame* (Case C-213/89), para 20). There would therefore be little point in obtaining such an opinion if the administrative authority was free to ignore it. The nature of remedies generally under Arts 8 and 9, Directive 64/221 must also be considered in the light of Art 13 of the European Convention on Human Rights, which provides that 'Everyone whose rights and freedoms … are violated shall have an effective remedy before a national authority notwithstanding that the violation has been committed by persons acting in an official capacity'. In *Johnston* v *RUC* (Case 222/84), the Court declared that Art 13 is to be applied when rights conferred by Community law are at issue, and it emphasised that the existence of effective judicial protection is a general principle of Community law.

Further reading

Arnull, A. (1990) *The General Principles of EEC Law and the Individual*, Leicester University Press, pp. 92–99.

Barav, A., 'Court Recommendations to Deport and the Free Movement of Workers in EEC Law' (1981) 6 EL Rev 139.

Connor, T.C., 'Migrant Community Nationals: Remedies for Refusal of Entry by Member States' (1998) 23 EL Rev 157.

Craig, P. and De Burca, G. (1998) *EU Law Text, Cases and Materials* (2nd edn), OUP, Chapter 18.

Handoll, J. (1995) *Free Movement of Persons in the European Union*, J. Wiley & Son, Chapter 7.

O'Neill, M., 'Note on Joined Cases C-6/95 and C-111/95 *R* v *Secretary of State for the Home Department, ex parte Shingara and Radiom*' (1998) 23 EL Rev 157.

Steiner, J. and Woods, L. (2000) *Textbook on EC Law* (7th edn), Blackstone Press, Chapter 22.

Vincenzi, C., 'Freedom of Movement in the Single Market: An Irish Solution?' (1990) NLJ 664.

Vincenzi, C., 'Deportation in Disarray: the Case of EC Nationals' [1994] Crim LR 163.

Chapter 16

FREE MOVEMENT RIGHTS
IN THE UNITED KINGDOM

THE BRITISH APPROACH TO FREE MOVEMENT:
THE ISLAND PROBLEM

The maintenance of strict immigration controls at the ports and airports of the United Kingdom has characterised UK immigration policy since the First World War. Even after the effective date for the creation of the Single Market at the beginning of 1993 had passed, the Government continued to maintain the need for strict frontier controls and nationality checks on all passengers coming from within the Community. It did not participate in the Schengen Agreement, an agreement reached outside the European Union between all continental EU states, which removed most controls over individuals at the land frontiers of those states, and has, with the Republic of Ireland, opted out of the common EU frontier control system set up by the Treaty of Amsterdam in 1997 (Art 69 EC Treaty and Protocol on the Position of United Kingdom and Ireland).

Successive UK Governments have used the port control system to give effect to Community law and in some areas, such as registration with the police under the Immigration (Registration with the Police) Regulations 1972 (SI 1972/1758), as amended, Community nationals benefit from a more relaxed regime. Community law would permit such registration, although not as a condition of residence (*Watson and Belmann* (Case 118/75)). The more relaxed internal system reflects a less intrusive policy of internal controls when compared to mainland Europe. In most continental Member States immigration controls have, for a great many years, been of a post-entry type, involving registration and identity cards, because borders with other Member States were largely unpoliced, except at road crossing points. The effect of the United Kingdom's island geography, however, has been that the emphasis has been very much on the entry process and the granting or refusing of leave at the point of entry.

The distinct position of those exercising Community free movement rights was finally addressed, more than 20 years after British entry, by the Immigration (European Economic Area) Order 1994, which came into effect in July 1994 (SI 1994/1895). The Order was made under s 2(2) of the European Communities Act 1972 and was intended to implement the free movement rights conferred by all the directives relating to entry and residence, including Directives 64/221, 68/360, 73/148, 90/364, 90/365 and 93/96 (Explanatory Note to the Order). Although this was its intention, the second edition of this book highlighted areas where the 1994 Order was deficient.

The 1994 Order was repealed by the Immigration (European Economic Area) Order 2000 (SI 2000/2326) (the 'EEA Order'). The EEA Order, which came into force on 2 October 2000, re-enacts, with amendments, the provisions of the 1994 Order. It applies to workers, self-employed persons, providers and recipients of services, self-sufficient persons, retired persons (who have pursued an activity as an employed or self-employed person (reg 3(1)(f))) and students. The EEA Order creates free-standing rights of appeal which (in contrast to the position under the 1994 Order) are no longer dependent upon rights of appeal arising under the statutory provisions which apply to persons not claiming rights under Community law. The EEA Order copies out many of the provisions of the various directives and regulations and is a far better attempt than its predecessor at complying with Community law. Its provisions will be discussed further below.

SCOPE OF THE IMMIGRATION (EUROPEAN ECONOMIC AREA) ORDER 2000

Nationality of beneficiaries

The Order applies to all 'EEA Nationals', i.e. to all nationals of states who were parties to the European Economic Area Agreement of 1992, which was incorporated into British law by the European Economic Area Act 1993. It therefore applies to all the Member States of the Community together with Iceland, Liechtenstein and Norway, except the United Kingdom; UK citizens are excluded, it would appear, because they already have an unqualified right of entry and residence under British law (s 1, Immigration Act 1971). This is unfortunate because Community law confers certain rights on EU citizens which are more beneficial to British citizens than the provisions of national law. However, one exception to this is reg 11, which provides limited rights of reunification for family members of UK nationals which are equivalent to those applying to family members of EEA nationals.

Other nationalities may benefit from more limited free movement rights under Community law. These include employees of companies based in other Member States which carry on economic activities here (*Van der Elst* v *OMI* (Case C-43/93)), and nationals of states which have association agreements with the Community (*Kziber* v *ONEM* (Case C-18/90); see Chapter 11). These are not covered by the EEA Order, and the beneficiaries will have to rely upon the direct effect of the relevant provisions of the Treaties.

Family rights

The EEA Order is more substantive than the 1994 Order in terms of the persons to whom it applies. Where the beneficiary is a student, it applies only to his spouse and dependent children. In all other cases, it applies to the beneficiary's spouse, descendants of the beneficiary or his spouse who are under 21 or dependent, and ascendants (parents, grandparents) of the beneficiary or his spouse who are dependent on them (reg 6).

This definition excludes some of the family members covered by Art 10(2), Regulation 1612/68 and Art 1(2), Directive 68/360. These two provisions cover other family members of the worker or self-employed person who are dependent on him or who live under his roof in the country of origin. In this instance, the host state must 'facilitate' their admission. Regulation 10 therefore provides a power for the issuing of, *inter alia*, a residency permit to persons who are dependent on the beneficiary or his spouse, or who lived as part of his household outside the United Kingdom. This provision applies only where the beneficiary is a worker, is self-employed or is a provider or recipient of services (i.e. it excludes those who are self-sufficient, retired or studying).

The term 'spouse' in the EEA Order 'does not include a party to a marriage of convenience' (reg 2(1)). There is no definition of a 'marriage of convenience' in the Order, but during the debate on the draft 1994 Order in the House of Lords, Earl Ferrers, on behalf of the Government, described such a marriage as 'entirely bogus, the purpose of which is simply to circumvent immigration control' (HL Debates Vol 557 No. 120 Col 116 (18 July 1994)). Governments may properly be concerned about abuses of Community free movement rights, but it is doubtful whether it is open to Member States to act unilaterally in this way by adding further qualifications to existing categories of Community beneficiaries. To benefit as a spouse of a Community worker, there simply has to be a subsisting marriage (*Diatta* v *Land Berlin* (Case 267/83)). It does not matter if the parties are no longer cohabiting and are even likely to divorce (see *R* v *Immigration Appeal Tribunal and Surinder Singh, ex parte Secretary of State for the Home Department* (Case C-370/90)). Whether or not a marriage is subsisting is a matter for national law, and it would seem that, under UK law at least, a marriage entered into purely for the purposes of remaining in England and to evade extradition may still be valid as a marriage (*Puttick* v *Attorney General* [1979] 3 WLR 542 at 556). The Immigration Appeal Tribunal has, however, decided that a marriage entered into with a Community worker for the purpose of remaining in the United Kingdom did not confer a right to remain under Community law (*Kwong* (1994) (10661) 11 February 1994 (unreported)).

The exercise of free movement rights in the United Kingdom: entry

All British ports and airports now have a route for British, EU and EEA nationals, and those arriving through the Channel Tunnel will be examined in transit (Channel Tunnel (Fire Services, Immigration and Prevention of Terrorism) Order 1990, SI 1990/ 2227). Examination will generally be confined to ensuring that a person is an EU citizen or a national of an EEA state, and any EU citizen or EEA national should be admitted simply on production of a valid identity card or passport (reg 12, EEA Order). People who enter as a family member and who are not themselves EU citizens or EEA nationals will have to produce (in addition to a valid identity card or passport) either a family permit, or a residence document or another document proving his status as a family member of the beneficiary (reg 12, EEA Order).

Regulation 21, EEA Order provides that a person can be denied admission on grounds of public policy, public security or public health, or if at the time of his arrival he is not a family member of the beneficiary.

The Immigration Service retains full powers of examination of EU and EEA citizens on entry. This can, under the EEA Order and the Immigration Act 1971, involve detention in custody, an oral examination, and a full physical (and medical) examination (reg 24(2), EEA Order; Schedule 2, Immigration Act 1971), although this will be a very rare occurrence, and indeed millions of Community nationals enter annually without examination. However, the power of examination is without precondition and there is no requirement under UK law for there to be a perceived threat, in an individual case, to public policy, public security or public health, and the powers are, probably, much wider than permitted by Community law (*Commission* v *Belgium (Re Belgian Passport Controls)* (Case 321/87); *Commission* v *Netherlands* (Case C-68/89)).

Residence

Under the EEA Order, a 'qualified person' is entitled to reside in the United Kingdom without the need to have 'leave' under UK law, as long as he remains a 'qualified person' (reg 14(1), EEA Order). The expression 'qualified person' covers anyone falling within one of the classes of beneficiaries of free movement rights either under the EC Treaty or under secondary legislation. It covers workers, self-employed people, providers of services, recipients of services, the self-employed who have ceased economic activity, retired people, students and the economically self-sufficient (reg 5(1), EEA Order). Work-seekers are not distinguished from workers. The Order simply refers to 'a worker within the meaning of Art 39 EC Treaty'. Workers clearly have a right to remain for the duration of that status, and the Order makes specific provision for loss of employment and confirms that a worker does not lose that status by virtue of temporary incapacity to work as a result of illness or accident, or involuntary unemployment (reg 5(2)). As far as work-seekers are concerned, Community law provides no time limit for that status. The Court of Justice has merely observed that six months is a reasonable period for a person to find work, but a longer time may, in some circumstances, be appropriate (*Antonissen* (Case C-292/89) (see Chapter 12)). No attempt is made to reflect this ruling in the Order. Generally, however, the provisions of the Order in this context do reflect Community law. There are, nevertheless, some omissions where individuals will have to rely on the direct effect of Community law.

'Students', for example, are defined only with regard to those undertaking vocational courses. They have to show that they have sufficient funds to maintain themselves and that they are covered by all-risks sickness insurance (reg 3(1)(g), EEA Order). This is in accordance with Directive 93/96. However, students who enter to take non-vocational courses also have a right of entry and residence, provided that they are studying outside the state system and are paying the full cost of the course. They should be treated as recipients of services and, as such, do not have to meet the means and insurance requirements (*Luisi* (Case 286/82); *Belgium* v *Humbel* (Case 263/86)).

A retired person (other than a self-employed person who has ceased activity (see reg 4, EEA Order)) must have pursued an activity as an employed or self-employed person. He has to show that he has an invalidity, early retirement, old-age, survivor's or industrial pension which is sufficient to avoid his becoming a burden on the social security system of the United Kingdom. This meets the requirement of Art 1, Directive 90/365 which relates to those who have spent their working life outside the United Kingdom. European Union citizens and EEA nationals who have worked in the United Kingdom for more than three years benefit from Regulation 1251/70 and do not have to have sufficient funds to maintain themselves. Regulation 8(1)(d), EEA Order therefore provides that a person who has rights under Regulation 1251/70 is to be regarded as a person who is in the United Kingdom without being subject under the immigration laws to any restriction on the period for which he may remain.

Residence permits

Residence permits must be granted to those who are qualified to reside in the United Kingdom as a 'qualified person' (reg 15(1), EEA Order). The Order does not specify what proof a person who claims that he has a right to reside must produce, except a valid identity card or passport and, in the case of a worker, confirmation from the employer. There is no need to produce the document with which the applicant entered the country (compare Art 3(3), Directive 68/360). It would seem that the Order takes into account the decision of the Court in *Giagounidis* (Case C-376/89) that, despite the clear wording of the directive, this is not required. The periods for the grant of residence permits and the terms on which they are to be granted, generally five years, reflect the requirements laid down in Arts 4–8 of Directives 68/360 and 73/148 (regs 16–20, EEA Order; see Chapters 12 and 13). Family members are entitled to permits on the bases laid down in the same Directives (reg 15(2), EEA Order, and see above commentary on reg 10, EEA Order).

Exclusion and removal

European Union citizens and EEA nationals may be excluded from the United Kingdom if that exclusion is justified on grounds of public policy, public security or public health. In addition, EU citizens and EEA nationals may be removed from the United Kingdom on ceasing to have a right of residence as a qualified person, or if the removal is justified on public policy, public security or public health grounds (reg 21, EEA Order). Residence permits may also be refused on public policy, public security or public health grounds under the Order, and withdrawn on the same grounds. They may also be revoked on the same grounds when a person ceases to be qualified to remain under Community law (reg 22, EEA Order). For the first time, the limitations on state action based on public policy, public security and public health set out in Arts 2–5, Directive 64/221 were set out, *in extenso*, in the 1994 Order (reg 17). This is also the case with the new EEA Order (reg 23).

Most of the provisions concerning exclusion and removal accurately reflect Directive 64/221. However, it is clear from the directive that a residence permit may not be revoked, nor may a person be removed on public health grounds, and in that respect reg 22, EEA Order would appear to be in conflict with Community law. However, reg 23(e), EEA Order does at least provide that 'a disease or disability contracted *after* a person has been granted a first residence permit or first residence document does not justify a decision to refuse to renew the permit or document or a decision to remove him' (emphasis added).

THE EFFECT OF CLAIMS TO SOCIAL ASSISTANCE

Prior to the coming into force of the 1994 Order, the residence rights of EU citizens and their families were made dependent upon them not claiming public funds (para 72, Immigration Rules HC 251). These conditions were too wide and consequently breached Community law. Many Community citizens will, after they have worked and gained worker status, be entitled to benefits such as 'social advantages' under Art

7(2), Regulation 1612/68 or, in some cases, under Regulation 1408/71 (see Chapters 12 and 14). Others, although not entitled under Community law to the benefits they claimed, should not have been required to leave. Expulsions of this kind are contrary to Art 2(2), Directive 64/221, which prohibits expulsions 'to service economic ends'.

This prohibition is reflected in reg 23(a), EEA Order, which provides that decisions taken on grounds of public policy, security or health 'must not be invoked to secure economic ends'. Nevertheless, there remains an important link between claims to public funds and the rights of residence of EU citizens. The link may operate in two separate, but related, ways: first, by denying the financial support which a Community national may require when he has insufficient resources to maintain himself; and, secondly, by providing evidence that he cannot support himself without recourse to social assistance.

Prima facie, a work-seeker or a beneficiary of the general right of residence under Directive 90/364, or a retired person under Directive 90/365, will have a right to remain as long as he satisfies the relevant requirements of Community law. He cannot, however, look to the United Kingdom's welfare system for any kind of assistance, unless it be for contributory benefits to which he may be entitled under Regulation 1408/71 (see Chapter 14). Income support, housing benefit and council tax benefit, for example, are conditional upon proof by a claimant who is a national of an EEA state or an EU citizen that he is 'habitually resident in the United Kingdom, the Republic of Ireland, the Channel Islands or the Isle of Man' (Income-related Benefits Schemes (Miscellaneous Amendments) (No. 3) Regulations 1994 (SI 1994/1807)). The test is not applied to those who have worker status or during the first six months in which a worker is looking for work (reg 21(3)(h), Income Support (General) Regulations 1987, SI 1987/1967), or to a person who has a right of residence as a self-employed person or as a recipient of services under Directive 73/148.

The second way in which the social assistance system may jeopardise a person's right to remain is by providing evidence that he is no longer self-sufficient. The residence rights conferred on students, retired people who have worked in another Member State, and people relying on their own resources are all conditional upon the beneficiaries not becoming a burden on the social assistance system of the host state (Art 1, Directives 90/364, 90/365 and 93/96). A claim to income support or to one of the benefits named in the above regulations is almost certain to fail, because the habitual residence test is difficult to satisfy. The details of the claim would then be forwarded to the Home Office, and, if the individual is not a worker or a self-employed person, or otherwise entitled to remain under the EEA Order, then he could be required to leave under reg 21(3)(a), EEA Order as someone who has 'ceased to be a qualified person'.

DEPORTATIONS

In the United Kingdom, deportations are carried out either by the Home Secretary on his own initiative or following a recommendation of the courts at the time when a sentence is imposed on an offender (ss 3(5) and (6), 5, Immigration Act 1971). The Home Secretary has a general power to deport a foreign national where he 'deems his deportation to be conducive to the public good' (s 3(5)(b), Immigration Act 1971). It was on this basis that deportations of Community nationals have been carried out, although both the Home Secretary and the courts have been obliged to make decisions on whether or not to deport or recommend deportation within the limits laid down by Directive 64/221. The Community criteria are much narrower than those allowed under UK immigration law, and the EEA Order lays down both the circumstances for removal and deportation and the Community criteria. The Court of Appeal has, however, said that Community law in this area 'simply mirrors the law and practice of this country' (R v *Jacobo Escavriaza* (1988) 9 Cr App R (S)542).

In R v *Secretary of State for the Home Office, ex parte Marchon* [1993] 2 CMLR 132, the appellant, a Portuguese national, who had been a general practitioner, was convicted of dealing in drugs. He was sentenced to a long term of imprisonment but not recommended for deportation by the trial court. The Home Secretary, nonetheless, issued notice of an intention to deport him. The Court of Appeal upheld the decision on the ground that 'the offence merits deportation ... it involves a disregard of the basic or fundamental tenets of society' (Dillon LJ). Concurring, Beldam LJ added that there should be no hint that society was prepared to tolerate the importation of and dealing in drugs: 'I say this *not simply because refusal to do so would act as a deterrent to others but rather because it serves to emphasise the grave and present danger from this threat*' (emphasis added). The decision is surprising, not least because it is clearly not wholly based on the conduct of the offender and the likelihood of his future offending, but on a clear intention by the Court to take deterrent or general preventive action because of a concern about offences of this type. Such an approach obviously conflicts with Art 3(1), Directive 64/221 and the decision of the Court of Justice in *Bonsignore* – Chapter 15.

Further reading

Macdonald and Blake (1995) *Macdonald's Immigration Law and Practice* (4th edn), Butterworths.

Vincenzi, C. (1995) 'Welcoming the Well and Wealthy: the Implementation of Directive 90/364 in the United Kingdom', in Daintith, T., *Implementing EC Law in the United Kingdom: Structures for Indirect Rule*, John Wiley & Sons.

Vincenzi, C. and Marrington, M. (1992) *Immigration Law: The Rules Explained*, Sweet & Maxwell.

Part III

THE FREE MOVEMENT OF GOODS

Chapter 17

CUSTOMS DUTIES AND INTERNAL TAXATION

INTRODUCTION

The Community set as one of its central tasks the creation of an internal market characterised by the abolition, as between Member States, of obstacles to the free movement of goods, persons, services and capital. This necessarily involved 'the prohibition, as between Member States, of customs duties and quantitative restrictions on the import and export of goods, and all other measures having equivalent effect' (Art 3(1)(a) EC Treaty). The European Community also bound itself, in Art 23 EC Treaty, to the maintenance of 'a customs union which shall cover all trade in goods and which shall involve the prohibition between Member States of customs duties on imports and exports and all charges having equivalent effect, and the adoption of a common customs tariff in their relations with third countries'. The object of these provisions is to create not only an internal free trade area within the Community, where there are no duties imposed on the internal borders, but also a customs union where there is a common external tariff. Goods entering the Community are subject to the same external tariff, irrespective of where they enter it. Once goods from third states have been subjected to the appropriate duties on crossing the external border of the Community, they are regarded as being in 'free circulation' and are to be treated like any other goods produced within the Community (Art 23 EC Treaty). Benefits are intended to accrue to producers in the opening up of new markets, the possibility of larger, and hence cheaper, product runs, and to consumers in the form of greatly increased choice in products at lower prices.

Tariff barriers between Member States have long since been removed. Border controls on goods were swept away by the Single European Act 1986. Much still remains to be done, however, to achieve a single undivided market in products, goods and services, such as exists, for example, between England and Scotland. The problems that still persist arise largely as a result of invisible barriers in the shape of different product and other standards and a whole range of national measures aimed at consumer and environmental protection. Until these different standards are harmonised it would be very difficult for, say, a French manufacturer of a bicycle to make a product which he knows with confidence he will be allowed to sell to any one of the 350 million consumers in the European Union. In the long term, these problems are being addressed by the creation of EU-wide standards through the approval of harmonising directives for a huge range of products (see Chapter 18). Until this massive task is achieved, however, producers will have to rely upon Arts 28 and 29 EC Treaty, and the intervention of the Court of Justice, to ensure that national rules do not have the effect of excluding their products (see Chapter 18). Although it also remains one of the objectives of the EC Treaty to harmonise rates of indirect taxation (Art 93), little progress has been made in this area, and obstacles to the creation of a genuine, undivided market continue to be caused by different rates of tax and other charges levied on goods by the Member States. The EC Treaty attempts to address these problems by the provisions of Arts 23 and 25 (prohibition of customs duties on imports and exports and all charges having equivalent effect) and the prohibition of discriminatory internal taxation (Art 90).

ARTICLE 25: THE ELIMINATION OF BORDER CHARGES AND FISCAL BARRIERS

When the Treaty of Amsterdam (ToA) came into force on 1 May 1999, it repealed, amended and renumbered the EC Treaty provisions regulating customs duties and charges having an equivalent effect to a customs duty. This necessitates an explanation of the provisions of the EC Treaty *before* and *after* the coming into force of the ToA.

Prior to the ToA coming into force, Arts 9–17 EC Treaty regulated the imposition of customs duties (and charges which had an equivalent effect) on imports and exports. Most of these provisions have been renumbered, amended and/or repealed.

Article 9(1) EC Treaty set out the objective of the Community; this has been renumbered Art 23(1) by the ToA:

> The Community shall be based upon a customs union which shall cover all trade in goods and which shall involve the prohibition between Member States of customs duties on imports and exports and of all charges having an equivalent effect, and the adoption of a common customs tariff in their relations with third countries. (Art 23(1) EC Treaty (formerly Art 9(1)))

The other relevant articles pre-ToA were 12, 13 and 16: Art 12 prohibited *new* customs duties from being introduced; Art 13 required *existing* customs duties on *imports* to be phased out; and Art 16 required the abolition of customs duties on *existing exports* by 31 December 1961. The last two provisions were superfluous, and therefore Art 12 was amended (and renumbered) to cover all three situations. The new Art 25 provides that:

> Customs duties on imports and exports and charges having equivalent effect, shall be prohibited between Member States. This prohibition shall also apply to customs duties of a fiscal nature.

The Court of Justice held that the former Art 12 had a direct effect (see, e.g., *Van Gend en Loos* v *Nederlandse Administratie der Belastingen* (Case 26/62)). There is little doubt that its mirror provision, the new Art 25, will likewise have direct effect.

We will now consider the case law of the Court of Justice with regard to these Treaty provisions.

Scope of the term 'goods'

The scope of the term 'goods' was explored by the Court of Justice in *Commission* v *Italy* (Case 26/62).

Italy imposed a tax on the export of articles of an 'artistic, historical, archaeological or ethnographic nature'. The Commission took infraction proceedings against Italy pursuant to Art 169 EC Treaty (now Art 226) alleging this tax was in breach of the former Art 16 which required the abolition of customs duties and equivalent charges on exports by 31 December 1961; the substance of this provision is now included within Art 25. Italy argued, *inter alia*, that the tax was being levied on 'cultural articles' which were being exported and such articles should not be regarded as goods. This argument was rejected by the Court of Justice.

Under Article 9 of the Treaty the Community is based on a customs union 'which shall cover all trade in goods'. *By goods, within the meaning of that provision, there must be understood products which can be valued in money and which are capable, as such, of forming the subject of commercial transactions.*

The articles covered by the Italian law, whatever may be the characteristics which distinguish them from other types of merchandise, nevertheless resemble the latter, inasmuch as they can be valued in money and so be the subject of commercial transactions. That view corresponds with the scheme of the Italian law itself, which fixes the tax in question in proportion to the value of the articles concerned. (emphasis added)

It follows from the above that the rules of the common market apply to these goods subject only to the exceptions expressly provided by the Treaty.

The Court thus held that goods, for the purpose of these provisions, will consist of 'products which can be valued in money and which are capable ... of forming the subject of commercial transactions'. The scope of 'goods' will therefore be very wide, but in *Jagerskiold* v *Gustafsson* (Case C-97/98) the Court of Justice was faced with a more difficult question.

On 29 May 1997 Mr Gustafsson (G) fished with a spinning rod in waters belonging to Mr Jagerskiold (J) in the commune of Kimoto in Finland. Two days earlier, on 27 May 1997, he had paid the fishing licence fee provided for in Finnish law, which allowed him to practise that type of fishing even in private waters. J brought an action before the national court for a declaration that G might not, without his permission, fish with a rod in his waters, notwithstanding the fact that J had paid the fishing licence fee provided for by Finnish law. In support of his action, J argued that the Finnish law, on which the right to fish with a rod was based, was contrary to the rules of the EC Treaty concerning, *inter alia*, the free movement of goods.

The Court has already defined goods, for the purposes of Article 9 [now Art 23] of the EC Treaty ... as products which can be valued in money and which are capable, as such, of forming the subject of commercial transactions.

J contends that fishing rights and fishing permits derived from them constitute 'goods' within the meaning of that case law, in so far as they can be valued in money terms and may be transferred to other persons as it is expressly provided for by [Finnish law] ...

As is clear from Council Directive 88/361/EEC of 24 June 1998, the Treaty provisions on the free movement of capital cover, in particular, operations relating to shares, bonds and other securities which, like fishing rights or fishing permits, can be valued in money and may be the subject of market transactions.

Similarly, the organisation of lotteries does not constitute an activity relating to 'goods', even if such an activity is coupled with the distribution of advertising material and lottery tickets, but must be regarded as a provision of 'services' within the meaning of the Treaty.

In that activity, the provision of services in question are those provided by the lottery organiser in letting ticket buyers participate in the lottery against payment of the price of the lottery tickets.

The same applies to the grant of fishing rights and the issue of fishing permits. The activity consisting of making fishing waters available to third parties, for consideration and upon certain conditions, so that they can fish there constitutes a provision of services which is covered by Article 59 *et seq.* of the EC Treaty (now, after amendment, Article 49 *et seq.*) if it has a cross-frontier character. *The fact that those rights or those permits are set down in documents which, as such, may be the subject of trade is not sufficient to bring them within the scope of the provisions of the Treaty relating to the free movement of goods.* (emphasis added)

The Court of Justice held that the granting of fishing rights and the issuing of fishing permits could be valued in money and were capable of forming the subject of commercial transactions. However, they were not a tangible product; they were an intangible benefit even if those rights were set out in a document. The granting of fishing rights and issuing of fishing permits could not therefore be considered to be 'goods', although they could constitute a service which would be regulated by what is now Art 49 EC Treaty (see Chapter 13).

Goods from third countries

Article 23(2) EC Treaty (formerly Art 9(2)) provides that:

> The provisions of Article 25 and of Chapter 2 of this Title shall apply to products originating in Member States and to products coming from third countries which are in free circulation in Member States.

Article 24 EC Treaty (formerly Art 10(1)) further provides that:

> Products coming from a third country shall be considered to be in free circulation in a Member State if the import formalities have been complied with and any customs duties or charges having equivalent effect which are payable have been levied in that Member State, and if they have not benefited from a total or partial drawback of such duties or charges.

These provisions provide that goods lawfully entering the common market from a third country will come within the provisions of Art 25 (and also 'Chapter 2 of this Title' (i.e. Arts 28–30, which are considered in Chapter 18)).

Duties and equivalent charges: the effect *not* the purpose

Whether or not Art 25 EC Treaty (formerly Art 12) will apply depends upon the *effect* of the duty or charge. It is irrelevant *why* the Member State imposed the duty/charge (i.e. *purpose* is irrelevant). A reconsideration of the *Italian Art* case (*Commission v Italy* (Case 7/68)), which concerned the former Art 16 (the substance of which now comes within the remit of the new Art 25) will serve to illustrate this.

This is the case where Italy imposed a tax on the export of articles of an 'artistic, historical, archaeological or ethnographic nature'. The Commission took infraction proceedings against Italy, alleging this tax was in breach of Art 16 EC Treaty (now Art 25). Italy argued, *inter alia*, that the *purpose* of the tax in question was not to raise revenue, but was designed to protect the artistic heritage of the country. This argument was rejected by the Court of Justice.

In the opinion of the Commission the tax in dispute constitutes a tax having an effect equivalent to a customs duty on exports and therefore the tax should have been abolished, under Article 16 [now Art 25] of the Treaty, no later than the end of the first stage of the common market, that is to say, from 1 January 1962. The defendant argues that the disputed tax does not come within the category, as it has its own particular purpose which is to ensure the protection and safety of the artistic, historic and archaeological heritage which exists in the national territory. Consequently, the tax does not in any respect have a fiscal nature, and its contribution to the budget is insignificant.

Article 16 of the Treaty prohibits the collection in dealings between Member States of any customs duty on exports and of any charge having an equivalent effect, that is to say, any charge which, by altering the price of an article exported, has the same restrictive effect on the free circulation of that article as a customs duty. *This provision makes no distinction based on the purpose of the duties and charges* the abolition of which it requires.

It is not necessary to analyse the concept of the nature of fiscal systems on which the defendant bases its argument upon this point, for the provisions of the section of the Treaty concerning the elimination of customs duties between the Member States exclude the retention of customs duties and charges having equivalent effect without distinguishing between those which are and those which are not of a fiscal nature.

The disputed tax falls within Article 16 [now Art 25] by reason of the fact that export trade in the goods in question is hindered by the pecuniary burden which it imposes on the price of the exported articles. (emphasis added)

The above case demonstrates that it is the *effect* of the tax and not its *purpose* which is of prime importance. To have decided otherwise would have considerably weakened the effect of the former Arts 9–17 (now Arts 23–25), the aim of which was to remove fiscal barriers from the borders of Member States which would otherwise have hindered the free movement of goods. In this case Italy had argued that it had a legitimate reason for imposing the export tax (i.e. the protection of its artistic, historic, and archaeological heritage) which should be recognised by the Court as a sufficient reason for it to declare that the tax fell outside the scope of the Treaty. If the Italian argument had been accepted by the Court, then it would have had to adjudicate in the future on what other legitimate reasons were sufficient to take them outside the Treaty (and thus afford the otherwise defaulting Member State a defence). In rejecting the Italian argument, and confirming that the reason for the charge is irrelevant, the Court has made a significant impact on removing the financial frontiers which could otherwise have remained in a disguised form and thus impacted upon the free movement of goods. As the Court of Justice stated in *Commission* v *Italy* (Case 24/68):

6. ... the purpose of the abolition of customs barriers is not merely to eliminate their protective nature, as the Treaty sought on the contrary to give general scope and effect to the rule on the elimination of customs duties and charges having equivalent effect, in order to ensure the free movement of goods.

7. It follows from the system as a whole and from the general and absolute nature of the prohibition on any customs duty applicable to goods moving between Member States that customs duties are prohibited independently of any consideration of the purpose for which they were introduced and the destination of the revenue obtained therefrom.

The justification for this prohibition is based on the fact that any pecuniary charge, however small, imposed on goods by reason of the fact that they cross a frontier constitutes an obstacle to the movement of such goods. (emphasis added)

This is further illustrated by *Sociaal Fonds voor de Diamantarbeiders v SA Ch. Brachfeld & Sons* (Cases 2 & 3/69), where it was submitted that a small levy imposed under Belgian law on imported diamonds could not be in breach of Art 9 (now Art 23) and Art 12 (now Art 25) because (1) it had no protectionist purpose as Belgium did not produce diamonds and (2) the levy's purpose was to provide social security benefits for Belgian diamond workers. The Court of Justice explained the sweeping nature of these provisions:

In prohibiting the imposition of customs duties, the Treaty does not distinguish between goods according to whether or not they enter into competition with the products of the importing country. Thus, the purpose of the abolition of customs barriers is not merely to eliminate their protective nature, as the Treaty sought on the contrary to give general scope and effect to the rule on elimination of customs duties and charges having equivalent effect in order to ensure the free movement of goods. It follows from the system as a whole and from the general and absolute nature of the prohibition of any customs duty applicable to goods moving between Member States that customs duties are prohibited independently of any consideration of the purpose for which they were introduced and the destination of the revenue obtained therefrom. *The justification for this prohibition is based on the fact that any pecuniary charge – however small – imposed on goods by reason of the fact that they cross a frontier constitutes an obstacle to the movement of such goods.* (emphasis added)

Charges having an equivalent effect

Article 25 EC Treaty prohibits not only customs duties but also *charges having an equivalent effect* to a customs duty (CEEs). If this phrase had been omitted Member States could quite easily have avoided the prohibition. The scope of CEEs was considered by the Court of Justice in *Commission v Italy* (Case 24/68).

Italy imposed a levy on goods which were exported to other Member States to finance the collecting of statistical data relating to trade patterns. The Commission challenged the legality of such a charge pursuant to its powers under the former Art 169 EC Treaty (now Art 226). The Court of Justice held as follows:

8. The extension of the prohibition of customs duties to charges having an equivalent effect is intended to supplement the prohibition against obstacles to trade created by such duties by increasing its efficiency.

The use of these two complementary concepts thus tends, in trade between Member States, to avoid the imposition of any pecuniary charge on goods circulating within the Community by virtue of the fact that they cross a national border.

9. Thus, in order to ascribe to a charge an effect equivalent to a customs duty, it is important to consider this effect in the light of the objectives of the Treaty, in the Parts, Titles and Chapters in which Articles 9, 12, 13 and 16 [now Arts 23 and 25] are to be found, particularly in relation to the free movement of goods.

Consequently, *any pecuniary charge, however small and whatever its designation and mode of application, which is imposed unilaterally on domestic or foreign goods by reason of the fact that they cross a frontier, and which is not a customs duty in the strict sense, constitutes a charge having equivalent effect* within the meaning of Articles 9, 12, 13 and 16 [now Arts 23 and 25] of the Treaty, *even if it is not imposed for the benefit of the State, is not discriminatory or protective in effect and if the product on which the charge is imposed is not in competition with any domestic product.*

10. It follows from all the provisions referred to and from their relationship with the other provisions of the Treaty that the prohibition of new customs duties or charges having equivalent effect, linked to the principle of the free movement of goods, constitutes a fundamental rule which, without prejudice to the other provisions of the Treaty, does not permit of any exceptions.

A customs duty, in the strict sense, comprises two elements:

- a tax or levy
- which is imposed simply because of the fact that the goods cross a frontier.

But, as the above case illustrates, the Treaty also forbids more discrete forms of charges which are levied at the border; these are termed 'charges having an equivalent effect to a customs duty' (referred to as CEEs). This was defined broadly by the Court at para 9 of its judgment. The Court of Justice perceived customs duties and CEEs as a barrier to the notion of a single common market. Article 25 prohibits them and the Court has strictly interpreted the predecessors of Art 25 (the former Arts 12, 13 and 16), allowing very few exceptions. But are there any exceptions?

Provision of a service – exception to the general rule?

In principle the Court of Justice has accepted that where the charge imposed is merely payment for a service which the Member State has rendered *directly* to the importer then the charge should not be regarded as a CEE, provided the charge levied is in proportion to the service provided. This is illustrated in *Commission* v *Belgium* (Case 132/82).

European Community rules allowed imported goods to be given customs clearance at public warehouses located inside a Member State rather than at the frontier. Belgium levied storage charges on goods stored temporarily at such warehouses at the request of the trader concerned. Charges were also levied on imported goods which simply attended the warehouse for customs clearance and were not in fact stored there. The Commission initiated infraction proceedings against Belgium, arguing that these charges were in breach of the former Arts 9, 12, 13 and 16 (now Arts 23 and 25). The Court of Justice held that:

---

8. It is appropriate to recall, in the first place, that according to the established case law of the Court, any pecuniary charge, however small and whatever its designation and mode of application, which is imposed unilaterally on the goods by reason of the fact that they

cross a frontier and which is not a customs duty in the strict sense, constitutes a charge having equivalent effect within the meaning of Articles 9, 12, 13 and 16 [now Arts 23 and 25] of the Treaty, even if it is not levied by the State. *The position is different only if the charge in question is the consideration for a service actually rendered to the importer and is of an amount commensurate with that service, when the charge concerned, as in this case, is payable exclusively on imported products.*

9. The prohibition of charges having an effect equivalent to customs duties, laid down in provisions of the Treaty, is justified on the ground that pecuniary charges imposed by reason or on the occasion of the crossing of the frontier represent an obstacle to the free movement of goods.

10. It is in the light of those principles that the question whether the disputed storage charges may be classified as charges having an effect equivalent to customs duties must be assessed. It should therefore be noted, in the first place, that the placing of imported goods in temporary storage in the special stores of public warehouses clearly represents a service rendered to traders. A decision to deposit the goods there can indeed be taken only at the request of the trader concerned and then ensures their storage without payment of duties, until the trader has decided how they are to be dealt with. Moreover the Commission does not dispute that the placing of goods in temporary storage may legally give rise to the payment of charges commensurate with the service thus rendered.

11. However, it appears ... that the storage charges are payable equally when the goods are presented at the public warehouse solely for the completion of customs formalities, even though they have been exempted from storage and the importer has not requested that they be put in temporary storage.

12. Admittedly the Belgian Government claims that even in that case a service is rendered to the importer. It is always open to the latter to avoid payment of the disputed charges by choosing to have his goods cleared through customs at the frontier, where such a procedure is free. Moreover, by using a public warehouse, the importer is enabled to have the goods declared through customs near the places for which his products are bound and he is therefore relieved of the necessity of himself either having at his own disposal premises suitable for their clearance or having recourse to private premises, the use of which is more expensive than that of the public warehouses. It is therefore legitimate, in the Belgian Government's view, to impose a charge commensurate with that service.

13. That argument cannot however be accepted. Whilst it is true that the use of a public warehouse in the interior of the country offers certain advantages to importers it seems clear first of all that such advantages are linked solely with the completion of customs formalities which, whatever the place, is always compulsory. It should moreover be noted that such advantages result from the scheme of Community transit introduced ... in order to increase the fluidity of the movement of goods and to facilitate transport within the Community. There can therefore be no question of levying any charges for customs clearance facilities accorded in the interests of the common market.

14. It follows from the foregoing, that *when payment of storage charges is demanded solely in connection with the completion of customs formalities, it cannot be regarded as the consideration for a service actually rendered to the importer.*

15. Consequently, it must be declared that, *by levying storage charges on goods which originate in a Member State or are in free circulation, and which are imported into Belgium, and presented merely for the completion of customs formalities at a special*

store, the Kingdom of Belgium has failed to fulfil its obligations under Articles 9 and 12 [now Arts 23 and 25] of the Treaty. (emphasis added)

In this case, the Court of Justice held that the charge will not constitute a CEE 'if the charge in question is the consideration for a service actually rendered to the importer and is of an amount commensurate with that service' (para 8). However, Belgium failed in this case, because the charge for the service (i.e. storage of goods at a public warehouse) was solely connected with the completion of customs formalities. It was accepted by the Court that charges levied in relation to private premises did not fall to be considered within the former Arts 9 and 12 (now Arts 23 and 25) EC Treaty (para 12); the Treaty provisions apply only to the state.

It is clear that an argument that the charge is consideration for a service actually rendered to the importer will be closely scrutinised by the Court. In its actual decisions, the Court has shown considerable reluctance in accepting that a particular charge is an appropriate fee outside Art 25. In *Ford Espania* v *Spain* (Case 170/88), the Court said that even if a specific benefit to the person or body paying the charge can be identified, the state imposing the charge will still fall foul of Art 25 if it cannot be shown that the sum demanded is proportionate to the cost of supplying the benefit. In this case, Ford received a demand for 0.165 per cent of the declared value of cars and other goods imported into Spain. The Spanish Government maintained that the sum related to services rendered in connection with clearing the goods through customs. The Court held that, even if a specific benefit conferred on Ford could be shown, the flat-rate way in which the charge was calculated was evidently not fixed according to the cost of the alleged service and was, accordingly, a breach of Art 25.

Another case which illustrates the Court's reluctance to find that a charge falls outside the remit of Art 25 is *Commission* v *Italy* (Case 24/68).

This case was considered above. The Italian Government had argued that the charge imposed was consideration for the collection of statistical information. It was argued that this information would provide importers with trade patterns and therefore give them a better competitive position in the Italian market. The Court of Justice held as follows:

---

15. The Italian Government further maintains that the disputed charge constitutes the consideration for a service rendered and as such cannot be designated as a charge having equivalent effect.

According to the Italian Government the object of the statistics in question is to determine precisely the actual movements of goods and, consequently, changes in the state of the market. It claims that the exactness of the information thus supplied affords importers a better competitive position in the Italian market whilst exporters enjoy a similar advantage abroad and that the special advantages which dealers obtain from the survey justifies their paying for this public service and moreover demonstrates that the disputed charge is in the nature of a *quid pro quo*.

16. The statistical information in question is beneficial to the economy as a whole and *inter alia* to the relevant administrative authorities.

Even if the competitive position of importers and exporters were to be particularly improved as a result, the statistics still constitute an advantage so general, and so difficult to assess, that the disputed charge cannot be regarded as the consideration for a specific benefit actually conferred.

17. It appears from the above mentioned considerations that in so far as the disputed charge is levied on exports it is contrary to Article 16 [now Art 25] of the Treaty.

In the above case, the Court of Justice held that the service (i.e. provision of statistics) was not *directly* rendered to the importers/exporters because it was 'beneficial to the economy as a whole and *inter alia* to the relevant administrative authorities' (para 16). Even where it is more direct, the Court may still be reluctant to rule that the charge is consideration for the service rendered. Consider *Bresciani* v *Administrazione Italiane delle Finanze* (Case 87/75).

The Italian authorities imposed a charge for compulsory veterinary and public health inspections carried out on the importation of raw cowhides. The case was referred by the domestic court pursuant to the former Art 177 EC Treaty (now Art 234) for a preliminary ruling on the question of whether the charge for the inspection constituted a CEE:

---

6. The national court requests that the three following considerations be taken into account:
    First, the fact that the charge is proportionate to the quantity of the goods and not to their value distinguishes a duty of the type at issue from charges which fall within the prohibition under Article 13 [now Art 25] of the EEC Treaty. Second, a pecuniary charge of the type at issue is no more than the consideration required from individuals who, through their own action in importing products of animal origin, cause a service to be rendered. In the third place, although there may be differences in the method and time of its application, the duty at issue is also levied on similar products of domestic origin ...

8. The justification for the obligation progressively to abolish customs duties is based on the fact that any pecuniary charge, however small, imposed on goods by reason of the fact that they cross a frontier constitutes an obstacle to the free movement of goods.
    The obligation progressively to abolish customs duties is supplemented by the obligation to abolish charges having equivalent effect in order to prevent the fundamental principle of the free movement of goods within the common market from being circumvented by the imposition of pecuniary charges of various kinds by a Member State.
    The use of these two complementary concepts thus tends, in trade between Member States, to avoid the imposition of any pecuniary charge on goods circulating within the Community by virtue of the fact that they cross a national frontier.

9. Consequently, any pecuniary charge, whatever its designation and mode of application, which is unilaterally imposed on goods imported from another Member State by reason of the fact that they cross a frontier, constitutes a charge having an effect equivalent to a customs duty. In appraising a duty of the type at issue it is, consequently, of no importance that it is proportionate to the quantity of the imported goods and not their value.

10. Nor, in determining the effects of the duty on the free movement of goods, is it of any importance that a duty of the type at issue is proportionate to the costs of a compulsory public health inspection carried out on entry of the goods. *The activity of the administration of the State intended to maintain a public health inspection system imposed in the general interest cannot be regarded as a service rendered to the importer such as to justify the imposition of a pecuniary charge. If, accordingly, public health inspections are still justified at the end of the transitional period, the costs which they occasion must be met*

by the general public which, as a whole, benefits from the free movement of Community goods. (emphasis added)

At para 10 the Court of Justice held that a public health inspection system was imposed to benefit the general public, and therefore was not a service rendered directly to the importer; it was there for the benefit of the general public and therefore it was the general public who would have to meet the costs incurred by the state in carrying out those inspections.

Even where EC law *permits* an inspection to be undertaken by the state, the national authorities cannot recover the cost from the importers (see *Commission* v *Belgium* (Case 314/82)).

However, if Community law *requires* an inspection to be carried out, the costs of such an inspection *may* be recoverable and will not be caught by the provisions of Art 25. This was decided by the Court of Justice in *Commission* v *Germany* (Case 18/87).

German regional authorities charged certain fees on live animals when they were imported into Germany. These charges were to cover the cost of inspections undertaken pursuant to Directive 81/389. The question before the Court of Justice was whether such charges constituted CEEs and were therefore prohibited:

5. It should be observed in the first place that, as the Court has held on a number of occasions, the justification for the prohibition of customs duties and any charges having an equivalent effect lies in the fact that any pecuniary charge, however small, imposed on goods by reason of the fact that they cross a frontier, constitutes an obstacle to the movement of goods which is aggravated by the resulting administrative formalities. It follows that any pecuniary charge, whatever its designation and mode of application, which is imposed unilaterally on goods by reason of the fact that they cross a frontier and is not a customs duty in the strict sense constitutes a charge having an equivalent effect to a customs duty within the meaning of Articles 9, 12, 13 and 16 [now Arts 23 and 25] of the Treaty.

6. However, *the Court has held that such a charge escapes that classification* if it relates to a general system of internal dues applied systematically and in accordance with the same criteria to domestic products and imported goods alike (judgment of 31 May 1979 in Case 132/78 *Denkavit* v *France* [1979] ECR 1923), *if it constitutes payment for a service in fact rendered to the economic operator of a sum in proportion to the service* (judgment of 9 November 1983 in Case 158/82 *Commission* v *Denmark* [1983] ECR 3573), *or again, subject to certain conditions, if it attaches to inspections carried out to fulfil obligations imposed by Community law* (judgment of 25 January 1977 in Case 46/76 *Bauhuis* v *Netherlands* [1977] ECR 5).

7. The contested fee, which is payable on importation and transit, cannot be regarded as relating to a general system of internal dues. Nor does it constitute payment for a service rendered to the operator, because this condition is satisfied only if the operator in question obtains a definite specific benefit (see judgment of 1 July 1969 in Case 24/68 *Commission* v *Italy* [1969] ECR 193), which is not the case if the inspection serves to guarantee, in the public interest, the health and life of animals in international transport (see judgment of 20 March 1984 in Case 314/82 *Commission* v *Belgium* [1984] ECR 1543).

8. *Since the contested fee was charged in connection with inspections carried out pursuant to Community provision*, it should be noted that according to the case law of the Court

(judgment of 25 January 1977 in *Bauhuis*, cited above; judgment of 12 July 1977 *Commission* v *Netherlands* [1977] ECR 1355; judgment of 31 January 1984 in Case 1/83 *IFG* v *Freistaat Bayern* [1984] ECR 349) *such fees may not be classified as charges having an equivalent effect to a customs duty if the following conditions are satisfied*:

(a) they do not exceed the actual costs of the inspections in connection with which they are charged;

(b) the inspections in question are obligatory and uniform for all the products concerned in the Community;

(c) they are prescribed by Community law in the general interest of the Community;

(d) they promote the free movement of goods, in particular by neutralising obstacles which could arise from unilateral measures of inspection adopted in accordance with Article 36 [now Art 30] of the Treaty.

9. In this instance these conditions are satisfied by the contested fee. In the first place it has not been contested that it does not exceed the real cost of the inspection in connection with which it is charged.

10. Moreover, all the Member States of transit and destination are required, under, *inter alia*, Article 2(1) of Directive 81/389/EEC, cited above, to carry out the veterinary inspections in question when the animals are brought into their territories, and therefore the inspections are obligatory and uniform for all the animals concerned in the Community.

11. Those inspections are prescribed by Directive 81/389/EEC, which establishes the measures necessary for the implementation of Council Directive 77/489/EEC of 18 July 1977 on the protection of animals during international transport, with a view to the protection of live animals, an objective which is pursued in the general interest of the Community and not a specific interest of individual States.

12. Finally, it appears from the preambles to the two abovementioned directives that they are intended to harmonise the laws of the Member States regarding the protection of animals in international transport in order to eliminate technical barriers resulting from disparities in the national laws (see third, fourth and fifth recitals in the preamble to Directive 77/489/EEC and the third recital in the preamble to Directive 81/389/EEC). In addition, failing such harmonisation, each Member State was entitled to maintain or introduce, under the conditions laid down in Article 36 [now Art 30] of the Treaty, measures restricting trade which were justified on grounds of the protection of the health and life of animals. It follows that the standardisation of the inspections in question is such as to promote the free movement of goods.

13. The Commission has claimed, however, that the contested fee is to be regarded as a charge having equivalent effect to a customs duty because, in so far as fees of this type have not been harmonised, such harmonisation, moreover, being unattainable in practice, their negative effect on the free movement of goods could not be compensated or, consequently, justified by the positive effects of the Community standardisation of inspections.

14. In this respect, it should be noted that since the fee in question is intended solely as the financially and economically justified compensation for an obligation imposed in equal measure on all the Member States by Community law, it cannot be regarded as equivalent to a customs duty; nor, consequently, can it fall within the ambit of the prohibition laid down in Articles 9 and 12 [now Arts 23 and 25] of the Treaty. (emphasis added)

An inspection fee levied on imported goods is therefore valid under Community law, provided the conditions laid down in para 8 above are satisfied. An important condition is that the inspection must be mandatory (i.e. compulsory) under Community law. The Court followed its previous judgment in *Bauhuis* v *Netherlands* (Case 46/76), where there was a challenge to a fee imposed by the Dutch Government for veterinary inspections of pigs imported into The Netherlands. Some of the checks were carried out to meet rules of national law. Others were made to meet the requirements of a Community directive. The Court held that, where such checks are mandatory under Community law and are part of the process of ensuring the free movement of goods, they are permitted under what is now Art 25. The fee must, however, be proportionate to the actual cost of the inspection. In *Commission* v *Netherlands* (Case 89/76), the question arose as to the compatibility with former Art 12 of plant inspections carried out under the International Plant Protection Convention 1951. This Convention was not a source of Community law, but it was binding in international law on those states who were signatories to it; it was designed to liberalise trade by replacing different checks in signatory states by a single check on which all states were able to rely. The Court drew a parallel with *Bauhuis*, and held that the charges imposed did not breach the then Art 12 (now Art 25).

Customs duty or internal taxation?

Since the Single European Act 1986 the opportunity for border checks and charges has been much diminished. Any processing or inspection of goods that may be necessary may now take place within the boundaries of the importing state, often many miles from the frontier.

Most charges which have been held to breach the prohibition in Arts 23 and 25 have been those levied directly on imported or exported goods. Charges which are levied indiscriminately on home-produced and imported goods will not, generally, breach Art 25 and will be lawful, provided they do not conflict with the prohibition in Art 90 against discriminatory taxation (see below). A breach of Art 23 or Art 25 may occur if the charge on the imported product is not imposed in the same way and determined according to the same criteria as the domestic product. In *Marimex* v *Italian Finance Administration* (Case 29/72), a veterinary inspection tax imposed on imported meat to ensure that it complied with national health standards was also imposed on domestic meat, but the inspections were conducted by different bodies applying different standards.

Where the charge is in the nature of a tax, care must be taken to determine whether it is in fact a charge in the nature of a customs duty or a provision of national taxation. If it is a charge equivalent to a duty, it is unlawful in its entirety. If it is a provision of national taxation, it is unlawful only to the extent that it is discriminatory or protective (*IGAV* v *ENCC* (Case 94/74)). The difficulty of distinguishing between charges equivalent to duties and taxation is illustrated by *Capolongo* v *Azienda Agricola* (Case 77/72). In this case a charge ostensibly levied on both imported and domestic products was claimed to be used to promote domestic products. The Court emphasised that the same charge could not both be equivalent to a customs duty and be a provision of internal taxation. It held that where a charge is levied both on imports and on domestic products, it can, nevertheless, constitute a charge equivalent to a customs duty when it is intended exclusively to support activities which specifically benefit the taxed domestic product. In *IGAV* v *ENCC* (above), the Court held that this was also the case where the domestic tax was remitted on the domestic product 'wholly or in part'. The Court later modified its position in *Fratelli Cucchi* (Case 77/76), where it held that apparent internal taxation can only constitute a charge equivalent to a customs duty: 'if it has the sole purpose of financing activities for the specific advantage of the taxed domestic product; if the taxed product and the domestic product benefiting from it are the same; and if the charges imposed on the domestic product are made good in full'. However, a much more probable conclusion is that a tax on imported and domestic products which gives a partial benefit to the taxed domestic product constitutes discriminatory internal taxation, contrary to Art 90, on the basis that it indirectly imposes a heavier burden on products from other Member States than on domestic products (*Commission* v *Italy* (Case 73/79)).

The Court did not follow this approach in *Haahr Petroleum Ltd* v *Abenra Havn* (Case C-90/94). In this case the claimant challenged a Danish law under which the port of Abenra and others charged an import surcharge of 40 per cent, which was levied in addition to duties on all imported goods loaded or unloaded within Danish commercial ports or in the deep-water approach channel to those ports. On a reference to the Court of Justice, it held that the amount paid formed part of a general system of internal taxes payable for the use of commercial ports and facilities. It had been argued by the Danish Government that the charge levied was lawful under what is now Art 25 EC Treaty because it constituted a charge for a service actually supplied to traders, and could not therefore also fall foul of the prohibition against discriminatory taxation under Art 95 (now Art 90) EC Treaty. Without accepting that the charge might be lawful under Art 25, the Court held that even if this was the case, it did not mean that the charge also escaped the prohibition against discriminatory taxation under Art 95 (now Art 90).

Figure 17.1 relates to Art 25 EC Treaty: customs duties and charges having an equivalent effect.

ARTICLE 90: DISCRIMINATORY AND PROTECTIONIST INTERNAL TAXATION

In the absence of a harmonised tax system in Member States, the Member States are entitled to take such measures as are necessary to make that system effective, even, it would seem, at the expense of fundamental rights under the Treaty, such as the right of establishment (*R* v *HM Treasury, ex parte Daily Mail* (Case 81/87)). Article 93 EC Treaty provides for the enactment of measures to harmonise legislation on turnover taxes, excise duties and other forms of indirect taxation, but because such legislation can only be adopted by the Council of Ministers acting unanimously there has been little movement. Until a fully harmonised Community tax regime is achieved, however, Member States retain their national prerogative in relation to internal taxation. This principle of national autonomy gives way to another fundamental principle, that of free movement of goods. Article 90 EC Treaty (previously Art 95) provides that:

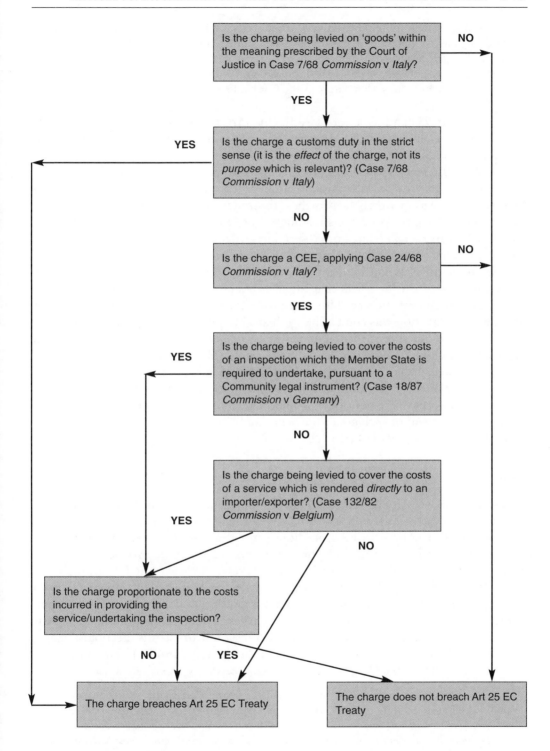

Figure 17.1 Article 25 EC Treaty: customs duties and charges having an equivalent effect

> No Member State shall impose, directly or indirectly, on the products of other Member States any internal taxation of any kind in excess of that imposed directly or indirectly on similar domestic products.
>
> Furthermore, no Member State shall impose on the products of other Member States any internal taxation of such a nature as to afford indirect protection to other products.

The former Art 95 (and as a corollary to this, Art 90) has been held to be directly effective by the Court since 1 January 1962 (see *Alfons Lutticke GmbH* v *Hauptzollamt Sarrelouis* (Case 57/65)).

Since Art 90 refers to 'products of other Member States' it might well be thought that discriminatory or protectionist taxation levied on goods coming from another Member State was permissible provided those goods originated from outside the Community. Unlike the provisions relating to the free movement of goods in Part III, Title I, EC Treaty, which relate both to products originating in the Community and 'to products coming from third countries which are in free circulation in Member States', there is no such application to the non-discriminatory tax rules (Art 23(2) EC Treaty). The Court therefore at first held that Member States were entitled to impose discriminatory or protectionist taxes on third-state products circulating freely in the Community, provided such taxation was compatible with any concessions made to that state in any association or other agreement (*Hansen* v *Hauptzollamt Flensburg* (Case 148/77)). It modified its position, however, in *Co-Frutta* (Case 193/85). In this case, which involved Italian taxation of bananas imported through other Member States, the Court accepted that the Common Customs Tariff and the Common Commercial Policy were intended to ensure a uniform treatment of goods imported from third states and the facilitation of the free movement of such goods once they had been legitimately imported into one of the Member States (see Usher, 1986).

The purpose of Article 90

As discussed above, Arts 23–25 EC Treaty are designed to prevent financial measures from being imposed as a result of a product *crossing a frontier*. The financial measure does not necessarily have to be protectionist in nature (*protectionist* means that the financial measure imposed has the effect of protecting domestic products from competition by foreign goods); however, it often is.

Articles 23–25 would be of little use if a Member State could impose taxes on foreign products (but not on the rival domestic product) once they were inside their territory; because the tax was not levied at the frontier it would not be caught by Arts 23–25. Article 90 seeks to prevent this where a discriminatory or protectionist charge is levied on the imported product but not on the domestic product. The purpose of Art 90 was set out by the Court of Justice in *Commission* v *Denmark* (Case 171/78):

> The ... provisions supplement, within the system of the Treaty, the provisions on the abolition of customs duties and charges having equivalent effect. *Their aim is to ensure the free movement of goods between the Member States in normal conditions of competition by the elimination of all forms of protection which result from the application of internal taxation which discriminates against products from other Member States.* As the Commission has correctly stated, Article 95 [now Art 90] must guarantee

the complete neutrality of internal taxation as regards competition between domestic products and imported products. (emphasis added)

Article 90 is aimed at two distinct, but sometimes overlapping, national taxation practices: first, the taxing of the same or similar imported and home-produced products in a different way; and secondly, the taxing of different but competing imported and home-produced products in such a way as to afford protection to the home-produced product. The two key concepts are therefore similarity and product competition (*Commission* v *France* (Case 168/78)). These two concepts will now be considered further.

Article 90(1): similar products

Article 90(1) does not require a Member State to adopt a particular system of internal taxation, just that whatever system is adopted must be applied without discrimination to similar imported products: i.e. it prohibits the imposition of internal taxes on products from other Member States which are greater than those levied on *similar* domestic products. Therefore, once the imported and domestic products are considered to be *similar*, Art 90(1) will apply.

In *Commission* v *France* (Case 168/78), the Court of Justice, at para 5, stated that it is necessary to consider as *similar* products which have

similar characteristics and meet the same needs from the point of view of consumers.

This has been subsequently applied by the Court of Justice in *John Walker* v *Ministeriet for Skatter* (Case 243/84). The issue before the Court was whether liqueur fruit wine was *similar* to whisky for the purposes of the former Art 95(1) (now Art 90(1)). The Court analysed the *objective characteristics* of the products, including their alcoholic contents, methods of production and consumer perceptions as to the nature of the products. The Court held that they were not similar: they had different alcohol contents and different manufacturing processes (whisky was distilled rather than fermented). Any scrutiny of the tax therefore had to be considered under the former Art 95(2) (now Art 90(2)).

Assessing the similarity of beverages was required in *FG Roders BV ea* v *Inspecteur der Inverrechten en Accijnzen* (Joined Cases C-367 and 377/93), where importers of French wine, Spanish sherry and Italian vermouth challenged the higher rates of excise duty that were charged on those products, as compared to fruit wines produced in the Benelux countries. The Court decided that they were. They are made from the same kind of agricultural products, and by the same process of natural fermentation. Both beverages possess the same kind of organoleptic properties, in particular taste and alcoholic strength, and meet the same needs of consumers, since they can be consumed for the same purposes, namely to quench thirst, to refresh, and to accompany meals.

Commission v *Italy* (Case 184/85) concerned the question of similarity between different types of fruit. Italy levied a consumption tax on bananas which amounted to about half their import price. The tax was not levied on other fruit (e.g. apples, pears, plums). Italy produced large amounts of fruit, other than bananas which it imported from France. The Commission took action against Italy alleging the tax infringed the former Art 95 (now Art 90). The Court first considered whether bananas and other fruit were *similar* for the purposes of the former Art 95(1) (now Art 90(1)). It held that they were *not* similar, taking into account the objective characteristics of the products. Any further examination of the tax had to proceed under the former Art 95(2) (now Art 90(2)).

If goods are *similar* under Art 90(1) then the tax will be unlawful if it is discriminatory: this can be either direct or indirect.

Direct discrimination

Different rates and methods of taxation applied to similar imported or domestic products are usually easily recognisable. For this reason direct discrimination of this kind is rare.

In *Lutticke GmbH v Hauptzollamt Saarlouis* (Case 57/65), an internal tax was levied on imported dried milk but not on domestically produced dried milk. The tax was directly discriminatory and breached the former Art 95(1) (now Art 90(1)).

In *Bobie Getränkvertrieb v Hauptzollamt Aachen-Nord* (Case 127/75), a German beer tax imposed a sliding scale on home-produced beer, varying between DM 12 and 15 per hectolitre, according to the size of the brewery. Small brewers paid only DM 12. Imported beers had a flat rate tax of DM 14.40 levied upon them. The Court of Justice held that the tax was discriminatory, since small foreign breweries could not avail themselves of the low rate available to domestic breweries. The Court repeated this formulation in *Haahr Petroleum Ltd v Abenra Havn* (Case C-90/94), where goods unloaded in harbours which originated in inland waterways paid a lower rate of harbour tax, compared to goods unloaded in harbours which originated in deep-water channels:

> A criterion for the charging of higher taxation which by definition can never be fulfilled by similar domestic products cannot be considered to be compatible with the prohibition of discrimination laid down in Article 95 [now Art 90] of the Treaty. Such a system has the effect of excluding domestic products in advance from the heaviest taxation. Likewise, the Court has held that such differential taxation is incompatible with Community law if the products most heavily taxed are, by their very nature, imported products.

The latter was the case in *Haahr Petroleum*, since the goods from the inland waterways were overwhelmingly the product of the home state, and the goods unloaded from the deep-water channel were from outside it.

The method for the collection of the tax may also involve discrimination, even if the criteria for its payment do not. In *Commission v Ireland* (Case 55/79), the Court held an Irish tax incompatible with Art 95 (now Art 90). The tax was payable according to the same criteria, irrespective of the origin of the goods. However, domestic producers were permitted several weeks' grace to pay the tax, whilst importers had to pay immediately on importation.

Indirect discrimination

Indirectly discriminatory internal taxation will be similarly caught by Art 90(1). On the face of it an internal tax rule may not differentiate between domestic and imported goods, but the actual effect of the tax may place a greater burden on the imported goods. An example of this is illustrated in *Humblot* v *Directeur des Services Fiscaux* (Case 112/84).

France imposed two different types of annual car tax. The key threshold between the two was the power rating (or fiscal horsepower) of the car. Below 16 CV the tax increased gradually in proportion to the car's fiscal horsepower, up to a maximum of 1,100 francs. Above 16 CV a flat rate tax of 5,000 francs was imposed. The way in which the fiscal horsepower was calculated was very complicated. It took into consideration: the number of cylinders; the bore in centimetres; the stroke in centimetres; and the rotation speed in revolutions per second. The result of applying this calculation was that no French car was given a fiscal horsepower rating above 16 CV, therefore only imported vehicles were subject to the higher flat rate tax. The effect of the fiscal horsepower calculation was such that a foreign car of similar characteristics to a French car (e.g. same engine size, similar specifications, etc.) would fall within a higher rating and therefore attract a higher level of annual tax.

M. Humblot was charged 5,000 francs on his imported car, which had been given a fiscal horsepower rating of 36 CV. He claimed the tax breached the former Art 95 (now Art 90) and sought a refund. As discussed above, the former Art 95 was directly effective, and, as a corollary to this, Art 90 will also be directly effective. The French court referred questions to the Court of Justice under the former Art 177 EC Treaty (now Art 234):

12. It is appropriate in the first place to stress that as Community law stands at present the Member States are at liberty to subject products such as cars to a system of road tax which increases progressively in amount depending on an objective criterion, such as the power rating for tax purposes, which may be determined in various ways.

13. Such a system of domestic taxation is, however, compatible with Article 95 [now Art 90] only in so far as it is free from any discriminatory or protective effect.

14. That is not true of a system like the one at issue in the main proceedings. Under that system there are two distinct taxes: a differential tax which increases progressively and is charged on cars not exceeding a given power rating for tax purposes and a fixed tax on cars exceeding that rating which is almost five times as high as the highest band of the differential tax. Although the system embodies no formal distinction based on the origin of the products it manifestly exhibits discriminatory or protective features contrary to Article 95 [now Art 90], since the power rating determining liability to the special tax has been fixed at a level such that only imported cars, in particular from other Member States, are subject to the special tax whereas all cars of domestic manufacture are liable to the distinctly more advantageous differential tax.

15. In the absence of considerations relating to the amount of the special tax, consumers seeking comparable cars as regards such matters as size, comfort, actual power, maintenance costs, durability, fuel consumption and price would naturally choose from among cars above and below the critical power rating laid down by French law. However, liability to the special tax entails a much larger increase in taxation than passing from one category of car to another in a system of progressive taxation embodying balanced differentials like the system on which the differential tax is based. *The resultant additional taxation is liable to cancel out the advantages which certain cars imported from other Member States might have in consumers' eyes over comparable cars of domestic manufacture, particularly since the special tax continues to be payable for years. In that respect the special tax reduces the amount of competition to which cars of domestic manufacture are subject and hence is contrary to the principle of neutrality with which domestic taxation must comply.*

16. In the light of the foregoing considerations the questions raised by the national court for a preliminary ruling should be answered as follows: Article 95 [now Art 90] of the EEC Treaty prohibits the charging on cars exceeding a given power rating for tax purposes of a special fixed tax the amount of which is several times the highest amount of the progressive tax payable on cars of less than the said power rating for tax purposes, where the only cars subject to the special tax are imported, in particular from other Member States. (emphasis added)

France subsequently amended its legislation, but the Court of Justice has been required to adjudicate on its compatibility with Community law on numerous occasions. See, for example:

- *Feldain* v *Services Fiscaux du Departement du Haut-Rhin* (Case 433/85)
- *Deville* v *Administration des Impôts* (Case 240/87)
- *Jacquier* v *Directeur Général des Impôts* (Case C-113/94)
- *Yves Tarantik* v *Direction des Services Fiscaux de Seine-et-Marne* (Case C-421/97).

Objective justification – a defence to indirect discrimination

While direct discrimination will never be justifiable, tax rules of a Member State which tend to favour the domestic product may be held not to breach Art 90(1) if there is some *objective justification* for the conduct complained of. This objective justification must be acceptable to the Court; if accepted it will prevent Art 90(1) from being applied too harshly. Consider *Chemial Farmaceutici* v *DAF SpA* (Case 140/79).

Italian internal taxation of *synthetic* ethyl alcohol was higher than taxation of *fermented* ethyl alcohol. The products were interchangeable in use. Italy produced very little of the higher taxed synthetic product, and therefore the tax system had a harsher impact upon importers. The rationale for the tax policy was to encourage the manufacture of the fermented product (the raw material of which was agricultural products), thus preserving the petroleum ingredients used to make the synthetic product for other, more economically important purposes. The Court considered the legitimacy of this policy choice:

13. ... the different taxation of synthetic alcohol and of alcohol produced by fermentation in Italy is the result of an economic policy decision to favour the manufacture of alcohol from agricultural products and, correspondingly, to restrain the processing into alcohol of ethylene, a derivative of petroleum, in order to reserve that raw material for other more important economic uses. *It accordingly constitutes a legitimate choice of economic policy to which effect is given by fiscal means.* The implementation of that policy does not lead to any discrimination since although it results in discouraging imports of synthetic alcohol into Italy, it also has the consequence of hampering the development in Italy itself of production of alcohol from ethylene, that production being technically perfectly possible.

14. As the Court has stated on many occasions, particularly in the judgments cited by the Italian Government, *in its present stage of development Community law does not restrict the freedom of each Member State to lay down tax arrangements which differentiate between certain products on the basis of objective criteria, such as the nature of the raw materials used or the production processes employed. Such differentiation is compatible*

with Community law if it pursues economic policy objectives which are themselves compatible with the requirements of the Treaty and its secondary law and if the detailed rules are such as to avoid any form of discrimination, direct or indirect, in regard to imports from other Member States or any form of protection of competing domestic products.

15. Differential taxation such as that which exists in Italy for denatured synthetic alcohol on the one hand and denatured alcohol obtained by fermentation on the other satisfies these requirements. It appears in fact that the system of taxation pursues an objective of legitimate industrial policy in that it is such as to promote the distillation of agricultural products as against the manufacture of alcohol from petroleum derivatives. That choice does not conflict with the rules of Community law or the requirements of a policy decided within the framework of the Community.

16. *The detailed provisions of the legislation at issue before the national court cannot be considered as discriminatory since*, on the one hand, it is not disputed that imports from other Member States of alcohol obtained by fermentation qualify for the same tax treatment as Italian alcohol produced by fermentation, and on the other hand, although the rate of tax prescribed for synthetic alcohol results in restraining the importation of synthetic alcohol originating in other Member States, *it has an equivalent economic effect in the national territory in that it also hampers the establishment of profitable production of the same product by Italian industry.* (emphasis added)

In this case the Court stated at para 16 that there was no *actual* discrimination, direct or indirect, because the tax would deter not only importers of the affected product but also national producers, even though there was very little domestic production of the affected product. The tax was applicable to both imported and domestic products, so it could only have the potential for being indirectly discriminatory (i.e. if the tax had a greater impact on the imported product than on the domestic product). If there is no actual discrimination then the tax is *per se* (i.e. automatically) outside Art 90. However, in this case the Court, in finding that there was no actual discrimination, was no doubt strongly influenced by the *reason* for the imposition of the tax (i.e. 'legitimate choice of economic policy' – see para 13). It is therefore considered that this case provides scope for a defence to an internal tax that is indirectly discriminatory. The defence will apply where the measure can be objectively justified; in this case on the ground that the imposition of the tax constituted a 'legitimate choice of economic policy'. Although the Court did not expressly state it constituted a defence, it was influenced by the reason when deciding not to impose a strict application of Art 90.

Similarly, in the course of Art 226 EC Treaty proceedings brought by the Commission against France, the Court held that a more favourable tax rate applied to natural sweet wine as compared to ordinary table wine was justified. The purpose of the tax was to assist the economy of areas that were heavily reliant on such wines, which were produced in difficult circumstances (*Commission v France* (Case 196/85)). Where such tax relief is applied, it must be operated indiscriminately, even where there is a legitimate and defensible objective. Thus, it has been held that an importer of spirits into Germany was entitled to take advantage of tax relief available, *inter alia*, in respect of spirits made by small businesses and collective farms. The Court accepted that such tax concessions could meet legitimate economic and social purposes, but Art 90 required that such preferential systems must be extended without discrimination to spirits coming from other Member States (*Hansen v Hauptzollamt Flensburg* (Case 148/77)).

Article 90(1) and (2) – the relationship

As discussed above, Art 90(1) prohibits the imposition of internal taxes on products from other Member States which are greater than those levied on *similar* domestic products. Therefore, once the imported and domestic products can be considered to be *similar*, Art 90(1) will apply and the taxes must be equalised.

Article 90(2) applies to other products which are not *similar*, but the effect of the tax is to afford *indirect protection* to some other domestic product: i.e. products which are not similar but which may otherwise be in competition with each other. For example, wine and beer may not be considered to be similar, however they may be in competition with one other. One of the questions which need to be addressed when considering whether the products are in competition with one another, is whether the two products have a cross-elasticity of demand; are the products interchangeable? Having established a competitive relationship between the two products, if the tax on wine is greater than that on beer, it could deter beer drinkers from switching to wine. If the Member State which has adopted this tax policy is a major producer of beer but produces only small amounts of wine, the vast majority of it being imported, the tax policy could afford an indirect protection to its domestic beer producers.

In *Commission* v *France* (Case 168/78), the Court of Justice, at paras 5 and 6, considered the scope of the former Art 95(1) and (2) (now Art 90(1) and (2)):

France had higher tax rates for spirits which were based upon grain (e.g. whisky, rum, gin, vodka) than those based upon wine or fruit (e.g. cognac, armagnac). France produced very little of the more heavily taxed grain-based spirits, but was a major producer of the wine/fruit-based spirits. The Commission took infraction proceedings against France pursuant to the former Art 169 EC Treaty (now Art 226) alleging the tax breached the former Art 95 (now Art 90):

---

4. [Article 95 (now Art 90) supplements] within the system of the Treaty, the provisions on the abolition of customs duties and charges having equivalent effect [i.e. Articles 9–17 (now Arts 23 and 25)]. Their aim is to ensure free movement of goods between the Member States in normal conditions of competition by the elimination of all forms of protection which result from the application of internal taxation which discriminates against products from other Member States. As the Commission has correctly stated, Article 95 [now Art 90] must guarantee the complete neutrality of internal taxation as regards competition between domestic products and imported products.

5. *The first paragraph of Article 95 [now Art 90], which is based on a comparison of the tax burdens imposed on domestic products and imported products which may be classified as 'similar', is the basic rule in this respect.* This provision, as the Court has had occasion to emphasise in its judgment of 10 October 1978 in Case 148/77, *H Hansenjun. & O.C. Balle GmbH & Co.* v *Hauptzollamt Flensburg* [1978] ECR 1787, must be interpreted widely so as to cover all taxation procedures which conflict with the principle of the equality of treatment of domestic products and imported products; it is therefore necessary to interpret the concept of 'similar products' with sufficient flexibility. *The Court specified in the judgment of 17 February 1976 in the REWE case (Case 45/75 [1976] ECR 181) that it is necessary to consider as similar products which have 'similar characteristics and meet the same needs from the point of view of consumers'. It is therefore necessary to determine the scope of the first paragraph of Article 95 [now Art 90] on the basis not of the criterion of the strictly identical nature of the products but on that of their similar and comparable use.*

6. *The function of the second paragraph of Article 95 [now Art 90] is to cover, in addition, all forms of indirect tax protection in the case of products which, without being similar within the meaning of the first paragraph, are nevertheless in competition, even partial, indirect or potential, with certain products of the importing country.* The Court has already emphasised certain aspects of that provision in its judgment of 4 April 1978 in Case 27/77 *Firma Fink-Frucht GmbH* v *Hauptzollamt Munchen-Landsbergerstrasse* [1978] ECR 223, in which it stated that for the purposes of the application of the second paragraph of Article 95 [now Art 90] it is sufficient for the imported product to be in competition with the protected domestic production by reason of one of several economic uses to which it may be put, even though the condition of similarity for the purposes of the first paragraph of Article 95 [now Art 90] is not fulfilled.

7. Whilst the criterion indicated in the first paragraph of Article 95 [now Art 90] consists in the comparison of tax burdens, whether in terms of the rate, the mode of assessment or other detailed rules for the application thereof, in view of the difficulty of making sufficiently precise comparisons between the products in question, the second paragraph of that article is based upon a more general criterion, in other words the protective nature of the system on internal taxation. (emphasis added)

This case, as with many of the 'Spirit' cases, was decided on the basis that there had been an infringement of the former Art 95 (now Art 90) without a detailed examination of the paragraphs separately. The reason why the Court was not unduly worried whether the infringement was based on the first or second paragraph of the former Art 95 (now Art 90) was explained by the Court as follows:

12. Two conclusions follow from this analysis of the market in spirits. First, there is, in the case of spirits considered as a whole, an indeterminate number of beverages which must be classified as 'similar products' within the meaning of the first paragraph of Article 95 [now Art 90], although it may be difficult to decide this in specific cases, in view of the nature of the factors implied by distinguishing criteria such as flavour and consumer habits. Secondly, even in cases in which it is impossible to recognise a sufficient degree of similarity between the products concerned, there are nevertheless, in the case of all spirits, common characteristics which are sufficiently pronounced to accept that in all cases there is at least partial or potential competition. It follows that the application of the second paragraph of Article 95 [now Art 90] may come into consideration in cases in which the relationship of similarity between the specific varieties of spirits remains doubtful or contested.

13. It appears from the foregoing that Article 95 [now Art 90], taken as a whole, may apply without distinction to all the products concerned. It is sufficient therefore to examine whether the application of a given national tax system is discriminatory or, as the case may be, protective, in other words whether there is a difference in the rate or the detailed rules for levying the tax and whether that difference is likely to favour a given national production ...

39. ... the Court deems it unnecessary for the purposes of solving this dispute to give a ruling on the question whether or not the spirituous beverages concerned are wholly or partially similar products within the meaning of the first paragraph of Article 95 [now Art 90] when it is impossible reasonably to contest that without exception they are in at least partial competition with the domestic products to which the application refers and that it is impossible to deny the protective nature of the French tax system within the second paragraph of Article 95 [now Art 90].

40. In fact, as indicated above, spirits obtained from cereals have, as products obtained from distillation, sufficient characteristics in common with other spirits to constitute at least in certain circumstances an alternative choice for consumers. ...

41. As the competitive and substitution relationships between the beverages in question are such, the protective nature of the tax system criticised by the Commission is clear. A characteristic of that system is in fact that an essential part of domestic production, ... spirits obtained from wine and fruit, come within the most favourable tax category whereas at least two types of product, almost all of which are imported from other Member States, are subject to higher taxation under the 'manufacturing tax'.

In this case, the Court considered that classification into the first or second paragraph of the former Art 95 (now Art 90) was difficult (para 12). It also stated that the end result would be the same. At para 39 the Court concluded that the tax would fail, notwithstanding that the spirits were not similar, because they were to some degree in competition with one another and the tax was protective. The Court therefore got around the problem of classification.

However, one problem of this failure by the Court is that the defaulting Member State will need to take remedial action to remedy the defect. If the tax is contrary to Art 90(1) then the tax must be equalised. However, where the tax is in breach of Art 90(2) the state is required to remove the protective effect; this may not require the tax to be equalised. We shall consider the concept of *protective effect* below. In later judgments the Court has distinguished between the two paragraphs.

Article 90(2): protective effect

One of the early 'alcohol' cases brought by the Commission was against the United Kingdom for the discriminatory taxation of wine in comparison with beer: *Commission v United Kingdom* (Case 170/78). There is quite clearly a greater difference between the objective characteristics of beer and wine than there is between two spirits. Beer and wine were not considered to be Art 95(1) (now Art 90(1)) *similar* and therefore the Court of Justice proceeded under the former Art 95(2) (now Art 90(2)). It adjourned the hearing for more information to be put before it, relating to the competitive relationship between the two products. This case provides an insight into how the Court approaches the application of the former Art 95(2) (now Art 90(2)).

The United Kingdom levied a tax on certain wines, which was about five times that levied on beer in terms of 'volume'. The tax on wine represented about 38 per cent of its sale price compared to 25 per cent for beer. The United Kingdom produced vast amounts of beer, but very little wine. The Commission took infraction proceedings against the United Kingdom pursuant to the former Art 169 EC Treaty (now Art 226) claiming the differential UK tax breached the former Art 95(2) (now Art 90(2)). Following an adjournment while further evidence was gathered relating to the competitive relationship between beer and wine, the Court gave its judgment:

---

8. As regards the question of competition between wine and beer, the Court considered that, to a certain extent at least, the two beverages in question were capable of meeting identical needs, so that it had to be acknowledged that there was a degree of substitution for one another. It pointed out that, for the purpose of measuring the possible degree of

substitution, attention should not be confined to consumer habits in a Member State or in a given region. Those habits, which were essentially variable in time and space, could not be considered immutable; the tax policy of a Member State must not therefore crystallise given consumer habits so as to consolidate an advantage acquired by national industries concerned to respond to them.

9. The Court nonetheless recognised that, in view of the substantial differences between wine and beer, it was difficult to compare the manufacturing processes and the natural properties of those beverages, as the Government of the United Kingdom had rightly observed. For that reason, the Court requested the parties to provide additional information with a view to dispelling the doubts which existed concerning the nature of the competitive relationship between the two products ...

11. The Italian Government contended in that connection that it was inappropriate to compare beer with wines of average alcoholic strength or, *a fortiori*, with wines of greater alcoholic strength. In its opinion, *it was the lightest wines with an alcoholic strength in the region of 9, that is to say the most popular and cheapest wines, which were genuinely in competition with beer*. It therefore took the view that those wines should be chosen for purposes of comparison where it was a question of measuring the incidence of taxation on the basis of either alcoholic strength or the price of the products.

12. The Court considers that observation by the Italian Government to be pertinent. In view of the substantial differences in the quality and, therefore, in the price of wines, *the decisive competitive relationship between beer, a popular and widely consumed beverage, and wine must be established by reference to those wines which are the most accessible to the public at large, that is to say, generally speaking the lightest and cheapest varieties. Accordingly, that is the appropriate basis for making fiscal comparisons by reference to the alcoholic strength or to the price of the two beverages ...*

19. It is not disputed that comparison of the taxation of beer and wine by reference to the volume of the two beverages reveals that wine is taxed more heavily than beer in both relative and real terms. Not only was the taxation of wine increased substantially in relation to the taxation of beer when the United Kingdom replaced customs duty with excise duty ... but it is also clear that during the years to which those proceedings relate, namely 1976 and 1977, the taxation of wine was, on average, five times higher, by reference to volume, than the taxation of beer; in other words wine was subject to an additional tax of 400% in round figures.

20. As regards the criterion for comparison based on alcoholic strength ...

21. In the light of the indices which the Court has already accepted, *it is clear that in the United Kingdom during the period in question wine bore a tax burden which, by reference to alcoholic strength, was more than twice as heavy as that borne by beer, that is to say an additional tax burden of at least 100%.*

22. As regards the criterion of the incidence of taxation on the price net of tax, the Court experienced considerable difficulty in forming an opinion, in view of the disparate nature of the information provided by the parties ...

26. After considering the information provided by the parties, the Court has come to the conclusion that, if a comparison is made on the basis of those wines which are cheaper than the types of wine selected by the United Kingdom and of which several varieties are sold in significant quantities on the United Kingdom market, it becomes apparent that

precisely those wines which, in view of their price, are most directly in competition with domestic beer production are subject to a considerably higher tax burden.

27. It is clear, therefore, following the detailed inquiry conducted by the Court – whatever criterion for comparison is used, there being no need to express a preference for one or the other – that the United Kingdom's tax system has the effect of subjecting wine imported from other Member States to an additional burden so as to afford protection to domestic beer production, inasmuch as beer production constitutes the most relevant reference criterion from the point of view of competition. Since such protection is most marked in the case of the most popular wines, the effect of the United Kingdom tax system is to stamp wine with the hallmarks of a luxury product which, in view of the tax burden which it bears, can scarcely constitute in the eyes of the consumer a genuine alternative to the typically produced domestic beverage.

28. It follows from the foregoing considerations that, by levying excise duty on still light wines made from fresh grapes at a higher rate, in relative terms, than on beer, the United Kingdom has failed to fulfil its obligations under the second paragraph of Article 95 [now Art 90] of the EEC Treaty. (emphasis added)

The Court of Justice carried out a two-stage process in determining whether the United Kingdom had breached the former Art 95(2) (now Art 90(1)):

- The Court sought to establish some competitive relationship between the two products to ascertain if the former Art 95(2) (now Art 90(2)) could be applicable at all (paras 8–12). In considering this point the Court took account of the extent to which the goods were substitutable for each other: i.e. whether they had a high or low degree of cross-elasticity.

  In considering whether or not the goods are substitutable the Court will ignore current consumer perceptions, because they can change over a period of time. Indeed the consumer may be affected because of the differential tax on the two products. This may deter the consumer from purchasing the more heavily taxed product. At para 27, the Court declared that the United Kingdom's taxation of cheap wine was to stamp it with the hallmark of a luxury product.

  If there is a competitive relationship between the two products the Court will also examine the nature of this competition. In this case the nature of the competition was held to be between beer and the cheaper, lighter wines (rather than the more expensive, heavier wines).

- Having established a competitive relationship between the two products, the Court will ascertain whether the tax system is in fact protective of beer.

  In this case it was quite clear that the differential rates had a protective effect on beer. Tax on wine was (a) 500% by reference to 'volume' and (b) 100% by reference to 'alcoholic strength', greater than that levied on beer.

  However, the difference in the level of taxation may not be that great. The Court may therefore be faced with a much more difficult task. Much will depend on the degree of cross-elasticity between the two products. If this is low then a small tax differential will probably make no difference, whereas if it is high, the level of taxation may be of critical importance to the consumer.

  Alternatively, although the rate of tax between the two products may be high in percentage terms, it may only be a very low proportion of the final selling price.

For example, in the UK beer and wine case, if the tax on beer had been 2p per litre compared to 10p per litre on wine then, by volume, the tax on wine is 500% greater than that on beer. However, the level of tax is low with respect to the final selling price of the products and therefore the level of taxation is unlikely to have a protective effect on the domestic beer producers (i.e. the tax difference alone would be unlikely to deter a beer drinker from switching to wine).

This two-stage process can be seen in other cases. In *FG Roders BV ea v Inspecteur der Inverrechten en Accijnzen* (Joined Cases C-367–377/93), although the Court of Justice conceded that fruit wine produced in the Benelux countries was not similar to imported sherry, madeira, vermouth and champagne, it recognised that these products might, nevertheless, be in competition with the fruit wine, and the differential tax structure might, therefore, favour the home-produced fruit wine. The Court observed that the existence of a competitive relationship between the products had to be considered to establish whether or not there was a breach of the second paragraph of Art 90. The essential question was whether the charge imposed was of such a kind as to have the effect, on the market in question, of reducing potential consumption of the imported products. The national court that has to make the final decision, must have regard to the difference between the selling prices of the products in question and the impact of that difference on the consumer's choice, as well as to changes in the consumption of those products.

The facts of *Commission v Italy* (Case 184/85) have been considered above (the Court of Justice decided that bananas were not similar to other fruit and therefore Art 90(1) did not apply). Having decided that there was a competitive relationship between bananas and other fruit, the Court went on to consider whether the Italian consumption tax levied on bananas, but not on other, home-grown fruit, had a protective effect. It held that it did, because the tax levied on the bananas was almost half their import price, while no tax was levied on almost all Italian grown fruit. This was clear evidence of protectionism.

However, as stated above, the fact that there is a tax differential between domestic and imported goods will not automatically result in protectionism being established. In *Commission v Belgium* (Case 356/85), Belgium levied a tax on beer which was produced in Belgium, and a tax on wine which was mostly imported. There was a 6 per cent difference in the tax levied, wine being taxed more heavily. The Court of Justice held that this did not have a protective effect because the cost of the two products differed substantially, and therefore a relatively minor difference in the tax rates would not serve to protect the Belgian beer producers.

The fact that tax is imposed on a product which is not produced in the importing state and for which there is no domestic equivalent may well mean that there is no breach of Art 90, since there will be no similar product in relation to which discrimination can be alleged or home market to be protected (*Fink-Frucht v HZA Munchen-Landsberger Strasse* (Case 27/67)).

Figure 17.2 relates to Art 90 EC Treaty: internal taxation.

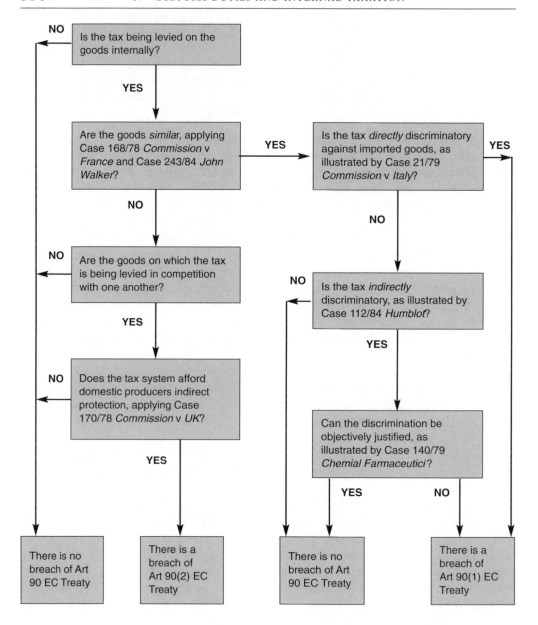

Figure 17.2 Article 90 EC Treaty: internal taxation

Further reading

Craig, P. and De Burca, G. (1998) *EU Law Text, Cases and Materials* (2nd edn), OUP, Chapter 13.

Danusso, M. and Denton, R., 'Does the European Court of Justice Look for a Protectionist Motive under Article 95?' (1991) 1 LIEI 67.

Easson, A.J., 'Fiscal Discrimination: New Perspectives on Article 95' (1981) 18 CML Rev 521.

Green, N., Hartley, T.C. and Usher, J. (1991) *The Legal Foundations of the Single Market*, Clarendon Press, Chapters 3 and 4.

Kuyper, P.J., 'Booze and fast cars: tax discrimination under GATT and the EC' [1996] LIEI 129.

Schwarze, J. (1988) 'The Member States' Discretionary Powers under Tax Provisions of the EEC Treaty' in Schwarze, J. (ed.) *Discretionary Powers of the Member States in the Fields of Economic Policies and their Limits under the EEC Treaty*, Nomos.

Steiner, J. and Woods, L. (2000) *Textbook on EC Law* (7th edn), Blackstone Press, Chapters 7–9.

Tillotson, J. (2000) *European Union Law: Text, Cases and Materials* (3rd edn), Cavendish Publishing, pp. 271–282.

Usher, J., 'The Single Market and Goods Imported from Third Countries' [1986] YEL 159, 167.

Weatherill, S. (2000) *Cases and Materials on EC Law* (5th edn), Blackstone Press, Chapter 6.

Chapter 18

THE ELIMINATION OF QUANTITATIVE RESTRICTIONS AND MEASURES HAVING AN EQUIVALENT EFFECT

INTRODUCTION

The elimination of any restrictions on the free movement of goods is central to the creation of an internal market in the Member States of the Community, and this is one of the main objectives of the Community (Art 3(1)(a) EC Treaty). Article 28 (previously Art 30) provides that:

> Quantitative restrictions on imports and all measures having equivalent effect shall be prohibited between Member States.

The prohibition of restrictions on *imports* in Art 28 is reflected by a matching prohibition on *export* restrictions in Art 29 (previously Art 34). Both prohibitions are, however, qualified by the right of Member States to impose limited restrictions on trade, if they can *justify* them under the criteria laid down in Art 30 (previously Art 36), or in some cases under the *Cassis* rule of reason (see below). The articles attempt to strike a balance between achieving a genuine free and competitive market in goods on the one hand, and the recognition of the need, in some circumstances, to protect essential public interests on the other. The process of harmonising national standards of consumer and environmental protection, through a programme of standardising directives for goods throughout the Community, is part of a programme to reduce the need for such national exceptions to the general Community right of free movement of goods. Much of the jurisprudence of the Court of Justice has been devoted to consideration of the extent to which such national measures infringe the relevant provisions of the Treaty or fall within the permitted derogations.

Articles 28 and 29 adopt the same approach as has been adopted for the prohibitions set out in Arts 23 and 25 (see Chapter 17). They are aimed at measures which are clearly directed at imports and exports to and from other Member States, but they also prohibit measures which have the same effect as such restrictions, even though there may be no intention by the Member State imposing them to have that effect. Articles 28 and 29 are directly effective. Any state measure breaching them can give rise to a claim in damages against the state concerned, provided that the criteria laid down by the Court of Justice in *Brasserie du Pêcheur* (Case C-46/93) in relation to imports and *R v Ministry of Fisheries and Food, ex parte Hedley Lomas Ireland Ltd*

(Case C-5/94) in relation to exports can be met (see Chapter 9). Articles 28 and 29 are directed at the state, therefore they cannot be used by private individuals against each other. They may, however, be used by individuals as a defence in civil proceedings where the national law is alleged to breach Arts 28 or 29: *Vereinigte Familiapress Zeitungsverlags und Vertriebs GmbH* v *Heinrich Bauer Verlag* (Case C-368/95).

The prohibition on restrictions affects all kinds of products, including agricultural produce, and it applies not only to goods which originate in the Member States but also to goods which come from outside the Community and are in free circulation in a Member State. Such goods are in free circulation when they have crossed the Common External Tariff wall with all import formalities complied with and duties and charges paid (Art 24 EC Treaty).

For the purposes of Arts 28–30, the Court has held that 'goods' are 'manufactured material objects' (*Cinéthèque* (Cases 60 & 61/84)). The term is wide enough to include not only plants, vegetables, fruit and livestock and a whole variety of animal products (*Société Civile Agricole* (Case C-323/93)), but also even covers generated electricity (*Commission* v *Netherlands* (Case C-157/94)). The context in which an item is applied, may, however, result in it being regarded not as a product in itself subject to the provisions of Arts 28–30, but as an incident to the provision of a service, and thus subject to Art 49 EC Treaty (*HM Customs and Excise Commissioners* v *Schindler* (Case C-275/92), para 23). Coins and banknotes or bearer cheques are not 'goods', as their transfer is subject to the rules on transfer of capital under Art 56 EC Treaty (*Aldo Bordessa and Others* (Joined Cases C-358 & 416/93)). However, in *R* v *Thompson* (Case 7/78), the Court held that old gold coins were 'goods' because they were not a normal means of payment.

STATE MEASURES

Articles 28 and 29 are directed at the governments of *Member States*; they apply only to measures adopted by the state and not those taken by private parties. However, the provisions of Art 28 have also been held by the Court of Justice to be binding on the institutions of the Community, and the Court has expressed the view that it would have been prepared to strike down a Council Regulation requiring Member States to gather information from importers and exporters, had it been satisfied that the regulation imposed a disproportionately heavy burden on the free movement of goods (*Rene Kieffer and Romain Thill* (Case C-114/96)).

We have already considered the prohibition of tariffs and discriminatory charges and taxes imposed by Member States in the previous chapter. Articles 28–30 form part of a larger strategy to free up trade and to prevent Member States from adopting covert protectionist policies. The same strategy also includes the regulation of state monopolies of a commercial character under Art 31 and state aids to nationalised industries under Arts 87–88. It underlies Council Directives 88/95 and 89/440 on public procurement, which are intended to prevent the governments of Member States from favouring national contractors in the award of public works contracts. For that reason, attempts by a private undertaking to persuade consumers to buy national products in, say, a 'Buy British' advertising campaign, will not breach Art 28, although such a campaign would infringe Art 28 if promoted by a public, or publicly sponsored, body (*Apple and Pear Development Council* v *K.J. Lewis Ltd* (Case 222/82) – see below).

So what exactly constitutes a *state* measure for the purposes of Arts 28 and 29? This question was considered by the Court of Justice in *Commission* v *Ireland* (Case 249/81).

The Irish Government embarked upon a 'Buy Irish' campaign. The Irish Government had introduced, in 1978, a three-year programme to help promote Irish products. The campaign was launched by a speech delivered by the Irish Minister for Industry, Commerce and Energy. A number of measures were adopted, of which two were carried out: the encouragement of the use of a 'Buy Irish' symbol for goods made in Ireland and the organisation of a publicity campaign by the Irish Goods Council in favour of Irish products, designed to encourage consumers to buy Irish products.

The Commission brought former Art 169 (now Art 226) proceedings against the Irish Government alleging the campaign was a measure equivalent to a quantitative restriction and therefore in breach of the former Art 30 (now Art 28). Ireland defended the action on the ground *it* had never adopted 'measures' for the purpose of the former Art 30; it was the Irish Goods Council. It argued that any financial assistance it had given to the Council should be judged under the former Arts 92–93 (aids granted by states – now Arts 87–88) and not under the former Art 30 (now Art 28). The members of the Irish Goods Council were appointed by the Irish Government and it was funded in proportions of 6:1 by the Government and private industry respectively.

The initial question to be considered by the Court of Justice was whether or not the campaign constituted a *measure* undertaken *by the state*:

15. It is thus apparent that the Irish Government appoints the members of the Management Committee of the Irish Goods Council, grants it public subsidies which cover the greater part of its expenses and, finally, defines the aims and the broad outline of the campaign conducted by that institution to promote the sale and purchase of Irish products. In the circumstances the Irish Government cannot rely on the fact that the campaign was conducted by a private company in order to escape any liability it may have under the provisions of the Treaty ...

21. The Irish Government maintains that the prohibition against measures having an effect equivalent to quantitative restrictions in Article 30 [now Art 28] is concerned only with 'measures', that is to say, binding provisions emanating from a public authority. However, no such provision has been adopted by the Irish Government, which has confined itself to giving moral support and financial aid to the activities pursued by the Irish industries ...

23. ... the campaign is a reflection of the Irish Government's considered intention to substitute domestic products for imported products on the Irish market and thereby check the flow of imports from other Member States.

24. It must be remembered here that a representative of the Irish Government stated when the campaign was launched that it was a carefully thought-out set of initiatives constituting an integrated programme for promoting domestic products; that the Irish Goods Council was set up at the initiative of the Irish Government a few months later; and that the task of implementing the integrated programme as it was envisaged by the Government was entrusted, or left, to that Council ...

28. Such a practice cannot escape the prohibition laid down by Article 30 [now Art 28] of the Treaty solely because it is not based on decisions which are binding upon undertakings. Even measures adopted by the government of a Member State which do not have binding effect may be capable of influencing the conduct of traders and consumers in that state and thus of frustrating the aims of the Community as set out in Article 2 and enlarged upon in Article 3 of the Treaty.

The Court of Justice considered the involvement of the Irish Government with the Irish Goods Council at para 15. At paras 21 and 28 the Court rebutted the Irish argument that only formally binding measures are caught by the former Art 30 (now Art 28).

This was followed by the Court of Justice in *Apple and Pear Development Council v K.J. Lewis Ltd* (Case 222/82), where there was a statutory obligation on the growers of fruit to pay a levy to the Development Council. This statutory underpinning was sufficient to render it public for Art 28 purposes. As the Court of Justice stated:

a body such as the Development Council, which is set up by the government of a Member State and is financed by a charge imposed on growers, cannot under Community law enjoy the same freedom as regards the methods of advertising used as that enjoyed by producers themselves or producers' associations of a voluntary character.

Article 28 imposed on the Council 'a duty not to engage in any advertising intended to discourage the purchase of products from other Member States or to disparage those products in the eyes of consumers. Nor must it advise consumers to purchase domestic products solely by reason of their national origin' (para 18).

Similarly, in *R v The Pharmaceutical Society, ex parte API* (Cases 266 & 267/87), the Society was an independent body which had the responsibility for the regulation of standards among UK pharmacists. In order to practise, a pharmacist had to appear on the Society's register. The Society had certain statutory functions under the Pharmacy Act 1954. The Court of Justice held that the Society had a sufficient measure of state support or 'statutory underpinning' to constitute it a state entity for the purposes of Art 28. Accordingly, the Society was bound by Art 28. The Court therefore held that rules of the society which required pharmacists to supply, under a prescription, only a named branded drug were, *prima facie*, in breach of Art 28.

It is, of course, not only the state and public bodies which may, either directly or indirectly, seek to exclude foreign competition. Articles 28–30 must also be considered in the light of Arts 81 and 82, which play an important part in preventing national cartels and national monopolies from using private economic power to keep goods from other Member States from entering national markets. Where the private body enjoys a monopoly conferred on it by the state, which enables it to restrict the import of foreign products by virtue of that monopoly, there may be an overlap between Arts 28 and 82. In such circumstances, the state may be liable for maintaining a situation which has the effect of excluding products from other Member States in breach of Art 28, or an unlawful state monopoly in breach of Art 31 (*Harry Franzen* (Case C-189/95) and *Société Civile Agricole v Coopérative d'Elevage de la Mayenne* (Case C-323/93), and see also Chapter 19).

QUANTITATIVE RESTRICTIONS

Direct restrictions, such as quotas and bans on certain products of other Member States, were abolished or phased out in the early days of the Community and during transitional periods following the admission of new Member States. The concept of 'quantitative restrictions' is straightforward enough:

> The prohibition on quantitative restrictions covers measures which amount to a total or partial restraint of, according to the circumstances, imports, exports, or goods in transit. (*Geddo* v *Ente Nazionale Risi* (Case 2/73))

The concept of quantitative restriction therefore applies to an outright ban (e.g. a French ban on British beef) or the imposition of a quota (e.g. a numerical restriction on the number of vehicles which can be imported into Spain each year from abroad).

Some national prohibitions do survive, such as the prohibition on the importation of obscene materials into the United Kingdom under the Customs Consolidation Act 1876. It was argued by the British Government in *R* v *Henn and Darby* (Case 34/79) that a ban on the import of pornographic material under the Act was not a quantitative restriction under Art 28. The Court of Justice, in an Art 234 reference, disagreed. It held that Art 28 'includes such a prohibition on imports in as much as this is the most extreme form of restriction'. The reference in Art 28 to 'quantitative restrictions' was to be read in the light of Art 30, which referred also to 'prohibitions' on imports. In the event, the Court held that the prohibition in this case was justified under Art 30. That aspect of the case will be examined below. Although a quantitative restriction is readily recognisable, measures having an equivalent effect to quantitative restrictions on imports have proved much more elusive and have resulted in a large, and growing, jurisprudence on the subject by the Court of Justice.

MEASURES HAVING EQUIVALENT EFFECT TO QUANTITATIVE RESTRICTIONS (MEQRs)

The *Dassonville* formula

Article 28 also prohibits 'measures having [an] equivalent effect' to quantitative restrictions (MEQRs). The Court of Justice, in *Procureur du Roi* v *Dassonville* (Case 8/74), considered the scope of what is now Art 28 in relation to MEQRs, and provided a very useful definition (referred to as 'the *Dassonville* formula') of exactly what constitutes an MEQR.

A Belgian importer of Scotch whisky was prosecuted for selling the whisky with false certificates of origin. He had imported the whisky from France and it had been difficult to obtain the certificates from the producers. He argued that the Belgian law infringed Art 30 (now Art 28), in that it made the importation of whisky from anywhere other than the state of origin more difficult. The Belgian court referred the case to the Court of Justice under the former Art 177 (now Art 234).

---

2. By the first question it is asked whether a national provision prohibiting the import of goods bearing a designation of origin where such goods are not accompanied by an official document issued by the government of the exporting country certifying their right

to such designation constitutes a measure having an effect equivalent to a quantitative restriction within the meaning of Article 30 [now Art 28] of the Treaty.

3. This question was raised within the context of criminal proceedings instituted in Belgium against traders who duly acquired a consignment of Scotch whisky in free circulation in France and imported it into Belgium without being in possession of a certificate of origin from the British customs authorities, thereby infringing Belgian rules.

4. It emerges from the file and from the oral proceedings that a trader, wishing to import into Belgium Scotch whisky which is already in free circulation in France, can obtain such a certificate only with great difficulty, unlike the importer who imports directly from the producer country.

5. *All trading rules enacted by Member States which are capable of hindering, directly or indirectly, actually or potentially, intra-Community trade are to be considered as measures having an effect equivalent to quantitative restrictions ...*

9. Consequently, the requirement by a Member State of a certificate of authenticity which is less easily obtainable by importers of an authentic product which has been put into free circulation in a regular manner in another Member State than by importers of the same product coming directly from the country of origin constitutes a measure having an effect equivalent to a quantitative restriction as prohibited by the Treaty. (emphasis added)

It is clear from the Court's definition of an MEQR in para 5 that the crucial element in proving the existence of an MEQR is its *effect*; a discriminatory *intent* is not required. This is a very broad definition ('the *Dassonville* formula'), which, as will be discussed below, indicates a determination by the Court of Justice to ensure that very few measures will be permitted to hinder the free movement of goods between Member States.

Directive 70/50/EEC

Directive 70/50/EEC, issued in December 1969, was intended to provide guidance on the kind of acts and activities which constituted 'measures' infringing Art 28, and which were in existence when the EC Treaty came into force. It was formally only of application during the Member States' transitional period, yet it has been very influential in representing the Commission's view of the scope of Art 28; it is still on occasion referred to by the Court of Justice. Although many measures will have been made since that time, and will be outside the directive's scope, it still has value in identifying prohibited acts or conduct.

Article 2 of the directive covers measures 'other than those applicable equally to domestic or imported products, which hinder imports which could otherwise take place, including measures which make importation more difficult or costly than the disposal of domestic products'. Article 2 is thus concerned with national measures which apply specifically to, or affect only, imported products. These are often called 'distinctly applicable' measures, because they distinguish between imported and domestically produced products. Article 2 of the directive contains a non-exhaustive list of the sort of measures applied to imported goods which would constitute MEQRs. They include:

- the laying down of minimum and maximum sale prices;

- the fixing of less favourable prices for imported than for domestically produced goods;
- the exclusion of prices for imported goods which reflect importation costs;
- the making of access to markets in the importing state dependent upon having an agent there;
- the laying down of conditions of payment in respect of imported products only, or the subjection of imported goods to conditions which are different from those laid down for domestic products and are more difficult to satisfy;
- requiring, for imported goods only, the giving of guarantees or the making of payment on account;
- subjecting only imported products to conditions in respect of shape, size, weight, composition, presentation and identification, or subjecting imported products to conditions which are different from those for domestic products and more difficult to satisfy;
- hindering the purchase by individuals of imported products only, or encouraging, requiring or giving preference to the purchase of domestic products only;
- the total or partial preclusion of the use of national facilities or equipment in respect of imported products only, or the total or partial confinement of such facilities to national producers;
- the prohibition or limitation of publicity in respect of imported products only, or the total or partial restriction of publicity to home-produced products.

The above list is indicative of the sorts of national measures which will constitute MEQRs, but the ability of Member States to introduce measures which are either intended to protect, or will have the effect of protecting, domestically produced goods can neither be anticipated nor underestimated, and the Court has laid down a number of general principles about measures which specifically affect imported goods and which constitute MEQRs. Each national measure will have to be assessed on these principles as and when it comes before national courts and before the Court of Justice. Article 3 of the directive also refers to measures which are non-discriminatory or *indistinctly applicable*, but which may, nonetheless, have the effect of impeding imports (see below).

DISTINCTLY APPLICABLE MEASURES

Distinctly applicable measures, as stated above, are measures which are applied only to imported or exported goods; the measure is not applied to domestically produced goods. Hence the reason for the label: distinctly applicable, i.e. measures which distinguish between domestic and foreign goods.

There are many examples where the Court of Justice has struck down national rules which apply only to imported or exported goods. Some specific categories will be considered further.

Import and export restrictions

In *International Fruit Company* v *Produktschap voor Grotenten en Fruit (No. 2)* (Cases 51–54/71), the Court of Justice held that import or export licences are caught by the former Arts 30 and 34 (now Arts 28 and 29) because, applying *Dassonville*, such a measure is 'capable of hindering, directly or indirectly, actually or potentially, intra-Community trade'. The necessity to apply for a licence before goods can be imported into a Member State, or exported out of a Member State, has a three-fold impact: first, until the licence application has been processed, goods cannot be imported or exported (and therefore this in effect constitutes a ban); secondly, the application could be rejected; and thirdly, the very fact of having to apply for a licence will require additional paperwork to be completed by the importer or exporter. Completing the paperwork will cost time and money, and this additional cost will have to be accounted for when determining the price of the goods. Increasing the cost of the goods could decrease their competitiveness with domestically produced goods, and therefore the measure is capable of affecting trade within the Community.

In *Commission* v *Italy* (Case 154/85), Italy had procedures and data requirements which applied only to the importation of cars, which meant that their registration was longer, more complicated and expensive, compared to the registration of domestic cars. The Court of Justice held that such procedures and requirements were prohibited under the former Art 30 (now Art 28).

In *Rewe-Zentralfinanz* v *Landwirtschaftskammer* (Case 4/75), phyto-sanitary inspections on imported apples contravened the former Art 30 (now Art 28) because there was no similar inspection of domestically grown apples. The Court of Justice stressed the fact that border inspections made imports more difficult or costly.

In *Procureur de la République Besancon* v *Bouhelier* (Case 53/76), the same approach was applied to discriminatory export rules. This case concerned a French rule which imposed quality checks on watches for export, but there was no similar inspection of those intended for the domestic market. The Court of Justice held this to contravene the former Art 34 (now Art 29).

The Court of Justice more recently held, in *Commission* v *France* (Case C-265/95), that a *failure to act* by a Member State could constitute an infringement of former Art 30 (now Art 28).

Fruit and vegetables imported into France from other Member States were targeted by French farmers, who would obstruct their passage, preventing them from reaching their final destination. For more than a decade, the Commission had received complaints concerning the inactivity of the French authorities in the face of violent acts by the French farmers. From April to July 1993 that campaign was directed particularly at strawberries originating in Spain. In August and September 1993 tomatoes from Belgium were treated in the same way. In 1994 the same type of action, involving threats against shopping centres and destruction of goods and means of transport, was directed against Spanish strawberries in particular. On 20 April 1995 further serious incidents occurred in the south west of France, in the course of which agricultural products from Spain were destroyed. On 3 June 1995 three lorries transporting fruit and vegetables from Spain were the subject of acts of violence in the south of France, without any intervention by the police.

At the beginning of July 1995 Italian and Spanish fruit were once again destroyed by French farmers. Further serious incidents of the same type occurred in 1996 and 1997. It was not denied by France that when such incidents occurred the French police were either not present on the spot, despite the fact that in certain cases the competent authorities had been warned of the imminence of demonstration by the French farmers, or they simply failed to intervene, even where the police far outnumbered the French farmers. As regards the numerous acts of vandalism committed between April and August 1993, the French authorities could cite only a single case of criminal prosecution.

The Commission took action against France, arguing that its failure to act impeded the free movement of goods imported from other Member States and constituted a breach of the former Art 30 EC Treaty (now Art 28). The Court of Justice held as follows:

> In the light of all the foregoing factors, the Court, while not discounting the difficulties faced by the competent authorities in dealing with situations of the type in question in this case, cannot but find that, having regard to the frequency and seriousness of the incidents cited by the Commission, the measures adopted by the French Government were manifestly inadequate to ensure freedom of intra-Community trade in agricultural products on its territory by preventing and effectively dissuading the perpetrators of the offences in question from committing and repeating them.
>
> Although it is not impossible that the threat of serious disruption to public order may, in appropriate cases, justify non-intervention by the police, that argument can, on any view, be put forward only with respect to a specific incident and not, as in this case, in a general way covering all the incidents cited by the Commission ...
>
> It must be concluded that in the present case the French Government has manifestly and persistently abstained from adopting appropriate and adequate measures to put an end to the acts of vandalism which jeopardise the free movement on its territory of certain agricultural products originating in other Member States and to prevent the recurrence of such acts ...
>
> By failing to adopt all necessary and proportionate measures in order to prevent the free movement of fruit and vegetables from being obstructed by actions by private individuals, the French Republic has failed to fulfil its obligations under Article 30 [now Art 28] of the EC Treaty.

Promotion of domestic goods

A state may promote or favour a domestic product to the detriment of competing imports, but this may be caught by Art 28. An obvious example of this is where a Member State engages in a campaign to persuade consumers to purchase domestic rather than imported products. This is illustrated in *Commission* v *Ireland* (Case 249/81).

The Irish Government (through the Irish Goods Council) embarked upon a 'Buy Irish' campaign. The aim of the campaign was to achieve 'a switch from imports to Irish products equivalent to 3% of total consumer spending'. The campaign was 'a carefully thought out set of initiatives that add up to an integrated programme for promoting Irish goods, with specific proposals to involve the producer, distributor and consumer'. A number of measures were adopted, of which two were carried out: the encouragement of the use of a 'Buy Irish' symbol for goods made in Ireland and the organisation of a publicity campaign by the Irish Goods Council in favour of Irish products, designed to encourage consumers to buy Irish products. The Commission brought former Art 169 (now Art 226) proceedings against the Irish Government, alleging the campaign was an MEQR. The Court of Justice held as follows:

> 22. The Irish Government goes on to emphasise that the campaign has had no restrictive effect on imports since the proportion of Irish goods to all goods sold on the Irish market fell from 49.2% in 1977 to 43.4% in 1980 ...

25. Whilst it may be true that the two elements of the programme which have continued in effect, namely the advertising campaign and the use of the 'Guaranteed Irish' symbol, have not had any significant success in winning over the Irish market to domestic products, it is not possible to overlook the fact that, regardless of their efficacy, those two activities form part of a government programme which is designed to achieve the substitution of domestic products for imported products and is liable to affect the volume of trade between Member States ...

27. In the circumstances the two activities in question amount to the establishment of a national practice, introduced by the Irish Government and prosecuted with its assistance, the potential effect of which on imports from other Member States is comparable to that resulting from government measures of a binding nature ...

29. That is the case where, as in this instance, such a restrictive practice represents the implementation of a programme defined by the government which affects the national economy as a whole and which is intended to check the flow of trade between Member States by encouraging the purchase of domestic products, by means of an advertising campaign on a national scale and the organisation of special procedures applicable solely to domestic products, and where those activities are attributed as a whole to the government and are pursued in an organised fashion throughout the national territory.

30. Ireland has therefore failed to fulfil its obligations under the Treaty by organising a campaign to promote the sale and purchase of Irish goods within its territory.

The Court's reasoning in this case illustrates that insofar as the former Art 30 (now Art 28) is concerned, it is more interested in *substance* than in *form*. At para 25, the Court rejected the argument that because the campaign appeared to fail Community law should be unconcerned with it. There is no need to prove that trade between Member States has been affected by the measure. All that is necessary is for there to be a *possibility* of such an effect (applying the *Dassonville* formula).

The Court of Justice remains very ready to assume that different treatment of imported goods may result in a reduced volume of sales. In *Lucien Ortscheit GmbH* v *Eurim-Pharm GmbH* (Case C-320/93), a German law prohibiting the advertising of foreign medicinal products which had not been authorised for sale in Germany but which could, nonetheless, still be imported into Germany, was held necessarily to fall within the scope of Art 28, since it did not have the same effect on the marketing of medicinal products from other Member States as on the marketing of national medicinal products. The Court added that the prohibition of advertising might restrict the volume of imports of medicinal products not authorised in Germany, since it deprived pharmacists and doctors of a source of information on the existence and availability of such products. It was, therefore, equivalent to a quantitative restriction.

In *Commission* v *Germany* (Case 12/74), the Court of Justice stated that it may be possible for origin-marking to be acceptable, where it implies a certain quality in the goods, that they were made from certain materials or by a particular form of manufacturing, or where the origin indicates a special place in the folklore or tradition of the particular region in question. However, this exception will be treated with caution by the Court, as illustrated in *Commission* v *Ireland* (Case 113/80).

This case concerned Irish legislation which required *imported* articles of jewellery which depicted motifs or which possessed characteristics which suggested they were souvenirs of Ireland (e.g. an Irish character, event or scene, a wolfhound, a round tower or a shamrock) to bear an indication of their country of origin or the word 'foreign'. The Court of Justice held as follows:

1. By an application lodged at the Court Registry on 28 April 1980, the Commission instituted proceedings under Article 169 [now Art 226] of the EEC Treaty, for a declaration that Ireland had failed to fulfil its obligations under Article 30 [now Art 28] of the EEC Treaty by requiring that the imported goods falling within the scope of the Merchandise Marks (Restrictions on Sale of Imported Jewellery) Order 1971 (SI No 306) ... and the Merchandise Marks (Restriction on Importation of Jewellery) Order 1971 (SI No 307) ... bear an indication of origin or the word 'foreign'.

2. According to the explanatory notes thereto, SI No 306 (hereinafter referred to as 'the Sale Order') prohibits the sale or exposure for sale of imported articles of jewellery depicting motifs or possessing characteristics which suggest that they are souvenirs of Ireland, for example an Irish character, event or scene, wolfhound, round tower, shamrock etc. and SI No 307 (hereinafter referred to as 'the Importation Order') prohibits the importation of such articles unless, in either case, they bear an indication of their country of origin or the word 'foreign'.

3. The articles concerned are listed in a schedule to each order. However, in order to come within the scope of the orders the article must be made of precious metal or rolled precious metal or of base metal, including polished or plated articles suitable for setting.

4. In the Commission's opinion, the restrictions on the free movement of the goods covered by the two orders constitute measures having an effect equivalent to quantitative restrictions on imports, contrary to the provisions of Article 30 [now Art 28] of the EEC Treaty; it also observes that according to Article 2(3)(f) of Directive 70/50/EEC ... 'measures which lower the value of an imported product, in particular by causing a reduction in its intrinsic value, or increase its costs' must be regarded as measures having an effect equivalent to quantitative restrictions, contrary to Article 30 [now Art 28] of the EEC Treaty ...

17. Thus by granting souvenirs imported from other Member States access to the domestic market solely on condition that they bear a statement of origin, whilst no such statement is required in the case of domestic products, the provisions contained in the Sale Order and the Importation Order indisputably constitute a discriminatory measure.

18. The conclusion to be drawn therefore is that by requiring all souvenirs and articles of jewellery imported from other Member States which are covered by the Sale Order and the Importation Order to bear an indication of origin or the word 'foreign', the Irish rules constitute a measure having equivalent effect within the meaning of Article 30 [now Art 28] of the EEC Treaty. Ireland has consequently failed to fulfil its obligations under the article.

However, not all measures which promote domestic goods will be caught by Art 28 EC Treaty. In *Apple and Pear Development Council* v *K. J. Lewis Ltd* (Case 222/82):

The Apple and Pear Development Council was set up by the UK Government. It was financed by a mandatory charge imposed on growers (the charge was calculated as a sum per hectare of land). Part of the Council's role was to market the goods. It brought actions against certain fruit growers who refused to pay the charge. The actions were defended on the basis that the charges were contrary to the former Art 30 (now Art 28) EC Treaty. The Court of Justice reiterated its decision in the above case, and then continued as follows:

> 18. ... such a body [as the Council] is under a duty not to engage in any advertising intended to discourage the purchase of products of other Member States or to disparage those products in the eyes of consumers. Nor must it advise consumers to purchase domestic products solely by reason of their national origin.
>
> 19. On the other hand, Article 30 [now Art 28] does not prevent such a body from drawing attention, in its publicity, to the specific qualities of fruit grown in the Member State in question or from organising campaigns to promote the sale of certain varieties, mentioning their particular properties, even if those varieties are typical of national production.

Therefore it will be perfectly in order for the government of a Member State to promote varieties of apples. The French may promote Golden Delicious apples, and may draw attention to the particular qualities of the apples. However, such promotion may overstep the boundary if the advertising is intended to discourage the purchase of imported products. This must be a fine line to draw in practice.

We have considered two forms of national favour (a national campaign to purchase domestic goods, and origin-marking). A third form, towards which the Court of Justice is equally harsh, occurs in the field of public procurement (i.e. public service contracts). In *Du Pont de Nemours Italiana SpA v Unità Sanitaria Locale No. 2 Di Cascara* (Case C-21/88), the Court of Justice held that a Member State which reserved a proportion of its public supplies to products which were made in a particular depressed region of the country automatically contravened the former Art 30 (now Art 28) in that it hindered the free movement of goods because it impeded imports:

> 11. It must be pointed out ... that such a system, which favours goods processed in a particular region of a Member State, prevents the authorities and public bodies concerned from procuring some of the supplies they need from undertakings situated in other Member States. Accordingly, it must be held that products originating in other Member States suffer discrimination in comparison with products manufactured in the Member State in question, with the result that the normal course of intra-Community trade is hindered.
>
> 12. That conclusion is not affected by the fact that the restrictive effects of a preferential system of the kind at issue are borne in the same measure both by products manufactured by undertakings from the Member State in question which are not situated in the region covered by the preferential system and by products manufactured by undertakings established in other Member States.
>
> 13. ... the fact remains that all the products benefiting by the preferential system are domestic products.

In *Campus Oil Ltd v Minister for Industry and Energy* (Case 72/83), Ireland had placed an obligation on importers to buy a certain proportion of their oil supplies (35 per cent) from Ireland's only state-owned refinery at prices fixed by the Government. The Court held this was clearly discriminatory and breached the former Art 30 (now Art 28).

Price-fixing regulations

Another way in which a state can treat imports less favourably than domestic products is by the fixing of prices so as to make it more difficult for an importer to market his goods within that Member State. If price fixing is applied only to the imported product, then clearly it will be caught by Art 28 (e.g. minimum price for imported apples £3 per kg).

INDISTINCTLY APPLICABLE MEASURES

Article 3, Directive 70/50 (see above) also covers measures which affect both home-produced and imported products. In other words, the measures do not distinguish between goods according to their origin, and are, therefore, referred to as 'indistinctly applicable' measures. Specifically, Art 3 refers to measures relating to the marketing of products dealing with shape, size, weight, composition, presentation, or identification 'which are equally applicable to domestic and imported products where the restrictive effect of such measures on the free movement of goods exceeds the effects intrinsic to trade rules'. This will be the case where the restrictive effects on the free movement of goods are out of proportion to their purpose and where the same objective can be attained by other means which are less of a hindrance to trade (an application of the 'proportionality test'). These criteria have been crucial in the development of the jurisprudence of the Court of Justice in relation to national measures which appear, at least, to apply indiscriminately to both imported and home-produced goods.

In a landmark decision on whether such national provisions could constitute MEQRs, the Court of Justice, in *Rewe-Zentrale AG* v *Bundesmonopolverwaltung für Branntwein* (Case 120/78) (usually called 'the *Cassis de Dijon* Case'), laid down an important principle:

The case concerned the proposed importation of a blackcurrant liqueur called 'Cassis de Dijon' into the Federal Republic of Germany. The importer applied for a licence to do so from the administrative authority in Germany, but it was refused because the liqueur did not meet the Federal Republic's requirement of a minimum alcoholic content of 25 per cent which was required for domestic Cassis. French Cassis was required only to have an alcoholic strength of between 15 and 20 per cent. The importer challenged the decision on the basis that the rule infringed the former Art 30 (now Art 28), and the case was referred to the Court of Justice under the former Art 177 (now Art 234).

The Court accepted that, in the absence of any common rules in the Community relating to the production and marketing of alcohol, it was up to Member States to regulate these activities in their own territories. However, it held that:

> 14. ... It ... appears that the unilateral requirement imposed by the rules of a Member State of a minimum alcohol content for the purposes of the sale of alcoholic beverages constitutes an obstacle to trade which is incompatible with the provisions of Article 30 [now Art 28] of the Treaty.
>
> There is therefore no valid reason why, provided that they have been lawfully produced and marketed in one of the Member States, alcoholic beverages should not be introduced into any other Member State; the sale of such products may not be subject to a legal

prohibition on the marketing of beverages with an alcohol content lower than the limits set by national rules.

This case reaffirms para 5 of the Court's judgment in *Dassonville* (see above). It is made clear that the former Art 30 (now Art 28) can apply to indistinctly applicable rules which apply equally to domestic and imported goods, but which nevertheless inhibit trade between Member States because the rules applied are different to those which apply in the product's country of origin. This imposes a dual burden on the foreign producer. The domestic producer will already comply with domestic laws and will therefore not be further disadvantaged; whereas in contrast the foreign producer will have to change the method of production to comply with the laws of the importing state, thus inhibiting intra-Community trade. In this case the German producers of Cassis would already be complying with the German law requiring the alcoholic content to be at least 25 per cent; whereas the French producers would have had to change their manufacturing processes in order to satisfy this requirement, thus increasing their costs and decreasing any competitive advantage French Cassis might otherwise have had over the German beverage. An additional point to be aware of is that other Member States could have different regulations: e.g. Denmark could have had a law requiring liqueurs to have a maximum alcoholic content of 10 per cent. France in this case would have had to employ different manufacturing processes for the respective Member States.

The rule of mutual recognition

The first *Cassis* principle, referred to as 'the rule of mutual recognition', is set out by the Court of Justice at para 14: once goods have been lawfully marketed in one Member State, they should be free to be marketed in any other Member State without restriction. Derogations from this general principle will be considered below.

Examples of indistinctly applicable measures

Following *Cassis*, there have been a number of cases applying the doctrine to a wide variety of different measures. Some examples follow.

Origin marking

In *Commission* v *United Kingdom* (Case 207/83):

UK legislation required that certain goods (including woollen clothing and cutlery) which were sold in retail markets had to be marked with their country of origin. The Commission took infraction proceedings against the United Kingdom under the former Art 169 (now Art 226), claiming this requirement was in breach of the former Art 30 (now Art 28) in that it constituted an MEQR. French manufacturers complained that goods for the British market had to be specially origin marked, which increased production costs. The Commission also argued that such origin marking encouraged consumers to exercise their prejudices in favour of national products and was likely to reduce the sale of Community-produced goods. The British Government defended the origin marking order on the grounds that the origin details gave important information to the consumer about the nature and quality of the product, and that the requirement of origin marking was non-discriminatory because it applied to both domestic and imported products.

Considering the second of the United Kingdom's arguments (i.e. that the measure applied equally to imported and national products), the Court of Justice stated:

> 17. … it has to be recognised that the purpose of indications of origin or origin-marking is to enable consumers to distinguish between domestic and imported products and this enables them to assert any prejudices which they may have against foreign products. As the Court has had occasion to emphasise in various contexts, the Treaty, by establishing a common market and progressively approximating the economic policies of the Member States, seeks to unite national markets in a single market, the origin-marking requirement not only makes the marketing in a Member State of goods produced in other Member States in the sectors in question more difficult; it also has the effect of slowing down economic interpenetration in the Community by handicapping the sale of goods produced as a result of a division of labour between Member States.

> 18. It follows from those considerations that the United Kingdom provisions in question are liable to have the effect of increasing the production costs of imported goods and making it more difficult to sell them on the United Kingdom market.

The Court was not persuaded that origin marking was a necessary consumer protection measure. It agreed with the Commission that it encouraged the exercise of national prejudices and therefore, applying *Dassonville*, the measure was capable of affecting intra-Community trade. Any distinctive national quality of the goods could be highlighted by individual retailers, but should not be the subject of national legislation.

National quality standard

In *Commission* v *Ireland* (Case 45/87):

The Commission brought an action under the former Art 169 (now Art 226) EC Treaty against the Irish Government for allowing a specification relating to a water supply contract in Dundalk which, it alleged, breached the former Art 30 (now Art 28). The specification stipulated for pipes which had been certified as complying with Irish Standard 188. Only one manufacturer, located in Ireland, made pipes of such a standard. This was an indistinctly applicable measure because the requirement applied to all pipes whether Irish or imported. One of the bids was based on the use of pipes not conforming to this standard, although it did comply with international standards. Dundalk Council refused to consider the bid for that reason.

The question before the Court of Justice was whether this specification constituted a barrier to the importation of pipes for this contract:

> 19. … it must first be pointed out that the inclusion of such a clause (as 4.29) in an invitation to tender may cause economic operators who produce or utilise pipes equivalent to pipes certified with Irish standards to refrain from tendering.

> 20. It further appears from the documents in the case that only one undertaking has been certified by the IRIS to IS 188:1975 to apply the Irish Standard Mark to pipes of the type required for the purposes of the public works contract at issue. That undertaking is located

in Ireland. Consequently, the inclusion of Clause 4.29 had the effect of restricting the supply of the pipes needed for the Dundalk scheme to Irish manufacturers alone.

21. The Irish Government maintains that it is necessary to specify the standards to which materials must be manufactured, particularly in a case such as this where the pipes utilised must suit the existing network. Compliance with another standard, even an international standard such as ISO 160:1980, would not suffice to eliminate technical difficulties.

22. That technical argument cannot be accepted. The Commission's complaint does not relate to compliance with technical requirements but the refusal of the Irish authorities to verify whether those requirements are satisfied where the manufacturer of the materials has not been certified by the IRIS to IS 188. By incorporating in the notice in question the words 'or equivalent' after the reference to the Irish standard, as provided for by Directive 71/305 where it is applicable, the Irish authorities could have verified compliance with the technical conditions without from the outset restricting the contract to tenderers proposing to utilise Irish materials.

Therefore, the Court of Justice held that whilst it was perfectly reasonable to specify the quality of pipes to be used for the transmission of drinking water, the attainment of that object could as well have been achieved by pipes produced abroad to a standard *equivalent* to the Irish standard.

In the above cases, the Court of Justice considers the *effect* of the national practice, rather than its legal form. This is quite clear in the following category.

Administrative practices

In *Commission* v *France* (Case 21/84):

The Commission alleged that France had violated Art 30 (now Art 28) by delaying a request to approve postal franking machines from other Member States. This was an indistinctly applicable measure because approval was required for both the domestic and imported machines; however, administrative practices resulted in the delay of approval of foreign machines. A British manufacturer had failed to secure the approval of the French authorities, despite repeated applications, and even after France had repealed an earlier law which explicitly stated a preference for domestic machines.

The Court of Justice held as follows:

11. The fact that a law or regulation such as that requiring prior approval for the marketing of postal franking machines conforms in formal terms to Article 30 [now Art 28] of the EEC Treaty is not sufficient to discharge a Member State of its obligation under that provision. Under the cloak of a general provision permitting the approval of machines imported from other Member States, the administration might very well adopt a systematically unfavourable attitude towards imported machines, either by allowing considerable delay in replying to applications for approval or in carrying out the examination procedure, or by refusing approval on the grounds of various alleged technical faults for which no detailed explanations are given or which prove to be inaccurate.

12. The prohibition on measures having an effect equivalent to quantitative restrictions would lose much of its useful effect if it did not cover protectionist or discriminatory practices of that type.

13. It must however be noted that for an administrative practice to constitute a measure prohibited under Article 30 [now Art 28] that practice must show a certain degree of consistency and generality. That generality must be assessed differently according to whether the market concerned is one on which there are numerous traders or whether it is a market, such as that in postal franking machines, on which only a few undertakings are active. In the latter case, a national administration's treatment of a single undertaking may constitute a measure incompatible with Article 30 [now Art 28].

14. In the light of those principles it is clear from the facts of the case that the conduct of the French postal administration constitutes an impediment to imports contrary to Article 30 [now Art 28] of the EEC Treaty.

15. It must therefore be concluded that by refusing without proper justification to approve postal franking machines from another Member State, the French Republic has failed to fulfil its obligations under Article 30 [now Art 28] of the EEC Treaty.

In this case the Court of Justice held that a law which on the face of it does not breach Art 28, could result in a breach if the method of its application results in a harsher impact on foreign goods.

Price-fixing regulations

Article 28 can also catch price-fixing regulations which apply to both imported and domestic goods, as was declared by the Court of Justice in *Openbaar Ministerie v Van Tiggele* (Case 82/77).

Dutch legislation provided for minimum selling prices for certain spirits. A seller sold spirits for less than this minimum and was prosecuted. In his defence he argued that the legislation breached the former Art 30 (now Art 28) and should therefore be inapplicable. The question referred to the Court of Justice was whether this minimum price constituted an MEQR within the former Art 30 (now Art 28):

---

12. For the purposes of this prohibition it is sufficient that the measures in question are likely to hinder, directly or indirectly, actually or potentially, imports between Member States.

13. Whilst national price-control rules applicable without distinction to domestic products and imported products cannot in general produce such an effect they may do so in certain specific cases.

14. Thus imports may be impeded in particular when a national authority fixes prices or profit margins at such a level that imported products are placed at a disadvantage in relation to identical domestic products either because they cannot profitably be marketed in the conditions laid down or because the competitive advantage conferred by lower cost prices is cancelled out.

The Court of Justice held that on the facts the Dutch law did contravene the former Art 30 (now Art 28). As a matter of Community law, price-fixing schemes must give the importer the opportunity to benefit from any competitive advantage the imported goods may possess (e.g. by the setting of a lower price than the competing domestic product), or to take account of any disadvantage they may possess (e.g. by setting a higher price). Schemes which exclude the importer's ability to achieve such flexibility are capable of violating Art 28.

Differentiation between dual-burden and equal-burden rules

Cassis, and many cases after it, concerned dual-burden rules. This would be the case where, for example, one Member State imposed certain rules relating to the manufacture of goods (e.g. margarine must be packaged in cube-shaped containers) and these rules applied equally to domestic and imported goods, even though the exporting producer would have had to comply with the relevant trade rules of his own Member State. This is said to put a dual burden on the exporting producer. *Cassis* would render such rules incompatible with Art 28 unless they could be saved by one of the mandatory requirements (or Art 30 (see below)).

Equal-burden rules, by contrast, again apply to all goods (domestic and imported); they regulate trade in some manner, but do not have a protectionist effect. Even though they may have an impact on the overall volume of trade, the impact is equal as between the sale of domestic products and imported products.

Whereas dual-burden rules have been held to fall within Art 28, there was some confusion as to whether equal-burden rules should also fall within Art 28, subject to the *rule of reason* defence (and Art 30 (see below)).

Equal-burden rules – outside Article 28

In a number of cases the Court of Justice held that rules which did not relate to the *characteristics* of the product and did not impose a dual burden on the importer, but only concerned the *conditions* under which the product was to be sold, were outside the remit of Art 28 (see, e.g., *Oebel* (Case 155/80), which concerned a national rule prohibiting the delivery of bakery products to consumers and retailers during the night; and *Quietlynn Ltd* v *Southend-on-Sea Borough Council* (Case C-23/89), which concerned a UK law restricting the sale of lawful sex products to shops that had been licensed by the local authority).

Equal-burden rules – within Article 28

In other cases, however, the Court of Justice held that such rules would fall within Art 28, but the Court would then seek to exclude them from the effect of Art 28 by applying the *rule of reason* or Art 30 defences (see below). In *Cinéthèque SA* v *Fédération Nationale des Cinémas Français* (Cases 60 & 61/84), French legislation prohibited the selling or hiring of film videos during the first year of the film receiving its performance certificate. The objective was to encourage people to go and watch the film at the cinema. The effect was that both domestic and imported films could not be sold during that first year. A distributor of videos used the former Art 30 (now Art 28) before French courts to challenge the law as a trade barrier. The Court of Justice held that although 'its effect is not to favour national production as against the production of other Member States ... the application of such a system may create barriers to intra-Community trade in video-cassettes'. In those circumstances it held that there was a *prima facie* breach of the former Art 30 (now Art 28).

The difficult question of whether equal-burden cases fell within the former Art 30 (now Art 28) was the issue in a series of UK *Sunday Trading* cases which came before the Court. In *Torfaen Borough Council* v *B&Q plc* (Case 145/88), B&Q was prosecuted for violation of Sunday trading laws which prohibited retail shops from selling goods on Sundays, subject to certain exceptions. B&Q claimed that these laws constituted an MEQR. The effect of the laws was to reduce turnover, but imported goods were in the same position as domestic goods; the reduction in turnover affected all goods equally. However, the Court of Justice held that this constituted a *prima facie* breach of Art 28.

The *Keck* judgment

This confused state of affairs was totally unhelpful. As we have seen, the Court of Justice has been inconsistent in its approach in dealing with equal-burden rules. In *Criminal Proceedings against Keck and Mithouard* (Cases C-267 & 268/91), the Court recognised that it was time to clear up some of the confusion and to adopt a *general rule* which would apply in these circumstances.

The defendants (Keck and Mithouard) were prosecuted in a French court for having resold goods at a loss, a practice that was forbidden under French law. In their defence they pleaded, *inter alia*, that this rule constituted an MEQR and was unlawful under the former Art 30 (now Art 28). The case was referred to the Court of Justice under the former Art 177 (now Art 234):

---

11. By virtue of Article 30 [now Art 28], quantitative restrictions on imports and all measures having equivalent effect are prohibited between Member States. The Court has consistently held that any measure which is capable of directly or indirectly, actually or potentially, hindering intra-Community trade constitutes a measure having equivalent effect to a quantitative restriction.

12. It is not the purpose of national legislation imposing a general prohibition on resales at a loss to regulate trade in goods between Member States.

13. Such legislation may, admittedly, restrict the volume of sales, and hence the volume of sales of products from other Member States, in so far as it deprives traders of a method of sales promotion. But the question remains whether such a possibility is sufficient to characterise the legislation in question as a measure having equivalent effect to a quantitative restriction on imports.

14. In view of the increasing tendency of traders to invoke Article 30 [now Art 28] of the Treaty as a means of challenging any rules whose effect is to limit commercial freedom even where such rules are not aimed at products from other Member States, *the Court considers it necessary to re-examine and clarify its case law on this matter.*

15. In 'Cassis de Dijon' ... it was held that, in the absence of harmonisation of legislation, measures of equivalent effect prohibited by Article 30 [now Art 28] include obstacles to the free movement of goods where they are the consequence of applying rules that lay down requirements to be met by such goods (such as requirements as to designation, form, size, weight, composition, presentation, labelling, packaging) to goods from other

Member States where they are lawfully manufactured and marketed, even if those rules apply without distinction to all products unless their application can be justified by a public-interest objective taking precedence over the free movement of goods.

16. However, *contrary to what has previously been decided, the application to products from other Member States of national provisions restricting or prohibiting certain selling arrangements is not such as to hinder directly or indirectly, actually or potentially, trade between Member States within the meaning of the Dassonville judgment ... provided that those provisions apply to all affected traders operating within the national territory and provided that they affect in the same manner, in law and fact, the marketing of domestic products and of those from other Member States.*

17. Where those conditions are fulfilled, the application of such rules to the sale of products from another Member State is not by nature such as to prevent their access to the market or to impede access any more than it impedes the access of domestic products. Such rules therefore fall outside the scope of Article 30 [now Art 28] of the Treaty.

18. Accordingly, the reply to be given to the national court is that Article 30 [now Art 28] of the EEC Treaty is to be interpreted as not applying to legislation of a Member State imposing a general prohibition on resale at a loss. (emphasis added)

There has certainly been a change of tack by the Court of Justice which now prefers a general rule to be applied.

The general rule

The Court distinguishes between *rules which relate to the goods themselves* in terms of packaging, composition, size, etc. (para 15), which clearly fall within the *Cassis* doctrine, and *rules relating to selling arrangements* (para 16), which do not fall within Art 28 *provided* the conditions set out in the second part of para 16 are met.

The reason why rules which fall within para 16 are outside Art 28 is that their *purpose* is not to regulate trade as such (para 12) and because their *effect and nature* do not prevent access to the market, or at least they do not make it any more difficult for importers to penetrate the market than national traders (para 17). They impose an equal burden on both domestic producers and importers; but remember that if the conditions set out in para 16 are not met, then the rule would fall within Art 28. The para 16 conditions are:

- the provisions of the rule apply to all traders operating within the national territory; and
- they affect in the same manner, in law and in fact, the marketing of domestic goods and imports.

Provided these two conditions are met, then a rule which relates to selling arrangements will not fall within the ambit of Art 28.

Commenting on the new test described in *Keck*, Advocate-General Jacobs has observed:

It seems to me ... that the *Dassonville* formula was indeed too broad – and illustrates the dangers in taking as a starting point a very broad proposition which subsequently has to be whittled down – but that the main body of the Court's case law on Art 30 [Art 28] was wholly satisfactory and that to introduce at this stage a notion of discrimination may raise more problems than it solves. (*The European Advocate* (1994/1995) 2, 4)

Post-Keck *case law*

One needs first to distinguish 'selling arrangements', which will not breach Art 28 at all, provided that they are non-discriminatory: this means that they must affect, in the same way, in law and in fact, domestic goods and goods from other Member States. If they do not affect domestically produced and imported goods in the same way and are liable substantially to restrict access to the national market, then they will breach Art 28. 'Selling arrangements' can cover a multiplicity of activities. The expression includes price restrictions, as in *Keck* itself, or any other national rules which govern the way products or services are sold or advertised.

The rule in *Keck* has been applied to a number of cases relating to the marketing of goods. In *Criminal Proceedings against Tankstationt' Heukske vof* v *JBE Boermans* (Cases C-401 & 402/92):

National rules provided for the compulsory closure of petrol stations. The Court applied the *Keck* general rule and held that the rules did not fall within the former Art 30 (now Art 28) because they related to selling arrangements which applied equally to all traders without distinguishing between origin. It was an equal-burden rule, affecting domestic traders and importers equally:

> Those conditions [in *Keck*] are fulfilled [in this case]. The rules in question relate to the times and places at which the goods in question may be sold to consumers. However, they apply to all relevant traders without distinguishing between the origin of the products in question and do not affect the marketing of products from other Member States in a manner different from that in which they affect domestic products.

In *Hunermund* (Case C-292/92) there was a prohibition by the German pharmacists association, preventing its members from advertising popular medicines outside their premises. The Court of Justice ruled that this was a 'selling arrangement' within the meaning of *Keck*, and consequently Art 28 did not apply. Two years later, in *Leclerc-Siplec* (Case C-412/93), the Court considered a French law which prevented Leclerc-Siplec from advertising unleaded petrol imported by them and sold in their supermarkets. The law applied to all advertisers, irrespective of the source of their product. The Court acknowledged that 'the prohibition may … restrict the volume of sales, and hence of products from other Member States, in so far as it deprives distributors of a particular form of advertising for their goods'. It decided that this was a 'selling arrangement' which affected all such goods sold equally, and Art 28 did not therefore apply.

By contrast, in *Mars* (Case C-470/93), the manufacturers challenged a national law in Germany which prohibited the selling of Mars bars marked '+10 per cent' (as part of a Europe-wide selling campaign). The Court held, in this case, that these requirements related to the presentation, labelling and packaging of the product lawfully manufactured and marketed in another Member State. They were, therefore, caught by what is now Art 28.

In *Vereinigte Familiapresse* (Case C-368/95) a German newspaper publisher was selling in the German and Austrian markets newspapers which offered readers the opportunity to take part in games with prizes. This practice breached the Austrian Unfair Competition Act 1992. A competitor tried to stop the imported German papers and the case was referred to the Court of Justice. The Court rejected the Austrian argument that this was merely a 'selling arrangement', since it affected the content of the newspaper and its access to the Austrian market. Potentially, therefore, it breached Art 30 (now Art 28):

> 11. The Court finds that, even though the relevant national legislation is directed against a method of sales promotion, in this case it bears on the actual content of the products, in so far as the competitions in question form an integral part of the magazine in which they appear. As a result, the national legislation in question as applied to the facts of the case is not concerned with a selling arrangement within the meaning of the judgment in *Keck* ...

> 12. Moreover, since it requires traders established in other Member States to alter the contents of the periodical, the prohibition at issue impairs access of the products concerned to the market of the Member State of importation and consequently hinders free movement of goods. It therefore constitutes in principle a measure having equivalent effect within the meaning of Article 30 [now Art 28] of the Treaty.

The Court of Justice recognised this for what it was, i.e. a dual-burden rule, and therefore it came within the scope of former Art 30 (now Art 28).

EXPORTS: ARTICLE 29

Most of the cases considered so far have involved national restrictions, or measures equivalent to restrictions, on imports. As discussed above, Art 29 (previously Art 34) applies in much the same way as Art 28, in that it prohibits quantitative restrictions and MEQRs, but in relation to *exports* rather than *imports*. The principles applicable to restrictions on exports are, broadly, the same. The more limited case law on measures affecting exports matches that for imports. In *Procureur de la République* v *Bouhelier* (Case 53/76), for example, a quality control charge imposed only on exports and not on goods sold on the domestic market was held to be a measure equivalent to a quantitative restriction on exports. However, the Court of Justice appears to look for some element of discrimination, either formal or material, in the case of exports. It emphasised that aspect in *Groenveld* (Case 15/79):

> [Article 29(1)] concerns national measures which have as their specific object or effect the restrictions of patterns of exports and thereby the establishment of a difference in treatment between the domestic trade of a Member State and its export trade in such a way as to provide a particular advantage for national production of the domestic market of the state in question at the expense of the production or of the trade of other Member States. This is not so in the case of a prohibition like that in question which is applied objectively to the production of goods of a certain kind without drawing a distinction depending on whether such goods are intended for the national market or for export. (para 7)

Whether or not there is discrimination is a matter both of national law and practice. Clearly, therefore, a national law requiring producers to deliver poultry offal to their local authority has been held, necessarily, to involve a ban on exports

(*Nertsvoederfabriek Nederland* (Case 118/86)). However, legislation applied to all producers of cheese in The Netherlands, affecting its content and quality, which put Dutch producers at a disadvantage in comparison to foreign producers who did not have to produce their cheese to the same standards, was held by the Court of Justice not to be a measure equivalent to a quantitative restriction on exports, although it made exporting more difficult for Dutch producers (*Jongeneel Kaas BV v Netherlands* (Case 237/82)). Here, the Court demonstrated its willingness to tolerate measures which, although not actually discriminating against exports, had an adverse effect on domestic producers, which it would not have been prepared to tolerate in relation to imports.

ARTICLE 30: JUSTIFICATIONS FOR DISTINCTLY AND INDISTINCTLY APPLICABLE MEASURES

Article 30 (formerly Art 36) EC Treaty permits Member States to derogate from their obligation to ensure the free movement of goods. It provides:

> The provisions of Articles 28 and 29 shall not preclude prohibitions or restrictions on imports, exports or goods in transit justified on grounds of public morality, public policy or public security; the protection of health and life of humans, animals and plants; the protection of national treasures possessing artistic, historic or archaeological value; or the protection of industrial and commercial property. Such prohibitions or restrictions shall not, however, constitute a means of arbitrary discrimination or a disguised restriction on trade between Member States.

These derogations comprise an exhaustive list and are interpreted strictly by the Court. Article 30 is most often pleaded by Member States in defence of distinctly applicable measures (*Commission* v *Ireland* (Case 113/80)). Article 30 is, however, equally applicable to indistinctly applicable measures:

> A measure which, in regard both to domestic products and imported products, imposes an obligation to verify conformity [with the rules in force on that market] on the person who first places the product on the market is, in principle, applicable without distinction to both categories of products. It may, therefore, be justified under Article 36 [now Art 30] and under Article 30 [now Art 28] as interpreted by the Court [in the *Cassis* case]. (*Wurmser* (Case 25/88))

Since the exceptions contained in Art 30 are treated as exhaustive, national measures not falling clearly within its terms are rejected by the Court.

The Art 30 exceptions can be advanced to justify national measures only in the absence of any relevant Community-wide provisions aimed at harmonising the legislation protecting the interest which the national measure seeks to protect. In *Lucien Ortscheit GmbH* v *Eurim-Pharm GmbH* (Case C-320/93), German legislation prohibited the advertising of foreign drugs which had not been authorised for use in the German market, but which could, under certain conditions, be imported into Germany. The Court was in no doubt that the measure was distinctly applicable and equivalent to a quantitative restriction. It noted, however, that the health and life of humans ranks foremost among the interests protected by Art 30, and at the present stage of harmonisation there was no procedure for Community authorisation or mutual recognition of national authorisations. In those circumstances, it was for

Member States, within the limits imposed by the Treaty, to decide what degree of protection they intend to ensure. In the circumstances, the Court was satisfied that the German measures were justified under Art 30. However, if there is relevant Community legislation, there will be no scope for national measures that are incompatible with it, or the application of Art 30. The Court reiterated its position in *R v Ministry of Agriculture, Fisheries and Food, ex parte Compassion in World Farming Ltd* (Case C-1/96). The applicants had attempted to argue that the Minister was entitled to ignore the effect of a new Council directive on the treatment of farm animals in transit, and stop the export of live animals in reliance on Art 36 (now Art 30), since the directive did not conform to an international convention on the humane treatment of animals. The Court rejected this argument, insisting that Art 36 could not be used to justify a national prohibition, since the directive was intended to deal exhaustively with the situation.

In *Société Agricole de la Crespelle* (Case C-323/93), French rules conferred a monopoly on a number of regional bovine insemination centres and, effectively, created a restrictive regime for the importation of bovine semen from other Member States. The Court was satisfied that the restrictive regime amounted to an MEQR, but could it be justified under former Art 36? It decided that it could not be:

> The Court has consistently held that where, in application of Article 100 [now Art 94] of the EEC Treaty, Community Directives provide for the harmonisation of the measures necessary to ensure, inter alia, the protection of animal and human health and established Community procedures to check that they were observed, invoking Article 36 [now Art 30] is no longer justified and the appropriate checks have to be carried out and protective measures adopted within the framework of the directive.

This rule applies where the Community has introduced a consistent and exhaustive set of measures to cover the type of importation in question (*Commission v Italy (Re Authorisation for Importation of Plants)* (Case C-296/92)). However, it does not preclude restrictions on imports where these are specifically authorised by the directive (*The State v Vitaret and Chambron* [1995] 1 CMLR 185 (French Cour de Cassation)).

Where Art 30 can be advanced as a justification for national measures, it is for the national government relying on it to provide evidence to support the grounds justifying its actions. This principle of casting the evidential burden upon the Member State taking the action applies not only in relation to the national measure itself, but also in relation to individual cases in which that national measure is applied. In *Officier van Justitie v Sandoz BV* (Case 174/82), Sandoz wished to sell confectionery in The Netherlands to which vitamin supplements had been added. The confectionery was freely sold in Belgium and Germany. The Dutch authorities refused permission for it to be sold, on the grounds that the vitamins were a risk to health. The case was referred to the Court of Justice under Art 177 (now Art 234). The Court was in no doubt that the measure breached Art 30 (now Art 28), but in the absence of Community harmonising measures on the kinds of additives which were acceptable, it was permissible under Art 36 (now Art 30) for the Member State to determine the kind and extent of protection to be given. However, the state had first to establish the existence of a risk:

> In as much as the question arises as to where the onus of proof lies when there is a request for authorisation [to market a foodstuff] … it must be remembered that Article 36 [now

Art 30] of the Treaty creates an exception, which must be strictly interpreted, to the rule of free movement of goods within the Community which is one of the fundamental principles of the Common Market. It is therefore for the national authorities who rely on that provision in order to adopt a measure restricting intra-Community trade to check in each instance that the measure contemplated satisfies the criteria of that provision ... Community law does not permit national rules which subject authorisation to market to proof by the importer that the product in question is not harmful to health. (paras 22, 24)

Where action may be justified under Art 30, measures taken by Member States will still have to meet two fundamental Community criteria. First, there must be no arbitrary discrimination between imported and domestic products and, second, any national measures must be proportionate to any risk and must not restrict trade any more than is necessary to protect the legitimate public interests recognised by Art 30. The operation of these principles can best be seen by an examination of the jurisprudence of the Court of Justice in relation to the specific exceptions.

Public morality

The concept of public morality will vary widely from state to state and is not elaborated in Art 30 or in any secondary legislation. The Court has, for example, refused to rule that termination of pregnancy is intrinsically immoral and cannot, therefore, constitute a service under Art 49 EC Treaty, because it is, in fact, lawfully carried out in several Member States (*Society for the Protection of the Unborn Child* v *Grogan* (Case C-159/90); and in *HM Customs and Excise Commissioners* v *Schindler and Others* (Case C-275/92)) it observed, with regard to gambling, that, 'Even if the morality of lotteries is at least questionable, it is not for the Court to substitute its assessment for that of the legislature where that activity is practised legally' (para 32). The Court may, however, have to assess whether or not national rules are applied proportionately and without discrimination (see Chapter 13). The issue first came before the Court in relation to Art 30 in an Art 177 (now Art 234) reference from the House of Lords. In *R* v *Henn and Darby* (Case 34/79), the defendants were convicted of being 'knowingly concerned in the fraudulent evasion of the prohibition of the importation of indecent or obscene articles' contrary to s 42 of the Customs Consolidation Act 1876 and s 304 of the Customs and Excise Act 1952. The articles involved in the charges formed part of a consignment of several boxes of obscene films and magazines which had been brought into the United Kingdom in 1975 on a lorry travelling on a ferry from Rotterdam. The six films and magazines referred to in the charges were all of Danish origin.

The House of Lords referred a number of questions to the Court of Justice. The first question related to whether a law of a Member State prohibiting the importation of pornographic articles is a measure having equivalent effect to a quantitative restriction. The Court was in no doubt that it was, since a prohibition on imports is 'the most extreme form of restriction' (para 12). However, it emphasised that Member States were free to take such action in appropriate circumstances:

In principle, it is for each Member State to determine in accordance with its own scale of values and in the form selected by it the requirements of public morality in its territory. In any event, it cannot be disputed that the statutory provisions applied by the United

Kingdom in regard to the importation of articles having an indecent or obscene character come within the powers reserved to the Member States by the first sentence of Article 36 [now Art 30].

The House of Lords was also concerned to know whether the fact that the prohibition imposed on the importation of pornography was different in scope from that imposed by the criminal law on the possession and publication of such material in the United Kingdom constituted a means of arbitrary discrimination or a disguised restriction on trade between Member States. In particular, there were (and are) differences in treatment of the possession and publication of pornography in different parts of the United Kingdom, and there are circumstances in which, under the Obscene Publications Act 1959, possession and publication may not be a criminal offence. The defences available in those circumstances have no application to the Customs and Excise Acts under which the defendants were prosecuted. The Court of Justice was satisfied that the differences, such as they were, were not significant:

> Whatever may be the differences between the laws on this subject in force in the different constituent parts of the United Kingdom, and notwithstanding the fact that they contain certain exceptions of limited scope, these laws, taken as a whole, have as their purpose the prohibition, or at least the restraining, of the manufacture and marketing of publications or articles of an indecent or obscene character. In these circumstances it is permissible to conclude, on a comprehensive view, that there is no lawful trade in such goods in the United Kingdom. A prohibition on imports which may in certain respects be more strict than some of the laws applied within the United Kingdom cannot, therefore, be regarded as amounting to a measure designed to give indirect protection to some national product or aimed at creating arbitrary discrimination. (para 21)

Another case in which goods had also been seized by HM Customs and Excise under s 42 of the Customs Consolidation Act 1976 came, on a reference under Art 177 (now Art 234) from the Queen's Bench Division to the Court of Justice in 1986. In *Conegate Ltd v HM Customs and Excise* (Case 121/85) the goods consisted of inflatable sex dolls and other erotic articles. The importers argued that the situation was different to that in *Henn and Darby* because sex dolls, although not permitted to be publicly displayed, could be lawfully sold throughout the United Kingdom. The Court of Justice agreed:

> 15. ... Although Community law leaves the Member States free to make their own assessments of the indecent or obscene character of certain articles, it must be pointed out that the fact that the goods cause offence cannot be regarded as sufficiently serious to justify restrictions on the free movement of goods where the Member State concerned does not adopt, with respect to the same goods manufactured or marketed within its territory, penal measures or other serious or effective measures intended to prevent the distribution of such goods in its territory.

> 16. It follows that a Member State may not rely on grounds of public morality in order to prohibit the importation of goods from other Member States when its legislation contains no prohibition on the manufacture or marketing of the same goods in its territory.

There is a striking similarity in the language used by the Court in this case to that employed by it, with regard to the free movement of workers, in *Adoui and Cornuaille* v

Belgium (Cases 115 & 116/81) (see Chapter 15). That case concerned the scope of the public policy exception in Art 39(3) EC Treaty. The Court, having accepted in *Van Duyn* v *Home Office* that the public disapproval of the Church of Scientology to which Ms Van Duyn belonged was sufficient to justify her exclusion, moved away from that position in *Adoui*. It held, in that case, that a Member State could not take action under the public policy exception against a European citizen unless it took some kind of 'repressive measures' against its own nationals for engaging in the same conduct on which the exclusion is based. A similar concept of equality of treatment underlies the requirement that the state excluding the goods must take 'penal measures or other serious or effective measures' in relation to the same kind of goods produced on its own territory.

Public policy and public security

Very few attempts have been made by national governments to justify restrictive measures on these grounds. Public policy, was, however, successfully advanced by the UK Government in *R* v *Thompson and Others* (Case 7/78). The defendants traded in coins, some of which were old British gold coins that were no longer legal tender. They were convicted in England of being knowingly concerned in the fraudulent evasion of the prohibition on importation of gold coins into England. They argued, on appeal, that the provisions under which they had been convicted breached Arts 28–29 EC Treaty. The UK Government defended the legislation on the ground that it was an important aspect of public policy to protect the national coinage and the Court agreed. It held that a ban on destroying old coinage with a view to it being melted down or destroyed in another Member State was justified on grounds of public policy under Art 30 because it was based on the need to protect the right to mint coinage which is traditionally regarded as involving the fundamental interests of the state.

It was put to the Court in *Cullet* (Case 231/83) by the French Government that national rules fixing retail selling prices for fuel was justified on grounds of public order and security which would arise in relation to retailers affected by unrestrained competition. The Advocate-General warned against the dangers of responding to public agitation:

> The acceptance of civil disturbance as a justification for encroachments upon the free movement of goods would … have unacceptably drastic consequences. If road-blocks and other effective weapons of interest groups which feel threatened by the importation and sale at competitive prices of certain cheap products or services, or by immigrant workers or foreign businesses, were accepted as justification, the existence of the four freedoms of the Treaty could no longer be relied upon. Private interest groups would then, in the place of the Treaty and Community (and, within the limits laid down in the Treaty), determine the scope of those freedoms. In such cases, the concept of public policy requires, rather, effective action on the part of the authorities to deal with the disturbances. (para 5.3)

The Court was equally sceptical about the incapacity of the French authorities in the face of rampaging fuel retailers on the streets of France. It remarked dryly:

> In that regard, it is sufficient to state that the French Government has not shown that it would be unable, using the means at its disposal, to deal with the consequences which an

amendment of the rules in question ... would have upon public order and security. (paras 32, 33)

In response to attempts by animal welfare groups to block the export of live animals, the issue was seen by Simon Brown LJ, expressly adopting the Advocate-General's Opinion in *Cullet*, above, as a straightforward issue of the rule of law, both Community and national (*R v Coventry City Council, ex parte Phoenix Aviation* [1995] 3 All ER 37 at 67; and see also *R v Chief Constable of Sussex, ex parte International Trader's Ferry Ltd* [1995] 4 All ER 364). Although the Court of Appeal did not uphold the decision of the Divisional Court, the Court of Justice has since reiterated that the Member States cannot prevent the import or export of products because of the 'views or behaviour of a section of the Community'. A failure to act, where persistent obstruction by private groups has been drawn to the attention of the authorities, will represent a breach of the state's obligation to uphold the law of the Community and will not be justified by Art 30: *Commission v France* (Case C-265/95).

The Irish Government had more success with the public security argument in *Campus Oil v Ministry for Industry and Energy* (Case 72/83). Irish legislation required importers of petroleum products to purchase up to 35 per cent of their requirements from Ireland's state-owned refinery at prices fixed by the Minister. There was no doubt that the requirement breached Art 30 (now Art 28). The Government, however, argued that the measure was necessary on the ground that the importance of oil for the maintenance of the life of the country made it essential to maintain fuel capacity in Ireland. The system it had adopted was the only means by which a fuel reserve could be built up. The Court agreed that petroleum products were of fundamental importance to the country's existence, since they were needed for the country's institutions, vital services and the survival of its inhabitants. The Court therefore accepted the public security justification. It did, however, warn the Irish Government that the purchasing obligation could be continued only if there was no less restrictive measure which was capable of achieving the same objective; nor should the quantities covered by the scheme exceed the minimum supply requirements without which the public security of the state would be affected. The scheme had, in other words, to be proportionate to the risk anticipated.

Public health

The same principle of proportionality has been prominent in the many decisions of the Court of Justice in which Member States have sought to rely on the exception relating to the health of humans, animals and plants. In this context, Art 30 attempts to strike a balance between the interests involved in the creation of a single market and the protection of health, and the Court is particularly careful to determine whether or not a measure is, in fact, a disguised form of protectionism. To be capable of justification as a health measure, it must form part of 'a seriously considered health policy'.

This was lacking in *Commission v United Kingdom (Re Imports of Poultry Meat)* (Case 40/82). There was evidence before the Court of Justice that, in the two years before the ban on the import of turkeys from France in September 1981 that was the subject of the proceedings, there had been a steep rise in turkey imports for the Christmas market from France and other Member States. This had been followed by a chorus of complaints about unfair competition from British poultry producers. The imposition of a sudden ban on the import of French turkeys was, ostensibly, because of the risk of the outbreak of Newcastle Disease, a serious poultry infection. There had, however, been no recent outbreak in France, and the main object of the UK Government's ostensible concern was imports into France of turkeys from Eastern European countries where there was a more serious risk. The Court was unconvinced by the British justification:

> Certain established facts suggest that the real aim of the 1981 measure was to block, for commercial and economic reasons, imports of poultry products from other Member States, in particular from France. The United Kingdom government had been subject to pressure from British poultry producers to block these imports. It hurriedly introduced its new policy with the result that French Christmas turkeys were excluded from the British market for the 1981 season ... The deduction must be made that the 1981 measures did not form part of a seriously considered health policy.
>
> Taken together, these facts are sufficient to establish that the 1981 measures constitute a disguised restriction on imports of poultry products from other Member States, in particular from France, unless it can be shown that, for reasons of animal health, the only possibility open to the United Kingdom was to apply the strict measures which are at issue in this case and that, therefore, the methods prescribed by the 1981 measures ... were not more restrictive than was necessary for the protection of poultry flocks in Great Britain.

The Court was satisfied that, on the evidence, there were much less restrictive methods available that were appropriate to the degree of risk. The United Kingdom had, therefore, breached Art 28. Subsequently, this successful action by the Commission led to a claim in the British courts by an importer affected by the ban (*Bourgoin* v *Ministry of Agriculture, Fisheries and Food (MAFF)* [1986] QB 716; see Chapter 10).

Many of the cases in which the health exception is raised turn on whether there is, in fact, any risk at all. The perception of risk may, quite genuinely, be different in different Member States. The Court, in these cases, will have to assess, on the best available scientific evidence, first whether there is, indeed, a risk to health, and secondly, if there is, whether the state taking the restrictive measures has responded appropriately. In *Commission* v *France* (Case 216/84), for example, French legislation prohibited the marketing of milk substitutes. The French Government attempted to justify the prohibition on the ground, first, that milk substitutes had a lower nutritional value, and secondly, that they were harmful to some people. The Court rejected both arguments. The fact that an imported food product had a lower nutritional value than milk products hardly constituted a health risk when consumers had so many other food products to choose from. Milk products themselves could pose a risk to some individuals with certain allergies or suffering from certain diseases. Labelling would provide consumers with the necessary information to enable them to make a properly informed choice.

Milk also figured in *Commission* v *United Kingdom (Re UHT Milk)* (Case 124/81). In this case, the Commission brought Art 226 proceedings against the United Kingdom for imposing a requirement that UHT milk should be marketed only by approved dairies or distributors. The Government argued that this was necessary to ensure that milk was free from bacterial or viral infections. The effect of the restriction was that all imported milk had to be repackaged and re-treated. The Court rejected these measures as inappropriate and unnecessary. There was evidence that milk in all Member States was of similar quality and subject to equivalent controls. The restriction was, therefore, unjustified. The Court has also held that German legislation, which prohibited the import from other Member States of meat products manufactured from meat not coming from the country of manufacture of the finished product, could not be justified on health grounds since there was no reason to believe that the risk of contamination increased simply because the fresh meat crossed a Community frontier (*Commission* v *Germany* (Case 153/78)).

Although the Court has held that the fact that testing has occurred in the country of origin should give rise to a presumption that the imported goods are safe to use, this is not the universal rule (*De Peijper* (Case 104/75); *Frans-Nederlandse* (Case 272/80)). In particular, differences in approach to food additives or medical products may justify additional testing by the importing state before authorisation to market the goods is given. In *Sandoz*, noted above, there was uncertainty about the point at which a large intake of vitamin additives in food could become harmful. The Court held that the importing state was entitled to carry out tests on the food before it was put on the market:

> Community law permits national rules prohibiting without prior authorisation the marketing of foodstuffs lawfully marketed in another Member State to which vitamins have been added, provided that the marketing is authorised when the addition of vitamins meets a real need, especially a technical or nutritional one. (para 20)

The position is similar for medical products. The Court has held that Member States are entitled, at the present stage of harmonisation and in the absence of a procedure for Community authorisation or mutual recognition of national authorisation, to exclude from other Member States medical products which have not been authorised by the competent national authorities (*Lucien Ortscheit GmbH* v *Eurim-Pharm GmbH* (Case C-320/93)).

Protection of industrial and commercial property

Industrial and commercial property rights are valuable rights relating to the protection and distribution of goods and services. Such rights are protected by patents, trade marks, copyrights and similar devices. Each Member State has devised its own system for protecting the investment, creativity and innovation which has gone into a new product or system. The period of protection may vary widely between Member States, and between different kinds of industrial property rights. In the United Kingdom, for example, the exclusive rights enjoyed under a patent endure for 20 years, indefinitely for trade marks, and the author's lifetime plus 50 years for copyright. Since each form of industrial property is defined under national law, it would seem, *prima facie*, not to be a matter within Community competence and, indeed, Art 295 EC Treaty appears to emphasise the exclusive competence of each Member State in this matter:

This Treaty shall in no way prejudice the rules in Member States governing the system of property ownership.

However, it is clear that a restrictive approach taken by the owners of industrial property rights could have a very significant effect on the free movement of goods. The different national rules on such property rights could be used, effectively, to partition the market for those products on a national basis, and prevent the achievement of one of the Community's primary aims. The Court has, therefore, drawn a distinction between rules affecting the ownership of such rights and their exercise. It has declared that the protection given to the different systems of property ownership in different Member States by Art 295 EC Treaty does not allow national legislatures to adopt measures relating to industrial and commercial property which would adversely affect the principle of free movement of goods within the common market (*Spain* v *Council* (Case C-350/92)). It has also emphasised that this Art 30 exception cannot 'constitute a means of arbitrary discrimination or a disguised restriction on trade between Member States'. National rules protecting patents and copyrights must therefore operate without discrimination. In *Collins* v *Imtrat* (Case C-92/92), the performer Phil Collins attempted to bring proceedings to stop the distribution in Germany of pirated tapes and illegal recordings taken at his concerts. Under German law, such relief was available only to German nationals. The Court of Justice held that, although Member States were still free to determine the nature and extent of protection provided by national copyright rules, such rules should be applied indiscriminately. On this basis it has also held that there is a breach of Art 28 when national rules require that a patent be exploited only on the territory where the patent is granted and which prohibit or restrict its development elsewhere, so that the patented goods may not be manufactured elsewhere and imported into the patent-granting state (*Commission* v *Italy* (Case C-235/89); *Commission* v *United Kingdom* (Case C-30/90)). There is a parallel here to the prohibition of discrimination in the acquisition of real property rights by those attempting to establish themselves under Art 43 EC Treaty (*Steinhauser* v *City of Biarritz* (Case 197/84); *Commission* v *Italy (Re Housing Aid)* (Case 63/86)).

The Court has tried to allow the property exception to operate only in relation to the essential core of property rights, although what those are in each case is sometimes difficult to determine. In the case of a patent, the Court said in *Centrafarm* v *Winthrop BV* (Cases 15 & 16/74):

> Article 36 [now Art 30] in fact only admits of derogations from the free movement of goods where such derogations are justified for the purpose of safeguarding rights which constitute the specific subject matter of this property.
>
> In relation to patents, the specific subject matter of the industrial property is the guarantee that the patentee, to reward the creative effort of the inventor, has the exclusive right to use an invention with a view to manufacturing industrial products and putting them into circulation for the first time, either directly or by the grant of licences to third parties, as well as the right to oppose infringements.

This right is enjoyed in the Member State in which the goods are patented. The patentee, under the Art 30 exception, can exclude goods which breach his patent. However, once the patented goods are circulated in another Member State, either by him or with his consent, his right to exclude those goods as the patentee is then said to be 'exhausted'. This principle is demonstrated by the facts of the *Centrafarm* case.

Sterling Drug Inc. held British and Dutch patents relating to a drug called NEGRAM. In both countries the drug was marketed either by Sterling Drug itself, or by companies which it had licensed to do so. Centrafarm, an independent Dutch company, bought supplies of the drug in both Britain and Germany, where it was much cheaper, as a result of price controls, and resold it in The Netherlands. Sterling Drug and its subsidiaries invoked their respective patent and trade mark rights before the Dutch courts to prevent NEGRAM being marketed in The Netherlands by Centrafarm.

The Dutch court referred a number of questions to the Court of Justice under Art 177 (now Art 234). The Court described the limits of national patent rights in this context:

> An obstacle to the free movement of goods may arise out of the existence, within national legislation concerning industrial and commercial property, of provisions laying down that a patentee's right is not exhausted when the product protected by the patent is marketed in another Member State, with the result that the patentee can prevent importation of the product into his own Member State when it has been marketed in another Member State. Whereas an obstacle to the free movement of goods of this kind may be justified on the ground of the protection of industrial property where such protection is invoked against a product coming from a Member State where it is not patentable and has been manufactured by third parties without the consent of the patentee and in cases where there exist patents, the original proprietors of which are legally and economically independent, a derogation from the principle of the free movement of goods is not, however, justified where the product has been put onto the market in a legal manner, by the patentee himself or with his consent, in the Member State from which it has been imported, in particular in the case of a proprietor of parallel patents. (paras 10 and 11)

The 'exhaustion of rights' principle has been applied by the Court with regard not only to patent rights, but also to trade marks, copyright and industrial design. It defined the proprietorial interest in relation to trade marks in *Centrafarm v Winthrop* (Cases 15 & 16/74):

> The specific subject matter of the industrial property is the guarantee that the owner of the trade mark has the exclusive right to use that trade mark for the purpose of putting products protected by the trade mark into circulation for the first time, and is therefore intended to protect him against any competitor wishing to take advantage of the status and reputation of the trade mark by selling products illegally bearing the trade mark.

Crucial to the application of the exhaustion principle is the meaning of 'consent' in this context. Consent is assumed where the owner markets the goods himself, where he does so through a subsidiary company or where the owner and the undertaking responsible for the first marketing are under common control. The limits of consent were explored in *Pharmon BV v Hoechst AG* (Case 19/84).

Hoechst owned a patent in Germany for the process to manufacture a drug called FRUSEMIDE. It also owned parallel patents on the process in The Netherlands and the United Kingdom. Although FRUSEMIDE was not manufactured by Hoechst or any of its subsidiaries in the United Kingdom, it was manufactured there by an independent company called DDSA under a compulsory licence granted under British legislation. As its name suggests, a compulsory licence does not require the consent of the owner of the patent, but royalties on sales are paid to him. The litigation in this case arose out of imports from the United Kingdom being placed on the Dutch market by Pharmon; because British prices for the drug were much lower, Pharmon stood to make a considerable profit at Hoechst BV's expense. Could Hoechst resist their marketing in The Netherlands? The question turned on whether the compulsory licensing and payment of royalties to Hoechst amounted to 'consent'. The Court of Justice, in an Art 177 (now Art 234) reference, did not think that it did:

> It is necessary to point out that where, as in this instance, the competent authorities of a Member State grant a third party a compulsory licence which allows him to carry out manufacturing and marketing operations which the patentee would normally have the right to prevent, the patentee cannot be deemed to have consented to the operation of that third party. Such a measure deprives the patent proprietor of his right to determine freely the conditions under which he markets his products. (para 25)

The Court went further in *IHT Internationale Heiztechnik GmbH* v *Ideal-Standard GmbH* (Case C-11/93), holding that action by an assignee under contract (as opposed to a subsidiary in another Member State) could not be regarded as carried out with 'consent' of the assignor in relation to the use of a trade mark on goods imported into another Member State, and the import could be restrained under the property justification in Art 30. The decision is surprising because it could be said that the assignment itself included a right to deal generally with the trade mark and the assignment would therefore exhaust the rights of the assignor. The Court, however, stressed that the free movement of the goods would undermine the essential function of the trade mark. Consumers would no longer be able to identify, for certain, the origin of the marked goods, and the proprietor of the trade mark could be held responsible for the poor quality of the goods for which he is in no way accountable. In this case, at least, the Court's concern for the proprietorial interest of the patentee seems to have outweighed its concern to secure the free movement of goods.

The importance of consent can be seen in two apparently similar cases involving copyright. In *Musik Vertrieb Membran GmbH* v *GEMA* (Case 55/80) the Court of Justice held that the performing rights society GEMA could not rely on its German copyright in sound recordings to prevent parallel imports of records from the United Kingdom which had been put on the market there with its consent. In *EMI Electrola* v *Patricia* (Case 341/87), the claimants owned the production and distribution rights in Germany of the musical works of Cliff Richard. The defendants sold records of Cliff Richard's songs in Germany which had been imported from Denmark, where the copyright protection had expired. The claimants applied for an order from the German courts to exclude these imports. The defendants resisted on the grounds that such an order would breach Art 28, since the records lawfully circulated in Denmark. The Court of Justice, in an Art 234 reference, did not agree. Lawful circulation was not equivalent to consent. The Court distinguished the *GEMA* case on the ground that the marketing in Denmark was due to the expiry of the protection period in another Member State, and not to the consent of the copyright owner or his licensee. This was an aspect of ownership and the different rights of copyright owners in different Member States. The problems caused by these difficulties would continue until these rules had been harmonised for the whole Community.

Harmonisation of industrial property rights

The Commission has two principal aims in this field. The first is that each Member State should employ, as far as possible, the same substantive industrial property rules. The second is that intellectual property monopolies should run the length and breadth of the Community, irrespective of the country of their origin. Some modest progress has been made towards both these aims (for an account, see Phillips and Firth, 1995). There are broadly similar rules in Member States governing criteria for patentability and the patent term. Registration is, however, undertaken according to different rules in different states. A Community Patent Convention, which would provide that one unitary patent would cover the entire territory of the Community, and that the Community would be treated as one country under the existing rules of the European Patent Convention, still awaits implementation. In the meantime, some specific measures have been approved, or are being considered, to give some protection in a few areas which are regarded as particularly important in the context of the Single Market. So, for example, a regulation has been approved to extend existing protection for pharmaceutical products (Regulation 1768/92), and a Community Plant Variety Regulation has been adopted to protect the rights of plant breeders (Regulation 2100/94).

There is more difficulty in harmonising legislation on copyright, because the United Kingdom and Ireland as common law countries have a very different approach to copyright to that prevailing in the other civil law states of the Community. An attempt in a Community Green Paper of 1988 to reconcile the civil *droit d'auteur* with the common law concept of copyright was not well received. As with patents, some progress has been made on individual measures to harmonise the law where the need seemed most pressing and there are now, for example, copyright directives on computer software, rental and lending rights, cable and satellite transmission (Directives 91/250, 92/100 and 93/83).

The area of industrial property law where there has been the most progress is in relation to trade marks and designs. The Trade Mark Approximation Directive 1988 laid down principles common to the Community's national or regional trade mark systems (Directive 89/104). In addition, the Community Trade Mark Regulation provides for a single standard of registrability for a trade mark which will grant protection to its proprietor throughout the Community (Regulation 40/94). Both were implemented in the United Kingdom by the Trade Marks Act 1994. The relationship between the Trade Mark Directive and the Court's existing case law on the protection of intellectual property rights and the scope of Art 30 was considered by the Court in *Bristol Myers Squibb* (Joined Cases C-427, 429 & 436/93). The context involved the repackaging of goods, but the principles involved covered a much wider area of intellectual property law. Repackaging of trade marked products presents a particular problem in reconciling the fundamental principle of free movement of goods with the EC Treaty's guarantee of protection of intellectual property rights. The problem of repackaging is particularly acute in relation to pharmaceutical products, where prices vary widely throughout the Community. The wide price differentials are, largely, because the pricing of medical products in each Member State is regulated through state health service provisions. Traders can exploit the price differentials by buying goods in a low-price state and then selling them in a high-price market for a figure which undercuts the recommended retail price in that state. The usual practice, in these cases, is for the goods to be repackaged to meet the requirements of the importing state. The manufacturer will frequently attempt to prevent these parallel imports on the basis that the repackaging infringes its trade mark. The Court was quite early in rejecting these attempts at restraining imports and effectively partitioning the market. In *Hoffman La Roche* v *Centrafarm* (Case 102/77), it declared that the trade mark owner could not resist repackaging if his marketing system contributed to the artificial partitioning of the market, if the repackaging could not adversely affect the original condition of the product, if he received prior notice of the marketing of the repackaged product and if the identity of the repackager was stated on the new packaging. The issue in *Bristol Myers Squibb* (Cases C-427, 429 & 436/93) was, essentially, whether, and if so, how far, the existing case law was still relevant after the coming into effect of the Trade Mark Directive. Article 7 of the directive gives legislative recognition to the idea of exhaustion of rights which, as we have seen in relation to all intellectual property rights, prevents the owners of a trade mark or patent from developing separate markets for their products in each Member State (see *Centrafarm* v *Sterling Drug* (Cases 15 & 16/74), above). The Court stressed that, since the directive was a harmonising measure, it had to be interpreted in the light of the EC Treaty rules on the free movement of goods. On that basis, it specifically reiterated the four rules set out in *Hoffman La Roche* (above) and affirmed that they continued to apply. However, although the directive had to be read in the light of Art 36 (now Art 30), it did not allow the repackager to treat the goods (including the way they were advertised) in such a way as to damage their market 'image'. In *Parfums Christian Dior SA* v *Evora BV* (Case C-337/95), the subject matter of the repackaging was high-prestige perfume. The Court held that Art 7 of the directive did allow the owner of the trade mark to take steps to ensure that the presentation and advertising 'did not affect the value of the trade mark by detracting from the allure and prestigious image of the goods in question and from their aura of luxury'.

Community legislation on intellectual property rights is likely never to be exhaustive, as modern technology continues to develop new products which raise new issues. There is an inevitable time lag between the evolution of the new product and the Community's response. The exception covering intellectual property rights in Art 30, and the Court's jurisprudence on the subject, will, therefore, continue to be important.

ARTICLE 30 AND UK IMPLEMENTATION OF THE FREE MOVEMENT OF GOODS

The implementation of Arts 28 and 29 and the Community's harmonising measures in the United Kingdom has involved a major legislative programme to give effect to the Community directives that were intended to complete the Single European Market by 1 January 1993. In terms of primary legislation, this has involved measures of a general kind, such as the Customs and Excise Management Act 1979, which imposes a general obligation on the UK customs authorities 'for the purpose of implementing Community obligations ... [to] co-operate with other customs services ... to give effect ... to any Community requirement or practice as to the movement of goods between countries'. More specific Acts of Parliament have been passed to implement major directives, such as the Product Liability Directive 85/374, which was put into effect by the Consumer Protection Act 1987. Other specific legislation has been enacted to put decisions of the Court of Justice into effect. For example, the Importation of Milk Act 1983 was passed to comply with the judgment in *Commission* v *United Kingdom (Re UHT Milk)* (Case 124/81) (above). In implementing the law relating to the free movement of goods, as with other Community provisions, the United Kingdom has, essentially, four options:

- where the requirements of a directive are already met in national law, no specific action may be necessary;
- where there is existing UK legislation, by creating the power to make appropriate national regulations;
- by delegated legislation under the European Communities Act 1972, s 2(2);
- through primary legislation.

Where legislation is adopted to implement a directive, it must give precise effect to the directive. It was thought by many writers that the Product Liability Directive, which created liability for the manufacturers of defective goods, had not been effectively implemented by the Consumer Protection Act 1987, and the Commission brought proceedings in the Court of Justice against the United Kingdom. This was because the Act provided a defence to manufacturers based on the state of knowledge existing at the time the goods were put into circulation in circumstances in which, the Commission argued, a manufacturer might escape liability by demonstrating that he had not been negligent if he was unaware of any potential risk. The directive itself imposed strict liability. The Court refused to accept the Commission's interpretation of the Act, and noted that there was 'nothing ... to suggest that the courts of the United Kingdom, if called upon to interpret [the Consumer Protection Act] would not do so in the light of the wording and the purposes of the Directive': *Commission* v *United Kingdom* (Case C-300/95).

THE *CASSIS* RULE OF REASON: JUSTIFICATIONS FOR INDISTINCTLY APPLICABLE MEASURES

The *Cassis* case was considered above, where the Court of Justice held that Art 28 applies to indistinctly applicable measures (i.e. measures which apply to *both* imported and domestic products) which impact upon the free movement of intra-Community trade. The first *Cassis* principle (the rule of mutual recognition) was discussed, which provides that once goods have been lawfully marketed in one Member State, they should be free to be marketed in any other Member State without restriction. However, this is subject to the second principle, the 'rule of reason', or the 'mandatory requirements defence'.

In the *Cassis* case, the applicant wished to import the liqueur 'Cassis de Dijon' into Germany from France. The relevant German authorities refused to allow the importation because the French drink was not of sufficient alcoholic strength to be marketed in Germany: under German law liqueurs had to have an alcoholic strength of 25 per cent, whereas that of the French drink was between 15 per cent and 20 per cent. The applicant argued that this rule was an MEQR, since it prevented the French version of the drink being marketed in Germany. The Court of Justice held as follows:

8. In the absence of common rules relating to the production and marketing of alcohol … it is for the Member States to regulate all matters relating to the production and marketing of alcohol and alcoholic beverages on their own territory.

Obstacles to movement within the Community resulting from disparities between the national laws relating to the marketing of the products in question must be accepted in so far as those provisions may be recognised as being necessary in order to satisfy mandatory requirements relating in particular to the effectiveness of fiscal supervision, the protection of public health, the fairness of commercial transactions and the defence of the consumer.

9. The Government of the Federal Republic of Germany, intervening in the proceedings, put forward various arguments which, in its view, justify the application of the provisions relating to the minimum alcohol content of alcoholic beverages, adducing considerations relating on the one hand to the protection of public health and on the other to the protection of the consumer against unfair commercial practices.

10. As regards the protection of public health the German Government states that the purpose of the fixing of minimum alcohol contents by national legislation is to avoid the proliferation of alcoholic beverages with a low alcohol content, since, in its view, such products may more easily induce a tolerance towards alcohol than more highly alcoholic beverages.

11. Such considerations are not decisive since the consumer can obtain on the market an extremely wide range of weakly or moderately alcoholic products and furthermore a large proportion of alcoholic beverages with a high alcohol content freely sold on the German market is generally consumed in diluted form.

12. The German Government also claims that the fixing of a lower limit for the alcohol content of certain liqueurs is designed to protect the consumer against unfair practices on the part of producers and distributors of alcoholic beverages.

This argument is based on the consideration that the lowering of the alcohol content secures a competitive advantage in relation to beverages with a higher alcohol content, since alcohol constitutes by far the most expensive constituent of beverages by reason of the high rate of tax to which it is subject.

Furthermore, according to the German Government, to allow alcoholic products into free circulation wherever, as regards their alcohol content, they comply with the rules laid down in the country of production would have the effect of imposing as a common standard within the Community the lowest alcohol content permitted in any of the Member States, and even of rendering any requirements in this field inoperative since a lower limit of this nature is foreign to the rules of several Member States.

13. As the Commission rightly observed, the fixing of limits to the alcohol content of beverages may lead to the standardisation of products placed on the market and of their designations, in the interests of a greater transparency of commercial transactions and offers for sale to the public.

However, this line of argument cannot be taken so far as to regard the mandatory fixing of minimum alcohol contents as being an essential guarantee of the fairness of commercial transactions, since *it is a simple matter to ensure that suitable information is conveyed to the purchaser by requiring the display of an indication of origin and of the alcohol content on the packaging of products.*

14. It is clear from the foregoing that the requirements relating to the minimum alcohol content of alcoholic beverages do not serve a purpose which is in the general interest and such as to take precedence over the requirements of the free movement of goods, which constitutes one of the fundamental rules of the Community.

In practice, the principal effect of requirements of this nature is to promote alcoholic beverages having a high alcohol content by excluding from the national market products of other Member States which do not answer that description.

It therefore appears that the unilateral requirement imposed by the rules of a Member State of a minimum alcohol content for the purposes of the sale of alcoholic beverages constitutes an obstacle to trade which is incompatible with the provisions of Article 30 [now Art 28] of the Treaty.

There is therefore no valid reason why, provided that they have been lawfully produced and marketed in one of the Member States, alcoholic beverages should not be introduced into any other Member State; the sale of such products may not be subject to a legal prohibition on the marketing of beverages with an alcohol content lower than the limits set by national rules. (emphasis added)

The rule of reason

Paragraph 8 of the judgment contains the second *Cassis* principle, the 'rule of reason':

... Obstacles to movement within the Community resulting from disparities between the national laws relating to the marketing of the products in question must be accepted in so far as those provisions may be recognised as being necessary in order to satisfy mandatory requirements relating in particular to the effectiveness of fiscal supervision, the protection of public health, the fairness of commercial transactions and the defence of the consumer.

There are four matters listed which may prevent a rule from being caught by Art 28:

- fiscal supervision
- public health
- fairness of commercial transactions
- protection of the consumer.

This list is not exhaustive. Any measure which satisfies the *rule of reason* will not be caught by Art 28. This is separate and distinct from the Art 30 derogations (considered above).

The state is placed upon the defensive. After asserting the right of the state to regulate, the Court provides that such indistinct rules which interfere with the free movement of goods will be lawful only insofar as they are justified under one of the heads of the rule of reason.

The mandatory requirement defence: 'the rule of reason'

We have already seen that Art 30 provides a defence to rules otherwise caught by Art 28. Although this defence can apply to both distinctly and indistinctly applicable measures, the Court has applied Art 30 very strictly so that a Member State cannot breach the principle of free movement of goods very easily. However, the Court has recognised that an indistinctly applicable rule which in some way restricts trade may be defended under the *Cassis* rule of reason.

The fact that the rule of reason applies only to an indistinctly applicable measure has been made clear by the Court of Justice on a number of occasions: see, e.g., *Italian State* v *Gilli and Andres* (Case 788/79). The Court held that it was only where national rules applied without discrimination to both national and imported products that they could be justified using the mandatory requirements derived from *Cassis*.

In *Commission* v *Ireland* (Case 113/80), when considering the nature of a distinctly applicable measure, the Irish Government, as part of its defence, argued that the distinctly applicable measure could be saved because it satisfied the *Cassis* rule of reason. The Court of Justice held that the rule of reason applied only to indistinctly applicable measures and therefore was not relevant to the facts of this particular case:

> 5. The Irish Government does not dispute the restrictive effects of these orders on the free movement of goods. *However, it contends that the disputed measures are justified in the interests of consumer protection and of fairness in commercial transactions between producers ...*

> 10. In this respect, the Court has repeatedly affirmed (in the judgments of 20 February 1979 in Case 120/78 *REWE* [1979] ECR 649, 26 June 1980 in Case 788/79 *Gilli and Andres* [1980] ECR 2071, 19 February 1981 in Case 130/80 *Kelderman* [1981] ECR 527) that 'in the absence of common rules relating to the production and marketing of the product in question it is for Member States to regulate all matters relating to its production, distribution and consumption on their own territory subject, however, to the condition that those rules do not present an obstacle ... to intra-Community trade' and that '*it is only where national rules, which apply without discrimination to both domestic and imported products, may be justified as being necessary in order to satisfy imperative requirements relating in particular to ... the fairness of commercial transactions and the defence of the consumer that they may constitute an exception to the requirements arising under Article 30 [now 28]*'.

> 11. *The orders concerned in the present case are not measures which are applicable to domestic products and to imported products without distinction but rather a set of rules which apply only to imported products and are therefore discriminatory in nature, with the result that the measures in issue are not covered by the decisions cited above which relate exclusively to provisions that regulate in a uniform manner the marketing of domestic products and imported products.* (emphasis added)

As discussed above, the Court set out a list of *mandatory requirements* in the *Cassis* case:

> 8. ... Obstacles to movement within the Community resulting from disparities between the national laws relating to the marketing of the products in question must be accepted in so far as those provisions may be recognised as being necessary in order to satisfy mandatory requirements relating in particular to *the effectiveness of fiscal supervision, the protection of public health, the fairness of commercial transactions and the defence of the consumer*. (emphasis added)

This list is not exhaustive (note the use of the words 'relating in particular to ...'). The Court has added others to that list. We shall now consider the application of some of the specific mandatory requirements.

Consumer protection

In *Commission* v *Germany* (Case 178/84), the Commission instituted former Art 169 (now Art 226) proceedings against Germany, alleging a breach of the former Art 30 (now Art 28). Germany prohibited the marketing on its territory of beer lawfully produced and marketed in other Member States if the beer failed to comply with the provisions of the *Biersteuergesetz* of 1952 (Beer Duty Act 1952). There were two provisions which the Commission wished to challenge. The first one was that the name 'Bier' could be used only for products brewed using malted barley, hops, yeast and water alone. The use of other ingredients such as maize did not prohibit the product being marketed, but it could not be called 'Bier'. The German Government sought to defend its law on the basis that it was necessary to protect the German consumer who associated the label 'Bier' with beverages made exclusively from the stated ingredients. The Court ruled that the law was a barrier to free trade and then considered whether it was necessary to protect consumers:

31. The German Government's argument that section 10 of the Biersteuergesetz is essential in order to protect German consumers because, in their minds, the designation 'Bier' is inseparably linked to the beverage manufactured solely from the ingredients laid down in section 9 of the Biersteuergesetz must be rejected.

32. Firstly, consumers' conceptions which vary from one Member State to the other are also likely to evolve in the course of time within a Member State. The establishment of the Common Market is, it should be added, one of the factors that may play a major contributory role in that development. Whereas rules protecting consumers against misleading practices enable such a development to be taken into account, legislation of the kind contained in section 10 of the Biersteuergesetz prevents it from taking place. As the Court has already held in another context (Case 170/78 *Commission* v *United Kingdom*), the legislation of a Member State must not 'crystallise given consumer habits so as to consolidate an advantage acquired by national industries concerned to comply with them'.

33. Secondly, in the other Member States of the Community the designations corresponding to the German designation 'Bier' are generic designations for a fermented beverage manufactured from barley, whether malted barley on its own or with the addition of rice or maize. The same approach is taken in Community law as can be seen from heading 22.03 of the Common Customs Tariff. The German legislature itself utilises the designation 'Bier' in that way in section 9(7) and (8) of the Biersteuergesetz in order to refer to beverages not complying with the manufacturing rules laid down in section 9(1) and (2).

34. The German designation 'Bier' and its equivalents in the languages of the other Member States may therefore not be restricted to beers manufactured in accordance with the rules in force in the Federal Republic of Germany.

35. *It is admittedly legitimate to seek to enable consumers who attribute specific qualities to beers manufactured from particular raw materials to make their choice in the light of that consideration. However, as the Court has already emphasised (Case 193/80 Commission v Italy) that possibility may be ensured by means which do not prevent the importation of products which have been lawfully manufactured and marketed in other Member States and, in particular, 'by the compulsory affixing of suitable labels giving the nature of the product sold'.* By indicating the raw materials utilised in the manufacture of

beer 'such a course would enable the consumer to make his choice in full knowledge of the facts and would guarantee transparency in trading and in offers to the public'. It must be added that such a system of mandatory consumer information must not entail negative assessments for beers not complying with the requirements of section 9 of the Biersteuergesetz. (emphasis added)

The Court therefore held that the German law breached the former Art 30 (now Art 28). Although there were some arguments in favour of Germany's 'consumer protection' claim, the Court looked at whether the action taken was necessary, or whether action which was less restrictive of intra-Community trade could have been taken (an application of the proportionality test). At para 35 the Court held that consumer interests could be met through better labelling rather than an outright ban.

Other cases have followed this approach. In *De Kikvorsch Groothandel-Import-Export BV* (Case 94/82), the Court of Justice again rejected a restrictive rule which was a barrier to free movement on the ground that better labelling could achieve the objective sought – protection of the consumer.

A similar result was achieved in *Ministre Public* v *Deserbais* (Case 286/86).

French legislation restricted the use of the name 'Edam' to cheese with a minimum fat content of 40 per cent. Mr Deserbais imported cheese into France from Germany, where it was lawfully produced with a fat content of 34.3 per cent. He marketed the cheese in France as 'Edam' cheese and was prosecuted. In his defence he argued that French law was not applicable because it contravened the former Art 30 (now Art 28). The matter was referred to the Court under the former Art 177 (now Art 234) for a preliminary ruling:

---

10. The national court starts from the premise that the cheese in question, containing 34% fat, has been lawfully and traditionally produced in the Federal Republic of Germany under the name 'Edam' in accordance with the laws and regulations applicable to it there, and that consumers' attention is adequately drawn to that fact by the labelling.

11. It must also be stated that at the present stage of development of Community law there are no common rules governing the various types of cheeses in the Community. Accordingly, it cannot be stated in principle that a Member State may not lay down rules making the use by national producers of a name for a cheese subject to the observance of a traditional minimum fat content.

12. However, it would be incompatible with Article 30 [now Art 28] of the Treaty and the objectives of a common market to apply such rules to imported cheeses of the same type where those cheeses have been lawfully produced and marketed in another Member State under the same generic name but with a different minimum fat content. *The Member State into which they are imported cannot prevent the importation and marketing of such cheeses where adequate information for the consumer is ensured.*

13. The question may arise whether the same rule must be applied where a product presented under a particular name is so different, as regards its composition or production, from the products generally known by that name in the Community that it cannot be regarded as falling within the same category. However, no situation of that kind arises in the circumstances described by the national court in this case …

Article 30 [now Art 28] et seq. of the Treaty must be interpreted as precluding a Member State from applying national legislation making the right to use the trade name of a type of cheese subject to the observance of a minimum fat content to products of the same type imported from another Member State when those products have been lawfully manufactured and marketed under that name in that Member State and consumers are provided with proper information. (emphasis added)

The Court of Justice held that the French indistinctly applicable rule was a restriction on trade in relation to cheese which had been lawfully produced and marketed in Germany. It was therefore in breach of the former Art 30 (now Art 28), unless the rule could be justified under one of the heads of the rule of reason (e.g. defence of the consumer). In this case the Court held that the consumer could be provided with adequate information on the fat content of the different 'Edam' cheeses and therefore the rule was not justified under the rule of reason.

However, the Court acknowledged in para 13 that a product may be so different (as regards composition or production) from products generally known by that name in the importing country that it could not be considered to fall within the same category.

In *Italian State* v *Gilli and Andres* (Case 788/79), Italian law required that vinegar had to be made from the fermentation of wine. Importers of apple vinegar from Germany into Italy were prosecuted for fraud. The importers relied on the former Art 30 (now Art 28) as a defence. There were no Community harmonisation rules on the issue. The Court adopted the *Cassis* reasoning and said that in the absence of harmonisation measures, a Member State could regulate the production and marketing of products within its territory, provided that such regulation did not constitute an obstacle, actually or potentially, to the free movement of intra-Community trade. This rule did hinder the free movement of goods and therefore it could be saved only if it could be justified under one of the heads of the rule of reason. The Court held that it could not be justified because once again the consumer could be protected by proper labelling of the products and in this case there was no danger to health.

The same approach was adopted by the Court in *Walter Rau Lebensmittelwerke* v *de Smedt PvbA* (Case 261/81). The claimants manufactured margarine and complained that a Belgian law, under which margarine had to be sold in Belgium in cube-shaped packs to distinguish it from butter, infringed former Art 30 (now Art 28). The Court, in an Art 177 (now Art 234) reference, agreed. Although the rule applied to all margarine sold in Belgium, foreign manufacturers wishing to import margarine into Belgium would have to establish a special production and packaging line for the Belgian market, which would increase their production costs. There was no consumer protection reason for the packaging requirement. The true nature of the product could just as well be conveyed to the consumer by effective labelling. The EC Treaty, as amended by the ToA, now specifically requires Community harmonising measures on the free movement of goods to contain provisions giving a right to information to consumers about matters relating to their health, safety and economic interests (Art 153). National measures should also always rely upon such information where possible, rather than on an outright prohibition against sale.

However, even labelling requirements themselves may not escape Art 28. In *Fietje* (Case 27/80) the Court of Justice stated:

10. Although the extension to imported products of an obligation to use a certain name on the label does not wholly preclude the importation into the Member State concerned

of products originating in other Member States or in free circulation in those States it may nonetheless make their marketing more difficult, especially in the case of parallel imports. As the Netherlands Government itself admits in its observations, such an extension of that obligation is thus capable of impeding, at least indirectly, trade between Member States. It is therefore necessary to consider whether it may be justified on the ground of public interest in consumer protection, which, according to observations of the Netherlands Government and according to 'Warenwet', underlies the rules in question.

11. If the national rules relating to a given product include the obligation to use a description that is sufficiently precise to inform the purchaser of the nature of the product and to enable it to be distinguished from products with which it may be confused, it may well be necessary, in order to give consumers effective protection, to extend this obligation to imported products also, even in such a way as to make necessary the alteration of the original labels of some of these products. At the level of Community legislation, this possibility is recognised in several directives on the approximation of the laws of the Member States relating to certain foodstuffs as well as by Council Directive 79/112/EEC of 18 December 1978 on the approximation of the laws of the Member States relating to the labelling, presentation and advertising of foodstuffs for sale to the ultimate consumer (Official Journal 1979, L33, p.1).

12. However, *there is no longer any need for such protection if the details given on the original label of the imported product have as their content information on the nature of the product and that content includes at least the same information, and is just as capable of being understood by consumers in the importing State, as the description prescribed by the rules of that State.* In the context of Article 177 [now Art 234] of the EEC Treaty, the making of findings of fact necessary in order to establish whether there is such equivalence is a matter for the national court. (emphasis added)

The Court held that labelling requirements (that a specific name had to appear on the label) may render it more difficult for an importer to market goods in another Member State and therefore it would fall within the former Art 30 (now Art 28) unless justified (e.g. protection of the consumer). The Court held the labelling requirement (that a specific name had to appear on the label) would not be justified if the necessary information required by the state of import was included on the original label (but not the specific name) and this was just as capable of being understood by consumers.

In *Neeltje* v *Houtwipper* (Case C-293/93), the compatibility with Art 28 of national legislation requiring the hall-marking of precious metals which are offered for sale was raised in criminal proceedings against the defendant. All such metals in The Netherlands, both home produced and imported, had to be hall-marked to show the content of precious metals. The measure thus appeared to be indistinctly applicable, but it meant, in practice, that it rendered importation of precious metals into The Netherlands more difficult and costly, because importers would have to have their products re-assayed and date-stamped to indicate the year of manufacture in accordance with the Dutch hall-marking law. In practice, therefore, the importers of precious metals were at a disadvantage. Although the Court accepted that hall-marking of precious metals was a mandatory requirement designed to ensure effective protection of consumers and the promotion of fair trading, it held that the way in which the system operated breached Art 28:

A Member State cannot require a fresh hall-mark be affixed to products imported from another Member State in which they have been lawfully marketed and hall-marked in accordance with the legislation of that state, where the information provided by that hall-mark, in whatever form, is equivalent to that prescribed by the Member State of importation and intelligible to consumers of that state.

Fairness of commercial transactions

This overlaps with the previous mandatory requirement, and both may be pleaded in the alternative. In the *Cassis* case, Germany argued, *inter alia*, that the rule that liqueurs must contain a minimum alcohol content of 25 per cent was justified under the rule of reason on the ground of fairness of commercial transactions. It was argued that French Cassis, with a lower alcohol content, gained an unfair competitive advantage because tax on alcohol content constituted the greatest proportion of the cost of the product. A liqueur with a lower alcohol content would be taxed at a lower rate and therefore its selling price would be less than those liqueurs with a higher alcohol content (which would be subjected to a higher level of taxation). This argument was rejected by the Court.

Public health

Public health is included in both Art 30 and the list of mandatory requirements. When faced with a rule which is being defended by the imposing state on the ground of public health, the Court may not be overly concerned with whether it falls to be considered under Art 30 or the *Cassis* list.

Commission v *Germany* (Case 178/84) has already been considered above, with regard to the German rule which banned using the term 'Bier' unless the beverage was made from certain prescribed ingredients. The Commission was also concerned with a provision under the German Foodstuffs Act 1974, which banned the marketing of beer containing additives. It was accepted that this indistinctly applicable rule constituted a barrier to intra-Community trade, as it banned beer lawfully produced and marketed in other Member States where such beer contained additives. The question before the Court was whether this rule could come within the former Art 36 (now Art 30) on public-health grounds:

41. The Court has consistently held (in particular in Case 174/82 *Criminal Proceedings Against Sandoz BV*) that 'in so far as there are uncertainties at the present state of scientific research it is for the Member States, in the absence of harmonisation, to decide what degree of protection of the health and life of humans they intend to assure, having regard to the requirements of the free movement of goods within the Community'.

42. As may also be seen from the decision of the Court (and especially the *Sandoz* case, cited above, in Case 247/84, *Motte*, and in Case 308/84, *Ministère Public* v *Muller*), in such circumstances Community law does not preclude the adoption by Member States of legislation whereby the use of additives is subjected to prior authorisation granted by a measure of general application for specific additives, in respect of all products, for certain products only or for certain uses. Such legislation meets a genuine need of health policy, namely that of restricting the uncontrolled consumption of food additives.

43. However, the application to imported products of prohibitions on marketing products containing additives which are authorised in the Member State of production but prohibited in the Member State of importation is permissible only in so far as it complies with the requirements of Article 36 [now Art 30] of the Treaty as it has been interpreted by the Court.

44. *It must be borne in mind, in the first place, that in its judgments in Sandoz, Motte and Muller, the Court inferred from the principle of proportionality underlying the last sentence of Article 36 [now Art 30] of the Treaty that prohibitions on the marketing of products containing additives authorised in the Member State of production but prohibited in the Member State of importation must be restricted to what is actually necessary to secure the protection of public health. The Court also concluded that the use of a specific additive which is authorised in another Member State must be authorised in the case of a product imported from that Member State where, in view, on the one hand, of the findings of international scientific research, and in particular the work of the Community's Scientific Committee for Food, the Codex Alimentarius Committee of the Food and Agriculture Organisation of the United Nations (FAO) and the World Health Organisation, and, on the other, of the eating habits prevailing in the importing Member State, the additive in question does not present a risk to public health and meets a real need, especially a technical one.*

45. Secondly, it should be remembered that, as the Court held in *Muller*, by virtue of the principle of proportionality, traders must also be able to apply, under a procedure which is easily accessible to them and can be concluded within a reasonable time, for the use of specific additives to be authorised by a measure of general application ... (emphasis added)

[It was then pointed out that the German rule prohibited all additives and there was no procedure whereby a trader could obtain authorisation to use a specific additive. Additives were allowed in other beverages. It was argued by the German Government that if the beer was manufactured in accordance with German law (i.e. section 9 of the Biersteuergesetz) additives would not be needed. The Court continued:]

51. It must be emphasised that the mere reference to the fact that beer can be manufactured without additives if it is made from only the raw materials prescribed in the Federal Republic of Germany does not suffice to preclude the possibility that some additives may meet a technological need. Such an interpretation of the concept of technological need, which results in favouring national production methods, constitutes a disguised means of restricting trade between Member States.

52. The concept of technological need must be assessed in the light of the raw materials utilised and bearing in mind the assessment made by the authorities of the Member States where the product was lawfully manufactured and marketed. Account must also be taken of the findings of international scientific research and in particular the work of the Community's Scientific Committee for Food, the Codex Alimentarius Committee of the FAO and the World Health Organisation.

53. Consequently, in so far as the German rules on additives in beer entail a general ban on additives, their application to beers imported from other Member States is contrary to the requirements of Community law as laid down in the case law of the Court, since that prohibition is contrary to the principle of proportionality and is therefore not covered by Article 36 [now Art 30] of the EEC Treaty.

The Court of Justice held that the German law breached the former Art 30 (now Art 28) because it was not proportionate. Although individual states have a margin of discretion in deciding what level of protection to provide to consumers, the Court, in determining whether such national measures are proportionate, will take into account the extent of current knowledge, particularly when assessing national provisions to protect the health of consumers. In *Proceedings against M Debus* (Cases C-13 & 113/91), the defendant was prosecuted for importing and marketing in Italy beer containing sulphur dioxide in a quantity permitted by the relevant French legislation but higher than that permitted in Italy. The defendant contested the prosecution on the basis that the Italian legislation breached former Art 30 (now Art 28) and the case was referred to the Court under former Art 177 (now Art 234). The Court had little difficulty in finding that the Italian rules led to 'a general and absolute prohibition of all beers containing more than 20 mg of sulphur dioxide per litre without any exception whatsoever'. There was uncontested evidence that the level of sulphur dioxide prohibited was far less than that found to constitute a risk by the World Health Organisation. It was an indistinctly applicable measure. The Court did not accept that, since there were other methods of preserving beer, the importing state was entitled to determine the method to be used, 'since such an interpretation of the concept of technological requirement, which leads to preference for domestic production methods, constituted a means of imposing a disguised restriction on trade between Member States' (see also *Sandoz BV* (Case 174/82); *Deserbais* (Case 286/86)).

Other mandatory requirements

As stated above, the *Cassis* list is not an exhaustive list. The list was left open so that it could be added to by the Court as its case law developed. The Court has accepted a wide range of national measures, many of them going well beyond measures designed to protect consumers or the specific exceptions permitted to Member States under Art 30.

In *Commission v Denmark* (Case 302/86), for example, the Commission challenged a Danish law under which all containers for beer and soft drinks must be returnable. *Prima facie*, this constituted a barrier because foreign manufacturers would not be geared up to selling drinks in such containers and would have to take special steps to do so to supply the Danish market. The Court recognised, citing the case of *Walter Rau* (above), that the rule constituted an obstacle to trade. Was it, however, a mandatory requirement? The Court accepted that protection of the environment is one of the Community's 'essential objectives', which may justify certain limitations to the principle of the free movement of goods (see, now, Art 2 EC Treaty, as amended by the ToA). Those limitations must not, however, 'go beyond the inevitable restrictions which are justified by the pursuit of the objective of environmental protection'. It was, therefore, necessary to examine whether all the restrictions which the contested rules imposed on the free movement of goods were necessary to achieve the objectives pursued by those rules.

The Court has shown a willingness to accept that restrictions aimed at protecting national, cultural and social values could also be mandatory requirements. In *Cinéthèque* (Cases 60 & 61/84), for example, the Court upheld a non-discriminatory French rule prohibiting the sale or hire of videos of films within a year of their first showing at a cinema. Although the rule had the effect of restricting the import of videos from other Member States, the Court held the restriction to be justified and not, therefore, in breach of Art 28. The Court accepted that the protection of the French cinema was a legitimate objective, presumably (although it was not stated) as a means of protecting national culture. The case can, perhaps, be compared to a case involving the free movement of workers, *Groener v Minister for Education* (Case 379/87), in which the Court accepted a requirement of a knowledge of Irish imposed on a Dutch teacher seeking employment in Ireland, although it was not needed for the subject she was to teach (see Chapter 12). The Court did so in recognition of the clear national policy of maintaining and promoting the language as a means of promoting national identity and culture.

The Court has also accepted as mandatory requirements national rules intended to protect the character of Sunday, and the limitation of workers' hours on that day, provided that national legislation did not go further than was necessary to achieve those legitimate aims. The Court laid down some general principles applicable to national restrictions on activities of this kind:

> It is therefore necessary in a case such as this to consider first of all whether the rules such as those at issue pursue an aim which is justified with regard to Community law. As far as that question is concerned, the Court has already stated in its judgment of 14 July 1981 in *Oebel* (Case 155/80) that national rules governing hours of work, delivery and sale in the bread and confectionery industry constitute a legitimate part of economic and social policy, consistent with the objectives of public interest pursued by the Treaty.
>
> The same consideration must apply as regards national rules governing the opening hours of retail premises. Such rules reflect certain political and economic choices in so far as their purpose is to ensure that working and non-working hours are so arranged as to accord with national or regional socio-cultural characteristics, and that, in the present state of Community law, is a matter for the Member States. Furthermore, such rules are not designed to govern the patterns of trade between Member States. (*Torfaen Borough Council v B & Q plc* (Case 145/88))

It should be noted, however, that *Cinéthèque* and *Torfaen Borough Council* have been overturned following the Court's judgment in *Keck* because they would be outside Art 28 *per se*, with no necessity to rely upon the defence of objective justification. However, this aspect of these two judgments is undoubtedly still good law.

OVERCOMING BARRIERS CREATED BY DIFFERING NATIONAL STANDARDS

The relationship between harmonising directives and Articles 28–30

Much of the jurisprudence of the Court of Justice relating to MEQRs concerns national measures enacted, ostensibly at least, for the protection of consumers or to promote other national concerns. It was apparent from the inception of the Community that such national provisions, including an enormously diverse range of standards, could be effectively tackled only by creating a Community-wide minimum standard binding on all Member States. In that way producers could have the advantage of large product runs, without having to go to the additional expense of having to tailor their products to the standards set in each Member State. Consumers could have a wider range of products at a lower cost. Article 94 was included in the Treaty specifically for this purpose. To facilitate the approximation of national legislation on a whole range of issues affecting the development of a common market, it enables the Commission, for example, on the advice of expert advisory committees, to draft directives on Community-wide standards on the safety of specific products, to be approved *unanimously* by the Council of Ministers.

Considerable difficulties were encountered in this harmonising process, not least because some Member States, not unnaturally, wished to ensure that their own high national standards were reflected in the Community standard. Member States were unwilling to accept a standard that represented the lowest common denominator. Procedures for agreeing common standards were time consuming and cumbersome, and since approval had to be unanimous, the opportunity for procrastination was great. The standards adopted were, in some cases, technically obsolete by the time they came into effect and the cost, in terms of lost intra-Community trade, was high.

Where, however, a common standard has been reached and the appropriate directive adopted, there is no further scope for national measures in the same field, and attempts to justify them either as mandatory requirements or under the specific exceptions in Art 30 will be rejected. In *Commission v Germany (Re Compound Feedingstuffs)* (Case 28/84), the Commission brought proceedings against the German Government because, the Commission contended, Council directives adopted in 1970, 1974 and 1979 constituted a complete and exhaustive set of rules covering the whole field of production and marketing of compound animal feedstuffs. The Court agreed and consequently held that German rules on the minimum and maximum levels of certain ingredients could not apply (see also *Société Civile Agricole v Coopérative d'Elevage du Departement de la Mayenne* (Case C-323/93)).

The new approach to harmonisation

The *Cassis de Dijon* case gave a new impetus to the harmonisation process. It led to a declaration by the Commission that it would concentrate on steps for the harmonisation of national laws which could still affect inter-state trade and which would have to be justified, in the absence of harmonisation, if at all, as mandatory requirements under the first *Cassis* principle or under one of the specific exceptions provided for in Art 30. It also led to a Council Resolution of 7 May 1985 on a new approach to technical harmonisation and standards. The resolution established four fundamental principles on which the new approach would be based:

1   Legislative harmonisation is limited to adoption, by means of directives based on Art 100 (now Art 94) EC Treaty, of the essential safety requirements (or other requirements in the general interest) with which products put on the market must conform, and which should therefore enjoy free movement throughout the Community.

2   The task of drawing up the technical specifications needed for the production and placing on the market of products conforming to the essential requirements

established by the directives, while taking into account the current stage of technology, is entrusted to organisations competent in the standardisation area.

3   These technical specifications are not mandatory and maintain their status of voluntary standards.

4   National authorities are obliged to recognise that products manufactured in conformity with harmonised standards (or, provisionally, with national standards) are presumed to conform to the 'essential requirements' established by the directive. (This signifies that the producer has the choice of not manufacturing in conformity with the standards, but that in this event he has an obligation to prove that his products conform to the essential requirements of the directive.)

In order that this system may operate it is necessary:

- on the one hand that the standards offer a guarantee of quality with regard to the 'essential requirements' established by the directives;
- on the other hand that the public authorities keep intact their responsibility for the protection of safety (or other requirements envisaged) on their territory.

There is a clear link between the resolution and the *Cassis de Dijon* principles, which is most apparent in the four fundamental principles, above. The new approach established a clear break with the past; instead of attempting to create a detailed technical specification for a 'Europroduct', which was a difficult and lengthy task, new directives would set only minimum safety and other standards (minimum requirements) which could be satisfied in a number of different ways in Member States, including different manufacturing methods. The emphasis was now on broad performance standards rather than compliance with detailed technical specifications. Once a Community directive is adopted under the new approach and after the implementation date in each Member State, performance is verified at Community level under a process monitored by the Commission. Where a directive has been adopted, Member States are obliged to assume that products purporting to conform to the essential requirements do, in fact, do so. Until new directives are adopted establishing Community-wide standards in other products, Member States should recognise (under the *Cassis* 'mutual recognition' principle) that those products meet appropriate essential requirements, unless there are indications that they do not.

Besides the adoption of a broader approach to essential requirements, agreement between Community institutions was further facilitated by the addition of Art 95 to the Treaty by the Single European Act 1986. Under Art 95, the Council now needs only to agree, on a *qualified majority* basis, 'codes of essential requirements' for broad, homogenous product areas or types of risk. This leaves manufacturers greater flexibility in meeting such requirements. Proof of conformity with essential requirements is satisfied by conformity with standards set by Europe-wide standards bodies, such as the European Committee for Standardisation (CEN) and the European Committee for Electrotechnical Standardisation (CENELEC). Products marked with the appropriate standards mark are presumed to conform. To satisfy those Member States who were concerned about the lowering of general product standards and the effect on specific products, in exceptional circumstances Member States may adopt higher standards than those laid down in the essential requirements. Under Art 95(4), (6) and (9) EC Treaty (as amended by the ToA):

> (4) If, after the adoption by the Council or by the Commission of a harmonisation measure a Member State deems it necessary to apply national provisions on grounds of major needs referred to in Article 30, or relating to protection of the environment or the working environment, it shall notify the Commission of these provisions as well as the grounds for maintaining them.
>
> ...
>
> (6) The Commission shall, within six months of the notification as referred to [above], approve or reject the national provisions involved after having verified whether or not they are a means of arbitrary discrimination or a disguised restriction on trade between Member States and whether or not they shall constitute an obstacle to the functioning of the internal market.
>
> ...
>
> (9) By way of derogation from the procedures laid down in Articles 226 and 227, the Commission or any Member State may bring the matter directly before the Court of Justice if it considers that another Member State is making improper use of the powers provided for in this Article.

Between 1984 and 1990 over 800 European product standards were adopted, which was three times as many as in the previous 20 years. Since 1986, when a target of more than 300 directives was set to lay the foundations for the Single Market on 1 January 1993, fewer than a dozen national provisions have been approved under the exception contained in Art 95. It remains, however, a valuable safety valve to deal with national concerns over specific products. More recently, directives have been adopted on cross-border credit transfers (Directive 97/9/EC) and the protection of consumers in distance contracts (Directive 97/7/EC). Overall, the new approach is widely regarded as having had considerable success in reducing national legal and technical barriers and in moving the Community towards a genuine Single Market.

Figure 18.1 relates to Art 28: quantitative restrictions and measures having an equivalent effect.

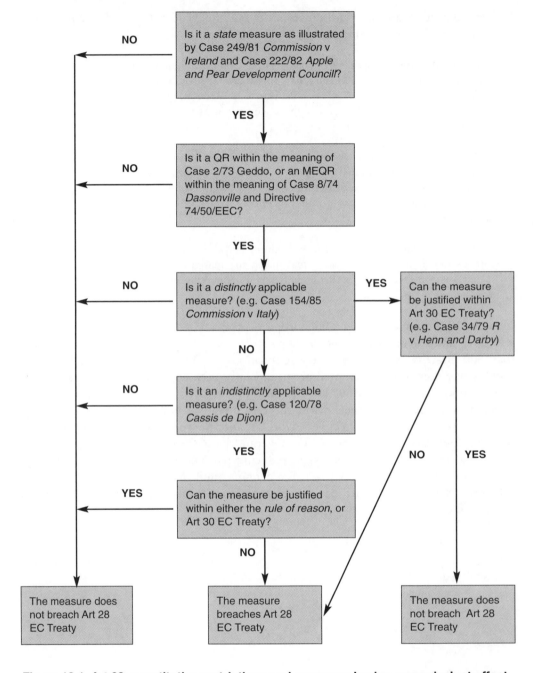

Figure 18.1 Art 28: quantitative restrictions and measures having an equivalent effect

Further reading

Alexander, W., 'IP and the Free Movement of Goods – 1996 Caselaw of the ECJ' (1998) 29 IIC 16.

Bentley, L. and Burrell, R., 'Copyright and the Information Society in Europe: A matter of timing as well as content' (1997) 34 CML Rev 1197.

Biondi A., 'The merchant, the thief and the citizen: The circulation of works of art within the European Union' (1997) 34 CML Rev 1173.

Burrows, N., 'Harmonisation of Technical Standards' (1990) 53 MLR 597.

Cecchini, P. (1988) *The European Challenge 1992, The Benefits of a Single Market*, European Commission.

Craig, P. and De Burca, G. (1998) *EU Law Text, Cases and Materials* (2nd edn), OUP, Chapter 14.

Ehlermann, C., 'The Internal Market Following the Single European Act' (1987) 24 CML Rev 361.

Green, N., Hartley, T.C. and Usher, J.A. (1991) *The Legal Foundations of the Single European Market*, Clarendon Press.

Hansen, H.C. (1996) *International Intellectual Property Law and Policy*, Sweet & Maxwell.

Kendall, V. (1995) *EC Consumer Law*, John Wiley and Sons.

McGee, A. and Weatherill, S., 'The Evolution of the Single Market – Harmonization or Liberalization?' (1990) 53 MLR 578.

Millet, T., 'Free Movement of Goods and Public Morality' (1987) NLJ 39.

Mortelmans, K., 'Article 30 of the EEC Treaty and Legislation Relating to Market Circumstances: Time to Consider a New Definition?' (1991) 28 CML Rev 115.

Oliver, P. (1996) *Free Movement of Goods in the European Community under Articles 30 to 36 of the Rome Treaty*, Sweet & Maxwell.

Phillips, J. and Firth, A. (1995) *Introduction to Intellectual Property Law*, Butterworths, Chapter 27.

Pinder, J. (1991) *European Community: The Building of a Union*, OUP, Chapter 4.

Reich, N., 'The November Revolution: *Keck, Meng, Audi* Revisited' (1994) 31 CML Rev 749.

Seville, C., 'Notes on Joined Cases C-427, 429 and 436/93 *Bristol-Myers Squibb and Others* v *Paranova A/S*' (1997) 34 CML Rev 1039.

Slot, P.J., 'Harmonisation' (1996) 21 EL Rev 378.

Steiner, J., 'Drawing the Line: Uses and Abuses of Article 30 EEC' (1992) 29 CML Rev 749.

Steiner, J. and Woods, L. (2000) *Textbook on EC Law* (7th edn), Blackstone Press, Chapters 10 and 11.

Tillotson, J. (2000) *European Community Law: Text, Cases and Materials* (3rd edn), Cavendish Publishing Ltd, Chapters 12 and 18.

Vicien, C.F., 'Why parallel imports of pharmaceutical products should be forbidden' (1996) 17 ECLR 219.

Weatherill, S., 'After *Keck*: Some thoughts on how to clarify the clarification' (1996) 33 CML Rev 885.

Weatherill, S. (2000) *Cases and Materials on EC Law* (5th edn), Blackstone Press, Chapters 7, 8 and 14.

Wils, W., 'The Search for the Rule in Art 30 EEC: Much Ado About Nothing?' (1993) 18 EL Rev 475.

Part IV

COMPETITION LAW

Chapter 19

STATE MONOPOLIES AND STATE AID

When the Community was formed, state ownership of major utilities played an important part in the economic and social policies of the founding states. It continues to do so, although state ownership is now less favoured, and subsidies and direct or indirect regulation of private undertakings providing important services have become more common. State intervention will continue to provide a safety net to industries in decline or facing sudden crises, and to support undertakings providing important public services. Although these activities by the state may well breach the Community's commitment to a Single Market, in which goods and services compete on an equal basis, the Community's own support for agriculture and agricultural products and its regional and social funds demonstrate an equal commitment to social, educational, health and cultural objectives supported by Community intervention. This support was continued and expanded both by the Treaty on European Union and the Treaty of Amsterdam (Arts 136–152 EC Treaty). The EC Treaty seeks to strike a balance between state intervention and the operation of the market. In Member States, the position of public ownership is, like private ownership, protected by Art 295 EC Treaty. The balance between public and private ownership is a matter for national policy, but state ownership is subject to similar constraints as private ownership. The title to that ownership is a matter of state policy, but the exercise of ownership rights, if it affects trade between Member States, is governed by the law of the Community. The Court of Justice has increasingly seen state intervention as a process that is, *prima facie*, likely to interfere with the creation and operation of a Single Market in the Community, and has shown a tendency to interpret provisions of Community law allowing state monopolies and subsidies in a restrictive manner, accepting only those seen as necessary to achieve certain clearly defined aims.

STATE MONOPOLIES

The position with regard to state monopolies is dealt with by Art 31 EC Treaty:

> Member States shall adjust any state monopolies of a commercial character so as to ensure that no discrimination regarding the conditions under which goods are procured and marketed exists between nationals of Member States.
>
> The provisions of this Article shall apply to any body through which a Member State, in law or in fact, either directly or indirectly supervises, determines or appreciably influences imports or exports between Member States. These provisions shall likewise apply to monopolies delegated by the state to others.

Article 31 must be read in conjunction with Art 86 EC Treaty. Article 31 is concerned with the procurement and marketing of goods while Art 86 is concerned with services. Article 86 provides:

1 In the case of public undertakings and undertakings to which Member States grant special or exclusive rights, Member States shall neither enact nor maintain in force any measure contrary to the rules contained in this Treaty, in particular to those rules provided for in Article 12 and Articles 81–89.

2 Undertakings entrusted with the operation of services of general economic interest or having the character of a revenue-producing monopoly shall be subject to the rules contained in this Treaty, in particular to the rules on competition, in so far as the application of such rules does not obstruct the performance, in law or in fact, of the particular tasks assigned to them. The development of trade must not be affected to such an extent as would be contrary to the interests of the Community.

Article 86(3) EC Treaty requires the Commission to enforce this Article by addressing, where necessary, appropriate directives or decisions to Member States.

The nature of 'state monopolies of a commercial character' referred to in Art 31 was considered by the Court of Justice in *Costa* v *ENEL* (Case 6/64). The case concerned the compatibility with Community law of the nationalisation of the Italian electricity industry:

One must consider … carefully paragraph (1) of Article 37 [now Art 31]. This prevents the creation not indeed of all national monopolies but only of those that present 'a commercial character' and even of these, insofar as they tend to introduce the discrimination aforesaid. It follows, therefore, that *to come within the terms of the prohibition of this Article, national monopolies and bodies must on the one hand have as objects transactions in commercial products capable of competition and exchanges between Member States; and on the other hand play a leading part in such exchanges.* (emphasis added)

Whether or not a state monopoly exists is a matter of law and fact. A claimant who proves the existence of a breach of Art 31 and loss caused by that breach may obtain an award in damages, since the provision is directly effective (*Hansen* v *Hauptzollamt Flensburg* (Case 91/78)).

The operation of a body enjoying a state monopoly may involve potential restrictions on the importation of goods into a Member State, thus breaching Art 28 EC Treaty, discrimination by such a body in relation to the provision of such goods and services, and the abuse of a monopoly position. An example of the interplay of these provisions was considered by the Court of Justice in *Société Civile Agricole de la Crespelle* v *Coopérative d'Elevage de la Mayenne* (Case C-323/93). In this case, under French law certain approved bovine insemination centres were granted exclusive rights within a defined area. Breeders established in those areas were, effectively, obliged to use their services. Such licensed centres enjoyed what the Court described as 'a contiguous series of monopolies territorially limited but together covering the entire territory of a Member State'.

The Court held, first, that the mere creation of such a dominant position by the granting of an exclusive right within the meaning of Art 86(1) EC Treaty was not as such incompatible with Art 82 EC Treaty (see Chapter 21). A Member State contravened the prohibitions contained in those two provisions only if, in merely exercising the exclusive right granted to it, the undertaking in question could not avoid abusing its dominant position. An undertaking abused its dominant position where it had an administrative monopoly and charged for its services fees which were disproportionate to the economic value of the services provided. Secondly, the Court held that national rules which required importers of bovine semen from a Member State to deliver it only to an approved insemination or production centre were in breach of Art 28 EC Treaty, but were in the circumstances saved by Art 30 EC Treaty as necessary for the protection of animal health (see Chapter 18). Although the point was not specifically dealt with in this case, the Court has held that an exclusive right, *inter alia*, to import particular goods falls within the scope of Art 31 (*Manghera* (Case 59/75)).

In *Hansen* v *Hauptzollamt Flensburg* (Case 91/78), the Court had to consider the extent to which the German state alcohol monopoly was compatible with Art 31. It held, first, that after the end of the transitional period, Art 31 remained applicable wherever the exercise by a state monopoly of its exclusive rights entailed a discrimination or restriction prohibited by that article. Secondly, that Art 31 prohibited a monopoly's right to purchase and resell national alcohol from being exercised so as to undercut imported products with publicly subsidised domestic products. Whilst Art 86(2) recognises that publicly owned undertakings can carry on revenue-producing economic activities, it specifically prohibits their operation in a way which would constitute an abuse of a monopoly position or which would distort the operation of the market. However, the public body is allowed to derogate from these rules, insofar as it is actually necessary to carry out the tasks assigned to it. The Court of First Instance has considered the position of the French Post Office in *FFSA and Others* v *Commission* (Case T-106/96). The 'task', in this case, was the maintenance of uneconomic postal services in rural areas. A body of insurers had unsuccessfully complained to the European Commission that the French Post Office was being unlawfully subsidised, contrary to Art 87(1). The CFI upheld the Commission's decision. Following the decision of the Court of Justice in *Corbeau* (Case 320/91), the Court held that the postal monopoly was necessary to enable the Post Office to subsidise the regional development of the postal service. It was only lawful, however, if 'the *sole* purpose of the aid was to offset the additional costs incurred' and 'the grant of the aid is necessary for the undertaking to perform its public service obligations under conditions of economic equilibrium' (emphasis added).

State undertakings and the need for transparency

Where an undertaking is state-owned, or directly or indirectly controlled by the state, it is subject to the provisions of Directive 80/723. This directive (the 'transparency Directive') was made under Art 86(3) EC Treaty and requires that financial relations between public authorities and public undertakings are transparent. 'Transparency' in this context means transparency to the Commission: Art 5, Directive 80/723. The particular matters requiring disclosure are the amount of public funds made available directly by public authorities to the public undertakings concerned, or through intermediaries, and the uses to which such public funds are put (Art 1, Directive 80/723). The extent and nature of such support may well be of concern to the Commission in determining whether or not unlawful state aids have been provided.

Directive 80/723 will be amended by Directive 2000/52, the substance of which has an implementation date of 31 July 2001. The aim of the amending directive is to achieve the basic objective of transparency by laying down rules requiring specified undertakings to maintain separate accounts relating to the different activities which they carry on. This is considered to be 'the most efficient means by which fair and effective application of the rules on competition to [public and private undertakings granted special or exclusive rights or entrusted with the operation of services of general economic interest ...] can be assured' (Preamble). The obligation of separate accounts will not apply to undertakings whose activities are limited to the provision of services of general economic interest and which do not operate activities outside the scope of these services of general economic interest.

STATE AIDS

There is no absolute prohibition of state aids in the Treaty. Rather, the prohibitions are directed against the use of state aids in ways that are not 'compatible with the common market'.

Article 87(1) EC Treaty provides:

> Save as otherwise provided in this Treaty, any aid granted by a Member State or through state resources in any form whatsoever which distorts or threatens to distort competition by favouring certain undertakings or the production of certain goods shall, in so far as it affects trade between Member States, be incompatible with the common market.

Article 87(1) is not concerned with how state aid is given. It is rather directed at aid given by the state or derived from state resources, which either distorts or may distort competition by favouring undertakings and affects trade between Member States. 'Aid' is a wide concept including, but not confined to, state subsidies:

> The concept of an aid is ... wider than that of a subsidy because it embraces not only positive benefits, such as subsidies themselves, but also interventions which, in various forms, mitigate the charges which are normally included in the budget of an undertaking and which would without, therefore, being subsidies in the strict sense of the word, be similar in character and have the same effect. (*Steenkolenmijnen* v *HA* (Case 30/59))

Aid may come in a large number of different guises and has been held to include: exemption from duties and taxes; exemption from parafiscal charges; preferential interest rates; guarantees of loans on especially favourable terms; making land or buildings available either for nothing or on especially favourable terms; provision of goods, services or personnel on preferential terms; indemnities against operating losses; and the purchase of shares of a company in financial difficulties (*Intermills* v *Commission* (Case 323/82); *Spain* v *Commission* (Joined Cases C-278–280/92); *Commission* v *Sytraval* (Case C-347/95)).

Despite the wide definition of aid favoured by the Commission, the Court has tended to insist that if it is to be regarded as 'aid' it must constitute a government measure 'involving a charge on the public account' of the state concerned (*Sloman Neptun* (Case C-72/91); *Kirsammer Hack* (Case C-189/91)). This was not, however, the view of the Advocates-General in both cases. Both decisions have been the subject of criticism for allowing too much scope for states to give unfair competitive advantages to undertakings in their territories by such devices as relaxing environmental and planning controls, or by making various beneficial administrative concessions (Slotboom, 1995).

Some types of aid are, *per se*, deemed to be compatible under Art 87(1):

The following shall be compatible with the common market:

(a) aid having a social character, granted to individual consumers, provided that such aid is granted without discrimination related to the origin of the products concerned;

(b) aid to make good the damage caused by natural disasters or exceptional occurrences;

(c) aid granted to the economy of certain areas of the Federal Republic of Germany affected by the division of Germany, in so far as such aid is required in order to compensate for the economic disadvantages caused by that division.

An example of aid of the kind referred to in (a) would be sales of basic food products such as bread, pasta and butter at a low, fixed price. In these cases the wholesaler might be compensated by the state for the loss of his profit. The proviso would, however, require that such support would be equally available to imported and home-produced products. The aid referred to in (b) is self-explanatory, and the aid to which Germany was entitled under (c) is now seen by the Commission as no longer necessary. However, it could be argued that the very considerable difficulties suffered by the Eastern territories of the Federal Republic on reunification were consequent upon the original division, and justified state subsidies to the Eastern industries to bring them up to Western standards, provided that the aid given is no more than is necessary to achieve that purpose.

Other types of aid are seen as potentially justifiable. Under Art 87(3), there are five categories of aid. Before a Member State commences or alters any of the aid projects falling within categories 1 to 5 below, it must notify the Commission in sufficient time to enable the Commission to comment. The Commission has the power to block the project or require its amendment (Art 88(2), (3)).

The categories are:

1 aid to promote the economic development of areas where the standard of living is abnormally low or where there is serious underemployment;

2 aid to promote the execution of an important project of common European interest or to remedy a serious disturbance in the economy of a Member State;

3 aid to facilitate the development of certain economic activities or of certain economic areas, where such aid does not adversely affect trading conditions to an extent contrary to the common interest;

4 aid to promote culture and heritage conservation, where such aid does not affect trading conditions and competition in the Community to an extent that is contrary to the common interest;

5 such other categories of aid as may be specified by decisions of the Council acting by a qualified majority on a proposal from the Commission.

1 The promotion of economic development of areas of low income or high underemployment (Art 87(3)(a))

In *Philip Morris* v *Commission* (Case 730/79) the Commission's criteria to determine whether or not an aid scheme should be approved received the support of the Court of Justice. First, the aid must promote or further a project that is in the Community interest as a whole. Aid which therefore promotes a national interest is unacceptable. Secondly, the aid must be necessary for promoting the first objective, and thirdly, the way in which the aid is provided must be proportional to the legitimate object, and must not be likely to affect trade between Member States and distort competition.

In the *Morris* case, the Netherlands Government proposed to grant the applicant capital assistance to enable it to increase cigarette production so that it would account for nearly 50 per cent of cigarette production in The Netherlands. Eighty per cent of that production would be exported to other Member States. There was the possibility that aid could have an effect, therefore, on trade between Member States. Philip Morris argued that Art 87(3) only required that the investment plan be compatible with the objectives set out in paragraphs (a), (b) and (c). It did not have to be shown that the aid would contribute to the attainment of one of those legitimate objectives. The development of cigarette manufacture was to take place in Bergen-op-Zoom, where underemployment was high and the per capita income was lower than the national average in the rest of The Netherlands. The company maintained that the Commission had been wrong to compare unemployment and income not with that prevailing elsewhere in The Netherlands but with that elsewhere in the Community.

The Court rejected the argument that trade with other Member States was not likely to be distorted:

> When State financial aid strengthens the position of an undertaking compared with other undertakings competing in intra-Community trade, the latter must be regarded as affected by that aid. In this case the aid which the Netherlands government proposed to grant was for an undertaking organised for international trade and this is proved by the high percentage of its production which it intends to export to other Member States. The aid in question was to help enlarge its production capacity and consequently to increase its capacity to maintain the flow of trade including that between Member States. On the other hand the aid is said to have reduced the cost of converting the production facilities and has thereby given the applicant a competitive advantage over manufacturers who have completed or intend to complete at their own expense a similar increase in the productive capacity of their plant.

The Court also refused to accept the company's argument that it was legitimate to look at unemployment and income levels only in The Netherlands, and that the Commission had been wrong to take a broader view of all the circumstances:

> These arguments put forward by the applicant cannot be upheld. It should be borne in mind that the Commission has a discretion the exercise of which involves economic and social assessments which must be made in a Community context. That is the context in which the Commission has with good reason assessed the standard of living and serious underemployment in the Bergen-op-Zoom area, not with reference to the national average in the Netherlands but in relation to the Community level ... The Commission could very well take the view, as it did, that the investment to be effected in this case was not 'an important project of Common European interest' ... since the proposed aid would have permitted the transfer to the Netherlands of an investment which could be effected in other Member States in a less favourable economic situation than that of the Netherlands, where the national level of unemployment is one of the lowest in the Community.

Although the Court has held that decisions of this kind involve the making of complicated economic assessments with which the Court will not readily interfere, when the Commission purports to be acting according to a stated economic policy, its decisions must be compatible with that policy (*Spain* v *Commission* (above)).

The Commission has issued guidelines on national regional aid (OJ 1998 C 74/9) outlining the circumstances in which aid will be considered to be in the interest of the Community. These guidelines do not have legal force, but they will undoubtedly be taken into account by the Court of Justice.

2 The promotion of the execution of a project of common European interest or to remedy a serious economic disturbance (Art 87(3)(b))

The sort of projects which have been approved by the Commission under this head are mostly ones in which there is cross-Community cooperation in some technological or environmental project. In this connection the Court stated in *Exécutif Régional Wallon and Glaverbel* v *Commission* (Case 62/87) that there will be no common European interest in a scheme 'unless it forms part of a transnational European programme supported jointly by a number of governments of the Member States, or arises from concerted action by a number of Member States to combat a common threat such as environmental pollution'. As a result, the Court found that a scheme under which modernisation aid was granted to Glaverbel, who were manufacturers of glass in Belgium, was not an important project of European interest, since it was not part of a transnational programme.

3 Aid to facilitate the development of certain economic activities or certain economic areas (Art 87(3)(c))

In its *First Report on State Aids* in the European Community published in 1989, the Commission reported a very large increase in the preceding 10 years of cases notified and investigated under Art 92 (now Art 87). A survey in the report indicated that over 108 billion Ecus were given in aid each year over that period, the majority of which went to manufacturing companies under the former Art 92(3)(c). In its *18th Report on Competition Policy*, published the same year, the Commission described its approach to applications made by Member States for approval of state aids in relation to the regional aspect of Art 92(3)(c) (now Art 87(3)(c)):

> Regions falling under Art 92(3) [now Art 87(3)(c)] are those with more general development problems in relation to the national as well as the Community situation. Often they suffer from the decline of traditional industries and are frequently located in the more central prosperous parts of the Community. In its Art 92(3)(c) method, the Commission has established a system which takes account of national regional problems and places them into a Community context.

The Commission has, in the context of Art 87(3)(c), operated on the basis of two primary indicators. The first is income (as measured by gross domestic product or gross value added) and the second is structural unemployment. In this context (unlike that with regard to the criteria applicable to Art 87(3)(a), above), the assessment of conditions is made in the national and the Community context. The better the position of the Member State in which the region is located in relation to the Community as a whole, the wider must be the disparity between the region concerned and the state as a whole, to justify the aid. Broadly, regions wanting to receive aid must, in relative terms, be worse off than regions in poorer Member States before aid is approved by the Commission. In addition, for approval of the Commission to be secured, any aid proposal must be linked to a major restructuring of the sector of the industry concerned. It should not be used either simply to 'prop up' an ailing concern, or to allow an undertaking to gain an unfair competitive advantage (*Spain* v *Commission* (Case C-42/93)). In 1998, the Commission approved a research and development grant to Rolls-Royce by the British Government to develop a new generation of aero engines in Derby. The grant was authorised under Art 87(3)(c) and what is now Art 158 (reduction of disparities between different regions); but it also took account of the need to enable the Community to compete in the worldwide aviation market (*Competition Policy Newsletter* (1998) No. 2, p. 85).

4 The promotion of heritage conservation (Art 87(3)(d))

This provision was added by the Treaty on European Union, and must be read in the light of Art 151(2) EC Treaty. This provides that:

> Action by the Community shall be aimed at encouraging cooperation between Member States and, if necessary, supporting and supplementing their action in ... conservation and safeguarding of cultural heritage of European significance.

Heritage conservation is closely linked to the promotion of tourism, the right of access to which is a primary service under Art 49 (*Luisi and Carbone* (Case 286/82); see Chapter 13), and to the obligation, in Title XII of the EC Treaty, of the Community to contribute to 'the flowering of the cultures of the Member States'. The Treaty of Amsterdam added the obligation of the Community 'to respect and promote the cultural diversity' of its members (Art 151(4) EC Treaty). This addition is intended to provide specific authorisation for the kind of aid approved by the Commission in the past to sustain the Greek film industry (Decision 89/441, OJ 1989 L 208/3).

5 Specific state aids approved by the Council (Art 87(3)(e))

A number of directives have been made under Art 87(3)(e), including Directive 90/684 on state aid to shipbuilding. Under the directive, state aid could be deemed to be compatible with the common market if it related to shipbuilding and ship conversion granted as development assistance to a developing country. The Commission had to verify the development content of the proposal in accordance with criteria laid down by an OECD Working Party. In October 1991 the German Government notified the Commission of its intention to grant aid to mainland China in the form of aid credit for three container vessels to be operated by a state-owned Chinese trading company, Cosco. The Commission informed the Federal Republic that the proposed aid could not be regarded as 'genuine development aid ... and is therefore incompatible with the common market'. It declared that it was not satisfied that the aid was any more than 'an operating aid to the German shipyards ... rather than a genuine aid to a developing country'. This decision was challenged by the German Government in an action to annul the decision under Art 173 (now Art 230) EC Treaty.

The Court of Justice upheld the Commission's decision. The directive conferred a discretion on the Commission which was required to satisfy itself that the aid complied with the OECD criteria. It also had to verify the particular development content of the project. It decided that Cosco was not a company that needed development aid in order to contribute to the general development of China. It was entitled to come to that decision and was well within its discretion to do so.

Block exemptions

Under Art 89 EC Treaty the Council, acting by a qualified majority and having consulted with the European Parliament, can adopt regulations proposed by the Commission concerning the application of Arts 87 and 88. Pursuant to Art 89, during 1998 the Council adopted Regulation 994/98, the purpose of which is to facilitate the operation of the state aid system. It provides for a block exemption system to be used for certain categories of aid. Pursuant to this regulation, the Commission has proposed three regulations for block exemptions as follows:

- state aid to small- and medium-sized undertakings (defined as those which: (1) employ fewer than 250 employees; (2) have an annual turnover not exceeding 40 million ECU *or* an annual balance sheet total not exceeding 27 million ECU; and (3) conform with the regulation's independence criteria);
- state aid of small amounts (*de minimis*), defined as not exceeding 100,000 ECU over a period of three years; and
- state aid to finance certain training activities.

THE COMMISSION'S ROLE OF MONITORING THE GRANT OF STATE AID

The Commission has a general obligation to keep all systems of state aid under review, both those which are, *prima facie*, lawful under Art 87(2) and those which have been approved under the Commission's discretionary powers under Art 87(3), to ensure that both continue to be operated in a way that is compatible with the Single Market. It is the Commission which has to decide whether any kind of state aid is compatible with Community law, except for those types of aid which have been given specific clearance by the Council under Art 87(3)(e).

To enable it to assess whether or not any new aid scheme is permitted under Art 87, there is a clearance procedure which must be followed by Member States. Under Art 88(3):

> The Commission shall be informed, in sufficient time to enable it to submit its comments, of any plans to grant or alter aid. If it considers that any such plan is not compatible with the common market having regard to Article 87, it shall without delay initiate the procedure provided for in paragraph 2. The Member State concerned shall not put its proposed measures into effect until this procedure has resulted in a final decision.

The Commission is required to decide quite quickly if a proposed measure is justified under Art 87. In *Germany* v *Commission* (Case 84/82), the Court declared that two months should suffice for this purpose. If at the end of that time the Commission has not defined its attitude towards the proposal, the Member State that has made the proposal could go ahead with it, but should notify the Commission of its intention to do so.

If the Commission decides that the proposed state aid is incompatible with the Treaty, or if aid which has previously been approved by it is being misused, it can inform the state concerned that the aid scheme should be abolished or altered within a timescale fixed by the Commission, and that the aid, together with interest, should be recovered by the state (*Commission v Italy* (Case C-348/93)). Failure to comply can result in that state being brought before the Court of Justice (Art 88(2)). Although it is not specifically provided for in Art 87, the Court has accepted that any aid which has been unlawfully paid may also be recovered by the Commission (*Commission v Germany* (Case 70/72)). Even though the aid may have been accepted by an undertaking in good faith, without any reason to believe that it had been paid in breach of Community law, that innocent receipt cannot found a legitimate expectation that the aid may be retained. The effect of doing so could be fatal to the effective operation of Arts 87 and 88:

> A Member State whose authorities have granted aid contrary to the procedural rules laid down in Article 93 [now Art 88] may not rely on the legitimate expectations of recipients in order to justify a failure to comply with the obligation to take the steps necessary to implement a Commission decision instructing it to recover the aid. If it could do so, Articles 92 and 93 [now Arts 87 and 88] of the Treaty would be set at naught, since national authorities would thus be able to rely on their own unlawful conduct in order to deprive decisions taken by the Commission under provisions of the Treaty of their effectiveness. (*Commission v Germany* (Case C-5/89))

The Court of Justice, in *Land Rheinland-Pfalz v Alcan Deutschland GmbH* (Case C-24/95) also made it clear that repayment had to be made even if it would be unlawful under state time-limit rules.

It is not only the Commission which will have an interest in the payment of state aids. Rival companies may also feel threatened by the actual or proposed distribution of state support and may wish to challenge a decision of the Commission approving it. In *ASPEC and AAC v Commission* (Case T-435/93), aid had been approved by the Commission under Arts 87 and 88 in relation to the production of starch in the Mezzogiorno region of Italy, which would have had the consequence of increasing production by some 7 per cent at Community level and of establishing a production level in Italy alone which would have exceeded the previous total production capacity of that country. The challengers would have been seriously affected by the decision and the Court recognised that they had a sufficient interest to mount a challenge under Art 173 (now Art 230) (see Chapter 8). Although the Court has held that the Commission enjoys a wide discretion in granting approval, its reasoning must be consistent with its declared policy, and it must adopt proper procedures in adopting its decision (see *Spain v Commission* (above)). In this case, the decision had never actually been taken by the full Commission but, in breach of its own procedures, had been delegated to Ray MacSharry, the then Agriculture Commissioner, on the eve of the Commission's annual holiday. The decision to approve the aid was, accordingly, annulled by the Court.

Lastly, it should be noted that damages can be awarded against the government of a Member State that has granted competition-distorting state aids without having notified these to the Commission for review (*Fédération National du Commerce* v *France* (Case 354/90)).

Regulation 659/1999

Regulation 659/1999 was adopted by the Council on 22 March 1999 and lays down detailed rules for the application of Art 88 EC Treaty. The aim of the regulation is to improve transparency and legal certainty by codifying and clarifying in a single text the procedural rules relating to state aid. This regulation will therefore take the place of the procedural matters discussed above, but, as stated, its purpose is to codify and clarify these matters rather than to replace them. The regulation sets out procedures regarding the following:

- notified aid
- unlawful aid
- misuse of aid
- existing aid schemes.

It also sets out the rights of interested parties and codifies monitoring mechanisms through a system of annual reports and on-site monitoring.

Further reading

Craig, P. and De Burca, G. (1998) *EU Law Text, Cases and Materials* (2nd edn), OUP, Chapter 25.

Evans, A., 'Privatisation and State Aid Control under EC Law' (1997) 18 ECLR 259.

Evans, A. (1997) *EC Law of State Aid*, Clarendon Press.

Evans, A. and Martin, M., 'Socially Acceptable Distortions of Competition: Community Policy on State Aid' (1991) 16 EL Rev 79.

Frazer, T., 'The New Structural Funds, State Aids and Interventions in the Single European Market' (1995) 32 CML Rev 3.

Green, N., Hartley, T.C. and Usher, J.A. (1991) *The Legal Foundations of the Single European Market*, OUP, Chapter 21.

Hancher, L., Ottervanger, T. and Slot, P.J. (1993) *EC State Aids*, Chancery.

Ross, M., 'Challenging State aids – the effect of recent developments' (1986) 23 CML Rev 867.

Schütte, M. and Hix, J.P., 'The application of the EC State aid rule to privatisations: the East German example' (1995) 32 CML Rev 215.

Slotboom, M., 'State Aids in Community Law: A Broad or a Narrow Definition?' (1995) 20 EL Rev 289.

Steiner, J. and Woods, L. (2000) *Textbook on EC Law* (7th edn), Blackstone Press, Chapters 12 and 13.

Stuart, E.G., 'Recent developments in EU Law and Policy on State Aids' (1996) 17 ECLR 226.

Chapter 20

CARTELS AND RESTRICTIVE AGREEMENTS

ARTICLE 81 EC TREATY
(FORMERLY ARTICLE 85)

COMPETITION LAW AND POLICY

In its *First Report on Competition Policy* the Commission emphasised the value of effective competition in the Community. Competition is the best stimulant of economic activity, since it guarantees the widest possible freedom of action to all. An active competition policy, pursued in accordance with the provisions of the Treaties establishing the Communities, makes it easier for the supply and demand structures continually to adjust to technological development. Through the interplay of decentralised decision-making machinery, competition enables enterprises continuously to improve their efficiency, which is essential for the steady improvement of living standards and employment prospects within the countries of the Community. From this point of view, competition policy is an essential means for satisfying to a great extent the individual and collective needs of our society.

Competition is not, however, regarded as an end in itself. It is one of the most important means by which a genuinely integrated market is achieved. Articles 81 and 82 EC Treaty match Arts 28 and 29 EC Treaty, in the sense that the latter are aimed at measures taken by Member State governments which have the effect of restricting the free movement of goods (see Chapter 18), while the former are concerned with restrictive and abusive practices by undertakings which have the effect of excluding or restricting goods or services from Member States. The distinction between state and private undertaking in this context is not, of course, absolute. States may run commercial monopolies and private undertakings, and may secure an unfair competitive advantage by injections of state capital and other state aids. Both practices are subject to restriction under the Treaty and have been examined in Chapter 19. Major sectors of the West European economy are dominated by large private business corporations, some of which have a bigger annual turnover than the gross domestic product of many small states. Abusive practices by such businesses may have more impact on cross-border trade than the actions of smaller Member State governments. Paradoxically, to create a genuinely free and competitive market, some restrictions are essential to ensure that the largest actors in the market place do not distort the working of the market to their own advantage and to the disadvantage of competitors and consumers.

The primary objective, therefore, of European competition policy has been market integration. A secondary one has been a form of equity or equality of competition, an aspect of 'the level playing field' to which many businesses aspire in the Community. The third aspect of competition policy is that espoused by the Commission in its First Report – the promotion of efficiency. Increasingly, this is viewed in the wider trading context of North and South America and the Pacific rim.

Competition law, more than any other area of Community law, is informed by economic factors. Conduct which may be lawful in one context, may be unlawful in another. The behaviour of business actors will have to be assessed in the light of prevailing economic circumstances, and the way in which particular markets may react. The pricing policy of a company which has a monopoly will be a subject of acute interest to consumers, whereas overpricing by a company in a highly competitive market will rapidly be corrected by the effect on that company of consumers taking their custom elsewhere. The behaviour of business undertakings in relation to competition law and policy must always, therefore, be viewed in the context of such matters as degrees of concentration and the relevance of market power, the importance of entry barriers and actual and potential competition.

Community competition policy, taking the objectives discussed above into account, is directed towards three kinds of anti-competitive activity:

1   Restricting trading agreements between otherwise independent business undertakings which may affect trade between Member States and which distort competition within the common market (Art 81 EC Treaty).
2   Abusive, anti-competitive practices of large undertakings which dominate markets for goods or services which affect trade between Member States (Art 82 EC Treaty).
3   Major mergers of undertakings resulting in positions of market dominance in the Community (Regulation 4064/89, as corrected by Corrigendum to OJ 1990 L 395/1 and amended by OJ 1994 C 241/57; Decision 95/1 (OJ 1995 L 1/1); and Regulation 1310/97 (OJ 1997 L 180/1)).

Each of these kinds of anti-competitive practice is subject to regulation and control by the Commission, and the national competition authorities and courts of the Member States. The powers of the Commission, and the national competition authorities and courts of the Member States, and the way in which these powers are interpreted and applied, will be examined in Chapter 22. The primary law on which the regulation of anti-competitive practices is based will be considered within this chapter and the next.

Over the past few years there have been major changes to the regulation and control of these anti-competitive practices. These changes have been implemented primarily through secondary Community instruments. In addition, in some instances, the Commission has issued guidelines on the application of the anti-competitive measures. The aim of these guidelines is to assist industry in making the regulation and control processes more transparent. These changes will be discussed throughout this and the next two chapters, where relevant.

The Commission's Competition website contains current primary and secondary legislation, together with proposals for the future. It also includes the full texts of non-binding guidelines. See: europa.eu.int/comm/competition/index_en.html.

ARTICLE 81

Article 81 EC Treaty is directed against cooperation between companies that operate in an anti-competitive way. Article 81(1) prohibits

> all agreements between undertakings, decisions by associations of undertakings and concerted practices which may affect trade between Member States and which have as their object or effect the prevention, restriction or distortion of competition within the common market.

A number of examples of the type of agreements covered by Art 81(1) are provided in Art 81(1)(a)–(e), i.e. those which:

1 directly or indirectly fix purchase or selling prices or any other trading conditions (Art 81(1)(a));
2 limit or control production, markets, technical development, or investment (Art 81(1)(b));
3 share markets or sources of supply (Art 81(1)(c));
4 apply dissimilar conditions to equivalent transactions with other trading parties, thereby placing them at a competitive disadvantage (Art 81(1)(d));
5 make the conclusion of contracts subject to acceptance by the other parties of supplementary obligations which, by their nature or according to commercial use, have no connection with the subject of such contracts (Art 81(1)(e)).

Article 81(2) provides that any agreement or decision prohibited by Art 81(1) shall be automatically void. Although the list in Art 81(1) is not exhaustive, it is indicative of the kind of practices which will breach the prohibition. It is primarily aimed at 'horizontal' cooperation between nominally competing companies – the classic cartel – but it is also designed to deal with restrictive agreements between manufacturers, wholesalers and retailers – i.e. 'vertical agreements' – which also affect the availability of goods and services and the terms on which they are supplied. The Commission remains free to identify other agreements or practices which are operated in an anti-competitive way. There are, in addition, a number of agreements, decisions and practices which may be declared not to breach the prohibition in Art 81(1). These are listed in Art 81(3):

> The provisions of paragraph 1 may, however, be declared inapplicable in the case of:
>
> – any agreement or category of agreements between undertakings;
> – any decision or category of decisions by associations of undertakings;
> – any concerted practice or category of concerted practices
>
> which contributes to improving the production or distribution of goods or to promoting technical or economic progress, while allowing consumers a fair share of the resulting benefit, and which does not:
>
> (a) impose on the undertakings concerned restrictions which are not indispensable to the attainment of these objectives;

(b) afford such undertakings the possibility of eliminating competition in respect of a substantial part of the products in question.

Undertakings

The term 'undertaking' includes every kind of natural or legal person engaged in economic or commercial activity; it must be established in order to make a profit. The Court has often had to consider the nature of 'undertakings' to which Arts 81 and 82 are applicable. In *Poucet* v *Assurances Générales de France* (Case C-159/91) the Court decided that regional social security organisations were not 'undertakings'. Complaints had been made alleging anti-competitive restrictions on market access for 'consumers' of social insurance 'services'. The Court distinguished between bodies pursuing economic activities as such and those activities which are based upon a principle of solidarity and which are pursued entirely without intention to make a profit. In *SAT* v *Eurocontrol* (Case C-364/92) the Court concluded that Eurocontrol, a body set up by treaty to recover fees payable by airlines for traffic control services, was not an 'undertaking'. It undertook the tasks assigned to it in the public interest with a view to assuring the maintenance and improvement of air transport. There was not a sufficient economic element in the work of Eurocontrol, which could not be held responsible for the amounts which it collected. The fees payable had been established by the states which were parties to the treaty by which it was established. Similarly, in *Diego Cali* v *SEPG* (Case C-343/95), the Court held that a body established under national law to collect harbour dues in the port of Genoa (intended to cover the cost of anti-pollution measures) was not an 'undertaking' within the meaning of Arts 81 and 82. The body performed 'a task in the public interest which forms part of the essential functions of the states as regards protection of the environment in maritime areas'. However, the fact that a body is state-owned or state-financed and provides a service usually provided by the state does not prevent it from being an 'undertaking' within Arts 81 and 82 if it is providing services 'of general economic interest' (*Job Centre Coop* (Case C-55/96)).

Agreement

Article 81 is applicable only if there is an 'agreement', a 'decision by an association of undertakings' or a 'concerted practice'. Agreements are not confined to binding contracts of whatever kind, but include understandings and 'gentlemen's agreements' (*ACF Chemiefarma* v *Commission* (Case 41/69)). The type of loose arrangement that may fall foul of Art 81(1) is demonstrated by the facts of *BMW Belgium* v *Commission* (Case 32/78). In this case an attempt was made by BMW's subsidiary in Belgium to discourage car dealers there from selling the cars to other Member States. BMW dealers in Belgium had received a circular from BMW Belgium urging them not to engage in such sales. They were asked to indicate assent to this policy by signing and returning a copy of the circular. It was made clear that this was not a contractual document, but the Court nonetheless held that it was an 'agreement' under Art 81(1). In *Tréfilenrope SARL* v *Commission* (Case T-148/89) the Court of First Instance declared that:

For there to be an agreement within the meaning of Article 85(1) [now Art 81(1)] of the

Treaty, it is sufficient for the undertakings in question to have expressed their joint intention to conduct themselves in the market in a particular way.

The 'agreement' does not have to be voluntary. In the *Volkswagen* case (*The Community v Volkswagen AG and Others* (Case IV/35.733)), the Commission concluded that there existed an 'agreement' between Volkswagen and its dealers in Italy where they complied with instructions (reinforced by heavy pressure from Volkswagen) not to sell to purchasers from outside Italy.

A decision by an association of undertakings

The commonest kind of decision at which Art 81(1) is aimed is that of a trade association which lays down standards for the activities of its members. Standardisation of pricing or the way in which a service may be supplied may well fall foul of the provisions of Art 81. Even an agreement to supply information about sales by competitors, although it is concerned with neither prices nor any anti-competitive arrangement, has been held to fall within Art 81, since it could enable the dominant suppliers to adopt strategies to resist market penetration by those competitors (*Fiatagri UK Ltd* v *Commission* (Case T-34/92)). The body concerned does not, however, have to be engaged in commercial activity itself. In *NV IAZ International Belgium and Others* v *Commission* (Case 96/82) two Belgian Royal Decrees provided that washing machines and dishwashers could be connected to the main water supply only if they satisfied Belgian standards. For the purpose of monitoring the conformity of washing machines or dishwashers with those Belgian standards, the manufacturers and sole importers of electrical appliances affiliated to certain trade organisations made an agreement with the national association of water suppliers (the 'ANSEAU-NAVEWA' agreement). Under this agreement, all appliances put into commercial distribution had to bear a label issued by a designated trade organisation. The Commission made a decision that certain provisions of the agreement infringed Art 81(1). In its view, the offending provisions excluded the possibility for importers other than the sole importers to obtain a conformity check for the washing machines and dishwashers which they imported into Belgium under conditions which did not discriminate against them. ANSEAU attempted to argue that the agreement did not fall within Art 81(1) as its member undertakings were not legally bound by the agreement and since ANSEAU did not itself carry on any kind of economic activity. The Court rejected both arguments:

> Article [81(1)] of the Treaty also applies to associations of undertakings in so far as their own activities or those of the undertakings affiliated to them are calculated to produce the results which it aims to suppress ... A recommendation, even if it has no binding effect, cannot escape Article [81(1)] where compliance with the recommendation by the undertakings to which it is addressed has an appreciable influence in the market in question.

However, the Court recognised a limit to the application of Art 81 where the nominees of trade organisations concerned with the fixing of prices were genuinely independent of their parent bodies. In *Germany* v *Delta Schiffahrts und Speditionsgesellschaft GmbH* (Case C-153/93) representatives of shippers and inland waterway ship operators were both represented on freight commissions which fixed inland waterway freight charges. The decisions of these commissions on relevant charges were approved by the Federal

Minister of Transport and were then compulsory. These charges were challenged by a shipper as contrary to Art 81 and the question was referred to the Court under Art 234 EC Treaty. The Court held that Art 81 did not preclude rules of a Member State from providing that tariffs for commercial inland waterways traffic might be fixed by the freight commissions comprised of individuals recommended by the businesses concerned, provided that they were genuinely independent of those businesses and provided that the public authority retained a power to override their decisions.

Concerted practice

This term means some kind of coordinated action which, although it may fall short of an agreement, knowingly substitutes practical cooperation for competition (*ICI* v *Commission* (Case 48/69)). In the *ICI* case, ICI was among a number of businesses producing aniline dyestuffs in Italy. It was the first to impose a price increase, but was shortly followed by other producers of similar products, accounting for more than 80 per cent of the market. A similar pattern of price increases had taken place among the 10 major producers of aniline dyestuffs who dominated the dyestuffs market in the Community. The Commission concluded from the circumstances that there had been a 'concerted practice' between the undertakings, and imposed fines on them. The undertakings challenged the Commission's decision, arguing that the price increases merely reflected parallel behaviour in an oligopolistic market where each producer followed the price leader. An oligopoly is a market in which a small number of suppliers supply the preponderant portion of demand (for a discussion on oligopolies, see Green, Hartley and Usher, 1991, Chapter 15). The Court considered the circumstances and the nature of a concerted practice in the context of Art 81:

> Article 85 [now Art 81] draws a distinction between the concept of 'concerted practices' and that of 'agreements between undertakings' or of 'decisions of associations'; the object is to bring within the prohibition of that Article a form of coordination between undertakings which, without having reached the stage where an agreement properly so called has been concluded, knowingly substitutes practical cooperation between them for the risks of competition.
>
> By its very nature, then, a concerted practice does not have all the elements of a contract but may inter alia arise out of coordination which becomes apparent from the behaviour of the participants. Although parallel behaviour may not by itself be identified with a concerted practice, it may, however, amount to strong evidence of such a practice if it leads to conditions of competition which do not correspond to the normal conditions of the market, having regard to the nature of the products, the size and number of the undertakings and the volume of the said market. (paras 64 to 66)

In the event, the Court decided that there was evidence of a concerted practice that breached Art 81. Concertation is difficult to prove, and the mere fact of parallel price increases is not conclusive. There must be 'a firm, precise and consistent body of evidence' on concertation to justify such a finding (*Åhlström Osakeyhito* v *Commission* (Joined Cases C-89, 104, 114, 116, 117 & 125–129/85)).

An agreement between undertakings

As we have seen above, the concept of an 'undertaking' is wide, and it includes all legal and natural persons involved in economic or commercial activity, such as companies, sole traders and state-owned public utilities. Undertakings may be engaged in the manufacture, sale or distribution of products or the provision of services and may comprise several companies which are owned or controlled by another one. There must be an agreement or concerted practice by two or more of such undertakings. There will be no agreement between 'undertakings' where it is within:

> one economic unit within which subsidiaries do not enjoy real autonomy in determining their course of action in the market. Where, as in this case, the subsidiary, although having a separate legal personality, does not freely determine its conduct on the market but carries out instructions given to it directly or indirectly by the parent company by which it is wholly controlled, Article 85(1) [now Art 81(1)] does not apply to the relationship between the subsidiary and the parent company with which it forms an economic unit. (*Viho Europe BV* v *Commission* (Case T-102/92))

The substantive requirements of Article 81

Having established the kind of agreement or arrangement which, potentially, may breach Art 81, what is the content of such a deal that will infringe Art 81? Not all agreements that affect trading relations between undertakings will breach Art 81. Clearly, the conferring of the power on the Commission to grant exemptions under Art 81(3) recognises that the potentially restrictive effect of some agreements may be outweighed by their beneficial effect. Before an assessment can be made of the grounds for exemption, however, it is necessary to isolate the constituent elements in Art 81 which will enable one to identify an offending agreement.

An agreement which may affect trade between Member States

Article 81(1)(a)–(e) (above) provide a non-exhaustive list of the sort of agreements which will, *prima facie*, breach Art 81, but they must be seen in a Community context. The kind of conduct at which Art 81 is primarily aimed is the conclusion of agreements or concerted practices between apparently competing producers or distributors who agree to give each other a 'free run' in specific national territories. Such horizontal agreements (e.g. between producer and producer; or between distributor and distributor) clearly continue to partition what should be a single market on a national basis, and attempt to defeat one of the primary aims of the Community. In *Suiker Unie* v *Commission* (Case 40/73), for example, sugar producers agreed to keep out of one another's territories; and in *ACF Chemiefarma* v *Commission* (Case 41/69) the undertakings concerned agreed (in a 'gentlemen's agreement') to share out domestic markets and to fix common prices of synthetic quinidine. Clearly, in these cases trade is affected, and the effect of these horizontal agreements is to deny consumers the benefit of competitive products from other Member States.

The possible effect on trade between Member States received careful examination by the Court in relation to a vertical agreement (e.g. between producer and distributor) in the landmark case of *Consten and Grundig* v *Commission* (Case 56/64). Here, as part of its international distribution network, the German manufacturer of electrical equipment, Grundig, came to an agreement with the French distributor, Consten, by which Consten was appointed as Grundig's sole representative in France, Corsica and the Saarland. Under that agreement Consten was authorised to use Grundig's name and trade mark, and Consten duly registered the Grundig trade mark 'GINT' in France. Consten then brought proceedings for infringement of a trade mark against a French company, UNEF, which had attempted to sell Grundig products in France which it had bought in Germany. The Commission, after an investigation, decided that the Consten–Grundig agreement breached Art 81, and Grundig and Consten applied to the Court of Justice for annulment of that decision under Art 230(2) EC Treaty. The applicants argued that the Commission had relied on a mistaken interpretation of the concept of an agreement which may affect trade between Member States, and had not shown that such trade would have been greater without the disputed agreement. The Court rejected the argument:

> The concept of an agreement 'which may affect trade between Member States' is intended to define, in the law governing cartels, the boundary between the areas respectively covered by Community law and national law. It is only to the extent to which the agreement may affect trade between Member States that the deterioration in competition caused by the agreement falls under the prohibition of Community law contained in Article 85 [Art 81]; otherwise it escapes the prohibition. In this connection, what is particularly important is whether the agreement is capable of constituting a threat, either direct or indirect, actual or potential, to freedom of trade between Member States in a manner which might harm the attainment of the objectives of a single market between States. Thus the fact that an agreement encourages an increase, even a large one, in the volume of trade between states is not sufficient to exclude the possibility that the agreement may 'affect' such trade in the above mentioned manner. In the present case, the contract between Grundig and Consten, on the one hand by preventing undertakings other than Consten from importing Grundig products into France, and on the other hand by prohibiting Consten from re-exporting those products to other countries of the common market, indisputably affects trade between Member States.

It was not necessary, moreover, to wait to see if trade was in fact affected by the way in which the agreement was intended to operate. The Court said that 'there is no need to take into account the concrete effects of an agreement *once it appears that it has as its object the prevention, restriction or distortion of competition*' (emphasis added).

The effect of the *Consten and Grundig* decision is that Art 81 applies not only to competing undertakings on a horizontal level, but also to vertical agreements between companies which are not themselves competing with each other but which aim to exclude competitors from the market, provided that the agreement is one that affects trade between Member States. Such vertical supply agreements can be caught by Art 81, as affecting trade between Member States, even if they are not in any way concerned to affect trade outside one Member State. Trade may, however, in fact be affected if the agreement, taken in the context of trading conditions in that state, is likely to affect trade into that state. This situation is most likely to occur in relation to 'sole supply' agreements between producers and retailers. In *Brasserie de Haecht SA* v *Wilkin (No. 1)* (Case 23/67) the proprietor of a café in Belgium obtained a loan from a Belgian brewery on the basis that he would obtain supplies of beverages exclusively from the brewery. The legality of the agreement in the context of Art 81(1) was raised in subsequent proceedings and referred by the Belgian court to the Court of Justice under Art 234 EC Treaty. The Court held that the validity of the agreement under Art 81 had to take into account not only the scope and effect of the agreement itself, but the trading conditions in the state in which it was made. The agreement, when viewed in isolation, as Advocate-General Roemer observed in the case, did not 'seem to be prejudicial to the common market in any way ... On the other hand it is possible for such an effect to occur as the result of the combined operation of all the beer distribution agreements in a Member State'. The Court agreed, and said:

> Article 85(1) [now Art 81(1)] implies that regard must be had to such effects in the context in which they occur, that is to say in the economic and legal context of such agreements, decisions and practices and where they might combine with others to have a cumulative effect on competition. In fact, it would be pointless to consider an agreement, decision or practice by reason of its effects if those effects were to be taken distinct from the market in which they are seen to operate and could only be examined apart from the body of effects, whether convergent or not surrounding their implementation.

In *Stichting Certificatie Kraanhuurbedrijf (SCK) and FNK and Another* v *Commission* (Joined Cases T-213/95 & T-18/96), FNK, an organisation of crane owners and hirers in The Netherlands which purported to maintain the quality of cranes hired out, published recommended prices for hire and prohibited members from hiring cranes from anyone except its members. The Commission declared these practices to be in breach of Art 85(1) (now Art 81(1)). SCK challenged the decision, arguing that, since its membership covered only 37 per cent of the market, the system of recommended hiring charges and restrictions on hiring could not affect trade between Member States. The Court of First Instance rejected this argument, stating that:

> even if the market share of FNK members was 'only' 37 per cent or 40 per cent of the Netherlands market, the applicants were large enough and had sufficient economic power for their practices ... to be capable of having an appreciable effect on trade between Member States.

The context within Member States may also have to take account of the actions of undertakings outside the Community, where those actions have an effect within Member States. In *Åhlström Osakeyhito* v *Commission* (*Re Wood Pulp*) (Joined Cases C-89, 104, 116, 117 & 125-129/85) concerted action by forestry undertakings in Finland, Sweden (then both outside the Community) and Canada was said to have had an effect on wood pulp prices in the Community. The undertakings submitted that Art 81 did not extend to regulate conduct restricting competition outside the Community merely because it had economic repercussions within it. The Court disagreed, holding that where wood pulp producers established outside the Community sell directly to purchasers established in the Community and engage in price competition in order to win orders from those customers, that constitutes competition within the common market. Where those producers concert on the prices to be charged to their customers in the Community and put that concertation into effect by selling at prices which are actually coordinated, they are taking part in concertation which has the object and effect of restricting competition within the common market within the meaning of Art 81 EC Treaty.

De minimis presumption

There is a *de minimis* presumption by the Commission, which was originally contained in a notice issued in 1986 and which was amended in 1994 (Notice on Agreements of Minor Importance (OJ 1986 C 231/2, as amended by OJ 1994 C 368/20)). In the notice (as amended), the Commission stated that in its opinion, agreements between undertakings engaged in the production or distribution of goods or in the provision of services generally would not fall within the prohibition of Art 81 if the goods and services which were subject to the agreement, together with other related goods and services of the participants, did not altogether represent more than 5 per cent of the total market for such goods or services in the area of the common market affected by the agreement. In addition, to come within this exception the undertakings must not have an aggregate turnover of more than 300 million ECUs. The notice raised only a presumption. It did not alter the law, and therefore it could be rebutted by evidence to the contrary. In *Distillers Company Ltd* v *Commission* (Case 30/78) the presumption was held to have been displaced by evidence of a distribution agreement of a product, the entire production of which was in the hands of a large undertaking.

The amended 1984 notice was replaced by the Commission in 1997 with a new Notice on Agreements of Minor Importance (OJ 1997 C 372/13). Under this new notice, an agreement will come within the exception if the total market share of all undertakings involved is not more than 5 per cent in the case of a horizontal agreement or 10 per cent in the case of a vertical agreement. Paragraph 19 of the notice provides that small- and medium-sized enterprises (as defined in Recommendation 96/280 (OJ 1996 L 107/4)) will be treated as coming within the exception even if they exceed the above market share thresholds. Once again, the notice raises only a presumption, which can be rebutted.

Commission notices: horizontal and vertical anti-competitive activities

As stated above, Art 81(1) applies to both horizontal and vertical anti-competitive activities. The Commission has issued two notices providing non-binding guidelines concerning (1) vertical restraints; and (2) horizontal cooperation agreements.

The Guidelines on Vertical Restraints (OJ 2000 C 291/01) are stated to be 'without prejudice to the interpretation that may be given by the Court of First Instance and the Court of Justice of the European Communities in relation to the application of Article 81 to vertical agreements' (para 1(4)). The Commission's aim in issuing these guidelines is to 'help companies to make their own assessment of vertical agreements under the EC competition rules' (para 1(3)). The guidelines are structured as follows:

- Section II describes vertical agreements which generally fall outside Art 81(1).
- Section III comments on the application of the Block Exemption Regulation 2790/99 on the application of Art 81(3) EC Treaty to categories of vertical agreements and concerted practices (see below).
- Section IV describes the principles concerning the withdrawal of the block exemption and the disapplication of the Block Exemption Regulation.
- Section V addresses market definition and market share calculation issues, primarily as regards the application of the *de minimis* rule as set out in the 1997 *de minimis* notice (OJ 1997 C 372/13 – see above).

- Section VI describes the general framework of analysis and the enforcement policy of the Commission in individual cases concerning vertical agreements (see Chapter 22, and below).

The Guidelines on Horizontal Cooperation Agreements (OJ 2001 C 3/02) are, like the vertical restraint guidelines, stated to be 'without prejudice to the interpretation that may be given by the Court of First Instance or the Court of Justice' in relation to the application of Art 81 to such agreements (para 16). The purpose of the guidelines is to 'provide an analytical framework for the most common types of horizontal cooperation', although it is recognised that 'given the enormous variety in types and combinations of horizontal cooperation and market circumstances in which they operate, it is impossible to provide specific answers for every possible scenario' (para 7). Chapters 2 to 7 of the guidelines are concerned with specific types of agreement; practical examples are included of situations where Art 81 would apply and where it would not. The specific types of agreement covered are as follows:

- agreements on research and development (chapter 2, paras 39–77);
- production agreements (including specialisation agreements) (chapter 3, paras 78–114);
- purchasing agreements (chapter 4, paras 115–138);
- commercialisation agreements (chapter 5, paras 139–158);
- agreement on standards (chapter 6, paras 159–178);
- environmental agreements (chapter 7, paras 179–198).

Both sets of guidelines are available on the Commission's website at: <u>europa.eu.int/ comm/competition/antitrust/legislation/entente3–en.html#nature</u>.

The object or effect of distorting competition

Article 81 prohibits both conduct which is *intended* to affect trade between Member States, and conduct which, although not based upon any such intention, in fact has, or is *likely* to have, such an effect. There is no need for both elements to be present; they are alternative, not cumulative (*Ferriere Nord SpA* v *Commission* (Case C-219/ 95P)). As we have seen, in *Consten and Grundig* (above), there will be a breach of Art 81 even if an agreement is likely to increase trade between Member States. Article 81 is, unlike Art 28 EC Treaty, aimed not at restrictions on trade between Member States as such, but at the use of restrictive agreements to partition markets and to distort the flow of trade which would normally take place in a genuine open market. The Court stated the underlying principle of Art 81 in *Züchner* v *Bayerische Vereinsbank AG* (Case 172/80):

> A basic principle of the EEC competition rules is that each trader must determine independently the policy which he intends to adopt on the common market and the conditions which he intends to offer to his customers. This does not prevent the traders adapting themselves intelligently to the existing or anticipated conduct of their competitors; it does, however, strictly preclude any direct or indirect contact between such traders the object or effect of which is to create conditions of competition which do not correspond to the normal conditions of the relevant market, in the light of the nature of

the products or services offered, the size and number of the undertakings and the size of the market.

In cases where there is an attempt to rig the market by price-fixing and market-sharing agreements there is no problem in concluding that the object of any agreement or concerted action is the prevention, restriction or distortion of competition. Difficulties arise in identifying situations where, although there is no such attempt at market distortion, the effect of an agreement may have the same, probably unintended, outcome. The intention of a sole-supply agreement may, for example, be that the supplier is repaid money that he may have lent the retailer and, at the same time, is guaranteed an outlet for his goods. A network of such sole-supply agreements across a Member State, even if concluded between a large number of different suppliers and retailers, may have the effect of denying penetration of that market to producers in other Member States of the goods which are subject to the agreements. This was the basis of the Court's reasoning in the *Brasserie de Haecht* case (see above) in relation to 'tied-houses' supplied by breweries in Belgium. In analysing the object and effect of an agreement the Court will look first to its content and then to its effect. Even if its terms do not indicate an intention to restrict or distort competition, its operation may have that effect. Factors such as the percentage of the market affected, and the duration and terms of the agreements will all have to be assessed. In *Langnese-Iglo GmbH* v *Commission* (Case T-7/93), the Court of First Instance found that the applicant held more than 30 per cent of the market share of ice-cream sold through shops. These outlets were protected by a series of exclusive purchasing agreements under which the retailers bound themselves to sell only the applicant's ice-cream for two-and-a-half years and to use the freezer cabinets lent by the applicant only for the applicant's products. The Court concluded that, in view of the strong position occupied by the applicant in the relevant market and, in particular, its market share, the agreements contributed significantly to the closing-off of the market. A network of sole-supply agreements across a Member State will, however, not automatically be regarded as providing an insurmountable barrier to market penetration from other Member States. In *Stergios Delimitis* v *Henninger Bräu* (Case C-234/89) the Court emphasised that it was important to look at the state of the market in question to determine 'whether there are real concrete possibilities for a new competitor to penetrate the bundle of contracts' (para 21). An exclusive supply agreement may even, in some circumstances, assist in opening up competition.

In *Société Technique Minière* v *Maschinenbau Ulm GmbH* (Case 56/65) Maschinenbau Ulm (MU) agreed to give Société Technique Minière (STM) the exclusive right to sell its earth-moving equipment in France, on condition that STM should not sell competing machinery. The validity of the agreement was disputed in a French court, which referred the issue to the Court of Justice for a preliminary ruling. The Commission argued in the proceedings that the agreement in question breached Art 81. The Court did not agree. It described the two stages through which it was necessary to go to determine whether or not Art 81 was infringed. 'Object or effect' in this context are alternative, not cumulative. It was first necessary to look at the precise purpose of the agreement, in the economic context in which it was to be applied. An intention to interfere with competition in the way prohibited by Art 81 was to be deduced, if at all, from the clauses of the agreement itself. If those clauses indicated an *intention* to restrict competition, the fact that the involvement of one of the participants had a negligible effect on competition was irrelevant (*Usines Gustave Boël SA* v *Commission* (Case T-142/89)). If the agreement disclosed no such intention, or an effect on competition that was not 'sufficiently deleterious', the consequences of the agreement would then have to be considered. A consideration of those consequences would include, in the case of an exclusive sale agreement, the nature and quantity, limited or otherwise, of the products covered by the agreement, the position and importance of the grantor and the concessionaire on the market for the product concerned, the isolated nature of the disputed agreement or, alternatively, its position in a series of agreements, the severity of the clauses intended to protect the exclusive dealership or, alternatively, the opportunities allowed for other commercial competitors in the same products by way of parallel re-exportation and importation. In this case the Court also took into account the fact that there was here an attempt at market penetration in another Member State, and it doubted whether there was an interference with competition if the agreement 'was really necessary for the penetration of a new area by an undertaking'.

The *Société Technique Minière* case thus not only defined the relationship between the intention and the consequences of an agreement, but also introduced the concept of *de minimis* in the context of promoting the desirable objective of market penetration (see above). In other words, a distributor of a new product in another Member State may need some protection in order to get that product launched in the state. Essentially, the Court recognised that a balance needs to be struck in the legal control of agreements which appear, on their face, to be restrictive of competition, but which may, in fact, assist in promoting market integration and product distribution. Thus the limited restrictive effect of an agreement may be outweighed by its more beneficial long-term consequences. This has been described as a 'rule of reason'. As long as an agreement does not have as its object the restriction of competition, its anti-competitive effect may be outweighed by its ultimate competitive advantages. The apparently conflicting priorities contained within this rule of reason were considered by the Court in *Nungesser* v *Commission* (Case 258/78). In this case, there was an attempt to protect, in an agreement, techniques of cultivating new types of maize. An agreement conferring exclusive rights to the technique on Nungesser was challenged by the Commission, which concluded that its terms must, inevitably, breach Art 81. The Court disagreed with the Commission's approach. It decided that some protection for the licensee of the new technique for hybrid maize seeds was a necessary precondition for penetration of the German market by INRA, the developers of the technique:

> The exclusive licence which forms the subject-matter of the contested decision concerns the cultivation and marketing of hybrid maize seeds which were developed by INRA after years of research and experimentation and were unknown to German farmers at the time when the cooperation between INRA and the applicants was taking shape ... In the case of a licence of breeders' rights over hybrid maize seeds newly developed in one Member State, an undertaking established in another Member State which was not certain that it would encounter competition from other licensees for the territory granted to it, or from the owner of the right himself, might be deterred from accepting the risk of cultivating and marketing that product; such a result would be damaging to the dissemination of new

technology and would prejudice competition in the Community between the new product and similar existing products. (paras 55 and 56)

Given that the launching of the new seed and cultivation technique called for some protection for the licensee, did that mean that total protection of the production and distribution of the seed was justified? The Court would not go so far, citing its view in *Consten and Grundig* that absolute territorial protection, granted to a licensee in order to enable parallel imports to be controlled and prevented, results in the artificial maintenance of separate national markets, in breach of the Treaty. It would, however, countenance the grant of an open exclusive licence, under which the grantor himself would not compete with the licensee in Germany and would not license anyone else there to do so. Such a licence should not, however, contain an assurance by the grantor that he would protect the licensee from parallel imports, by preventing licensees in *other* Member States from exporting to Germany. A limited approval by the Court has also been given to apparently restrictive franchise agreements, provided that the restrictions are no more than those which are strictly necessary to ensure that the know-how and assistance provided by the franchisee do not benefit competitors, or which establish the control necessary for maintaining the identity and reputation of the network identified by the common name or symbol. However, provisions which share markets between the franchisor and the franchisee, or between franchisees, do breach Art 81 (*Pronuptia de Paris GmbH* v *Pronuptia de Paris Irmgaard Schillgalis* (Case 161/84)).

The list of agreements likely to breach Article 81(1)

Article 81(1) contains a list, in paragraphs (a) to (e), of the kind of agreements which will be prohibited. The cases examined so far range far beyond those described in that list, and it provides no more than a guide to the sort of agreements which will fall foul of the prohibition. However, with the help of the list and the case law of the Court of Justice, it is possible to come to some conclusions as to the type of agreement which may breach Art 81. A list indicative of the types of offending agreements could include:

- exclusive distribution agreements
- exclusive purchasing agreements
- exclusive licences of intellectual property rights (such as patents, copyright and trade marks)
- selective distribution agreements
- franchise agreements
- research and development agreements
- joint ventures on development
- joint sale and buying agencies
- information-sharing agreements.

All of these types of agreement have been held at some time or other to be actually or potentially in breach of Art 81. If they are found to breach Art 81(1), they are, by Art 81(2), automatically void. The effect of this finding is that they cannot, for example, form the basis of a claim or a defence in contract in national courts. Article 81 was used in this way in both the *Brasserie de Haecht* and the *Société Technique Minière* cases (above). In many cases, the Court is obliged to give an indication, on the basis of the facts in the relevant market (as found by the Commission), and after weighing up all the relevant circumstances, of whether the agreement actually breached the prohibition. If it does breach Art 81(1), there always remains the possibility that it may nonetheless be granted exemption by the Commission under Art 81(3).

The grant of exemptions under Article 81(3)

The object of Art 81(3), set out at the beginning of this chapter, is to provide criteria for the grant of exemption by the Commission. Essentially, exemption may be granted in cases where the anti-competitive effects of an agreement or concerted practice are outweighed by the economic benefit to consumers or the public at large. Exemption may result either from an individual decision of the Commission pursuant to Regulation 17/62, or as a consequence of an agreement falling within a type to which a block or group exemption has been granted (see below). In order to obtain an exemption, undertakings which have entered into restrictive agreements must either make a formal application to the Commission pursuant to Regulation 17/62, or draft their agreements to comply with one of the block or group exemption regulations which have been specifically drawn up by the Commission. In the latter instance, if the agreement complies with one of the regulations, it will automatically obtain exemption without the necessity for a formal application to the Commission.

The grant of exemption will depend on the applicants satisfying four conditions:

1   The agreement must contribute to the improvement of the production or distribution of goods, or the promotion of technical or economic progress.
2   The agreement must allow consumers a fair share of the resulting benefit.
3   The agreement must not impose upon the undertakings concerned restrictions which are not indispensable to the attainment of the above objects.
4   The agreement should not provide the undertakings with the possibility of eliminating competition in respect of a substantial part of the product in question.

These are all linked conditions which must, in each case, be satisfied (Commission Decision 73/323 *Prym-Werke*). Each agreement must be notified to the Commission and exemption obtained under the procedure established for the purpose under Arts 4, 19 and 21, Regulation 17/62. Exemptions may be granted only for specific periods, conditions may be attached and the exemption may be renewed or revoked. As a result of the delays of two or three years that may ensue following an application, and the practical problems attending the requirement that a fully reasoned decision must be given in each case, the Commission has tended to try to avoid formal decisions, which are normally reserved for what are seen as important cases. In other cases a *comfort letter* will be issued after informal meetings with the parties concerned stating that, in the Commission's view, the agreement that has been notified does not infringe Art 81(1) at all or is of a type which falls within an exempt category. The file is then closed, although it may be reopened if the legal, material or factual circumstances change. The parties are then entitled to rely upon the letter and enjoy a legitimate expectation that the Commission will take no further action. Comfort letters have only a limited legal status and, as they are not 'Decisions', cannot be challenged in Art 230 EC Treaty proceedings before the Court of Justice (*SA Lancôme* v *ETOS BV* (*'Perfumes'*) (Case 99/79)). Nor are opinions expressed in such letters 'binding on the national courts but constitute a factor which the latter may take into account in examining whether or not the agreements are in accordance with the provisions of Article 85 [now Art 81]'. The reliance which the parties can place on a comfort letter depends very much on the circumstances in which the letter was issued remaining the same. Any change in those circumstances, or any misrepresentation, may result in the reopening of the file (*Langnese-Iglo* v *Commission* (Case T-7/93)).

Besides meeting the formal requirements set out in **1** to **4** above, applications for exemption will also be examined in the light of the Commission's broader policy objectives in relation to agreements between undertakings. The Commission's aim is to encourage those agreements which favour the introduction of new technology resulting in better production methods, economies of scale, the faster or more effective development of new products or the process of change in older industries. Agreements which are highly unlikely to secure exemption are price-fixing agreements, agreements limiting production or controlling markets, or agreements which are aimed at retaining dominance in a national market. An example of an application that met both the specific and general criteria can be seen in *Prym-Werke* [1973] CMLR D250, [1981] 2 CMLR 217 (see also the *ACEC/Berliet* decision [1968] CMLR D35; *Re Vacuum Interrupters (No. 2)* [1981] 2 CMLR 217). In *Prym-Werke*, Prym agreed to give up making needles and instead to buy them from Beka, who agreed to supply Prym. Beka could then specialise in needle production. The Commission explained the approach it had adopted in its decision:

> The concentration of manufacturing agreed on by Prym and Beka has, from the point of view of the improvement of production, favourable effects analogous to those of specialisation; it causes an increase of at least 50 per cent in the quantity of needles to be manufactured at the European factory, which makes it possible to make more intensive use of the existing plant and to introduce production-line manufacture.

The sort of application that will not attract approval from the Commission was considered by the Court of First Instance in *SPO* v *Commission* (Case T-29/92). In this case the applicants were a group of associations of building contractors in The Netherlands. Since 1952 they had had a body of rules with a view to organising competition. The rules were intended to 'promote and administer orderly competition, to prevent improper conduct in price tendering and to promote the formation of economically justified prices'. From 1980, these rules became binding on all contractors belonging to the member associations of the SPO. In 1988 the SPO notified its amended rules with a view, *inter alia*, to obtain an exemption under Art 81(3). The Commission rejected the application for exemption and found the SPO rules in breach of Art 81(1). The Court upheld this decision. It had no hesitation in finding that the provision of information to SPO by contractors submitting tenders for contracts which enabled other contractors to adjust their commercial behaviour and their prices amounted to unlawful concertation in the Netherlands building market affecting not just Dutch contractors but contractors wishing to tender from other Member States. It therefore breached Art 81(1). The Court, applying the four criteria for exemption, also found the rules wanting. The applicants had argued that an open tendering system would necessarily lead to ruinous competition which would ultimately have adverse repercussions on contract awarders. The Court observed dryly that it was impossible to distinguish between normal competition and ruinous competition as, potentially, any competition is ruinous for the least efficient undertakings. That is why, by taking action to counteract what they regard as ruinous competition, the applicants necessarily restrict competition and therefore deprive consumers of its benefits.

Commission proposal to replace Regulation 17/62

In April 1999 the Commission adopted a White Paper concerning the modernisation of the rules implementing Arts 81 and 82 (Commission Programme No. 99/027, Brussels, 28 April 1999). Subsequent to this, on 27 September 2000 the Commission proposed a regulation extensively to amend the system for the implementation of Arts 81 and 82 (COM (2000) 582 final). The proposal intends to strengthen competition in the Community and will extend to national competition authorities and courts the power to apply Community competition law in full. It is therefore proposed that the Commission will no longer have the sole power to apply Art 81(3). Part of the reasoning for this change is due to the lengthy delays currently being experienced by undertakings which apply for clearance under Art 81(3) (see above). The Commission acknowledges that it does not have sufficient resources to continue to apply Art 81(3), and the situation would further deteriorate once the Community is enlarged. Therefore it is proposed that national authorities and courts will be able to apply Art 81(3) as well as Art 81(1). The new regulation will replace Regulation 17/62 (see above); this will be further considered in Chapter 22.

Block exemptions

The four criteria for exemption are reflected in the Block Exemption Regulations. Block exemptions have come about as a result of the huge burden placed on the Commission by the requirement in Regulation 17/62 to investigate each application before delivering a decision (although see above on the Commission's proposal to replace Regulation 17/62). The delays caused great uncertainty for business, and as a result the Commission has increasingly relied on its power to grant block exemptions by means of regulations.

The value of block exemptions is that undertakings can make their own assessment as to whether or not the agreement to which they are a party falls within the terms of an apparently relevant block exemption regulation. If the agreement is clearly within it, they do not need to notify it to the Commission and may treat it as *prima facie* valid and enforceable. If it falls outside any existing exemption they will have to apply to the Commission for individual exemption. The Commission does, however, remain free to decide that agreements which purport to fall within an existing block exemption do in fact fall outside it, and to take the necessary action against the participants.

A number of block exemption regulations have been issued since 1983, some of which have been amended or replaced by subsequent regulations. For example:

- Technology Transfer Regulation 240/96 (OJ 1996 L 31/2), which replaced the Patent Licensing Block Exemption Regulation 2349/84 (OJ 1984 L 219/15) and the Know-how Licensing Block Exemption Regulation 556/89 (OJ 1989 L 61/1);
- Vertical Restraints Regulation 2790/99 (OJ 1999 L 326/21), which replaced the block exemptions for exclusive distribution agreements (Regulation 1983/83 (OJ 1983 L 173/1)), exclusive purchasing agreements (Regulation 1984/83 (OJ 1983 L 173/15)), and franchising agreements (Regulation 4078/88 (OJ 1988 L 359/46));
- Specialisation Agreements Regulation 2658/2000 (OJ 2000 L 304/3), which replaced Regulation 417/85 (OJ 1985 L 53/1), the latter having expired on 31 December 2000;
- Research and Development Agreements Regulation 2659/2000 (OJ 2000 L 304/7), which replaced Regulation 418/85 (OJ 1985 L 53/5), the latter having expired on 31 December 2000.

The pattern of block exemption regulations is similar. They reflect both the content of Art 81(3) and the decisions of the Court of Justice in relation to individual applications concerning the activities covered by the regulation. However, the last two regulations in particular have moved away from the approach of listing clauses in an agreement which would be exempted from Art 81(1), and instead place a greater emphasis on defining the categories of agreements which are exempted up to a certain level of market power and on specifying the restrictions or clauses which are not to be contained in such agreements.

The fact that an agreement falls within the terms of a block exemption regulation does not confer immunity under Art 81(1) on everything purported to be done under that agreement. If, for example, the operation of the agreement in practice excludes parallel imports, the effect of the agreement would still be to restrict competition (*P Automobiles Peugeot SA* v *Commission* (Case C-322/93)). On this basis, the Commission decided that Regulation 123/85 (block exemption regulation on selective distribution in the motor vehicle sector) did not allow Volkswagen to prohibit its dealers in Italy from selling to consumers and motor agencies outside Italy (*The Community* v *Volkswagen AG and Others* (Case IV/35.733) (1998)). The decision demonstrates the way in which an agreement, ostensibly lawful as within the block exemption, can work to the disadvantage of customers and lead to the partitioning of the market.

Further reading

Barr, F., 'The New Commission Notice on Agreements of Minor Importance: Is Appreciability a Useful Measure?' [1997] ECLR 207.

Bellamy, C. and Child, G., (Roth P.M., ed.) (1996) *Common Market Law of Competition*, Sweet & Maxwell, Chapters 1–6.

Craig, P. and De Burca, G. (1998) *EU Law Text, Cases and Materials* (2nd edn), OUP, Chapter 20.

Ehlermann, C.D., 'The Contribution of EC Competition Policy to the Single Market' (1992) 29 CML Rev 257.

Frazer, T., 'Competition Policy after 1992: the next step' (1990) 53 MLR 609.

Green, N., 'Article 85 in Perspective' (1988) 9 ECLR 190.

Green, N., Hartley, T.C. and Usher, J.A. (1991) *The Legal Foundations of the Single Market, Pt III*, OUP.

Kirkbride, J. and Tao Xiong, 'The European Control of Joint Ventures: An Historic Opportunity or a Mere Continuation of Existing Practice?' (1998) 23 EL Rev 37.

Lidgard, H.H., 'Unilateral Refusal to Supply: An Agreement in Disguise?' [1997] ECLR 352.

Steiner, J. and Woods, L. (2000) *Textbook on EC Law* (7th edn), Blackstone Press, Chapter 15.

Tillotson, J. (2000) *European Community Law; Text, Cases and Materials* (3rd edn), Cavendish Publishing Ltd, Chapter 14.

Weatherill, S. (2000) *Cases and Materials on EC Law* (5th edn), Blackstone Press, Chapter 11.

Whish, R. (1993) *Competition Law*, Butterworths, Chapter 1.

Chapter 21

ABUSE OF A DOMINANT POSITION

ARTICLE 82 EC TREATY
(FORMERLY ARTICLE 86)

Article 82 EC Treaty provides that:

Any abuse by one or more undertakings of a dominant position within the common market or in a substantial part of it shall be prohibited as incompatible with the common market in so far as it may affect trade between Member States. Such abuse may, in particular, consist in:

(a) directly or indirectly imposing unfair purchase or selling prices or other unfair trading conditions;

(b) limiting production, markets or technical development to the prejudice of consumers;

(c) applying dissimilar conditions to equivalent transactions with other trading parties, thereby placing them at a competitive disadvantage;

(d) making the conclusion of contracts subject to acceptance by the other parties of supplementary obligations which, by their nature or according to commercial usage, have no connection with the subject of such contracts.

There are three key elements in Art 82. There must be:

1 a dominant position;
2 an abuse of that position; and
3 the abuse must affect trade between Member States.

Whereas Art 81 is directed at cooperation between nominally competing businesses, which has the effect of diminishing or distorting competition, Art 82 is aimed at the position and conduct of one undertaking. Essentially, Art 82 is not concerned with the *fact* of monopoly power in the Community, but with *abuse* of that monopoly or dominant position. To determine whether or not that has occurred, each of the key elements mentioned will have to be analysed and applied to the relevant circumstances.

A dominant position

The concept of dominance must be viewed in the context of the relevant market for the goods or services produced or distributed by the undertaking the conduct of which is in question. The Court of Justice, in *United Brands Co v Commission* (Case 27/76), at para 65, defined a dominant position as:

> A position of economic strength enjoyed by an undertaking which enables it to hinder the maintenance of effective competition on the relevant market by allowing it to behave to an appreciable extent independently of its competitors and customers and ultimately of consumers.

To determine whether or not an undertaking is 'dominant' one has, therefore, to look at the relevant product market. A useful example for this exercise is the case of *United Brands Co v Commission* (Case 27/76). United Brands Co (UBC), at the time of the Commission's investigation, was a conglomerate which handled 40 per cent of the EC banana trade. In some Member States – the Benelux countries, Germany, Denmark and Ireland – its share of the banana market was much greater. The Commission accordingly concluded that it enjoyed a dominant position in the banana market which, on the facts, it was abusing. UBC challenged the decision on a number of grounds, *inter alia*, that it did not enjoy a dominant position in the fruit market, which was the proper context for the examination of its position. Bananas compete with other fresh fruit in the same shops, on the same shelves, at prices which can be compared, satisfying the same needs: consumption as a dessert or between meals. On the other hand, the Commission contended that there is a demand for bananas which is distinct from the demand for other fresh fruit, especially as the banana is a very important part of the diet of certain sections of the Community, especially the very young and the very old. The specific qualities of the banana influence customer preference and induce him not readily to accept other fruits as a substitute. The Court accepted the Commission's argument that the relevant market was in bananas, and not in fruit generally:

> For the banana to be regarded as forming a market which is sufficiently differentiated from other fruit markets, it must be possible for it to be singled out by such special features distinguishing it from other fruits that it is only to a limited extent exchangeable with them and is only exposed to their competition in a way that is hardly perceptible.
>
> The ripening of bananas takes place the whole year round without any season having to be taken into account. Throughout the year production exceeds demand and can satisfy it at any time. Owing to this particular feature the banana is a privileged fruit and its production and marketing can be adapted to the seasonal fluctuations of other fresh fruit which are known and can be computed. There is no unavoidable seasonal substitution since the consumer can obtain this fruit all the year round ... It follows from these considerations that a very large number of consumers having a constant need for bananas are not noticeably or even appreciably enticed away from the consumption of this product by the arrival of other fresh fruit on the market and that even the seasonal peak periods only affect it for a limited period of time and to a very limited extent from the point of view of substitutability.
>
> Consequently the banana market is a market which is sufficiently distinct from the other fresh fruit markets. (paras 22–26, and 34–35)

The most noticeable feature of this part of the judgment is the way in which the Court focuses on *product-substitution* as a primary determinant in isolating bananas as a separate market. There are two kinds of substitutability: (1) demand-side substitutability; and (2) supply-side substitutability.

Demand-side substitutability determines which products compete with each other from the perspective of the consumer. The Commission normally refers to the criteria of price, quality and intended use as the determining factors. In the *UBC* case the relatively constant price and lack of seasonal variation, and the suitability and intended use for children and the elderly meant that other fruits could not be readily substituted for bananas. This test can result in a very narrow market definition in appropriate cases. In *Hugin Kassaregister AB* v *Commission* (Case 22/78), the Commission held Hugin in breach of Art 82 for its refusal to supply spare parts for Hugin cash registers to Liptons. It defined the relevant product market as consisting of spare parts for Hugin machines required by independent repairers. This finding was rejected by Hugin as too narrow. It insisted that the relevant market was the very competitive cash register market. The Court, however, accepted the Commission's market definition in relation to the independent repairers of Hugin machines:

> The role of those undertakings [the repairers] on the market is that of businesses which require spare parts for their various activities. They need such parts in order to provide services for cash register users in the form of maintenance and repairs and for the reconditioning of used machines intended for re-sale or renting out ... It is, moreover, established that there is a specific demand for Hugin spare parts, since those spare parts are not interchangeable with spare parts for cash registers of other makes. (para 7)

The Court has accepted that there was dominance in an equally narrow market of information on the content of BBC and RTE television programmes in *RTE and ITP* v *Commission* (Cases C-241/91 & C-242/91P); and, subsequently, in *Deutsche Bahn AG* v *Commission* (Case T-229/94), the Court of First Instance held that there was a *distinct sub-market* in the carriage of maritime containers by rail and, in assessing dominance, the Commission was justified in not taking into account other services provided by rail transport operators, road hauliers and inland waterway operators.

Supply-side substitutability is concerned with the ability of a manufacturer to switch his production system from product A to product B, and therefore constitutes a test of whether the manufacturer of product A is a rival to the manufacturer of product B. In *Tetra-Pak International SA* v *Commission* (Case T-83/91), the Court rejected Tetra-Pak's argument that there were separate markets for aseptic cartons and the related packing machinery and non-aseptic cartons and packaging machinery because of the relative ease with which the manufacturer could switch from one to the other. Also, in *Europemballage and Continental Can* v *Commission* (Case 6/72), the issue involved packaging containers and the scope of the market. The Court held that, in order to be regarded as constituting a distinct market, the products must be individualised, not only by the mere fact that they are used in packing certain products, but by the peculiar characteristics of production which make them specifically suitable for this purpose:

> Consequently, a dominant position on the market for light metal containers for fish and meat cannot be decisive, as long as it has not been proved that competitors from other sectors of the market for light metal containers are not in a position to enter this market, by a simple adaptation, with sufficient strength to create a serious counterweight.

Whether or not supply-side substitutability exists is a matter of fact to be investigated by the Commission. In *Instituto Chemioterapico Italiano SpA and Commercial Solvents Corporation* v *Commission* (Cases 6 & 7/73), an American company, CSC, and its Italian subsidiary cut off supplies of aminobutanol to another Italian company, Zoja. Aminobutanol is an effective and cheap raw material used in the production of ethambutol, a drug used for treating tuberculosis. The Commission alleged that CSC had an almost worldwide monopoly in aminobutanol, and was considering manu-facturing ethambutol in Italy, through its subsidiary there. There were other drugs for the treatment of tuberculosis, but they were based on different but less effective raw materials. The Court of Justice decided that the relevant product market was the supply of aminobutanol, and not the production of ethambutol. It could not accept that Zoja could readily adapt its production facilities to other raw materials for the manufacture of ethambutol. Only if other materials could be substituted without difficulty could they be regarded as acceptable substitutes.

The geographical market

In order to decide whether or not the dominant position is held in a substantial part of the common market, it is necessary to look not only at the geographical extent of the market in question but also at the economic importance of the area as defined, the pattern and volume of the production and consumption of the relevant product, and the habits of producers and consumers in that area. An area can be defined by factors which promote its geographical isolation. Factors tending to emphasise that isolation might be lack of transport facilities, or the cost of transportation relative to the value of a product, giving an unchallengeable advantage to local producers. The transport cost factor was held in *Suiker Unie* v *Commission* (Case 40/73) to be very significant in defining the geographical market. Conversely, in *Tetra-Pak International SA* v *Commission* (Case T-83/91) the Court of First Instance supported the Commission's finding that the geographical market consisted of the whole of the Community, because, *inter alia*, the very low cost of transport for cartons and machines meant that they could be easily and readily transported between states. Sometimes the geographical market can be readily identified as lying within the borders of a Member State. In *NV Nederlandsche Banden-Industrie Michelin* v *Commission* (Case 322/81) the Court found that tyre companies operated in the Dutch market through local subsidiaries, to which local dealers looked for their supplies. It therefore upheld the decision of the Commission to regard The Netherlands as the area in which the competition facing NBIM was located.

Another factor identifying a separate geographical market is its homogeneity. Article 9(7) of Merger Regulation 4064/89 recognises this factor:

> The geographical reference market shall consist of the area in which the undertakings concerned are involved in the supply and demand of products and services, in which the conditions of competition are sufficiently homogenous and which can be distinguished from neighbouring areas because, in particular, conditions of competition are appreciably different in those areas.

These features were significant in the *United Brands* case (see above) when the Court considered the geographical market. Looking at the banana market throughout the Community, the Commission had identified three states which had distinctive rules for the import and sale of bananas: Italy, which operated a national system of quota restrictions; the United Kingdom, which had a system of Commonwealth preference; and France, which had a similar preferential system favouring the African francophone states. Only the then remaining six Member States had a completely free market in bananas. France, Italy and the United Kingdom were therefore excluded from the analysis by the Commission and the other six states were identified as the relevant geographical market. The Court supported this finding on the basis that 'although the applicable tariff provisions and transport costs are of necessity different but not discriminatory ... and ... the conditions of competition are the same for all ... [t]hese six states form an area which is sufficiently homogenous to be considered in its entirety' (paras 52 and 53). The Court went so far, in a case involving the application of Regulation 4064/89, as to hold that, for the purposes of the production of potash and rocksalt, the whole Community, apart from Germany, was 'sufficiently homogenous to be regarded overall as a separate geographical market' (*France* v *Commission* (Joined Cases C-68/94 & C-30/95)).

Dominance in fact

Besides the ability to operate independently of its rivals, another indicator of dominance is the extent of market share. The larger this is, the more likely, and well-founded, will be an acceptance of dominance. In *Hoffman La Roche* v *Commission* (Case 85/76), the company's market shares over a three-year period of 75 per cent to 87 per cent were held to be so large that they were, in themselves, evidence of a dominant position; whereas, in *United Brands*, a market share of between 40 and 45 per cent did not 'permit the conclusion that UBC automatically controls the market'. However, in *Tetra-Pak* (above), the company's 90 per cent share of the market in aseptic cartons and the relevant packaging machines made it 'an inevitable partner for packers and guaranteed it the freedom of conduct characteristic of a dominant position'.

Besides market share, there are a number of other factors indicative of actual dominance of the market. These will include ownership of, or ready access to, massive financial resources. In addition, a firm's ability to establish and maintain a lead in product development or technical services may well contribute to the maintenance of a dominant position. The process of using financial resources or a technical advantage to maintain a dominant position could well, however, also constitute an abuse of that position.

Abuse of a dominant position

Article 82(a)–(d) provide a non-exhaustive list of the sort of conduct which will constitute an abuse of a dominant position, primarily concerned with unfair trading practices, such as imposing unfair purchase or selling prices, restricting production to create an artificial shortage and discriminating unfairly between different trading partners. It was originally thought that Art 82 applied exclusively to practices which constituted an abuse of market power, rather than to activities intended to gain or maintain dominance. However, in *Continental Can* (above), the Court rejected such a narrow interpretation of Art 82 and declared that 'the provision is not only aimed at practices which may cause damage to consumers directly, but also at those which are detrimental to them through their impact on an effective competitive structure, such as is mentioned in Article 3(f) of the Treaty'. Article 3(f) (now Art 3(g)) EC Treaty speaks of 'a system ensuring that competition in the internal market is not distorted':

> Abuse may therefore occur if an undertaking in a dominant position *strengthens such position in such a way that the degree of dominance reached substantially fetters competition* i.e., that only undertakings remain in the market whose behaviour depends on the dominant one. (emphasis added)

In *Continental Can* the conduct complained of was an agreement by Continental Can to buy a competitor in the food packaging market that would, in the Commission's view, have enabled it to achieve absolute dominance in its sector of the market. The Court accepted, in principle, that this sort of conduct could breach Art 82, but decided, on the facts of the case, that the Commission had chosen the wrong relevant product market.

It should, however, be noted that gaining or maintaining dominance is not, *per se*, in breach of Art 82. In *Gottrub Klim Grovvareforening* v *Dansk Landbrugs Grovvaresel* (Case C-250/92) the Court held that the conduct of a cooperative of growers that dominated the market of purchasers for certain agricultural supplies was not in breach of Art 82. The cooperative had strengthened its own statutes to reduce competition from members who had left the cooperative. The Court held that 'neither the creation nor the strengthening of a dominant position is in itself contrary to Article 86 [now Art 82] EC Treaty'. 'The activities of cooperative purchasing organisations may actually encourage more effective competition on some markets, provided that the rules binding members do no more than is necessary to ensure that the cooperative functions properly and maintains its contractual power in relation to producers'.

What is important is the effect of achieving or maintaining dominance. The Court explored the concept further in *Hoffman La Roche* v *Commission* (Case 85/76), where it stated:

> The concept of abuse is an objective concept relating to the behaviour of an undertaking in a dominant position where, as a result of the very presence of the undertaking in question, the degree of competition is weakened and which, through recourse to methods different from those which condition normal competition in products and services on the basis of the transactions of commercial operators, has the effect of hindering the maintenance of the degree of competition still existing in the market or the growth of that competition.

Specific abuses

Article 82 contains a number of examples of the type of conduct by an undertaking in a dominant position which constitutes an abuse. The list is exemplary and not exhaustive, but it provides a useful starting point for an examination of abusive practices.

(1) The imposition of unfair purchase or selling prices

The most obvious abuse by a supplier in a monopoly position is the imposition of extortionate prices on consumers. There is an element of subjectivity in any assessment of what is a fair price, but in *United Brands* the Court declared that a price is excessive where 'it has no reasonable relation to the economic value of the product supplied'. In determining the economic value, one had to take into account the difference between the costs actually incurred and the price charged. A price may also be excessive if it is not attributable to ordinary market conditions. In *Tetra-Pak*, the Court of First Instance found that the very great disparity in charges between the prices paid by Italian purchasers and those paid elsewhere in the Community could not be explained by additional market or transport costs in Italy, but were derived simply from Tetra-Pak's dominance in that country. The prices charged in Italy were, essentially, discriminatory.

In relation to prices for services, an undertaking would be abusing its dominant position if it charged fees which were disproportionate to the economic value of the service provided. In *Société Civile Agricole de la Crespelle* v *Coopérative d'Elevage de la Mayenne* (Case C-323/93), artificial insemination centres providing bovine semen which enjoyed a virtual monopoly under national legislation in each region of France were held by the Court to be abusing their position if they were to charge additional costs over and above those actually incurred in obtaining and conserving semen imported from other Member States. The Commission has applied this decision to price-fixing for dock-work in a series of local port monopolies established by national law throughout Italy (*Re Italian Ports Employment Policy: The Italian Community* v *Italy* (Case 97/94)).

Unnaturally low prices may also amount to an abuse, where they are intended to drive an actual or potential competitor from the market. This practice is normally called 'predatory pricing'. A good example of this is the case of *AKZO Chemie BV* v *Commission* (Case C-62/86). Here, the Commission found that AKZO occupied a dominant position in the market for flour additives and for organic peroxides used in the making of plastics. Another company, ECS, which was already in the flour additives market, wished to enter the peroxide for the plastics market in the United Kingdom. The Commission found that AKZO had made direct threats to ECS, had systematically offered and supplied flour additives to ECS's customers at abnormally low prices and had also offered them products which it did not normally supply at below cost price. The Court repeated its previously stated position that Art 82 prohibits a dominant undertaking from eliminating a competitor and thus reinforcing its position by means other than competition on merit. In that sense, not all price competition can be regarded as legitimate:

> Prices lower than the average total costs by which a dominant undertaking seeks to eliminate a competitor must be regarded as an abuse. A dominant undertaking has no interest in offering such prices except to eliminate its competitors in order then to raise its prices again on the basis of its monopolistic position, since every sale involves it in a loss, namely all the fixed costs and at least a part of the variable costs relating to the unit produced.

(2) Exclusive supply

It is not uncommon for suppliers to give discounts to customers who place large orders with them, and indeed there is nothing wrong, in principle, with such arrangements. But if the discount is tied to a requirement that the purchaser purchase all or a very large part of his supplies from the dominant undertaking, the arrangement may very well fall foul of Art 82. In *Hoffman La Roche* (Case 85/76) the investigation by the Commission revealed that the company, which was the largest producer of pharmaceuticals in the world, occupied a dominant position in markets for a number of vitamin products. It sold these products on the basis that customers were bound by an exclusive or preferential purchasing commitment in favour of the company for all or a large proportion of their requirements. This was achieved either by an express exclusive purchase agreement, or as a result of 'fidelity rebates'. The Court rejected these arrangements, since the discounts did not reflect any real cost saving as a result of a bulk purchase (i.e. transport, storage, etc.) but were a direct attempt to 'buy' the exclusive custom of the purchaser.

Similarly, in *Michelin* v *Commission* (Case 322/81), the company gave target bonuses to its dealers according to their marketing efforts. Dealers were not given a clear indication of the basis on which such bonuses were calculated. The Commission found that the system had the effect of ensuring that the dealers remained attached to Michelin in the hope of receiving the often unknown, but hoped-for, bonuses. The Court accepted the Commission's finding and ruled that discounts had to be justified by a benefit conferred on the supplier which reduced the supplier's costs and enabled the supplier to pass on the benefit in terms of reduced prices. Across-the-board discounts on a range of products are also an abuse, because they make it more difficult for other suppliers who may not have a similar range of products to compete for an opportunity to supply.

(3) Tied sales

These are specifically prohibited by Art 82(d), which forbids 'making the conclusion of contracts subject to acceptance by the other parties of supplementary obligations which, by their nature or according to commercial usage, have no connection with the subject of such contracts'. Typically, this applies to an arrangement under which the supplier requires the purchaser to purchase its requirements of a second product (the 'tied' product) as a condition of being able to buy a first product (the 'tying' product). In *Tetra-Pak* (Case T-83/91), the Commission had found that Tetra-Pak held approximately 90 per cent of, *inter alia*, the market of machines for making aseptic cartons for liquids. Purchasers of such machines were required to obtain their supplies of cartons exclusively from Tetra-Pak or from a supplier designated by it. The Court declared:

> It is clear that the tied-sale clauses [in the agreements with purchasers] ... went beyond their ostensible purpose and are intended to strengthen Tetra-Pak's dominant position by reinforcing its customers' economic dependence on it. Those clauses are therefore wholly unreasonable in the context of protecting public health and also go beyond the recognised right of an undertaking in a dominant position to protect its commercial interests. Whether considered in isolation or together, they were unfair.

(4) Refusal to supply

Whether or not a dominant undertaking's refusal to supply another undertaking is an abuse or not will be very much a matter of fact, depending on the circumstances of the refusal and the previous dealings of the parties. In *Commercial Solvents Corporation* v *Commission* (Cases 6 & 7/73), the Corporation had decided to discontinue sales of aminobutanol to another manufacturer, Zoja, because it had decided to manufacture its derivative, ethambutol, itself. The Court held that the decision to manufacture ethambutanol itself did not justify a refusal to supply the raw material to a potential rival. To do so would effectively eliminate one of the principal manufacturers of etham-butanol in the Community. There may, however, be objectively justifiable reasons for not supplying a commodity.

In *BP* v *Commission* (Case 77/77), BP refused to sell oil to an intermittent purchaser during the oil crisis in the early 1970s. There was, effectively, an oil embargo of Western Europe and BP had drawn up a list of regular customers whom it would continue to supply, and others whom it would not, or would supply only as and when it was able. The Court of Justice held that, in such a supply crisis, a refusal to supply was justified. There must, however, be an objective justification for a refusal. In *United Brands* v *Commission* (Case 27/76), the issue, it will be remembered, was the nature of the banana market (see above) and a number of alleged abuses by UBC. One of these was refusal to supply certain, hitherto regular, customers. One of these, Olesen, had participated in an advertising campaign run by one of UBC's rivals, and it was this participation that UBC wished to 'punish'. The Court rejected this attempted justifi-cation of a refusal to supply:

> Although it is true, as the applicant points out, that the fact that an undertaking is in a dominant position cannot disentitle it from protecting its own commercial interests if they are attacked, and that such an undertaking must be conceded the right to take such reasonable steps as it deems appropriate to protect its said interests, such behaviour can-not be countenanced if its actual purpose is to strengthen this dominant position and abuse it.
>
> Even if the possibility of a counter-attack is acceptable, that attack must still be pro-portionate to the threat taking into account the economic strength of the undertakings confronting each other.
>
> The sanction consisting of a refusal to supply by an undertaking in a dominant position was in excess of what might, if such a situation were to arise, reasonably be contemplated as a sanction for conduct similar to that for which UBC blamed Olesen.

Another example of a refusal to supply being used to retain dominance in a market occurred in a case which did not go to the Court of Justice: *British Brass Band Instruments* v *Boosey and Hawkes* [1988] 4 CMLR 67. In this decision, the Commission found that Boosey and Hawkes produced and sold 90 per cent of the market in British brass band instruments. The BBBI wished to import and distribute brass band instruments originating in other parts of the Community. Boosey and Hawkes refused to continue to supply the BBBI with British instruments until it desisted in its importation and sale of Continental brass band instruments. The Commission found the discontinuance of supply abusive. Where an undertaking has a monopoly of information, a refusal to supply that information to a potential publisher of television programmes can constitute a refusal to supply under Art 82(b) (*RTE & ITP* v *Commission* (Cases C-241/91P & C-242/91P)).

(5) Other abusive practices

The ingenuity of undertakings seeking to extend their dominance and to exclude competitors makes it impossible to provide more than some examples of common abusive practices. In *Tetra-Pak International SA v Commission* (Case T-83/91), for example, besides the tying agreements and excessive and predatory pricing which have already been considered, Tetra-Pak was found by the Commission to have engaged also in the following abusive practices: buying back competitors' machines with a view to withdrawing them from the market; obtaining an undertaking from one of the dairies with which it did business not to use two machines it had acquired from competitors of Tetra-Pak; eliminating in Italy all Resolvo aseptic packaging machines developed by a rival company; and finally, appropriating advertising media by obtaining an exclusive rights agreement with an Italian milk industry journal under which Tetra-Pak's rivals would not be allowed to advertise in the journal.

Affecting trade between Member States

As with Art 81, there must be some effect on trade between Member States for Art 82 to apply. To satisfy this condition, it is not necessary that the effect on trade should be of a particular kind. Typically, it would meet the requirement if the effect of the conduct would be to partition markets in the Community. In *Greenwich Film Production v SACEM* (Case 22/79), SACEM was an association formed to collect royalties arising out of the performance of artistic and other works in France and elsewhere. SACEM demanded payment of royalties arising out of the performance of music in films distributed in France. Greenwich argued that SACEM effectively had a monopoly of such rights in France and was abusing its position. SACEM contended, *inter alia*, that even if this was so, it did not affect trade between Member States. The Court, however, accepted that there might be some effect. It recognised that in certain Member States organisations such as SACEM were entrusted by composers to supervise performances of their work and to collect royalties. It held that it is possible in those circumstances that 'the activities of such associations may be conducted in such a way that their effect is to partition the common market and thereby restrict the freedom to provide services which constitutes one of the objectives of the Treaty'.

This will not be the case where the activities are exclusively directed at part of a Member State. In *Hugin v Commission* (Case 22/78), the Commission had found that Hugin, the Swedish manufacturers of cash registers, had refused to supply spare parts of their machines to a London-based firm, Liptons. Liptons serviced, repaired and reconditioned such machines. Their business was essentially local, and they did no work outside the United Kingdom. The Court concluded that the abuse did not have the effect of preventing Liptons from carrying out their servicing in other Member States or affect the trade in parts between Member States, because those requiring the parts would normally obtain them direct from the manufacturers in Sweden (which was not, then, of course, in either the Community or the European Economic Area).

Relationship between Articles 81(1) and 82: collective dominance?

It is clear that many undertakings in a dominant position will endeavour to reinforce that position by various kinds of loyalty, tying and other agreements. Such agreements in themselves may infringe Art 81(1), or they may also constitute forms of abusive behaviour which breaches Art 82. On the other hand, agreements between undertakings and subsidiaries may not breach Art 81 simply because they are subsidiaries, and their action is seen as the action of one and the same entity: *VIHO Europe BV* v *Commission* (C-73/95P). In such circumstances, the agreement between a parent company and subsidiaries may, however, where it is intended to drive or exclude a competitor from the market, constitute an abuse of a dominant position. In *Instituto Chemioterapico Italiano and Commercial Solvents Corporation* v *Commission* (Cases 6 & 7/73), it was CSC, the controlling company, which had instructed its subsidiary ICI not to supply aminobutanol to Zoja.

An agreement between several undertakings, each of which has a powerful position in a particular market, may come close to creating dominance which may then be subject to abuse by them. Article 82, indeed, refers to abuse by 'one or more undertakings'. However, the undertakings involved are more likely to be penalised for a breach of Art 81(1) than a breach of Art 82 (Commission decision on *Italian Flat Glass* [1990] 4 CMLR 535). The nearest the Court had come to accepting a breach of Art 82 where there is a linkage of several undertakings was in the case of an actual or proposed merger of those undertakings (see, e.g., *Continental Can* (Case 6/72)). Tacit collusion between major undertakings comprising, in effect, a tight oligopoly, may be difficult for the Commission to deal with. In *Hoffman La Roche* (Case 85/76), the Court declared (in response to Advocate-General Lenz's observation that there was a problem in knowing where a collective monopoly ends and an oligopoly begins):

> A dominant position must also be distinguished from parallel courses of conduct which are peculiar to oligopolies in that in an oligopoly the courses of conduct interact, while in the case of an undertaking occupying a dominant position the conduct of the undertaking which derives profits from that position is to a great extent determined unilaterally.

In the absence of clear evidence, a concerted practice breaching Art 81(1) may not be demonstrable. If that is the case, then, *a fortiori*, an abuse by connected undertakings cannot be shown to breach Art 82. Evidence of some judicial movement in relation to the concept of collective dominance came first when the Court of First Instance considered the decision of the Commission in *Italian Flat Glass* (*SIV* v *Commission* (Joined Cases T-68, 77 & 78/89)). The CFI held that Art 86 (now Art 82) was capable of applying to independent firms which, because of the economic links between them, held a collective dominant position on the relevant market. Nevertheless, on the facts of the case, it decided that there was insufficient evidence to support a finding of collective dominance. However, in *Compagnie Maritime Belge* (Joined Cases T-24–26 & 28/93), the CFI held that the members of a shipping conference had abused the collective dominant position they held as a result of close relations between them. The Court of Justice had already, by then, accepted in principle that Art 86 (now Art 82) was capable of applying to collective dominance (*DIP and Others* v *Commune di Bassano del Grappa* (Joined Cases C-140–142/94)). The basis of these decisions is the fact that Art 82 applies to 'one or more undertakings'. This may, originally, have been intended by the draftsmen of the Treaty to refer only to a primary undertaking and its subsidiaries, as in *VIHO* v *Commission* (Case C-73/95P), but the difficulty of proving the existence of a concerted practice in Art 81(1) seems to have led the Court to take a more sympathetic view of collective dominance, in order to bring the activities within Art 82, and to bridge the apparent gap between Arts 81 and 82.

Mergers

A merger takes place when two or more undertakings which were formerly independent are brought under common control. As a result of the decision of the Court of Justice in *Continental Can* (above), it was clear that a merger between undertakings could, in appropriate circumstances, breach Art 82. What those circumstances were became the subject, after prolonged discussions, of a Council regulation on mergers (Council Regulation 4064/89, on the control of concentrations between undertakings). Under the regulation, the Commission is given sole competence to take decisions with regard to 'concentrations with a Community dimension'.

Such concentrations may be viewed from two perspectives. On the one hand, the combined economic strengths of fully merged undertakings, or the cooperation between undertakings which have partly merged, may produce a degree of market control and distortion of competition that is detrimental to the effective operation of the market. On the other hand, the merger may produce economies of scale, and result in the creation of an undertaking whose size and strength may enable it to compete effectively on world markets. In considering the effect of a merger under the regulation, the Commission has to strike a balance between competing objectives.

Article 2(1) of the regulation requires the Commission to make an appraisal of the proposed merger, taking into account:

(a) the need to maintain and develop effective competition within the common market in view of, amongst other things, the structure of all the markets concerned and the actual or potential competition from undertakings located either within or outwith the Community;

(b) the market position of the undertakings concerned and their economic and financial power, the alternatives available to suppliers and users, their access to suppliers or markets, any legal and other barriers to entry, supply and demand trends for the relevant goods and services, the interests of the intermediate and ultimate consumers, and the development of technical and economic progress provided that it is to the consumers' advantage and does not form an obstacle to competition.

Concentrations which do, or do not, create or strengthen a dominant position impeding or limiting competition are to be declared by the Commission to be compatible with the common market, or incompatible, according to the facts as found by the Commission (Art 2(2), (3)).

The Community dimension of a merger is achieved when the aggregate worldwide turnover of all the undertakings concerned is more than 5,000 million ECU and the aggregate Community-wide turnover of at least two of the undertakings involved is more than 250 million ECU, unless each of the undertakings concerned achieves more than two-thirds of its aggregate Community-wide turnover in one and the same Member State (Art 1(2)).

Regulation 1310/97, which amended Regulation 4064/89, introduced a new Art 1(3) into the latter regulation, which provides that where a concentration does not meet the above thresholds, it will still have a Community dimension where:

(a) the combined aggregate worldwide turnover of all the undertakings concerned is more than ECU 2,500 million;

(b) in each of at least three Member States, the combined aggregate turnover of all the undertakings concerned is more than ECU 100 million;

(c) in each of at least three Member States included for the purpose of point (b), the aggregate turnover of each of at least two of the undertakings concerned is more than ECU 25 million; and

(d) the aggregate Community-wide turnover of each of at least two of the undertakings concerned is more than ECU 100 million;

unless each of the undertakings concerned achieves more than two-thirds of its aggregate Community-wide turnover within one and the same Member State.

The regulation has not, to date, constituted much of a barrier to mergers and the vast majority of the mergers notified to the Commission have obtained clearance. The Commission seems to see mergers as a way of reducing national control of undertakings and promoting the strength of large Community undertakings on the world market. Less attention appears now to be paid to the possible adverse effects on consumers in the Community. One case where the Commission denied clearance, *Aerospatiale-Alenia/de Haviland* [1992] 4 CMLR M2, on the grounds that the merger would have had an unacceptable impact on customers' freedom of choice and the balance of competition in the Community, was widely criticised by governments, many with clear political interests in a different outcome than that resulting from the decision.

In *France v Commission* (Cases C-68/94 & C-30/95), the Court gave the merger regulations a new cutting edge, holding that they applied to a situation of collective dominance which fell short of an actual merger (see Editorial (1998) 23 EL Rev 199, 'Collective dominance: trump card or joker?'). Under the consolidated Merger Regulation 1310/97, which amends Regulation 4064/89, cooperative aspects of joint ventures by undertakings which fall within the turnover threshold will have to be notified to the Commission, and assessed for compatibility with Art 81(1).

Further reading

Andrews, P., 'Is Meeting Competition a Defence to Predatory Pricing? The Irish Sugar Decision Suggests a New Approach' [1998] ECLR 49.

Art, J.-Y. and van Liederkerke, D., 'Developments in EC Competition Law in 1996 – An Overview' (1997) 34 CML Rev 895.

Brittan, Sir Leon, 'The Law and Policy of Merger Control in the EEC' (1990) 15 EL Rev 351.

Brown, A., 'Distinguishing between concentrative and co-operative ventures: Is it getting any easier?' (1996) 17 ECLR 240.

Craig, P. and De Burca, G. (1998) *EU Law Text, Cases and Materials* (2nd edn), OUP, Chapters 21 and 22.

Downes, T.A. and Ellison, J. (1991) *The Legal Control of Mergers in the European Communities*, Blackstone Press.

Goyder, D.G. (1993) *EEC Competition Law* (2nd edn), OUP.

Korah, V. (1997) *EC Competition Law and Practice*, Hart Publishing.

Plender, R. and Usher, J. (1993) *Cases and Materials on the Law of the European Communities*, Butterworths, Chapter 11.

Sanders, A.K. (1997), *Unfair Competition Law*, Clarendon Press.

Soames, T., 'An Analysis of the Principles of Concerted Dominance: A Distinction without a Difference?' [1996] ECLR 24.

Steiner, J. and Woods, L. (2000) *Textbook on EC Law* (7th edn), Blackstone Press, Chapter 16.

Tillotson, J. (2000) *European Community Law: text, cases and materials* (3rd edn), Cavendish Publishing Ltd, Chapters 15 and 16.

Weatherill, S. (2000), *Cases and Materials on EC Law* (5th edn), Blackstone Press, Chapter 12.

Whish, R. (1993) *Competition Law*, Butterworths, Chapter 8.

Chapter 22

ENFORCEMENT OF COMPETITION LAW: POWERS AND PROCEDURES

INTRODUCTION

The European Commission has a general duty, imposed on it by Art 85(1), 'to ensure the application of the principles laid down in Articles 81 and 82'.

Article 85(1) requires that:

> On application by a Member State or on its own initiative, and in co-operation with the competent authorities in the Member States, who shall give it their assistance, the Commission shall investigate cases of suspected infringement of these principles. If it finds that there has been an infringement, it shall propose appropriate measures to bring it to an end.

Under Art 85(2), if the infringement is not brought to an end, the Commission is required to record details of the infringement in a reasoned decision and to authorise Member States to take the necessary measures to remedy the situation.

Article 85 enables the Commission to make the appropriate decision, but it does not confer specific investigative powers, define the investigative process or prescribe any means of enforcement by the Commission. These powers and duties are conferred on the Commission by Regulation 17/62, and, with the exception of transport (subject to a special process under Regulation 141/62), they apply to all investigations by the Commission.

On 27 September 2000, the Commission proposed a regulation to replace Regulation 17/62. This proposal is considered at the end of the chapter.

INITIATING ACTION BY THE COMMISSION

Where an apparent breach of Art 81 or Art 82 has come to the notice of the Commission through, for example, a question by a member of the European Parliament, or a report in the press, the Commission can, under the general power conferred on it by Art 85, commence an investigation. Article 3, Regulation 17/62 provides that Member States and 'natural and legal persons who claim a legitimate interest' may apply to the Commission to decide whether or not there has been an infringement. Since, however, the Commission has its own residual power to commence such an investigation, even a person who does not have a claim to a legitimate interest can bring details of a possible breach of Art 81 or Art 82 to the attention of the Commission with an expectation that it will be investigated (see Hunnings, 1987 (Adams' complaint ultimately resulted in a decision against his former employers); *Hoffman La Roche*

(Case 85/76); and a claim against the Commission itself – *Adams v Commission* (Case 145/83)).

Although the Commission is not obliged to investigate every complaint it receives, it must, when it does decide to open an inquiry, do so 'with the required care, seriousness and diligence in order to evaluate, in full knowledge, the elements of fact and law submitted for its assessment' (*Asia Motor France v Commission (No. 2)* (Case T-7/92)). The element of care involves showing proper regard for the interests of both the complainant and the respondent in the proceedings. A growing number of decisions made by the Commission have, in recent years, been struck down by the Court of Justice and the Court of First Instance because proper procedural requirements have not been met. This has occurred partly because Regulation 17/62 is not at all specific as to how the rights of the parties should be respected during consideration of a complaint and the subsequent investigation. The regulation has, therefore, been 'fleshed' out by the Court, drawing on a variety of sources, including the European Convention on Human Rights, the International Covenant of Civil and Political Rights and the domestic constitutional systems of Member States (*National Panasonic v Commission* (Case 136/79); *Orkem v Commission* (Case 374/87)). The Commission has had to learn by a process of trial and error whether its procedures met the evolving standards of the Court. The other reason for the failure of the Commission to meet the Court's procedural requirements has been the chronic shortage of resources which has, on occasion, compelled it to take short cuts in the process, and to rely increasingly on national anti-trust agencies and national courts to deal with infringements of competition law where there is both a national and a Community dimension (see Shaw, 1995).

If the Commission decides to reject a complaint, it is required by Art 253 to give reasons for that decision. In *Tremblay and Others v Syndicat des Exploitants de Lieux de Loisirs (SELL)* (Case T-5/93), the Commission had received a number of complaints against the Société des Auteurs, Compositeurs et Editeurs de Musique (SACEM). The complainants, who ran discotheques throughout France, alleged that SACEM, which manages copyright in musical works in France, had infringed Arts 81 and 82. In response to the complaints, the Commission undertook an investigation and subsequently informed the complainants that its investigation provided no basis 'for concluding that the conditions for the application of Article 86 [now Art 82] are fulfilled with regard to the level of tariffs at present applied by SACEM'. In relation to Art 81, the Commission told the complainants that the practices of which they complained were essentially national, there was no Community interest involved and the issues raised were, in any event, already before a number of French courts. The Court found that the Commission had not provided the complainants with the grounds for rejecting their complaint as to the alleged partitioning of national markets by reciprocal representation contracts made between various copyright management societies in different Member States. It rejected the challenge to the Commission's finding of a lack of a sufficient Community interest and held that the fact that a national court or national competition authority is already dealing with a case concerning the compatibility of an agreement or practice with Art 81 or Art 82 is a factor which the Commission may take into account in evaluating the extent to which a case displays a Community interest (see *Automec Srl v Commission (Automec No. 2)* (Case T-24/90); Shaw, 1993; Friend, 1994).

A complainant has no right to insist that the Commission adopt a final decision as to the existence or otherwise of an alleged infringement. Where the Commission does not propose to initiate infringement proceedings, it is required by Art 6, Regulation 99/63 to inform any complainants of its reasons and to fix a time limit within which they may submit further comments in writing. In such a case, if the Commission then decides that further investigation is unwarranted or unnecessary, it should provide a sufficiently reasoned decision to the complainant to enable its legality to be challenged in judicial review proceedings under Art 230 EC Treaty (*Ladbroke Racing (Deutschland) GmbH* v *Commission* (Case T-74/92)).

APPLICATIONS BY PARTIES TO A POSSIBLE INFRINGEMENT

Article 2, Regulation 17/62 enables undertakings concerned with agreements which may breach Art 81(1) or Art 82 to apply to the Commission for negative clearance. This may be followed by a formal grant of clearance. This consists of a decision by the Commission certifying that, on the basis of the facts in its possession, there are no grounds for action to be taken in respect of the agreement or conduct in question. The chief advantage of obtaining clearance is that activity can continue under an agreement or practice until the Commission makes a decision (Art 15(5), Regulation 17/62). If clearance is obtained, it provides a bar to action by the Commission while it is extant. The full facts must, however, be disclosed to the Commission. Failure to disclose them could result in revocation of the clearance and the imposition of a fine on the defaulting undertaking (Art 15(1)(a), Regulation 17/62).

Article 4, Regulation 17/62 provides for the notification to the Commission of agreements, decisions and concerted practices defined by Art 81(1) EC Treaty and for which the parties seek a declaration under Art 81(3) that the agreement or practice is not subject to Art 81(1). A decision of this kind will be for a fixed period, but it may be renewed if the requirements of Art 81(3) continue to be satisfied (see above, Chapter 20). The Commission can revoke or amend its decision, or prohibit certain acts by the parties where there has been any change in the facts which formed the basis of the decision, where the parties have breached a condition attached to the decision, where the decision was based on incorrect information or was induced by deceit, or where the parties abuse the exemption conferred on them by the decision (Art 8(3), Regulation 17/62).

The effect of application for negative clearance or for exemption under Art 81(3) may result in refusal of clearance or the granting of an exemption by the Commission, or precipitate a demand for more information or even a full investigation.

The provision of information to the Commission

Article 11, Regulation 17/62 is intended to assist the Commission in obtaining the information necessary to investigate a suspected infringement. Under it the Commission can obtain all necessary information from the governments of the Member States and from undertakings and associated undertakings (Art 11(1)). The Commission is required, when making a request for information, to state the legal basis and the purpose of the request and also the penalties under Art 15(1)(b) for supplying incorrect information. The undertakings are under a legal obligation to supply the full information required, with a penalty for failure to do so (Arts 11(4) and (5), 15(1)(b) and 16(1)(c)). Non-cooperation in the supply of information can take the form of unhelpful replies to questions as well as an outright refusal to answer them. In *Scottish Football Association* v *Commission* (Case T-46/92), the Court of First Instance held that the Commission was under no obligation either to pursue lengthy informal correspondence or to engage in oral discussions with the applicant, who had provided only half the information requested. It could simply, as it had done in this case, demand the information on the basis of Art 11(5), on pain of a penalty of ECU 500 per day for non-disclosure.

The request for information must specify the kind of anti-competitive practice to which it relates, and details of the request must be sent to the government of the Member State in which the principal office of the undertaking is based (Art 11(2) and (3)).

In *Société General* v *Commission* (Case T-34/93), the Commission was making inquiries into the operation of the so-called Helsinki Agreement which fixed a differential system of charges made to payees of Eurocheques. This followed an investigation which had already resulted in the imposition by the Commission of heavy fines on other parties to the agreement and the abandonment of the agreement by French banks: Commission Decision 92/212 OJ 1992 195/50 (*Groupement Bancaire and Europay* v *Commission ('Eurocheques')*). It sent a letter to Société General requesting information about an apparently discriminatory charge imposed on a private payee and about the operation of another inter-bank agreement called the Package Deal Agreement. Société General refused to supply the information, even after the Commission had explained how it related to its investigation, and argued that a reply on the application of the Package Deal would infringe its rights as a defendant. The Court rejected both arguments, accepting that the Commission had adequately explained its purpose in requiring the information on charging practices. It held that the answers requested were purely factual and could not be regarded as capable of requiring the Société General to admit an infringement of the rules on competition.

The obligation to cooperate with the Commission in its inquiries extends to the provision of all relevant information, even that which might support a finding of an infringement. However, informants are not obliged to incriminate themselves. The issue of possible self-incrimination was raised in *Solvay* v *Commission* (Case 27/88) and *Orkem* v *Commission* (Case 374/87). The applicants in these cases argued that the Commission decisions requiring them to provide information under Art 11 sought to force them to incriminate themselves. The Court noted that Regulation 17/62 recognises no such right of non self-incrimination, but instead calls for active cooperation from the party investigated. The Court did, however, look at the issue in the context of the fundamental rights to which all Community law is subject. It decided that there was no such right in relation to legal persons (companies) where infringements of economic law are in issue. This distinction was criticised by the European Court of Human Rights in *Funke* v *France* (Case A/256-A) (in relation to the application of Art 6.1 ECHR) and it is doubtful if the *Orkem* decision is still good law (see also *Société Stenuit* v *France* (1992) 14 EHRR 509 (a decision of the Human Rights Commission that fines imposed by the European Commission for breaches of competition law were of a criminal nature)).

Whatever the extent of the application of the right against self-incrimination, the rules on the right of the defence do have the effect of not requiring those being investigated to make any admissions of infringement:

> While ... the Commission is entitled to oblige the company to furnish all necessary information relating to facts of which it is aware and, if necessary, to communicate to it the relevant documents in its possession even if these may be used to prove anti-competitive behaviour by it or another company, *it may not, by a request for information, compromise the rights of defence of a company. Thus, the Commission may not oblige a company to furnish replies by which it would be induced to admit the existence of the infringement which it is for the Commission to prove.* (*Solvay*, paras 31 and 32) (emphasis added)

In *Société General* (above) the Court accepted that those under investigation were not obliged to accept the existence of an infringement of the rules of competition. However, there may well be a very fine line between admission of the facts which constitute the infringement and admission of the infringement itself.

THE COMMISSION'S POWERS OF INVESTIGATION

The Commission can take a more pro-active role in the conduct of its inquiries by carrying out investigations in the territory of Member States. Under Art 14, Regulation 17/62 the Commission is authorised to undertake all necessary investigations of undertakings and associations of undertakings. To this end the officials authorised by the Commission are empowered:

1   to examine the books and other business records;
2   to take copies of or extracts from the books and business records;
3   to ask for oral explanations on the spot;
4   to enter any premises, land, and means of transport of undertakings. (Art 14(1))

Officials who are authorised by the Commission to act in relation to these powers are entitled to exercise them on production of an authorisation in writing, specifying the subject matter and purpose of the investigation and the penalties for not supplying or for supplying incomplete books and other business records. Undertakings are obliged to submit to investigations ordered by a decision of the Commission. In good time before the investigation the Commission has to inform the relevant authority in the host state and identify the officials concerned (Art 14(2) and (3)). Before the decision to conduct an investigation of this kind is made, the Commission must consult the relevant authority in the host state. That authority is bound to give every assistance to the Commission officials, especially where the undertaking concerned is opposing the investigation (Art 14(4), (5) and (6)).

In *Hoechst* v *Commission* (Case 46/87), two Commission investigators conducted a 'dawn raid' (during office hours!) on Hoechst in Germany on 15 January 1987, armed with the necessary decision under Art 14(3), for the purpose of investigating various suspected infringements relating to price fixing and market sharing in the market for PVC and polyethylene. Hoechst refused to submit to the investigation, on the grounds that it was a search which was illegal in the absence of a judicial warrant. On 17

January the investigators tried again, accompanied by two officials of the Federal Cartel Office and two policemen. Hoechst again refused to submit, for the same reason. A third attempt also failed. The Commission eventually obtained access following the issue of a search warrant to the Commission by the German Court. A year later the Commission imposed a fine of 55,000 ECUs on Hoechst for its refusal to submit to the investigation. Hoechst appealed to the Court of Justice.

The Court reaffirmed its earlier rulings that fundamental rights, and the European Convention on Human Rights in particular, are part of the general principles of law. In interpreting Art 14, Regulation 17/62 particular regard must be given to the rights of the defence. It held that some rights of the defence, especially those relating to legal representation and the privileged nature of correspondence between solicitor and client, had to be recognised from the preliminary inquiry stage of an investigation. Having said that, the Court emphasised the importance of the Commission's investigative powers, and the need to secure access where its inquiries were thwarted:

> That right of access would serve no useful purpose if the Commission's officials could do no more than ask for documents or files which they could identify precisely in advance. On the contrary, such a right implies the power to search for various items of information which are not already known or fully identified. Without such a power, it would be impossible for the Commission to obtain the information necessary to carry out the investigation if the undertakings concerned refused to cooperate or adopted an obstructive attitude.

The Court made it clear that, where the Commission's entry is opposed, Commission officials cannot force an entry without first seeking the assistance of national courts. Those courts must, however, ensure that the Commission's actions are effective, and cannot substitute their own assessment of whether or not the investigation ordered by the Commission is necessary, since that function is the exclusive prerogative of the Commission, subject only to review by the Court of Justice itself. In these circumstances, therefore, the Commission requires a national warrant but the national courts are more or less obliged to grant it! The decision is, in many ways, an uncomfortable compromise between fundamental principles of national law and the need for effective Commission powers. In such cases there is an inevitable conflict between the need to give adequate notice to the person or body concerned of the purpose of the search (under Art 14(3)) on the one hand and, on the other, the difficulty of knowing precisely what is in the hands of the suspected undertaking and ensuring that it remains there when the officials arrive (for comment, see Forrester and Norall, 1989; Shaw, 1990; for parallel problems in English law, see *IRC* v *Rossminster* [1980] AC 952 (Lord Wilberforce)).

Information obtained in the course of an investigation must be used only for the purpose of the relevant request or investigation. The Commission is bound to publish its decisions, but it must make sure that it takes into account the legitimate interest of undertakings in the protection of their business secrets (Arts 20 and 21, Regulation 17/62). Although the Commission has a general obligation to send copies of the most important documents to Member States, where an undertaking has expressly raised the confidentiality of a particular document containing business secrets with the Commission, the Commission may have to decide not to send a particular document or set of documents to the relevant Member State (*Samenwerkende Elektriciteits-produktiebedrijven NV* v *Commission* (Case C-36/92P)). The obligation of secrecy is owed not only to undertakings under investigation, but also to informants and complainants (*Adams* v *Commission* (Case 145/83)).

THE RIGHT TO A HEARING

Before it adopts a decision applying Art 81 or Art 82, the Commission must, under Art 19, Regulation 17/62, give the undertakings concerned the opportunity of being heard on the matters to which the Commission has taken objection. If the Commission or the relevant authorities in the Member States consider it necessary, they can also hear representations from other legal or natural persons, provided they can show a sufficient interest. Under Regulation 99/63 such representations will normally be in writing, although under Art 7, Regulation 99/63 undertakings may, if they have requested it in their written submissions, or if the Commission proposes to impose a fine on them or a periodic penalty, put forward their arguments orally.

To enable undertakings to exercise their right to make representations effectively, they must be informed of the facts and considerations on the basis of which the Commission is minded to act (Art 2(1), Regulation 99/63; *NTN Toyo Bearing Company and Others* v *Council and Commission (Ballbearings)* (Case 113/77) (A-G Warner)).

In *Hoffman La Roche* v *Commission* (Case 85/76), the Court ruled that undertakings must be afforded 'the opportunity during the administrative procedure to make known their views on the truth and relevance of the facts and circumstances alleged and on the documents used by the Commission to support its claim that there has been an infringement'.

The duty of disclosure is not, however, absolute. There is a *class* of documents, including correspondence with Member States and purely internal Commission documents, which are regarded as confidential and which do not have to be disclosed. Other documents, such as correspondence with third-party undertakings, might legitimately be withheld where disclosure might lead to retaliation against those third parties by the undertaking involved in the proceedings (*BPB Industries plc and British Gypsum Ltd* v *Commission* (Case C-310/93P)). Previous practice has been formalised by Commission Decision 94/90, incorporating its Code of Conduct of 6 December 1993 (see now Art 255 EC Treaty as amended by the Treaty of Amsterdam). Under the Code, the Commission is obliged to give public access to any document it holds. That right must, however, be denied by the Commission 'where disclosure could ... undermine ... the protection of the public interest (public security, international relations, monetary stability, court proceedings, inspections and investigations)'. If access is refused, the Commission is required, under Art 253 EC Treaty, to specify, in the case of *each category of documents*, how the public interest might be damaged if the documents are disclosed: *Interporc Im-und Export GmbH* v *Commission* (Case T-124/96).

THE DECISION

There is a general principle of Community law contained in Art 253 EC Treaty that 'decisions shall state the reasons on which they are based'. They should also be made by the Commission according to the proper procedure and according to the proper form. Failure to observe these principles may render the decision a nullity from the start. In *Commission* v *BASF AG and Others* (Case C-137/92P), the Court of First Instance had declared non-existent a Commission decision under which the applicants and others had infringed Art 81 in relation to the production of PVC (Commission Decision 89/190/EEC of 21 December 1988). The Court of First Instance had found that the original decision had been altered after it had been adopted by the Commissioners 'by persons who were clearly not Commissioners'. The CFI also found that the contested decision had adopted the decision only in its English, German and French versions, leaving it to the Commissioner then responsible for competition, Mr Sutherland, to adopt the text of the decision in the other official languages of the Community. The CFI noted that Mr Sutherland had no competence to do this and held that the measure was 'vitiated by particularly serious and manifest defects rendering it non-existent in law'.

The Commission appealed against this decision, and the appeal was allowed by the Court of Justice. The Court pointed out that, as a general rule, acts of the Community institutions are presumed to be lawful and productive of legal effects even if affected by irregularities, until such time as they are annulled or withdrawn. There was, however, an exception to that rule in relation to acts

> ... tainted by an irregularity whose gravity is so obvious that it cannot be tolerated by the Community legal order. [Such acts] ... must be treated as having no legal effect, even provisional, that is to say that they must be regarded as legally non-existent. The purpose of this exception is to maintain a balance between two fundamental, but sometimes conflicting, requirements with which a legal order must comply, namely stability of legal relations and respect for legality.

The Court emphasised the collegiate nature of the Commission's decision-making process. It rejected the Commission's argument that in the decision-making process the college of Commissioners can confine itself to making clear its intention without having to become involved in the drafting and finalisation of the act giving effect to its intention. After the final form of the decision had been approved by the Commissioners as a body, only simple corrections of spelling and grammar could be made to the text. In the event, however, the Court of Justice thought that the CFI had gone too far in holding the decision to be non-existent. It was, however, annulled on the same procedural grounds on which the CFI decision had been based.

If the Commission decides that there has been an infringement of Art 81 or Art 82, the Commission may, under Art 3(1), Regulation 17/62, adopt a decision ordering the infringement to be brought to an end. Under Article 16 it can impose a periodic penalty payment of 50 to 1,000 units of account per day, from the date of the decision until the infringement is brought to an end. It can also impose fines on the undertakings concerned.

FINES

The Commission has the power, by decision, to impose fines for intentionally or negligently supplying incorrect or misleading information, or for refusing to submit to an investigation (Art 15(1), Regulation 17/62). In cases where the Commission has found a breach of Art 81 or Art 82, it may, by decision, impose on an undertaking or association of undertakings fines from 1,000 to 1,000,000 units of account, or a sum in excess of that figure, provided that this is no more than 10 per cent of the turnover in the preceding year of each of the undertakings participating in the infringement. Fines can be imposed only where the undertakings have acted intentionally or negligently. The criteria for the appropriate level of fine should, the Court has stated, take into account in particular the nature of the restrictions on competition, the number and size of the undertakings concerned, the relative proportions of the market controlled by them and the situation in the market where the infringement was committed (*ACF Chemiefarma* v *Commission* (Case 41/69)).

The Commission's policy on fines can be seen in *Welded Steel Mesh* (OJ 1989 L 260/1). In this case 14 companies in France, the Benelux, Germany and Italy shared markets between themselves, fixed prices and volumes and took action to enforce their cartel. The activities of the participants amounted to 'a sustained effort, carried on for a long period covering at least five years … to frustrate … one of the main aims of the Treaty, namely the creation of a common market, by interference in the price mechanism, restrictions on import penetration of one another's domestic markets, quantity restrictions and market sharing'. Mitigating factors were taken into account: namely, the parties sometimes did not respect the price and quota regime they had established; the welded mesh sector had not been profitable; welded mesh was subject to competition from reinforced bars, which exercised price-restraint on the cartel; some companies had financial problems; one company gave the Commission some assistance in its investigations. All in all, the Commission decided not to impose 'very large' fines, and to set the fines 'considerably below the level which would normally be justified'. The fines imposed ranged from 1,375,000 ECUs to 13,000 ECUs (see Forrester and Norall, 1989). One of the companies in the *Welded Steel Mesh* cartel was, however, successful in obtaining a reduction of the fine imposed on it, on the basis that the Commission had by its conduct given the appellant cause to believe that the agreement was not unlawful (*Baustahlgewebe GmbH* v *Commission* (Case T-145/89)).

In January 1998 the Commission imposed a fine of 102 million ECUs on Volkswagen for preventing its dealers in Italy from selling to consumers and agencies in other Member States. The conduct of Volkswagen was regarded as having been aggravated by its failure to respond to repeated warnings by the Commission, and by the fact that the breaches had continued over a period of more than 10 years (*The Community* v *Volkswagen AG and Others* (Case IV/35.733)). In the same month, the Commission published a Notice laying down a new method of determining the amount of fines (OJ 1998 C 9/3). The fines notice sets out clear rules regarding the level of fines: the greater the negative impact on the Single Market, the larger the fine. There is now a consensus among the Member States that for serious infringements of the competition rules extremely high fines are justified, no matter the size and nationality of the firm. Even minor infringements may attract a fine as high as 1,000,000 ECUs.

JUDICIAL REVIEW OF COMMISSION DECISIONS

Like any other legal act of the institutions, decisions made by the Commission in relation to alleged infringements, including findings of infringements and the imposition of fines and periodic penalties, are subject to judicial review. The Court of First Instance may review such acts under Art 230 EC Treaty. There is an appeal on a point of law to the Court of Justice itself in relation to decisions of the CFI. The Court of First Instance, in reviewing the legality of the decision of the Commission, has the power not only to quash any decision, but to reduce or increase any fine imposed by the Commission (Art 229 EC Treaty; Art 17, Regulation 17/62).

THE ROLE OF THE COMMISSION IN RELATION TO NATIONAL COURTS

As discussed above, the Commission is obliged, under Art 10, Regulation 17/62, to transmit to the authorities responsible for competition policy in the Member States copies of any applications made to the Commission about the conduct of undertakings or, for example, for exemption under Art 81(3) EC Treaty in relation to agreements or concerted practices. The Commission is assisted by an Advisory Committee on Restrictive Practices and Monopolies composed of officials, drawn from a number of Member States, competent in restrictive practices and monopolies. The Commission is under an obligation to carry out its procedures in close cooperation with the competent authorities in Member States. These authorities have the right to express an opinion about the procedures adopted by the Commission during the course of an investigation (Art 10, Regulation 17/62).

The competition authorities in Member States may also be asked by the Commission to assist in the carrying out of investigations initiated by the Commission. Under Art 13, Regulation 17/62, national officials may be called upon to gather information on behalf of the Commission under Art 14, and may be assisted by Commission officials while doing so, if the Commission so requests. There is a general assumption that national authorities will cooperate with the Commission in the enforcement of competition law. National courts are also expected to cooperate with the Commission, as the Court explained in *Stergios Delimitis* v *Henninger Brau* (Case C-234/89):

> It should be noted in this context that it is always open to a national court, within the limits of the applicable national procedural rules and subject to Article 214 [now Art 287] of the Treaty [prohibiting the disclosure of confidential business information], to seek information from the Commission on the state of any procedure which the Commission may have set in motion and as to the likelihood of its giving an official ruling on the agreement in issue pursuant to Regulation 17. Under the same conditions, the national court may contact the Commission where the concrete application of Article 85(1) or Article 86 [now Art 81(1) or Art 82] raises particular difficulties, in order to obtain the economic and legal information which the institution can supply to it. Under Article 5 [now Art 10] of the Treaty, the Commission is bound by a duty of sincere co-operation with the judicial authorities of the Member State, who are responsible for ensuring that Community law is applied and respected in the national legal system. (para 53)

In an important notice issued in 1993 on cooperation between national courts and the

Commission in applying Arts 81 and 82 of the EC Treaty (OJ 1993 C 39/5), the Commission expressed the view that, by encouraging more effective participation by national courts in the day-to-day application of Community competition law, it will free up the Commission to 'perform its administrative task, namely to steer competition policy in the Community' (para 34). Although the Commission accepts that national courts cannot grant exemptions under Art 81(3), it envisages that where an agreement or concerted practice is apparently in breach of Art 81(1), but may nonetheless attract exemption under Art 81(3), or fall within some existing block exemption regulation, the court can stay the proceedings to enable the Commission to reach a decision. It was not clear how this process of cooperation was intended to work in practice. In 1997, the Commission issued a notice on the process (Final version of the Notice OJ 1997 C 313/3, 15 October 1997). The notice is not, however, legally binding. The division of competence between national courts and the Commission and the criteria to be applied in deciding whether or not a national court should refer a case to the Commission were considered by the Court of Justice in *Fonderies Roubaix-Wattrelos* (Case 63/75):

> The direct applicability of those provisions [Arts 81 and 82 EC Treaty] may not, however, lead the national courts to modify the scope of the exemption regulations by extending their sphere of application to agreements not covered by them. Any such extension, whatever its scope, would affect the manner in which the Commission exercises its legislative competence.
>
> ... It now falls to examine the consequences of that division of competence as regards the specific application of the Community competition rules by national courts. Account should here be taken of the risk of national courts taking decisions which conflict with those taken or envisaged by the Commission in the implementation of Articles 85(1) [Art 81(1)] and 86 [Art 82] and also of Article 85(3) [Art 81(3)]. Such conflicting decisions would be contrary to the general principles of legal certainty and must, therefore, be avoided when national courts give decisions on agreements or practices which may subsequently be the subject of a decision by the Commission. [Para 47]
>
> ... The national court may have regard to the following considerations in applying Article 85. If the conditions for the application of Article 85(1) are clearly not satisfied and there is, consequently, scarcely any risk of the Commission taking a different decision, the national court may continue the proceedings and rule on the agreement in issue. It may do the same if the agreement's incompatibility with Article 85(1) is beyond doubt and, regard being had to the exemption regulations and the Commission's previous decisions, the agreement may on no account be the subject of an exemption decision under Article 85(3). [Para 50]

The question of whether or not to stay proceedings in an English court where an application has been made to the Commission for an exemption under Art 81(3) may raise difficulties for the court. In *MTV Europe v BMG Records (UK) Ltd* [1995] 1 CMLR 437, the claimant brought an action in damages for breach of Art 81. Although the agreement in issue had been notified to the Commission, no decision had yet been delivered on whether it attracted exemption under Art 81(3), and one was not likely for some time. The Commission's decision would be retrospective to the extent that the agreement could be validated from the date of notification, but that validation could not be effective *prior* to notification. There was still a prospect that the claimant could recover damages in relation to that time. The court (Evans-Lombe J), in interlocutory proceedings, decided to continue with the case, despite the involvement of the Commission. It decided that the proceedings should continue until they reached the point of setting down for trial. If that point was reached before the Commission's decision, proceedings should at that point be stayed, and the stay should remain in effect until one month after the Commission's decision.

The Commission foresees that, although it will retain its overall function in competition law, and will cooperate with national courts and national authorities in supplying both factual and advisory information, individual claims alleging breaches of Community law by those who have suffered loss will increasingly be dealt with by national courts, and will, in its view, be better served by them. The reasons for preferring national courts (besides the lessening of the Commission's investigative burden) are:

1   The Commission cannot award compensation for loss suffered as a result of an infringement of Arts 81 or 82. Such claims may be brought only before national courts. Companies are more likely to avoid infringements of the Community competition rules if they risk having to pay damages or interest in such an event.
2   National courts can usually issue interim orders to stop the infringement more quickly than the Commission.
3   Claims for breaches of Community law in national courts can usually be coupled with claims for breaches of national law. This cannot be done in procedures before the Commission.
4   In those Member States where the successful party is awarded costs, these can be awarded in a claim for breach of Community law. A successful complainant in administrative procedures before the Commission has no such right, although if the proceedings are taken to the Court of First Instance, costs may be awarded in relation to that Court.

The argument in favour of national courts as the primary forums for individual complaints is not, however, as clear-cut as the Commission has maintained. As Riley has argued:

> A complaint to the Commission can be very cheap. A complaint can be anonymous. Anonymity is of great importance when the complainant is one of a number of small businesses who are threatened by the practice of much larger competitors. In addition, the Commission has considerable fact-finding powers culminating in its power to carry out on-the-spot inspections under Art 14 of Regulation 17. (Riley, 1993)

Whether the national courts are to have such an increasing role will depend, in the absence of Community legislation, on complainants' willingness to use them and on the degree to which the Court of Justice supports the Commission's approach. This may be seen in the Court's case law on the application of Arts 81 and 82 in those courts and in the allocation of functions between the Commission and national courts.

THE ROLE OF NATIONAL COURTS IN THE ENFORCEMENT OF COMMUNITY COMPETITION LAW

The Court has demonstrated some sympathy for the Commission's attempt to leave individual complaints which have a largely national dimension, although potentially affecting trade between Member States, to the courts of the state most affected. In *Automec and Asia Motor France* v *Commission* (Cases T-24 & 28/90), the Court of First Instance held that the Commission was not under an obligation to commence proceedings to determine whether or not a violation of Community law had occurred. Where the national court would be able to rule on the compatibility of a national distribution agreement for cars under Art 81(1) and provide the appropriate remedies if there was a breach, there was no need for Commission intervention. In *Tremblay* v *Commission* (Case T-5/93), the Commission had declined to investigate further an alleged abuse of a monopoly position enjoyed by the Société des Auteurs, Compositeurs et Editeurs de Musique (SACEM) in relation to musical copyrights on the grounds, *inter alia*, that the effects of the alleged infringements outside France were limited and that several cases raising the same issues were pending before the French courts. The Court supported this approach:

> The fact that a national court or national competition authority is already dealing with a case concerning the compatibility of an agreement or practice with Articles 85 and 86 [now Arts 81 and 82] of the Treaty is a factor which the Commission may take into account in evaluating the extent to which a case displays a Community interest. ... The Court considers that where the effects of the infringement alleged in a complaint are essentially confined to the territory of one Member State and where proceedings have been brought before the courts and competent administrative authorities of that Member State by the complainant against the body against which the complaint was made, the Commission is entitled to reject the complaint through lack of any sufficient Community interest, provided however that the rights of the complainant or its members can be adequately safeguarded, in particular by the national courts.

Article 81(1) and Art 82 are both directly effective in national courts and may be used both offensively and defensively. The availability of remedies for private parties in national courts on the basis of Community competition rules arises from the decision of the Court of Justice in *BRT* v *SABAM* (Case 127/73). In this case, the Court held that Arts 81 and 82 are both horizontally and vertically effective. As a result of this decision, a party may claim that an agreement is void under Art 81(2), that an injunction should be granted to enforce the competition rules, and that damages are payable for breach of Art 81 or Art 82.

The Court noted in *Tremblay* (above) that the national court was a satisfactory forum, provided the rights of complainants can be adequately safeguarded. This may not always be the case. In this context, Community law may have to eschew subsidiarity and provide, for example, that national courts should operate on the basis of legal presumptions against defendants or deeming certain conduct to be an infringement of the competition rules, subject to rebuttal by the defendant, if they are to be as effective as the Commission under the powers conferred by Regulation 17/62.

RELATIONSHIP BETWEEN COMMUNITY AND NATIONAL COMPETITION LAW

The potential for conflict between national competition rules and those of the Community was addressed by the Court in *Walt Wilhelm* v *Bundeskartellamt* (Case 14/68). The case related to a dyestuffs cartel. The Court held that, since their objectives are different, national competition rules may be applied in parallel with those of the Community, but not so as to prejudice the uniform application of Community rules throughout the common market. In practice, this means that there must be a set-off between any fines which are imposed by the national courts and the Commission, so that the later sanctions take account of earlier ones:

> The case-law of the Court of Justice has accepted the possibility of concurrent sanctions resulting from two parallel procedures pursuing different ends, the acceptability thereof deriving from the special system of sharing jurisdiction between the Community and the Member States with regard to cartels. However, the Court of Justice has established that, by virtue of a general requirement of natural justice, the Commission must take account of penalties which have already been borne by the same undertaking for the same conduct, where they have been imposed for the infringement of the cartel law of a Member State and, consequently, have been committed on the Community territory. (*Sotralenz SA* v *Commission* (Case T-149/89))

Conduct which infringes Art 81 or Art 82, but which does not infringe national law, cannot be held to be lawful in that state. However, there may be situations where an agreement or prohibited conduct does not infringe Art 81 or Art 82 because it does not affect trade between states, but it may still breach national competition law, and an agreement or concerted practice which has been exempted by the Commission under Art 81(3) may be lawful, even if it breaches national competition rules (Competition Report 1974, p. 29).

IMPLEMENTING COMMUNITY COMPETITION LAW IN THE ENGLISH COURTS

Article 81, since it is directly effective, may be used in English courts both as a defence to a claim for breach of contract and, for example, as the basis for a claim that an unlawful agreement between competitors has damaged an undertaking that is not a party to that agreement (*MTV Europe* v *BMG Records (UK) Ltd* (above); *Society of Lloyds* v *Clementson* [1995] 1 CMLR 693). In *Cutsworth* v *Mansfield Inns* [1986] 1 CMLR 1, for example, the claimants had for many years, under an agreement with the tenants, supplied coin-operated amusement machines to more than 50 public houses in the Humberside area. The public houses were taken over by Mansfield Inns in 1985, and, not long after this, the defendants gave to their tenants a list of suppliers of amusement machines from whom tenants were permitted to purchase. The claimants (who were not on that list) applied for an injunction to restrain the defendants from restricting their tenants from buying from them. They claimed that there was a seriously arguable case that the covenant in the licensees' tenancy agreement had the object or effect of distorting competition and potentially affected trade between Member States, contrary to Art 81(1) EC Treaty. This argument was accepted by the national court and the injunction was granted (see also *Holleran and Evans* v *Daniel Thwaites plc* [1989] 2 CMLR 917). It now seems clear that a declaration that an agreement breached Art 81(1) would not be sufficient. Under Community law, the national court would have to make an award of damages (*H.J. Banks and Co Ltd* v *British Coal Corporation* (Case C-128/92)). Article 81 can also be used defensively. In

Société Technique Minière v *Maschinenbau Ulm* (Case 56/65), the defendant distributors were held to be able to plead the invalidity of the distribution agreement in the national courts as a defence to breach of contract (see also *Brasserie de Haecht* v *Wilkin (No. 1)* (Case 23/67)).

Article 82 can also provide the basis for a claim for damages in the English courts. The leading case is *Garden Cottage Foods Ltd* v *Milk Marketing Board* [1984] AC 130. In this case an application was made for an interlocutory injunction to restrain the defendants from refusing to supply milk to the claimants. The refusal to supply was alleged by the claimants to be an abuse of a dominant position by the board, and much of the case is concerned with whether or not it was appropriate, in the circumstances, to grant an interlocutory injunction. In determining this point, the House of Lords had to consider whether or not an award of damages would be available if the claimants were successful in the substantive proceedings. Lord Diplock, who delivered the principal speech, thought that damages could be awarded under English law for a breach of Art 82:

> This article of the Treaty of Rome (the EEC Treaty) was held by the European Court of Justice in *Belgische Radio en Televisie* v *SV SABAM* (Case 127/73) to produce direct effects in relations between individuals and to create direct rights in respect of the individuals concerned which the national courts must protect. This decision of the European Court of Justice is to the effect that Art 86 [Art 82] is one which s 3(1) of the European Communities Act 1972 requires your lordships to follow. The rights which the article confers upon citizens in the United Kingdom accordingly fall within s 2(1) of the Act. They are without further enactment to be given legal effect in the United Kingdom and enforced accordingly. A breach of the duty imposed by Art 86 [Art 82] not to abuse a dominant position in the common market or in a substantial part of it, can thus be categorised in English law as a breach of statutory duty that is imposed not only for the purpose of promoting the general economic prosperity of the common market but also for the benefit of private individuals to whom loss or damage is caused by breach of that duty.

There is little case law on successful claims for damages for breach of Art 82 as a breach of statutory duty, but the principle has been applied in the Divisional Court and affirmed in the Court of Appeal. In *An Bord Bainne Co-operative Limited (The Irish Dairy Board)* v *The Milk Marketing Board* [1984] 2 CMLR 584 CA, Neill J declared that the speeches of their Lordships in the *Garden Cottage* case provided 'compelling support for the proposition that contraventions of EEC regulations which have "direct effects" create rights in private law which national courts must protect'. Article 82 could also provide a defence to an action that, for example, an exclusive supply agreement was entered into by one party while being subject to abuse of a dominant position by another undertaking. Thus, the United Kingdom purchasers of Tetra-Pak drinks packaging machines who were required to buy only Tetra-Pak cartons for use in those machines, would be free to buy other cartons and could use the breaches of Arts 81 and 82 found by the Court of First Instance as a defence to any action for breach of contract in the courts of England and Wales (*Tetra-Pak International SA* v *Commission* (Case T-83/91)).

FUTURE REFORM: PROPOSED REGULATION AMENDING THE SYSTEM FOR IMPLEMENTATION OF ARTICLES 81 AND 82

The Commission undertook a review of the application of Arts 81 and 82, which culminated in the adoption of a proposed regulation which, if adopted by the Council of Ministers, will result in, *inter alia*, the replacement of Regulation 17/62.

The Explanatory Memorandum to the proposed regulation sets out in full the history surrounding its adoption by the Commission and the impact it will have on the current powers and procedures. This Memorandum is set out below. Although some of the matters are related to the constitutional side of Community law, they are included insofar as they provide a timely review of Part I of this book. Developments concerning the proposed regulation can be followed by visiting the Commission's website at: http://europa.eu.int/comm/competition/index_en.html.

PROPOSED REGULATION AMENDING THE SYSTEM FOR IMPLEMENTATION OF ARTICLES 81 AND 82: EXPLANATORY MEMORANDUM

1. GENERAL

A. Context

The Community competition rules were established in its founding Treaty of 1957. Article 81 sets out the rules applicable to restrictive agreements, decisions and concerted practices, while Article 82 concerns abuses of dominant positions.

In 1962, the Council adopted Regulation No 17, which sets out the rules of procedure for the application of Articles 81 and 82 of the Treaty which have been applied till today without any significant modifications. Regulation No 17 was based on direct applicability of the prohibition rule of Article 81(1) and prior notification of restrictive agreements and practices for exemption under Article 81(3). While the Commission, national courts and national competition authorities can all apply Article 81(1), the power to apply Article 81(3) was granted exclusively to the Commission. Regulation No 17 thus established a highly centralised authorisation system for all restrictive agreements requiring exemption. In contrast, Article 82 has always been enforced in parallel by the Commission, national courts and national authorities.

This system was well suited for a Community of six Member States in which there was little competition culture. It allowed the development of Community competition law and its consistent application throughout the Community. However, today the context has changed fundamentally. The European Union now has 15 Member States, whose markets have already been extensively integrated, 380 million inhabitants, and 11 official languages. National competition authorities have been set up in the Member States and national competition laws have been enacted, many reflecting the content of Articles 81 and 82.

In this new context, the current system presents two major deficiencies. First, it no longer ensures the effective protection of competition. The Commission's monopoly on the application of Article 81(3) is a significant obstacle to the effective application of the rules by national competition authorities and courts. And in a wide Community, the Commission alone cannot bear the responsibility for enforcing the competition rules throughout the Union. Furthermore, the notification regime no longer constitutes an effective tool for the protection of competition. It only rarely reveals cases that pose a real threat to competition. In fact, the notification system prevents the Commission's resources from being used for the detection and punishment of serious infringements.

The second deficiency of the current system is that it imposes an excessive burden on industry by increasing compliance costs and preventing companies from enforcing their agreements without notifying them to the Commission even if they fulfil the conditions of Article 81(3). This is particularly detrimental to SMEs for whom the cost of notification and in the absence of notification, the difficulty of enforcing their agreements can constitute a competitive disadvantage compared with larger firms.

The perspective of the enlargement of the Community makes it even more urgent to proceed with a reform of Regulation No 17. A Union with 25 or even more Member States is now in prospect. A notification system with prior authorisation by one administrative body would be completely unsustainable in an enlarged Community, since, potentially, thousands of agreements would require administrative clearance in order to be enforceable. Direct application of Article 81(3) would ensure that agreements fulfilling the conditions of that provision were legally enforceable without recourse to an administrative body being necessary.

B. The White Paper and the consultation process

In order to prepare Community competition law for the challenges of the coming years, the Commission initiated the reform process by adopting and publishing in 1999 a White Paper on modernisation of the rules implementing Articles 81 and 82 of the EC Treaty.

The White Paper examines various options for reform and proposes the adoption of a fundamentally different enforcement system called a directly applicable exception system. Such a system is based on the direct applicability of the exception rule of Article 81(3), implying that the Commission and national competition authorities and courts would apply Article 81(3) in all proceedings in which they are called upon to apply the prohibition rule of Article 81(1), which is already directly applicable.

The White Paper was adopted on 28 April 1999. Interested parties were invited to submit comments by 30 September 1999. The European Parliament organised a public hearing on 22 September 1999. It adopted a resolution on 18 January 2000. The Economic and Social Committee adopted an opinion on 8 December 1999. The Commission has received and carefully examined submissions from all Member States and more than 100 interested parties, including submissions from EFTA countries, the ESA, and competition authorities from Estonia, Hungary and the Czech Republic. A working group composed of Commission officials and experts from the national competition authorities has discussed the content of the White Paper in a number of meetings.

The European Parliament and the Economic and Social Committee support the Commission's proposal while insisting on the importance of ensuring consistent application of Community competition law in a system of parallel powers and of maintaining an adequate level of legal certainty.

The positions of industry associations and lawyers are varied. Many welcome the Commission's approach as a more efficient and less bureaucratic alternative to the present system of implementation, which is almost universally considered unsatisfactory. However, many also stress the need to ensure that the reform does not lead to inconsistent application and renationalisation of Community competition law and that the reform does not reduce legal certainty for companies.

The proposal for a new regulation is in its main parts based on the White Paper, taking due account, however, of the major preoccupations expressed in the consultation process. The question of extending the procedures of the Merger Regulation to partial-function production joint ventures, that was also raised in the White Paper (nos. 79–81), will be further examined in the context of forthcoming reflections on the revision of that regulation.

2. PROPOSAL FOR A NEW COUNCIL REGULATION

A. Subject

The subject of the proposal is the reform of the implementing regulations for Articles 81 and 82 of the EC Treaty, i.e. Regulation No 17 and the corresponding transport regulations. It is proposed to create a new enforcement system referred to as a 'directly applicable exception system'. In such a system, both the prohibition rule set out in Article 81(1) and the exception rule contained in Article 81(3) can be directly applied by not only the Commission but also national courts and national competition authorities. Agreements are legal or void depending on whether they satisfy the conditions of Article 81(3). No authorisation decision is required for enforcing agreements complying with Article 81 as a whole. This is already the existing enforcement system for Article 82 of the EC Treaty.

B. Legal basis

The legal basis for the present proposal is Article 83 of the EC Treaty. Article 83 empowers the Council to lay down the appropriate regulations or directives to give effect to the principles set out in Articles 81 and 82. In a non-exhaustive list, Article 83(2) mentions elements that should in particular be covered by implementing rules created on this basis.

The legal basis in Article 83 covers the application of Articles 81 and 82 in general. In particular, it is not limited to the application of the rules by specific decision-makers. The Community legislature, within the limits of the general principles of the Treaty, is therefore empowered to lay down rules on the application of Articles 81 and 82 by bodies other than the Community institutions as well as rules on the interaction between the different decision-makers. Accordingly, the proposed Regulation provides for certain rules to be respected by national competition authorities and/or courts when applying Articles 81 and 82 as well as rules on cooperation between them and with the Commission.

Article 83(2)(b) expressly provides for the Community legislature to lay down detailed rules for the application of Article 81(3), taking into account the need to ensure effective supervision on the one hand, and to simplify administration to the greatest extent possible on the other. The legal basis in Article 83 thereby enjoins the Community legislature to fill a lacuna left by Article 81. Leaving aside Article 81(2), Article 81 is divided into a prohibition rule (Article 81(1)) and a rule according to which the prohibition may be declared inapplicable if stated conditions are satisfied (Article 81(3)). It does not, however, lay down by what procedure the prohibition may be declared inapplicable, and by whom. In particular, the words 'may be declared inapplicable', unlike the words 'the High Authority shall authorise' used by the ECSC Treaty (see Article 65 of the ECSC Treaty), do not define a specific procedure.

The existing Regulation No 17 granted exclusive power to the Commission to apply Article 81(3) in the framework of an administrative procedure aiming at an authorisation decision. Article 81(3) is however suitable for direct application. While leaving a certain margin of appreciation as to its interpretation, Article 81(3) does not imply discretionary powers that could only be exercised by an administrative body. A limited margin of appreciation does not make a Treaty provision unsuitable for direct application, as is clear from the case-law on for instance Article 81(1) and Article 82, which are already directly applied by national courts.

There is no indication in the Treaty to contradict this conclusion. In particular, the words 'to simplify administration to the greatest extent possible' in Article 83(2)(b), while imposing on the legislature the objective of a minimum of procedural bureaucracy, do not exclude the application of Article 81(3) by courts in addition to administrative bodies. Under the powers granted to it by Article 83, the Community legislature can choose an implementing system that is based on direct application of Article 81(3).

Article 83(2)(e) states that the Community legislature is also empowered to define the relationship between national laws and the Community rules on competition. Regulation No 17 refrained from regulating this relationship, which has led to long-standing debates and to legal uncertainty. The Court of Justice was able to clarify some of the issues involved by applying the principle of primacy of Community law over national law. Given the specificity of Article 81 in particular, the solutions found on that basis do not, however, cover the entirety of cases in which conflicts can arise. In addition, the change to a new implementing system risks reopening the debate and creating new legal uncertainties as to this fundamental issue. The proposed Regulation therefore lays down a rule regulating the relationship between Community competition law and national law.

Finally, Article 83 is also the appropriate legal basis for regulating the application of Articles 81 and 82 to the transport sector. This was not yet clear when Regulation (EEC) No 1017/68 was adopted: it had two legal bases, the former Articles 75 and 87, now Articles 71 and 83. However, the Court of Justice has since held that the Community competition rules apply in full to the transport sector (see Joined Cases 209 to 213/84 *Nouvelles Frontières* [1986] ECR 1425 and Case 66/86 *Ahmed Saeed* [1989] ECR 803). The Community legislature can therefore provide that the application of Articles 81 and 82 to agreements and decisions presently governed by Regulation (EEC) No 1017/68 is integrated into the proposed Regulation on the legal basis of Article 83. The same goes for the application of Articles 81 and 82 to the maritime transport sector presently governed by Regulation (EEC) No 4056/86. The latter regulation, although adopted subsequently to the abovementioned case-law of the Court of Justice, and in contrast to the Commission proposal (based on Article 87 (now 83) alone), was also based by Council on the former Article 84(2) (now 80(2)), owing to the inclusion of Article 9 of that Regulation concerning relations with third countries. The difference of opinion between the Council and the Commission does not need to be resolved in the present instance, as the proposed Regulation leaves Article 9 of Regulation (EEC) No 4056/86 untouched.

C. Characteristics of the proposed system

1. More efficient protection of competition
The proposal aims at increasing the protection of competition in the Community. This will be achieved by the proposal in three ways.

(a) More enforcers
The proposed system will result in increased enforcement of Community competition rules, as in addition to the Commission, national competition authorities and national courts will also be able to apply Articles 81 and 82 in their entirety.

National competition authorities, which have been set up in all Member States, are generally well equipped to deal with Community competition law cases. In general, they have the necessary resources and are close to the markets.

As regards the applicant countries, considerable progress has already been made in establishing national competition authorities. Even if initially they may not all possess sufficient resources to ensure the effective protection of competition, the proposed reform will allow the Commission to step up enforcement in those parts of the enlarged Community. The proposed discontinuation of the notification and exemption system ensures that all available resources can be used for the effective protection of competition.

It is a core element of the Commission's proposal that the Commission and the national competition authorities should form a network and work closely together in the application of Articles 81 and 82. The network will provide an infrastructure for mutual exchange of information, including confidential information, and assistance, thereby expanding considerably the scope for each member of the network to enforce Articles 81 and 82 effectively. The network will also ensure an efficient allocation of cases based on the principle that cases should be dealt with by the best placed authority.

National courts will also play an important and enhanced role in the enforcement of Community competition rules. Unlike national authorities or the Commission, which act in the public interest, the function of national courts is to protect the rights of individuals. They can grant damages and order the performance or non-performance of contracts. They are the necessary complement to action by public authorities.

The Commission's proposal aims at promoting private enforcement through national courts. Both Article 81(1) and Article 81(3) confer rights on individuals, which should be protected by national courts. The present division of powers under Article 81 is not in line with the important role that national courts play in the enforcement of Community law in general. In the present Regulation No 17 the authorisation system and the Commission's monopoly on the application of Article 81(3) make application of Article 81(1) by national courts very difficult. The fact that the elimination of this obstacle may lead to more application of Article 81 and thereby increase the case load on national courts is not a valid argument against the reform. Such considerations should not be allowed to hamper the implementation of a reform that aims at strengthening the enforcement of the rules and at enhancing the protection of individual rights.

(b) Refocusing the Commission's action

The second way in which the proposal will increase the protection of competition is by allowing the Commission to concentrate on the detection of the most serious infringements. Experience in the last decades has shown that notifications do not bring to the attention of the Commission serious violations of the competition rules. The handling of a large number of notifications prevents the Commission from focusing on the detection and the punishment of the most serious restrictions such as cartels, foreclosure of the market and abuses of dominant positions. In the proposed system, the abolition of the notification and authorisation system will allow the Commission to focus on complaints and own-initiative proceedings that lead to prohibition decisions, rather than establishing what is not prohibited. The Commission intends to issue a notice providing potential complainants with guidance on the treatment of complaints. The notice will *inter alia* set a deadline within which the Commission should inform the complainant whether it intends to deal with its complaint.

(c) Increased powers of investigation for the Commission

In order to guarantee the protection of competition, it is also necessary to ensure that the Commission's powers of investigation are sufficient and effective. Under the existing Regulation No 17, the Commission can conduct inspections on the premises of companies and make written requests for information. It can fine companies for infringements of substantive and procedural rules and impose periodic penalty payments.

Three main improvements of the current system are required to ensure a more effective application of Articles 81 and 82.

First, the rules governing the obtaining of judicial orders at national level in order to overcome any opposition on the part of an undertaking to an inspection should be codified. This will clarify the intervention of national judges in accordance with the limits established by the Court of Justice.

Secondly, it is necessary to adapt the powers vested in Commission officials during inspections: they must be empowered, subject to judicial authorisation, to search private homes if professional documents are likely to be kept there. The experience of the national competition authorities and the Commission shows that incriminating documents are ever more frequently kept and discovered in private homes. Commission inspectors should also be empowered to seal cupboards or offices in order to ensure that documents are not removed and destroyed. Finally, they should be entitled to ask oral questions relating to the subject matter of the inspection.

Thirdly, the fines for breaches of procedural rules and the periodic penalty payments, which were set in absolute terms in the sixties, must be increased. A system based on turnover percentage figures is considered the appropriate solution.

2. More level playing field

Competition laws have an immediate impact on the commercial activities of companies, as they have to adapt to the prevailing standard in any given area. For companies that engage in activities having cross-border effects it is therefore important that there be a level playing field throughout the European Union, allowing them to reap the full benefits of the single market.

The present proposal will create a more level playing field in two ways. First, Community competition law will be applied to more cases, thereby limiting the scope for inconsistencies caused by differences in national competition laws. Secondly, a number of measures will ensure that Articles 81 and 82 are applied in a consistent manner by the various decision-makers involved in their application.

(a) More application of Community competition law

In the present enforcement system, several national systems of competition law and Community competition law may apply concurrently to the same transaction to the extent that an agreement or practice is capable of affecting trade between Member States. The application of national law is constrained only by the principle of primacy of Community law.

Several national systems of competition law have been modelled on Articles 81 and 82. However, no formal harmonisation is in place, and differences remain both in law and practice. Such differences can lead to different treatment of agreements and practices that affect trade between Member States.

In order to promote a level playing field for companies that engage in agreements or practices that have a cross-border effect, it is necessary to regulate the relationship between national law and Community law, as provided in Article 83(2)(e) of the EC Treaty. Accordingly, Article 3 of the proposed Regulation provides that only Community competition law applies when an agreement, decision or concerted practice within the meaning of Article 81 or abusive conduct within the meaning of Article 82 is capable of affecting trade between Member States. This rule ensures in a simple and effective way that all transactions with a cross-border effect are subject to a single body of law.

The proposal not only creates a level playing field throughout the European Union, it also facilitates an efficient allocation of cases within the network of competition authorities, the aim being that cases should be dealt with by the best placed authority. In several Member States the competition authority, once seized of a case, is obliged to come to a formal decision. Such obligations may hinder reallocation of cases to a better placed authority. To overcome this problem in respect of the application of Articles 81 and 82 the Regulation empowers a competition authority to suspend a proceeding or reject a complaint on grounds that another competition authority is dealing with or has dealt with the case. However, the scope of this provision is limited to the application of Community competition law. Article 3 of the proposed Regulation ensures that an efficient allocation of cases is not hindered by simultaneous application of national law in respect of which a national competition authority may remain bound to come to a formal decision. Parallel application of national and Community competition law should be avoided because it leads to unnecessary parallel proceedings.

(b) Consistent application of Community competition law

The application of the same law and policy will in itself promote consistency throughout the single market. The application of Articles 81 and 82 by national competition authorities and courts will be subject to Community block exemption regulations, creating safe harbours for defined categories of agreements. Further guidance will be provided by guidelines adopted by the Commission.

Application by national competition authorities and courts will also be subject to the case-law of the Court of Justice of the European Communities and the Court of First Instance as well as the administrative practice of the Commission. In the latter respect, it is proposed in Article 16 of the proposed Regulation to impose on national competition authorities and courts an obligation to use every effort not to contradict a Commission decision.

More decision-makers also mean more case-law and administrative decisions, which will further clarify the scope of the Community competition rules.

Moreover, there will be a number of additional instruments aiming at ensuring that Articles 81 and 82 are applied in a consistent manner.

The application of the Community competition rules by national courts will be subject to the preliminary reference procedure of Article 234 of the EC Treaty. The Court of Justice of the European Communities will play the same important role in ensuring consistency as it has done and continues to do in other areas of Community law. As the proposal aims at increasing the level of private enforcement before national courts, an initial increase in Article 234 references can be expected. A significant increase, however, is unlikely, as it is expected that most litigation before national courts will concern areas where the law has been clearly established.

Article 15 of the proposed Regulation codifies the existing obligation of the Commission, based on Article 10 of the Treaty, to cooperate with national courts. This cooperation includes a right for national courts to ask the Commission for information in its possession or for its opinion on questions concerning the application of the Community competition rules. It is expected that the importance of this mechanism will increase once national courts are empowered to apply Article 81(3) as well.

Article 15 also proposes to vest in the Commission the power to submit written or oral submissions to national courts at its own initiative and in the Community public interest. This will allow the Commission to contribute to the consistent application of Community competition law by national courts. It is also proposed that the national competition authorities be empowered to make oral and written submissions to the courts of their Member State.

With regard to the national competition authorities, the creation of a network in which all members apply the same law and policy will greatly promote consistency and a level playing field throughout the single market. The formal basis for establishing the network is found in Article 11 of the proposed Regulation, according to which the national competition authorities and the Commission are to apply the Community competition rules in close cooperation. The details of this cooperation will be developed in a notice. The network will foster the development of a common competition culture throughout the Community.

In addition, certain formal mechanisms are established to ensure consistent application, including a consultation procedure for certain types of decisions adopted by national competition authorities (see Article 11(4) of the proposed Regulation). This provision requires national competition authorities to consult the Commission prior to the adoption of prohibition decisions, decisions accepting commitments and decisions withdrawing the benefit of a block exemption regulation. All such decisions have direct repercussions for the addressees. It is therefore important to ensure that these decisions are consistent with the general practice of the network. In case of substantial disagreement within the network, the Commission retains the power to withdraw a case from a national competition authority by itself initiating proceedings in the case.

It is not necessary for consistency purposes to provide for prior consultation in respect of other types of decisions adopted by national competition authorities, such as rejections of complaints and decisions to take no action. These decisions bind only the deciding authority, and do not preclude subsequent action by any other competition authority or before national courts.

As regards decisions adopted by the Commission, it is proposed to maintain the present obligation for the Commission to consult the Advisory Committee on Restrictive Practices and Dominant Positions.

3. An adequate level of legal certainty for companies and a reduction of bureaucracy

Under the existing Regulation No 17 an agreement or decision caught by Article 81(1) can become valid, i.e. enforceable before a civil court, only if it is notified to the Commission and is exempted by the Commission. In practice, most notified cases are closed by a non-binding administrative letter from the Commission services (a 'comfort letter').

The proposed Regulation removes the bureaucratic obstacles connected with the notification and authorisation procedure while maintaining an adequate degree of legal certainty.

In particular, the proposed Regulation provides that agreements and decisions which satisfy the conditions of Article 81(3) are valid and enforceable *ab initio* with no administrative decision being required to that effect. Undertakings can therefore rely on civil enforceability as an element of improved legal certainty independently of any action by an administration.

The proposed Regulation does not remove the necessity for undertakings to assess their business transactions to verify whether they are in compliance with the competition rules. Under the present Regulation No 17, this analysis is carried out by undertakings when preparing a notification. The proposal assimilates the application of the Community competition rules to other areas of law where undertakings are required to ascertain themselves that their behaviour is legal.

In the field of Community competition law, companies' task of assessing their behaviour is facilitated by block exemptions and Commission notices and guidelines clarifying the application of the rules. As a complementary element of the current reform, the Commission commits itself to an even greater effort in this area. Article 28 of the proposed Regulation confers on the Commission a general power to adopt block exemption regulations. This power will ensure that it is in a position to react with sufficient speed to new developments and changing market conditions.

In addition, under the new system, with the larger number of decision-makers applying Article 81(3), case-law and practice on its interpretation will rapidly develop where they do not yet exist, thereby inherently reinforcing the framework for assessment.

The Commission will further contribute to this development by continuing to set policy through its own decisions in individual cases. In addition to prohibition decisions, the proposed Regulation provides that in cases where it is in the Community public interest to do so the Commission, acting on its own initiative, can adopt decisions finding that no infringement has been committed. This will permit the Commission to set out its position in a landmark case so as to clarify the law for all companies that find themselves in similar situations.

Finally, the Commission will remain open to discuss specific cases with the undertakings where appropriate. In particular, it will provide guidance regarding agreements, decisions or concerted practices that raise an unresolved, genuinely new question of interpretation. To that effect, the Commission will publish a notice in which it will set out the conditions under which it may issue reasoned opinions. Any such system of opinions must not, however, lead to companies being entitled to obtain an opinion, as this would reintroduce a kind of notification system.

3. SUBSIDIARITY AND PROPORTIONALITY

In the interest of the single market, the proposed Regulation ensures that Community competition law should be applied to agreements and practices capable of affecting trade between Member States, thereby creating a level playing field throughout the Community. At the same time, the proposal ensures that the application of that law takes place at the most efficient level. Under the proposal, the Commission shares the power to apply Article 81(3) with national competition authorities and national courts, thereby enabling these bodies to apply Articles 81 and 82 effectively.

The scope for effective intervention at national level is substantially increased by the cooperation mechanisms contained in Articles 12 and 21 of the proposed Regulation, which empower national competition authorities to exchange confidential information and to assist each other in respect of fact-finding. As a result of market integration evidence and information will increasingly be located in several Member States. Enhanced horizontal cooperation will make it easier for national competition authorities to obtain all the relevant facts.

The Commission's proposal is thus fully in line with the principle enshrined in Article 5 of the Treaty, according to which action should be taken at the most efficient level. While promoting the Community interest in a level playing field throughout the single market, the proposal ensures that national competition authorities and courts can apply Articles 81 and 82 fully and effectively to all cases in respect of which intervention at national level is more efficient.

The Commission, being the only authority that can act throughout the European Union, will necessarily continue to play a central role in the development of Community competition law and policy and in ensuring that it is applied consistently throughout the single market, thereby preventing any renationalisation of Community competition law. The development and application of the law and policy will, however, be a concern of all the competition authorities involved in the enforcement of Articles 81 and 82. Policy issues will be the subject of discussion within the network.

The proposal does not go beyond what is necessary to achieve the objectives of the Treaty. The Treaty aims, *inter alia*, to create an internal market and a system of undistorted competition. The very objective of the present proposal is to enhance the protection of competition and to create a level playing field throughout the Community.

The proposal to exclude the application of national competition law to agreements and practices that affect trade between Member States is necessary in order to ensure that such agreements and practices are subject to a single set of rules. This is essential in order to ensure that competition in the internal market is not distorted as a result of differences in the legal framework and to ensure that cases can be allocated efficiently within the network.

Effective case allocation also makes it necessary that the members of the network should inform each other of all new cases and exchange relevant case-related information. Moreover, provision must be made for prior consultation by the national competition authorities in respect of prohibition decisions, decisions accepting commitments and decisions withdrawing the benefit of a block exemption regulation.

Inconsistencies in respect of these types of decisions would be detrimental to the single market and the objective of creating a level playing field throughout the Community. Such decisions also have important implications for the common competition policy of the network. The Commission will associate the other members of the network in the consultation process. The functioning of the network will be further elaborated upon in a notice on cooperation between competition authorities.

The present proposal is based on the premise that national competition authorities will apply Articles 81 and 82 in accordance with their respective national procedural rules. It is not necessary for the implementation of the reform to embark on a full-scale harmonisation of national procedural laws. On the other hand, it is necessary to regulate at Community level a limited number of issues that have a direct impact on the proper functioning of the proposed system.

First and foremost, it is necessary to oblige the Member States to empower their national competition authorities to apply Articles 81 and 82.

It is also necessary to stipulate the content of the decisions that national competition authorities may adopt in the application of Articles 81 and 82 (see Article 5 of the proposed Regulation), in order to ensure a full and effective implementation of the directly applicable exception system. No competition authority forming part of the network can be empowered to adopt constitutive exemption decisions when applying the Community competition rules.

Article 13 of the proposed Regulation empowers national competition authorities and the Commission to suspend or terminate proceedings on the ground that another member of the network is or has been dealing with the case; this is necessary to ensure an efficient allocation of cases and use of resources within the network. It is, however, neither necessary nor appropriate to oblige other competition authorities to suspend or terminate their proceedings. It is the task of the network to ensure in practice that resources are used efficiently.

The proposed Regulation provides a legal basis for the exchange of information and assistance between national competition authorities. Such horizontal cooperation is necessary in order to enable them to apply Articles 81 and 82 effectively.

The power of the Commission to make written and oral submissions in the Community public interest before national courts hearing a case on the application of Articles 81 and 82 (see Article 15) is necessary in order to allow the Commission to contribute to their consistent application. Divergent application of Community competition law by national courts would pose a threat to the proper functioning of the single market and the coherence of the system. In accordance with the principle of subsidiarity it is proposed that the power to make submissions before the courts be shared between the Commission and the national competition authorities. Furthermore, submissions will be made in accordance with the procedural rules in force in the Member State in question. Thus, the proposal does not purport to harmonise national procedural law, except that it grants the Commission and the national competition authorities the power to make submissions on their own initiative. In order to enable the Commission and the national competition authorities to exercise this proposed new power effectively, it is necessary to oblige national courts to furnish, upon request, relevant information pertaining to cases before them in which the Commission or a national competition authority is considering making a written or oral submission or has decided to do so.

Further reading

Chiti, E., 'The right of access to Community information under the Code of Practice' (1996) 2 EPL 363.

Craig, P. and De Burca, G. (1998) *EU Law Text, Cases and Materials* (2nd edn), OUP, Chapter 23.

Davidson, J., 'Action for Damages in the English Courts for Breach of EEC Competition Law' (1985) 34 ICLQ 178.

D'Sa, R. (1994) *European Community Law and Civil Remedies in England and Wales*, Sweet & Maxwell, Chapter 10.

Forrester, I.S. and Norall, C., 'Competition Law' (1989) 9 YEL 271, 286, 300.

Friend, 'Rights of Complainants in EC Competition Proceedings' (1994) 110 LQR 209.

Harris, B., 'Problems of Procedure in EEC Competition Law' (1989) NLJ 1452.

Hunnings, N.M., 'The Stanley Adams Affair or the Biter Bit' (1987) 24 CML Rev 65.

Kerse, C., 'Enforcing Community Competition Policy under Arts 8 and 89 of the EC Treaty – New Powers for UK Competition Authorities' [1997] ECLR 17.

Korah, V. (1997) *EC Competition Law and Practice*, Hart Publishing.

Lang, J.T., 'Duties of National Authorities under Community Constitutional Law' (1998) 23 EL Rev 109.

Marsden, P.B., 'Inducing Member States' Enforcement of European Competition Law: A Competition Policy Approach to Anti-trust Federalism' (1997) 18 ECLR 234.

Riley, A.J., 'More Radicalism, Please. The Notice on Cooperation between National Courts and the Commission: Applying Articles 85 and 86 of the EEC Treaty' (1993) 3 ECLR 91.

Shaw, J., 'Competition Complaints: a Comprehensive System of Remedies?' (1993) 18 EL Rev 427.

Shaw, J., 'A Review of Recent Cases on Articles 85 and 86 EC: Procedural Issues' [1995] EL Rev 83.

Steiner, J. and Woods, L. (2000) *Textbook on EC Law* (7th edn), Blackstone Press, Chapter 17.

Tillotson, J. (2000) *European Community Law: Text, Cases and Materials* (3rd edn), Cavendish Publishing Ltd, Chapter 17.

Van der Woude, M., 'Hearing officers and EC anti-trust procedures: the art of making subjective procedures more objective' (1996) 33 CML Rev 531.

Weatherill, S., (2000) *Cases and Materials on EC Law* (5th edn), Blackstone Press, Chapter 13.

Wils, W.P.J., 'The Commission's New Method for Calculating Fines in Anti-trust Cases' (1997) 22 EL Rev 125.

INDEX